Women Remembered

Women Remembered

A GUIDE TO LANDMARKS OF WOMEN'S HISTORY IN THE UNITED STATES

Marion Tinling

GREENWOOD PRESS
NEW YORK • WESTPORT, CONNECTICUT • LONDON

Library of Congress Cataloging-in-Publication Data

Tinling, Marion, 1904–
Women remembered.

Bibliography: p.
Includes index.
1. Women—United States—Monuments—Guide-books.
2. Historic sites—United States—Guide-books.
3. United States—Description and travel—1981– —
Guide-books. I. Title.
E159.T56 1986 917.3'04927 85–17639
ISBN 0–313–23984–3 (lib. bdg. : alk. paper)

Library of Congress Catalog Card Number: 85–17639
ISBN: 0–313–23984–3

First published in 1986

Greenwood Press, Inc.
88 Post Road West
Westport, Connecticut 06881

Printed in the United States of America

The paper used in this book complies with the Permanent Paper Standard issued by the National Information Standards Organization (Z39.48–1984).

10 9 8 7 6 5 4 3 2 1

Dedicated to my creative and adventurous friend Linda Ruffner-Russell, who first thought of presenting women's history in this way, and to the many helpful and knowledgeable librarians, scholars, and curators of historical collections who provided information and encouragement.

CONTENTS

PREFACE

Women may be slighted by those who write history books, but feminist history can be found all across the land, chiseled in stone and engraved in brass. Women who played a part in history are commemorated in the preservation of their birthplaces and homes; the erection of monuments; the naming of parks, schools, buildings, and streets; and the placing of historical markers. Some women left their own monuments when they established hospitals, art galleries, colleges, or business enterprises.

Sarah Orne Jewett, a great admirer of the Brontë sisters' novels, once visited the Yorkshire home of the Brontës. She wrote enthusiastically to a friend at home: "Nothing you ever read about them can make you know them until you go there . . . . Never mind people who tell you there is nothing to see in the place where people lived who interest you. You always find something of what made them the souls they were, and at any rate you see their sky and their earth."

Jewett would be surprised to know that admirers of her writings now visit her home in South Berwick, Maine, to experience her sky and earth and feel her unseen presence.

Every year thousands of Americans and travelers from foreign countries make pilgrimages to historical sites. The nation has made a strong effort to seek out such places, to restore and mark them, and to interpret their meaning and value. Such visits to the past illuminate history. They connect us to the network of previous lives. Standing in a spot where some great event took place or where some admired person was born, lived, loved, and worked puts us in touch with our own roots. Statues and buildings may be only brick or granite, marble or bronze, but they can evoke powerful tribal memories.

Monuments also reflect the attitudes of those who erect them. Anthropologists take seriously totem poles, cave drawings, and pyramids, not as art forms alone but as symbols communicating beliefs. Today even graffiti are studied as a way of understanding those who produce them. Can we understand the American attitude toward women through a study of the memorials to them?

Monuments are erected by governments, by relatives or family associations, or by historical societies. Patriotic, fraternal, and professional groups commemorate those who seemed significant to their contemporaries or now assume value to their descendants. Memorials are set up most often well after the event, so that the importance of the person or happening seems to have increased in time. Homes of the famous, fallen into oblivion, are rediscovered and restored. Graves go unmarked until someone realizes that the person buried there is deserving of remembrance.

One of the earliest historical site markers we know of in America was put up by a woman (in Reading, Vermont, sometime between 1799 and 1810). It commemorated an Indian captivity, as did many of the first memorials. Heroines of the American Revolution were remembered, many with markers put in place by the Daughters of the American Revolution. Monuments to the women of the Confederacy were erected in the South and statues of the pioneer woman across the West. While statues of male heroes graced every public building, it was not considered at first quite proper to erect statues of real women.

One of Aesop's fables concerns a lion and a man engaged in a dispute over which was the more powerful. As they passed a statue of a man strangling a lion, Man claimed it as proof that he was dominant. Lion replied, "Let the lions make the statues, and we will see who is stronger."

When women began studying women, monuments to forgotten heroines, such as Sacajawea, were raised. Statuary Hall in the National Capitol, established in 1864 to honor national heroes, had no women represented until 1905. The Hall of Fame in New York City, which began selecting honorees in 1900, chose its first women in 1905. An American Women's Hall of Fame was established in 1968, and in Seneca Falls, New York, the site of the first convention called by American women to discuss their legal and civil rights is now recognized as a National Women's Rights Historical Park. Of late, homes of notable women have been nominated for the National Register of Historic Places. The list of such sites grows yearly and encourages us to believe that our foremothers are not without honor in their own communities, let historians write what they will.

While we have these tangible reminders of the presence of achieving women all about us, one could miss the experience of visiting them for lack of a guide to their locations. This guide is designed to provide access to a wealth of feminist history in the United States.

Women included are memorable for contributions to society, for acts of heroism, or as participants in some historical event. No living women are included. Omitted are women described chiefly in relation to great men—wives, daughters, mothers—and this includes most presidential wives. Also omitted are generic statues to pioneers, nurses, nuns, and other heroines without names.

Many of the most noted women in American history are not represented here because no memorials to them could be found. On the other hand, many women remembered locally are not in our history books, nor have their names been included in biographical compilations. Women who seem to have made significant contributions have been so neglected by history that little could be found about them, not even the dates of birth and death, nor, for a few married women, their own names.

As for the sites, they are public—something that can be visited: a statue or marker; a home that is identified as a historical site or is open to the public; an institution founded by a woman or a group of women; a place (town, park, school, building) named for a historical woman; or public artwork created by a woman. A few women are so well remembered that their names are attached to places all across the country. Grave markers are included only in special cases, generally when marked long after the death as a special remembrance.

Groups who erect monuments often forget and neglect them. Marble and stone fall prey to weather, pigeons, and vandals. Historical plaques are defaced or stolen. Markers are moved from one place to another to make room for new roads and buildings. Some are removed for safety and stored out of sight. Historical buildings have burned down or been demolished. Every effort has been made to include only sites that can still be viewed.

The guide is divided into five geographic regions: New England, the South, the Mid-Atlantic, the Midwest, and the West. Such divisions, though arbitrary, have some validity in terms of the historical experience and social values of their inhabitants, and an attempt is made in introductory passages to elucidate the differences between them. Since a geographic guide necessarily ignores chronology, the individual entries include not only the dates of birth and death (if known) of the biographee but dates that place her in historical context. A list of dates significant to women's history is supplied as an appendix.

The entries are arranged within each region by state, within a state by city or town, and within the city in alphabetical order of the name of the woman commemorated. The exceptions are memorials to a group of women, such as a hall of fame, in which case that entry leads the rest in a city. Cross-references rescue women's names who might thus be overlooked. The names given are the first, maiden, and married name; in cases of those professional women generally known by their maiden names, the married name follows in parenthesis. Pen names, chosen names of nuns, and such designations as Calamity Jane are also given in parenthesis. The initials NAW or NAWM following a name indicate that a biography appears in *Notable American Women, 1607–1950* or *Notable American Women, The Modern Period*, the standard biographical guides to American women, published by Harvard University Press in 1971 and 1980. In some cases other initials indicating honorees of a state hall of fame are also included.

The initials HABS, NR, or NHL following a site designation indicate that the building or site is included in the Historical American Buildings Survey, the National Register of Historic Places, or is designated a National Historic Landmark. A few states and cities also have landmark designations. Where sites are difficult to find, directions are included in the entry. For sites open to the public at designated times only, hours are given as accurately as possible, but these are subject to change. It is wise to inquire locally before planning a visit. Historical homes privately owned and occupied are so described. Although the owners may be receptive to requests to visit by persons with a special interest, their privacy should be respected.

Sources of information and of quotations, or suggestions for further reading about the women are given in notes following each state's entries. The notes omit references to the books and articles listed in the full bibliographies following entries in *NAW* or *NAWM*. They do not include the usual guidebooks, standard references, or general history books. They do cite recent publications, particularly articles in popular historical journals easily available to readers. The author's debt to state and local historical societies and libraries is great; all are listed, even in cases where the information supplied could not be used.

Cross-references are included in entries for women who are commemorated in more than one city, but they are referenced only within the region. Women represented in more than one region may be traced through the index.

The literature of women's history is so vast that it would be impossible to attempt any full bibliography, but the bibliographic essay at the end of the guide includes works considered the most useful keys to further study. It is hoped that the biographical vignettes in the guide will stimulate others to look more deeply into the lives of these women. Their own words are in some cases available in the form of letters, autobiographies, lectures, and essays. Biographies by others illuminate the lives, as do interpretations of significant groups, movements, and institutions in which the women were involved.

In a work of this scope and so long in writing, it is inevitable that errors will exist. In many instances it has been necessary to depend on sources such as newspaper accounts, memoirs, and articles that do not measure up to strict standards of historical accuracy, but within those limitations the material presented is as close to the truth as can be ascertained.

The author is grateful to a number of state libraries that checked lists of women and sites, and does not hold them responsible for her errors. Sylvia Zeiss read most of the copy, helped clear up some of the ambiguities, and corrected some of the mistakes. It is hoped that readers will feel free to communicate any corrections or additions that might be made.

Women Remembered

REGION I

New England

The six New England states constitute an easily defined region—geographically, historically, and psychologically. Although the 1607 Virginia settlement predated the arrival of the Plymouth colonists, New England is generally thought of as the cradle of the nation, the battleground of independence. The experiences of its first inhabitants made them self-sufficient, hardworking, thrifty, and independent—qualities that typify the New England character.

The women who came to settle New England had been taught from childhood to be submissive. Obedience to God, to authority, and to parent or husband was the first rule of behavior. Married women were governed by a strict interpretation of the biblical "Thy desire shall be to thy husband and he shall rule over thee." Such submission was not only a religious duty but a legal one. William Blackstone's statement of English common law made it clear: "By marriage, the husband and wife are one person in law; that is, the very being or legal existence of the woman is suspended during marriage."

Whatever autonomy a woman had was within the context of her duties as a wife, mother, mistress of a household, supervisor of servants, and neighbor to others in the community. She achieved satisfaction and was given praise according to how well she fulfilled these various roles. Since most women by custom had the same day-to-day routines, there was little opportunity for one to stand out as an individual, except in unusual circumstances. Captivity by Indians or triumph over disaster made her a heroine. Loss or absence of a husband forced on her a broader role, and many women entered farm management, business, or even a profession in this way.

Unmarried adult women and widows had somewhat more freedom but few options. They generally made their homes with relatives as unpaid household helpers and caretakers. A woman could teach, sew, or acquire enough medical knowledge to be a midwife. Colonial women ran small shops and a surprising number became printers.

The Revolution had its impact on women. With men joining the fighting forces, women had to take over many male duties. For perhaps the first time women were involved politically. If Loyalists, they might lose their property. If rebels, they gave up British imports. Battles often came close to their homes, and some women became heroines for the part they played in the war. It was after the war, however, when a new government was being formed, that women like Abigail Adams wondered how much independence women had won. Would girls have access to the same education their brothers had? Would women have a voice in political decisions? Would they be allowed or even encouraged to become doctors, lawyers, or ministers?

The answers were slow in coming. In 1792 an English writer, Mary Wollstonecraft, published *A Vindication of the Rights of Women*, and a few women in New England, such as Judith Sargent Murray, who had been thinking about women's rights, took heart from what was said. They began to demand access to education. As the subsistence economy gave way to commercial enterprise, a woman's domestic sphere narrowed and she needed education for the enjoyment of more leisure, if nothing else. Men then discovered that women were the educators of their children and thus ought to be given opportunities to acquire the needed intellectual training.

By 1850, when the first national women's rights convention was held in Worcester, Massachusetts, New England women had begun to broaden their horizons. They took part in discussions of abolition, or temperance or utopianism. They talked of kindergartens, social reforms, and women's rights. They wrote books and they began to publish women's newspapers. They organized women's clubs. A few became physicians, ministers, and, in time, lawyers. Most of them realized that reforms depended not on talk but on political power, and they worked for suffrage. During the Civil War their campaigns were abandoned while they gathered supplies for the army, sent nurses to army hospitals, and supplied volunteers to teach freed Negroes in the South. New England men and women established female seminaries, some the predecessors of today's great women's (now coeducational) colleges.

The establishment of textile mills in New England brought employment outside the home to many women and with it came the need to band together for something more immediate than the vote, the right to a fair wage and decent working conditions. Leadership came from within the working class itself. Women who had means and some power had little interest in the industrial strife going on under their noses until late in the nineteenth century, when Denison House, a Boston, Massachusetts, settlement house, became a meeting place for labor groups; its directors took part in the bitter textile strike in Lawrence, Massachusetts, in 1912.

The new feminism of the 1970s unexpectedly focused on the very center of New England's pride—the great women's colleges. Betty Friedan's *The Feminine Mystique* (1963) called attention to the dilemma of well-educated women for whose ability and energy society found no real use. Critics charged the colleges with channeling women's energies back into the domestic sphere from which they had once escaped. While men's colleges assumed the purpose of education was to create leadership, women's schools apparently proposed to create followers, specifically home and community servants. Instead of preparing women to meet society's needs for the best brains of both sexes, they offered training for semiskilled, short-term careers or dilettante community service. They retained "the vicious self-perpetuating circle that has kept women second-class citizens."

Under the pressure of such criticisms, the great bastions of male supremacy, the men's colleges, began to admit women, and the women's colleges to admit men. Educated women were once again encouraged to assume places in the professions, in politics, in business. New England women may retain the old-fashioned qualities of thrift, dedication to the work ethic, and decorum that one associates with the region, but they are definitely in step with the world of today.

NOTES

See Laurel T. Ulrich, *Good Wives* (New York: Alfred A. Knopf, 1982) for a full discussion of colonial New England women. Criticism of the colleges is quoted from Doris L. Pullen, "The Educational Establishment: Wasted Women," in *Voices of the New Feminism*, ed. Mary Lou Thompson (Boston, Mass.: Beacon Press, 1970).

CONNECTICUT

AVON

Riddle, Theodate Pope, 1868–1946, Architect

Avon Old Farms School

Theodate Pope Riddle was a registered architect in New York and Connecticut by 1910. Among the Connecticut buildings she designed are Hill-Stead Museum in Farmington, q.v., and the Westover School in Middlebury. She also did the restoration of the Theodore Roosevelt home in New York City. She founded and designed Avon Old Farms and regarded it as the culmination of her architectural career. No modern building methods were used in its construction, which went on between 1922 and 1927. She brought in English craftsmen who used sixteenth-century hand tools, and she insisted that only unskilled and nonunion laborers who could be taught to use such tools be hired for the work force. Her educational ideas were equally individualistic; the school was a protest against conventional education. The graduates of boys' schools she had met she believed to be without strength of character, yet because of their wealth or social standing they would grow up to occupy positions needing real ability and stamina. Avon was designed to give boys backbone. It was not until after the founder's death that administrators were free to relax some of her overly rigid rules. The school still gives boys what is needed.[1]

BERLIN

Willard, Emma Hart, 1787–1870, and Her Sister Almira Hart Lincoln Phelps, 1793–1884, Educators; NAW

Marker, Lower Lane and Norton Road. Emma Hart Willard School, 1088 Norton Road

Emma Hart Willard and Almira Hart Lincoln Phelps were two of seventeen children in the family of Samuel Hart, whose farm was in this vicinity. Wool from sheep raised on the farm was divided into three parts: the best for the father, the next best for the men, and the poorest third for the women. The father, however, did not always treat his daughters with the scorn this tradition indicated. He recognized that they had brains; he discussed his liberal views of politics and religion with them; he allowed them to attend Berlin Academy and even to teach classes at home.

Emma married, at twenty-two, John Willard, of Middlebury, Vermont, q.v. He was a widower with four children and he, too, believed in educating girls. With his encouragement, Emma opened a school in her home, emphasizing subjects like science and mathematics. She appealed to the legislature of New York State for funds to open a girls' academy. Although they turned her down, she went to the state anyway and opened in 1821 the pioneer Troy Female Seminary. She educated hundreds of young women for homemaking and teaching before she retired in 1838. She is honored by inclusion in the Hall of Fame in New York City.

Almira, youngest of the Harts, also became a distinguished teacher and the author of books on botany and chemistry. She was married twice: to Simeon Lincoln, a Hartford, Connecticut, newspaper editor; and to John Phelps, a lawyer of Guilford, Vermont. The latter joined her in running a school in Ellicott's Mills, Maryland, offering to southern women courses of collegiate quality. Almira and her sister both opposed votes for women, and for some time Almira was an officer of the Woman's Anti-Suffrage Association. Her science textbooks led to her election to the American Association for the Advancement of Science in 1859 at a time when only one other woman—Maria Mitchell of Nantucket, Massachusetts—belonged to that august body.

No one knows the exact location of the house in which these two famous women were born. The stone marker was placed at the approximate site in 1913 by the Emma Hart Willard Chapter of the Daughters of the American Revolution.[2]

BLOOMFIELD

Smith, Virginia Thrall, 1836–1903, Social Worker; NAW

Plaque, First Congregational Church, 10 Wintonbury Avenue

The memorial plaque, in the hall outside the minister's study, was placed in the church by Virginia Thrall Smith's sons. It reads: "She consecrated her life to the cause of the poor, and led the way toward bringing happiness to homeless and crippled children." Smith was born and grew up in Bloomfield. Moving to Hartford, Connecticut, after her marriage, she established the Hartford City Mission Association, which developed into the Children's Aid Society (see Newington, CT).[3]

BRISTOL

Gaylord, Katherine Cole, 1745–1840, Pioneer Heroine

Monument, Federal Hill Green

Katherine Cole Gaylord was widowed when her husband, Aaron Gaylord, was scalped and murdered by Indians in the Wyoming Massacre of July 3, 1778. The family had only two years earlier left their Connecticut home to join other New Englanders in the fertile northern Pennsylvania valley. While many of the men were away in the Revolutionary forces, the settlers were attacked by the British and then most of the survivors were murdered by Indians. On learning of her husband's death, Gaylord saddled a horse, loaded another with provisions, and set off in the dark of night with three children to make her way to her father's home in Bristol. Many weeks later the ragged little group trudged into the familiar streets of home. The indomitable Gaylord joked, before bursting into tears, "Well, we are the worst looking lot you ever saw." The symbol of motherly heroism, she lived to be ninety-five and saw the arrival of twenty-two grandchildren. In 1895 the Daughters of the American Revolution chapter that took her name erected the monument to her.[4]

CANTERBURY

Crandall, Prudence (Philleo), 1803–1890, Abolitionist Educator; NAW

Prudence Crandall House, Junction of State Routes 14 and 169; HABS, NR

In 1832 Prudence Crandall opened a school for the daughters of substantial citizens of Canterbury. She accepted, among others, Sarah Harris, daughter of a respectable black farmer. When other parents objected to having their children in a school with a black girl, Crandall closed the school, then opened it again for Negro girls only, soliciting pupils from Boston, Massachusetts, Providence, Rhode Island, and New York State. Most of the friends of black people in town favored colonization in other countries, not equal treatment in Connecticut, and Crandall at once found herself in trouble. Merchants would not sell her food. Vandals threw manure into her well. Townspeople insulted her pupils. The legislature passed a law barring persons of color from outside the state from attending Connecticut schools, and Crandall was jailed for breaking the law. In spite of support from the Unitarian minister and from William Lloyd Garrison's abolitionist paper, Crandall was forced out after neighbors attacked the house, breaking windows and almost battering it to pieces with blocks of wood. Crandall married Calvin Philleo and they moved to Illinois. Fifty years later the state voted her a small pension in recompense for damages. Sarah Harris, later Fayerweather, remained a lifelong friend (see Kingston, RI). The site of Crandall's school has been restored. Operated by the Connecticut Historical Commission, it is open Jan. 15–Dec. 15, Wed.-Sun. 10–4:30; adm. See Hope Valley, RI.[5]

ENFIELD

Abbe, Penelope Terry, 1729–1818, Midwife

Memorial Bench, Old Cemetery, Enfield Street

Penelope Terry Abbe studied medicine with her father, Enfield's first physician, and went on to practice for thirty-three years. Present at the birth of 1,389 children, she heard the first angry bellowing of a couple of generations of Enfield inhabitants. She also bore eleven children of her own and left many descendants, some still living in Enfield. The local Daughters of the American Revolution chapter took Abbe's name. Her husband, Thomas Abbe (or Abbey), a soldier in the French and Indian wars and a captain in the Revolution, is memorialized by a statue on the green facing the old town hall. It is the work of Sherry Edmundson Fry (b. 1879), a sculptor from Iowa who had a studio in Kent, Connecticut. Her works are found in several cities of the United States.[6]

FARMINGTON

Porter, Sarah, 1813–1900, Educator; NAW

Miss Porter's School, Main Street and Mountain Road; NR

Many of the notable women of the late nineteenth and twentieth centuries began their education at Miss Porter's School, and it is still graduating New England girls imbued with Sarah Porter's love of learning and zest for life. Born in the family homestead on Main Street, Porter was the daughter of a Yale-educated minister who encouraged her studies. She was the first girl to attend Farmington Academy, where she received the same instruction as her brothers. In 1843, after teaching at the academy, she started her own school, and to it she devoted the rest of her life. Students were offered instruction in Latin, French, German, chemistry, natural philosophy, mathematics, and music, all taught in a noncompetitive atmosphere. Her pupils were offered concerts by leading musicians and lectures by outstanding men. Porter loved Farmington and twice saved its tree-shaded central streets from being invaded by railroad tracks and trolley wires. The area around the school is part of Farmington Historic District.[7]

Riddle, Theodate Pope, 1868–1946, Architect

Hill-Stead Museum, 671 Farmington Avenue

Theodate Pope Riddle, daughter of a wealthy Cleveland, Ohio, family, was sent to Miss Porter's School, and after graduation she was allowed to return to

Farmington, where she purchased a cottage and forty-two acres. Here she ran a little tea room, "The Gundy," next to her house, and a shop, "Odds and Ends," patronized by Miss Porter's pupils. The profits went to support a visiting nurse for the community. Some years later, Riddle persuaded her parents, Alfred Atmore and Ada Brooks Pope, to build Hill-Stead to house their growing collection of fine Impressionist paintings. She helped design the house, which resembles Mount Vernon, and it was built to her designs by McKim, Mead, and White. She continued to study architecture and to design other buildings (see Avon, CT). After 1920, both her parents having died, she and her husband, diplomat John W. Riddle, lived in Hill-Stead. It was opened to the public in 1947 in accordance with her will. The museum has a wealth of paintings, including works by Degas, Manet, Monet, Matisse, Whistler, Durer, and Cassatt. It is open Wed.-Sun. 2–5; closed holidays and Jan. 15–Feb. 15; adm.[8]

GLASTONBURY

Smith, Hannah Hadassah Hickock, 1767–1810, and Her Daughters Julia Evelina Smith, 1792–1886, and Abby Hadassah Smith, 1797–1878, Women's Rights Advocates; NAW (under Abby Smith)

Kimberly Mansion, 1625 Main Street (Private); NHL

Hannah Hadassah Hickock Smith, a student of French, Latin, and Italian, wrote one of the first antislavery petitions sent to Congress. It was signed by forty women of Glastonbury and presented to Congress by Abigail Adams's son, former president John Quincy Adams. Smith's five daughters were all advanced thinkers.

Julia and Abby, the youngest, were already elderly when they made their historic strike for women's rights. They refused payment of taxes on their farm because, as women, they had no voice in levying the taxes nor in spending them. Their cows were seized and sold by the sheriff, as was part of the farm, and a lengthy court case ensued. The story was recounted by Julia with spirit and humor in *Abby Smith and Her Cows, With A Report of the Law Case Decided Contrary to Law* (1877). Widely circulated, the book focused attention, as no suffrage tract could, on the inequity of women's status. Abby became a favorite speaker for suffrage. Julia had translated the Bible from original languages and published it at her own expense in 1876 as an example of what women could do. In existence are twelve volumes of a diary kept by Hannah and fifteen volumes of one kept by Julia, hers in French. When Julia was eighty-seven, she married an elderly judge, Amos Parker. At ninety-one, she addressed the state woman's suffrage association.

HARTFORD

Auerbach, Beatrice Fox, 1887–1968, Businesswoman; NAWM

A.S.K. House, 1040 Prospect Avenue

Beatrice Fox Auerbach succeeded her father in 1938 as president of Hartford's leading department store, G. Fox & Company. Employees were soon put on a five-day week, something that raised eyebrows in the merchandising world. They also enjoyed paid medical care, participated in retirement plans, ate in nonprofit lunchrooms, and when things got tough could apply for loans. As a result of enlightened employee relations and innovative merchandising methods, G. Fox became one of the largest department stores in the country. Auerbach sponsored a program at Connecticut State College that trained women for management positions in retailing, and black women had a part in it.

Her interests were not confined to business. The Beatrice Fox Auerbach Foundation trained women in community and international affairs and its Service Bureau for Women's Organizations served as a clearinghouse for the civic concerns of women of the state. Her home was donated to the University of Hartford; it is used for offices and for many seminars and meetings. The *A* in A.S.K. stands for Auerbach, *S* and *K* for the names of her two married daughters.[9]

Beecher, Catharine. See Stowe, Harriet

Cogswell, Alice, 1805–1830, Deaf Pupil

Gallaudet Statue, Gallaudet Square

Young Alice Cogswell was totally deaf, with little hope for an education. No school existed in the Western Hemisphere for teaching the deaf, and no studies were known of methods that might be used. Thomas Hopkins Gallaudet, a graduate of Andover Theological Seminary, tried to teach the child the names of objects, and recognizing her intelligent effort to learn, urged her father, Mason Cogswell, to give her some education. Cogswell and some of his friends raised money to send Gallaudet abroad to study institutions and methods of educating the deaf. When he returned they opened, in 1817, the first free American school for the deaf. Alice was its first pupil.

The statue, showing Gallaudet's hands holding the young woman, was commissioned by the National Association for the Deaf, executed by Frances Wadsworth, and dedicated in 1953. It is near the Hartford Insurance Company Headquarters, where the school was situated from 1821 to 1921. The school has moved to West Hartford, Connecticut, q.v.[10]

Day, Katharine Seymour, 1870–1964, Artist and Civic Reformer

Katharine S. Day House, 77 Forest Street; NR

Katharine Seymour Day was the granddaughter of Isabella Beecher Hooker of Hartford, q.v. To be a Beecher, the family that included the great Calvinist minister Lyman Beecher, the silver-tongued Brooklyn pastor Henry Ward Beecher, as well as famed author Harriet Beecher Stowe and educator Catharine Beecher, was a formidable inheritance. Day managed to uphold the tradition of her family as artist, civic reformer, and philanthropist. She studied painting in New York City with William Merrit Chase and spent time working in studios in Paris, France. In her fifties she moved to Nook Farm to study the records of the charmed circle of writers and reformers who had lived here. At her death she left her extensive collection of books and manuscripts to the Stowe-Day Foundation, which she endowed. It was chartered by the state in 1941 as the Stowe, Beecher, Hooker, Seymour, Day Memorial Library and Historical Foundation. The foundation owns not only the Day House, containing the library and offices, but the restored Harriet Beecher Stowe House. The library, a treasure trove of Victorian literary, social, and architectural history, is open to any serious student Mon.-Fri. 9–4:30. Among its unexpected treasures are paintings by Harriet Beecher Stowe.[11]

Hewins, Caroline Maria, 1846–1926, Librarian; NAW

Caroline Maria Hewins Collection, Hartford Public Library, 500 Main Street

Caroline Maria Hewins, librarian of a private library at the Young Men's Institute—which later became the Hartford Public Library—dared to invite boys and girls to use the books hitherto reserved for adult readers. She read to children, talked to them, and took them on field trips. She compiled lists of books for children, an innovation in the library field. In 1895 she began a small branch library specifically for children in the Hartford Social Settlement, where she lived for twelve years. To honor her as the principal founder of library work with children in America the Caroline M. Hewins Lectureship was established by the editor of *Publishers Weekly*. Some of her friends started a scholarship in her name for students planning to enter this phase of library work.

The collection named for her consists of foreign children's books. A large collection of Hewins' own materials, more than 3,650 books and pamphlets and 1,000 children's periodicals, is at the Connecticut Historical Society, 1 Elizabeth Street.[12]

Hooker, Isabella Beecher, 1822–1907, Suffragist; NAW

Nook Farm, Farmington Avenue and Forest Street

Isabella Beecher Hooker, half sister of Catharine and Harriet Beecher (later Stowe), married John Hooker and in the 1850s the couple and another family bought a hundred acres of woodland outside of Hartford. They built homes for themselves and sold sites to friends and relatives, including the Stowes, Charles Dudley Warner, and later Mark Twain. Nook Farm became the center of literary and intellectual activity. Hooker, won over to the woman's suffrage movement by reading John Stuart Mill's *The Subjection of Women*, was one of the founders of the New England Woman's Suffrage Association. She recognized, however, that women's attitudes must change before they were worthy of voting or holding office. "I am persuaded," she wrote, "that women are quite as much responsible for the present condition of affairs as men, and that they . . . will be the last to be convinced of their duty in the matter of good citizenship." The house once occupied by the Hookers is now an apartment house.[13]

Sigourney, Lydia Howard Huntley, 1791–1865, Poet; NAW

Tablet, Christ Church, 45 Church Street. Sigourney Street

Lydia Howard Huntley Sigourney was called the sweet singer of Hartford, and for years she poured forth a flood of poems, sketches, and biographies eagerly bought by the periodicals of the day. Few of them outlasted their early publication. Their themes were historical, moral, and religious, stressing piety and duty. She was one of the first American women to make a successful career of writing. The tablet, on the north wall of the church, quotes the Bible—"She openeth her mouth with wisdom and in her tongue was the law of kindness"—and a laudatory verse by John Greenleaf Whittier.[14]

Stowe, Harriet Beecher, 1811–1896, Abolitionist Author; NAW

Harriet Beecher Stowe House, 73 Forest Street; NR

Harriet Beecher Stowe's *Uncle Tom's Cabin* is a sentimental novel that can still bring tears to the eyes of its readers. When published in 1852, it was a sensation. The book's story of cruelty, suffering, and privation and its wholesale condemnation of southern civilization won thousands to the cause of abolition. During the Civil War, when President Abraham Lincoln met Stowe, he reportedly said, "So this is the little lady that made this big war." By the time Stowe moved to Nook Farm, next door to Mark Twain, she was an established and wealthy writer. Here in the congenial atmosphere of culture, affluence, and good living, she spent much of the last quarter of her life.

For a few years in the late 1860s and early 1870s Stowe's sister Catharine

Beecher (1800–1878) lived with the Stowes in Hartford. The two women collaborated on *The American Woman's Home*. It is interesting that of the four Beecher sisters only Catharine, the one who believed a woman's place was in the home or in school teaching family values, never married or had a home of her own. When she wrote that "heaven has appointed to one sex the superior, and to the other subordinate station," there was no doubt in her mind which sex was subordinate. Catharine's claim to fame was in the many schools for women she established, including the Hartford Female Seminary. She wrote twenty-five books and many articles expounding her views on women and their role.

The Stowe House is open June 1–Aug. 31, daily 10–4:30; Sept. 1–May 31, Tues.-Sat. 9:30–4, Sun. 1–4; closed some holidays; adm. See Litchfield, CT, and Brunswick, ME.[15]

LITCHFIELD

Pierce, Sarah, 1767–1852, Educator; NAW

Plaque at Site of Academy, North Street

Sarah Pierce opened in 1792 what is considered the first institution in America for the higher education of women. Later known as the Litchfield Female Seminary, it was for over sixty years a leader in women's education. Pierce wrote *Sketches of Universal History* to liven up the teaching of her favorite subject. The famous Beechers, Catharine and Harriet, were pupils here.[16]

Stowe, Harriet Beecher, 1811–1896, Abolitionist, Author; NAW

Signpost on Lawn, North and Prospect Street

When Harriet Beecher Stowe was born here, the seventh child of minister Lyman Beecher, her life seemed preordained: she would get as much education as was good for a woman, perhaps teach school, become a wife, and mother sturdy children to carry on the Beecher tradition. She was certainly not to write an inflammatory novel like *Uncle Tom's Cabin* that would stir irrepressible emotions in her fellow citizens, help propel them into a civil war, and in the end emancipate the slaves. She attended Sarah Pierce's seminary, then taught in her sister Catharine's Western Female Institute in Cincinnati, Ohio. She married Calvin Stowe, and when they left Ohio to return to New England (see Brunswick, ME), she had six children. But she had found time to write. Calvin said, when she worried about combining a literary career with maternal duties, "God has written it in His book that you must be a literary woman, and who are we that we should contend against God?" On the village green in Litchfield is a boulder with a bas-relief of Stowe and of her brother Henry Ward Beecher. See Hartford, CT.

NEW HAVEN

Ilg, Frances Lillian, 1902–1981, Child Behaviorist

Gesell Institute of Child Development

Frances Lillian Ilg (M.D. 1929, Cornell Medical School) was in 1932 made visiting pediatrician at the Clinic of Child Development at Yale University, headed by Arnold Gesell. From that time Ilg was concerned less with pathology than with normal child development. The clinic was the leading laboratory in the nation for the study of infant behavior. From facts gathered by close observation of children at work, play, meals, and asleep, Gesell and Ilg and their associates settled on theories that have had a profound impact on the way children are brought up today. Gesell retired in 1950, and Ilg, with Louise Bates Ames, founded the Gesell Institute of Child Development. They began a newspaper column answering questions from worried mothers, and they followed this up with helpful books on children in different age groups.[17]

Troup, Augusta Lewis, c. 1848–1920, Labor Leader; NAW

Augusta Lewis Troup Junior High School, 259 Edgewood Avenue

Both Augusta Lewis Troup and her husband, Alexander Troup, publisher of the prolabor *New Haven Union*, had been active before their marriage in the labor movement in New York City. She had supported herself for some years by newspaper work and then by typesetting. Becoming aware of the job discrimination and inequality of pay suffered by women of her craft, she organized women typesetters in 1868 and was president of the Women's Typographical Union No. 1. Later the (men's) Typographical Union voted to admit women and in 1870 elected her corresponding secretary. She was the first woman elected to a national union office. After her marriage, she settled in New Haven, had a large family, and supported woman's suffrage and local causes, especially in the Italian community. A tablet in the school's hallway commemorates her as the "Little Mother of the Italian Colony."[18]

NEW LONDON

Blunt, Katharine, 1876–1954, College President; NAWM

Katharine Blunt House, Connecticut College

While marching in a suffrage parade down Fifth Avenue, Katharine Blunt and Marion Parker Whitney began a friendship that lasted for many years. As a member of the committee to select a new president for Connecticut College in 1929, Whitney proposed her friend's name. Blunt was then an established nutrition expert and professor of home economics at the University of Chicago.

The third president and first woman president of Connecticut College, she served until 1943 and was recalled for 1945–46. In her inaugural address she expressed the hope that women should not merely look on at the world but shape it. Her aim was to destroy the ivory tower and to so motivate graduates that their desire for public service would not "evaporate into vague benevolence, but develop into well-considered action." The residence hall named for her and informally called KB was dedicated in 1946.[19]

Branch, Anna Hempstead, 1875–1937, Poet; NAW

Hempsted House, 11 Hempstead Street; NR

Anna Hempstead Branch was born here in the house that had been in her mother's family for ten generations. She grew up, however, in New York City, returning to New London for the summers. Her mother, Mary Lydia Branch (1840–1922) was a writer of verse and children's books. Anna was a poet and a friend of the leading poets of her day. She has been called a minor Christina Rossetti and is said to have had a pre-Raphaelite beauty. At Christadora House, a settlement house in New York City's lower east side, she organized some of her literary friends into a poets' guild, which for some years brought to the young people of the settlement classes in literature, drama, and art. After her father's death in 1909 Anna and her mother remained in New London, although she kept her ties with Christadora House all her life. She pioneered playgrounds in New London. The house is open May 15–Oct. 15, Tues.-Sun. 1–5; adm.[20]

Hamilton, Edith, 1867–1963, Scholar, and Her Sister Alice Hamilton, 1869–1970, Toxicologist; NAWM

Edith and Alice Hamilton Dormitory, Connecticut College

Working in widely different fields, Edith and Alice Hamilton left the world considerably better and richer than they found it. They grew up in their family's home in Fort Wayne, Indiana, and were taught at home. Both came to Connecticut to attend Miss Porter's School in Farmington, which their aunts had attended before them, and both went abroad (after Edith earned an M.A. at Bryn Mawr College in Pennsylvania and Alice an M.D. at the University of Michigan) for further study. From that point they pursued separate careers, each remaining the other's firm admirer.

Edith taught school for some years, then turned to writing. Her two books, *The Greek Way* and *The Roman Way*, brought the spirit of the past to thousands of readers and belong in every well-chosen library. They were selected by the Book of the Month Club as a summer dividend in 1957, although they had been published a quarter of a century earlier. That was Edith's year for honors. She appeared on national television; she was elected to the American Academy of

Arts and Letters; and, most heartwarming to her, she was made an honorary citizen of Athens, Greece.

Alice joined Jane Addams as a resident of Hull House in Chicago, Illinois, where she remained for over two decades while pursuing a career in science. After years of trying to reconcile the overwhelming problems of Chicago's poor through medical research, it began to seem "remote and useless." Reading *Dangerous Trades*, a book by an English author on industrial poisons, she found that there was almost complete ignorance in America of the dangers to which industrial workers were exposed and that there were no laws to protect the workers' health and no workmen's compensation to help the family when the wage earner became incapacitated. She began an investigation of American factories where bathtubs were enameled, storage batteries made, and ink manufactured. Her discoveries of lead poisoning and other effects on the body suffered by workers in such plants led to the adoption of laws protecting workers from toxic gases, fumes, and dust. In 1919 she became the first woman on the faculty of Harvard University, where she taught medicine associated with industrial diseases. When she was ninety, the School of Health established a fund in her name. She is in the National Women's Hall of Fame.

Alice lived in a stately old house in Hadlyme, on the Connecticut River. She spent her years of retirement there, although she continued her studies and was also active in working for human rights, world peace, and justice. Edith, too, established a New England residence—a summer home on Mount Desert Island. Connecticut College honored the two by naming the dormitory for them in 1962.[21]

NEWINGTON

Smith, Virginia Thrall, 1836–1903, Social Worker; NAW

Newington Children's Hospital, 181 E. Cedar Street

Virginia Thrall Smith was appointed in 1882 to the Connecticut State Board of Charities. When she visited local almshouses, she was horrified to find twenty-five hundred handicapped children housed with the senile, the mentally ill, and the criminally insane. Many physically handicapped individuals were considered also retarded and families had no place for them. Doubting her report of conditions, officials investigated and found not twenty-five hundred but twice as many unwanted children lodged in poorhouses. In May 1883 they passed a law establishing temporary county homes for them. A few years later local authorities accused Smith of "baby-farming"—because she was placing children in adoptive homes—and of making Hartford a dumping ground for out-of-state paupers. They forced her resignation. Friends who defended her helped form the Connecticut Children's Aid Society, with Smith as director, and raised funds for a home for handicapped children. The first home, established in Newington in 1898, had room for only ten children, but it was the small beginning of the Children's Hospital, which has achieved national recognition for its medical, surgical, and rehabilitative care for those with handicapping disorders. See Bloomfield, CT.[22]

NORWALK

Rudkin, Margaret, 1897–1967, Businesswoman; NAWM

Pepperidge Farm, Inc.

Margaret Rudkin began to bake bread because her asthmatic son needed a special diet. Soon she was supplying the bread to other of his doctor's patients, then sending loaves to market. People who moved away from the neighborhood had her send them bread by mail. She built up a great bakery on the premise that some people prefer bread that is not "homogenized, fortified, energized, vitaminized, or atomized" and are willing to pay for it. Furthermore, her bread was definitely touched by human hands: 90 percent of her employees were women, many of them dough kneaders. She began the business at her home in Fairfield, using her own kitchen, then the converted stables and garage. In 1963 she published her *Margaret Rudkin Pepperidge Farm Cookbook.*[23]

NORWICH

Caulkins, Frances Manwaring, 1795–1869, Historian; NAW

Marker, Village Green

Frances Manwaring Caulkins, a native of New London, Connecticut, is honored as a careful historian. She wrote the *History of the Town of Norwich* (1845) and the *History of New London* (1852), both classics of local history based on original town records. She was the first woman, and the only one for many years, to be elected to the renowned Massachusetts Historical Society (in 1849). The New London County Historical Society owns a large collection of her literary and historical manuscripts.

OLD LYME

Griswold, Florence, 1850–1937, Artist and Art Patron

Florence Griswold Museum, 96 Lyme Street

Florence Griswold, descendant of two Connecticut governors, was called the patron saint of the artist colony. The last of her family, she began taking artists as boarders in her stately home in 1900. One artist said he came to "Miss Florence's" because she served four different vegetables at her table. In general, they were attracted by her keen encouragement of the arts and the stimulation of being with fellow artists. Many of the prominent boarders left souvenirs behind them on doors and walls: Childe Hassam painted bathing nudes; Henry W. Ranger did moonlit scenes; Will E. Howe, cattle; and Henry W. Poore, a hunting scene. The pioneer art colony was enlivened with evening musicales, picnics, improvised games, and theatrical performances. Annual exhibits were held to which art lovers thronged. In 1936 Griswold's friends purchased the house, cared for her until the end of her life, and then established a museum. Today the house is headquarters of the Lyme Historical Society. It is open June 1–Labor Day, Tues.-Sat. 10–5, Sun. 1–5; Sept.-May, Wed.-Sun. 1–5; adm.[24]

OLD SAYBROOK

Fenwick, Lady Alice Apsley Boteler, d. c. 1646, Gardener

Monument, Cypress Cemetery, Main Street (Route 154)

Lady Alice Apsley Boteler Fenwick, the wife of Colonel George Fenwick (and relict of Sir John Boteler Fenwick), came to Saybrook in 1639 from England. Her home was within the grim walls of Saybrook Fort, of which George was governor, but she brightened it with roses, daffodils, poppies, and herbs brought from home. A contemporary has left a charming word picture of ''Merry Lady Alice . . . most often seen amidst her flowers singing blithely old madrigals.'' After seven years of life in the wilderness, she died in childbirth. Her tombstone, probably the oldest monument to a female in the state (erected about 1679) was first on Tomb Hill in the old fort but in 1870 was removed to the cemetery. Professor Samuel Hart called her death ''the romantic event in the history of the town. For long years there was something touching in the sight of the massive tombstone standing alone in the field on the spot where the first settlers lived.''[25]

WATERFORD

Harkness, Mary Stillman, 1874–1950, Philanthropist; NAW

Harkness Memorial State Park, Goshen Point

Mary Stillman Harkness was financially independent when she married Edward Harkness, son of a wealthy Standard Oil investor, and during a marriage of thirty-five years the couple gave away millions of dollars. The park consists of their summer estate at Waterford. Many of Harkness's gifts went to Connecticut institutions, including Connecticut College, the Marine Historical Association of Mystic, and Yale University. The memorial park comprises 231 acres, half devoted to a rehabilitation center for the handicapped, and the mansion, which displays life-size watercolor paintings of birds by Rex Brasher. The grounds are open daily. The mansion is open May 29–Labor Day, daily 10–5; adm.

WEST HARTFORD

Cogswell, Alice, 1805–1830, Deaf Pupil

Gallaudet Statue, American School for the Deaf, 139 Main Street

The statue of Thomas Hopkins Gallaudet and his first deaf-mute pupil, Alice Cogswell of Hartford, Connecticut, q. v., is a replica of the Daniel Chester French sculpture which stands in front of Gallaudet College in Washington, D.C. The duplicate was contributed to the American School in 1925.[26]

WINDSOR

Longman, Evelyn Beatrice (Batchelder), 1874–1954, Sculptor

Founders Monument, Palisado Green, Palisado Avenue

Evelyn Beatrice Longman, who also sculptured the Spanish War Memorial in Hartford, Connecticut, studied at the Chicago Art Institute and with Daniel Chester French. She is represented in the Metropolitan Museum of Art by a bronze figure of a man in classical dress entitled *Victory*. A small replica was chosen to be awarded for athletic competence by the Atlantic Fleet of the U.S. Navy. Also among her works are bronze doors at the U.S. Naval Academy and at Wellesley College and the Allison monument in Des Moines, Iowa. She was married to Nathaniel H. Batchelder, headmaster at Loomis School. The Founders Monument lists settlers who arrived in 1630 on the *Mary and John*.[27]

NOTES

In addition to the sources cited below, the following have supplied information: Department of Commerce, State of Connecticut; Connecticut State Department of Education; Clara N. Hamernick, Town Clerk, Burlington; Farmington Town Clerk; City of Bristol; Congregational Church of Brookfield; Milford Historical Society; Old Lyme–Phoebe Griffin Noyes Library Association; the Canton Public Library, Collinsville; Jackson F. Eno, Hartford National Bank and Trust Company; and Harkness Memorial State Park.

1. Brooks Emeny, *Theodate Pope Riddle* (Middlebury, Ct.: Avon Old Farms School, 1977); correspondence, Avon Old Farms School and Westover School, Middlebury.

2. Florence Crofut, *Guide to the History and the Historic Sites of Connecticut* (New Haven, Ct.: Yale University Press, 1937); correspondence, Berlin Free Library Association.

3. Correspondence, First Congregational Church, Bloomfield.

4. Crofut, *Guide*; George R. Perry, "Builders of Bristol: Katherine C. Gaylord," *Bristol Press*, Apr. 23, 1975; Mary P. Root, *Chapter Sketches, Connecticut, Daughters of the American Revolution* (n.p.: Judd, 1901); correspondence, Public Library of Bristol.

5. Crofut, *Guide*; correspondence, Connecticut Historical Commission, Hartford.

6. *Memorial of Captain Thomas Abbey* (East Orange, N.J.: Abbey Printshop, n.d.); correspondence, Enfield Central Library.

7. Crofut, *Guide*; John N. Pearce, ''Miss Porter's Houses: A School Preserves Its Surroundings,'' *Historic Preservation* 23 (Oct.-Dec. 1971).

8. Brooks Emeny, op. cit.; Nancy La Roche, ''The Hill-Stead Museum: A Victory for the Muses,'' *Artnews* 74 (Dec. 1975).

9. Correspondence, Mortensen Library, University of Hartford.

10. Marion Hepburn Grant, *In and About Hartford: Tours And Tales* (Hartford, Ct.: Connecticut Historical Society, 1978); Donald F. Moores, *Educating the Deaf* (Boston, Mass.: Houghton Mifflin Co., 1978).

11. David McCullough, ''The Unexpected Mrs. Stowe,'' *American Heritage* 24 (Aug. 1973); correspondence, Connecticut Historical Society and Stowe-Day Foundation.

12. Correspondence, Connecticut Historical Society.

13. Isabella Beecher Hooker, *A Mother's Letter to a Daughter on Woman Suffrage* (Hartford, Ct.: Press of Cas Lockwood & Brainard, 1870); Olympia Brown, *Acquaintances Old and New, Among Reformers* (Milwaukee, Wis.: S. E. Tate Printing Co., 1911); Milton Rugoff, *The Beechers: An American Family in the Nineteenth Century* (New York: Harper & Row, 1981).

14. *Contributions to the History of Christ Church* (Hartford, Ct.: Belknap & Warfield, 1895); correspondence, Connecticut Historical Society.

15. Milton Rugoff, op. cit.

16. Crofut, *Guide*; see *The Americas* 29 (June-July 1977).

17. *Current Biography*, 1956.

18. Barbara Mayer Wertheimer, *We Were There: The Story of Working Women in America* (New York: Pantheon Books, 1977).

19. *Connecticut Teacher* 14 (March 1947); *New York Times*, July 30, 1954; correspondence, Connecticut College Library.

20. *Twentieth Century Authors*, ed. Stanley Kunitz and Howard Haycroft (New York: H. W. Wilson Co., 1924); Christina Tree, *How New England Happened* (Boston, Mass.: Little, Brown & Co., 1976); correspondence, Hempsted House and New London County Historical Society.

21. Madeleine P. Grant, *Alice Hamilton, Pioneer Doctor in Industrial Medicine* (London: Abelard-Schuman, 1967).

22. Correspondence, Newington Children's Hospital.

23. John Bainbridge, ''Striking a Blow for Grandma,'' *New Yorker*, May 22, 1948; correspondence, Pepperidge Farm, Inc.

24. John J. Tarrant, ''Florence Griswold, Old Lyme, and the Impressionists,'' *Smithsonian* 12 (Jan. 1982); Lyme Historical Society, ''Florence Griswold House'' (brochure).

25. Crofut, *Guide*; Andrew Kull, *New England Cemeteries: A Collector's Guide* (Brattleboro, Vt.: Stephen Greene Press, 1975).

26. Correspondence and clippings, American School.

27. *New York Times*, Mar. 11, 1954.

MAINE

ANDOVER

Locket, Molly, d. 1816, Midwife

Marker, Andover Cemetery

Molly Locket, the wife of the Pequawket chief Sabattus, served the settlers in Andover as a midwife. The Ladies Aid Society of Andover remembered her after her death with a gravestone inscribed: ''Mollocket baptised Mary Agatha, Catholic, died in the Christian Faith, August 2, A.D. 1816. The Last of the Pequakets.''

BRISTOL

Carson, Rachel, 1907–1964, Ecologist; NAWM

Rachel Carson Salt Pond Preserve, Route 32 at New Harbor

Rachel Carson's book *Silent Spring* is a landmark in the development of America's ecological consciousness. She predicted an environmental disaster, endangering not only bird species but man himself, unless the indiscriminate use of herbicides and pesticides throughout the world was halted. When the book was published in 1962 it caused a furor. Farmers and chemical supply firms disputed her conclusions, but the scientific community, on the whole, agreed with her. The book led to governmental control of the poisons.

Carson had worked as an aquatic biologist for the U.S. Bureau of Fisheries (later the Fish and Wildlife Service), and her first books grew out of her work there and her summer studies at Woods Hole, Massachusetts. Those books gave her enough income to leave her job and move from Washington, D.C., to a cottage at West Southport, Maine. She helped to found the Maine Chapter of the Nature Conservancy and was its honorary president until her death. She left a fund to be divided between the Sierra Club and the conservancy to buy coastal properties, preferably in Maine. The conservancy has decided that all such property touching salt water shall be called the Rachel Carson Seacoast. In 1966 it acquired the salt ponds where she had studied the tide pools and in 1970 it placed a plaque honoring her at the beginning of the trail into the preserve. It is open to visitors, who are warned that the pond is a natural area and must be treated with care.[1]

BRUNSWICK

Stowe, Harriet Beecher, 1811–1896, Author; NAW

Harriet Beecher Stowe House, 63 Federal Street; NHL

During her short residence in Brunswick (1850–52), Harriet Beecher Stowe wrote *Uncle Tom's Cabin*, the book that brought her fame and fortune. Her husband, Calvin Stowe, taught at nearby Bowdoin College. For the first years of their marriage they had lived in Cincinnati, Ohio, where Stowe began to write, finding that it was far more congenial to put together a story than to care for babies and do the housekeeping. What she earned went toward the salary of a maid to do the household chores. She arrived in Brunswick with six children and ready to bear a seventh. About this time she described herself in a letter: "I am a little bit of a woman,—somewhat more than forty, about as thin and dry as a pinch of snuff; never very much to look at in my best days, and looking like a used-up article now."[2]

The Brunswick house was an inn before she lived here and is one again, named Harriet's Place. It is open daily. Some of her furnishings can be seen in her former study. A pew at the First Parish Congregational Church, where Calvin preached, bears her name. Stowe is in the Hall of Fame in New York City. See Hartford and Litchfield, CT.

CAMDEN

Millay, Edna St. Vincent, 1892–1950, Poet; NAW

Monument, Camden Hills State Park

Edna St. Vincent Millay grew up in Camden and began writing here the lyrics that were to bring her fame. The monument is placed at the spot overlooking the seacoast view which inspired lines in *Renascence*, a poem written in 1911. The bronze plaque quotes its opening lines. A room at the Whitehall Inn (where she first read the poem to friends) is dedicated to Millay.

DOVER-FOXCROFT

Stevens, Lillian Ames, 1844–1914, Temperance Worker; NAW

Marker, Lawn of House at 191 South Street (Private)

Lillian Ames Stevens, who became national president of the Woman's Christian Temperance Union (WCTU) and vice president of the world WCTU, was born in Dover and lived here until her marriage to Michael Stevens, when she moved to Portland, Maine, q. v. She followed Frances E. Willard into the WCTU presidency after that great leader died in 1898. Under Stevens' aggressive leadership the organization built up a large membership and endorsed progressive measures that had little to do with liquor control, including the federal Pure Food and Drug Act of 1906 and the Mann Act of 1910.

ELLSWORTH

Stanwood, Cordelia, 1865–1958, Ornithologist

Stanwood Homestead (Birdsacre Sanctuary), State 3; NR

Cordelia Stanwood found life and health in the woods around this sanctuary and left a rich heritage of ornithological data. Before she was forty, and after a quarter of a century spent teaching school, she crept home to her parents' house so emotionally drained that life held no meaning. Slowly she began to explore her surroundings. Then she undertook a serious study of natural history. Over the next half century she spent long days in the woods, waiting patiently for the birds to mate, nest, and bring their young along. She studied, observed, and filled many pages with valuable notes. Needing photographs to illustrate her articles on wildlife, she learned photography and took thousands of pictures of birds. She would even carry tiny birds home to her studio to be photographed, returning them to the nest so carefully that the mother birds accepted her without terror. In 1974 her valuable glass plates were discovered in the Acadia National Park and returned to Birdsacre.

The Stanwood Wildlife Sanctuary consists of some one hundred acres of woodland, open fields, pasture, rocky hillsides, swamps, streams, and forests—an ideal place for all varieties of birds. The sanctuary is open all year. The museum is open June 15–Oct. 15, daily 10–4; adm.[3]

FARMINGTON

Norton, Lillian (Nordica), 1857–1914, Opera Singer; NAW (under Nordica)

Nordica Homestead Museum, Holly Road, Off State 27; NR

Lillian Norton was born in this typical Maine farmstead to a family that loved music. She studied voice at the New England Conservatory of Music and after years of study and singing engagements she reached her goal—operatic roles. During the period 1894–1909 she was a popular singer, known abroad and in the United States for Wagnerian roles and in concert and oratorio singing. Her Italian coach changed her name to one more pronounceable to Italians—Giglio Nordica ("Lily of the North"). Although she enjoyed the perquisites of fame—diamonds and a private railway car—she never lost touch with her Yankee roots. Her sisters restored and furnished the old farmhouse as a gift to Nordica. After her death the Farmington citizens bought it and opened it to the public in 1928 as a museum where some of Nordica's possessions, including music, gowns by Worth, and jewels by Tiffany, are displayed. Open June 1–Labor Day, Tues.-Sun. 10–12 and 1–5; Sept. and Oct. by appointment; adm.[4]

GARDINER

Richards, Laura Howe, 1850–1943, Author; NAW

House, 3 Dennis Street (Private); NR

Laura Howe Richards wrote almost all her life, producing nearly eighty books, many of them written for the amusement of her seven children. But she produced more solid fare, including a two-volume edition of her father's papers, *The Letters and Journals of Samuel Gridley Howe*. In collaboration with her sister, Maude Howe Elliott, she wrote a biography of their mother, Julia Ward Howe, and won the first Pulitzer Prize given for biography. Richards was buried in Christ Church yard, near the grave of her sister-in-law, Ellen Swallow Richards (see Cambridge, MA).

HAMPDEN

Dix, Dorothea, 1802–1887, Humanitarian; NAW

Dorothea Dix Park, Route 1A

In 1843 mentally ill patients were kept in "cages, closets, cellars, stalls, pens; chained, naked, beaten with rods and lashed into obedience." So stated Dorothea Dix in a *Memorial to the Legislature of Massachusetts*. She knew, for she had just completed a thorough study of the jails, almshouses, and workhouses in Massachusetts. Dix was born in Hampden on the old Isaac Hopkins farm, while this was still part of Massachusetts. She began her work for the mentally ill when she was asked to teach a Sunday school class for women in jail. Among them were a number of women who were there only because they were of unsound mind; they were given no care at all, and they were believed by the insensate jailer to be unaware of the cold and filth. Her investigation and report of conditions aroused the state to provide hospitals for the insane. Other states and European countries followed.

A plaque on one side of the stone archway leading into the park reads: "In memory of Dorothea Lynde Dix who by devoted care to sick and wounded soldiers during the Civil War earned the gratitude of the Nation, and by her labors in the cause of prison reform and of humane treatment of the insane won the admiration and reverence of the civilized world. 1802–1887. Her birthplace.'' The park was dedicated in 1899 by the Dorothea Dix Memorial Association. Dix is in the National Women's Hall of Fame.

HOG ISLAND, MUSCONGUS BAY

Todd, Mabel Loomis, 1856–1932, Naturalist and Writer, and Her Daughter, Millicent Todd Bingham, 1880–1968, Geographer; NAW (under Mabel Loomis Todd)

Todd Wildlife Sanctuary

Though remembered principally for her work in editing the first of Emily Dickinson's poems to be published, Mabel Loomis Todd had a career in nature study. The wife of David Peck Todd, an astronomer on the faculty of Amherst College, she often went on expeditions with him and collected native artifacts in various parts of the world. Some of the artifacts are now in the Peabody Museum in Salem, Massachusetts.

Millicent Todd Bingham, her only daughter, also went on some of the expeditions. She inherited an interest in and taste for editing and writing as well as science. She earned a Ph.D. in geography from Harvard University, wrote a number of books on geography, and edited Dickinson poems left unpublished by her mother. With the advent of the atomic bomb she began to crusade for the conservation of natural resources. ''Man can now be ranked,'' she wrote, ''with earthquakes and tidal waves as a geological agent of destruction, one potentially even more powerful.''

Hog Island was bought by Todd in 1909 to protect it from loggers. In 1936 it was made a wildlife sanctuary and the Audubon societies held the first Audubon Nature Camp here. In a ceremony marking the fiftieth anniversary of Todd's acquisition of the island, her daughter gave it in her name to the society.[5]

HOLLIS

Wiggin, Kate Douglas Smith, 1856–1923, Writer; NAW

Quillcote, Off State 4A, Salmon Falls (Private); NR

Kate Douglas Smith Wiggin spent much of her childhood in Hollis, moving to California in 1873 and establishing in a San Francisco slum the city's first kindergarten. When she married Samuel Wiggin, her sister Nora Archibald Smith took over the kindergarten, and Wiggin, to raise money for its support, wrote *The Story of Patsy* and *The Birds' Christmas Carol*. The Wiggins moved to New York in 1884 but just five years later Wiggin's husband died. She continued her writing, sometimes in New York, sometimes back in Maine, and at times traveling abroad. Her most popular work was *Rebecca of Sunnybrook Farm*, published in 1903, later converted into a play and then into a screen version starring Mary Pickford. Kate's play, *The Old Peabody Pew*, is presented each August at the old Tory Hill Meeting House, Bar Mills, Buxton, Maine.

JONESBORO

Weston, Hannah, 1758–1855, Revolutionary War Heroine

Memorial Tablet at Grave

The tablet, erected in 1902 by the Hannah Weston Chapter, Daughters of the American Revolution (DAR), reads in part: "She was a woman of great courage and bravery. She manifested it during the battle at Machias in 1775 by collecting ammunition and carrying it through the wilderness to aid the citizens in defense of the town." Weston was seventeen when she and her sister Rebecca Weston helped win the first naval engagement of the Revolutionary War, the capture of the British ship *Margaretta*, by carrying fifty pounds of lead and powder from Jonesboro to the port of Machias. The DAR headquarters in the Burnham Tavern at Machias contains materials belonging to the famous sisters. In Dexter, Maine, the DAR chapter is named for Rebecca. Hannah's grave is at the north end of Jonesboro, near the highway.[6]

KITTERY POINT

Pepperrell, Mary Hirst, Lady, d. 1789, Loyalist

Lady Pepperrell House, State 103; NHL

In this beautiful house behind the great front door with its heavy knocker—Sarah Orne Jewett said that it frightened her as a child—lived the widowed Lady Mary Hirst Pepperrell in some seclusion for the last twenty-nine years of her life. Her husband, Sir William Pepperrell, owned great quantities of Maine land in Saco and Scarborough. He was created a baronet by the British government for his successful campaign against Louisbourg in 1745. He was on the governor's council and was chief justice until his death in 1759. Lady Pepperrell, whom he married in 1723, was related to many of Boston's first families. Shortly after Sir William died, his widow built the mansion, choosing a location near the church, which meant much to her.

When the Revolution began, the widow of a baronet, pensioned by the British government, could not but remain loyal to the Crown. In 1778, as a result, the property left by Sir William was confiscated along with that of all Loyalists. Lady Pepperrell was able to purchase the mansion and to continue living there. In 1789 George Washington visited the parson of the church, but he walked past the Pepperrell house without stopping to call on the old lady. The home now belongs to the Society for the Preservation of New England Antiquities. It is not open to the public.[7]

LUBEC

Roosevelt, (Anna) Eleanor, 1884–1962, Humanitarian; NAWM

Roosevelt-Campobello International Park, Campobello Island, New Brunswick

When Anna Eleanor Roosevelt became the First Lady in 1932, her public activities were roundly criticized as unbefitting the wife of the U.S. president. By the time her husband ran for a third term, she had more admirers than did he. After his death, she was honored by appointment as a U.S. delegate to the United Nations. She had become the best-known and most admired woman, perhaps, in the world. Her folksy, neighborly newspaper column, *My Day*, was read by millions. Young people thought highly of her; she understood them. Low-income people knew she was on their side. Black people adored her—especially after she publicly withdrew from the Daughters of the American Revolution because of their slight to black singer Marian Anderson in refusing the use of their hall for a concert. A woman of great energy, wisdom, and kindliness, Eleanor will long be remembered. Campobello was the summer house of the Roosevelts. It is open to the public in the summer, reached from Lubec by the FDR Memorial Bridge. The park is a memorial to international friendship between the United States and Canada. Open late May to early Oct., daily 9–5.

NORRIDGEWOCK

Clarke, Rebecca Sophia (Sophie May), 1833–1906, Writer; NAW

Sophie May House, Sophie May Lane; NR

Writing under the name of Sophie May, Rebecca Sophia Clarke produced more than forty books for children, many set in her native Norridgewock. The Little Prudy series (six volumes) and the Dotty Dimple series (six volumes) were her first successes. They appealed to children because of their homely realism and humor, a welcome change from the purely didactic and moralizing tales then generally offered the young. The writer made a comfortable living and had money to give away. One of her gifts was a building to be used as the town library. The home, a large brick house with four white columns, is privately owned but occasionally open to visitors.

ORONO

Patch, Edith Marion, 1876–1954, Entomologist

The Patch House, 500 College Avenue

A sign at the house, now used by students of the University of Maine as a cooperative residence, tells us that it was the home of Edith Marion Patch. She organized the Department of Entomology at the Maine Agricultural Experiment Station and headed it from 1903 to 1937. During her years of teaching and research she wrote many scientific articles in learned journals and was active in numerous professional organizations. In addition, she made a significant contribution to the future of science by writing on the subject for boys and girls. Beginning in 1920 with *Hexapod Stories* in the Little Gateway to Science Series, she produced some fifteen books on nature and science for children.[8]

Warren, Constance, 1880–1971, College President

Television Station, University of Maine

Constance Warren was president of Sarah Lawrence College from 1929, the year after its founding, until 1945, and helped to shape this new venture in education, where flexibility replaced a rigid curriculum. A native of New Hampshire, Warren had degrees from many colleges in New England and New York. She had also taught at a number of colleges and had formed convictions about women's education and education in general. She wrote *A New Design for Women's Education* and viewed teaching as one of the most important jobs in the world. She wrote that she had little concern "that my name should be remembered, but I hope that I may have accumulated a little anonymous Treasury which will filter down through succeeding generations." Her credo, expressed in an essay written for Edward R. Murrow, was sealed in the cornerstone of a new Student Art Center at Sarah Lawrence in 1952.

At the age of eighty-two Warren was given her last college degree, honorary Doctor of Humane Letters from the University of Maine. The television studio was given her name in recognition of her work in educational television.[9]

PORTLAND

Payson, Joan Whitney, 1903–1975, Philanthropist and Sportswoman

Joan Whitney Payson Gallery of Art, Westbrook College

Heiress to the Payne Whitney fortune, Joan Whitney Payson gave generously to medical, art, and other civic institutions, and she collected art masterpieces for over half a century. She was best known to the public as the owner of the New York Metropolitan Baseball Club and coowner with her brother Jock Whitney of the Greentree Stable. Her mother founded the racing and breeding stable, which produced many Kentucky Derby winners. Payson's interest in baseball began early. For many years she was a fixture at the New York Mets' home games, and when the team moved to California in 1958, she helped to finance a new stadium and got the club back, celebrating with them their world championship in 1969.

She was the wife of Charles Shipman Payson, of a wealthy Portland family, and was mother of five children. She served on the boards of several hospitals and museums and was president of the Helen Hay Whitney Foundation, named for her mother. For all her wealth and power, she struck people who knew her as singularly unaffected, warm, generous, and direct. In 1977 her son John Payson and his wife gave Westbrook College a new art gallery to house, on permanent loan, her art collection. It includes works by modern artists—Marc Chagall, Edgar Degas, Henri Rousseau—as well as earlier masters such as Sir Joshua Reynolds and Americans Andrew Wyeth and Winslow Homer.[10]

Stevens, Lillian Ames, 1844–1914, Temperance Worker; NAW

Fountain, Courtyard of Public Library, 5 Monument Square

"The streets of Portland," wrote temperance leader Frances E. Willard, "have not a sight more familiar, and surely none more welcome to all save evil-doers, than Mrs. Stevens in her phaeton rapidly driving her spirited horse from police station to Friendly Inn; from Erring Woman's Refuge to the sheriff's office." Lillian Ames Stevens followed Willard as president of the national Woman's Christian Temperance Union (WCTU). She had founded the Maine WCTU in 1875 and was its lifelong president. Maine already had prohibition and she helped to get the ban on liquor written into its constitution. The fountain, "The Little Cold Water Girl," is a replica of one commemorating Willard in Chicago, Illinois. See Dover-Foxcroft, ME.[11]

SABBATHDAY LAKE

Lee, Ann, 1736–1784, Religious Founder; NAW

Shaker Village, Near State 26; HABS, NHL

Ann Lee brought the Shaker society (United Society of Believers in Christ's Second Appearance) to the New World in 1774. They worshipped by singing, dancing, shouting, shaking, and speaking in tongues. They were also celibate, which guaranteed the eventual demise of the community. Under Lee's magnetic leadership eleven communal settlements of Shakers were established in New York and New England before her death. She was an early feminist, advocating the equality of the sexes and the sharing of rights and responsibilities. Of the original communities, a few remain as museums, others adapted to a different use. The site at Alfred, Maine, is now occupied by the Christian Brothers.

In 1982 six surviving sisters remained here, joined by new, young recruits. Three other eldresses were living in Canterbury Shaker Village, New Hampshire. The village here consists of a brick central dwelling house; seventeen hundred acres of forest, field, and lakeshore; and sixteen wooden buildings and structures dating from the late eighteenth and nineteenth centuries. Open May 30-Labor Day, Tues.-Sat. 10–4:30; adm. See Hancock, MA, and Canterbury, NH.[12]

SOUTH BERWICK

Jewett, Sarah Orne, 1849–1909, Writer; NAW

Jewett House, 101 Portland Street (State 236); HABS, NR

When Sarah Orne Jewett was a girl she rode the rounds with her country doctor father through the inland towns and coast villages of Maine, and when she came to write she wisely wrote about the people and places she knew. She also read voraciously from her father's well-chosen library, gaining a wide knowledge of humane letters. Her best work, *The Country of the Pointed Firs*, has taken its place as a classic of American literature. She lived in this house almost all her life, though she was no recluse. She had many friends among artists, writers, and readers in America and Europe who loved and admired her. The Sarah Orne Jewett Creative Arts Center is in the Berwick Academy. Her birthplace on Portland Street is now the public library. The Hamilton House, on Vaughan's Lane, off I–91 and State 236, is the scene of her novel *The Tory Lover*. Both the Jewett House and the Hamilton House belong to the Society for the Preservation of New England Antiquities and are open June 1–Oct. 15, Tues., Thurs., Sat., and Sun. 12–5; adm.

THOMASTON

Knox, Lucy Flucker, c. 1756–1824, Hostess

Montpelier, High Street (Off US 1)

Lucy Flucker Knox was an heiress of distinguished ancestry, her father a Crown appointee. When she married in 1774 Henry Knox, son of an Irish immigrant and a self-educated revolutionary, it was against her family's wishes. The couple had met in the bookstore Henry kept in Boston. The first years of the marriage were difficult, as her husband was away most of the time helping George Washington fight the Revolution. After Henry became a major general and was made the first secretary of war, they lived in New York City (the first national capital) and Philadelphia, Pennsylvania, where Lucy was in the center of all official activity. Both the Knoxes were fat: she weighed 250 pounds, he a mere 230. They lived and dressed well, spending far more than he made. Lucy's parents, being Tories, lost their property, and she, the only "patriot" in the family, got it. In 1794 the Knoxes finally settled down and built Montpelier, a princely mansion; it was her money that paid for it. The original house was demolished in 1872 and much later (in 1930) the Knox Memorial Association built this replica on another site. It is open May 30–Labor Day, Wed.-Sun. 9–5; adm.[13]

WAYNE

Cary, Annie Louise, 1841–1921, Opera Singer; NAW

Annie Louise Cary Memorial Library, Morrison Heights Road

Annie Louise Cary was called one of the noblest contraltos in the world. She was born in Wayne and grew up here and in Yarmouth and Gorham. She had planned to teach school until someone heard her sing and advised her to study voice instead. Her operatic debut took place in 1868 in Copenhagen. Two years later she was invited to join a concert company in New York City. Thereafter she was kept busy singing in America and Europe in concerts and opera. She loved above all the great oratorios with their religious messages. At the age of forty she married a New York banker, Charles Raymond, and retired to Norwalk, Connecticut. She devoted much time to charity, especially to the work of the New York Diet Kitchen. When she died she left a bequest to the People's Symphony Concerts of New York to fund chamber music recitals. Displays related to her life are in the Baxter House, South Street, Gorham, Maine. The library is open Mon. 8:30–12:30, Wed. 2–7, and Sat. 11–5.

YORK

Bulman, Mary, 1715–1790, Needleworker

Crewel Hangings, Emerson-Wilcox House

Mary Bulman is the wonder of needlework experts who view her crewel bedspread and hangings displayed in one of the rooms here. Made in 1745, they are the first-known crewel embroideries in the state and the only complete set of such bed hangings in the country. The valances carry a poem of Isaac Watts, "Meditation in a Grove." Mary married Alexander Bulman, who had come to York in 1727, the town paying him one hundred British pounds to establish a medical practice here. Her family had lived in the area, and part of the coastline near the mouth of the York River, "Swett's Point," still bears her family name. Alexander served as an army surgeon during the Louisbourg campaign and died in Canada. Mary then married the Reverend Thomas Prentice and moved to Massachusetts but she returned to her York home, widowed a second time, some ten years before her death. Maintained by the Old York Historical Society, this and several other historical houses are open mid-June through mid-Oct., Mon.-Sat. 10:30–5, Sun. 1:30–5; adm.[14]

YORK HARBOR

Wood, Sally Sayward Barrell Keating, 1759–1855, Novelist; NAW

Sayward-Wheeler House, 79 Barrell Lane; NR

Sally Sayward Barrell Keating Wood was Maine's first woman novelist. Her first husband, Richard Keating, died in 1783, leaving her with three children to raise. It was then that she turned to writing, producing four sentimental novels, all published anonymously, during twenty-one years of widowhood. In her preface to *Julia and the Illuminated Baron*, she was careful to report that she had not sacrificed or postponed "one social, or one domestic duty" to write, and she felt that her pen had "smoothed many *melancholy*, and sweetened many *bitter* hours." Sally was born in this house, the opulent home of her maternal grandfather, Judge Jonathan Sayward. The judge was a Loyalist during the Revolution, as was Sally's father, Nathaniel Barrell, but Sally herself approved of the rebellion. She was married again in 1804 and moved with her husband, General Abiel Wood, to Wiscasset. Her status as an author was no secret, and as "Madam Wood" she was a celebrity at social gatherings. The Sayward house in which she spent many of her productive years now belongs to the Society for the Preservation of New England Antiquities and is open June 1–Oct. 15, Tues., Thurs., Sat., and Sun. 12–5; adm.[15]

NOTES

In addition to the sources mentioned below, I have had assistance from the following: the Maine State Development Office; the Brewer Public Library; the Public Library of East Baldwin; the Ellsworth City Library, the Annie Louise Cary Memorial Library in Wayne; and the Society for the Preservation of New England Antiquities.

The Victorian Mansion, Park and Danforth Streets, Portland, is the home of the Victoria Society of Maine Women, which honors outstanding women of the state. The library is dedicated to Zilpah Longfellow, mother of Henry Wadsworth Longfellow, and the music room is dedicated to four musical artists of Maine. Other Maine women of achievement have been elected to an honor court.

Also worthy of note is the Maine Women's Writers Collection, established by Westbrook College in Portland to collect books by and about women writers with Maine connections.

1. Correspondence, Maine Chapter, Nature Conservancy.
2. Edward Wagenknecht, *Harriet Beecher Stowe* (New York: Oxford University Press, 1965).
3. Chandler S. Richmond, *Beyond the Spring: Cordelia Stanwood of Birdsacre* (Ellsworth, Maine: Latona Press, 1978); correspondence, Stanwood Homestead.
4. James and Constance Camner, "On a Hillside in Maine: Visiting the Nordica Homestead," *Opera News* 46 (July 1981); brochures, Nordica Homestead Museum.
5. *Current Biography*, 1961.
6. Correspondence, Porter Memorial Library, Machias.

7. Edward S. Stackpole, *Old Kittery and Her Families* (Lewiston, Maine: n.p., 1903); John E. Frost, *Colonial Village* (Kittery Point, Maine: Gundalow Club, Inc., 1947); Usher Parsons, *The Life of Sir William Pepperrell* (Boston, Mass.: Little Brown & Co., 1855); correspondence, Rice Public Library, Kittery.

8. Correspondence, University of Maine.

9. *New York Times*, June 16, 1971; Edward R. Murrow, *This I Believe*, vol. I (New York: Simon & Schuster, 1952); *Maine Alumnus*, June-July 1962; correspondence, University of Maine.

10. *Current Biography*, 1972; correspondence, Westbrook College.

11. Correspondence, Portland Public Library.

12. Jane Holtz Kay, "Last of the Shakers," *Historic Preservation* 34 (Mar.-Apr. 1982); brochure, Shaker Village.

13. Diana Forbes-Robertson, "Lady Knox," *American Heritage* 17 (Apr. 1966); Sally S. Booth, *The Women of '76* (New York: Hastings House, 1973); correspondence, Maine State Bureau of Parks and Recreation.

14. Correspondence, Old York Historical Society and Old Gaol Museum.

15. Richard Nylander, "The Jonathan Sayward House, York, Maine," *Antiques* 116 (Sept. 1979); correspondence, Doris Ricker Marston.

MASSACHUSETTS

ADAMS

Anthony, Susan Brownell, 1820–1906, Suffrage Leader; NAW

Quaker Meeting House, Maple Street; HABS, NR

When Susan Brownell Anthony was born on her father's farm in Adams (the house still exists on East Road and East Street), nobody would have predicted that the United States would someday use her likeness on a coin; or that her birthday would be celebrated by feminists throughout America every year; or that Gertrude Stein would write an opera about her; or that she would be elected to the national Hall of Fame, as well as the Women's Hall of Fame, and honored as Susan B. Anthony of the World. She has been called the Napoleon of the Woman's Rights Movement and the Mother of Us All. Yes, Anthony was loved, respected, and revered in her later years and is today, but during her career this suffrage leader was ridiculed, caricatured, reviled, and insulted. One of the nicer things said about her was that she had "the proportions of a file and the voice of a hurdy-gurdy." She was once arrested for the crime of voting.

Anthony lived in Massachusetts only six years. She attended the Quaker Meeting House with her father, where she may have heard that in the eyes of God women are the equals of men.

AMESBURY

Eddy, Mary Baker, 1821–1910, Religious Founder; NAW

Mary Baker Eddy Historic House, 277 Main Street

Mary Baker Eddy, the founder of the Church of Christ, Scientist, lived here during two periods between 1868 and 1870. She was then the wife of Daniel

Patterson and had not yet written her famous *Science and Health.* She had, however, been initiated into the ideas of divine healing through Phineas Quimby. She had also experienced a significant instance of mental healing in 1866 when she fell, seriously injuring her spine, and cured herself by prayer and Bible reading.

This house was the home of Sarah Bagley, a spinster gentlewoman in reduced circumstances who made a meager living by sewing. She took in Eddy when she had no place to go, cared for her lovingly, and was to benefit greatly from her brief association with the spiritual leader, for she became herself a healer and earned a living through this work. Followers of Eddy have preserved a number of her residences (see Boston, Lynn, Stoughton, and Swampscott, MA, and Rumney, NH). The house is open May 1–Oct. 31, Tues.-Sat. 11–4, Sun. 1–4; closed July 4; open Nov.-Apr. by appointment; adm.

AMHERST

Dickinson, Emily, 1830–1886, Poet; NAW

Emily Dickinson Home, 280 Main Street (Private); NR

The world took little note of the genius of Emily Dickinson, the reclusive poet who lived here. Few of her poems were published until after her death, and she was generally thought of as an eccentric minor female poet. Dickinson's niece, Martha Dickinson Bianchi (1866–1943), who lived in a house just across the street, began to publish Dickinson's poems in the 1920s and in 1932 wrote a biography of the poet which reached a new and receptive audience, not only in the United States but abroad. Subsequent publications established Dickinson's rightful claim to a place in English literature. She used the English language in a fresh way. She described herself thus to a friend: "I had no portrait, now, but am small, like the Wren, and my Hair is bold, like the Chestnut Bur—and my eyes, like the Sherry in the Glass, that the Guest leaves."

The Dickinson house is owned by Amherst College and is used as a faculty house. It may be visited once or twice a week by reservation made through the secretary of Amherst (413–542–2321). The Jones Library, 43 Amity Street, has a room devoted to Amherst authors, including Dickinson. She is in the National Women's Hall of Fame.

AYER

Rogers, Edith Nourse, 1881–1960, Congresswoman; NAWM

Parade Ground, Fort Devens

Although Edith Nourse Rogers was first elected to Congress in 1925 to fill the office vacated by her husband's death, she continued to be reelected for eighteen terms. She had already made veterans' rights a major concern; since 1922 she had served as a dollar-a-year inspector of veterans' hospitals and was apt to pop up any time to ask the boys what they needed. One of her first major bills appropriated $15 million to build more hospitals for veterans. She sponsored the GI Bill of Rights of 1944 and encouraged the creation of a volunteer women's Army Corps. See Bedford, MA.

BEDFORD

Farmer, Fannie, 1857–1915, Cook; NAW

Miss Farmer's School of Cookery, 4 Preston Court

Fannie Farmer believed that "progress in civilization has been accompanied by progress in cookery." When she first learned to cook, it was by the old-fashioned method, "a pinch" of this, a "handful" of that, and it occurred to her that level measurements might produce more reliable results. She enrolled in the Boston Cooking School, soon becoming its director. When in 1902 the Boston School became part of Simmons College, Farmer opened her own school, where she taught society women and housewives as well as professional cooks and teachers of cookery. She had written the *Boston Cooking School Cookbook* (1896), but the publisher made her pay for it before he would proceed with so risky a proposition. Now entitled *The Fannie Farmer Cookbook*, it is still in print and still one of the best-selling cookbooks. Farmer went beyond family meals to study diets and nutrition and considered her *Food and Cookery for the Sick and Convalescent* (1904) her best work.[1]

Rogers, Edith Nourse, 1881–1960, Congresswoman; NAWM

Veterans' Hospital

During World War I Edith Nourse Rogers went to France and joined other Red Cross volunteers caring for wounded soldiers. She helped at the Young Men's Christian Association's Eagle Hut in London. On her return to Washington, D.C., she became the first Gray Lady in the capital and earned the name of the Angel of Walter Reed Hospital. Her husband died in 1925 while serving his seventh term in the House of Representatives, and she was chosen to fill out his term (see Ayer, MA). Her interest in veterans continued to be a major concern as she was reelected year after year, serving in Congress until her own death. The Veterans' Hospital is named in her honor.

BOSTON

Alcott, Louisa May, 1832–1888, Author; NAW

Marker on House, 20 Pinckney Street (Private)

Best known for *Little Women*, Louisa May Alcott was a prolific writer of juvenile literature, books that reflected the values of the American middle-class home. Their popularity brought her fame and helped her family out of poverty. She did much of her writing in Boston, away from her family. The Pinckney Street house, where she lived in 1853–54, is marked "Louisa May Alcott once lived here." She later owned the house at 10 Louisbourg Square, and also lived for a time at the Bellevue Hotel. See Concord and Harvard, MA.

Bates, Katharine Lee, 1859–1929, Author; NAW

Tablet, The Fenway

Katharine Lee Bates is best remembered as the author of "America the Beautiful," a poem she wrote while visiting Colorado. She said it was inspired by the view from Pikes Peak: "As I was looking out over the sealike expanse of fertile country spreading away so far under those ample skies, . . . the opening lines of the hymn floated into my mind." A graduate of Wellesley College, she was identified with the school as a teacher of English literature for most of her life. Memorials to her at Wellesley include murals illustrating her anthem in the Blue Lounge at Green Hall, a fund for poetry readings, a chair of English literature, and her portrait. The bronze tablet near a road and footpath in the Fenway was paid for by public subscription. Designed by John Francis Paramino, it contains the first stanza of "America the Beautiful." See Falmouth, MA.[2]

Blackwell, Alice Stone. See Stone, Lucy

Crabtree, Lotta, 1847–1924, Actress; NAW

Fountain, Banks of Charles River, near Boston University

Lotta Crabtree, who began her stage career as a child performer in California's gold country, became a favorite comedienne, for a time the highest-paid performer on the American stage. After her retirement she lived in Boston at the Brewster Hotel, which she owned. Much of her time was spent planning for the disposition of her wealth, valued at some $4 million. Half went to veterans of World War I, and a large sum went to the Lotta Crabtree Dumb Animal Fund to provide for domestic horses and dogs. She had donated a drinking fountain to San Francisco, California, where Lotta's Fountain is a landmark, and this Boston fountain was another of her benefactions. By the time her estate was settled, horses for transportation were being replaced by the automobile, and the

Lotta Crabtree, popular comedienne, died in Boston, Massachusetts, worth some $4 million. Much of it went to World War I veterans, and a substantial sum went to the Lotta Crabtree Dumb Animal Fund for fountains such as this one on the Charles River in Boston.
Courtesy Estate of Lotta M. Crabtree, Boston.

fund was used mainly to support agricultural students, many of them interested in animal husbandry.

Crocker, Lucretia, 1829–1886, Science Teacher; NAW

School, Jamaica Plain

In 1873, when Lucretia Crocker and three other women were elected to the Boston School Committee with the help of the New England Woman's Club, the male members refused to seat them, believing it was illegal for women to hold the office. New legislation opened the way so that the following year Crocker and five other women were seated. In 1876 she was elected to the board of supervisors, a post she held until her death. Using the considerable authority given her, she virtually revolutionized science teaching in the Boston public schools, emphasizing geography, zoology, and mineralogy. In 1880 she was elected to the American Association for the Advancement of Science. See Framingham, MA.

Dudley, Helena Stuart. See Scudder, Vida

Dyer, Mary, d. 1660, Martyr; NAW

Statue, State House Grounds

The seated figure of "Mary Dyer, Quaker, Witness for Religious Freedom, Hanged on Boston Common 1660," was authorized by the Massachusetts General Court three centuries after the court ordered her execution and almost as many years after the court repealed the law banishing Quakers from Massachusetts Bay Colony. The repeal resulted from the willingness of Dyer and others to perish for their faith. She was banished the first time when she openly supported another nonconformist, Anne Hutchinson, whose statue stands opposite hers at the State House. Dyer returned to New England again as a convert to the Society of Friends and was promptly jailed. Her husband had her released and took her to Connecticut, but she came back to visit two condemned Quakers held in jail. The two men and Dyer were marched to the gallows on October 27, 1659; the men were hanged but at the last moment Dyer was reprieved. The following year, back in Boston to get the unjust law against Quakers repealed, she was not so lucky. Boston has several streets named Dyer.[3]

The statue is the work of Sylvia Shaw Judson (later Haskins, 1897–1978). In her sculpture, which can be seen in gardens throughout the country, Judson captures the quiet, thoughtful moments of individuals or animals. She was born in Illinois and studied in Chicago, Illinois, and Paris, France. Her work is displayed, among other places, at the Art Institute of Chicago, the National Academy of Design, and the First Lady's Garden at the White House. She was the wife of Clay Judson, 1921–60, and of Sidney Haskins after 1963.

Eddy, Mary Baker, 1821–1910, Religious Founder; NAW

Christian Science Church Center, Huntington and Massachusetts Avenues. Eddy House, 400 Beacon Street, Chestnut Hill

By the time the Mother Church was dedicated in 1895, Mary Baker Eddy had been for some years developing and expounding her religion of Divine Science, with its basic tenet that "matter and death are mortal illusions." She had written *Science and Health*, a book still read every Sunday from Christian Science pulpits throughout the world. In 1908 the church began publishing the *Christian Science Monitor*, acknowledged by readers in and out of the faith as a great newspaper. The center, world headquarters of Christian Science, comprises the Mother Church built in 1894 and the Italian Renaissance extension added in 1904. In the garden of the museum is a bronze statue of Eddy by Cyrus Dallin.

The center is open May–Oct., Mon.-Fri. 8–4, Sat. and some holidays 9–4, Sun. 12–4:45; Nov.-Apr., shorter hours. The house in Chestnut Hill is open May-Oct., Wed.-Sat. 11:30–4, Sun. 2–5; rest of year by appointment. The Longyear Historical Society and Museum, 120 Seaver Street, Brookline (with Eddy displays but no official connection with the church) is open year round, Tues.-Sat. 10–4:15, Sun. 1–4:15; adm. See Amesbury, Lynn, Stoughton, and Swampscott, MA, and Rumney, NH.

Gardner, Isabella Stewart, 1840–1924, Art Collector; NAW

Isabella Stewart Gardner Museum, 280 The Fenway

New Yorker Isabella Stewart Gardner came to Boston as the bride of Jack Gardner, but wealth, education, and a tour of Europe were not enough to guarantee acceptance by the Boston Brahmins. Ill and despondent after the loss of a child, she left Boston for a tour of European capitals. On the voyage she made a remarkable recovery and spent the next eighteen months viewing art galleries and purchasing Worth gowns. On her return, the dashing young matron took Boston by storm and became the hostess whose invitations were most prized. With her houses on Beacon Street and in Brookline bulging with paintings and art objects, and assisted in her selection of paintings by Bernard Berenson, she planned an art gallery. Fenway Court, a highly personal art collection, was opened to the public in 1903. Gardner lived for two decades in quarters on the fourth floor. Her will dictated that no item in the collection might be moved from the spot where she had placed it. The gallery is open Tues. 12–9, Wed.-Sun. 12–5, except during July and Aug., when it is closed Tues. evenings; adm.

Howe, Julia Ward, 1819–1910, Writer; NAW

House, 13 Chestnut Street (Private); NHL

After she had been married twenty years, Julia Ward Howe wrote in her journal: "In the course of that time I have never known my husband to approve of any act of mine which I myself valued. Books—poems—essays—everything has been contemptible in his eyes because not his way of doing things. . . . God help me if I did wrong in not carrying out my intentions, remember that I feared to do wrong in disobeying one who has a husband's authority.'' She was a wealthy and talented member of New York society when she married Samuel Gridley Howe, Boston's respected teacher of the blind. Almost twice her age, Samuel controlled his wife's money and her life. He disapproved of women's rights, of his wife's writings, and even of any participation in his work as director of the Perkins Institution for the Blind. Julia became famous when she wrote the ''Battle Hymn of the Republic,'' which, set to the tune of ''John Brown's Body,'' became a national hymn. Samuel's disapproval dimmed somewhat, and Julia was allowed to participate in the woman's suffrage movement with Lucy Stone. After Samuel's death in 1876 she blossomed into an active feminist, author, and worker for peace.[4]

Hutchinson, Anne, 1591–1643, Dissenter; NAW

Statue, State House Grounds. Plaque, near Old Corner Bookstore, School and Washington Streets

In Anne Hutchinson's day and in New England, thinking for oneself and encouraging others to do so was heresy. The Puritan orthodoxy, challenged by Hutchinson's religious teachings and baffled by her steadfast refusal to submit to their dogma, banished her from the Massachusetts Bay Colony in 1637. She went first to Narragansett Bay (see Portsmouth, RI). After her husband died she went to New York, where she settled in the wilderness. Defenseless and alone, she and her five children were massacred by Indians.

The monument, by Cyrus Dallin, was erected in 1920, when public sentiment had undergone a radical change. It reads: ''Anne Marbury Hutchinson, Baptized at Alford, Lincolnshire, England, 20 July 1591, Killed by the Indians at East Chester New York 1643. A courageous exponent of civil liberty and religious toleration.'' The plaque at the Old Corner Bookstore reads: ''On this site stood the house of Anne Hutchinson, a religious leader, brilliant, fearless, unfortunate. Banished to Rhode Island 1637. Killed by Indians 1643.''[5]

Judson, Sylvia Shaw (Haskins). See Dyer, Mary

Kitson, Theo Alice Ruggles, 1871–1932, Sculptor

Statue of Thaddeus Kosciuszko, Boston Public Gardens

Theo Alice Ruggles Kitson specialized in sturdy war memorials, heroic statues, and portrait busts. She was born in Brookline, Massachusetts, and studied in Paris, France, and New York City. In 1893 she married Henry Hudson Kitson, also a sculptor. They maintained a studio in Boston, where she produced the statue of the Polish patriot who fought in the American Revolution. Her equestrian *Victory* is in Hingham, Massachusetts, and a number of her busts of Civil War heroes are at Vicksburg battlefield in Mississippi. Near the gates to the Arlington National Cemetery, Virginia, is *The Hiker*, a memorial to Spanish-American War veterans. She also executed the memorial to Mother Bickerdyke, the Civil War nurse, in Galesburg, Illinois.[6]

Nichols, Rose Standish, 1872–1960, Landscape Architect

Nichols House Museum, 55 Mount Vernon Street

For eighty years this four-story brick building was the home of Rose Standish Nichols, a member of a wealthy and civic-minded Boston family. She studied and practiced garden architecture, and for some time she was a director of the Boston Society of Decorative Art and the Cooperative Building Society. She wrote *English Pleasure Gardens*. On her death she left Boston the house, designed by Charles Bulfinch, as an example of early nineteenth-century architecture, complete with furnishings. It now houses the Boston Council for International Visitors and is open Mon., Wed., and Sat. 1–5; adm.[7]

Palmer, Sophia French, 1853–1920, Nurse; NAW

Palmer-Davis Library, Massachusetts General Hospital School of Nursing

Sophia French Palmer entered this school, then called the Boston Training School for Nurses, in 1876. In her day, caring for others in childbirth, illness, age, and disablement was considered women's work, and all women were expected to perform nursing duties for members of their families, regardless of aptitude, training, or inclination, yet training as a nurse and entering the field as a vocation was looked upon as not quite nice. Palmer did much to change the public's view of trained nurses by developing professional organizations for nurses, setting standards of practice and training, and promoting legislative regulation. As editor of the *American Journal of Nursing*, from its inception in 1900 until her death, she exerted a powerful influence for nursing reform.

Peabody, Elizabeth Palmer, 1804–1894, Humanitarian; NAW

Elizabeth Peabody House, 357 Charles Street

Van Wyck Brooks called Elizabeth Palmer Peabody "the salt of Boston." William James called her "the most dissolute woman in Boston." Henry James used her as the model for Miss Birdseye in *The Bostonians*. William Ellery Channing told the Blackwell sisters, "You must not be frightened by her rough manners . . . or hair not so smooth as might be—but if you can get beyond that she is an angel—and I sometimes wonder how people will wonder when they see her in the other world with her wings on.''[8]

Elizabeth Peabody was the oldest of three sisters, all of whom achieved fame (Sophia Peabody as the wife of Nathaniel Hawthorne and Mary Peabody as the wife of Horace Mann). Elizabeth was the most energetic and resourceful one. In 1840 she opened a bookshop at 19 West Street where her father sold homeopathic remedies and her mother helped sell foreign books and literary periodicals. For ten years the shop was the liveliest spot in Boston, an intellectual center where Margaret Fuller held her famous ''Conversations.'' It was the rendezvous for the transcendentalists, and the literary Tories called it the Hospital for Incapables. Peabody closed the shop in 1850 and took up, among other causes, Friedrich Froebel's theories of early childhood education. In 1860 she opened one of the first kindergartens in America.

The Peabody House is a settlement house established as a memorial to her in 1896; it occupied several sites before it moved in 1913 to Charles Street.

Scudder, Vida, 1861–1954, Teacher and Social Reformer; NAWM

Denison House, 584 Columbia Road, Dorchester

Vida Scudder, a distinguished member of the Wellesley College faculty, worked in the College Settlements Association. Denison House was opened in Boston's South End in 1893, and for years, Scudder wrote, ''The center of my social living was at that dear House . . . where fifteen hundred people a week were presently passing through our pretty Green Room.'' In 1912, however, a textile strike at Lawrence, Massachusetts, widened her view of poverty and its causes. There she made an impassioned speech, saying, ''I would rather never again wear a thread of woolen than know my garments had been woven at the cost of such misery as I have seen. . . . If the wages are of necessity below the standard to maintain man and woman in decency and in health, then the woolen industry has not a present right to exist in Massachusetts.'' Her radicalism impelled the Boston *Transcript* to call for her resignation from Wellesley. The college did not request it nor did Scudder offer it. She did, however, resign from Denison House, knowing that her socialistic views were unacceptable to many of the board members. She remained a radical, a scholar, and a believer in peace all her life.[9]

Helena Stuart Dudley (1858–1932, NAW) was the first director of Denison House and was one of the most important leaders, after Jane Addams of Hull House in Chicago, in the settlement movement. Her first year at Denison was a year of financial panic, and Dudley was kept busy with relief work. The house organized clubs, classes, and extension courses; held art exhibitions; and had a gymnasium. But Dudley, as well as Scudder, began to realize that such well-meant efforts were merely palliatives to poverty. What workers needed was a living wage and protection against economic disasters. She, too, took part in the Lawrence textile workers' strike, then left Denison House to work for the cause of world peace.

Shaw, Pauline Agassiz, 1841–1917, Educator; NAW

North Bennett Street Industrial School, 39 N. Bennett Street

Pauline Agassiz Shaw believed the greatest problem of the race was the proper rearing of the children. She established a number of kindergartens in the Boston area, day nurseries for the children of working mothers, and classes in hygiene and sewing for the mothers. Her compassion for Boston's rootless immigrants and her abhorrence of racial discrimination led her to expand the nurseries into settlement houses serving the urban poor. The industrial school, established in 1881, gave school children the practical classes—in cooking, printing, metal, and woodworking skills—that public schools failed to provide.

Stone, Lucy (Blackwell), 1818–1893, Women's Rights Leader; NAW

Chapel, Forest Hills Cemetery

Lucy Stone was born at her father's farm on Coy's Hill, near West Brookfield, Massachusetts. The night before the birth her mother had to milk eight cows and get supper for the menfolks. Perhaps rebellion at the lot of women was born in Lucy; it was certainly reinforced by many of her early experiences. Her mother's hard lot, the Bible injunction that men should rule (which she believed a mistranslation), the denial of a voice for women in the church, the disparity between her pay as a teacher and that given a man, her father's refusal to pay anything toward her expenses at Oberlin College, the college administrators' refusal to let her read her commencement address because she was a female—all made her a natural ally of the first women's rights activists. When she consented to marry Henry Blackwell, she insisted on keeping her own name. (For a long time women who kept their maiden names after marriage were called Lucy Stoners.) Her whole life was dedicated to the cause of equality for women. Always an innovator, she was the first person in New England to be cremated. Her ashes are here in the cemetery where the chapel is her memorial.

The ashes of Stone's only child, Alice Stone Blackwell (1857–1950, NAW) were also placed in the columbarium here. Alice became Lucy's disciple and assistant in editing the *Woman's Journal*, organ of the American Woman's Suffrage Association and the voice of woman's liberation. Lucy began its publication in 1869 and after two years under the editorship of Mary Livermore it continued under Lucy, Henry, and Alice for an unbroken forty-seven years. Alice took a leading part in healing the breach between the American and the

National Woman's Suffrage Associations. In 1890, when the two organizations merged, she became recording secretary of the National American Woman's Suffrage Association and held the post for almost two decades. After Lucy's death and after women finally won the vote, Alice found many other groups needing support: Armenians mistreated in Turkey, Russian freedom fighters, blacks discriminated against in college, Sacco and Vanzetti, and a host of others. She was a radical where her mother had been a conservative, but she was like her mother in fighting for what she believed in, never too much of a lady to attend protest meetings.

Vincent, Mary Ann Farlow, 1818–1887, Actress; NAW

Vincent Memorial Hospital, Massachusetts General Hospital

Mary Ann Farlow Vincent, the popular actress known throughout her acting career as Mrs. J. R. Vincent, became a Boston institution, loved for her merry personality and good works as well as for her acting. She performed at the Boston Museum from 1852 until 1887, and after her death her many admirers continued her good works by raising money to build the hospital in her memory. She had come from England as a young woman, lost her husband soon afterward, and remained to give her considerable talents as a comedienne to the American stage.

Wheelock, Lucy, 1857–1946, Kindergartner; NAW

Wheelock College, 200 the Riverway

Lucy Wheelock intended to prepare herself to enter Wellesley College, but when she went to Chauncy Hall School, she saw a kindergarten for the first time. She felt as though "the gates of heaven were opened and I had a glimpse of the kingdom where peace and love reign." On Elizabeth Peabody's advice she went to the Kindergarten Training School and spent the ten years after graduation happily teaching at Chauncy Hall. The city then incorporated kindergartens into the public school system and Wheelock began to train teachers. She founded her own teacher-training school, a forerunner of Wheelock College, in 1896. She was one of the foremost women in the national kindergarten movement.

Whitney, Anne, 1821–1915, Sculptor; NAW

Statues of Samuel Adams, Adams Square, in Front of Faneuil Hall, and of Leif Ericsson, Commonwealth Avenue

Approached by the Board of Lady Managers for the World's Columbian Exposition in 1893 to contribute some pieces to the Woman's Building, Anne Whitney, a strong feminist, replied that she would not think of exhibiting her work with quilts, draperies, needlework, and other woman's rubbish. She did not believe in segregating women's art from men's. However, she yielded to entreaties and sent not only her Leif Ericsson statue and a fountain for the Woman's Building but also busts of Harriet Beecher Stowe and Lucy Stone. She had won the commission from Massachusetts to make the statue of Adams for Statuary Hall in the National Capitol in 1873, after returning from four years of study in Rome. The statue in Boston is a replica. Among her sculptures are many busts of famous men and women who were crusaders for social justice, as well as symbolic pieces expressive of her liberal views. More than a hundred of her sculptures have been cataloged, and she is considered one of the distinguished sculptors of Victorian America.[10]

Winslow, Mary Chilton, d. 1679, Pioneer

Memorial, Spring Lane, at Devonshire Street

The bronze tablet gives all the known facts of Mary Chilton's life: ''Mary Chilton, the only Mayflower passenger who removed from Plymouth to Boston, died here in 1679. John Winslow and Mary Chilton were married at Plymouth about 1624, came to Boston about 1657, and bought a house on this site in 1671. John Winslow died here in 1674. As a passenger on the Mayflower in 1620 Mary Chilton came to America before any other white woman who settled in Boston.''

CAMBRIDGE

Memorials, Radcliffe College

A number of memorials at Radcliffe College perpetuate the names of women connected with the institution. A hall is named for Elizabeth Cary Agassiz (1822–1907, NAW). Since Harvard University would not admit women to classes, she and other women banded together to start a school for women taught by Harvard professors. First known as the Harvard Annex, then as the Society for the Collegiate Instruction of Women, the institution became in 1892 Radcliffe College. Agassiz, widow of the great naturalist Louis Agassiz, was president of the school from its beginning in 1882 until 1903.

A hall in Cabot House is named for Ada Comstock (1876–1973, NAWM), president of Radcliffe from 1923 until 1943. She did a great deal to establish Radcliffe as a strong woman's college in its own right rather than as a poor relation to Harvard. After her resignation she became the wife of Wallace Notestein (see Smith College, in Northampton, MA).

The Cronkhite Graduate Center, opened in 1956, commemorates Bernice Brown Cronkhite (1893–1983), dean of Radcliffe, 1923–34, and the first dean of the Radcliffe Graduate School of Arts and Science. Constance Smith (1922–1970) gave her name to a conference room at the Radcliffe Institute for Independent Study. She was chosen to direct the institute when it began in 1961, during the presidency of Mary I. Bunting.

In addition to these women who as administrators created Radcliffe's greatness, a number of alumnae are honored. The first was Alice Mary Longfellow (1850–1928), daughter of Henry Wadsworth Longfellow and the "grave Alice" of his poem, "The Children's Hour." Alice Mary Longfellow Hall is now part of the School of Education at Harvard.

A dormitory is named for Mabel Daniels (1878–1971, NAWM), class of 1900, who became a successful composer. Her cantata *The Song of Jael* was performed in the Worcester Municipal Auditorium, with, as she said, "the sound and fury of Old Testament combat." She was the dean of U.S. women composers.

A world-famous graduate was Helen Keller (1880–1968, NAWM), who despite the double handicap of blindness and deafness completed the full course of studies. Assisting her throughout was Anne Sullivan (later Macy, 1866–1936, NAW), who "read" to Helen in finger language all the assignments. A garden at the school is named for Keller and its fountain for Sullivan.

A tree on the campus commemorates Sara Murray Jordan (1884–1959, NAWM), a 1904 graduate who won honor in the field of medicine. She specialized in gastroenterology and was cofounder of the Lahey Clinic in Boston, Massachusetts.[11]

Baldwin, Maria, 1856–1922, Educator; NAW

Maria Baldwin House, 196 Prospect Street (Private); NHL

Maria Baldwin, the first black woman school principal in Massachusetts, was born in Cambridge, the daughter of a Haitian seaman. She taught at the Agassiz Grammar School near Harvard from 1882 and was made principal in 1889. In 1916 she was made master, the only Negro in New England to hold such a position. The twelve teachers she supervised and almost all of the children in the school were white. She had many friends in Boston's intellectual circles and belonged to several clubs, including the Woman's Era Club. Her home was a center for literary activities; she was a popular lecturer on historical and literary subjects. A memorial tablet was placed in the school's auditorium and a scholarship established in her honor. A girls'dormitory at Howard University (Washington, D.C.) was named for her.

Cannon, Annie Jump. See Draper, Mary

Draper, Mary Ann Palmer, 1839–1914 (NAW), and Other Astronomers

Henry Draper Memorial, Harvard Observatory

Our knowledge of the stars owes much to Mary Ann Palmer Draper's interest in astronomy. It began with her marriage to Henry Draper, a science professor at the University of the City of New York. She joined in his fascination with nebular and lunar photography, working with him in his personal observatory at Hastings-on-Hudson, New York. Widowed in 1882, she was eager to carry on Henry's pioneering work. After visiting the Harvard Observatory, she donated to it his eleven-inch telescope and established the Henry Draper Memorial to finance studies of the stellar spectra.

Two women astronomers, Williamina Stevens Fleming and Annie Jump Cannon, benefited from the Draper Memorial. The former compiled the first *Draper Catalog of Stellar Spectra* (1890); the latter carried the total classification to 359,000 stars in eleven further volumes.

Fleming (1857–1911, NAW) came to her career by a fluke. When her marriage broke up and she was left without resources, the Scotchwoman took a job as a domestic in the household of Edward Pickering of the Harvard Observatory. One day Pickering, annoyed by the inefficiency of a male assistant, fired him, saying that his maid could do better. She joined the staff in 1881 and did so well that Pickering continued to employ women as research assistants. Fleming not only did her own research and writing but edited all the observatory's publications and supervised the young women who served as computers. She was officially appointed curator of astronomical photographs in 1898—the first appointment of a female by the Harvard Corporation.

Cannon (1863–1941, NAW), who came from Delaware, studied astronomy while a student at Wellesley College, though she had become acquainted with the science at home under the influence of her mother. She studied also at Radcliffe College and began work as an assistant to Pickering in 1896. Her association with the observatory spanned forty-five years, and when Fleming died, Cannon took over the job as curator of astronomical photographs. She received many honors for her accomplishments and herself established the Annie J. Cannon Prize of the American Astronomical Society, given triennially to a woman rendering distinguished service to astronomy.

Fleming, Williamina Stevens. See Draper, Mary

Fuller, Margaret (Ossoli), 1810–1850, Feminist Writer; NAW

House, 71 Cherry Street; NHL

Margaret Fuller was the most intensely feminist woman of her day, author of *Woman in the Nineteenth Century* (1843), a classic manifesto of the woman's rights movement. Highly intellectual, she led the transcendentalists and edited their quarterly magazine, the *Dial*, which published the work of great thinkers, men and women. She held "Conversations" at Elizabeth Peabody's bookstore in Boston, discussing mythology, ethics, art, education, and philosophy. She went to New York City to write for Horace Greeley's *Tribune* and was sent to Europe as a foreign correspondent. There she met and married a young Roman nobleman, Giovanni Angelo, Marchese d'Ossoli, who was involved in radical politics. On their return to America in 1850, the ship was wrecked in New York harbor. Fuller's body and Ossoli's were never found. The body of their child was washed up on the beach at Fire Island and subsequently buried in Mount Auburn Cemetery, where a memorial was erected.

The Fuller house is now a settlement house. The house in which she lived in 1832, at 42 Brattle Street, is now the Cambridge Center for Adult Education. See West Roxbury, MA.

Irwin, Agnes. See Schlesinger, Elizabeth

McCormick, Katharine Dexter, 1875–1967, Philanthropist; NAWM

McCormick Halls, Massachusetts Institute of Technology

Margaret Sanger fought throughout her life for the right of men and women to plan their families, but it was her friend Katharine Dexter McCormick who made possible the development of the birth-control pill, thus consummating Sanger's dream of a physiological, woman-controlled contraceptive. McCormick earned a degree in biology from the Massachusetts Institute of Technology (MIT) in 1904. She married Stanley McCormick, of the International Harvester Company, who soon after the marriage became mentally deranged. For the rest of his life (until 1947) she sought a cure for him and saw that he was cared for. In her search for the cause of his illness she became interested in endocrinology, an interest that was important to the development of an oral contraceptive.

After meeting Sanger, McCormick became convinced that knowledge of birth-control methods was one of the kindest gifts that could be brought to women. When the Worcester Foundation for Experimental Biology was working on synthetic steroid compounds, she gave them funds for development of the pill. Enovid went on the market in 1960. When McCormick died seven years later she left $5 million to Planned Parenthood, $1 million to the Worcester Foundation, and the bulk of her $30 million estate to MIT.[12]

Parsons, Emily Elizabeth, 1824–1880, Nurse; NAW

Parsons Building, Mount Auburn Hospital, 330 Mount Auburn Street

Although she was almost blind, her hearing was impaired, and she limped as a result of a leg injury, Emily Elizabeth Parsons was determined to volunteer as a nurse during the Civil War. She entered Massachusetts General Hospital as a student and volunteer nurse, then went to a military hospital near New York City in charge of a ward of some fifty patients. At the invitation of Jessie Benton Frémont she moved to St. Louis, Missouri, to work with the Western Sanitary Commission. In 1863 she was appointed supervisor of nurses at Benton Barracks, the largest military hospital in the West. It was one of the most important appointments given to a woman during the Civil War. After the war she returned to Cambridge to open a hospital for destitute women and children, the forerunner of the Cambridge (now Mount Auburn) Hospital.

Richards, Ellen Swallow, 1842–1911, Scientist; NAW

Plaque, Building 4, Massachusetts Institute of Technology

Ellen Swallow Richards was the first woman graduate of the Massachusetts Institute of Technology (MIT), its first female faculty member, and the first woman to become a science consultant to industry. After she earned her B.S. degree at MIT, she married a science professor, Robert H. Richards, and settled down to help in his metallurgical studies. Both were pleased when she became the first woman elected to the American Institute of Mining and Metallurgical Engineers. Robert in turn helped his wife's scientific career. She worked with the Woman's Education Association of Boston to expand science education for women and for a woman's laboratory at MIT. The laboratory closed after six years, when women became full-fledged students of the institute, and Ellen was appointed to the faculty as instructor in the new field of sanitary chemistry. She tested wallpapers and fabrics for arsenic content, studied water pollution, experimented on commercial oils, and studied adulteration of household foods and cleaning supplies. Gradually her interests shifted to home economics. She instituted the school lunch, worked with hospitals on diets, and wrote bulletins on nutrition for the U.S. Department of Agriculture. She was the first president of the American Home Economics Association.

Schlesinger, Elizabeth, 1886–1977, Historian, and Agnes Irwin, 1841–1914, College Administrator; NAW (under Agnes Irwin)

Arthur and Elizabeth Schlesinger Library, Radcliffe College

Elizabeth Schlesinger marched with the suffragists when in her twenties and in the Vietnam War protests when in her eighties. Her husband, historian Arthur Schlesinger, was one of the first to point out the neglect of women in standard histories and to advocate the study of women's history. Elizabeth was one of a small group of scholars pioneering such studies. She wrote articles for scholarly journals on many nineteenth-century women, including Fanny Fern, Jennie June, and Abigail May Alcott.

The women's archives at Radcliffe College began in the 1940s when Maud Wood Park, first president of the League of Women Voters, gave her papers to the college. At the time there was little interest in the history of women, no college women's studies programs, and few scholarly books written on women. Consequently, very little use was made of the archives. The resurgence of feminism in the 1960s changed all that. In 1965 the Schlesinger name was given to the collection, now one of the foremost centers in America for the study of women's past and present.[13]

The Agnes Irwin Room in the library is named for the first dean of the newly chartered Radcliffe College. She and Elizabeth Cary Agassiz, the president, worked well together, though most of the administrative work fell on Irwin's shoulders. She had been for twenty-five years director of the Agnes Irwin School in Philadelphia, Pennsylvania, and she carried over to the college the headmistress approach to social behavior. Radcliffe girls were to wear hat and gloves when off the campus and were not to enter Harvard Yard without an invitation from a young man to one of the college events open to women. Irwin was an excellent college administrator, raising funds to build residence halls, a gymnasium, an administration building, and a library. When Agassiz retired as president, Irwin was bitterly disappointed in not being given the title. A man was chosen instead. She remained as dean, however, until 1909.

CONCORD

Alcott, Louisa May, 1832–1888, Author (NAW), and Other Tenants

The Wayside, 455 Lexington Road, in Minute Man National Historic Park; NHL

This historical house has had a series of remarkable women as tenants, including the writer, Louisa May Alcott; the artist Sophia Hawthorne, wife of Nathaniel Hawthorne; their daughter, religious founder Rose Hawthorne Lathrop; and the writer Harriet Lothrop.

Alcott was thirteen when her family moved here in 1845. The house was then called Hillside. They were here only a few years, struggling to live on what Bronson Alcott could earn by teaching and lecturing. They were hard years, the family often living on boiled rice and apples, but as Alcott looked back on those years with her three sisters, they had been happy, made so by a loving, wise, and hardworking mother. Alcott was to tell the family story in *Little Women*, the book that launched her successful career as a writer. Soon after they moved into this house she wrote in her journal, "I have at last got the little room I have wanted so long, and am very happy about it." The Alcotts also lived in Orchard House, q.v. See Boston and Harvard, MA.

The Wayside was purchased in 1852 by Nathaniel and Sophia Hawthorne. Sophia Amelia Peabody Hawthorne (1809–1871) was the youngest sister of Elizabeth Peabody, of Boston, Massachusetts. Considered an invalid, Sophia had been protected and dosed to the point of suffocation by her mother. When allowed to, she painted and studied sculpture. Elizabeth introduced her to Hawthorne, bringing that shy writer out of seclusion and saving her sister from a life of invalidism. The frail Sophia became her husband's protector, keeping the world away so that he could write. She illustrated some of his books. The first four years after their marriage were spent in the Emerson House, the Old Manse, q.v. In 1853 they went to Liverpool, England, where Nathaniel was American consul. After travel in France and Italy, they returned to the Wayside in 1860. Sophia stayed on for a few years after Nathaniel's death in 1864, editing his notebooks for publication. She sold the home in 1868 and moved to Dresden, Germany, then to London, where she died.

Rose Hawthorne Lathrop (1851–1926, NAW), the Hawthorne's youngest child, saw little of the Wayside until she was twelve. Her father's death was one of the most tragic events of her young life. The move to Dresden when she was seventeen gave her and her sister Una an opportunity to study music and art. She met George Parsons Lathrop there, and she was married in London at the age of twenty. The couple returned to Boston and in 1878 bought her old home, the Wayside, only to move a few years later to New York City, saddened by the death of a child. Rose became a Catholic and in 1900 took vows as Sister Mary Alphonsa, a lay sister of the Dominican Order. She founded the Dominican Congregation of St. Rose of Lima, which worked to make the last days of indigent cancer victims as comfortable as possible—the first hospice program.

In 1883 the Wayside was purchased by Daniel Lothrop and Harriet Mulford Stone Lothrop (1844–1924, NAW). Harriet, using the pen name of Margaret Sidney, had been writing stories about the Five Little Peppers for *Wide Awake*, a children's magazine published in Boston. One day Daniel, the publisher, stopped by to see what Margaret Sidney looked like. He found Harriet to be as warmhearted and lively as her stories, and the interest was mutual. They were married in 1881. After Daniel died Harriet continued to write and for some time to manage the publishing firm. The twelve volumes about the Five Little Peppers were favorites with children.

The Wayside is furnished in the style prevalent when the Lothrops lived here. Tours are conducted mid-Apr.–Oct. 31, Fri.-Tues. 10–5:30; adm.

Alcott, Louisa May, 1832–1888, Writer; NAW

Orchard House, 399 Lexington Road; HABS, NHL

Louisa May Alcott's journal records that in 1858 "an old house near R. W. E[merson]'s is bought with Mother's money and we prepare to move." While the house was being readied for them, the family (parents Bronson and Abigail May Alcott; Louisa; her sister Anna, soon to be married; Lizzie, who was dying of tuberculosis; and May) lived in a wing of the Wayside, which thirteen years earlier had been their home. Louisa thought Orchard House—which she called Apple Slump—looked pleasant, "though I never want to live in it." She was twenty-five years old, living in Boston, Massachusetts, and writing short fiction and verse, hoping to earn enough money to help the family finances. She returned to Orchard House in 1868 to care for her mother, and *Little Women* was written here.

When in 1902 Orchard House was to be torn down, Harriet Lothrop bought it and looked after it until the Louisa May Alcott Memorial Association was formed. It is open to the public Apr. 1–Sept.15, Mon.-Sat. 10–4:30, Sun. and holidays 1–4:30; Sept. 16–Oct. 31, daily 1–4:30; winter, groups by reservation; adm.

Hawthorne, Sophia Peabody, 1809–1871, Artist, and Sarah Alden Bradford Ripley, 1793–1867, Scholar; NAW

The Old Manse, Monument Street at Old North Bridge; HABS, NHL

The Old Manse has had more than one famous tenant. It was the Emerson home, where Ralph Waldo Emerson spent his boyhood. After Nathaniel Hawthorne and Sophia Peabody Hawthorne were married, they rented the house for four years. Nathaniel described it in his *Mosses from an Old Manse*. Sophia was happy here. She brightened up the old house with paintings. On the window in the study the Hawthornes inscribed with a diamond ring their names, the date, and ''Man's accidents are God's purposes.'' The original pane is put away for safekeeping, that on view being a facsimile.

After the Hawthornes moved to Salem, Massachusetts, the Old Manse was occupied by Samuel Ripley and his wife, Sarah Alden Bradford Ripley. Samuel had grown up in the house, as his father, Ezra Ripley, married the widow of its first owner, William Emerson. In the intervening years Samuel and Sarah had run a boarding school in Waltham, Massachusetts. Sarah was considered one of the most learned women in America. When as a young girl she suggested to her father that she would like to study Latin, he replied, ''Latin! A girl study Latin! Certainly. Study anything you like.'' With this approval, she studied not only languages but mathematics, botany, chemistry, and philosophy. In the boarding school, she had done the housekeeping, taught the boys, and maintained her own studies. Samuel died soon after their return to the Old Manse, but Sarah continued to live here until her death. She was a considerable influence on her nephew, Ralph Waldo Emerson. A portrait of Sarah hangs on the wall.

The Old Manse now belongs to the Trustees of Reservations. Tours are conducted June 1–Oct. 31, Mon. and Thurs.-Sat. 10–4:30, Sun. and holidays 1–4:30; mid-Apr. to May 31, Sat., Sun., and holidays only 1–4:30; adm.

Roberts, Elizabeth Wentworth, 1871–1927, Artist

Concord Art Association, 37 Lexington Road

Elizabeth (''Elsie'') Wentworth Roberts was a painter trained in Philadelphia, Pennsylvania, France, and Italy. She came to New England after the turn of the century and formed a close friendship with Grace Keyes, a resident of Concord. Roberts thereafter made this her permanent winter home, and the two women remained close companions. Finding it difficult to get artistic exposure for her work because of her sex, Elsie began to organize, with other artists, small exhibits, and in 1916 founded the Concord Art Association. She purchased a house and transformed it into a gallery. Much of her time was spent in arranging exhibits of fine works of art, for which she compiled carefully documented catalogs. She willed the gallery to the art association. It is open Tues.-Sat. 11–4:30, Sun. 2–4:30; generally closed Dec. 15–Feb. 1; adm. for nonmembers.[14]

DANVERS

Nurse, Rebecca, 1621–1692, Witchcraft Persecution Victim; NAW

Rebecca Nurse Homestead, 149 Pine Street

Early in 1692 a number of young girls and women in Danvers, then called Salem Village, began to have mysterious fits of hysterics. Puritan theology identified the trouble as caused by witches, and the Salem witchcraft trials began, with numbers of accused, mostly women, being brought to defend themselves. When it was over, more than twenty were dead; others lived but were scarred by the nightmarish trials and imprisonments.

Rebecca Nurse, a respected older woman, dared to criticize the trials and in spite of efforts by her family and friends, she was hanged on Gallows Hill, then buried with four other victims in a common grave. Her sons dug up the body secretly and buried it near the house. Two granite shafts mark the site, one bearing a verse by John Greenleaf Whittier. The home is operated by the Danvers Alarm List Company, Inc., a recreated eighteenth-century militia unit, and is open June–Oct. 15, Tues.-Sat. 1–4:30, Sun. 2–4:30; adm.

DUXBURY

Alden, Priscilla Mullins, b. 1602?, Pioneer; NAW

Alden House, 105 Alden Street

Priscilla Mullins Alden was the only survivor in her family of the terrible first winter in the Plymouth Colony after the *Mayflower* brought them from England. Her marriage to John Alden sometime between 1621 and 1623 was one of the first in the colony. The legend is that Myles Standish, a widower, got John (who was more prepossessing) to propose to Priscilla for him. When she matter-of-factly asked, "John, why do you not speak for yourself?" that sealed the fates of all three. Historians say there is not a shred of evidence to substantiate the story, but it is true that Priscilla married John, bore him eleven children, and helped him found the town of Duxbury. Nobody knows just when she died, but her grave is in the Old Burying Ground, Chestnut Street, out of Hall's Corner, South Duxbury.

The house, built in 1653 by Jonathan Alden, third son of John and Priscilla, is said to have been their last home. The Alden Kindred of America maintain the house, which is open from the last Saturday in June to Labor Day, Tues.-Sun. 10–5; adm.

EVERETT

Mahoney, Mary Eliza, 1845–1926, Nurse; NAW

Monument, Woodlawn Cemetery, 302 Elm Street

Mary Eliza Mahoney was the first black graduate nurse. She received her diploma from the New England Hospital for Women and Children in 1879, one of four graduates in a class that began with eighteen. She always maintained that thc training she received was the most thorough ever given for nurses. By 1899 the school had five Negro alumnae. She was a charter member of the National Association of Colored Graduate Nurses, established in 1908 to raise standards and fight racial bias in the profession. In 1936 a medal was established in her honor by the association. When it merged with the American Nurses Association in 1951, the award was continued and is given to those who make a contribution to intergroup relations. A reproduction of the medal appears on the back of the monument, which was erected in 1974.

FALMOUTH

Bates, Katharine Lee, 1859–1929, Poet; NAW

Katherine Lee Bates House, 16 Main Street

"To have put the expression of the highest and deepest patriotism into the mouths of a hundred million Americans is a monument so noble and so enduring that it seems as if no poet could possibly ask or expect anything more complete." This tribute to Katharine Lee Bates, poet, teacher, and author of America's unofficial anthem "America the Beautiful," was the conclusion of her obituary in the Wellesley *Townsman*. Bates was one of the earliest graduates of Wellesley College and spent most of her life teaching English literature to its students. The Falmouth Public Library now owns her collection of books, most of them poetry. Her birthplace, with its parlor furnished in Victorian style, is owned by the Falmouth Historical Society and is open June 15–Sept. 15, Mon.-Fri. 2–5; adm. See Boston, MA.

FRAMINGHAM

Crocker, Lucretia, 1829–1886, Science Teacher, and Abigail Williams May, 1829–1888, Reformer; NAW

Buildings, State College

Lucretia Crocker and Abigail Williams May were interested in having women vote in school elections and represented on school boards. In 1874 both were elected, along with four other women, to the Boston School Committee. Crocker later became a member of the board of supervisors, with much responsibility for the teaching of science in the public schools (see Boston, MA). Though not a practicing scientist, she was in 1880 elected to the American Association for the Advancement of Science.

May (a first cousin of Louisa May Alcott's mother) served on the State Board of Education from 1879 until shortly before her death. She was interested in many reforms—including abolition, dress reform, and suffrage—and was a founder of the New England Woman's Club. Crocker Hall and May Hall are named in honor of the two women.

Fuller, Meta Vaux Warrick, 1877–1968, Sculptor; NAWM

Storytime, *Sculpture at Framingham Center Library*

Although an accomplished sculptor, educated at the Philadelphia Academy of Fine Arts, l'École des Beaux Arts and the Colarossi Academy, Meta Vaux Warrick Fuller's color was a barrier to sales and exhibitions in her native city, Philadelphia, Pennsylvania. In 1907 she submitted to the Jamestown Tercentennial Exhibition tableaux of 150 figures illustrating the progress of blacks in America, for which she won a gold medal. The award brought her to the attention of the art world. Two years later she moved to Framingham as the wife of Solomon Fuller, a Liberian by birth, who became a noted psychiatrist. This was her home for the rest of her life. She brought up three sons here and managed to continue her artistic career, working first in her home and later in a studio. Most of her earlier pieces were destroyed by fire in 1910, but many of her later pieces are in major U.S. collections. A bronze plaque of a doctor and two nurses is at Framingham Union Hospital, where Solomon practiced.

May, Abigail Williams. See Crocker, Lucretia

GLOUCESTER

Murray, Judith Sargent Stevens, 1751–1820, Feminist; NAW

Sargent-Murray-Gilman-Hough House, 49 Middle Street

Judith Sargent Stevens Murray heard much discussion of human rights and freedom during the Revolutionary period. Like Abigail Adams, she began to question why women should not have the same rights and freedoms men were claiming. Under the name Constantia, she began writing essays on the status of women. In 1790 (when she was the wife of John Murray), the *Massachusetts Magazine* published her essay "On the Equality of the Sexes." It compared the education of boys and girls: "How is the one exalted and the other depressed, by the contrary modes of education which are adopted: the one is taught to aspire, and the other is early confined and limited. As their years increase, the sister must be wholly domesticated, while the brother is led by the hand through all the flowery paths of science."

The Gloucester house, built by her father, Winthrop Sargent, was occupied by Judith and both of her husbands (John Stevens, the first, died in 1786). It is open June-Sept., Tues., Thurs., and Sat. 1–5; rest of year by appointment (617–281–2432); adm.[15]

GREAT BARRINGTON

Anderson, Erica Collier, 1914–1976, Photographer

Albert Schweitzer Center, Hurlburt Road

Erica Collier Anderson, an Austrian photographer, left Vienna during the threatening days of Hitler's warlike preparations. In 1950 she met Albert Schweitzer, and during the next fifteen years she took more than thirty-three thousand photographs of him, although he at first flatly refused to have her around. Five years were spent making a documentary film on the great physician at his hospital in Lambaréné, Gabon, and in his home in Alsace, France. The film, first shown in 1957, won an Academy Award. Among other documentaries she made are *Grandma Moses* and *Henry Moore, Sculptor*. She moved to the Berkshires in 1965 and converted a barn on her property as a depository for her papers and Schweitzer memorabilia. She founded the center with the help of ten thousand dollars left her by Schweitzer. Its purpose is not to keep the great man's memory alive but to carry on his philosophy of reverence for life by means of seminars, lectures, concerts, and counseling. The center is open to the public year-round; in very cold weather, by appointment only. Hours in June and Aug., Tues.-Sat. 10–4, Sun. 12–4; rest of year, Thurs.-Sat. 10–4, Sun. 12–4.[16]

HANCOCK

Lee, Ann, 1736–1784, Religious Founder; NAW

Hancock Shaker Village, US 20, Five Miles South of Pittsfield; HABS, NHL

No Shakers—a sect that retreated from secular life to self-sufficient communities dedicated to religion—live here now. During the 1780s, when the village was established, Mother Ann Lee was still alive; in the 1830s some three hundred men and women lived here. Now only the superb buildings and handcrafted articles remain: some twenty buildings and a thousand acres of woodland. Among the architectural treasures is a round stone barn. Guided tours, lectures, films, and craft programs interpret the Shakers' way of life. Open June–Oct., daily 9:30–5; adm. See Sabbathday Lake, ME, and Canterbury, NH.[17]

HARVARD

Alcott, Louisa May, 1832–1888, Author; NAW

Fruitlands Farmhouse, Prospect Hill Road; NHL

Louisa May Alcott lived at the Fruitlands farmhouse as a child when her father, Bronson Alcott, was active in the transcendentalist movement. The utopian experiment in communal living was not a success. When Bronson went off during the harvest season to give lectures, Louisa's mother had to bring in the crops and preserve them so that the family could eat. Louisa later described the commune with humor in "Transcendental Wild Oats." In her journal she recorded her worries: "More people coming to live with us; I wish we could be together and no one else. I don't see who is to clothe and feed us all, when we are so poor now." The farmhouse, restored and furnished with heirlooms, is part of the Fruitlands Museums. It is open May 30–Sept. 30, Tues.-Sun. 1–5, and Oct. weekends and holidays through Columbus Day; adm. See Boston and Concord, MA.

Sears, Clara Endicott, 1863–1960, Preservationist

Fruitlands Museums; Prospect Hill

Clara Endicott Sears, a descendant of Governor John Winthrop, was a writer and agriculturist. Her country home overlooked Fruitlands, and when the famous house was falling to pieces she undertook to restore it, with some of its original furnishings, as a memorial to the Concord, Massachusetts, philosophers. She wrote several books about the history and people of the area and was also involved in the preservation of the Wayside in Concord. In addition to the Fruitlands farmhouse, the museums include a Shaker house from the Harvard Shaker Village, an American Indian museum, and a picture gallery of American art. All are open May 30–Sept. 30, Tues.-Sun. 1–5, and Oct. weekends and holidays through Columbus Day; adm.[18]

HATFIELD

Smith, Sophia, 1796–1870, College Founder; NAW

Sophia Smith Homestead, 75 Main Street

Sophia Smith never saw the college she founded. It was chartered in 1871 and opened in 1875 in Northampton, Massachusetts, q.v., using her bequest of

$395,105 and her ''Plan for a Woman's College.'' Her will expressed the opinion that ''by the higher and more thoroughly Christian education of women, what are called their 'wrongs' will be redressed, their wages will be adjusted, their weight of influence in reforming the evils of society will be greatly increased; as teachers, as writers, as mothers, and members of society, their power for good will be incalculably enlarged.'' The homestead in which Smith spent her entire life was purchased and refurbished by alumnae of Smith College in 1915. It is not open to the public.[19]

HAVERHILL

Duston, Hannah, 1657–1736?, Indian Captive; NAW

Statue, GAR Park, Main and Summer Streets

If Hannah Duston (or Dustin) were able to write, which seems unlikely, she could have provided one of the most gruesome stories of Indian captivity. She and another woman and a young boy captured here in 1697 were taken to an island near Boscawen, New Hampshire. The Indians had dashed her newborn infant to death before her eyes, and they held out to the captives the prospect of being ''stript, and scourg'd, and run the *gantlet* through the whole army of Indians.'' While their captors slept, the two women and the boy bashed in their heads. A few escaped, but Duston returned home with the scalps of ten. The statue shows Duston with musket, scalping knife, and tomahawk in hand. Today it is the subject of controversy, one group claiming that a murderer should not be honored, others saying she was a heroine for defending herself and managing the escape. In her day she was the most famous of New England women. Cotton Mather saw her heroism as a means of rallying and chastising a nation which had begun to lose its sense of destiny. He talked to her, preached a sermon about her, and wrote her story in *Humiliations follow'd with deliverances . . . with a narrative, of a notable deliverance lately received by some English captives, from the hands of cruel Indians* (1697). The Haverhill Historical Society, 240 Water Street, has relics of Duston (including what is said to be the original tomahawk). See Boscawen and Nashua, NH.[20]

IPSWICH

Bradstreet, Anne, 1612–1672, Poet; NAW

Plaque, 33 High Street

Anne Bradstreet was New England's first woman poet. Her first volume was published in England years after she emigrated to New England (1630) with her father and husband, both officials of the Massachusetts Bay Colony. She lived in Ipswich for a few years before moving to North Andover, Massachusetts, in 1644. She wrote her poems while keeping house at the edge of the wilderness for her husband and eight children. That she was sometimes criticized for spending her time writing is evidenced by the verses carved on this plaque: "I am obnoxious to each carping tongue Who says my hand a needle better fits."[21]

LANCASTER

Rowlandson, Mary White, c. 1635–after 1678, Indian Captive; NAW

Tablet, on Hill above Ropers Brook

On the 10th of February, 1676, the frontier settlement at Lancaster was attacked by Indians. Mary White Rowlandson, one of the settlers, afterward described the events of "the dolefulest day that ever mine eyes saw": the burning houses, men, women, and children shot and brutally butchered, wallowing in blood, while the Indians "ranting and insulting," destroyed everything. She and twenty-three others, including two daughters and a son, were taken captive. They spent a miserable three months trudging from place to place, suffering cold and hunger. One child died and the others were separated from her. Her abiding faith in God's goodness carried her through the ordeal, and from some of her captors she met with kindness. Her skill at sewing and knitting won her favor. When her husband raised a ransom of twenty British pounds, she was allowed to return home unmolested. Later her remaining children reached safety. Her graphic account of her troubles, the earliest account of a New England captivity, made her famous. Reprinted some thirty times under various titles, the narrative was one of the best-selling books in American publishing. The tablet marks the site of her home.[22]

LENOX

Kemble, Frances Anne, 1809–1893, Actress; NAW

Kemble Street

The English-born actress, Frances (Fanny) Anne Kemble, lived in the Perch, a cottage on Kemble Street, in the 1850s, while she gave readings from Shakespeare. She first came to the Berkshires shortly after her American debut in 1832 to be near her friend Catharine Sedgwick. She left the stage on her marriage to Pierce Butler in 1834 and moved to his Georgia plantation. She was horrified by the filth and violence associated with slavery. At length she separated from Butler and he divorced her. Her *Journal of a Residence on a Georgian Plantation*, which she waited to publish until 1863, threw a blazing light on the miserable life of the slaves and helped cool English sympathies with the South during the Civil War. Because she was divorced and connected with the theater, many old New Englanders shunned her, but she numbered among her Lenox friends Sedgwick, Nathaniel Hawthorne, Herman Melville, and other famous residents. She made donations to the local library and gave a clock to the Congregational church.[23]

Tappan, Caroline Sturgis, 1819–1888, Poet; NAW

Tanglewood, State 183

Caroline Sturgis Tappan and her sister, Ellen Sturgis Hooper, transcendental poets, were friends of Ralph Waldo Emerson and regular attendants at Margaret Fuller's "Conversations" in Boston, Massachusetts. Tappan's husband, Lewis Tappan, was a walking companion of Thoreau. She had boarded with Nathaniel and Sophia Hawthorne at the Old Manse in Concord, Massachusetts. They in turn lived in Lenox in 1850–51 in the "Little Red House" on the Tappan estate, first called Highwood and later Tanglewood. Hawthorne's *House of Seven Gables* was written here and his *Tanglewood Tales* made it famous.

The two-hundred acre estate, given to the Boston Symphony Orchestra by Tappan's daughters, is the scene of the annual Berkshire Music Festival. The Little Red House burned in 1891 but has been rebuilt in exact replica. It is used for practice rooms by musicians of the Berkshire Music Center. Concerts are given on weekends from July 28 to Aug. 26, 7 P.M. Fri., 8:30 P.M. Sat., and 2:30 Sun. The grounds are open daily.

Wharton, Edith, 1862–1937, Novelist; NAW

The Mount, Plunkett Road (US 7); NHL

The Pulitzer Prize–winning novelist Edith Wharton grew up a member of the New York aristocracy in what she later called the Age of Innocence. It was, said Janet Flanner, "a hard hierarchy of male money, of female modesty and morals," in which a lady did not write books. Wharton became a Bostonian by marriage to Edward Wharton. They lived first in a Newport, Rhode Island, mansion, then built the Mount. It was here that Wharton began to write. Her first major novel, *The House of Mirth*, was published when she was in her forties. In this and later works, her favorite targets were the idle urban rich and the parvenus who tried to emulate them. She has been called the female Henry James because of her skill in dissecting the foibles of society. She was, indeed, a favorite of James, who addressed her as "Dearest Edith," and introduced her to his London set. The Whartons moved to France in 1910, three years before their divorce. Wharton continued to live in France for the rest of her life. A U.S. postage stamp honoring her was issued in 1980.

The Mount became a girls school, then, acquired by the National Trust, was transferred to Shakespeare and Company, a performing and training school for professional actors. Performances are given on weekend evenings from July to Labor Day.[24]

LOWELL

Larcom, Lucy, 1824–1893, Mill Worker; NAW

Lucy Larcom Park, Adjacent to St. Anne's Church, Merrimack

It is not surprising that the only one of the Lowell mill girls to be memorialized by name here was one who was never involved in any of the "turnouts"—strikes—or complaints against long hours and low wages in the textile mills. Lucy Larcom worked here from 1835 to 1845, living in the boardinghouse her mother ran for young women employees. She was of the first generation of American girls recruited from the farms and she found the mill something like "a rather select industrial school for young people." After a thirteen-hour day at the looms, the women picked up an education through reading and attending lectures. Larcom was a contributor to the *Lowell Offering, A Magazine by Females Actively Employed in the Mills*. Manufacturers were fond of exhibiting this magazine as proof that the employees were healthy, educated, and morally clean young women. About the time Larcom left, the farm girls were being replaced by more easily exploitable immigrant women, and mill labor was a far cry from an industrial school. A monument to the Lowell mill girls was erected in the Lowell Cemetery at the behest of Louisa M. Wells, a mill worker who died in 1886.

LYNN

Eddy, Mary Baker, 1821–1910, Religious Founder; NAW

Mary Baker Eddy House, 12 Broad Street

Mary Baker Eddy bought this little house in 1875. Neighbors stared curiously at the sign, "Christian Scientists' Home." Two years after she moved into the house the book that had occupied so many years of her time, *Science and Health*, was published. Many readers found it over their heads, but among those who approved was Bronson Alcott. He wrote the author: "I hail with joy any voice speaking an assured word for God and Immortality. And my joy is heightened the more when I find the blessed words are of woman's divinings." While she lived here, Mary married Asa Gilbert Eddy, who was to support her dedication to Christian Science until his death in 1882. See Amesbury, Boston, Stoughton, and Swampscott, MA, and Rumney, NH. The house is open May 1–Oct. 31, Wed.-Sat. 11:30–4, Sun. 2–5; rest of year by appointment.

NANTUCKET

Mitchell, Maria, 1818–1889, Astronomer; NAW

Mitchell House, 1 Vestal Street; NHL. Science Library, 2 Vestal Street. Museum of Natural Science, 7 Milk Street. Aquarium, 28

Washington Street. Observatories, Adjacent to House and on Milk Street Extension

On the night of October 1, 1847, Maria Mitchell was on the roof of the Pacific Bank in Nantucket watching the skies through her father's two-inch telescope. She saw a comet, one not yet known to science. Her proud father announced it to the world and the comet was named for her. Nantucket was the greatest whaling port in the world, and as Mitchell explained, people who lived here "quite generally are in the habit of observing the heavens." She came to her love of astronomy through her father and got her formal education in the science through working with him and reading books in the Nantucket Athenaeum, where she was librarian for twenty years.

When Vassar College opened in 1865, Mitchell was invited to be the first teacher of astronomy, a job she was reluctant to accept because of her lack of academic credentials. She was found to be an excellent teacher, as well as a great astronomer, inspiring many young women to enter the field of science. "Nature made woman an observer," she said, "many of the natural sciences are well fitted for woman's power of minute observations." She was elected to the Hall of Fame in New York in 1905.

Mary Watson Whitney (1847–1921, NAW) was a student in Vassar's first classes and when she met Mitchell she chose to major in astronomy. Some thirteen years after graduation and further studies at Harvard University (where no women were yet officially admitted), as well as in Chicago, Illinois, and Zurich, Switzerland, she came back to Vassar as Mitchell's assistant. She succeeded her mentor in 1888 as professor of astronomy and director of the college observatory. Women trained in her program were soon in demand in leading observatories. A feminist, like Mitchell, she is said to have remarked: "I hope when I get to Heaven I shall not find the women playing second fiddle." In 1907 Whitney became president of the Maria Mitchell Association of Nantucket, founded that year as a living memorial to the great astronomer.

Mitchell's childhood home, with its roof walk and gardens, is furnished with family heirlooms. It is open June 15–Sept. 15, Tues.-Sat. 10–12 and 2–5. The library is open the same hours as the home in summer and Mon.-Thurs. 2–4 in winter. In summer the observatory on Milk Street Extension is open on Wed. evenings after dark for viewing the sky; adm. to Mitchell House, Aquarium, and Museum of Natural Science.

NORTH EASTON

Ames, Blanche Ames, 1878–1969, Artist and Women's Rights Advocate; NAWM

Borderland State Park

Blanche Ames Ames was a founder of the Birth Control League of Massachusetts. She was a leader also in the state Woman's Suffrage League and used her artistic talent to produce a series of prosuffrage cartoons. She married botanist Oakes Ames—no relation though with the same name—and for years they collaborated on the study of orchids, Blanche doing the drawings and etchings to illustrate Oakes's text. These are preserved in the Ames Orchid Herbarium at Harvard University. Borderland was the Ames' home, where they raised cattle and where she had a studio, still intact. It is open for tours at irregular intervals.[25]

NORTH OXFORD

Barton, Clara, 1821–1912, Red Cross Founder; NAW

Clara Barton Homestead, Clara Barton Road; NR

North Oxford was the birthplace and early home of Clara Barton. When she was eleven, her older brother was ill and for two years she was his nurse and constant companion, an experience which helped her later in life. As the Civil War broke out, she began collecting from citizens first-aid supplies, medicines, and food, which she took to army hospitals in Maryland and Virginia, commandeering mules and wagons from the army for transport. To soldiers she befriended she was the Angel of the Battlefield. After the war she prepared for the information of relatives lists of soldiers killed in action or dead of wounds or disease. Later she organized an American branch of the International Red Cross and supervised relief activities in many cases of floods, fires, and other disasters. An American heroine, she has memorials in many states.

The monument on her grave, in the North Cemetery, is topped by a red stone cross. The grounds surrounding the homestead host a conference center and a camp for diabetic girls. The house is open Apr.1–Nov. 30, Tues.-Sun. 1–5; rest of year by appointment.[26]

NORTHAMPTON

Smith College

In the years after the Civil War one of the links in the chain of myths that constricted the lives of women was the idea that higher education for women was dangerous to their health. Edward Clarke of Harvard University gave it as his opinion that college training would divert a female's blood supply from her reproductive organs to her brain, with disastrous results for the future of the race. One woman who did not believe this was Sophia Smith (1796–1870, NAW), of Hatfield, Massachusetts, q.v. Her will directed that her dream college be located at Northampton, a larger town than Hatfield. Smith College opened five years after Smith's death. It became one of the largest resident women's colleges in the country, thanks to its strong faculty members and supporters. Many of these have been honored by naming buildings on the campus for them.

Berenson Studio (a dance studio) is named for Senda Berenson (1868–1954),

Smith's first instructor in physical education. Her major contribution to sports was the devising, in 1892, of women's basketball, modified from the men's game and introduced at Smith. Her version of the game remained standard for seventy years. She was married in 1911 to Herbert V. Abbott, professor of English at Smith.[27]

A residence hall is named for Ada Comstock (1876–1973, NAWM), dean of Smith from 1912 to 1923. During 1917–18, in the absence of a president, she ran the college, but because she was a woman the trustees would not give her the title of acting president, an insult to herself and womanhood she never really forgave. She left to become president of Radcliffe College, continuing a distinguished career (see Cambridge, MA). At the age of sixty-six she married for the first time, becoming the wife of Yale professor emeritus Wallace Notestein.[28]

A hall bears the name of a beloved professor, Mary Ellen Chase (1887–1973), who taught English at Smith from 1926 to 1955, meanwhile writing novels, essays, textbooks, and stories. Many deal with Maine life, including her autobiographical *A Goodly Heritage* (1932) and *A Goodly Fellowship* (1939).[29]

The Studio Theater is named for Hallie Flanagan (1890–1969, NAWM), who came to Smith in 1942 as dean and then headed the theater department until 1955. Her involvement in the little theater movement began with the Federal Theater Project, started during the 1930s depression as a relief measure for destitute theater workers. Under Flanagan, a small, redheaded, dynamic woman, the project became a lively institution bringing drama of social significance to millions of Americans—until the House Committee on Un-American Activities decided it was too "free, adult, uncensored" and Congress withdrew its support. She was in private life the wife of Philip Davis.[30]

Sabin-Reed Hall at the Clark Science Center honors two Smith graduates who made names for themselves in the field of medicine. Florence Rena Sabin (1871–1953, NAWM) was a Colorado native. She followed her Smith years with medical training at Johns Hopkins Medical School and then became the first woman appointed to its medical faculty. She is one of the few women honored with a statue in Statuary Hall, Washington, D.C.

Dorothy Reed (1874–1964, NAWM) graduated from Smith in 1895 and then joined Sabin at Johns Hopkins. She researched Hodgkin's disease and demonstrated that a particular blood cell was characteristic of the disease. She married Charles Mendenhall and moved to Wisconsin. She was a medical officer for the U.S. Children's Bureau, 1917–36, and made a study of midwifery in Denmark which led to a recommendation for training of midwives on the Danish model.

Rogers, Harriet Burbank, 1834–1919, Teacher; NAW

Plaque, Entrance to Hubbard Hall, Clarke School for the Deaf

As a young woman, Harriet Burbank Rogers was asked to teach a deaf child, although she had no training or experience in working with the hearing-impaired.

She read of a school in Germany where the deaf were taught to speak by feeling the teacher's breath patterns and voice vibrations in the throat and chest. Using this method, she successfully taught the child speech. At that time the only other method in use was signing. With the help of Gardiner Hubbard, she opened a school in Chelmsford, Massachusetts, to teach the deaf by articulation and lip-reading. When John Clarke endowed the Clarke Institution for Deaf Mutes in 1867, he brought Rogers to Northampton as director.

From 1873 onward Rogers was assisted by Caroline A. Yale (1848–1933, NAW). Yale remained as associate director until 1886, as principal until 1922, and as teacher-training director until her death. The school developed the widely used Northampton Vowel and Consonant Charts, which came to be employed not alone for work with the deaf but also to teach reading to children of normal hearing.

PITTSFIELD

Coolidge, Elizabeth Sprague, 1864–1953, Music Patron; NAWM

South Mountain Concert Hall, New South Mountain Road; NR

The South Mountain Concert Hall, founded in 1918 by Elizabeth Sprague Coolidge, is one of the country's most distinguished musical centers. Concerts are performed in the rustic wooden building with pewlike seats on Saturdays during June, July, and August, and on Sundays in September and October. Coolidge, who also established the Coolidge Foundation at the Library of Congress to support music, was herself a musician and often performed at the early concerts. Many modern composers, including Ottorino Resphigi, Arnold Schönberg, and Paul Hindemith, were commissioned to write compositions premiered at South Mountain.[31]

PROVINCETOWN

Glaspell, Susan (Cook), 1876?–1948, Novelist and Playwright; NAW

Provincetown Playhouse

In 1913, shortly after her marriage to George Cram Cook, Susan Glaspell, a successful Iowa writer, visited Provincetown, and two years later the couple founded the Provincetown Players. An experimental theater, it provided an outlet for some of the most talented young writers in American drama, including Eugene O'Neill and John Reed. In the summer the group worked here, and in winter they migrated to Greenwich Village in New York City, where they organized the Playwright's Theater. The original playhouse in Provincetown, also called the Theater on the Wharf, was destroyed by fire in 1977, but the group still performs, producing at least one of O'Neill's plays each year.[32]

QUINCY

Adams, Abigail Smith, 1744–1818, Feminist; NAW

Abigail Adams House (John Quincy Adams Birthplace), 141 Franklin Street; HABS, NR. Adams National Historic Site, 135 Adams Street

When Abigail Smith married John Adams, it was the beginning of a life as equals and friends for two of the great figures in American history. For the first twenty years of marriage, their home was the small saltbox cottage at 141 Franklin Street. Here Abigail bore five children, one of whom, John Quincy Adams, was the sixth U.S. president. Abigail's husband went off to the Continental Congress in 1774 and the separation continued intermittently for almost ten years. While John served his country, Abigail capably ran the farm. Her sprightly letters to John kept him abreast of domestic affairs and gave him advice on politics. One of America's earliest advocates of sex equality, she cautioned him in making the nation's laws to "remember the ladies" (see Weymouth, MA).

After several years with John in Europe and London, Abigail returned to the mansion at 135 Adams Street. It was a good deal smaller than it is today. In fact, Abigail wrote to her daughter, "In height and breadth it feels like a wren's house." John called the house Peacefield; the family referred to it as the Old House. Abigail was again left alone to run the household much of the time when he was the first vice president and then second president of the United States. She died in the mansion and is now buried in the churchyard of the First Parish Church, 1306 Hancock Street. A cairn opposite 353 Franklin Street marks the spot where Abigail prayed for the revolutionists at Bunker Hill. Part of the Abigail Adams House is open Apr. 19–Oct. 15, daily 9–5; the mansion is open Apr. 19–Nov. 10, daily 9–5; adm.[33]

ROXBURY

Dimock, Susan, 1847–1875, and Marie Zakrzewska, 1829–1902, Physicians; NAW

Dimock Community Center, 55 Dimock Street

Susan Dimock was a student in 1866 at the New England Hospital for Women and Children, predecessor of the community center that now bears her name. It had been founded four years earlier by Marie Zakrzewska. "Dr. Zak" was an Austrian midwife who came to America because she believed it would be easier for a woman to get a medical education here than in Europe. Elizabeth Blackwell, America's pioneer woman M.D., arranged for her to study English and attend the medical department of Western Reserve College in Cleveland, Ohio. She graduated in 1856 and joined Elizabeth and Emily Blackwell at their New York Infirmary for Women and Children. From there she went to Boston, Massachusetts, and with the help of a few Boston women established the New England Hospital, staffed with women physicians. Later she moved the hospital to Roxbury, where the original main building was given her name.

Dimock wished further training after completing the course here and applied to the University of Zurich's medical school. When she returned she was one of the best trained of the early women physicians and she organized the hospital's training school for nurses, the first in the country. Just at the beginning of what seemed a brilliant career, Dimock was drowned off the coast of England. Her family endowed a bed at the hospital in her name. When the hospital's name was changed, so was its orientation. No longer a women's hospital, it now ministers to the health needs of the entire community.

SALEM

Witch Museum, 19-½ Washington Square North

Salem is where men and women were tried for witchcraft in 1692 and many condemned to hang (see Danvers, MA). The museum is devoted to victims of the trials. It is open daily 10–5; later in the summer months; closed some holidays; adm. The Witch House, 310-½ Essex Street, was the home of Jonathan Corwin, judge of the Witchcraft Court. It is open June 1–Labor Day, daily 10–6; Labor Day–Dec. 1 and Mar.-May, daily 10–5; adm.

Crowninshield, Louise du Pont, 1877–1958, Preservationist

Crowninshield-Bentley House, Grounds of Essex Institute

Before Social Security, widows often had to subsist on gifts from the wealthy. The Widows' Society of Boston was organized early in the nineteenth century to dispense such charity, and a hundred years later it was still performing this duty. One of the Ladies Bountiful who visited the widows was Louise du Pont Crowninshield, of the rich and philanthropic Delaware du Ponts. She became a Bostonian by marriage to Francis Boardman Crowninshield in 1900 and, according to a biographer, at once "put her unflagging energy and abilities into the work of various charitable organizations." She is chiefly remembered, however, as a great and knowledgeable collector of antiques and a tireless advocate of historical preservation. She made large contributions to the work of the National Trust for Historic Preservation and to the saving of historical homes of Salem.

The old house that was once the home of John Crowninshield and later of the minister William Bentley was moved from its former site to the Essex Institute in 1960 and restored as a memorial to Louise. The Peabody Museum of Salem, which also benefited from her concern, has a Louise Crowninshield Memorial Room. The Crowninshield-Bentley House is open June 1–Oct. 31, Tues.-Sat. 10–4, Sun. 1–4:30; closed holidays.[34]

SHARON

Sampson, Deborah (Gannett), 1760–1827, Revolutionary War Soldier; NAW

Deborah Sampson Road

In 1804 Paul Revere became acquainted with a woman of some fame: Deborah Sampson Gannett had fought with the Fourth Massachusetts Regiment through three years of the Revolution disguised as a soldier and using the name of Robert Shurtleff. Only when hospitalized with a fever was her sex discovered, and then she was discharged from the army. Revere found her, with her husband, Benjamin Gannett, and three children, almost destitute. In appealing to the Massachusetts authorities in her behalf, he wrote: "When I heard her spoken of as a Soldier, I formed the idea of a tall, masculine female, who had a small share of understanding, without education & one of the meanest of her sex—When I saw & discoursed with her I was agreeably surprised to find a small affeminate conversable Woman, whose education entitled her to a better situation in life." Massachusetts voted her a pension as did the federal government; and after she died, Congress took the unusual step of granting her husband a widow's pension. One wing of the memorial to Sharon's war dead, in Rockridge Cemetery, is devoted to Deborah Sampson Gannett, "revolutionary soldier."[35]

SOUTH HADLEY

Mount Holyoke College

Some years before any organized movement for women's rights got under way in America, Mary Lyon (1797–1849, NAW) contributed to the feminist cause by giving women credit for brains worth developing. "My heart so yearned over the adult female youth in the common walks of life," she wrote, "that it has sometimes seemed as if there was a fire, shut up in my bones." Lyon founded Mount Holyoke, which began as a female seminary, accepting youngsters of twelve and over. She found that men were generally unwilling to give money to build schools for women, so she traveled about Ipswich, Massachusetts, where she was teaching, and then throughout New England soliciting funds from women. The school opened its doors in 1837, and she was its president until her death. It became a college in 1893. One of its halls is named for Lyon; she is buried on the campus. In 1905 she was honored by election to the Hall of Fame in New York.

Several other buildings on the campus bear the names of women associated with the college. A science laboratory was named for Cornelia Maria Clapp

(1849–1934, NAW), who graduated from Mount Holyoke and then taught here from 1872 until her retirement in 1916. She began by teaching math and gym, but soon, influenced by Lydia Shattuck, q.v., she was drawn to natural history. She went to the Anderson School at Woods Hole and carried back to her teaching the enthusiasm for natural science engendered there by Harvard University's Louis Agassiz. She discarded the old texts on natural history and taught by means of laboratory experiments and observations of nature.

Lydia White Shattuck (1822–1889, NAW) graduated from the seminary in 1851, then stayed on as science teacher. Her own training in science had been sparse, but she made up for it by a love for nature, travel, keen observation, wide reading, and association with other scientists. She was one of fifteen women chosen to attend the Anderson School of Natural History at Woods Hole in its first summer, 1873, and was later a member of the Woods Hole Biological Laboratory Corporation. She built up the Mount Holyoke herbarium to include thousands of botanical specimens. In the 1890s a new chemistry and physics building was given her name. It was demolished in 1954 and the name transferred to a later physics building.

Mary Woolley Hall is named for Mary Woolley (1863–1947, NAW), Mount Holyoke's president from 1901 to 1937. If Lyon's philosophy of education formed the basis for the school's strength, it was Woolley's leadership that established the college as one of the great American institutions for women's education. Newspapers made much of the fact that she was the youngest college president in the country when she was inaugurated. In addition to building up the college in every way, Woolley was active outside the academic world. She was appointed a delegate to the Geneva Conference on Reduction and Limitation of Arms in 1932.

SPRINGFIELD

Sanderson, Julia (Crumit), 1887–1975, Actress

Julia Sanderson Theater (Paramount Theater), 1676–1708 Main Street; NR

Julia Sanderson, a native of Springfield, and her husband, Frank Crumit, were perhaps the first husband-wife team to reach radio stardom. They first performed for radio in 1929 and were popular for more than a decade. A five-foot-three-inch beauty, Sanderson had previously been successful in musical comedy. She played the title role in *No! No! Nanette!* and *Sunshine Girl*. In 1915 the West Point yearbook was dedicated to Sanderson. Among her admirers was a graduate of that year, Dwight D. Eisenhower. She married Crumit, her leading man, in 1927, and for years they lived in a lavish country estate in Longmeadow, Massachusetts. After his death in 1943 she retired and lived quietly in Springfield. She contributed to the renovation of the theater which now bears her name.[36]

STOCKBRIDGE

Choate, Mabel, 1871–1958, Art Collector and Philanthropist

Naumkeag, Prospect Hill; NR

Mabel Choate was the daughter of Joseph H. Choate, once ambassador to the Court of St. James, who built Naumkeag as a summer residence in 1885. She inherited the house and fashioned it into a sumptuous home filled with art and rich furnishings. Some, including a large collection of China-trade porcelains and ceramics, were gathered on her many trips to the Orient. The grounds she transformed into a fairyland of terraces, fountains, and groves. She gave the beautiful estate to the Trustees of Reservations in 1958. It is maintained as a museum, open June 23–Labor Day, Tues.-Sun. 10–4:15; Labor Day–Columbus Day and Memorial Day–June 22, weekends only; adm.[37]

Cresson, Margaret French, 1889–1973, Sculptor

Chesterwood, Off Route 183; NHL

Chesterwood was the summer home and studio of the famous sculptor, Daniel Chester French. He died in 1931, leaving the estate to his daughter, Margaret French Cresson, who donated it in 1969 to the National Trust for Historic Preservation. Cresson was herself a sculptor in the traditional style of the 1920s. Her works included bronze busts, reliefs, portrait heads, and memorial plaques. She was married to William Penn Cresson, writer, diplomat, and architect, who died in 1932. Much of her time was given to serving as a trustee for art museums and writing on art for popular magazines. She wrote three books on her father's work. Chesterwood is open May 1–Oct. 31, daily 10–5; adm.[38]

Freeman, Elizabeth (Mumbet), c. 1744–1829, Freed Slave

Monument, Sedgwick Family Plot

The stone reads: "Elizabeth Freeman known by the name of Mumbet died Dec. 28, 1829. Her supposed age was 85 years. She was born a slave and remained a slave for nearly thirty years. She could neither read nor write yet in her own sphere she had no superior or equal. She neither wasted time nor property. She never violated a trust nor failed to perform a duty. In every situation of domestic trial, she was the most efficient helper and the tenderest friend. Good mother farewell." In 1781 Elizabeth Freeman won her freedom in the court under the new Massachusetts Constitution declaring that "all men are created equal." She was the first of her race to achieve freedom by this means. Her lawyer was Theodore Sedgwick. She worked in his household for a generation. Among the children she cared for was his daughter Catharine Sedgwick (1789–1867), novelist, who called Freeman "the main pillar of our household." A portrait of Freeman is in the Massachusetts Historical Society.[39]

STOUGHTON

Eddy, Mary Baker, 1821–1910, Religious Founder; NAW

Mary Baker Eddy House, 133 Central Street (State 1A)

This was the home of Alan and Sally Wentworth, who invited Mary Baker Eddy to stay with them in 1868. She was a poor, lonely, and homeless wanderer, giving lessons in the science of divine healing in exchange for board and room. Eddy lived with the family for eighteen months, teaching Sally and writing her interpretations of the Bible. The house is open May 1–Oct. 31, Tues.-Sat. 10–4, Sun. 1–4; rest of year by appointment. See Amesbury, Boston, Lynn, and Swampscott, MA, and Rumney, NH.

SWAMPSCOTT

Eddy, Mary Baker, 1821–1910, Religious Founder; NAW

Mary Baker Eddy Historical House, 23 Paradise Road

Mary Baker Eddy, before her marriage to Asa Eddy, came to live in the second floor apartment of this house in 1865. It was a bad time for her. Her father died, leaving her one dollar. Her husband, dentist Daniel Patterson, was a philanderer. January, 1866, brought the death of her mentor, Phineas Quimby, from whom she had learned much about spiritual healing. February brought further disaster, when Eddy fell on the ice and suffered severe internal injuries, inducing spasms of intense pain. It was thought that her spine was broken and that she would never walk again. She was determined to recover, and so she did. In a moment of vision, she saw what she felt was the ultimate truth—that all being was spirit. There was no room for what men call matter. It was the decisive moment in her life that led to the founding of Christian Science as a world religion.

The house is open May 15–Oct. 31, Mon.-Sat. 10–5, Sun. 1–5; Nov. 1–May 14, Tues.-Sun. 1–4; adm. See Amesbury, Boston, Lynn, and Stoughton, MA, and Rumney, NH.

WAKEFIELD

Boit, Elizabeth Eaton, 1849–1932, Businesswoman; NAW

Boit Home for Aged Women, 5 Bennett Street

The part played by New England women in the textile industry is well known, but they are remembered as "mill girls," not as entrepreneurs. Elizabeth Eaton Boit stands out as an early factory administrator. She started working in the offices of a hosiery mill at the age of eighteen and became a manufacturer herself in 1888 when with Charles N. Winship she founded the Harvard Knitting Mill. At its height, the firm occupied a floor space of eight and a half acres, numbered 850 employees, and turned out men's, women's, and children's underwear at the rate of 2,000 garments a day. Boit was a good employer, treating the women and girls in the mills with fairness. On a rainy day she would order a streetcar to take them home. She was treasurer of the Wakefield Home for Aged Women, which took her name in recognition of her aid. The knitting mill still stands at 168 Albion Street, its next use possibly housing.[40]

WALTHAM

Heller, Florence, 1897–1966, Philanthropist

Florence Heller Graduate School for Advanced Studies in Social Welfare, Brandeis University

Florence Heller, the wife of Walter Heller, was elected president of the National Jewish Welfare Board in 1964. At that time she spoke of her fear that not enough social workers were being trained, which meant deprivation for those dependent on their services. Three years earlier this niece of Julius Rosenwald had taken a step toward remedying the situation. She founded the school which bears her name at Brandeis and gave it one million dollars for administrative expenses.[41]

WATERTOWN

Hosmer, Harriet, 1830–1908, Sculptor; NAW

Sculptures, Watertown Public Library, 123 Main Street

Watertown was the birthplace of Harriet Hosmer. She set up a studio at home for drawing and modeling, but as no medical school would teach anatomy to a woman, private lessons were arranged in St. Louis, Missouri. Later Hosmer went to Rome, Italy, to study. There she worked hard and began to win public commissions for statues—from the state of Missouri, the city of Dublin, Ireland, and the city of San Francisco, California, among others. While working on her colossal figures she dressed in a mannish jacket, shirt, and cravat, and sometimes in trousers. Her charm and energy disarmed criticism and won her many friends in Rome, including Robert and Elizabeth Browning and Nathaniel and Sophia Hawthorne. Her last years, like her first, were spent in Watertown.

WELLESLEY

Wellesley College

Wellesley College has named a number of buildings to honor women important to its history. Margaret Clapp Library memorializes Margaret Clapp (1910–1974,

NAWM) who served as president of the college from 1949 until 1966. A historian, she had won the Pulitzer Prize in 1948 for *Forgotten First Citizen, John Bigelow*, which started as her Ph.D. thesis. Only thirty-nine when she took the presidency, she brought vigor and a new approach to the job. College women were still expected to prepare themselves first of all for marriage and motherhood; Clapp felt that they should be educated for full participation in citizenship. Her own life served as an example. After resigning from Wellesley she went to South India and served as principal of a liberal arts college in Mandurai. In 1968 she was made cultural attaché in India for the U.S. Information Agency. "I became increasingly convinced," she wrote, "that people should move outside their own culture at some time in their lives. You see your own culture freshly when you see a culture with a different set of assumptions and traditions."[42]

Margaret Clay Ferguson (1863–1951, NAWM) designed the Wellesley greenhouses named for her and also raised funds to build them and a botany building, completed in 1927. Under her administration, the department of botany became a leading center for the study of plant science by undergraduates.

Mary Hemenway Hall was named for Mary Hemenway (1820–1894, NAW), a philanthropist who had founded the Boston Normal School of Gymnastics. Wellesley took over this school. Hemenway was a moderately wealthy woman of Boston, Massachusetts, with wide-ranging interests. Typical of the projects she supported were schools for blacks in the South, training in manual and household arts in Boston schools, the Hemenway Southwestern Archaeological Expedition, and preservation of the Old South Meeting House in Boston.

A memorial in the college chapel honors Alice Freeman Palmer (1855–1902, NAW), the second and much-loved president of Wellesley. During her six-year tenure she shaped the basic structure for the administration. She left on her marriage to George Palmer, who taught at Harvard University, but she continued working for women's advancement as a volunteer on public and private boards. In 1920 she was elected to the Hall of Fame in New York.

Observatory House was the home of Sarah Frances Whiting (1847–1927, NAW), appointed teacher of physics when Wellesley first opened its doors. She set up the first physics laboratory in a woman's college, and two years later introduced, under the name of "applied physics," a course in astronomy. A Wellesley trustee with a similar name, Mrs. John C. Whitin, donated an observatory and next to it built Observatory House as a home for Whiting. Whiting retired from teaching physics but remained as director of the Whitin Observatory until almost seventy.

WEST ROXBURY

Fuller, Margaret, 1810–1850, Feminist; NAW

Cottage, Brook Farm, 670 Baker Street; NHL

None of the original buildings of the famous utopian community remain here except the small cottage named for Margaret Fuller (see Cambridge, MA). The community was established by a group of transcendentalist philosophers in 1841 as a place where they could renew contact with the soil and live by cooperative labor. Called the Brook Farm Institute of Agriculture and Education, it began with Sophia Dana Ripley and her husband and eventually included Ralph Waldo Emerson, Bronson Alcott, Georgiana Bruce, and Elizabeth Peabody, among others. The community in Nathaniel Hawthorne's *Blithedale Romance* bears a striking resemblance to Brook Farm. Fuller, whose "Conversations" in Boston, Massachusetts, were a major influence in the development of the philosophy, visited the community but did not live here. The association was formally disbanded after only six years, an economic failure.

The property has had a checkered history since then. Sold to the town of Roxbury, it was used as a poor farm. During the Civil War it was lent to an infantry regiment and the troops cut down the trees in Piney Woods for fuel. Later it was a children's home. In 1966 it was named a National Historic Landmark with a view to its preservation. The grounds are open by way of a nature trail leading from the cemetery. It contains a 168-acre wildlife refuge and eventual historical museum. The West Roxbury Public Library has research materials on the community.[43]

WEYMOUTH

Adams, Abigail Smith, 1744–1818, Feminist; NAW

Abigail Adams Birthplace, North and Norton Streets, E. Weymouth

Abigail Smith Adams' words to her husband, John Adams, when he was in Congress in 1776, are often quoted with relish by today's feminists: "Remember the Ladies, and be more generous and favourable to them than your ancestors. Do not put such unlimited power into the hands of Husbands. Remember all Men would be tyrants if they could. If particular care and attention is not paid to the Laidies [sic] we are determined to foment a Rebelion [sic], and will not hold ourselves bound by any Laws in which we have no voice, or Representation." Her warning to John had little enough effect, but that did not keep her from often repeating her strong opinions against oppression or discrimination on the grounds of sex, creed, or color.

Abigail lived in this house for the first twenty years of her life. It was the parsonage of the First Congregational Church of Weymouth. Though she had no formal schooling, she had access to a good library. She taught herself to read French and read voraciously Shakespeare, Milton, Pope, and books of sermons. John courted her for two years, during which they carried on a startlingly uninhibited correspondence. In 1764 she became his wife and partner for life (see Quincy, MA). The house is maintained by the Abigail Adams Historical Society and is open in July and Aug., Tues.-Sat. 1–4; adm. Adams is in the National Women's Hall of Fame.

WORCESTER

Foster, Abigail Kelley, 1810–1887, Abolitionist; NAW

Abigail Kelley and Stephen S. Foster Home, 116 Mower Street (Private); NR

Abigail Kelley Foster made her first public speech in May 1838. The circumstances were anything but auspicious. The Anti-Slavery Convention of American Women was meeting in Philadelphia's Pennsylvania Hall. Reformers who had found it almost impossible to rent space for meetings on abolition and other unpopular topics had erected the hall for that use. Two days after opening ceremonies of this monument to free speech, a noisy and violent crowd surrounded the building. As Maria Chapman, Angelina Grimké, and Foster spoke, bricks crashed through the windows; the shouting and stamping outside almost drowned out their voices; men threatened to burst open the doors. After Foster's speech, Theodore Weld, newly wedded to Angelina Grimké, told Foster she must become an antislavery lecturer. "Abby, if you don't," he said, "God will smite you." For many years thereafter Foster was one of the most powerful and effective abolitionist speakers, but never again in Pennsylvania Hall. The mob had burned it to the ground. Abby married Stephen S. Foster and they lectured for the cause together. In 1847 they bought the farm in Worcester. Years later they began to dramatize the issue of discrimination against women by refusing to pay taxes on the farm, on the grounds that Abby was taxed without representation.[44]

Workman, Fanny Bullock, 1859–1925, Mountaineer; NAW

Monument, Rural Cemetery, 180 Grove

After five climbing expeditions into the mountain ranges of Tibet, Fanny Bullock Workman and William Hunter Workman had not intended to return. "But we had breathed the atmosphere of that great mountain-world, had drunk of the swirling waters of its glaciers, and feasted our eyes on the incomparable beauty and majesty of its towering peaks," wrote Fanny—and they could not resist another visit, and still another. The couple's first of seven climbs was made in 1898, their last in 1912, when Fanny was fifty-three and William sixty-five, hardly in the first flush of youth. When William retired from his Worcester medical practice because of ill health in 1889, Fanny's cure consisted of several years of energetic long-distance bicycle trips, followed by even more strenuous mountaineering. The bicycle trips took them through Algeria and Spain, then Ceylon, Java, Sumatra, and Cochin China—to use the old names—and India. The climbing made them famous. Fanny took a fierce pride in having reached a greater height than any woman (23,300 feet, a record in 1906). An ardent feminist, she was once photographed on a glacier with a newspaper headlined "Votes for Women." Between trips they collaborated on eight books detailing

Abigail Kelley Foster, lecturer on women's rights, of Worcester, Massachusetts. An engraving from a daguerreotype of 1846.
Courtesy Library of Congress.

their adventures. Fanny died in France and William brought her ashes back to Massachusetts for burial in her native city. He lived to be a hardy ninety-one. The stone over their graves reads: "Pioneer Himalayan Explorers."[45].

NOTES

In addition to the correspondents below, I have been assisted by the following: Framingham Historical Society; Massachusetts Audubon Society; Old Corner Bookstore; The Trustees of Reservations of Massachusetts; Schlesinger Library; Eldredge Public Library, Chatham; Nantucket Historical Association; Conant Free Public Library, Sterling; Salem Cross Inn; Amherst College; Abigail Adams Historical Society; Alden Kindred of America, Inc.; Isabella Stewart Gardner Museum; The First Church of Christ, Scientist, Boston; Minute Man National Historical Park in Concord; The Adams National Historic Site; Maria Mitchell House; Louisa May Alcott Memorial Association; Rebecca Nurse Homestead.

1. Kathleen A. Smallzried, *The Everlasting Pleasure: Influences on America's Kitchens, Cooks and Cookery, from 1565 to the Year 2000* (New York: Appleton-Century-Crofts, 1956).

2. Dorothy Burgess, *Dream and Deed: The Story of Katharine Lee Bates* (Norman: University of Oklahoma Press, 1952).

3. Deborah Crawford, *Four Women in a Violent Time* (New York: Crown Publishers, 1970).

4. Louise Hall Tharp, *Three Saints and a Sinner* (Boston, Mass.: Little, Brown & Co., 1956).

5. Wellington Newcomb, "Anne Hutchinson versus Massachusetts," *American Heritage* 15 (June 1974); Crawford, *Four Women*.

6. Charlotte S. Rubinstein, *American Women Artists* (New York: Avon Books, 1982).

7. Nicholas Zook, *Houses of New England Open to the Public* (Barre, Mass.: Barre Publishers, 1968); correspondence, Boston Public Library.

8. Elinor Rice Hays, *Those Extraordinary Blackwells* (New York: Harcourt, Brace & World, 1967); Van Wyck Brooks, *The Flowering of New England* (New York: E. P. Dutton, 1936).

9. Vida Scudder, *On Journey* (Philadelphia, Pa.: Richard West, 1937).

10. Elizabeth R. Payne, "Anne Whitney: Art and Social Justice," *Massachusetts Review* 12 (Winter 1971); Jeanne M. Weimann, *The Fair Women: The Story of The Woman's Building, World's Columbian Exposition* (Chicago, Ill.: Academy Chicago, 1981).

11. Clippings and correspondence, Radcliffe College.

12. Emily Taft Douglas, *Margaret Sanger: Pioneer of the Future* (New York: Holt, Rinehart and Winston, 1970); *New York Times*, Jan. 13, 1968.

13. "Preface," *Notable American Women, 1607–1950*, ed. Edward T. James and others (Cambridge, Mass.: Belknap Press of Harvard University Press, 1971); *New York Times*, June 1, 1977; Christina Robb, "Barbara Haber, Arbiter of Women's History," *MS Magazine*, Sept. 1982.

14. Gladys E. H. Hosmer, "Some Notable Concord Women," *Concord Journal*, Nov. 9 and 16, 1961; correspondence, Concord Art Association.

15. *The Feminist Papers: From Adams to Beauvoir*, ed. Alice Rossi (New York:

Columbia University Press, 1973); correspondence, Sargent-Murray-Gilman-Hough House Association.

16. *New York Times*, Sept. 25, 1976; correspondence and brochures, Albert Schweitzer Center.

17. Jane Holtz Kay, "Last of the Shakers," *Historic Preservation* 34 (Mar.-Apr. 1982); June Sprigg, "Hancock's Shaker Village, 'The City of Peace,' " *Antiques* 120 (Oct. 1981); correspondence, Hancock Shaker Village.

18. Undated, unsigned MS obituary, Schlesinger Library; correspondence and brochure, Fruitlands Museums.

19. Correspondence, Smith College.

20. Duston's story is printed in *We Were New England: Yankee Life By Those Who Lived It*, ed. Barrows Mussey (New York: Stackpole Sons, 1937); Laurel T. Ulrich, *Good Wives* (New York: Alfred A. Knopf, 1982), part 3 discusses her story and its significance in feminist terms.

21. Ann Stanford, "Ann Bradstreet, Dogmatist and Rebel," *New England Quarterly* 39 (Sept. 1966).

22. *We Were New England* also prints Rowlandson's narrative, and Ulrich discusses it in *Good Wives*.

23. *Life and Letters of Catharine M. Sedgwick*, ed. Mary E. Dewey (New York: Harper & Bros., 1872).

24. Richard Anthony, "The Endangered Properties Program: Last Hope for Landmarks," *Historic Preservation* 33 (Jan.-Feb. 1981); Janet Flanner, "Dearest Edith," *New Yorker* 5 (Mar. 1, 1929); Harry F. Waters, "Wharton's Gilded Age," *Newsweek*, Nov. 2, 1981.

25. Correspondence, Ames Free Library of Easton.

26. Patrick F. Gilbo, "Candid, 'Cranky' Clara Barton Gave Us the Red Cross," *Smithsonian* 12 (May 1981).

27. *Liberty's Women*, ed. Robert McHenry (Springfield, Mass.: G. & C. Merriam Co., 1980).

28. Susan Margot Smith, "Ada Comstock Notestein," in *Women of Minnesota*, ed. Barbara Stuhler and Gretchen Kreuter (St. Paul: Minnesota Historical Society Press, 1977).

29. *Current Biography*, 1940; *New York Times*, July 30, 1973.

30. *New York Times*, July 24 and Aug. 3, 1969.

31. Stephanie L. Johnson, *The Best of the Berkshires* (Chester, Conn.: Globe Pequot Press, 1979); correspondence, South Mountain Concert Hall.

32. "Iowa Writers and Painters," *Annals of Iowa* 42 (Spring 1974); Emilie Harting, *A Literary Tour Guide to the United States: Northeast* (New York: William Morrow & Co., 1978).

33. Margaret Coit, "Dearest Friends," *American Heritage* 19 (Oct. 1968); M. A. DeWolfe Howe, *Who Lived Here?* (New York: Bramhall House, 1952).

34. Walter Whitehill, *Analecta Biographica: A Handful of New England Portraits* (Brattleboro, Vt.: Stephen Greene Press, 1969); correspondence, Essex Institute.

35. Esther Forbes, *Paul Revere and the World He Lived In* (Cambridge, Mass.: Houghton Mifflin Co., 1942; Sally Smith Booth, *The Women of '76* (New York: Hastings House, 1973); Ann McGovern, *The Secret Soldier: The Story of Deborah Sampson* (New York: Four Winds Press, 1975).

36. Irving Settel, *A Pictorial History of Radio* (New York: Citadel Press, 1960);

Springfield *Sunday Republican*, Feb. 1, 1978; Springfield *Union*, Jan. 20, 1975; correspondence, Springfield City Library.

37. Anne D. and Warren C. Moffett, "Naumkeag, A Berkshire Landmark," *Antiques* 120 (July 1981); *New York Times*, Dec. 19, 1958; correspondence, Naumkeag.

38. *New York Times*, Oct. 2. 1973; correspondence, Chesterwood Studio Museum.

39. Harold W. Felton, *Mumbet: The Story of Elizabeth Freeman* (New York: Dodd, Mead & Co., 1970); Sylvia G. L. Dannett, *Profiles of Negro Womanhood*, vol. 1 (Yonkers, N.Y.: Educational Heritage, 1964).

40. Correspondence, Lucius Beebe Memorial Library, Wakefield.

41. Jacob R. Marcus, *The American Jewish Woman, 1654–1980* (New York: Ktav, 1981); *New York Times*, Jan. 6, 1966.

42. *New York Times*, May 4, 1974; *Current Biography*, 1948.

43. Edith Roelker Curtis, *A Season in Utopia: The Story of Brook Farm* (New York: Thomas Nelson & Sons, 1961).

44. Gerda Lerner, *The Grimké Sisters from South Carolina* (New York: Schocken Books, 1971).

45. William Hunter Workman and Fannie Bullock Workman, *The Call of the Snowy Hispar* (New York: Charles Scribner's Sons, 1911).

NEW HAMPSHIRE

BOSCAWEN

Duston, Hannah, 1657–1736?, Indian Captive; NAW

Statue, Duston Island, Confluence of the Merrimack and Contoocook Rivers

Hannah Duston (see Haverhill, MA) was brought here as the captive of a band of Indians in 1697. She and another woman and a young boy captured earlier conspired to kill the Indians, who had threatened to torture and enslave them. The boy had been shown by an Indian how they scalped whites, and after he and Duston had killed most of their captors, they scalped ten of the victims. The Massachusetts General Court paid her a bounty of fifty British pounds for the scalps. Time has so changed attitudes toward Native Americans that many now wish to have the statues removed. But a group of Duston's descendants, the Duston-Dustin Family Association, annually honors her as a frontier heroine. See Nashua, NH.[1]

CANTERBURY

Lee, Ann, 1736–1784, Religious Founder; NAW

Shaker Village, Fifteen Miles North of Concord; NR

In 1982 only three elderly women remained here of nine surviving Shakers. Ten years earlier the three women turned over the twenty-two buildings and six hundred acres to a nonprofit organization, Canterbury Shaker Village. Regarded as one of the most significant historical properties in the country, it was founded in 1792 by followers of Mother Ann Lee, who believed in the imminent coming of Christ. Members withdrew into self-sustaining celibate communities, following Lee's creed, "Put your hands to work and give your hearts to God." Here they made wooden boxes and washing tubs, capes, and cloaks, produced vegetable and herb seeds, and made maple sugar. Of the eighteen original settlements across the country, most of them in New York and New England, almost all have been turned over to other uses. Canterbury is dedicated to research and preservation of Shaker history and craftsmanship. It is open for guided tours May 15–Oct. 20, Tues.-Sat. 10–4; adm. See Sabbathday Lake, ME, and Hancock, MA.[2]

JAFFREY

Cather, Willa, 1873–1947, Writer; NAW

Marker, Old Town Burial Ground

Willa Cather, whose writings so clearly interpreted the frontier life of the Great Plains, grew to love the area around Jaffrey. She retreated here for a few weeks each summer to write undisturbed, and she asked to be buried here in the shadow of Mount Monadnock. Parts of *My Antonia* (1918) and *One of Ours* (1922), which won the Pulitzer Prize, were written here. The tombstone bears this quotation from *My Antonia*: "That is happiness; to be dissolved into something complete and great."

Davis, Hannah, 1784–1863, Boxmaker

Marker, State 124

The marker, about two miles west of the junction with State 202, tells us that "Aunt" Hannah Davis was a "resourceful and beloved spinster who made, trademarked and sold this country's first wooden bandboxes." Her house, at 249 Main Street, is now privately owned. Davis's sprucewood boxes, covered with brightly colored wallpaper, are now in museum collections.

MILFORD

Cutter, Carrie Eliza, 1842–1862, Civil War Nurse

Memorial, Old Cemetery, Elm Street

Young Carrie Eliza Cutter, a native daughter of Milford, was an early casualty of the Civil War. She traveled with the Twenty-first New Hampshire Regiment to Maryland and North Carolina, and she died of fever contracted while nursing the troops. She is not buried here; the memorial was placed near her mother's grave. It is claimed that "she was the first female to enter the service of her country in the Civil War, the first that fell at her post, and the first to form organized efforts to supply the sick of the army."[3]

NASHUA

Duston, Hannah, 1657–1736?, Indian Captive; NAW

Tablet, Alldst and Fifield Streets

The pioneer heroine Hannah Duston (see Boscawen, NH) is said to have spent the first night after her escape from Indian captivity in 1697 here, in a cabin owned by John Lovewell. See Haverhill, MA.

NEWPORT

Hale, Sarah Josepha Buell, 1788–1879, Writer and Editor NAW

Memorial, State 103

The tablet, on a grass island between town and state roads near the post office, records that Sarah Josepha Buell Hale, ''prominent humanitarian, poet and author,'' was born and taught school in Newport. Her greatest claim to fame is not the composition of ''Mary Had a Little Lamb'' nor the establishment of Thanksgiving as a national holiday or Mount Vernon as a national shrine. It is her long career as the editor of *Godey's Lady's Book* from 1837 to 1877. Hale was far from a radical feminist. She believed with others of her time that marriage and motherhood comprised women's destiny. But she did recommend that every young lady acquire a skill or practice an art or profession that could support her in case of need. She herself entered on her writing career when her husband died and left her with four children and expecting a fifth. She advocated greater educational opportunities for women, and she approved of women physicians because it would mean that females could get medical attention without loss of delicacy.

PETERBOROUGH

MacDowell, Marian Nevins, 1857–1956, Musician; NAWM

MacDowell Colony; NHL

The MacDowell Colony has for six decades offered a quiet retreat where creative artists work undisturbed. Many now world-famous figures in literature, art, and music are thankful for the opportunity they were given to live in one of its tranquil studios for a time. The nucleus of the colony was the summer home of Edward MacDowell, the composer, and his wife, Marian Nevins MacDowell. The establishment and success of the colony is almost entirely due to her efforts over the years after Edward's death in 1908, until age and ill health forced her to abandon her activities there in 1945. She gave concerts in her husband's memory, raised funds, supervised construction of roads and cottages, and made the colony one of the great cultural institutions of America. Some two hundred artists a year work at MacDowell. Among its "graduates" are more than thirty Pulitzer Prize winners. In 1949 Marian was honored by a grant from the National Institute of Arts and Letters for distinguished service to the arts. Grounds open Mon.-Sat. 2–5. A sign at the entrance says, "Visitors most welcome, save on Sunday."[4]

RUMNEY

Eddy, Mary Baker, 1821–1910, Religious Founder; NAW

Mary Baker Eddy Historic House, Stinson Lake Road

Mary Baker Eddy, then the wife of Daniel Patterson, lived in Rumney between 1860 and 1862, first in a boardinghouse, then in the house Patterson bought. When war broke out, Daniel went South, commissioned to take funds from New Hampshire to sympathizers of the Union cause. He was captured and taken to prison, leaving his poor wife without support. She was so ill with a spinal inflammation that she had to be carried up and down the stairs. She arranged to go for medical treatment to Phineas Quimby, in Portland, Maine. It proved a turning point in her life, for it introduced her to Quimby's principles of science and health, which she adopted in founding the Christian Science church. The house is open from May through Oct., Tues.-Sat. 10–5, Sun. 1–5; adm. Other memorials to Eddy are in Amesbury, Boston, Lynn, Stoughton, and Swampscott, MA.

STAR ISLAND, ISLES OF SHOALS

Thaxter, Celia Laighton, 1835–1894, Poet; NAW

Thaxter Room, Vaughn Memorial Building

> To feel the wind sea-scented on my cheek,
> To catch the sound of dusky flapping sail,
> And dip of oars, and voices on the gale,
> Afar off, calling softly, low and sweet.

Most of Celia Laighton Thaxter's poems, like this first one printed in the *Atlantic Monthly* in 1861, center around her love for the Isles of Shoals, off the Maine–New Hampshire coast. She grew up here on White Island, where her father was the lighthouse keeper, and lived for some years and many summers on Appledore, where her family ran a famed summer hotel. For most of her married years, however, she lived on the mainland because her husband took a dislike to the sea. She was for long one of the better-known New England poets. Gifted with a happy and outgoing personality, she was hostess to many contemporary writers, including John Greenleaf Whittier, Annie Fields, and Sarah Orne Jewett.

Star Island, ten miles from Portsmouth, is now a religious conference center and can be reached by ferry during the summer.[5]

NOTES

In addition to sources noted below, I have had help from the New Hampshire Historical Society, Concord, and the State Division of Economic Development, Concord.

1. *We Were New England: Yankee Life by Those Who Lived It*, ed. Barrows Mussey (New York: Stackpole Sons, 1937).

2. Jane Holtz Kay, "Last of the Shakers," *Historic Preservation* 34 (Mar.–Apr. 1982).

3. Andrew Kull, *New England Cemeteries: A Collector's Guide* (Brattleboro, Vt.: Stephen Greene Press, 1975).

4. William F. Claire, "Yaddo and MacDowell," *Smithsonian* 8 (July 1977).

5. Thaxter's "Land-Locked" appeared anonymously in the *Atlantic Monthly* 7 (March 1861); Lyman V. Rutledge, *The Isles of Shoals in Lore and Legend* (Barre, Mass.: Barre Publishers, 1965).

RHODE ISLAND

COVENTRY

Greene, Catherine Littlefield, 1755–1814, Plantation Manager; NAW

Home, 50 Taft Street, Anthony Village; HABS, NHL

Catherine (Kitty) Littlefield Greene, born in Rhode Island, married, in 1774, Nathanael Greene, who was to join the Revolutionary forces. They built this house and occupied it until 1783, although Nathanael's military duties gave him little time at home. Kitty was a delightful, animated young woman who followed her husband to his quarters on the Schuylkill and at Morristown, New Jersey, in the grim winter of 1777–78 and won the respect of Washington and other officers. She bore three children during the war years and two more after peace was won.

As a reward for his leadership during the Revolution, General Greene was given land in Georgia. In 1785, after the family had moved to the plantation, Mulberry Grove, he died, leaving his young widow with a debt-ridden estate, managed by Phineas Miller, the children's tutor. They were joined by Eli Whitney. With Greene's encouragement and at her suggestion, Whitney devised a machine to strip the seeds from cotton, an invention that revolutionized the process of growing and preparing cotton. That Greene was the real inventor of the cotton gin is not exactly true, but certainly it was her confidence and support, moral and financial, that helped Whitney to manufacture the device. Greene and Miller were married in 1795.

Greene maintained her ties with Rhode Island, returning every summer for some years. The house is now a museum with Greene furnishings and memorabilia. It is open Mar.-Nov., Wed., Sat., and Sun. 2–5; adm.[1]

HOPE VALLEY

Crandall, Prudence (Philleo), 1803–1890, Abolitionist and Educator; NAW

Monument, Town Park

Prudence Crandall, who was born in Hopkinton, Rhode Island, opened a school for girls in Canterbury, Connecticut, q.v. When she took Sarah Harris, the daughter of a French West Indian farmer, as a pupil, the people of Canterbury objected to the presence of a black girl with their daughters. The objections grew so violent that Crandall was forced to give up the school. She married Calvin Philleo, a minister who had supported her fight, and eventually moved West. About the same time Sarah Harris married George Fayerweather. The two women remained in touch with each other all their lives. Toward the end of Crandall's life, when she was a widow, the people of Connecticut considered compensating her for the damage to her property. Writing to Harris in 1886, Crandall said: "I do not want anyone to give me one cent, but I do want the state that injured me so unjustly to pay me a little for destruction of property, and the cutting off of every prospect and hope that lies before us when young."[2]

KINGSTON

Fayerweather, Sarah Harris, 1812–1878, Abolitionist

Fayerweather Craft Center, Mooresfield Road. Fayerweather Hall, University of Rhode Island

Sarah Harris Fayerweather's role in the tragedy of Prudence Crandall's school in Connecticut ensured that she would be involved in a lifelong crusade on behalf of black citizens. Some time after her marriage to George Fayerweather, she moved to Kingston. Here George took up the blacksmith business his father, an Afro-Indian, had established late in the eighteenth century. Their home became a center for antislavery activity. Great abolitionist leaders William Lloyd Garrison and Frederick Douglass visited them.

When the old Fayerweather cottage was restored recently, a packet of letters was discovered that throws light on Sarah's life and on the friendship between Prudence Crandall and the Fayerweathers. The home is now the craft center, open May-Dec., Tues.–Sat. 11–4. Fayerweather Hall, a dormitory at the university, was dedicated to Sarah in 1970. See Canterbury, CT, and Hope Valley, RI.[3]

LITTLE COMPTON

Pabodie, Elizabeth Alden, 1623–1717, Pioneer

Monument, Commons Burial Ground

Elizabeth Alden Pabodie was the daughter of the legendary lovers, John and Priscilla Alden (see Duxbury, MA). The count of Pabodie's progeny (12 children, 82 grandchildren, and 556 great-grandchildren by the time of her death at age 93) perhaps explains how so many persons can claim *Mayflower* ancestry. She was one of eleven Alden children, one of whom, oddly enough, married the son of Myles Standish. Elizabeth and her husband, William Pabodie, came to Little Compton in 1684. In 1882 a local poet, George Burleigh, wrote a long narrative poem telling in romantic vein the story of her life. Four lines are carved on her memorial:

> A bud from Plymouth's Mayflower sprung,
> Transplanted here to live and bloom,
> Her memory, ever sweet and young,
> The centuries guard within this tomb.[4]

NARRAGANSETT

Davis, Varina Anne (Winnie), 1864–1898, Writer

Memorial Window, St. Peter's-by-the-Sea

Varina Anne (Winnie) Davis, the daughter of Jefferson Davis, was born during the Civil War in Richmond, Virginia. In 1886 a veterans' group gave her the title of the Daughter of the Confederacy. Later her engagement to a northerner, grandson of the noted abolitionist Samuel J. May, caused such pain and anguish to southerners that the match was called off. Davis never married. She took to writing, producing two novels before her death at thirty-four. The stained-glass window was placed in this unlikely spot because she died while vacationing at Narragansett Pier.[5]

NEWPORT

International Tennis Hall of Fame, Newport Casino, 194 Bellevue Avenue; HABS, NR

The International Tennis Hall of Fame is a museum of tennis, a site for tennis tournaments, and the home of the National Tennis Hall of Fame. Each year since 1956 it has elected outstanding players, many of them female. Men were at first inclined to regard tennis as effeminate, because it was introduced into the United States by a woman (Mary Ewing Outerbridge, of Staten Island, New York) and was played by society women on grassy lawns of country villas. They wore dresses with long, full skirts (over corsets and petticoats), long-sleeved and high-necked; their complexions were protected by brimmed hats. It is a tribute to the spirit and ambition of women players that, so encumbered, they went at the game with vigor and joy. Men, without the same strictures as to costume and behavior, soon found the game both invigorating and challenging. They instituted tennis clubs and tournaments and, finally, the Tennis Hall of Fame.

The first woman elected was May Sutton (later Bundy, 1887–1975), one of four sisters, all excellent players, who dominated women's tennis in southern California. She was the first American woman to win at Wimbledon, where she won the singles championship in 1905. She had the previous year won both U.S. singles and doubles.

Many others elected were pioneers who began playing in tournaments before the end of the nineteenth century. Two were members of the Philadelphia "Big Four": Ellen Forde Hansell (later Allerdice, 1869–1937) won the first U.S. women's singles championship, 1887; and Bertha Townsend (later Toulmin, 1869–1909) won the title in 1888 and again in 1889. Ellen C. Roosevelt (1868–1954) defeated her sister to win the 1890 singles championship as well as the doubles and won the mixed doubles three years later. Juliette P. Atkinson of Brooklyn, New York, won thirteen championship titles between 1894 and 1902. Elisabeth H. Moore (1876–1944) began her winning career in 1896 and won a number of titles before 1905.

California women were among the great players. Hazel Hotchkiss (later Wightman, 1886–1974) began playing championship games in California and won the U.S. singles, doubles, and mixed doubles in 1909. Between that time and 1928 she chalked up numerous victories. Known as the Queen Mother of Tennis, she sponsored international tournaments and instituted the Wightman Cup for women's tennis. Elizabeth Ryan (1892–1979), of Anaheim, California, excelled in doubles. Between 1926 and her retirement in 1933 she had won more than six hundred events, nineteen titles at Wimbledon. Maureen Connolly (later Brinker, 1934–1969), of southern California, was known as Little Mo. She won the grand slam of tennis in 1953: the Australian, French, English, and U.S. singles titles.

Among eastern players was sportswoman Eleanora Sears (1881–1968), of Boston, Massachusetts, who excelled in many sports and began winning tennis titles in 1911. She helped to change the restrictions on dress. Marie Wagner (1883–1975) was a popular player in metropolitan New York. Maud Barger Wallach (1871–1954) began winning titles in 1908 and long continued a strong interest in tennis.

Two players from abroad influenced the game. Molla Bjurstedt (later Mallory, 1892–1959) came from Norway and later became a U.S. citizen. She won many titles between 1915 and 1928. In 1916 she published *Tennis for Women*, the first book on the subject written by a woman playing in America. Suzanne Lenglen (1899–1938), the dashing and temperamental Frenchwoman, was the darling of tennis, drawing crowds wherever she played. She shocked spectators at Wimbledon in 1919 by appearing in a one-piece sleeveless dress. Teamed

Elisabeth H. Moore, who began winning tennis tournaments in 1896, did not let long skirts hamper her game.
Courtesy International Tennis Hall of Fame, Newport, Rhode Island.

with Elizabeth Ryan, she won five women's doubles championships at Wimbledon, besides two mixed doubles titles.

The hall is open May-Oct., daily 9:30–5:30; Nov.-Apr., daily 11–4.[6]

Belmont, Alva Smith Vanderbilt, 1853–1933, Suffragist; NAW

Marble House, Bellevue Avenue; NR

Early in the twentieth century the suffrage cause won support—financial, social, and militant—from a most unexpected source. Alva Smith Vanderbilt Belmont, divorced wife of William K. Vanderbilt and widow of Oliver H. P. Belmont, was a wealthy society woman. Up to the time of Oliver's death in 1908 she had seemed thoroughly immersed in living ostentatiously and lavishly on her husbands' wealth and controlling her three children's lives. Then, influenced by Anna Howard Shaw, she became an ardent suffragist and began to entertain women's groups at Marble House. She rented the entire floor of an office building in New York City as headquarters for the National American Woman's Suffrage Association. She arranged a lecture tour for the English suffrage leader Christabel Pankhurst. When Alice Paul and Lucy Burns formed the militant National Woman's Party, Alva gave thousands of dollars to purchase the headquarters' building in Washington, D.C. She was president of the party in 1921. She also endorsed strikes of garment workers and even contributed money to the Socialist paper, the *Masses*, to prevent its bankruptcy.

Marble House is open Apr. 1–Oct. 31, daily 10–5; July 1 to mid-Sept. also Fri. 5–7 P.M.; winter, Sat. and Sun. 10–4; adm.

NEWPORT HARBOR

Lewis, Ida, 1842–1911, Lighthouse Keeper; NAW

Ida Lewis Yacht Club, Lime Rock

Ida Lewis began her duties as keeper of the lighthouse here when her father, the official keeper, suffered a stroke and needed her help. At sixteen she rescued four men from a capsized boat and in the following years she saved many other lives. News accounts of her bravery and skill brought her fame, but not until 1879, seven years after her father's death, did the federal government officially name her lighthouse keeper. Congress gave her a gold medal; the Carnegie Hero Fund gave a monthly pension; and the American Cross of Honor Society gave an award. Best of all, the grateful people of Newport gave her a boat, the *Rescue*. The boat and her medals are preserved by the Newport Historical Society. A memorial to Lewis was erected at the Common Burying Ground, Farewell Street, corner of Warner Street, Newport. The granite monument is marked with the emblem of an anchor crossed with oars, the inscription reading: "the Grace

Darling of America, Keeper of Lime Rock Lighthouse, Newport Harbor, Erected by her many kind friends.''[7]

PORTSMOUTH

Hutchinson, Anne, 1591–1643, Dissenter; NAW

Tablet, on Pudding Rock, Founders' Brook off Boyd's Lane

Rhode Island's second settlement, originally called Pocasset, was established here on Aquidneck Island in 1638 by a group of Massachusetts men and women seeking religious freedom, among them Anne Hutchinson. They had in fact been banished by the General Court for sedition and Hutchinson had been excommunicated for heresy (see Boston, MA). Her heresy had consisted in having and expressing her own beliefs. Her husband, William Hutchinson, died in 1642 and Anne moved to New Netherland (New York) with several of her children. There she and all but one of the children were murdered by Indians. The bronze tablet commemorating the founders of Portsmouth is inscribed with the ''Portsmouth compact,'' which established the settlement's democratic form of government.

PROVIDENCE

Doyle, Sarah, 1830–1922, Educator; NAW

Tablet, Pembroke Hall, Brown University

In 1895 President Elisha Benjamin Andrews of Brown University invited a few people to tea to discuss the problem of the experimental women's college tenuously attached to the university. Among the guests was Sarah Doyle, for years the principal of the girls' department of Providence High School, a founder of the coeducational Rhode Island School of Design, and then, retired from teaching, much involved in the woman's suffrage movement. The result of the meeting over teacups was the establishment of a committee, the Rhode Island Society for the Collegiate Education of Women, with Doyle as president. She was a whirlwind fund-raiser; within two years Pembroke Hall, built and paid for, housed the Women's College, and soon the school (later renamed Pembroke College) was accepted as a department of Brown University. Doyle remained as president until 1919, in the meantime working for women's opportunities through the State Federation of Women's Clubs. Her definition of a woman's sphere was ''one with an infinite radius.'' Her portrait hangs on the wall of Pembroke Hall.

Goddard, Sarah Updike, c. 1700–1770, Printer; NAW

Shakespeare's Head, 21 Meeting Street

Sarah Updike Goddard became a printer when her son William Goddard started Providence's first newspaper, the *Providence Gazette*, in 1762. He was not very successful financially and left Providence within three years. Sarah continued the printing business under the imprint "S. and W. Goddard" and then revived the *Gazette* under the auspices of "Sarah Goddard and Company." For her first venture into book publishing she chose the letters of a famous Englishwoman, Lady Mary Wortley Montague. Its title was given as *Letters of the Right Honorable Lady M——y W——y M——e*. One of Sarah's partners was John Carter, who built this house. He bought out her interest in 1768 when her son persuaded her to move to Philadelphia, Pennsylvania. Carter ran a print shop and bookstore here "at the sign of Shakespeare's head." It is now headquarters for the Providence Junior League. The back garden is open to the public.[8]

Rockefeller, Abby Aldrich, 1874–1948, Art Collector and Patron; NAW

Aldrich House, 110 Benevolent Street; HABS, NHL

Senator Nelson Aldrich had eight children, one of whom, Abby Aldrich Rockefeller, was destined to have a far-reaching influence on modern art in America, not as an artist but as a collector. She was a founder of the Museum of Modern Art in New York City, and her collection of folk art fills a museum named for her in Williamsburg, Virginia. She married John D. Rockefeller II, only son of the Standard Oil Company founder, and moved to his New York City home. In the 1920s she became interested in modern art, especially in French and American artists. John did not particularly care for paintings, so she used Aldrich money to buy works by Winslow Homer, William Zorach, and John Marin and to commission work which kept such young artists from starving. As her collection began to outgrow her private gallery (the children's old nursery), she and two other women organized the new Museum of Modern Art. It opened its doors in an office building in 1929, the year of the stock market crash, and ten years later went into its present building. Many of Abby's favorite paintings are there; others went to colleges and museums. Her childhood home in Providence is now the property of the Rhode Island Historical Society. Its Museum of Rhode Island History is open Tues.-Sat. 11–4; Sun. 1–4; adm.[9]

Yandell, Enid, 1870–1934, Sculptor

Carrie Brown Memorial Fountain, City Hall Park

Carrie Brown Bajnotti, a member of the prominent family for whom Brown University is named, is memorialized by this fountain, a gift to the city by her widowed husband. Enid Yandell, the artist, won the commission against a number of leading sculptors in 1901. She was born in Louisville, Kentucky, studied in Chicago, Illinois, and New York City, and won a medal for her work at the 1893 Columbian Exposition in Chicago. She moved in later life to Edgartown, Massachusetts, where she continued to work and teach.[10]

NOTES

In addition to the correspondents mentioned below, I have had assistance from the Rhode Island Historical Society in Providence, and the Newport Historical Society.

The Rhode Island Heritage Hall of Fame, founded in 1965, honors those whose efforts have added significantly to the illustrious heritage of the state. Most of the electees have been men, and most are still living. Information can be obtained from the *Providence Journal* Company, Fountain Square, Providence.

1. Sally Smith Booth, *The Women of '76* (New York: Random House, 1973).
2. Carl R. Woodward, "A Profile in Dedication: Sarah Harris and the Fayerweather Family," *New-England Galaxy* 15 (Summer 1973); correspondence, Old Sturbridge Village, Sturbridge, Massachusetts.
3. Woodward, op. cit.; correspondence, University of Rhode Island.
4. Correspondence, Little Compton Historical Society.
5. Leah A. Strong, "The Daughter of the Confederacy," *Mississippi Quarterly* 10 (Fall 1967).
6. Angela Lumpkin, *Women's Tennis: A Historical Documentary of the Players and Their Game* (Troy, N.Y.: Whitston Publishing Co., 1981); *Official Encyclopedia of Tennis* (New York: Harper & Row, 1981); brochures and correspondence, International Tennis Hall of Fame.
7. Andrew Kull, *New England Cemeteries: A Collector's Guide* (Brattleboro, Vt.: Stephen Greene Press, 1975). Grace Darling was a famous English heroine.
8. Nancy Fisher Chudacoff, "Women in the News, 1762–1770: Sarah Updike Goddard," *Rhode Island History* 32 (Nov. 1973).
9. Aline B. Saarinen, *The Proud Possessors* (New York: Random House, 1958).
10. Charlotte S. Rubinstein, *American Women Artists* (New York: Avon Books, 1982).

VERMONT

ARLINGTON

Fisher, Dorothy Canfield, 1879–1958, Writer; NAWM

Community House, Main Street

Dorothy Canfield Fisher's roots were in Vermont, although she was born and educated in the West, and except for summers with relatives in Arlington she did not live in Vermont until after her marriage to John Fisher. The couple chose a frugal and peaceful life in the country so that both could have freedom to write. Dorothy had begun with magazine fiction and for the rest of her days she produced a steady stream of fiction and nonfiction, many with a strong Vermont flavor. Both John and Dorothy were much involved in community affairs. She was the first woman appointed to the Vermont Board of Education; several of her books were on education and child rearing. She established the Dorothy Canfield Fisher Children's Book Award, given for books chosen by the school children themselves. She was on the first selection board of the Book-of-the-Month Club, which, among other things, gives an award to libraries in small communities. The first went to the Martha Canfield Library in Arlington. It now occupies one wing of the community house, the former Canfield home, which Dorothy donated to the town; it is named for her Aunt Mattie, who kept the first library in her living room.

BENNINGTON

Moses, Anna Mary Robertson (Grandma Moses), 1860–1961, Artist; NAWM

Schoolhouse, Bennington Museum, W. Main Street

Grandma Moses, a farm wife with little education and less art training, began to produce paintings when she was seventy-eight years old. On panels of Masonite cut to fit old frames, with cans of house paint accumulated in the barn, she painted familiar country scenes: carrying in the Christmas tree, making maple sugar, skating on icy ponds. A New York art dealer happened to see them at a Woman's Exchange near her home, bought some, and showed them at the Museum of Modern Art's "Contemporary Unknown American Painters." A one-woman show in 1940 launched her on a dizzying public career: television interviews with Edward R. Murrow, a White House visit, a documentary film of her life, and exhibits in America and abroad. As she worked to fill the demand for her paintings, her artistic skill developed. In 1969, the United States issued a Grandma Moses postage stamp. The old schoolhouse, which had been used as a museum in Eagle Bridge, New York, her home, was purchased by the Bennington Museum and moved here after her death. It is open Mar.-Nov., daily 9–5; adm.

BURLINGTON

Fletcher, Mary Martha, 1830–1885, Philanthropist

Mary Fletcher Hospital, Medical Center

Mary Martha Fletcher was the sole heir of an estate of $400,000. Her father, state senator Thaddeus Fletcher, had built up the estate as a merchant and investor in western land. He and his wife had given large sums to charities, including the Home for Destitute Children and the Essex Classical Institute. After his death, Mary and her mother gave funds to establish the Fletcher Free Library. They had all discussed founding a hospital, but at that time people were not hospital-minded. Folks feared they might become subjects of medical experimentation; hospitals were for the dying; only strangers and paupers were hospitalized. Nevertheless, Mary agreed with her parents' views and was determined to see the hospital established during her lifetime. Seriously ill with tuberculosis herself, she began making arrangements for the formation of a nonprofit institution, the purchase of property, and the construction of a building.

The hospital opened in 1879, and Mary then turned to organizing the Mary Fletcher Training School for Nurses. The first such school to be connected with a small-town hospital, it took in its first class of twelve students in 1882. Mary, almost never seen in public because of ill health and personal taste, could not attend the opening ceremonies of either institution and died soon afterward. In fact, most of the townsfolk who benefited from her generosity had never seen her.[1]

CALAIS

Kent, Louise Andrews, 1886–1969, Writer

Kent Museum, Kents' Corner

Louise (Lulu) Andrews Kent, the wife of Ira Rich Kent, wrote many books for children and some for adults, including a number of cookbooks, while bringing up three children here and in Brookline, Massachusetts. In addition she gardened, restored antiques, photographed, painted, and made a wide circle of friends. The heroine of many of her books is a bouncy New England matron, Mrs. Appleyard, who bears a strong resemblance to the author herself and was the inventor of such delicious Vermont specialties as apple cider jelly, tomato chutney, and tomato conserve. The museum building, an 1837 former tavern, was given to the Vermont Historical Society by A. Atwater Kent. Miniature rooms carefully made by Lulu are displayed, along with other memorabilia. To reach it from Montpelier, follow Main Street north, then ten miles on a country road to Maple Corner, then right half a mile, avoiding the mud season. It is open July and Aug. and on "foliage weekends," Tues.–Sun. 12–5; adm.[2]

GUILFORD

Tyler, Mary Palmer, 1775–1866, Writer

Marker, US 5, at Guilford Center Road

Young Mary Palmer Tyler was swept off her feet by the older, eccentric author Royall Tyler and agreed to keep their marriage secret because his mother opposed it. He returned to his Vermont home, leaving her in Farmington, Massachusetts, until the impending birth of her son forced her to reveal the secret. At length he brought her to Guilford, where they lived for five years before moving to Brattleboro, Vermont. Apparently she bore him no resentment for the odd beginning of their life together. In her reminiscences, written between 1858 and 1863 (after Royall's death), she always spoke of him with affection. The memoirs, a remarkable record of the years after the Revolution and the War of 1812, were published by descendants. *Grandmother Tyler's Book* (1925) gives us details of manners, customs, and events as seen through the eyes of a woman. She tells of the sheep raising, wool spinning, flax growing, weaving, and sewing—all the myriad productive activities of a farm household in the early nineteenth century.[3]

MARLBORO

Stark, Elizabeth Page, c. 1737–1814, Revolutionary War Figure

Molly Stark State Park, State 9

Elizabeth (Molly) Page Stark played little part in history, yet her name is known in New England because of a remark made by her husband, General John Stark. He led a militia company to battle the British in 1777, declaring, "There stand the redcoats. Today they are ours, or Molly Stark sleeps this night a widow." A monument in Bennington, Vermont, commemorates his victory over the British, and the trail from Bennington to Brattleboro, Vermont, has been named the Molly Stark Trail. The park is open from the last week of May until Oct. 12.[4]

MIDDLEBURY

Willard, Emma Hart, 1787–1870, Educator; NAW

Emma Willard House, Middlebury College Campus; NHL.
Plaque on Upper Village Green. Monument on Lower Green

At twenty-one, Emma Hart Willard came to Middlebury from her home in Connecticut to be preceptress of the female academy. Not just a pretty girl, she was a knowledgeable and experienced teacher who showed a good deal of spunk when denominational jealousies threatened to disrupt her school. One of her supporters was a local doctor, John Willard. He and Emma were married the following year. Although he was almost thirty years her senior and had four children, the union was fortunate. He encouraged her when in 1814 she opened a school in their home for young women. Middlebury College refused to let her attend classes, so she taught herself the classics and science, subjects then considered the sole province of men.

In 1819 she wrote an impassioned plea for public support of female education, which she presented to the legislature of New York. John accompanied her when she opened her Female Seminary at Troy, New York, in 1821 (without the support of the legislature). The school is recognized as the pioneer effort to educate women in serious intellectual subjects above the level of secondary education. It still exists as the Emma Willard School. Emma's honors include representation in the Hall of Fame in New York City. The Willard house on the campus is used as an administrative office. See Berlin, CT.

NORTH DANVILLE

Willard, Mary Thompson Hill, 1805–1892, Pioneer

Monument, Near Stanton School

Mary (Polly) Thompson Hill Willard was born at this site. After her marriage to Josiah Willard, she moved to New York and then to Ohio, where Josiah attended Oberlin College. Eager to be more than a farm wife, Polly joined a study group of women there who tried to keep pace with their husbands and brothers at the college. In 1846 the family—with three children— moved West, Polly driving one of three emigrant wagons, and settled in Janesville, Wisconsin Territory. As there were practically no schools, Polly taught her daughters herself. When they needed better educational opportunities, they moved to Evanston, Illinois. Her eldest daughter, Frances Willard, became famous as the dynamic organizer and longtime president of the Woman's Christian Temperance Union (WCTU). Frances was very close to her mother. By 1878 the younger daughter,

Mary, the son, and the father had all died, leaving only Polly and Frances. "I thank God for my mother as for no other gift," wrote Frances, "My nature is so woven into hers that I think it would almost be death to have the band severed." Five years after Polly's death two memorial trees were planted at her birth site, with Frances Willard present. The WCTU erected the monument in 1937.[5]

READING

Johnson, Susannah (Hastings), 1730–1810, Indian Captive

Indian Stones, State 106 Near Knapp Brook; NR

The Indian Stones, the oldest historical site markers in Vermont and possibly in America, commemorate an Indian captivity. James and Susannah Johnson, their three children, and several others from an English settlement in New Hampshire known as Number Four were taken by Abenaki Indians in August 1754. On the second day of a forced march across Vermont to Canada, Susannah bore a child. All but one of the captives were sold in Canada to French residents and by various means each returned to New England by 1760. Many years later Johnson published a graphic account of her captivity. She also revisited the sites of the first Indian encampment and of the birth of her child. Sometime between 1799 and 1810 she had a stone cutter make the slate markers, with the story of the capture and birth. This is the first time known in Vermont history that an individual considered a historical event worth such commemoration. In 1918 a descendant had the two slabs set into a single block of granite.

In the Pike Cemetery in Concord, Vermont, is a marker dedicated to Susannah Johnson Wetherbee, who was the four-year-old daughter captured with the Johnsons. She survived, grew up, married, bore fifteen children, and lived to be seventy-two.[6]

ROYALTON

Hendee, Hannah Hunter, c. 1753–after 1818, Pioneer Heroine

Memorial Arch, South Royalton Village Green

A band of Caughnawaga Indians led by British spies destroyed Royalton on October 16, 1780. Most of its three hundred inhabitants were left homeless, their houses and barns burned and looted, their livestock slaughtered, most of the men and boys captured. Hannah Hunter Hendee fled with her two children, but in her flight the Indians snatched seven-year-old Michael Hendee. Determined to rescue her son, Hendee followed the armed men to an encampment on the White River. She pleaded with the Indians and a British officer to release Michael and they agreed. Encouraged by her success, she then talked them into giving up eight other frightened little boys, on the grounds that they were weak and

Believed to be the first memorial to a woman erected in America, the ''Indian Stones'' in Reading, Vermont, were memorials to Susannah Johnson, an Indian captive. Photography by Courtney Fisher.
Courtesy Vermont Division for Historic Preservation.

would only hinder their progress. Again they agreed. Hendee, still with her little daughter in her arms, formed the lads into a chain and led them across the river safely. Years later one of the Royalton men who had returned home after two years of captivity interviewed many who had been in the town in 1780 and published the story. Among those mentioned was Hendee, since widowed, remarried, and again widowed, who was remembered by her townspeople as the heroine of the occasion.[7]

SHELBURNE

Webb, Electra Havemeyer, 1888–1960, Art Collector and Patron

Shelburne Museum, US 7, South of Burlington; NR

Electra Havemeyer Webb grew up in her art-collecting parents' New York mansion, which was decorated by Tiffany Studios, its walls hung with paintings, most of which are now in the Havemeyer Collection at the Metropolitan Museum of Art. Mary Cassatt had been her mother's friend and advisor. It was a shock to Electra's mother, then, when Electra began *her* collection of art by lugging home a cigar-store Indian. What she liked and collected avidly was Americana, including weather vanes, dolls, quilts, and toys. After she married J. Watson Webb, they moved from New York to Vermont. Electra expanded her collecting to such full-scale items as a covered bridge, a lighthouse, a jail, a schoolhouse, a country store, a locomotive, and—to top it all off—the last sidewheeler in the world, the SS *Ticonderoga*.

Instead of ignoring Electra's squirrel-like propensities, her husband encouraged her. They bought acreage at Shelburne on which to display a large number of carriages and other vehicles. Before they were finished they had some thirty-five buildings or other structures on forty-five acres. They were caught up in a movement which began in the mid–1920s to save the American crafts heritage and recreate the past through outdoor museums. Their Shelburne Museum, opened to the public in 1952, is actually a collection of museums. One is an art gallery, bearing the name of Electra Havemeyer Webb, for the display of American paintings. All are open May 15–Oct. 15, daily 9–5; adm.[8]

WEST SALISBURY

Story, Ann Goodrich, 1742–1817, Revolutionary War Figure

Monument, on an Island in Otter Creek

The monument reads: "Ann Story, in grateful memory of her services in the struggle of the Green Mountain Boys for independence." Ann Goodrich Story was the widow of Amos Story, who was killed in felling a tree to build a new home in the wilderness. She packed up her belongings and trudged, with her five children (the eldest thirteen), the 150 miles to the new homestead. An old-timer described her as "a busting great woman who could cut off a two-foot log as quick as any man in the settlement." In 1776, Indians burned the cabin. Story and the children rebuilt it, but they took the precaution to hide at night in a cave dug in the bank of the creek, entered by canoe. Her home became a communications center for the Green Mountain Boys, supplied by news Story picked up from Royalists passing through. When the monument to her was dedicated, a justice of the Supreme Court of the District of Columbia spoke of her as "brave and strong. . . . What her mind approved her arm did not tremble to execute."[9]

NOTES

In addition to the correspondents mentioned below, I have had help from the Vermont Historic Preservation Division, Agency of Development and Community Affairs; Bennington Museum; and Vermont Historical Society.

1. Lilian Baker Carlisle, "Humanities' Needs Deserve Our Fortune: Mary Martha Fletcher and the Fletcher Family Benevolences," *Vermont History* 50 (Summer 1982).

2. Madeleine Kunin and Marylyn Stout, *The Big Green Book: A Four-Season Guide to Vermont* (Barre, Mass.:Barre Publishers, 1976); Marjorie Ryerson, "Mrs. Appleyard & Company," *Vermont Life* 32 (Autumn 1977); correspondence and brochure, Kent Museum.

3. Mary Palmer Tyler, *Grandmother Tyler's Book*, ed. Frederick Tupper and Helen Tyler Brown (New York: G. P. Putnam's Sons, 1925).

4. Charles Edward Crane, *Let Me Show You Vermont* (New York: Alfred A. Knopf, 1950); correspondence, Vermont Historical Society.

5. *A Woman of the Century*, ed. Frances E. Willard and Mary A. Livermore (Detroit, Mich.: Gale Research Co., 1967; repr. of 1893 ed.).

6. Gilbert A. Davis, *Centennial Celebration Together with a Historical Sketch of Reading, Windsor County, Vermont* (Bellows Falls, Vt.: Press of A. N. Swain, 1874); Mary Billings French, *A New England Pioneer: The Captivity of Mrs. Johnson* (Woodstock, Vt.: Sun Tree Press, 1926); Susannah Johnson, *A Narrative of the Captivity of Mrs. Johnson* (Windsor, Vt.: 2nd ed., Alden Spooner, 1807, first published 1797 as *The Captive American*); notes in *Vermont History* 22 (Jan. 1954), pp. 56–57, and 23 (Jan. 1955), p. 72. Johnson's name is also given as Susanna Johnson Hastings, indicating a second marriage.

7. *Women and the American Revolution*, comp. Mollie Somerville (National Society, Daughters of the American Revolution, 1974); Evelyn M. Lovejoy Wood, *History of Royalton, Vermont* (Burlington, Vt., 1911).

8. Aline B. Saarinen, *The Proud Possessors* (New York: Random House, 1958); Walter Karp, "Electra Webb and Her American Past," *American Heritage* 33 (Apr.–May 1982); correspondence, Shelburne Museum.

9. Dorothy Canfield Fisher, "Ann Story," *Vermont History* 18 (July 1950).

REGION II

The South

The South as a region is generally defined as including those states who seceded from the Union. But it is less politics than geography that makes it distinctive. The mild climate, easily cultivated soil, and network of broad rivers make it predominantly suited for agriculture. The division of the land into large plantations, the early adoption of slave labor, and the reliance on a few exportable crops set its economic pattern. Its social system and its domestic policies grew naturally out of that pattern.

Its first settlers brought with them from England the ideas of the patriarchal family and its defined role of women. The plantation system, with its vast stretches of land and scarcity of labor, made large families desirable. Sons of the more prosperous planters were set up on plantations of their own; when daughters married, premarital agreements were often made, not to protect the wife but to protect her family's estates. A married woman's chief duty was to bear and bring up many children. When a wife was worn out or died in childbirth, as happened often, the widower married again and the succeeding wife brought up not only her own but all his other children. In spite of a high rate of infant mortality, households were large. Married women had their hands full. When the system of slavery began, plantation mistresses had plenty of help, but they also had to supervise the many untrained and uneducated servants, who themselves needed care in sickness and childbearing.

The southern housewife, unlike her New England and frontier sisters, did little weaving and spinning, for the southern economy was based on trade with Europe, and clothing was imported in exchange for cotton and tobacco. When the trade was broken off by war, slaves were taught to spin and sew. In the frontier settlements, of course, women were much more self-sufficient, and their households were simple and servantless. Yet they too were governed by the social mores of the planter class.

If early New England women modeled themselves after the goodwives of the Bible, southern women measured their goals against a standard of "true womanhood.'' This was an ideal held up in the mid-nineteenth century by novelists, women's magazine writers, preachers, lecturers, and politicians. In 1966 Barbara Welter studied the concept and described it as a ''cult,'' whose attributes were ''divided into four cardinal virtues—piety, purity, submissiveness, and domesticity.'' All American women were judged by the extent to which they exhibited these virtues. In the South men subscribed to a code of chivalry that elevated women a bit higher than elsewhere, and women constantly had to measure themselves against this male standard of the pure woman. Women's common sense in time rescued them from subscribing wholeheartedly to this impossible standard, but in the South it took longer than elsewhere. In fact, some southern politicians still invoke the image whenever their women want to run for office or get a fair share of educational facilities.

On the other hand, southern society put less emphasis on puritanical religious observances than did New England. Southern women were allowed to enjoy each other's company, eat well, dance, and flirt. Southern belles were kept on pedestals but they were permitted to enjoy it. Perhaps that is why it took them longer to rebel.

In spite of the rigid tradition of domesticity, many colonial women supported themselves by keeping shops or taverns, teaching dancing or music, nursing, or serving as midwives. Some were planters. Some participated in public life. Women who had to earn a living most often did so as teachers, and most of the educational choices open to girls well into the twentieth century were small schools established and taught by women. The curriculum was almost always designed around the skills of homemaking.

The Civil War was devastating for women of the South. Almost all of them lost husbands, fathers, brothers, or sons, many lost their homes, property, and means of livelihood. The whole economy was turned upside down with the freeing of slaves. It was equally tragic in its immediate consequences for white women and black. The latter were often left with no protection, no skills, no land. It is heartening to read of the attempts made by white northerners to educate freedmen and equally heartening to find so many black women dedicated to the elevation of their race through education and industrial training.

As southern women achieved access to better education, they campaigned for reforms and social changes in much the same way as their counterparts in the North. Cities had their settlement houses and community services. Women led the movement to preserve and develop handicrafts, as well as the folklore, songs, and dances of the mountain people. The scars left by Civil War, Reconstruction, and desegregation are healing, and the southern economy differs little now from that of the rest of the country. The charm and hospitality for which its women have been noted remain a characteristic of the region.

NOTE

The groundbreaking study of southern colonial women is Julia Cherry Spruill's *Women's Life and Work in the Southern Colonies* (New York: W. W. Norton & Co., 1972, first publ. 1938). Anne Firor Scott, *The Southern Lady: From Pedestal to Politics* (Chicago, Ill.: University of Chicago Press, 1970), studies women from 1830 to 1930. Barbara Welter's ''Cult of True Womanhood'' was first published in *American Quarterly* 18 (Summer 1966) and reprinted in her *Dimity Convictions* (Athens, Ohio: Ohio University Press, 1976).

ALABAMA

ANDALUSIA

Wallace, Lurleen Burns, 1926–1968, State Governor; AWHF[1]

Lurleen B. Wallace State Junior College

When Lurleen Burns Wallace was elected in 1966 to fill the office her husband, George Wallace, had held, she was the first woman chosen to govern Alabama and the third woman state governor in the country. Before her marriage she had planned to go into nursing, and it was natural for her to take a special interest in the needs of the mentally and physically handicapped. During her short term, before she succumbed to cancer, she initiated legislation to make the lives of mental patients easier. In 1967 she was awarded an honorary Doctor of Humanities degree from Judson College and was also chosen one of the Ten Most Admired Women of the World. Among other honors are the naming for Wallace of a Fine Arts Center at Florence State University, a building at Livingston University, a school of nursing at Jacksonville State, a library at Troy State, a state park near Tuscaloosa, and several centers for the care of the mentally retarded, one at Decatur, Alabama. See Montgomery, AL.[2]

BIRMINGHAM

Cahalan, Mary A., d. 1906, Teacher

Monument, Woodrow Wilson Park

Mary A. Cahalan was a teacher and then principal of Powell Public School from 1883 right up until the year of her death. Many men and women of Birmingham knew and loved her as their mentor and their children's inspiration. On the day she died all the schools in the city were closed in mourning. In 1908 friends raised a subscription to erect the monument, a seated figure with a book in her hand.[3]

Fletcher, Pauline Bray, 1884–1970, Nurse

Monument, Kelly Ingram Park

Pauline Bray Fletcher was the first black registered nurse in Birmingham. She came here in 1909 as health coordinator for the United Charities. Concerned about the effect of air pollution, she became a nurse with the Jefferson County Anti-Tuberculosis Association. She conceived the idea of establishing a fresh-air camp for the increasing number of blacks afflicted with tuberculosis. The camp, in the Shades Valley area near Bessemer, Alabama, was opened in 1926, named for Margaret Murray Washington (see Tuskegee, AL). It was later given the name Camp Pauline Bray Fletcher. Many admirers contributed to a fund to erect a monument recognizing her contributions to the city. It was unveiled in 1979 in a park which has special significance and sacredness for black people because of its role during the civil rights struggle of the 1960s.[4]

Mallory, Kathleen, 1879–1954, Churchwoman; AWHF

Conference Room, Woman's Missionary Union National Offices

Kathleen Mallory assumed leadership of Southern Baptist missions programs in 1908 and led the Woman's Missionary Union to power. In 1921 she was instrumental in having the national offices moved from Baltimore, Maryland, to Birmingham. She raised millions of dollars for missions and instituted countless progressive social services in the South. As editor of the monthly magazine *Royal Service*, she reached into thousands of homes with her inspiring messages. A hospital in China was named for her. An annual missions offering for the Alabama Baptist State Convention also bears her name, as does the headquarters conference room.

Tuggle, Carrie A., 1858–1924, Humanitarian; AWHF

Monument, Kelly Ingram Park. Carrie Tuggle School, 412 12th Court, N.

The school was originally Tuggle Institute, which had its humble beginnings when Carrie A. Tuggle, touched by the homeless black children who appeared before the courts, began to take some of them into her own home. After a long, uphill battle to raise funds and arouse interest, she and her supporters opened a school and residence for orphaned black boys (in one room) in 1903. The school and orphanage grew under "Granny," as the children called Tuggle, and "Old Lady Tuggle," as she was affectionately known to adults, and became a significant force in the advancement of blacks in Birmingham. During the depression the school was forced to close, and then the Board of Education bought it, changed its name to Enon Ridge School, and finally restored Tuggle's name. The monument in Kelly Ingram Park was erected in 1979, a companion to the monument to Pauline Fletcher, q.v.[5]

BLOUNTSVILLE

Murphree, Celia, 1841–1899, and Her Sister, Winnie Mae Murphree, 1844–1896, Civil War Heroines

Marker, State 26, at Royal Crossing

On May 1, 1863, Celia Murphree and Winnie Mae Murphree, teenaged sisters, were looking after a newly delivered mother and her baby here. Three Union soldiers burst into the house, looking for medical supplies and horses. Noticing a jug of whiskey which had been brought to ease the birth pains of the young mother, they demanded drinks. Winnie Mae laced their mint juleps with toothache medicine, which had the effect of putting the already wearied men to sleep. The sisters stealthily removed the guns of the sleeping Yankees and afterward marched them to General Nathan Bedford Forrest's headquarters. The girls were rewarded with mares recently in the possession of the Union's General Abel D. Streight. The highway marker commemorating the event was erected by the state in 1963.[6]

FORT McCLELLAN

Rogers, Edith Nourse, 1881–1960, Congresswoman; NAWM

Rogers Museum, U.S. Women's Army Nurse Corps Center

Edith Nourse Rogers represented Massachusetts in the U.S. House of Representatives from the 69th to the 86th Congresses, a stretch of public service spanning thirty-five years. Before election she had been interested in World War I veterans and was appointed (at a dollar a year) an inspector of veterans' hospitals. Most of the bills she introduced in Congress had something to do with veterans, including the bills to establish the Women's Army Corps and the G.I. Bill of Rights. The museum, displaying army history, is open daily.[7]

GADSDEN

Sansom, Emma, c. 1848–1900, Civil War Heroine

Monument, 1st and Broad Streets. Emma Sansom High School, Meighan Boulevard (US 278). Marker, US 278

Emma Sansom was sixteen when the Civil War came close to her home. First the Yankees came, asked for water, and burned the bridge across Black Creek.

Then Confederate General Nathan Bedford Forrest rode up and asked how his men could get across the creek. Sansom offered to show him a ford and, riding behind the general on his horse, guided him to the spot. The Union forces were ready; gunfire burst about them; the general left Sansom in a safe shelter and continued on to capture the federal troops. Sansom was so thrilled at meeting Forrest that she forgot to be frightened by the danger. "He asked me my name, and asked me to give him a lock of my hair," she recollected. He also remembered her, sending "my highest regards to Miss Emma Sansom for her gallant conduct." Sansom soon married a soldier and after the war moved to Texas. The monument, a life-size statue of young Sansom, was erected in 1907 by the United Daughters of the Confederacy.[8]

GREENSBORO

Gorgas, Amelia Gayle, 1826–1913, Librarian; AWHF

Tunstall House (Private)

The Tunstall house was the residence of John Gayle, sixth governor of Alabama, and the reputed birthplace of his daughter, Amelia Gayle Gorgas. She was a pioneer in the field of education for women and a longtime librarian at the University of Alabama in University, Alabama, q.v. She married General Josiah Gorgas, and was the mother of William Crawford Gorgas, U.S. surgeon general, who freed the Canal Zone of yellow fever.

HUNTSVILLE

Weeden, (Marie) Howard, 1847–1905, Poet and Artist

Marker at Home, 300 Gates Avenue (Private); HABS, NR

The poet who was born and lived in this house all her life was once considered the most famous of Alabama writers. Howard Weeden's verses describing slaves her family owned were published in a few slim volumes, illustrated with her watercolor and oil portraits of the blacks. Though highly regarded in her day, Weeden is now all but forgotten.

LIVINGSTON

Tartt, Ruby Pickens, 1880–1974, Folklorist and Writer; AWHF

Ruby Pickens Tartt Public Library

Ruby Pickens Tartt spent all the time she could spare studying the folklore of the blacks in Sumter County, which was in her day 79 percent Negro. Her work became known to others, including Carl Carmer, whose *Stars Fell on Alabama*

(1934) drew largely from her studies. He later wrote *Miss Ruby, My Most Unforgettable Character* (1975). John Lomax, noted folklorist and ballad collector, came to Livingston as national advisor for the Works Progress Administration's Writers' Project in 1936, the same year Tartt went to work for the Alabama Project. He paid her several visits and recorded a large number of the old songs performed by Tartt's friends. The records are now in the Library of Congress. Lomax said of Tartt that "without her a generation of black geniuses who have made life in this country so much more livable and more beautiful by their wit and by their music would have been lost to us." Tartt was librarian for Sumter County for thirty-six years and the year after her death the Livingston Public Library was given her name.[9]

Tutwiler, Julia Strudwick, 1841–1916, Educator and Reformer; NAW, AWHF

Julia Tutwiler Library, Livingston University. Marker, College Campus

Julia Strudwick Tutwiler was fortunate in having a father who believed in educating girls. She was given the same education as her brothers and was sent to Vassar College (where she remained only half a year) and spent three years in advanced study in Germany and a year in Paris, France. In 1881 she was made coprincipal of the Livingston Female Academy. The academy was later made a state normal school and she served as its president from 1888 until 1910. She worked for the admission of women to the University of Alabama and was one of the first to advocate prison reform. Memorials to her may be found in Montevallo, Montgomery, University, and Wetumpka, AL.

MARION

Alabama Women's Hall of Fame, Judson College

One of the first colleges in the nation to offer higher education to women, Judson College was founded in 1838 as Judson Female Institute. In 1970 it established the Alabama Women's Hall of Fame (AWHF), electing annually women who have made significant contributions to the state. Each one is represented by a bronze portrait medallion in the college's Bowling Library.

Many of the electees are noted elsewhere in this guide, designated by the initials AWHF. Others are: Tallulah Brockman Bankhead (1903–1968), a member of a prominent Alabama family and a talented actress; Ruth Robertson Berrey (1906–1973), who followed up a successful practice in pediatrics with many tours of duty as a medical missionary to Nigeria; Anne Mathilde Bilbro (1870–1958), a composer and teacher honored by *Etude* magazine as one of America's leading musicians; Mary Myrtle Brooke (1872–1948), who made the University of Montevallo the training center for social work in Alabama; Annie Forney Daugette (1875–1939), a clubwoman who persuaded Congress to pass a resolution designating the Civil War as the War between the States; Loula Friend Dunn (1896–1977), from 1937 to 1948 state commissioner of public welfare, then executive director of the American Public Welfare Association; Hallie Farmer (1891–1960), a faculty member of the University of Montevallo and a crusader for penal reform; and Agnes Ellen Harris (1883–1952), dean of women at the University of Alabama, 1927–52.

Pattie Ruffner Jacobs (1875–1935), one of the state's strongest suffragists, was responsible for prodding the state to change its child labor laws. She founded the Birmingham Equal Suffrage Association and for a decade worked for suffrage on the local, state, and federal levels. Her portrait, unveiled in 1938, hangs in the state capitol. Sister Chrysostom Moynahan (1863–1941), the first registered nurse licensed in Alabama, was administrator of Birmingham's St. Vincent's Hospital, founded its school of nursing, served abroad as head of a nursing unit during World War I, and administered hospitals in various cities of the Midwest, including Providence Hospital in Mobile, Alabama. Annie Lola Price (1903–1972) was the first woman to serve on a high court in Alabama. She was appointed a judge of the Court of Appeals in 1951 and reelected for four successive terms; from 1969 until 1972 she was presiding judge of the Court of Criminal Appeals. Loraine Bedsole Tunstall (1879–1953), first director of the Alabama Child Welfare Department, held this post from 1923 until her retirement in 1935 and was a national leader in the development and application of sound social work practices.[10]

MOBILE

Wilson, Augusta Evans, 1835–1909, Writer; NAW, AWHF

Marker at Home, Georgia Cottage, 2558 Spring Hill Avenue (Private); NR

The plaque of white marble reads: "Girlhood home of Augusta Evans Wilson, famed Mobile authoress." The writer was Augusta Evans when she built this cottage from the proceeds of her first book, *Inez: A Tale of the Alamo*, published anonymously when she was twenty. She lived here, constantly writing, until her marriage in 1868 to Colonel Lorenzo Madison Wilson, a widower with grown children. She was at the height of popularity, having two years earlier published her most famous book, *St. Elmo*, one of the best-selling novels of the nineteenth century. The story was adapted for the stage and as late as 1923 a film version was produced. Wilson was a disciplined writer who spent regular hours at her desk; she was one of the first American women to earn a substantial income from her writing. A village on US 90 in Mobile County is named Mt. Elmo. Georgia Cottage is open during the spring Iron and Lace Classic Columns Tour. See Columbus, GA.

MONTEVALLO

Tutwiler, Julia Strudwick, 1841–1916, Educator; NAW, AWHF

Tutwiler Hall, University of Montevallo

In 1878 Julia Strudwick Tutwiler (see Livingston, AL) went to France, and while there she visited vocational schools for girls. She became convinced that similar training was needed for women in Alabama and after a long campaign she succeeded in getting the state to establish, in 1893, the Alabama College for Women, now the University of Montevallo. See Montgomery, University, and Wetumpka, AL.

MONTGOMERY

Fitzgerald, Zelda Sayre, 1900–1948, Writer and Artist

Fountain, Fitzgerald Park, Felder and Dunbar Streets

Zelda Sayre Fitzgerald was the Golden Girl of America's Jazz Age, a southern belle who married the talented F. Scott Fitzgerald. The two became symbols of carefree youth. Scott was a successful writer whose books are of lasting fame. Zelda also wrote, and much of what she wrote was published under Scott's name. Publishers paid for the name. Zelda never begrudged him his fame and she more than helped to spend the money. She lived life lavishly and fully, but below her vibrant joy of life lurked a tragic strain of madness. Her last years were spent in her mother's home in Montgomery and in mental hospitals. In one of them she died when fire swept the building.[11]

Owen, Marie Bankhead, 1869–1958, Historian; AWHF

Alabama Department of Archives and History, 624 Washington Avenue

At her eighty-fifth birthday celebration, Marie Bankhead Owen (Miss Marie) was described as "an Alabama institution, as much a part of the state as the Alabama River, the blue skies and the rugged mountains." Her husband, Thomas M. Owen, established the Department of Archives and History in 1902. Marie assisted Thomas during his years as director, and after his death in 1919 she stepped into his place and for over three decades devoted herself to the preservation of the state's history. She lobbied for federal funds and Works Progress Administration labor to erect the current building, gaining a reputation at the state house for knowing just what she wanted, when she wanted it, and how she wanted it delivered. The magnificent edifice, though it does not bear her name, is a memorial to her work and dedication.[12]

Tutwiler, Julia Strudwick, 1841–1916, Educator and Reformer; NAW, AWHF

Plaque, Alabama Department of Archives and History, 624 Washington Avenue

The marble plaque was dedicated in 1933 in honor of Julia Strudwick Tutwiler, "teacher, poet, prison reformer, patriot, lover of humanity, beauty and truth. Pioneer for Industrial and University Education for Women in America." In addition to exerting her influence in education for women and other social changes, Tutwiler wrote the Alabama state song. See Livingston, Montevallo, University, and Wetumpka, AL.

Wallace, Lurleen Burns, 1926–1968, State Governor; AWHF

Lurleen B. Wallace Museum, 725 Monroe Street. Bust, State Capitol

Alabama has honored its first woman governor in many ways. Though Lurleen Burns Wallace's term was cut short by cancer, she exerted a lasting influence for good throughout the state, principally in sponsoring hospitals for the mentally handicapped. See Andalusia, AL.

SELMA

Gibbs, Henrietta M., 1879–1960, Church and Clubwoman; AWHF

Gibbs Hall, Selma University

Henrietta M. Gibbs was a chartered trustee of Selma University and a leader in the support of the institution. As president of the Alabama Federation of Colored Women's Clubs from 1936 to 1943, she was a strong voice for the establishment of an institution for delinquent youth at Mt. Meigs. For many years she was an active member of her church, the Dexter Avenue Baptist Church in Montgomery, Alabama, a trustee and treasurer of the church, and a Sunday school teacher. Her civic interest led to the ministry among women of the Julia Tutwiler Prison in Wetumpka, Alabama.

Parrish, Clara Weaver, 1861–1952, Artist; AWHF

Stained-Glass Windows, St. Paul's Episcopal Church and First Baptist Church

Clara Weaver Parrish was a writer, artist, and philanthropist whose Weaver-Parrish Memorial Trust helps many needy persons and provides scholarships for

Selma High School graduates. She began working on mosaics and stained glass after visiting the cathedrals of Europe. As an affiliate of Louis Tiffany she designed windows in churches of New York City. Churches in Uniontown and Tuscaloosa also have windows of her design.

THEODORE

Bellingrath, Bessie Morse, 1878–1943, Collector and Philanthropist

Bellingrath Gardens and Home; NR

Bessie Morse Bellingrath, of Mobile, was married to Walter Bellingrath, a pioneer in the Coca-Cola bottling industry. In 1917 they bought the semitropical jungle on the Isle-Aix-Oies River as a fishing lodge. Bessie began planting azaleas on the property. She and her husband were inspired by the beauty of the setting to transform the woodlands into one of the major gardens of the world. The gardens were opened to the public in 1932 and have delighted thousands of visitors ever since. The mansion was built in 1935. Before Walter died he created the Bellingrath-Morse Foundation to channel the income from the operation of the gardens and mansion to a number of Alabama colleges and churches. The gardens are open daily from 7 until dusk. The house, displaying the Bessie Morse Bellingrath Collection of art objects, is open from 8 until an hour before dusk; high adm. for both.[13]

TUSCALOOSA

Clay-Clopton, Virginia Tunstall, 1825–1915, Society Leader and Writer; NAW

Marker, Friedman Home (Friedman Civic and Cultural Center), 1010 Greensboro Avenue; HABS, NR

According to the marker, the house was once the residence of Virginia Tunstall Clay-Clopton. It was built in 1835 by Clay-Clopton's uncle, Alfred Battle. She lost her mother when only three and was brought up by various relatives, including Battle, a wealthy planter, in Tuscaloosa. When she was seventy-five, she published her memoirs, *A Belle of the Fifties*, in which she described her meeting with Clement Claiborne Clay, her marriage to him, the social life in antebellum Alabama and Washington, D.C., and the harrowing days of the Civil War. Clement died in 1882 and Virginia married David Clopton, whom she outlived by over two decades. She might be pleased to know that the house where she was a carefree belle is now a cultural center.

Dix, Dorothea, 1802–1887, Mental Health Crusader; NAW

Marker, Bryce Hospital

Dorothea Dix was one of the first, if not the first, in the United States to become outraged at the way mentally deranged persons were treated. In Massachusetts she found men and women caged, chained, isolated, and treated like animals simply because they were mentally ill. In an angry but well-studied memorial to the legislature she pleaded for institutions where such persons could be nursed and cared for. Successful in her home state, she went to other states and persuaded many of them to establish hospitals for the insane. Alabama's state hospital was completed and opened in 1861. The marker gives Dix credit for inspiring its founding. See Raleigh, NC.

TUSCUMBIA

Keller, Helen, 1880–1968, Blind Worker for the Blind (NAWM, AWHF), and Her Teacher, Anne Sullivan Macy, 1866–1936 (NAW)

Ivy Green, 300 W. North Commons; NHL

The birthplace of Helen Keller, one of America's most famous women, has been preserved as a shrine to her and her teacher. Keller was born a normal child but at nineteen months lost not only her sight but also her hearing and consequently was mute. Anne Sullivan (later Macy) was brought to Tuscumbia to try to teach the child a better way of communicating with her world than by means of grunts, cries, and physical action. It took a long time to reach through Keller's isolation, but suddenly she grasped that the way Sullivan was touching her fingers meant something. She learned to give and receive messages in this way and progressed rapidly. With Sullivan's help she graduated from college, developed enough speaking ability to give lectures, and wrote books and articles, helping and inspiring other handicapped persons. The two women lived closely together for much of their lives, even after Sullivan married John Macy. It was here at Ivy Green that Sullivan finally succeeded in her attempts to reach Keller's bright young mind. A play based on the incident, *The Miracle Worker*, is presented at Ivy Green each summer. The house and memorial garden are open daily 8:30–4:30, Sun. 1–4:30; adm. Keller is in the National Women's Hall of Fame.[14]

TUSKEGEE

Goldthwaite, Anne Wilson, 1869–1944, Painter; NAW

Mural, Tuskegee Post Office, 302 S. Main Street

Anne Wilson Goldthwaite was born in Montgomery, Alabama, and might have remained in the South, but the loss of a suitor (killed in a duel) led to her moving

Helen Keller, whose triumph over the handicaps of deafness and blindness was an inspiration to all, was born in this tiny cottage in Tuscumbia, Alabama.
Courtesy State of Alabama Bureau of Tourism and Travel.

to New York City. She studied art and soon followed other American artists to Paris, France. One day she saw a friend in the Luxembourg Gardens with another woman "who looked something like an immense dark brown egg," dressed in a brown wrap, a flat hat on her head, and flat sandals on her feet. When invited to tea with the woman, she was amazed to see a charming room furnished in valuable antiques and decorated with a fascinating display of modern paintings. The woman was Gertrude Stein. Goldthwaite was swept up into the circle around Stein and Pablo Picasso. On her return to the United States she took a teaching job at the Art Students League and began a productive career. Her paintings are in some of the leading art collections. She remained in New York City but returned often to her native state and reflected in many of her paintings the color and life of rural Alabama. She painted two murals for post offices in the state, one in Atmore and one in Tuskegee.[15]

Washington, Margaret Murray, 1865–1925, Educator; AWHF

The Oaks, Old Montgomery Road, US 80

Margaret Murray Washington, a native of Macon, Mississippi, was a graduate of Fiske University (1889), who came to Tuskegee to teach and became the third wife of Booker T. Washington. She started Saturday meetings for women and children and began a rural settlement program on a rundown plantation nearby. In a short period she raised enough money to buy land and build a house on the plantation. She exerted profound influence in founding rural schools, improving prisons, and encouraging industrial education. She is described as a woman of great compassion, intelligence, and judgment. The first president of the National Federation of Colored Women's Clubs, she was one of the greatest forces among Negro leaders and thinkers of her time. The Oaks, home of the Washingtons, is operated by the National Park Service and is open Mon.-Fri. 8–12 and 1–4:30.[16]

UNIVERSITY

Gorgas, Amelia Gayle, 1826–1913, Librarian; AWHF

Amelia Gayle Gorgas Library, University of Alabama. Gorgas Home, University Campus; HABS, NR

Amelia Gayle Gorgas was the first woman faculty member and the first woman librarian at the University of Alabama, taking her post in 1883, ten years before women were admitted as students. She was librarian for twenty-four years, setting her imprint firmly on the growing institution. The Gorgas home, northwest corner of the Quadrangle, was originally designed as a hotel. It became the residence of Gorgas and her husband, General Josiah B. Gorgas, after he retired as university president, and has become a shrine to the family. Gorgas's son, William Gorgas, helped rid the Canal Zone of yellow fever and served as surgeon general of the U.S. Army during World War I. The Gorgas Library, the first building on the campus named for a woman, was completed in 1925. The United Daughters of the Confederacy, Amelia Gorgas Chapter, erected a commemorative plaque and a stained-glass window in the library. The Gorgas home is open Mon.-Sat. 10–12 and 2–5, Sun. 3–5. See Greensboro, AL.

Tutwiler, Julia Strudwick, 1841–1916, Educator and Prison Reformer; NAW, AWHF

Julia Tutwiler Hall, University of Alabama

The University of Alabama named its first dormitory for Julia Strudwick Tutwiler, who was instrumental in getting women admitted to the institution in 1893. The first ten women admitted were graduates of Livingston Normal (now Livingston University), which she headed. See Livingston, Montevallo, Montgomery, and Wetumpka, AL.

WETUMPKA

Tutwiler, Julia Strudwick, 1841–1916, Educator and Prison Reformer; NAW, AWHF

Julia Tutwiler Prison for Women

Julia Strudwick Tutwiler's interest in penal reform started in 1880 when she helped a young woman who had been jailed; she was shocked to see the conditions that prevailed. She organized a benevolent association to work for reform and undertook a study of county jails. Her reports were publicized, resulting in legislation to provide separate quarters for men and women prisoners and to plan for a woman's prison. Although unable to get the infamous convict lease system changed, she did succeed in getting a prison school established. See Livingston, Montevallo, Montgomery, and University, AL.

Edwina Donnelly Mitchell (1894–1968, AWHF) was made superintendent of the prison in 1951. She had been assistant state attorney general and a member of the Pardon and Parole Board, for which she wrote the enacting legislation. A realist who recognized that the women in her charge were criminals, she nevertheless believed each had a spark that could be made to glow. Since most of them would be released into society, she tried to help them achieve dignity and self-respect so as to be able to live normal, productive lives.

NOTES

In addition to the sources listed below, I have had help from the Montgomery City-County Public Library; Marshall County Cooperative Library in Arab; Mildred Johnson

Memorial Library, Jacksonville; the Alabama Historical Commission; and the Landmarks Foundation in Montgomery.

1. AWHF indicates that the individual is an electee to the Alabama Women's Hall of Fame, in Marion, Alabama. Biographical notes on all women in the hall were supplied by Judson College.

2. *Mothers of Achievement in American History, 1776–1976*, comp. American Mothers Committee (Rutland, Vt.: Charles E. Tuttle Co., 1976).

3. Notes from Birmingham Public Library, Tutwiler Collection of Southern History.

4. *Birmingham News*, Oct. 27, 1978 and May 21 and Oct. 2, 1979.

5. Ibid.

6. Correspondence, Blount County Historical Society.

7. Hope Chamberlin, *A Minority of Members: Women in the U.S. Congress* (New York: New American Library, 1974).

8. Katharine M. Jones, *Heroines of Dixie* (New York: Bobbs-Merrill, 1955).

9. Virginia P. Brown and Laurella Owens, *Toting the Lead Row: Ruby Pickens Tartt, Alabama Folklorist* (University: University of Alabama Press, 1982).

10. Hall of Fame correspondence, Judson College, Marion, Alabama.

11. Nancy Milford, *Zelda, A Biography* (New York: Harper & Row, 1970).

12. Correspondence and clippings, Alabama Department of Archives and History.

13. Fred W. Holder, *Bellingrath Gardens and Home* (Theodore, Ala.: Bellingrath-Morse Foundation, 1974); brochures, Bellingrath Gardens.

14. Brochures, Helen Keller Home.

15. Charlotte S. Rubinstein, *American Women Artists from Early Indian Times to the Present* (New York: Avon Books, 1982); correspondence, postmaster, Tuskegee.

16. Robert G. Sherer, *Subordination or Liberation? The Development of Conflicting Theories of Black Education in Nineteenth Century Alabama* (University: University of Alabama Press, 1977).

ARKANSAS

BENTONVILLE

Thaden, Louise McPhetridge, 1906–1979, Aviator

Louise Thaden Airport

Louise McPhetridge Thaden was born in Bentonville and lived as a child in the McPhetridge home, 616 W. Central Street. She won the first Woman's Air Derby in 1927, and she held simultaneously three international flying records for solo endurance, altitude, and speed. In 1929 she was in Pennsylvania employed by the Pittsburgh Aviation Industries Corporation. She organized the Women's Division of the Penn School of Aviation. In 1936 she won the Harmon Trophy as the outstanding woman flier of the United States. In private life she was the wife of Herbert Von Thaden, aeronautical engineer and manufacturer, and was the mother of two children. She served as secretary, treasurer, and president of the Ninety-Nines, a women's aviation organization, and was a captain in the Women's Air Reserve. In 1980 she was elected to the Arkansas Aviation Hall of Fame. Her *High, Wide and Frightened* tells of her experiences.[1]

CLOVER BEND

French, Alice (Octave Thanet), 1850–1934, Writer; NAW

Markers at Alice French House (Private); NR

Alice French established a winter home at Clover Bend in 1884–85, and used the plantation locale in her first novel, *Expiation* (1890), and several others. The house, originally called Thanford, was built in 1896 to replace the original mansion, which had burned down. With her lifelong friend Jane Crawford, French spent many winters here at her desk. She began her writing career from her home in Davenport, Iowa, with stories and articles signed Frances Essex or

Octave Thanet. About the turn of the century she reached the peak of her career, but later years brought illness and near poverty. Her books are little read now; George L. McMichael titled his biography of her *Journey to Obscurity*. Yet there is still interest in her life, and the house, on the bank of Black River, is occasionally open to visitors. It is six miles west of Mentura on State 228.[2]

EUREKA SPRINGS

Nation, Carry Moore, 1846–1911, Antisaloon Crusader; NAW

Hatchet Hall, 19 Bridge Street; NR

Carry Moore Nation, remembered for her penchant for smashing up saloons with a hatchet, was born in Kentucky and lived in Missouri and Texas before she began her antisaloon activities in Kansas. Her first husband proved to be an incurable alcoholic, and her second, David Nation, was much her senior and not a very loving man. Carry once said she had been denied a happy home so that she could be a home defender for other women. It was in 1899 that she started going to saloons, where she would sing hymns, then break up bottles, mirrors, pictures, and furniture, effectively closing up many such establishments. David divorced her and she took to the lecture circuit to support herself, handing out hundreds of miniature hatchets engraved "Carry Nation, Joint Smasher." Too lively for the Women's Christian Temperance Union, as time went on she was charitably considered insane. She lived in Eureka Springs for the last few years of her life and next door to her house ran a school for young prohibitionists, a project abandoned after her death. It is now a museum, open Mar. 1–Nov. 30, Mon.-Sat. 9–5; adm. See Belton, MO, and Lancaster, KY.[3]

FAYETTEVILLE

Fulbright, Roberta Waugh, 1874–1953, Publisher and Businesswoman

Roberta Fulbright Library (Fayetteville Public Library), 217 E. Dickson Street

Roberta Waugh Fulbright and her husband, Jay Fulbright, moved to Fayetteville in 1906 and a few years later acquired the newspaper which eventually became the *Northwest Arkansas Times*. After Jay's death in 1923 Roberta took over the newspaper, finally becoming president and full owner. Her column, "As I See It," appeared whenever she had something to say and she never hesitated to address what she considered the important issues—important not only to the city but to Arkansas and the nation. In addition to the newspaper business, Roberta succeeded to the active management of Jay's other interests and was president of a lumber company, a Coca-Cola bottling company, a couple of banks, and several other businesses. A strong Democrat and supporter of Franklin D. Roosevelt, she encouraged her son J. William Fulbright (one of six children) to run for public office and avidly followed his career in Congress. In 1947 she was chosen Arkansas Mother of the Year. The family gave the land for the library as a memorial.[4]

Marshall, Ann James, 1813–1910, Teacher

Marker in Churchyard, Mount Comfort

The historical marker indicates that Far West Seminary once occupied this spot, and among those who taught here was ''Miss Annie James, principal of the girls' school.'' Ann James Marshall was in fact the owner and principal of her own school, the Mount Comfort Female Seminary, begun in 1849, one of several small educational establishments in the area. Soon after she began the school, she married the Reverend Lewis S. Marshall, an Arkansas minister, and then had to give up her school to go with her husband to a new assignment. She remained in Arkansas, however, for the rest of her life. When she was eighty-four, *The Autobiography of Mrs. A. J. Marshall* was published, an account of her early experiences as a missionary teacher.[5]

JONESBORO

Caraway, Hattie Wyatt, 1878–1950, U.S. Senator; NAW

Marker, Craighead County Courthouse, Main Street

Hattie Wyatt Caraway's husband, Senator Thad Caraway, died in November 1931, and the governor gave her an interim appointment as his successor. The term was to expire in March 1933 and in the special election in January she ran uncontested. Since the cost of elections in Arkansas was financed by filing fees, there was no money to pay officials and judges, so the men suggested that as the only candidate was a woman, women should raise money and serve as volunteer officials. The women did, and they liked it so much they continued an active political force, a result unforeseen by the men. The male establishment got another jolt when at the end of the term Caraway declined to step down and announced her intention to seek another term, a full six-year term. She won, not only once, but twice.

In Congress she worked hard, made few speeches, and sought legislation to help working people hit by the depression. She was not a strong feminist but in 1943 she became a cosponsor of the Equal Rights Amendment. In 1944 she lost her Senate seat to William Fulbright. See Little Rock, AR.[6]

LITTLE ROCK

Babcock, Bernie Smade, 1868–1962, Museum Director

Museum of Science and History, McArthur Park

The Museum of Science and History was founded by Bernie Smade Babcock, and she was for twenty-five years its director and curator. A prolific writer, her books on Arkansas and on Abraham Lincoln established her early literary reputation. During the depression Babcock was chosen assistant supervisor of the Arkansas Writers Project which produced the Arkansas contribution to the American Guide Series. She used fiction and nonfiction to express her liberal religious and feminist beliefs. She published one of the state's earliest magazines, *The Sketch Book*. The museum is open Mon.-Sat. 9–4:30, Sun. 1–4; closed holidays; adm.[7]

Caraway, Hattie Wyatt, 1878–1950, U.S. Senator; NAW

Senator Hattie Caraway Room, Statehouse Convention Center, Markham and Main Streets

When Hattie Wyatt Caraway went to Washington in 1931 as the nation's first elected woman senator, she got an unusual amount of attention. There were still many, in Congress and elsewhere, men and women, who thought no woman should be in politics. A steady stream of visitors and reporters came through her office, and numerous articles were written describing her unfashionable black dresses and housewifely appearance. Nobody expected her to do more than occupy a seat until a man could be elected (see Jonesboro, AR). She felt challenged to prove that women did belong in politics, and although she spoke so little that she earned the name of Silent Hattie, she had her own opinions and voted them. She served two full terms. In 1983 Little Rock's new convention center opened with a room dedicated to Caraway.[8]

Terry, Adolphine Fletcher, 1882–1976, Feminist and Civil Rights Activist

Pike-Fletcher-Terry House, 7th and Rock Streets; HABS, NR

When Governor Orval Faubus, with his stubborn belief that states' rights nullified U.S. Supreme Court decisions, closed the city's high schools, Adolphine Fletcher Terry organized the Women's Emergency Committee to Open Our Schools. Terry, matriarch of the Fletcher family, had marched in every progressive movement from the day in 1902 she graduated from Vassar College. She started the state library program, founded a Young Women's Christian Association branch for black women, organized the first juvenile court in the state, and was a prime mover in getting a community chest and a county tuberculosis association under way. Her biography of Little Rock's first black teacher, Charlotte Stephens, was published when Terry was ninety-two.

Terry spent most of her life in this mansion, which her father bought from the celebrated Albert Pike in 1889. Its front parlor was the scene of her wedding in 1910 to David Terry, later a congressman. John Gould Fletcher, the poet, was her brother. The Terrys lived in the house throughout their married life, raising five children. In 1964 she and her sister deeded the house to the city of Little Rock for the benefit of the Arkansas Art Center, reserving a life tenancy. After Terry's death plans were initiated to convert the house to the Terry Center for the Decorative Arts.[9]

NOTES

In addition to the sources mentioned below, I have corresponded with the following: Professor Michael Dowgan, State University; Professor Diane Blair, University of Arkansas; Arkansas Historical Association, University of Arkansas; Arkansas Historical Commission, Little Rock; Torreyson Library, University of Central Arkansas.

1. Correspondence, Arkansas Women's Historical Institute, Little Rock.

2. Ethel W. Hanft, *Outstanding Iowa Women, Past and Present* (Muscatine, Iowa: River Bend Publishing, 1980); correspondence, Nancy Phillips, Alicia, Ark.; nomination form, National Register of Historic Places, from Arkansas Historic Preservation Program.

3. *Arkansas Historical Quarterly* 42 (Winter 1983).

4. Clippings and correspondence, Fayetteville Public Library; *New York Times*, Jan. 12, 1953.

5. Deane G. Carter, "A Place in History for Ann James," *Arkansas Historical Quarterly* 28 (Winter 1969).

6. *Silent Hattie Speaks: The Personal Journal of Senator Hattie Caraway*, ed. Diane D. Kincaid (Westport, Ct.: Greenwood Press, 1979); correspondence, Greater Jonesboro Chamber of Commerce.

7. *Arkansas Historical Quarterly* 39 (Spring 1980); *Mothers of Achievement in American History, 1776–1976*, comp. American Mothers Committee (Rutland, Vt.: Charles E. Tuttle Co., 1976).

8. *Silent Hattie Speaks*.

9. *Mothers of Achievement*; Harry A. Ashmore, *Arkansas* (State and the Nation Series, New York: Norton, 1978); correspondence, C. Allan Brown, Little Rock.

FLORIDA

BROOKSVILLE

Robins, Margaret Dreier, 1868–1945, Labor Reformer and Conservationist; NAW

Chinsegut Hill Migratory Bird Sanctuary

Margaret Dreier Robins and her husband, Raymond Robins, social workers and labor reformers in Chicago, Illinois, moved in 1924 to Chinsegut Hill, a two-thousand-acre estate where they had spent vacations. It did not mean retirement from public life for either. She was vice president of a bank and manager of a bookstore, while continuing work with such organizations as the Young Women's Christian Association, the Red Cross, and the League of Women Voters. She was appointed by President Herbert Hoover to the planning committee for the White House Conference on Child Health and Protection in 1929, but several years later she deserted the Republican ranks to support President Franklin D. Roosevelt, whose New Deal policies appealed to her. Raymond traveled in 1933 some eight thousand miles in Soviet Russia studying collective farming, industry, and education. He and Margaret, both horticulturists, gave Chinsegut Hill to the U.S. Department of Agriculture for use as a wildlife refuge and forest conservation and experimental station.[1]

CROSS CREEK

Rawlings, Marjorie Kinnan, 1896–1953, Writer; NAWM

Marjorie Kinnan Rawlings House Museum, County 325 Near Hawthorne; HABS, NHL

It was after Marjorie Kinnan Rawlings and her husband, Charles Rawlings, came to Florida that she began writing about the people of the Florida scrub and piney woods, stories that would bring her fame and fortune. Charles did not share her enthusiasm for living in the isolated orange groves and they were subsequently divorced, but Marjorie continued to live at Cross Creek for some years. In 1933 her first book, *South Moon Under,* was selected by the Book of the Month Club. In 1939 *The Yearling* won the Pulitzer Prize for fiction. *Cross Creek* is a memoir of her life in the woods. Her books, with their strong regional flavor, are popular everywhere, for their themes are timeless and placeless. Her rural home has been restored and is open daily 9–5; adm.[2]

DAYTONA BEACH

Bethune, Mary McLeod, 1875–1955, Educator, Civil Rights Activist; NAWM

Bethune-Cookman College. Mary McLeod Bethune House, 2nd Avenue, Between McLeod and Lincoln Streets; NHL

For many years Mary McLeod Bethune was the most influential black woman in the United States. The daughter of parents freed from slavery by the Emancipation Proclamation, she grew up in poverty but with a strong determination to get an education. As a young woman she applied to the Presbyterian Mission Board for an assignment to Africa, only to be told that black missionaries were not sent to Africa. She went to teach at Lucy Laney's school in Augusta, Georgia, q.v., and some years later she made up her mind to open a school in Daytona Beach for black girls who had little access to education. With $1.50, some wooden boxes for benches, a strong character, and faith in God, she opened her school in 1904. "I haunted the city dump," she wrote, "retrieving discarded linen and kitchenware, cracked dishes, broken chairs, pieces of old lumber." So began the school that grew into the Daytona Normal and Industrial Institute and eventually became Bethune-Cookman College.

In 1936 Bethune began a second career in Washington, D.C., where she was close to President and Mrs. Franklin D. Roosevelt and was appointed to a high post in the National Youth Administration. As a charismatic leader, a spokesperson for her race, founder of the National Council of Negro Women, foremost advocate of civil rights, she was widely respected and admired. In 1949 she returned to Daytona Beach and transformed her home into an educational foundation. See Mayesville and Myrtle Beach, SC.

FORT GEORGE ISLAND

Jai, Anna Madgigaine, fl. 1817–1868, Princess

Kingsley Plantation State Historic Site; NR

The Kingsley house is one of the oldest in the state. It was the home of Zephaniah Kingsley, a white planter, and Anna Madgigaine Jai, a Senegalese princess.

Though married, they were not allowed by Florida law to live in the same house because of her color. Ma'am Anna's house was a separate two-room house in the rear. She was a tall, slender, dignified woman, mother of Kingsley's four children. Social pressure finally forced the family to move to Haiti. The island is available by ferry from Mayport or by State A1A. The plantation site is open daily, 8–5, with tours at regular intervals; adm. to tours.

FORT LAUDERDALE

Stranahan, Ivy Cromartie, 1881–1971, Teacher

Stranahan Park

Ivy Cromartie Stranahan and her husband, Frank Stranahan, are known as the founders of Fort Lauderdale. They were married in 1900 and lived at the Indian trading post he established. The town's first schoolteacher, Ivy taught for sixteen years in the Fort Lauderdale public schools. For another fifteen years she taught Seminole children on an informal basis. She founded the Friends of the Seminoles. Her interests included the Audubon Society, suffrage, and park development. Frank, who died in 1929, gave the sites for the Memorial Hospital and Stranahan Park.[3]

JACKSONVILLE

Alderman, Carlotta Townsend, 1882–1967, Civic Worker

Alderman Park. Alderman Road. Townsend Boulevard. Carlotta Road

Jacksonville recognized the civic accomplishments of Carlotta Townsend Alderman by naming a number of streets for her. She was a Georgian who came to Florida in 1908. Her husband, a realtor, died in 1927 and during her many years of widowhood she devoted herself to the betterment of the community. She was president of the Democratic Women's Club of Jacksonville and as a school board member innovated school cafeterias. She donated the site for the general headquarters of the state Chamber of Commerce in Jacksonville, and part of the building is named for her.

Connor, Jeanette Thurber, d. 1927, Historian

Florida State Historical Society

Jeanette Thurber Connor was a cofounder of the historical society and one of the world's foremost authorities on the early Spanish history of Florida. When Washington Everett Connor married her, he took her to see some old Spanish ruins he had bought at New Smyrna. She became so fascinated in tracing their history that he gave them to her and launched her on a lifetime study. She located the sites of forty-four original Spanish missions in the state and the names of the friars in charge of each one. She and John B. Stetson, Jr., between them collected photocopies or transcripts of all the documents in the Spanish archives in Seville relating to the early Florida settlements. She edited Jean Ribault's *Whole and True Discovery of Terra Florida* (1927, republished 1964) and *Colonial Records of Spanish Florida* (1925).[4]

Cummer, Ninah May Holden, 1875–1958, Art Collector

Cummer Gallery of Art, 829 Riverside Avenue

Ninah May Holden Cummer and her husband, Arthur Gerrish Cummer, were longtime residents of Jacksonville. Ninah began collecting art after the death of her only child in 1906. By the terms of her will, most of her estate, including her collections, went to the creation of a gallery of art which would contribute to the cultural life of Jacksonville. It was to be operated by the DeEtte Holden Cummer Museum Foundation, named for the lost child. The gallery was built on the site of the Cummer house and retains the original formal gardens on the St. John's River. Since its opening in 1961, gifts from many others have increased the original magnificent collection of paintings, sculpture, graphics, and decorative arts. The museum is open Tues.-Fri. 9–4, Sat. 12–5, and Sun. 2–5.[5]

White, Eartha Mary Magdalene, 1876–1974, Humanitarian; NAWM

Clara White Mission. Harriet Beecher Stowe Community Center. Eartha M. White Nursing Home

The daughter of a black woman and a white man, Eartha Mary Magdalene White was adopted as an infant by Clara and Lafayette White, who gave her a great gift: pride in her Afro-American heritage. When the child was twelve the family left Jacksonville for New York City. There she studied hairdressing and music, joined the Oriental-American Opera Company, and toured America, Europe, and the Orient with the company for a year. Back in Jacksonville, she taught school and then ran several small businesses. An admirer of Booker T. Washington, she joined in a number of organizations working for civil rights and did what she could to alleviate problems faced by blacks in her own neighborhood. She operated the first orphanage for black children in the county, raised funds for the Colored Old-Folks' Home, conducted Bible classes at the county prison, provided a recreation director at a Jacksonville park, and established the Harriet Beecher Stowe Community Center.

In 1928 she established a mission, named for her adoptive mother, which was Jacksonville's counterpart of Chicago's Hull House. During the depression it was the center for relief efforts and for Works Progress Administration projects.

A child placement center, an orphan home, and a maternity home were among the many institutions that grew out of the mission. In 1967 the Eartha M. White Nursing Home was opened, a modern 120-bed facility for which White raised much of the money. Jacksonville recognized her humanitarian efforts with many awards and honors. In 1970, when she was presented with a $5,000 Volunteer Award by the Lane Bryant department store, she was asked what she would do with it. ''I want it to serve humanity,'' she replied. ''The money is to God, not to me.''[6]

MANDARIN

Stowe, Harriet Beecher, 1811–1896, Antislavery Writer; NAW

Marker, Community Building. Memorial Window, Episcopal Chapel

It is surprising that the Yankee author of *Uncle Tom's Cabin*, once anathema to southerners, should be able to live quietly in the South while the memory of the Civil War was still fresh. The choice of Mandarin as a winter home was made partly out of a desire to be useful to the black people and partly to benefit the health of the Stowes' son Fred. Harriet Beecher Stowe and her husband, Calvin Stowe, taught in the Episcopal Chapel, but for the most part she basked ''like a lizard'' in the sun. A slight book, *Palmetto Leaves,* was written here, attracting other northerners to visit Florida. Passenger steamboats on the St. Johns River used to pause so that the curious could catch a glimpse of the famed author, and there is a legend that the steamboat company paid her a fee to sit on the front porch. After a time her admirers invaded the Stowe paradise, grabbing oranges from her trees and even clothes from her clothesline. The Stowes left in 1884. The house has since burned down, but the carriage house remains, now a private dwelling. The Tiffany window in the chapel was contributed by popular subscription under the sponsorship of the magazine *Outlook*.[7]

MIAMI

Earhart, Amelia (Putnam), 1897–1937, Aviator; NAW

Plaque, Lobby of Miami International Airport

On June 1, 1937, Amelia Earhart set off from the municipal airport, with Captain Frederick Noonan as copilot, to encircle the globe. They were flying Earhart's Lockheed Electra. The trip was planned for speed and to study the reactions of the human body and the mechanical performance of the plane at high altitudes and extreme temperatures. The plane was last heard from on July 2, near Howland Island in the Pacific. No trace of the plane or the pilots has ever been found. Admirers of ''Lady Lindy'' mourned her disappearance. An airmail stamp in her honor was issued in 1963. The marker at the Miami airport was dedicated in 1939 by the Dade County Federation of Women's Clubs.

Tuttle, Julia, 1848–1898, City Developer

Julia Tuttle Causeway

In 1891 Julia Tuttle took possession of a large plantation in Miami, but it was too isolated from the rest of the world to be a profitable enterprise. She induced Henry M. Flagler to construct the Florida East Coast Railroad south to Miami from West Palm Beach, giving every alternate lot to him to induce settlement. She thus changed Miami from a small fishing village to a modern city with connections to the North. The story goes that in the winter of 1894–95, when a hard freeze had devastated Florida groves and crops as far south as Palm Beach, Tuttle sent Flagler a bouquet of fresh flowers from untouched Miami, and this persuaded Flagler to build the railroad, though he still thought Miami would serve as nothing more than a fishing spot for his Palm Beach hotel guests.

ORLANDO

Hurston, Zora Neale, 1901?–1960, Writer and Folklorist; NAWM

Zora Neale Hurston Building (Florida State Office Building)

Zora Neale Hurston was a prolific writer, an anthropologist who participated in the life of the people she studied, and the most outstanding Afro-American woman of letters in her time. Yet she realized few of the rewards of authorship, often worked as a maid, had difficulty entering the academic profession, and died penniless. She was born in Eatonville, Florida, the first incorporated all-black town in America, where her father was several times the mayor and her mother urged her to "jump at de sun." Her mother's death in Hurston's ninth year and her father's remarriage changed the family atmosphere, and she left home at fourteen. In New York City she worked as a secretary and chauffeur for the novelist Fannie Hurst, won a scholarship and studied anthropology at Barnard College, and was the first black to graduate from the college (1928). Her autobiography, *Dust Tracks on a Road* (1942), and the novel *Their Eyes Were Watching God* (1937) are perhaps the best keys to her life and her writing, the value of which is only now being recognized. In 1973 another black writer, Alice Walker, found that Hurston's grave in the Garden of the Heavenly Rest, 17th Street in Fort Pierce, Florida, was unmarked. She ordered a marker erected and supplied the wording: "Zora Neale Hurston, 'A Genius of the South,' Novelist, Folklorist, Anthropologist." She also located Zora's Fort Pierce home, at 1734 School Court Street.[8]

PALMETTO

Atzeroth, Juliann (Madame Joe), fl. 1843–1880, Pioneer Storekeeper

Marker, 300 Block of 10th Avenue

Juliann (Madame Joe) Atzeroth acquired the property here in 1850. A log cabin under the six oaks about sixty yards southwest of the house was used as a store by Madame Joe and later became Palmetto's first public school. The first religious services were held there. See Terra Ceia Island, FL.

SARASOTA

Ringling, Mable Burton, 1875–1929, Art Collector and Circus Figure

Ringling Museums, US 41; NR

It was an architect's dream—to design a palatial home on one of the most beautiful waterfront estates in Florida, money no object. But it is said that architect James Baum blanched when Mable Burton Ringling told him what she wanted in a residence: a combination of the facade of the Doge's Palace in Venice and the tower of the old Madison Square Garden in New York City. He designed the residence, called Ca'd'Zan, which was completed in 1926. Mable, wife of circus king John Ringling, had only a few years to enjoy it before her death. The other parts of the Ringling Museums complex were added later, but all were part of the couple's wish to enrich the state of Florida with a showcase of circus memorabilia, art, and theater.

Little is known of Mable before she married John in Hoboken, New Jersey, in 1905, except that she was born in Fayette County, Ohio, and was named Armilda E. Burton. John and Mable were rarely separated during their quarter century of partnership. They came to Sarasota in 1909 in search of a country home. It was a tiny fishing town, population 763, since grown into a thriving city and center for the arts. When John died in 1936 he willed his entire estate to the people of Florida. The museum, recognized as one of the great art galleries of the country, is open Mon.-Fri. 9–7, Sat. 9–5, and Sun. 11–6; adm.[9]

Selby, Marie Minshall, 1885–1971, Gardener and Philanthropist

The Marie Selby Botanical Gardens, 800 S. Palm Avenue

A mecca for orchid lovers and serious students of tropical plants, the Selby Gardens are known around the world. Research is carried on here on the endangered plants of the Western Hemisphere. The Orchid and Bromeliad Identification Centers serve hobbyists and commercial growers alike.

Marie Minshall Selby started the gardens surrounding her own modest home (now the book and gift shop). She and her husband, William Selby, began coming to Sarasota every winter early in the twentieth century. Summers were spent at the Selby Ranch in Montana. Marie was adventurous and self-reliant. In 1909, shortly after her marriage, she and William outfitted a touring automobile for camping and drove from New York to Seattle at the time of the first transcontinental auto race. They took six days less than the car that won the race and Marie was heralded as the first woman to cross the country by automobile. Until well in her seventies she drove alone from Florida to Montana each summer, returning in time to supervise the gardening.

The Selby name is sprinkled through Sarasota, thanks to generous gifts from Marie and the Selby Foundation. The gardens are open every day in the year except Christmas, 9–5; adm.[10]

TALLAHASSEE

Murat, Catherine Dangerfield Willis, Princess, 1803–1867, Plantation Mistress

Bellevue, Adjacent to Junior Museum at Lake Bradford

Catherine Dangerfield Willis Murat was a great-grandniece of George Washington, and her husband, Achille Murat, was prince royal of the Two Sicilies before the overthrow of his father, the king of Naples (Napoleon Bonaparte's son). The princess named their home in Tallahassee Bellevue for a hotel in Brussels where they had spent many happy days. Achille never lived in the house, but Catherine spent her last days here on an annuity from Louis Napoleon. She was a patriotic American, raising thousands of dollars for the purchase of Mount Vernon, home of George Washington. In 1967 her house was moved from its original location and is now part of the Junior Museum. Open Tues.-Sat. 9–5 and Sun. 2–5; adm.

TERRA CEIA ISLAND

Atzeroth, Juliann (Madame Joe), fl. 1843–1880, Pioneer Storekeeper

Marker, Site of Atzeroth House, 728 Bay Shore Drive (Private)

Juliann and Joe Atzeroth were the first permanent settlers on Terra Ceia Island, arriving here in 1843. In 1880 she received a ten-dollar award for growing the first pound of coffee in this country. See Palmetto, FL.

WINTER PARK

Russell, Annie, 1864–1936, Actress; NAW

Annie Russell Theater, Rollins College

After years of acting in frothy popular plays, the English-born actress Annie Russell began a crusade for better theater. She decried the poor taste of American theater audiences who wanted only light entertainment and the managers who catered to that taste. For a short time she presented plays as the Annie Russell Old English Comedy Company, and she appealed to American clubwomen to support productions designed to elevate and educate the playgoing public. Mary Louise Curtis Bok of Philadelphia, Pennsylvania, a longtime friend of Russell, gave the playhouse to Rollins College, and Russell's final performance was given at its opening in 1932. She taught theater arts at Rollins from that time until her death.

Woolson, Constance Fenimore, 1840–1894, Writer; NAW

Woolson House, Rollins College

Over the door of the house named for Constance Fenimore Woolson are inscribed the words "Dean of Florida Writers." Woolson was one of the first northern writers to treat the postwar South in a sympathetic and nonsentimental way. She was noted for her travel sketches and local-color stories of the Great Lakes Region, the Ohio Valley, and the area around Cooperstown, New York. She was a grandniece of the novelist James Fenimore Cooper. She began visiting the South in the 1870s and a few of her sketches and novels have a southern background. The small house at Rollins College, erected by a niece, is sometimes used for literature classes.

NOTES

In addition to the sources mentioned below, I have had correspondence with the following: Florida Department of State, Division of Cultural Affairs; Stuart Area Branch, American Association of University Women, Stuart; Miami-Dade Public Library, Miami; Office of Visitor Inquiry, Florida Division of Tourism; State Department of Commerce; and the Florida Division of Archives, History and Records Management.

1. Sandra Conn, "Three Talents: Robins, Nestor, and Anderson of the Chicago Women's Trade Union League," *Chicago History* 9 (Winter 1980–81).

2. Stephanie Kraft, "The Nonfiction World of Writers," *Historic Preservation* 29 (Apr.-June 1977); Marcella Thum, *Exploring Literary America* (New York: Atheneum, 1979).

3. Henry S. Marks, *Who Was Who in Florida* (Huntsville, Ala.: Strode, 1973); *New York Times*, May 24, 1929.

4. Marks, op. cit.; *New York Times,* June 11, 1927.

5. Brochure, Cummer Gallery.

6. *New York Times,* Dec. 4, 1970.

7. Allen Morris, *Florida Place Names* (Coral Gables, Fla.: University of Miami Press, 1974).

8. Correspondence, Orlando Public Library.

9. Correspondence and brochures, Ringling Museums.

10. Correspondence and clippings, Marie Selby Botanical Gardens.

GEORGIA

ANDERSONVILLE

Barton, Clara, 1821–1912, Red Cross Founder (NAW), and Lizabeth A. Turner, d. 1907, Civil War Nurses

Monuments, Andersonville National Historic Site

The historical park, nine miles northeast of Americus on State 49, includes Andersonville Prison, where some thirteen thousand Union soldiers died during the Civil War. Heat, crowding, disease, and malnutrition took a grim toll of the thirty-three thousand men imprisoned here. The site also includes the cemetery where the victims were buried. Acquired by the Georgia Grand Army of the Republic after the war, the site was in 1896 turned over to the Woman's Relief Corps, an auxiliary of the Daughters of the American Revolution. They beautified the grounds, planting rose bushes sent from almost every state, and erected a caretaker's house. The park now belongs to the nation.

Clara Barton, best known as the founder of the American Red Cross, was a nurse during the war, and it was she who undertook the grim task of identifying the dead at Andersonville and marking their graves. A memorial sundial was erected in 1915 as a monument to her. Lizabeth A. Turner also cared for the wounded, and after the war, as treasurer of the Relief Corps, was active in the development of the park. She died while it was being prepared and her colleagues erected the monument.

ATHENS

Lumpkin, Mary Bryan Thomas, 1857–1932, Garden-club Pioneer

Founders Memorial Garden, 325 Lumpkin Street. Marker at Lumpkin House, 973 Prince Street

In December 1891 twelve women met at the home of Mary (Mamie) Bryan Thomas Lumpkin to form perhaps the first organized garden club in the nation, the Ladies' Garden Club of Athens. It had permanent officers, a constitution and bylaws, and held flower and vegetable shows. Lumpkin, whose iris garden was known throughout the state, was its first vice president. The club's successor, the Garden Club of Georgia, designed the gardens at the edge of the campus of the University of Georgia as a memorial to the founders, and in 1964 a house in the garden was dedicated as the state headquarters of the Garden Club. The gardens are open daily 7–5:30, and the headquarters building is open Mon.-Fri. 1–4.[1]

Lyndon, Mary Dorothy, 1877–1924, Educator

Lyndon Hall, University of Georgia South Campus

Mary Dorothy Lyndon was the first woman to graduate from the University of Georgia, by completing work in summer courses for the master of arts degree (1914). In 1918, after much opposition, the university officially opened its doors to women. When the board of trustees began to look about for an associate professor of education and dean of women, they found her in Lyndon. She proved a perfect choice. She encouraged students to participate in activities outside of their studies and organized the Pioneer Club (originally for women not taking home economics). She started a basketball team, a rifle team, a dramatic club, and an honorary sorority. Her objective—which she achieved—was to gain for women students an equal and responsible place in a man's world. A portrait of "Miss Mary" by an Atlanta, Georgia, artist, Kate Edwards, hangs in the hall of the dormitory bearing her name.[2]

Michael, Moina Belle, 1869–1944, Educator and Humanitarian

Moina Michael Park, Broad Street. Moina Michael Auditorium (Allen R. Fleming, Jr., Post 20, American Legion). Moina Michael Highway (US 78, Athens to Monroe)

Moina Belle Michael once told an interviewer that she had done everything in her lifetime but plow. At the end of the Civil War, when her family's finances crumbled, she worked to educate younger siblings and help out her parents, teaching school at the age of sixteen. She presided over an orphan's home, was principal at Bessie Tift College, and was from 1913 to 1938 social director of Winnie Davis Hall, Georgia State Teachers College. During World War I Moina served with the Young Women's Christian Association in Rome, Italy. Her chief claim to fame is in originating the idea of selling poppies on Memorial Day to aid disabled soldiers and their families. The movement spread nationwide and overseas, and by the time of her death some $200 million had been raised for this cause in the United States alone. The "Poppy Lady" was given many honors. A Liberty ship was named for her. Athens issued a commemorative stamp in her honor and gave her name to a tiny park. The state legislature named a stretch of highway for her in 1969. See Good Hope, GA.[3]

ATLANTA

Barrett, Kate Waller, 1857–1925, Humanitarian; NAW

Barrett Hall, Florence Crittenton Services, 3913 N. Peachtree Road

Kate Waller Barrett's awakening to the need for aid to unwed mothers came when a young unmarried woman knocked at her door and asked for help. Compassionate and motherly, Barrett responded by taking the girl into her home. She was surprised to find, when she talked to her guest, that it was not a case of degradation or depravity but of misfortune. She realized with a shock that any woman might have found herself in a like situation. Out of this realization she resolved to establish shelters for these social outcasts where they would be treated with justice and decency. In a Victorian age, such a determination took courage.

When Barrett's husband, Robert Barrett, was transferred from Richmond, Virginia, to Atlanta as dean of St. Luke's Cathedral, she enrolled in the Women's Medical College. While attempting to establish a rescue home in Atlanta, she contacted Charles N. Crittenton, who had devoted himself to the rehabilitation of prostitutes and had established several homes, naming them for a daughter who died at a young age. He gave Barrett five thousand dollars, and the city gave a piece of land (once a city dump). The Florence Crittenton Home of Atlanta opened a year after Barrett got her medical degree. Barrett remained active in establishing homes, and after Crittenton died she succeeded him as president of the National Florence Crittenton Missions. See Williamsburg and Alexandria, VA.[4]

Butler, Selena Sloan, 1872?–1964, Community Leader; NAWM

Selena Butler Park

Selena Sloan Butler's greatest achievement was the founding of the National Congress of Colored Parents and Teachers. Although she was a college graduate (Spelman College, 1888) and the wife of a successful physician and businessman, she found it difficult to find a preschool for her son because of their race. She set up a school in her own home and when the children went to the Yonge Street school she started there the first black parent-teacher organization in the country. (The school is now named for her husband, Henry Rutherford Butler.) The organization became statewide in 1920, nationwide in 1926. She worked harmoniously with the Congress of Parents and Teachers, which had been founded many years earlier by Alice Birney and Phoebe Hearst, and when that group became integrated in 1970, Butler was recognized as a cofounder of the organization. Though much of her energy went into the promotion of interracial understanding and child welfare, Butler gave time to many other civic programs. Atlanta regarded her as one of its outstanding citizens and had her portrait painted for the state capitol, as well as naming a park for her.[5]

Giles, Harriet. See Packard, Sophia

Hearst, Phoebe Apperson, 1842–1919, Philanthropist; NAW

Phoebe Hearst Hall, Oglethorpe University, 7200 Peachtree Road

Phoebe Apperson Hearst, who is known best as the benefactor of the University of California at Berkeley and for various philanthropies in Washington, D.C., was one of the founders of the National Congress of Parents and Teachers. Wife of a wealthy mining engineer, she used her fortune to subsidize many causes that took her interest, from archeological expeditions to kindergartens. In 1929 her son, William Randolph Hearst, gave the Silver Lake Estates, four hundred acres of forest surrounding a lake, to the adjoining Oglethorpe University, thus enlarging the campus and protecting it from urban encroachment. See Anaconda, MO.

High, Harriett Harwell Wilson, 1862–1932, Art Patron

High Museum of Art, Atlanta Memorial Arts Center, 1290 Peachtree Street, N.E.

Harriett Harwell Wilson High was a leading Atlanta hostess and civic worker, and for some years after her husband died she continued to operate his department store, the J. M. High Company. Much of her time was occupied with the orphanages, hospitals, libraries, and art and music committees which she supported. In 1926 she gave her home to the city to be used as an art museum as long as it bore the family name. At that time Atlanta was a provincial town and for years the city's first art museum showed gifts and bequests of no particular distinction. But today, thanks to Robert Woodruff, Coca-Cola magnate, and many enthusiastic art lovers, a dazzlingly modern art museum, still bearing the High name, has risen in the place of the old mansion.[6]

McCullar, Bernice Brown, 1905–1975, Journalist

Memorial Tree, State Capitol Grounds

Bernice Brown McCullar was a popular journalist, a respected publicist for the State Department of Education, a writer, a speaker, and a radio and television personality. When she came to Atlanta in 1954 to become director of information for the Department of Education, she had a rich personal and professional background. She was a member of the Georgia bar; coeditor with her husband of the *Milledgeville Times* and later the *Milledgeville News*; teacher; trustee of Mercer College; and after 1942, when Claudius McCullar died, the sole support of herself and two children. Her contributions to the state did not go unrecognized. In 1974 her birthday was proclaimed Bernice McCullar Day. A scholarship was established in her name by the alumni association of Georgia College. A dogwood tree, of a variety known as Cloud Nine, was planted in her memory following her death.[7]

McLendon, Mary Latimer, 1840–1921, Temperance and Suffrage Leader

Marble Fountain, State Capitol

Younger sister of Rebecca Latimer Felton (see Cartersville, GA), Mary Latimer McLendon is remembered as the mother of suffrage work in Georgia. Unlike many of her coworkers, McLendon lived to see the Nineteenth Amendment to the federal Constitution passed. She joined the Woman's Christian Temperance Union in the 1880s and in 1892, with one other Atlanta woman, she joined the new Georgia Women's Suffrage Association. These two causes, intermingled, occupied her heart and mind for the rest of her life. They encompassed many other programs to benefit women and children, such as opening state colleges to women, abolishing child labor, and establishing compulsory education. She gathered signatures for a six-foot-long petition in behalf of a scientific temperance instruction law to educate school children about the effects of alcohol and then presented it to the legislature in 1894. It was finally signed into law in 1901. Georgia women erected the fountain to her memory two years after her death.[8]

Mitchell, Margaret (Marsh), 1900–1949, Novelist; NAW

Margaret Mitchell Memorial Library, Atlanta Historical Society, 3101 Andrews Drive, N.W. Margaret Mitchell Room, Atlanta Public Library, 126 Carnegie Way, N.W. Plaque on Office Building at Site of Home, 1401 Peachtree Street, N.E.

Margaret Mitchell began writing sections of a novel based on the Civil War about 1926, with no particular plans for publishing it. In 1935 a friend who knew of Mitchell's preoccupation with the writing mentioned it to a visiting Macmillan editor, who asked to see the manuscript. At first she refused, but at the last minute changed her mind and brought the mass of papers to his hotel. The book was accepted at once, which meant that she had to spend many hours revising the manuscript and verifying its minute historical details, but in 1936 *Gone with the Wind* appeared. Despite its bulk (1,057 pages), readers loved it.

From the day of publication, the novel was a best-seller. It won the Pulitzer Prize, was translated into many languages, and as a movie with Vivian Leigh and Clark Gable it continues to earn millions. The book brought sudden fame and wealth to its author and her husband, John Robert Marsh, who acted as her business agent. Mitchell herself did not consider the book a work of great literary merit and she never wrote another novel. See Fayetteville and Jonesboro, GA.

Moore, Martha McDonald, 1884–1964, Lecturer and Churchwoman

Chapel, Protestant Radio and Television Center, 1727 Clifton Road, N.E.

The chapel bears the names of Martha McDonald Moore and her husband, Bishop Arthur J. Moore, who lived in Atlanta for many years. She was once called the "power behind the Bishop." Before their marriage, she was a country schoolteacher and he a "backsliding Baptist," read out of the church on a charge of dancing. The young couple began to attend church and Methodist meetings, at one of which he experienced a great awakening and began his preaching career without benefit of theological training. He gave Martha the credit for bringing him back into the fold. A woman impressed by his zeal put up the money to send him to Emory University. Martha herself was in great demand as a speaker for churches and missionary outposts. Another chapel named for her is at Magnolia Manors (South Georgia Methodist Home for the Aging), Lee Street Road in Americus, Georgia.[9]

Packard, Sophia, 1824–1891, and Harriet Giles, 1833–1909, Educators; NAW (under Packard)

Packard Hall and Giles Hall, Spelman College, 320 Spelman Lane, S.W.

In 1881 two elderly ladies came from Massachusetts to Atlanta to start a school for Negro women and girls. Sophia Packard and Harriet Giles had been fellow teachers and close friends for many years and had organized the Woman's American Baptist Home Missionary Society, which agreed to sponsor the proposed school. On arrival they opened the school in a church basement with eleven pupils. In a few months there were eighty. The seminary grew rapidly, and by the time Packard died, ten years after her arrival in Georgia, it was a flourishing institution with almost five hundred students. Giles succeeded her friend as president and continued to build its strength and influence. In 1924 the institution became Spelman College; in 1929 it affiliated with Morehouse, a neighboring college for Negro men, and with Atlanta University.

The school early won the support of Lucy Henry Spelman, whose two daughters, Laura and Lucy Spelman, had attended Oread Institute in Worcester, Massachusetts, while Packard and Giles were teaching there. Laura married John D. Rockefeller, who visited the struggling college and, along with the Spelmans, was its main support—thus the Spelman name. Buildings on the campus are named for other members of the family: Rockefeller Hall, Abby Aldrich Hall (for the wife of John D. Rockefeller, Jr.), Bessie Strong Nurses Home (daughter of John D. Rockefeller, Sr.), Laura Spelman Rockefeller Memorial, and the Sisters Chapel (for Laura and Lucy Spelman). The Florence Matilda Read (Health and Recreation) Building was named for Spelman's president emerita. Read was president from 1927 until 1953, and for another twenty years continued an active life in education. She wrote *The Story of Spelman College*.[10]

AUGUSTA

Laney, Lucy Craft, 1854–1933, Educator; NAW

Lucy Laney High School, 1339 Gwinnett Street

The Lucy Laney High School stands on the site of Haines Normal and Industrial Institute, established by Lucy Craft Laney in 1886 for the education of southern Negro youth, who at that time had little opportunity to prepare themselves for college. Laney believed that the black community's hope lay partially in the hands of educated Afro-American women who would be teachers and lecturers. She herself had been fortunate in having parents (both born into slavery) who encouraged her to study and sent her to Atlanta University. In addition to supervision of the struggling school, Laney had to work industriously to raise funds for its support. One of her early sympathizers and supporters was Francina Haines, whose name was given to the school. Financial help came from missionary societies and wealthy northern benefactors,and encouragement came from dedicated teachers in the school, among whom was Mary McLeod Bethune, who later founded her own school in Daytona Beach, Florida. After many years of service to Negro youth, Haines Institute was closed in 1949 and its buildings razed, to be replaced by the modern high school bearing Laney's name. Her portrait hangs in the state capitol.[11]

LeVert, Octavia Celeste Walton, 1811–1877, Social Leader; NAW

Meadow Garden, 1320 Nelson Street; NR

Octavia Celeste Walton LeVert was born in Augusta and spent some of her childhood years in Meadow Garden, the home of her grandmother. Her grandfather, George Walton, who died some years before her birth, was one of the signers of the Declaration of Independence. Her grandmother, Dorothy Camber Walton, was the proud daughter of an English gentleman. Octavia, the darling of an ambitious and aristocratic family, was educated at home by her mother,

her grandmother, and tutors, who taught her that she was destined for greatness. When the Marquis de Lafayette visited America in 1825, she was presented to him. Two years later she met Edgar Allan Poe, who wrote a poem "To Octavia." She toured the northern states in 1833–34 and became acquainted with political figures in Washington, D.C.

In 1836 Octavia married Henry LeVert, a physician of Mobile, Alabama, and began a thirty-year social career there. She was known as Madame LeVert, hostess and patron of culture. She wrote a two-volume travel book which established her as a writer. Tributes to her beauty and charm were legion. The Civil War ended her reign as social queen; she was the last of the southern belles.

Meadow Garden, after some years of neglect, was purchased by the National Daughters of the American Revolution, restored by the Augusta chapter, and officially opened in 1901 as a museum. It is open Mon.-Sat. 10–4; adm.[12]

Tubman, Emily Thomas, 1794–1885, Emancipator

Tablet, First Christian Church, 629 Greene Street

Emily Thomas Tubman freed her slaves twenty-seven years before President Abraham Lincoln's Emancipation Proclamation. She was born in Virginia and moved to the new state of Kentucky as a child. After her father died, nine-year-old Emily's legal guardian was the famous orator and statesman, Henry Clay. After marriage to an Englishman living in Georgia, Richard C. Tubman, Emily entered Augusta society. Richard died in 1836, leaving a will in which he expressed a wish to have the legislature allow his wife to emancipate her slaves.

Emily, searching for a place were the blacks could go if freed, heard about the federal government's plan to establish a home for freedmen in Africa, naming it Liberia. She gave her people the choice of going there or remaining with her. She chartered a ship in 1844 and sent to the new country the sixty-nine who chose to emigrate. A community in Liberia was named Tubmantown. In 1961, 107 years after she sent her slaves to Africa, the president of Liberia came to the United States. He was William V. S. Tubman, a descendant of slaves she had freed. See Frankfort, KY.[13]

BUTLER ISLAND

Kemble, Frances (Butler), 1809–1893, Actress and Writer; NAW

Marker, at Site of Pierce Butler Plantation, US 17

The marker, placed by the Georgia Historical Commission, reads: "During a visit here with her husband in 1839–40, Pierce Butler's wife, the brilliant English actress, Fanny Kemble, wrote her *Journal of a Residence on a Georgian Plan-*

tation, which is said to have influenced England against the Confederacy." The visit was actually made in 1838–39, and while the *Journal* is a powerful indictment of slavery, its publication in 1863 was too late to influence the course of the war, though it did change British sentiment toward emancipation.

When Frances Kemble married the wealthy Philadelphian, Pierce Butler, she was hardly aware that his fortune rested on a foundation of slavery. Shortly after the birth of her second daughter, she visited the Butler plantations here and on St. Simons Island, Georgia, q.v. She was horrified to find hundreds of slaves living in wretched, unsanitary, and hopeless conditions. She did what she could to alleviate their misery, until her unsympathetic husband forbade her to transmit any more of their petitions. She felt especially for the women, who were always carrying children and were forced to work in the fields shortly after giving birth. After one session with them, she reports, "I had my cry out for them, for myself, for *us*. All these women had had large families, and *all* of them had lost half their children, and several of them had lost more."

The marriage grew increasingly unhappy; Fanny returned to the stage; and finally, in 1849, Pierce divorced her, retaining custody of their children. From a sense of loyalty to him she did not at once publish her journal of the year she spent in Georgia, a year surrounded by "pride, profligacy, idleness, cruelty, cowardice, ignorance, squalor, dirt, and ineffable abasement." In 1863, when England was debating whether to throw its weight against the Union by a cotton loan, Fanny decided to add her voice to those of her abolitionist friends in the North by publishing the book.[14]

CARTERSVILLE

Felton, Rebecca Latimer, 1835–1930, U.S. Senator; NAW

Marker, Site of Felton Home, US 411

Rebecca Latimer Felton was the first woman seated in the U.S. Senate. Appointed in 1922 to fill the place of a deceased senator, she sat in the Senate for two days before her successor took office. This would seem to indicate that she rose from obscurity and after a moment of glory fell back into the shadows. As a matter of fact, she had been active in politics for many years. When her husband, William Harrell Felton, ran for Congress on the Independent ticket in 1874, Rebecca was his campaign manager. While William served in the U.S. Congress and then in the Georgia legislature, Rebecca was closely involved in all he was doing. She and her husband began a newspaper in Cartersville, which she ran while he was in the legislature. She wrote a column for the *Atlanta Journal* for twenty years, wrote several books, and was involved in many reform movements. In 1914 and 1915 she went before a state legislative committee to speak on behalf of woman's suffrage. The Felton home, which was listed in the National Register, recently burned to the ground. See Decatur, GA.[15]

Harris, Corra White, 1869–1935, Novelist; NAW

Marker, Memorial Chapel, US 411 at Pine Log

In 1909 the *Saturday Evening Post* published serially a novel by Corra White Harris entitled *A Circuit-Rider's Wife*. It took the Methodist church to task for meager pay and burdensome duties laid upon its itinerant ministers. The author spoke from personal experience, for her husband, Lundy Howard Harris, had spent years traveling from place to place ministering to rural communities. He suffered from melancholia and a year after her book appeared he took his own life. Harris continued writing, bringing out an average of one book a year until 1927. After 1914 she did most of her writing in a log cabin at Pine Log, which, according to legend, was once owned by an Indian chief. Twice she was sent to Europe by the *Saturday Evening Post*, once to write articles on the women of Europe and again to cover the beginnings of World War I. *A Circuit-Rider's Wife* was her most popular novel. In 1951 it was the basis of the movie *I'd Climb the Highest Mountain*. After her death three of her nephews erected the memorial chapel at her burial place.[16]

CLAYTON

Neel, Isa-Beall Williams, 1861–1953, Churchwoman

I. B. Neel Prayer Room, Memorial Chapel, Camp Pinnacle

For almost twenty years the annual offering for Baptist missions in Georgia was named for Isa-Beall Williams Neel, longtime president of the Baptist Woman's Missionary Union (WMU). After her marriage to W. J. Neel she and her husband formed a team in Baptist church life and civic work in Rome and Cartersville, Georgia. She was a major factor in the decision of the WMU to build a school for girls in Blue Ridge, and she led the organization to donate thousands of dollars to endow Bessie Tift College. While she was president, the union contributed to the building of a hospital and school in China and a school in Japan. After she resigned from the WMU presidency, at the age of seventy-two, she went to Bessie Tift College in Forsyth, Georgia, as instructor in foreign languages, where she remained until she was eighty. The WMU, which owns Camp Pinnacle near Clayton, gave her name to the prayer room.[17]

COLUMBUS

Ellis, Lizzie Rutherford, fl. 1860s, Clubwoman

Marker, 2nd Avenue and 11th Street

The marker commemorates the founding of Southern Memorial Day by the Ladies' Memorial Association of Columbus in 1866. Lizzie Rutherford Ellis is credited with initiating the custom of decorating the graves of Confederate soldiers each year on April 26. Mary Williams, as secretary of the association, wrote letters to the *Columbus Times* and other representative newspapers urging that the day be set apart throughout the South to remember the Confederate dead. "We cannot raise monumental shafts and inscribe thereon their many deeds of heroism," she wrote, "but we can keep alive the memory of the debt we owe them by dedicating at least one day in each year, to embellishing their humble graves with flowers."[18]

Fox, Susie MacDonald, 1879–1928, Educator

Susie MacDonald Fox School, 3720 5th Avenue

When Susie MacDonald Fox was made principal of the North Highlands School, she learned that children had to pay a small tuition fee, and those whose parents could not afford the fee were considered charity cases. She disapproved of this state of affairs and saw to it that such children were given small tasks, for which she paid them; then she collected the fee. This gave the youngsters a sense of pride. She also quietly provided food for those who were hungry, clothes or shoes for the poorly dressed, and even baths when needed, all with love and a sense of humor that robbed her philanthropy of the "Lady Bountiful" taint. She was principal of the school for the eight years preceding her death. Nineteen years later when the Board of Education renamed the school in her memory, the children who had attended the school, and their parents, were gratified.[19]

Johnson, Johnnie Pearl Patrick, 1878–1946, Civic Leader

Johnson School

Johnnie Pearl Patrick Johnson organized the first parent-teacher association in Columbus in 1905. She was elected to the Board of Education in 1922 and served for many years as advocate for teachers and protector of their interests. She also fought for a somewhat unpopular cause, racial understanding and equal opportunity for black and white children. In the fall of 1948 a new elementary school was dedicated to Johnson.[20]

Stewart, Euphan Collier, d. 1942, Art Patron

Euphan Collier Stewart Gallery, Columbus Museum of Arts and Crafts, 1251 Wynnton Road

Euphan Collier Stewart was the daughter of a prominent painter, Miles Collier, and it was natural for her to take an interest in art. She was a founding member of the Columbus Art Association and a leader in the development of the arts in Columbus. In 1924 she and a friend were responsible for bringing the first exhibit of outstanding paintings to Columbus. It was shown in the library, for lack of an art gallery. The Columbus Museum of Arts and Crafts, opened in 1953, was initiated by a large bequest from Stewart's sister, Georgia Collier Comer of Savannah, Georgia, in memory of Stewart. The museum is open for guided tours, Mon.-Sat. 10–5 and Sun. 1–5; closed holidays.[21]

Turner, Hallie, 1897–1981, Educator

Hallie Turner Private Schools

Hallie Turner began teaching some of her friends' children in her home, and during the depression she tutored in Latin. From that small private school grew the Turner Schools, with branches in Opelika and Dothan, Alabama, and Macon and Columbus, Georgia. Turner worked with the Quota Club, an organization of business and professional women, and through this society she helped to establish in 1952 the Girls' Clubs. The Girls' Clubs of America gave her its highest honor, the Service Award, in 1977.[22]

Wilson, Augusta Evans, 1835–1909, Writer; NAW

Marker, Wildwood, Garrard Street and Wildwood Avenue (Private). St. Elmo, 2810 St. Elmo Street (Private); HABS, NR

Wildwood was the birthplace of Augusta Evans Wilson, who later settled in Mobile, Alabama. She visited Columbus occasionally and while with her aunt at St. Elmo (then called El Dorado) she was inspired to write what became her most famous novel, *St. Elmo*. See Mobile, AL.[23]

Wood, Edwina, 1876–1965, Kindergartner

Edwina Wood Elementary School

Edwina Wood was the mother of kindergartens in Columbus. She began teaching in a private kindergarten in 1898, after graduating from a course offered by the Free Kindergarten Association. She was able to get kindergartens established for both black and white children as part of the public school system, and she directed the program for the city until 1921. For twenty years she was on the Board of Education in Columbus, much of the time supervising the recreation activities of the city. In 1962 an elementary school was given her name to recognize her lifetime of service to education, recreation, and church activities in the city. Her portrait hangs in the school vestibule.[24]

CRAWFORDVILLE

Montgomery, Roselle Mercier, 1874–1933, Poet

Marker, Taliaferro County Courthouse

The Georgia Historical Commission's plaque, erected in 1956, honors Roselle Mercier Montgomery, born on this site, as ''Georgia's best and one of America's finest poetesses.'' One of her poems, ''Evening on a Village Street,'' was written about this corner of town. Another speaks of her love for her native state: ''The ruddy hills that compassed me about were friends of mine; they shut the strange world out.''[25]

DECATUR

Felton, Rebecca Latimer, 1835–1930, U.S. Senator; NAW

Marker, Welburne Road, US 278

Rebecca Latimer Felton was born near here and among her earliest recollections, she wrote, were the Indians who then lived in the forests around the plantation. Later, when they were driven out of north Georgia, she was distressed ''to see them sent into exile from the forests their ancestors had lived in for centuries . . . pawns in the hands of destiny.'' Felton, the first woman to sit in the U.S. Senate (see Cartersville, GA), fought for justice throughout her career.[26]

FAYETTEVILLE

Mitchell, Margaret (Marsh), 1900–1949, Novelist; NAW

Margaret Mitchell Library, 195 Lee Street

The library has collections relating to Margaret Mitchell's famous novel *Gone with the Wind*. They were donated by the author herself, who met and admired the civic-minded women who started the library. The building is adjacent to the site of Fayetteville Academy, supposedly attended by Scarlett O'Hara before the Civil War. The library is open daily. See Atlanta, GA.[27]

FORSYTH

Tift, Bessie Willingham, 1860–1936, Churchwoman

Tift College

In 1905 Bessie Willingham Tift and and her husband, Henry Tift, attended a convention at which the president of what was then Monroe College made an urgent plea for funds. Unless they could find $37,000, the school must close. Henry, who sat some distance from his wife, sent her a note by an usher, "Bessie, you may give the $37,000." Bessie in turn sent an usher to the rostrum with a note: "Mr. Tift says he will give the $37,000." Two years later the school (founded in 1847 as Forsyth Female Collegiate Institute) became Bessie Tift College. Bessie was not only a supporter of the school but a trustee of Tallulah Falls School and of the Woman's Missionary Union Training School in Louisville, Kentucky. In 1950 the college, in accordance with general practice, dropped the "Bessie" and became Tift College, part of the Southern Association of Colleges.[28]

GOOD HOPE

Michael, Moina Belle, 1869–1944, Educator and Patriot

Marker at Birthplace, State 83

Moina Belle Michael conceived the idea of selling small artificial poppies to raise money for World War I veterans. Thanks to her, poppy sales by disabled veterans earn millions of dollars annually for charity. Several memorials have been erected to her in Athens, Georgia, q.v. In 1931 the Georgia legislature designated her a "Distinguished Citizen," and six years later the American Legion Auxiliary placed a marble bust of her in the state capitol.[29]

HARTWELL

Hart, Nancy, 1735?–1830, Revolutionary War Heroine; NAW

Nancy Hart Monument, Town Square. Sculpture, Hartwell High School. Nancy Hart Park

During the Revolution Nancy Hart was said to have captured Loyalists wherever she found them. Her most famous exploit concerned some British soldiers who appeared at her house and demanded dinner. She fed them, and after they had all fallen into a drunken slumber she grabbed their rifles and held them until the Whigs arrived and dispatched them. The story, never documented, grew into a legend, and Georgia has celebrated Hart's fame, deserved or not, by erecting markers and naming a county and a park for her. She was described as a "six-foot, cross-eyed sharp-shooter." The aluminum sculpture in the school's gymnasium-auditorium, by Julian Harris, depicts the capture of the hapless British soldiers.

The state park, south of Hartwell on the Nancy Hart Highway, has a reproduction of Hart's log cabin.[30]

JONESBORO

Mitchell, Margaret (Marsh), 1900–1949, Novelist; NAW

Margaret Mitchell Park, Carnegie Drive

Memorials to Margaret Mitchell, author of the best-selling *Gone with the Wind*, are found in Fayetteville, Georgia, and several in her native Atlanta, Georgia, q.v.

KNOXVILLE

Troutman, Joanna, 1818–1880, Flag Designer

Monument, Courthouse Square

In 1835 Joanna Troutman learned that a Georgia battalion had been formed to aid Texas in its fight for independence. The romantic sixteen-year-old made a flag for them to carry and presented it to the volunteers on their way through Knoxville. The following year the flag, white silk with one blue star, was raised over Fort Goliad to signify that Texas had been recognized as an independent republic. The flag, with its colors reversed, became the official emblem of the republic and later of the Lone Star State. Troutman, the wife of Vinson Troutman, died at the age of sixty-two and was buried in Crawford County. In 1913 Texas officials, who had not forgotten Troutman's contribution, got permission to remove her remains to the state cemetery at Austin, Texas, q.v., where a bronze statue was erected in her memory.[31]

LINDALE

Perkerson, Medora Field, 1892–1960, Journalist

Marker, Lindale Auditorium

On Christmas Eve in 1917 a young reporter, Medora Field Perkerson, disguised herself in cheap clothes, and went about to houses of prominent citizens asking for food for her "desperate family." All she could collect was $2.45 and a few baskets of food, which she gave to a local charity. Her story of public indifference to need appeared in a Rome, Georgia, newspaper and created a sensation. She expanded the story and sold it to the *Woman's Home Companion*. Angus Perkerson, founder and editor of the *Atlanta Journal Magazine*, was so impressed that he hired her, sight unseen, as a feature writer. Two years later they were married. Medora wrote for the paper for twenty years, using the pen name of Marie Rose in an advice column that was one of the paper's most popular features. She also wrote novels, including a best-selling mystery, *Who Killed Aunt Maggie?*, and a book of Georgia tales, *White Columns in Georgia*, which is still in print. Friends and admirers erected this memorial near the site of her birthplace.[32]

MARIETTA

Birney, Alice McLellan, 1858–1907, Founder of the National Congress of Mothers (PTA); NAW

Memorial, Marietta High School, Winn Street

Alice McLellan Birney was convinced that many children led lives warped by well-meaning but ignorant parents. She dreamed of a congress of mothers who would have access to advanced knowledge of child development. With the aid of Phoebe Apperson Hearst she called, in 1897, a meeting of mothers in Washington, D.C., expecting perhaps fifty to respond. Over two thousand swamped the meeting, necessitating a move to another hall. Shortly the National Congress of Mothers was formed. The name was changed several times and is now the National Congress of Parents and Teachers—PTA to its over a million members.

Birney was born in Marietta.The Birney house served for a time as the rectory of St. James Episcopal church. The building was then dismantled and moved to Kennesaw Avenue and its future is uncertain. The monument at the school is a sun court with a marble arch entry, sundial, and rose garden. It is inscribed: "This sun court is dedicated to a great woman who made a great dream come true. . . . From the seed of faith she planted has come the flowering of a new era of hope and promise for America's children." Stones sent from every state are incorporated in the monument. The garden is maintained by the Marietta Men's Garden Club. In 1972 a U.S. commemorative stamp was issued in recognition of the founding of the PTA.[33]

MILLEDGEVILLE

Atkinson, Susie Cobb Milton, c. 1861–c. 1941, Politician and Businesswoman

Atkinson Hall, Georgia College; NR

Susie Cobb Milton Atkinson's interest in giving the women of Georgia the same right men enjoyed to a state-supported institution of higher learning led to the founding in 1889 of the Georgia Normal and Industrial School for Girls. From a Florida family which had for generations been involved in state and national politics, she attended Lucy Cobb Institute at Athens, Georgia, and there met William Y. Atkinson. After their marriage and while he served as a member of the Georgia legislature and as governor, she was his secretary. She led other women in advocacy of a bill to support the college, and afterward, as chairman of the board of women visitors, she favored offering business and industrial training to fit women for vocations then opening in commercial fields. She herself entered the insurance business after William's death in 1899, then served as postmistress at Newnan for sixteen years. The school became the Georgia State College for Women and later Georgia College.

O'Connor, Flannery, 1925–1964, Writer; NAWM

O'Connor Room, Ina Dillard Russell Library, Georgia College

Flannery O'Connor began writing while a student at Georgia College, contributing to the college literary magazine and editing the senior yearbook. Graduating in 1945, she went next to the University of Iowa, where she developed her own literary style and began to publish. Her first novel, *Wise Blood*, was almost finished when she developed lupus erythematosus, the disease that had killed her father when she was fifteen. Under a rigorous regimen of medication and rest, she remained at home with her mother, who operated a dairy farm near Milledgeville, and continued to write. Another novel and a number of short stories were published before her death, others posthumously, all marking her as a highly original writer dealing with the fundamentals of religious faith in carefully crafted prose. The O'Connor Room contains original manuscripts, letters, and part of O'Connor's private library.[34]

MOUNT BERRY

Berry, Martha, 1866–1942, Educator and Humanitarian; NAW

Berry College and Academy; NR. Martha Berry Museum and Art Gallery, US 17

Martha Berry's tombstone, at the side of the log cabin in which she started her famous school, is inscribed "Not to be Ministered Unto, but to Minister." Born into a well-to-do family, she devoted her life and her inheritance to opening up the world of learning to the children of poor rural families. At her cabin retreat on Mount Berry she began reading Bible stories to a few children, and each week more showed up to listen. Not just children but adults came, adults who had never gone to school and could not read or write.

Berry started a Boys Industrial School at the cabin in 1902. Tuition was paid in part by manual labor, required of all students, although considered by many Georgians as degrading. Her neighbors and even some of her own family were critical of Berry's efforts, but the families who sent their children to the school adored her. One mother gave the family cow so that her son could get an education. Another family gave their best plow and sent their son to plow the school gardens. Soon a girls' school was added, then a college, and Berry's work became known nationally. The school now occupies thousands of acres with hundreds of buildings, many contributed by Henry Ford. The college is open Mon.-Fri. 8–5, weekends 1–5. The Museum and Art Gallery is in Oak Hill, Berry's birthplace; it is open Mon.-Fri. 10–5, weekends 2–5.[35]

RABUN GAP

Hambidge, Mary Crovatt, 1885–1973, Weaver

The Hambidge Center; NR

Mary Crovatt Hambidge learned to weave from Greek women in 1920–21. After the death of her husband, Jay Hambidge, she returned to Georgia, her native state, and revived the traditional mountain craft of weaving, from sheep raising to shearing, dying, carding, spinning, and weaving the wool. In the 1930s she bought eight hundred acres on Betty's Creek, where she developed the Hambidge Center. Noted for weaving and other crafts, it evolved into a retreat for artists, writers, and other creative workers from around the world. The Rabun weavers' products have been exhibited at the Museum of Modern Art, the Smithsonian, and abroad.[36]

RINCON

Greene, Catherine Littlefield, 1755–1814, Plantation Manager and Inventor; NAW

Marker, State 21, at Site of Mulberry Grove, North of Port Wentworth; NR

The invention of the cotton gin, which revolutionized the whole economy of the South, took place at Mulberry Grove Plantation, a homestead which had been given to General Nathanael Greene after the Revolution. The Greenes settled here in 1785 but Nathanael died within months, leaving Catherine Littlefield Greene with five small children and a rundown estate. She gave over management of the property to Phineas Miller, the children's tutor, and he in turn brought Eli Whitney, a Yale University graduate, into the household. One day a visitor remarked that there would be a fortune in store for someone who would invent a machine for separating the cotton from the seed. Catherine, who admired Whitney's abilities as a tinkerer and watch repairer, suggested that he invent such a machine. He constructed a device with wire teeth on a revolving cylinder, but, with no way to throw off the lint after it was separated from the seed, it clogged the teeth. Catherine seized a clothes brush and solved the problem, thus becoming coinventor of the cotton gin for which Whitney was long given sole credit.

Catherine later married Miller, and neither she nor Whitney made the predicted fortune from the invention. Whitney was engaged in constant lawsuits against others who claimed patent rights. He worked on the machine in secret; according to an early historian, he allowed only women to examine his machine, "as they were not supposed to be capable of betraying the secret to builders—an opinion for which modern females of the strong-minded school, will no doubt bear him a grudge—and not altogether without reason when we consider the material assistance he received from a woman in perfecting his invention.'' The Greene house was burned by General William Tecumseh Sherman in 1864–65 and a rebuilt mansion was destroyed by a storm in the early 1900s, so little remains to be seen.[37]

ST. SIMONS ISLAND

Cate, Margaret Davis, 1888–1961, Historian and Preservationist

Margaret Davis Cate Memorial Library, Fort Frederica National Monument

Margaret Davis Cate spent much of her lifetime studying the history and folklore of the Golden Islands, centering on the old fort on St. Simons which had been built in 1736 and was vital to the defense of the English against Spain. She was one of the founders of the Fort Frederica Association, which raised nearly one hundred thousand dollars to purchase the site and then gave it to the National Park Service. In the course of her researches, she interviewed many ex-slaves, collected folk stories, studied folk medicine, recorded the details of crafts such as basketmaking and woodcarving, and collected over ten thousand items of historical documentation (now in the Georgia Historical Society in Savannah). In 1958 the museum at Fort Frederica was dedicated, and after Cate's death the library was built as an annex. The monument is open daily in summer 8:30–5:30, rest of year 8–5.[38]

Leigh, Frances Butler, 1838–1910, Plantation Manager

Marker, Site of Pierce Butler Plantation, Hampton

Frances Butler Leigh and her sister were left to the custody of Pierce Butler when he divorced their mother, the actress Fanny Kemble (see Butler Island, GA). After the Civil War, Butler, like others planters, was almost ruined. He and his daughter came here to try to reestablish his plantation. Butler soon died, leaving Leigh to manage the operation. It was a task few women—and few men—could have accomplished in a ruined economy. It took all her ingenuity and force of character to deal with the workers and raise and sell the crops. Even after she married the Reverend James Wentworth Leigh, she remained in Georgia until the plantation was on a paying basis, then moved with him to England. There she published her account of the remarkable enterprise, *Ten Years on a Georgia Plantation Since the War*.[39]

SAVANNAH

Low, Juliette Gordon, 1860–1927, Founder of Girl Scouts of the U.S.A.; NAW

Juliette Gordon Low Birthplace, 10 Oglethorpe Avenue; HABS, NHL

Juliette Gordon Low spent her childhood in this home and returned to it after school to make her debut. In 1886 she married William Low, an English aristocrat, and moved to England. She was widowed in 1905. A few years later she met Sir Robert Baden-Powell and his wife, who introduced her to the Scouting movement. She returned to Savannah, where she called a friend and announced, "I've got something for the girls of Savannah, and all America, and all the world, and we're going to start it tonight." The American Girl Guides, begun in 1912, soon became the Girl Scouts of the United States. Low gave much of her fortune and most of her time to developing the organization.

In 1953 the Girl Scouts purchased the Wayne-Gordon House, Low's birthplace and family home, and restored it as a national program center. It is open Feb.-Nov., Mon.-Tues, Thurs.-Sat. 10–4 and Sun. 1:30–4:30; adm. Low is in the National Women's Hall of Fame.[40]

Martus, Florence, 1868–1943, Lighthouse Resident

Statue, The Waving Girl, *River Bluff*

The statue is by Felix de Weldon. The inscription on the tablet, erected by the Georgia Historical Commission in 1958, tells the story: "For 44 years, Florence Martus (1868–1943) lived on nearby Elba Island with her brother, the lighthouse keeper, and no ship arrived for Savannah or departed from 1887 to 1931 without her waving a handkerchief by day or a lantern by night. Throughout the years, the vessels in return watched for and saluted this quiet little woman. Few people ever met her yet she became the source of romantic legends when the story of her faithful greetings was told in ports all over the world. After her retirement the Propeller Club of Savannah, in honor of her seventieth birthday, sponsored a celebration on Cockspur Island. A Liberty ship, built in Savannah in 1943, was named for her."[41]

Taylor, Charlotte de Bernier Scarbrough, 1806–1861?, Entomologist

Scarbrough House, 41 W. Broad Street; HABS, NHL

Charlotte de Bernier Scarbrough Taylor had a curiosity about bugs, particularly the boll weevil that was so destructive to the South's chief crop, the silkworm from which came the thread for her dresses, and even the spider. A self-taught entomologist, she was knowledgeable enough to write articles about these creatures that were published by *Harper's New Monthly Magazine* between 1857 and 1864. They were written in a charming literary style and illustrated with painstakingly exact drawings. She hoped southern farmers would read and benefit from her advice: "It is enough to make one laugh and cry both," she wrote, "to go through the country and see the poor forlorn whitewashed, swathed and bandaged, lime-trodden, ashes-heaped, soap-sudded, train-oiled, bottle-hung trees and fields." The only way to rid the fields of pests, she wrote, was to burn the stubble. "I trust this advice will not be lost upon our intelligent farmers in all parts of the country, that there will be some to credit my words." At the approach of the Civil War, Taylor went to England and began a book describing plantation life, a project cut short by her death, which according to family tradition occurred on the Isle of Man in 1861, though some of her articles were published later than that.

Scarbrough House, the family home which had descended to Taylor, was in 1872 the first public school for blacks in Savannah. For almost ninety years it was known as the West Broad Street School. It has been restored by Historic Savannah Foundation and is open Mon.-Sat. 10–4, except Nov.-Feb., when it is closed Sat.; adm.[42]

SOUTH NEWPORT

Musgrove, Mary (Bosomworth), c. 1700–1763, Indian Leader; NAW

St. Catherine's Island; NHL

Mary Musgrove was born in the Creek Nation, the daughter of an Indian woman by an English settler. Her mother's brother was Old Brim, so-called emperor of the Creek Nation. Her father took her to South Carolina, where he saw that she was educated and instructed in the principles of Christianity. On her return to the Creek territory she married John Musgrove, a North Carolinian whose mission was to form a treaty of friendship and trade with the Indians. In 1733 when James Oglethorpe came from England to found the colony of Georgia, the Musgroves were running a profitable trading post. Mary's friendliness and knowledge of English made her of great value in forming amicable relationships between the Indians and the colonists, and later in keeping the Creeks loyal to the British against the Florida Spaniards. When Oglethorpe left Georgia ten years later he acknowledged Mary's help by giving her a diamond ring and a sum of money.

Had that been the end of the story, Mary Musgrove would go down in history as a heroine. But man's greed betrayed her. After John died, Mary was married twice more, her last husband, Thomas Bosomworth, proving to be a fortune seeker. At his instigation, Mary laid claim to three of the coastal islands, plus a tract near Savannah used as Creek hunting grounds, as well as a large sum of money she said Oglethorpe had promised her for her services as an interpreter. When this was refused, she led a band of warriors to Savannah and terrorized the town, which held out against the threat. The Bosomworths even went to England to press her claims. A few years later the government gave in and granted the Bosomworths St. Catherine's Island and over two thousand English pounds, which the colony had to pay.[43]

WASHINGTON

Andrews, Eliza Frances, 1840–1931, Writer and Botanist; NAW

Marker at Memorial Tree

In 1982 the Washington Women's Club erected a marker inscribed: "This tree planted 1930 honoring Eliza Frances Andrews, 'Miss Fannie,' Teacher, Author, Renowned Botanist." Andrews lived at Haywood plantation near Washington. She went through the Civil War and Reconstruction, then lost her father and his estate through a dishonest advisor. Past thirty and unmarried, she turned to teaching, first in Mississippi, then in Washington and Macon, Georgia. From 1898 to 1903 she taught botany in the Washington High School. She had meanwhile been writing and publishing novels and short stories. Still read is her *War-Time Journal of a Southern Girl*, a revealing record of her own experiences during the war and afterwards. In her later years she wrote mostly on botany and produced two textbooks on that subject, in which she noted the interdependence of the plant world and the man-made environment.[44]

NOTES

In addition to the sources mentioned below, I have had correspondence with the following: Atlanta Public Library; Georgia Historical Society Library, Savannah; Augusta Regional Library; Rabun County Library, Clayton; New Echota State Park; Mercer University, Macon; Atlanta Historical Society Library; Georgia State Library, Atlanta; Historic Augusta; and Historic Savannah Foundation.

1. Beth Abney, in *Dictionary of Georgia Biography*, ed. Kenneth Coleman and Charles S. Gurr (Athens: University of Georgia Press, 1983). The *Dictionary of Georgia Biography* is hereafter cited as *DGB*. Each biography in this excellent compilation is accompanied by a bibliography.

2. Susan B. Tate, in *DGB*.

3. Beth Abney, in *DGB; New York Times,* May 11, 1944.

4. Helen C. Smith, "She Befriended 'Unthinkables,' " *Atlanta Journal*, Jan. 18, 1976. This is one of a series of biographies of "Georgia's 25 Historic Mothers," written by Smith from material prepared by students under the supervision of Julia Voorhees Emmons, Emory University Division of Librarianship, and published during the centennial year; I am indebted to Emmons and the *Atlanta Journal* for copies of the biographies.

5. Darlene Roth, in *DGB*; Phillip T. Drotning, *A Guide to Negro History in America* (Garden City, N.Y.: Doubleday & Co., 1968).

6. Roberta Dixon, in *DGB*; Robert Wernick, ''Atlanta's New High Art Museum,'' *Smithsonian* 13 (Jan. 1984).

7. John Rozier, in *DGB*.

8. Ann Wells Ellis, in *DGB*; A. Elizabeth Taylor, ''The Origin of the Woman Suffrage Movement in Georgia,'' *Georgia Historical Quarterly* 18 (June 1944).

9. Helen C. Smith, ''Power Behind the Bishop,'' *Atlanta Journal*, May 30, 1976; correspondence, Lake Blackshear Regional Library, Americus.

10. Florence M. Read, *The Story of Spelman College* (Atlanta, Ga.: n.p., 1961).

11. Jeanne L. Noble, *The Negro Women's College Education* (New York: Teachers College, Columbia University, 1956).

12. *Sketch of Meadow Garden*, comp. Martha B. Benton (Augusta, Ga.: National Society Daughters of the American Revolution, 1922); Martha J. Craven, ''A Portrait of Octavia,'' *Richmond County History* 4 (Summer 1972); correspondence, Augusta-Richmond County Public Library, Augusta.

13. Edith Deen, *Great Women of the Christian Faith* (New York: Harper & Bros., 1959).

14. Frances Anne Kemble, *Journal of a Residence on a Georgian Plantation*, ed. John A. Scott (New York: New American Library, 1975).

15. Rebecca Latimer Felton, *The Romantic Story of Georgia's Women* (Atlanta, Ga.: Atlanta Georgian and Sunday American, 1930); Helen C. Smith, ''Rebecca Felton Breaks Barriers,'' *Atlanta Journal*, Feb. 1, 1976.

16. Helen C. Smith, ''Popular Novelist,'' *Atlanta Journal*, Mar. 7, 1976.

17. Dorothy Pryor, in *DGB*.

18. Lucian Lamar Knight, *Georgia's Landmarks, Memorials and Legends*, vol. 2 (Atlanta, Ga.: Byrd Printing Co., 1913), pp. 156–57 and 164–65.

19. Correspondence and clippings, Chattahoochee Valley Regional Library, Columbus.

20. Ibid.

21. Ibid.

22. Ibid.; Columbus *Saturday-Enquirer and Ledger*, Feb. 14, 1981.

23. Knight, *Georgia's Landmarks*, vol. 1, pp. 234–35.

24. Correspondence and clippings, Chattahoochee Valley Regional Library; Columbus *Ledger-Enquirer*, Sept. 10, 1972.

25. Clippings and correspondence, Bartram Trail Regional Library, Washington, Georgia, including quotations from *Oglethorpe Book of Georgia Verse*.

26. See note 15.

27. Correspondence, Flint River Regional Library, Griffin.

28. Eugenia Stone, *Yesterday at Tift* (Daraville, Ga.: Foote & Davies, 1969); *New York Times*, Dec. 9, 1936; correspondence, Hardin Memorial Library, Tift College.

29. See note 3.

30. Helen C. Smith, ''Nancy Hart: Bane of the British,'' *Atlanta Journal*, Apr. 11, 1976; Sally S. Booth, *The Women of '76* (New York: Hastings House, 1973).

31. Knight, *Georgia's Landmarks*, vol. 1, pp. 34–35. William M. Jones, *Texas History Carved in Stone* (Houston, Tex.: 1958).

32. Andrew Sparks, in *DGB*.

33. Helen C. Smith, ''Born Ahead of Her Time,'' *Atlanta Journal*, Jan. 4, 1976; correspondence and clippings, Cobb County Library System, Marietta.

34. Correspondence, Ina Dillard Russell Library and Susan B. Connor, Department of History, Georgia College.

35. Harnett Kane and Inez Henry, *Miracle in the Mountains* (Garden City, N.Y.: Doubleday & Co., 1956).

36. *New York Times*, Sept. 16, 1973; *Atlanta Journal and Constitution Magazine*, Mar. 21, 1976; brochures, Hambidge Center.

37. Knight, *Georgia's Landmarks*, vol. 1, pp. 125–29.

38. J. Ray Shurbutt, in *DGB*.

39. Caroline Bird, *Enterprising Women* (New York: New American Library, 1976).

40. Clippings, brochures, and correspondence, Juliette Gordon Low Girl Scout National Center.

41. Correspondence, Georgia State Department of Natural Resources.

42. Helen C. Smith, ''Aristocratic Belle Studied Bugs,'' *Atlanta Journal*, May 16, 1976; Raymond E. Davis, in *DGB; Harper's New Monthly Magazine*, vols. 15–29, quotation from ''Insects Destructive to Wheat,'' vol. 20, p. 52; brochure, Historic Savannah Foundation.

43. Helen C. Smith, ''She Was a Go-Between for Indians, Colonials,'' *Atlanta Journal*, May 23, 1976; Julia C. Spruill, *Women's Life and Work in the Southern Colonies* (New York: Norton, 1972; first publ. 1938), pp. 242–43.

44. Barbara B. Reitt, in *DGB*; correspondence, Bartram Trails Regional Library.

KENTUCKY

BEDFORD

Webster, Delia Ann, 1818–1904, Abolitionist

Marker, US 421 and State 1255

Delia Ann Webster, a Vermont native, ran the Lexington Female Academy in Lexington, Kentucky, and also a station on the underground railroad. In 1844 she and a minister, Calvin Fairbank, pretended to elope in a horse-drawn buggy. Instead they picked up a slave family working at the Phoenix Hotel and took them to safety in Ohio. Webster and Fairbank were caught; he was sentenced to fifteen years in the penitentiary, she to two. Although the governor said Webster had "desecrated" her sex, he soon pardoned her—but she went on helping escaping slaves, though jailed again, until she herself had to flee Kentucky.[1]

BRENT

Inglis (Ingles), Mary Draper, 1729–1813, Indian Captive

Marker, State 8

In 1755 Mary Draper Inglis, her two small boys, and a sister-in-law were captured by Shawnee Indians from their Virginia frontier home. The captives were soon separated and Inglis was alone with her captors. The Indians moved to Big Bone Lick (now Boone County, Kentucky). Inglis was strong and athletic, used to the rugged life of the frontier, and she never stopped looking for a chance to escape. She finally succeeded, and with a companion, an old Dutch woman, began the long journey home. The old woman became crazed by hunger and exposure and tried to kill Inglis, who went on alone. After forty days of travel, Inglis reached the vicinity of her home in Virginia and sent a rescue party back to the Dutch woman. Five years later her brother ransomed his wife. Someone who met Inglis twenty years later said that "terror and distress had left so deep an impression on her mind that she appeared absorbed in a deep melancholy." State Highway 10, along the Ohio River from South Portsmouth to Vanceburg, closely follows the trail she took in escaping from the Indians and has been named the Mary Ingles Trail. See Radford, VA.[2]

CLOVERPORT

Sacajawea, c. 1786–1812, Shoshoni Indian Guide; NAW

Sacajawea Festival

A four-day festival is held here on the first Sunday through Thursday in August to celebrate the legend of Sacajawea. She was the young woman made famous when she accompanied the Lewis and Clark Corps of Discovery to the Pacific Coast in 1805–6. See Charlottesville, VA, and Anadarko and Tulsa, OK.[3]

DANVILLE

Crawford, Jane Todd, c. 1763–1842, Survivor

Monument, Garden of Ephraim McDowell House, 125–127 S. 2nd Street; HABS, NHL

In 1809 Jane Todd Crawford, who lived in Greensburg, Kentucky, was afflicted with an ovarian tumor. No doctor had successfully removed such a tumor and Crawford faced a life of constant pain ending in early death. Ephraim McDowell consented to operate, and Crawford rode sixty-four miles on horseback to his surgery. With no anesthetic, the doctor removed an enormous tumor while the patient recited psalms and men held her arms and legs to prevent movement. Crawford recovered enough in five days to be out of bed and in three weeks to ride home. The pioneering doctor's home and apothecary shop, restored by the Kentucky Medical Association, is open Mon.-Sat. 10–12 and 1–4, and Sun. 2–4, except between Nov. 1 and Mar. 1, when it is closed Mon.; closed some holidays; adm. See Greensburg, KY.

FRANKFORT

Boone, Rebecca, 1739–1813, Frontierswoman

Marker and Monument, Frankfort Cemetery, E. Main Street

Rebecca Boone was the wife of Daniel Boone, and with him she moved from place to place, always westward, forerunners of the mountaineers who settled Kentucky. Although she and Daniel died in Missouri, their bodies were in 1845 removed to Kentucky and buried here, where a limestone monolith was erected over their graves. It has on its four sides marble panels depicting scenes from the life of the frontier couple.

Tubman, Emily Thomas, 1794–1885, Emancipator

Marker, First Christian Church, 316 Ann Street

Emily Thomas Tubman grew up in Frankfort and from the age of nine, when her father died, she was the ward of Kentucky's Henry Clay. After her marriage she moved to Augusta, Georgia, where in 1844 she freed many of her slaves who chose to go to the new republic of Liberia (see Augusta, GA). She often returned to Frankfort for visits, gave generously to Transylvania University, and donated money for the second edifice of the Ann Street church, part of which is incorporated in the present building.[4]

GREENSBURG

Crawford, Jane Todd, c. 1763–1842, Survivor

Marker, State 61 (Jane Todd Crawford Trail). Jane Todd Crawford Library, Greensburg Courthouse. Jane Todd Crawford Hospital

Jane Todd Crawford, who made medical history by surviving the first successful ovariotomy (see Danville, Ky), lived well into her seventies.

HINDMAN

Pettit, Katherine, 1868–1936, Settlement Worker; NAW

Hindman Settlement School, State 160

At the turn of the century the Cumberland plateau of eastern Kentucky was inhabited by people isolated from towns and living much as their Scotch-Irish ancestors had 150 years before, preserving the speech and songs of those early settlers. They scratched a living from the soil of the narrow valleys. They had poor one-room schools and no churches or medical services. Katherine Pettit, who grew up on a large farm near Lexington, Kentucky, took an interest in these people and when the State Federation of Women's Clubs received a plea that someone be sent to help the women, she and May Stone, a Louisville friend, held a six-week camp meeting at Hazard. They entertained the children with songs and stories, helped women with cooking and sewing, and gave health instruction. The mountain people were intrigued by the "queer women" who thus reached out to them. The following year a similar meeting was held in Hindman, and in 1901 the two went to Sassafras, Kentucky.

The idea of a permanent settlement, with the obligation of raising funds to buy land and erect buildings, was a challenge to Pettit and Stone, one they met with courage and hard work. In spite of disasters—their first buildings burned down twice—the school survived, and still survives. In addition to academic subjects, the curriculum included handicrafts and domestic science.

The settlement attracted the notice of social workers, including Linda Neville (1873–1961), who visited the school and discovered the high incidence of trachoma among the mountaineers. She worked to found the Kentucky Society for the Prevention of Blindness. A doctor who came to hold clinics interested the U.S. Public Health Service in making a medical survey of the area. Lucy Furman (1870–1958) taught at the school for twenty years and wrote of Pettit in *The Quare Women* (1923).

In 1913 Pettit left Stone in charge and went to Pine Mountain, Kentucky, (q.v.) to establish a settlement there. Stone was born in Owingsville, Kentucky, and attended Wellesley College. Between 1931 and 1934 she was vice president of the Confederation of Mountain Workers.

HYDEN

Breckinridge, Mary, 1881–1965, Nurse and Social Worker; NAWM

Mary Breckinridge Hospital. Wendover (Frontier Nursing Service), Off State 80; NR. Marker, Courthouse Lawn, US 421

Mary Breckinridge established the Frontier Nursing Service, which brings health care to the isolated rural inhabitants of eastern Kentucky's mountains. The nurses ride horses, bringing their supplies in saddlebags, and are called angels on horseback.

Personal tragedy—the death of her first husband and of her two children, the breakup of an unhappy second marriage—led Breckinridge to dedicate her life to helping children. She chose the children of this area and to prepare herself went to England to study midwifery. She began her work in Leslie County in 1925 and for the first three years used her own funds to support it. A few years after the nursing service was started, the hospital was opened in Hyden, followed by the Frontier Graduate School of Midwifery.

Breckinridge was much loved by the mountaineers, who called her the "blessed old gray-haired critter." When she died the *New York Times* wrote of her as "Kentucky's Samaritan of the Hills." Wendover was her home.[5]

LANCASTER

Nation, Carry Moore, 1846–1911, Antisaloon Crusader; NAW

Carry A. Nation House, Fisher Ford Road (Private); NR

Carry Moore Nation was born here and spent the first few years of her life in this house. To Nation, alcohol was the root of all evil, and she chopped at it with the hatchet that became her token, smashing saloons all through the Midwest. Her tactics embarrassed the Woman's Christian Temperance Union, but there is no doubt that they aroused public opinion to the evils of the demon rum more effectively than the more ladylike approach. The house is west of town on Herrington Lake near Pope's Landing. See Eureka Springs, AR, and Belton, MO.[6]

LAWRENCEBURG

Kavanaugh, Rhoda Caldwell, d. 1959, Educator

Kavanaugh Academy, 241 Woodford Street (US 62); NR

Rhoda Caldwell Kavanaugh founded this school as Kavanaugh Academy in 1904 and was its principal for forty-one years. Known affectionately as Mrs. K. and sometimes as the Old Lady, she made the school one of the nation's foremost preparatory schools for boys aspiring to enter Annapolis or West Point. A marker quotes the school's motto: "The sun never sets on Kavanaugh." Naval and army officers who got their first rigorous mental and physical training here have gone all over the world in pursuit of their careers. The marker lists the names of graduates of Annapolis and West Point who were also alumni of Kavanaugh. The school was incorporated into the public system in 1909 and until 1920 it was called Anderson County High School.[7]

LEXINGTON

Breckinridge, Madeline McDowell, 1872–1920, Social Reformer; NAW

Ashland (Henry Clay House), 1400 Block of Richmond Road (US 60); NHL

When Madeline McDowell Breckinridge was ten her father came into possession of the historic home of Henry Clay, her great-grandfather. An ancestor on her father's side was Ephraim McDowell, who made medical history by performing the first successful ovariotomy (see Jane Todd Crawford of Danville, Kentucky). Breckinridge grew up in a home where education was respected and public service, even from women, was expected. In 1898 she married Desha Breckinridge, whose sister, Sophonisba, was beginning an outstanding career in social work in Chicago, Illinois. Desha edited the *Lexington Herald*.

One of the first civic projects Breckinridge undertook was a mountain settlement near Proctor, Kentucky. She then turned to urban needs and helped to establish a settlement in Lexington's slum area and to found the Lexington Associated Charities. Because she herself was tubercular, her greatest efforts were directed toward the care of sufferers from consumption. The Blue Grass

Sanitarium was built in 1916, with funds she shamed out of the county administrators and fifty thousand dollars she raised herself.

She was long the central activist in the Kentucky Equal Rights Association. It was largely due to her leadership that Kentucky ratified the suffrage amendment early in 1920. In spite of a frail constitution, Breckinridge made a very large contribution to Lexington, to Kentucky, and to the nation.

Ashland was preserved and is operated by a foundation in whose establishment Breckinridge had a part. Her portrait hangs in the mansion, which is open daily 9:30–4:30.[8]

Desha, Mary, 1850–1911, Clubwoman

Marker, Maxwell and Mill Streets

Mary Desha was born in Lexington and taught for twelve years in the Lexington public schools. In 1886 she went to Washington, D.C., to take a government position and there joined other women in founding the Daughters of the American Revolution (DAR). She was assistant director of the DAR hospital corps which furnished a thousand trained nurses during the Spanish-American War. She was active also in the Mary Washington Memorial Association and the Pocahontas Memorial Association.[9]

LONDON

Bennett, Sue, 1842?–1892, Home Missionary

Sue Bennett Memorial School Building, College Street; NR

The school was originally a high school established in 1897 by Belle Harris Bennett (see Nashville, TN) and named for her older sister, Sue Bennett, who had dreamed of bringing education to the people of southeast Kentucky. Sue served on the central committee of the Methodist Woman's Parsonage and Home Mission Society (later the Woman's Home Mission Society). After Sue's death, Belle took her place on the committee and rose to the presidency of the society. She financed the Sue Bennett Memorial School herself for its first five years. It is now Sue Bennett College, a junior college.

LOUISVILLE

Ingram, Frances MacGregor, 1875?–1954, Social Worker

Neighborhood House, 225 N. 25th Street

Frances MacGregor Ingram started her thirty-four years as head resident of Neighborhood House in 1905, when its chief concern was the assimilation of newcomers to the country. During her years of service she guided the settlement's programs of social work to meet the changing needs of a rapidly growing city. She was active in many local and national professional organizations dealing with children and youth, a member of the Tenement House Commission and of a commission to investigate working conditions of women in Kentucky. In 1933 she was a leader in the White House Conference on youth problems.

When Neighborhood House opened in two rooms over a saloon in 1896, it was the first settlement house south of the Ohio River and west of the Allegheny Mountains. In 1962 it moved to its present location. It is now a community house, with clubs for everyone from toddlers to senior citizens.[10]

Marshall, Louise, 1889–1981, Social Worker

Cabbage Patch Settlement, 1413 S. 6th Street

As a young woman, Louise Marshall accompanied her parents to a mission church in the Louisville slum known as the Cabbage Patch. Upset by the sad conditions she saw there, she persuaded her father to purchase a lot in the area. With help from friends, a two-story building was erected and the neighbors were invited to participate in efforts to upgrade Cabbage Patch. Marshall remained the only full-time volunteer for most of her life. The settlement expanded and moved forward as the neighborhood and the city changed. Marshall loved to tell of the great work others were doing—a woman who gave college scholarships to youths, another who paid to enlarge the boys' locker rooms, many who donated television and stereo sets, clothing, and equipment. But all knew that the warm and compassionate atmosphere of Cabbage Patch was due to Marshall's loving nature. She never thought of retiring. When she was eighty-two, she said her life was full. "So many of my friends are really afraid of life and that's why they get incapacitated and senile. I can do twice as much work as anybody here. It's interest that keeps you going."[11]

When Marshall established the settlement, Alice Hegan Rice (1870–1942, NAW) was a supporter and member of the board. She was also a member of the Authors Club of Louisville and had written a novel based on the life of one of the slum dwellers, *Mrs. Wiggs of the Cabbage Patch* (1901). It portrayed a widow bringing up five children in dire poverty but meeting life's crises with indomitable courage, humor, and faith.

Semple, Ellen Churchill, 1863–1932, Geographer; NAW

Ellen C. Semple School, 724 Denmark Avenue

The school perpetuates the name of a Louisville native who won distinction in the field of geography. Ellen Churchill Semple's interest in the subject began after she graduated from Vassar College and met an American who had studied with a great German geographer, Friedrich Ratzel, at Leipzig. She got admitted to Ratzel's class, though not permitted to enroll, and absorbed his theory that environment determines human development. Back home, she started a girls' school, the Semple Collegiate Institute, where she taught for two years. She joined the Authors Club of Louisville along with Alice Hegan Rice. One of her first articles came from her study of the people of the Kentucky highlands. "The Anglo-Saxons of the Kentucky Mountains," published in the *Geographical Journal* in June 1901, established her scholarly reputation. Other books followed and she was invited to lecture at Oxford and the University of Chicago. For nine years she was a professor at the graduate school of geography at Clark University in Massachusetts. In 1921 she was the first woman elected president of the Association of American Geographers.[12]

Speed, Hattie Bishop, 1858–1942, Museum Founder

J. B. Speed Art Museum, 2035 S. 3rd Street

Hattie Bishop Speed, the wife of James Breckinridge Speed, studied music with American, German, and Italian masters and was active in Louisville's musical, cultural, and philanthropic circles. She appeared in public concerts as a pianist and gave recitals and organ concerts in her private music room. Among her donations to the city were the Louisville Health Clinic and the nurses' home at the Red Cross Hospital for Colored People. She also maintained four scholarships at the University of Kentucky. She gave the art museum to the city in 1925 and acted as its president and director. The first and largest art museum in Kentucky, it contains both modern and old master paintings and sculpture, including paintings by Kentucky artists. It is open Tues.-Sat. 10–4, Sun. 2–6; closed holidays.[13]

Yandell, Enid, 1870–1934, Sculptor

Daniel Boone Statue and Hogan Fountain, Cherokee Park, Eastern Parkway. Confederate Monument, S. 3rd and Shipp Streets

Enid Yandell was born in Louisville. She attended the Cincinnati Art School in Ohio and studied art in New York City and with MacMonnies and Rodin in Paris, France. When in 1891 the Board of Lady Managers for the World's Columbian Exposition to be held in Chicago, Illinois, were seeking women sculptors, Yandell's friends in Kentucky suggested her name. She was invited to go to Chicago. There she lived in an apartment with two other talented young women, Laura Hayes and Jean Loughborough. They were celebrated in Hayes's *Three Girls in a Flat* (later renamed *The Story of the Woman's Building*), which became a bestseller at the fair.

Yandell won a medal at the exposition, and her plaster statue of Daniel Boone, exhibited at the Kentucky Building, was later cast in bronze and purchased by C. C. Bickel for the city of Louisville. The Kentucky Women's Confederate Monument Association commissioned the Confederate Monument, which was unveiled in 1895. The Hogan Fountain was a gift, in 1905, of Mr. and Mrs. William Hogan. She executed sculptures for many other cities and was the first woman admitted to the National Sculpture Society.[14]

MOREHEAD

Stewart, Cora Wilson, 1875–1958, Educator

Cora Wilson Stewart Moonlight School, Morehead State University Campus. Marker, Across from Post Office, US 60

Appalled by the number of rural adults who could neither read nor write, Cora Wilson Stewart, Rowan County superintendent of schools, began to think about ways to offer them basic education. The day schools were overcrowded with children, and most of the adults were obliged to work in the daytime. Opening the schools by night was no answer, for most of the pupils would have to walk over bad roads, crossing gullies and unbridged streams to reach the school and many feared to venture out in the darkness. It was decided to open the schools on moonlit nights and let the moon light their way. The teachers of Rowan County volunteered their time, after teaching through the day, to return at night.

The first session opened on September 5, 1911. The teachers had estimated that perhaps 150 would attend, but, as Stewart wrote, they were overwhelmed by the response: "They came singly or hurrying in groups, they came walking for miles, they came carrying babes in arms, they came bent with age and leaning on canes, they came twelve hundred strong!" They ranged in age from eighteen to eighty-six. The experiment was such a success in reducing adult illiteracy that the idea spread to other counties and other states. Stewart headed state, national, and international commissions on illiteracy from 1914 to 1933 and served on the executive committee of the National Education Association.[15]

PADUCAH

Barton, Clara, 1821–1912, Founder of American Red Cross; NAW

Marker, 2nd and Broadway

The marker commemorates the visit in March 1884 of Clara Barton, who came to help direct relief work during the Ohio River Flood. Assistance in cases of domestic catastrophes such as floods, train wrecks, tornadoes, and fires was an extension of the Red Cross rescue efforts which Barton regarded as equal in importance to its work in time of war. This was the first flood relief operation of the American Red Cross. See Andersonville, GA.

PARIS

Duncan, Anne, fl. 1788–1850, Tavern Proprietor

Anne Duncan House and Duncan Tavern, 323 High Street; NR

Major Joseph Duncan died about 1800, leaving his wife Anne Duncan with six young children. She leased out his tavern and built a house next door to it for herself and the children. The tavern, which was built about 1788 and is said to have been frequented by Daniel Boone and other frontiersmen, was profitable enough to allow her to educate the children. All of her five sons went on to useful careers, one becoming governor of Illinois. The restored house and the tavern on the public square are open for tours Tues.-Sat. 10–12 and 1–5, Sun. 1:30–5; adm.

PEWEE VALLEY

Johnston, Annie Fellows, 1863–1931, Writer; NAW

Marker, Old L and N Depot

When Annie Fellows Johnston settled in Pewee Valley in 1898, she was a widow with the responsiblity of three stepchildren. She had visited Pewee Valley some years earlier, when it was called Smith's Station. She based her book, *The Little Colonel*, on an old Confederate colonel and his saucy granddaughter who lived here. The book was the forerunner of some fifty more children's books written during her lifetime. She built her home, the Beeches, near here in 1911 and much of her writing was done there, standing at a high desk. During her lifetime, Johnston's books sold well over a million copies and delighted innumerable young readers.

PINE MOUNTAIN

Pettit, Katherine, 1868–1936 (NAW), and Ethel DeLong Zande, 1878–1928, Settlement Workers

Pine Mountain Settlement School, State 510, Near Bledsoe; NR

In 1912 Katherine Pettit, who had founded Hindman Settlement School on Troublesome Creek a decade earlier, left Hindman, Kentucky, q.v., to establish a similar rural school in Harlan County. With her came Ethel DeLong Zande, a Smith College graduate who had taught at Hindman for two years. They found here a remarkable mountaineer, William Creech, who gave them 250 acres of virgin forest and helped them clear space and put up buildings. "I have heart and cravin that our people may grow better. I have deeded my land to the Pine

Mountain Settlement School to be used for school purposes as long as the Constitution of the United States stands,'' he wrote.

The school was the center of many activities reaching out to the people: an extension program to benefit one-room schools, health centers to treat trachoma and hookworm, farmers' institutes to upgrade agricultural methods, and encouragement of handweaving and other crafts and of old-time ballad singing and folk dancing. The two women also worked for the building of roads and railroads to reduce the isolation of the mountain settlements and open them up to markets. Both women were much loved by the highlanders. Zande was described in a *New York Times* editorial as ''a woman of rare talents, who rejoiced in devoting them to an underprivileged people in a remote mountain settlement. When she died she was laid to rest on a little rise of ground where the view encompassed the valley she loved.''[16]

Pettit, a frank and free-spoken woman, resigned after her friend's death to work among the Harlan County men who had sold their land to work in the coal mines. When the mines closed, they were destitute. She urged them to return to the land, where she taught them better farming methods.

PIPPA PASSES

Lloyd, Alice Geddes, 1876–1962, Educator; NAWM

Alice Lloyd College. Markers at Garner on State 80 and on State 899

Alice Geddes Lloyd, a newspaper writer and publisher from Boston, Massachusetts, came here with her mother in 1916 seeking relief for partial paralysis. In the impoverished area near Caney Creek she met a mountaineer who wanted education for his children so that they would be ''unliken the hog'' and who gave fifty acres for a start. She established Caney Creek Community Center, dedicated to the preservation of the best of the Appalachian way of life while educating the young people to be leaders in their communities. In 1922 she started Caney Creek Junior College, where tuition was free and all students had to work. Lloyd ran the college for thirty-nine years and raised more than $2 million for it. She never found the health for which she had come to Kentucky; she remained stooped and crippled all her life. She avoided publicity and was abashed when she was made the subject of a ''This Is Your Life'' television segment in Hollywood, California. The show brought in $50,000 for the school. During her lifetime more than two hundred Caney graduates were sent on to universities on fully paid scholarships. Most returned to serve their Appalachian neighbors. After Lloyd's death the grateful mountain people renamed the college for her.[17]

PRESTONBURG

Wiley, Jenny Sellards, 1760–1831, Indian Captive

Jenny Wiley State Park, off US 23

The son of Jenny Sellards Wiley recounted, "Before her marriage she had killed bears, wolves, panthers and other wild animals." She was to owe her life to her ability to survive in the woods. In 1787, she lived with her husband, Thomas Wiley, and four children at Harmon Station. There she was captured by Cherokees, who scalped three of the children, brutally killed the youngest, then killed another child born on the trail. They were ready to burn her at the stake when a Cherokeee chief saved her. After eleven months of captivity she managed to escape by wading through streams and slipping through the woods. Reunited with her family, she lived on for twelve more years in Virginia and Kentucky, bearing five more children. Her heroism and ability to survive are commemorated by the state park, four miles east of Prestonburg, and a marker near her grave in River, Kentucky, at US 23 and 460.[18]

RICHMOND

Clay, Laura, 1849–1941, Suffragist; NAW

White Hall State Shrine, Clay Lane, off US 25; NR

Laura Clay was born and brought up here in the home of her father, Cassius Clay. For years while her father was away as ambassador to Russia, Laura saw her mother struggling to keep the plantation afloat. When he came home in disgrace and with an illegitimate son, her mother returned to her family home in Lexington, Kentucky. Cassius divorced her for desertion, and she got nothing for her years of hard work. This and her father's early strong interest in abolition gave Laura both a hatred of oppression and sympathy for women. "Our own unhappy domestic life has left my eyes unblinded to the unjust relations between men and women," she wrote.

When the Kentucky Woman's Suffrage Association was formed in 1881, Laura was elected president. At the time, suffragists were referred to by the press as "silly-sallies," "crazy Janes," and "red-nosed angels." Laura ignored such epithets and served with the group and its successor until 1912, working for the repeal of discriminatory statutes. She traveled and lectured on behalf of suffrage; while she found it exhausting, she wrote that it was "jolly interesting."

She was also committed to states' rights and white supremacy in politics and when the federal suffrage amendment passed Congress she fought against its ratification.

White Hall, which is south of Lexington and northwest of Richmond off Interstate 75 and US 25 and 421, is operated by the Kentucky Department of Parks. One room is devoted to Laura Clay and her suffrage activities. It is open

Apr. 1–Labor Day, daily 9–5; after Labor Day to Oct. 31, Wed.-Sun. 9–5; adm.[19]

SHELBYVILLE

Tevis, Julia Ann Hieronymous, 1799–1880, Educator

Marker at Former Science Hill School, Washington Street; NR.
Monument, Grove Hill Cemetery

Julia Ann Hieronymous Tevis founded Science Hill School for girls in 1825 and directed it for fifty-four years. She wrote of her educational philosophy and practice in *Sixty Years in a Schoolroom: Autobiography of Mrs. Julia A. Tevis* (1878). A marker at the school calls it an outstanding preparatory school and records that her successor, W. T. Poynter, was principal for the next thirteen years and his wife and daughter succeeded him. The school was closed in 1939 and since the death of Juliet and Harriet Poynter has become the Wakefield-Scearce Antiques Gallery. The cemetery monument to Tevis was unveiled in 1884, in a ceremony lauding her as having "a life and character, as grand in woman's sphere as it was prolonged and useful."[20]

NOTES

In addition to the sources mentioned below, I have had help from the Historical Marker Program, Kentucky Historical Society; the Lincoln Trail Development District, Elizabethtown; and the Harrodsburg Historical Society.

1. Helen Deiss Irvin, *Women in Kentucky* (Frankfort: University Press of Kentucky, 1979).
2. Ibid.
3. Brochure, Sacajawea Festival.
4. Irvin, op. cit.
5. Carol Crowe-Carraco, "Mary Breckinridge and the Frontier Nursing Service," *Register of the Kentucky Historical Society* 76 (July 1978); *New York Times*, May 17, 1965.
6. Irvin, op.cit.
7. *Louisville Courier-Journal*, May 28, 1959; correspondence, Anderson Public Library, Lawrenceburg.
8. Sophonisba P. Breckinridge, *Madeline McDowell Breckinridge, A Leader in the New South* (Chicago, Ill.: University of Chicago Press, 1921).
9. Mary Simmerson Logan, *The Part Taken by Women in American History* (New York: Perry-Nalle, 1972).
10. Correspondence, Louisville Free Public Library; *Louisville Times*, Sept. 24, 1971.
11. *Lousiville Courier-Journal and Times*, May 16, 1971; clippings and correspondence, Louisville Free Public Library.
12. Correspondence, Louisville Library.
13. Ibid.; *Louisville Times*, Sept. 15, 1942.
14. Charlotte S. Rubinstein, *American Women Artists* (New York: Avon Books, 1982);

Altrusa Club of Louisville, *Cut, Cast, Carved* (Louisville, Ky.: Louisville Area Chamber of Commerce, 1974).

15. Irvin, op. cit.; Cora Wilson Stewart, *Moonlight Schools for the Emancipation of Adult Illiterates* (New York: E. P. Dutton, 1922).
16. *New York Times*, Apr. 8, 1928.
17. Irvin, op. cit.
18. Ibid.
19. Ibid.
20. *Shelby Sentinel*, May 19, 1884; correspondence, Shelby County Library.

LOUISIANA

BATON ROUGE

Culver, Essae Martha, 1882–1973, Librarian

Memorial, Louisiana State Library

In 1925 Louisiana had only five free public libraries, none serving rural people. The state Library Commission received a three-year Carnegie grant to develop library facilities, and fortunately Essae Martha Culver, a professional librarian with some years of experience in public library administration, was available to take on the challenging task. Enlisting the support of political leaders, women's groups, and men's service clubs, Culver was able to accomplish most of her objectives between the time of her acceptance of the library position and her retirement in 1962. A network of parish and regional libraries, locally supported, served the state; the Library School of Louisiana State University was established; and the State Library had its own building on the state capitol grounds.

Culver was not satisfied to reach the people of Louisiana alone. In 1940, as president of the American Library Association, she issued a Call for Action, asking members to "work together toward the goal of freedom and opportunity to read for all the people" and to eradicate bookless portions of America. The Louisiana Library Association established in 1962 the Essae M. Culver Award for distinguished service to librarianship, and in 1974 the Essae Martha Culver Memorial was dedicated.[1]

BERMUDA

Metoyer, Marie Therèse (Coincoin), 1742?–1816?, Plantation Operator

Maison de Marie Therèse (Private); NR

Marie Therèse Metoyer was for many years a slave of the man who founded Natchitoches. After his death she remained a slave in his family until 1778 when she was purchased and freed by her lover, Thomas Metoyer. They had several children before the alliance ended, and he gave her the land on which the Maison de Marie Therèse was built. She industriously operated the small plantation here and was able to free several of her children and grandchildren who were still in slavery. She left them an estate of over a thousand arpents of land and sixteen slaves, along with a legacy of determination, frugality, and mutual assistance. The remarkable group of buildings at Melrose, Louisiana, q.v., was developed by her sons and daughters.

The maison, a five-room raised, hip-roofed Creole cottage, is at the end of a dirt road off State 494 about a mile northwest of Bermuda.[2]

CLOUTIERVILLE

Chopin, Kate O'Flaherty, 1851–1904, Writer; NAW

Kate Chopin House (Bayou Folk Museum), State 1; NR

Kate O'Flaherty Chopin's observations of Creole life began about 1880 when she and her husband, Oscar Chopin, and their six children came to this house to live while Oscar managed two plantations and a general store. Following his death in 1882 Kate took over management of the land for more than a year. She then returned with her children to her native St. Louis, Missouri. Her first novel, *At Fault*, was published in 1890. *Bayou Folk* (1894) and *A Night in Acadie* (1897) collected short stories that first appeared in magazine form. *The Awakening*, a sensitive story, brilliantly written, of the sexual and artistic awakening of a young married woman, was published in 1899. Its theme was unpalatable to the Victorian taste of readers and the book was unfavorably reviewed. Kate never wrote another book. A recent revival of interest in her work has led to republication of her stories and a new awareness of their excellence.

The Cloutierville house was for a time the home and office of Eleanor Mendell Worsley, first woman doctor in Natchitoches Parish. In 1964 another remarkable woman, Mildred McCoy, bought the property, restored it, and filled it with things typical of a way of life that existed in the Cane River country over the past century. She opened it to the public in 1965 as the Bayou Folk Museum. Since then it has been designated a Louisiana Landmark and listed in the National Register. In 1978 McCoy and her son gave the museum to Northwestern State University. It is open June 1–Aug. 15, Tues.-Fri. 10–5, Sat.-Sun. 1–5; fall and spring, weekends only; closed Dec.-Feb., except first weekend in Dec.; adm.[3]

JACKSON

Dawson, Sarah Morgan, 1842–1909, Writer

Linwood Plantation (Private); NR

During the Civil War Sarah Morgan Dawson and several other women in her family moved from their home in Baton Rouge, Louisiana, to Linwood to escape the ravages of war. It was here that Dawson began a diary, later published as *A Confederate Girl's Diary*, which gives historians a vivid picture of the effect of the war on its civilian victims. The family home in Baton Rouge was destroyed by the war. In 1873 Dawson went to Charleston, South Carolina, where she was invited to write editorials for the *News*. She subsequently married the editor, Captain Francis Dawson. Except for eleven months of elementary schooling, Dawson was self-educated through reading in both English and French, yet she expressed herself so clearly and forcefully as to attract the attention of the literary world. Her Civil War diary, considered one of the greatest wartime diaries, was published in 1913, after her death, with a biographical preface by her son.[4]

Dixon, Margaret Richardson, 1908–1970, Editor

Dixon Correctional Institution

It takes skill to understand Louisiana's complicated political scene, and Margaret Richardson Dixon, managing editor of the Baton Rouge *Morning Advocate*, earned the respect of her colleagues of the press for her savvy. She covered the legislative news for years. She could handle other types of stories also and had great sympathy for the underprivileged and a righteous indignation at wrong-doing. At the time of her death the Louisiana House of Representatives established the Margaret Dixon Memorial Scholarship Fund, which supports one or more scholarships at the Louisiana State University School of Journalism, from which she graduated. One of her long-term interests was penal reform, and in 1975 the prison at Jackson was given her name in recognition of her efforts in this field.[5]

MELROSE

Metoyer, Marie Therèse (Coincoin), 1742?–1816?, Plantation Operator

Melrose Plantation House, State 119; HABS, NHL

Originally known as Yucca Plantation, Melrose contains what may well be the oldest buildings of African design built by blacks, for the use of blacks, in the United States. Included in the complex are Yucca House, the African House, the Big House, and the Ghana House. Metoyer, original mistress of the plantation, was a wealthy businesswoman at a time when most women of her color were slaves and most white women had no identity apart from their husbands (see Bermuda, LA). She was proud of her African heritage and passed on this pride to her children, who followed her example in working hard and building up large estates. Most of the Melrose buildings were erected by her offspring.

Melrose was sold to Hippolyte Hertzog, who conveyed it to Joseph Henry. His son, John Hampton Henry, married Carmelite (Cammie) Garrett (1871–

1948). Cammie lived here for almost half a century. She was widely known as a friend of artists and writers, whom she entertained at the plantation. She gathered and filed historical documents and made her valuable collection available to students. The Cammie G. Henry Louisiana Room in the Watson Library, Northwestern State University at Natchitoches, perpetuates her name.

Recently acquired by the Association of Natchitoches Women for the Preservation of Historic Natchitoches, the plantation now serves as a museum of Afro-American history. It is open daily except Mon. and Wed., 2–4:30; adm.[6]

NEW ORLEANS

Bass, Mary Elizabeth, 1876–1956, Physician; NAWM

Elizabeth Bass Collection on Women in Medicine, Matas Medical Library, Tulane University, 1430 Tulane Avenue

Mary Elizabeth Bass's brother Charles graduated from medical school in 1899 and encouraged Elizabeth and her sister Cora to study medicine. Since no medical school in the South admitted women, the sisters went to the Woman's Medical College in Pennsylvania. Back in New Orleans with their M.D.'s, they found that no clinical or hospital facilities in New Orleans were open to women physicians. In 1905 Elizabeth and five other women established a free dispensary, meeting a long-felt need for assistance to women and children of limited means, as well as giving female doctors a place to practice. It expanded into the New Orleans Hospital and Dispensary for Women and Children (later the Sara Mayo Hospital, named for one of its founders).

In 1911 Bass and Edith Ballard became the first women on the faculty of the School of Medicine at Tulane University. By 1914 the school admitted women medical students (with a push from the Equal Rights Association of New Orleans, of which Bass was a member). She remained at Tulane for thirty years, teaching pathology, clinical medicine, and bacteriology. Her extraordinary collection of material by and about women in medicine, which she drew upon for articles on outstanding women physicians, is now at Tulane. Her friends at the university established in her name a medical student loan fund.

Correjolles, Coralie, 1844–1931, Humanitarian

Maison Hospitalière, 822 Barracks Street

Coralie Correjolles founded in 1893 this nonsectarian, nonprofit home for elderly women, working with her Societé des Dames Hospitalières. It is located in historical buildings in the Vieux Carré of New Orleans. In 1984 the women of Louisiana chose a number of women to be honored at the Women's Pavilion of the Louisiana World Exposition. Correjolles was one.[7]

Goldsmith, Grace Arabell, 1904–1975, Physician; NAWM

Tulane School of Public Health and Tropical Medicine

When Grace Arabell Goldsmith, M.D., began teaching at Tulane School of Medicine in 1936, vitamin deficiency diseases were a serious problem. Pellagra and malnutrition sent many patients to charity wards. Goldsmith had been interested in nutrition and metabolism and began serious studies of vitamin C deficiency, the B-complex vitamins, and other aspects of the relationship between food and health. She instituted in the early 1940s the first nutritional training for medical students anywhere in the world. In 1967 she was instrumental in founding the Tulane School of Public Health and Tropical Medicine. She served as dean of the school for some years and remained on the faculty until her death. She was herself a superb example of energy and efficiency, an active sportswoman, dancer, gardener, and gourmet cook.

Gordon, Jean Margaret, 1865–1931, and Her Sister Kate Gordon, 1861–1932, Social Reform and Suffrage Leaders; NAW

Memorial Window, Children's Chapel, First Unitarian Church, Jefferson Avenue and Donnell Street. Jean Gordon School, 6101 Chatham Drive

Jean Margaret Gordon and Kate Gordon helped to establish New Orleans' Era Club (Equal Rights Association) to work for suffrage. They found, however, that they could not wait for the vote to get some things in their own community corrected. Kate's first municipal effort was to reform the inadequate sewage and drainage system. She learned that the constitution gave taxpaying women the vote on tax questions, and with the help of the club she organized a systematic campaign to pass a bond issue for the construction of a needed sanitation system. For some time a bronze plaque was displayed in the Sewage and Water Building crediting the Era Club and the Women's League for Sewerage and Drainage for helping to secure "the great public necessities of water, sewerage and drainage." When the building was razed, the plaque was stored away, but the water system remains a memorial to Kate's efforts of 1899.

Jean became concerned about the plight of working children and began a campaign to get the child labor laws enforced. It took her years to persuade the legislators to act, but in 1906 a modern child labor law was passed and women were allowed to be factory inspectors. Jean was one of the first to be appointed.

Both sisters were ardent suffragists but they were against a federal amendment, which would give the vote to black as well as white women. They feared the precedent if the federal government rather than individual states controlled voting requirements. Kate organized the Southern States Woman Suffrage Conference to press for states' rights. When it appeared that the federal amendment would be passed, they fought against ratification. In this, they were in tune with many other southern women.

Haughery, Margaret Gaffney, 1813–1882, Charitable Worker; NAW

Statue, Margaret Haughery Park, Camp and Prytania Streets. Margaret Haughery School, 2009 Palmyra

Margaret Gaffney Haughery was an unlettered Irish immigrant. She was also one of New Orleans' greatest benefactors, its most successful entrepreneur, and its best-loved woman citizen. On the day of her funeral her many friends began collecting funds for the erection of a statue, which was unveiled in 1884.

Haughery turned her personal tragedy, the loss of her husband and only child, into love for other children. Without family or funds, she worked as a domestic. Then she bought a few cows and started a dairy, peddling her milk through the streets and giving away as much as she sold. She exchanged this occupation for a bakery, which she developed into a large export business. All this time she had been giving away what she earned to help found orphanages and shelters for poor women, living herself in one of the orphanages, St. Vincent's. At her bakery she gave out advice, sympathy, and tangible help to those who sought her out. She was called the bread woman. Her many benefactions were given without publicity, and only at her death did the city learn how much she had done for its people. She left generous gifts to ten institutions and left the bakery to a young man she had brought up and trained to succeed her.

Keyes, Frances Parkinson, 1885–1970, Writer

Beauregard-Keyes House, 1113 Chartres Street; HABS, NR

The 1826 house occupied by Confederate General P. G. T. Beauregard after the Civil War was purchased and restored by Frances Parkinson Keyes. She made this her winter home and set some of her novels in New Orleans, notably *Dinner at Antoine's* (1948) and *Victorine* (1958). Her summer residence was in New Hampshire, where her husband, Henry Wilder Keyes, served as state governor from 1917 to 1919.

Keyes was a prolific writer, an editor for *Good Housekeeping* and for the Daughters of the American Revolution magazine. She turned out novels at the rate of almost one a year. Criticized for a flabby style, flat characters, and "uncorseted" plots, she nevertheless appealed to many readers for her stories' rich local color and glimpses into the life of the wealthy and aristocratic. She did extensive research for her books, traveled all over the world, and spoke Spanish, French, and German with competence. She was given awards for her writings on Catholic subjects and received many honors from the French for

Margaret Haughery, philanthropist of New Orleans known as the Bread Woman, is commemorated by this statue. It was erected in Margaret Haughery Park, New Orleans, Louisiana, in 1884.
From the collection of the Library of Congress.

work in France, including aid in the reconstruction of the Abbey of the Benedictines at Lisieux.

Beauregard House and its walled garden has guided tours on the hour, Mon.-Sat. 10–4; adm.[8]

King, Grace, 1853?–1932, Writer; NAW

Grace King High School, 4301 Grace King Place, Metairie

Grace King was a native of New Orleans, and her short stories, novels, and historical works document the Creole past of Louisiana. Beginning in the 1880s she was regularly published in northern magazines until about the turn of the century. This brought her into contact with other writers, and for some time she entertained at popular Friday afternoon receptions, with her mother and sisters superintending household duties. For many years she worked as recording secretary for the Louisiana Historical Society and was on the advisory board of its *Quarterly*. Some of her historical works, including *New Orleans: The Place and the People* (1895), are still of value to the historian, for she was writing of the place and people she knew intimately.

McMain, Eleanor, 1866–1934, Settlement House Worker; NAW

Kingsley House Settlement, 914 Richard Street. Eleanor McMain Magnet School, 5712 S. Claiborne Avenue

In 1901 Eleanor McMain was asked to be head resident of Kingsley House, a settlement established the year before. To prepare herself she spent the summer in Chicago, Illinois, studying the settlement movement at the Chicago Commons and Jane Addams' Hull House. She began her thirty-year career at Kingsley by organizing a vacation school and setting up a clinic where New Orleans' first women doctors, barred from male-dominated medical facilities, could treat patients. The settlement spread its influence in all directions: playgrounds, anti-tuberculosis campaigns, summer camps, day nurseries, courses for the blind, and numerous classes, all robbed of institutionalism by McMain's warm capacity for friendship.

McMain, as one might guess, belonged to the Era Club started by Kate and Jean Gordon, q.v., and to other progressive women's clubs. In 1920 New Orleans expressed its regard for her by awarding her the *Times-Picayune* loving cup, given annually for outstanding service to the community.

Newcomb, Josephine LeMonnier, 1816–1901, Philanthropist; NAW

H. Sophie Newcomb College, Tulane University, 6823 St. Charles Avenue

From the time of her birth, Harriet Sophie Newcomb was the idol of her parents. Her father, a successful businessman, died when she was eleven, and her mother's whole time and attention was given to providing her the best care and education possible. Then, at the age of fifteen, the young girl succumbed to diphtheria. Josephine LeMonnier Newcomb, who successfully carried on her husband's business in New York, was much preoccupied through the years with establishing a suitable memorial for her daughter Sophie. On a suggestion from a friend in New Orleans, where she had lived for some time before marriage, she decided in 1888 to fund a women's college in connection with the newly founded Tulane University. She wanted it to be given her daughter's name and to be an independent college, with its own faculty and buildings. She gave a moderate amount to begin with but continued her support throughout her life and even established legal residence in the state and spent her winters here so that she could watch the progress of the school. She left her entire estate to the college.

Pontalba, Micaëla Almonester, Baroness, 1795–1874, Builder

Pontalba Buildings, St. Ann and St. Peter Streets, Facing Jackson Square

Baroness Micaëla Almonester de Pontalba, daughter of Don Almonester, built the two Pontalba Buildings in 1850–51. Having a low opinion of architects and builders and a high opinion of her own ability, the baroness presented the builder, Samuel Stewart, with drawings and specifications of one architect, James Gallier, and drawings from her designs by another, Henry Howard, none of them compatible with the actual site conditions. Surprisingly, the result was eminently successful. The three-story buildings, with iron railings brought from France, proved a "pacesetting example of urban amenity." The baroness selected every detail, checked every expenditure, supervised construction, and designed some of the ornamental cast-iron work, including the initials AP (Almonester Pontalba). She also promoted the landscaping of Jackson Square and in 1856 helped finance the bronze statue of General Andrew Jackson.

After the Civil War, the houses gradually deteriorated into slum tenements, divided into apartments. They have been rehabilitated. The Upper Building belongs to the city, the Lower Building to the state. The latter is part of the Louisiana State Museum. Now completed and furnished as it might have been when new, it is open Tues.-Sun. 10–6; tours Mon. and Thurs. 11–3; adm.[9]

Seebold, Nettie Kinney, c. 1900–1966, Art Patron

Women's Guild, New Orleans Opera Association, 2504 Prytania Street

Nettie Kinney Seebold gave her home and its art treasures as headquarters for the Women's Guild. She and her husband, Herman Seebold, collected much of the woodwork and furnishings for the home from the Hamilton Palace in Lanarkshire when it was being dismantled in 1923. Other pieces were purchased from Paris chateaux and an Italian palace. They collected art of the Barbizon School, Limoges, Dresden and Sèvres pieces, and Tiffany windows. The gift stipulated that the guild could not dispose of any of the collection and must maintain the building for future generations to enjoy. Seebold was a dedicated member of the opera association and the house has become a rallying point for opera enthusiasts. Tours are offered daily.[10]

Stern, Edith Rosenwald, 1895–1980, Philanthropist

Longue Vue House and Gardens, 7 Bamboo Road

Edith Rosenwald Stern came from Chicago, Illinois, to New Orleans as the bride of Edgar Bloom Stern, a cotton broker. She was a daughter of Julius Rosenwald, of Sears, Roebuck, and had been brought up to believe that with great wealth went social responsibility. It was just before World War I and New Orleans seemed to her a city remarkably lacking in social consciousness, entrenched in laziness and bigotry. As a Jew she was excluded from the Mardi Gras Carnival balls.

She began to change the city by building a palatial Greek revival house in the midst of acres of formal gardens, where she entertained lavishly. The Sterns soon became leaders of society. When her children were of an age for school, Stern founded Newcomb Nursery School and later the Metairie Park Country Day School. Becoming involved with City Hall over building codes, she did a little investigating in city politics and made public what she found—corruption, voter fraud, disenfranchisement of blacks. She set up a voters service and was soon joined by other women intent on sweeping out the rascals. She entertained the black artist Marian Anderson and was made a trustee of Dillard, a black college. Her philanthropies were widespread. The art museum and symphony could always call on her for support. She contributed heavily to the state of Israel. She and her husband established the Stern Fund to distribute funds to worthy causes.

Longue Vue, with its furnishings and gardens and a $5 million endowment, was left to the city Stern had done so much to change. New Orleans honored her. Flags were flown at half-staff on her funeral day. The *New Orleans Times-Picayune* had given her one of their prized loving cups for civic participation. Longue Vue is open Tues.-Fri. 10–4:30, Sat.-Sun. 1–5; closed holidays; adm.[11]

Wisner, Elizabeth, 1894–1976, Social Work Educator

Elizabeth Wisner Social Welfare Research Center for Families and Children, Tulane University School of Social Work, 6823 St. Charles Avenue

A pioneer in social work, Elizabeth Wisner served as director and dean of Tulane's School of Social Work, the first such school in the South, from 1932 to 1958. Soon after she began, the new Social Security Act of 1935 was passed, and many trained workers were needed to administer its provisions. Under her guidance more than a thousand social workers graduated to become leaders in their field. At least six became deans in schools of social work elsewhere. Throughout her career, Wisner received honors for distinguished service to human welfare. In 1982 the research center was given her name.[12]

Wright, Sophie Bell, 1866–1912, Educator and Welfare Worker; NAW

Sophie Bell Wright Junior High School, 1426 Napoleon Avenue

Sophie Bell Wright was crippled as the result of an accident in childhood, but she went through high school and then, at the age of fifteen, opened a school of her own in her family's house. The school was chartered as the Home Institute, and there young women were instructed in academic subjects. When a young man who needed to pass a civil service examination sought her help, Wright became aware than many young working men had no access to education. She opened up a night school where employed men and boys could come, free. She used volunteer teachers and supported the night school with profits from the Home Institute. The night school ultimately grew to an enrollment of fifteen hundred and in 1909 the city opened its own night schools and relieved Wright of the burden.

Until the time of her death this frail woman continued to run her school and to participate in many charitable and civic activities. She was considered New Orleans' "First Citizen," and was awarded the *Times-Picayune* loving cup in 1903.

ST. GABRIEL

Hunt, Elayn, 1925–1976, Public Official

Hunt Correctional Institute

Elayn Hunt was the first of her sex to be appointed director of the Louisiana Department of Corrections (1972) and the second woman in the United States to hold such a position. She had been a police reporter, won degrees in journalism and law, practised law, and was a corporate executive. Married to John M.

Eicher, she had four children. During her term of office, which lasted until her death from cancer, she abolished the use of convicts as prison guards and opened the Louisiana Training Institute at Bridge City and the women's prison at St. Gabriel later named for her. She reorganized the department, improved the pay of correctional officers, and instituted reforms to protect prisoners' rights. During her newspaper days she had covered five executions, which caused her to develop a strong stand against capital punishment. She had also found a twelve-year-old boy jailed along with hardened adults because there were no separate facilities for juveniles; she took him home with her until he could be sent to relatives. She won numerous honors for her contributions to prison reform, drug prevention, and rehabilitation. In 1976 she was acclaimed Woman of the Year.[13]

ST. MARTINVILLE

Labiche, Emmeline, fl. 1755, Legendary Heroine

Evangeline Statue, St. Martin de Tours Catholic Church, 133 S. Main Street

Three women are memorialized here: Evangeline, the heroine of Henry Wadsworth Longfellow's poem; Emmeline Labiche, who is thought to be the real person on whom he modeled Evangeline; and Dolores del Rio, donor of the statue. The poem tells the story of the Acadians, who in 1755 were banished from Nova Scotia by the British and sent to various parts of New England and the South. Many came to this area, and St. Martinville is rich in memories of the French-speaking settlers. Labiche and her lover, Louis Arceneaux, were separated. After many years she found him, but he had married another, and Labiche died of a broken heart. In 1929 a silent film, *Evangeline*, was made here, with Dolores del Rio as the star, and she donated the statue of Evangeline, which has the features of del Rio, to mark Labiche's grave.

SALINE

Dormon, Caroline Coroneos, 1888–1971, Naturalist

Briarwood, State 9, Between Saline and Campti

Briarwood was the home of Caroline Coroneos Dormon, a self-taught botanist and writer on the trees, birds, and flowers of Louisiana. She had no particular interest in science, as such, and at Judson College studied literature and art. For some years she was one of a group of writers and artists in the Natchitoches area who gathered at Melrose plantation, where, according to one writer, "no one struck brighter sparks than Carrie." She never took a college course in forestry but won national recognition in the field because of her close study of the world of nature. She worked for the establishment of Kisatchie National Forest and was employed by the State Forestry Division until she became disenchanted with bureaucracy. She served the State Highway Department as a beautification consultant, battling nurserymen who wished to replace native trees and shrubs with more exotic plants.

At Briarwood she developed a wild garden appealing to botanists and horticulturists interested in plants indigenous to the South. The place was willed to the Foundation for the Preservation of the Caroline Dormon Nature Preserve. The gardens and the log house which served as her home for over fifty years are open every weekend in Apr., May, and Aug. and the first two weekends in Nov., Sat. 9–5, Sun. 12–5; adm.[14]

VILLE PLATTE

Dormon, Caroline Coroneos, 1888–1971, Naturalist

Caroline Dormon Lodge, Louisiana State Arboretum, State 3042, Adjacent to Chicot State Park

Caroline Coroneos Dormon was one of the first to suggest a state arboretum and was instrumental in its founding. The lodge houses a library and displays herbarium specimens and laminated leaves of native plants found in the arboretum. The latter is a 301-acre tract with nature trails leading past more than a hundred species of plants native to the state and other parts of the South. Grounds are open daily in summer 8–7, winter 8–5; lodge open daily 9–5.[15]

NOTES

In addition to the sources mentioned below, I have had assistance from the Louisiana State Department of Art, History, and Cultural Preservation, the Louisiana Office of Tourism, the Louisiana State University, and The Historic New Orleans Collection.

1. *Dictionary of American Library Biography*, ed. Bohdan S. Wynor (Littleton, Colo.: Libraries Unlimited, Inc., 1978); *Current Biography*, 1940; clippings, Louisiana State Library.
2. Nomination form, National Register of Historic Places; clippings from State Library.
3. Nomination form, National Register; brochure, Bayou Folk Museum.
4. Sarah Dawson, *A Confederate Girl's Diary* (Bloomington: Indiana State University Press, 1960; first publ. 1913); nomination form, National Register.
5. Newspaper clippings, State Library.
6. Nomination form, National Register; clippings, State Library; Louisiana Pen Women, *Vignettes of Louisiana History* (Baton Rouge, La.: Claitor's Publishing Division, 1967).
7. Nomination form, Artifacts Committee, Women in the Mainstream, for the Women's Pavilion of the Louisiana World Exposition '84, courtesy of Ernestine Thurman, Ph.D., New Orleans.
8. *New York Times*, July 4, 1970.
9. Nomination form, National Register.
10. Nomination forms, National Register and the Artifacts Committee.
11. Stephen Birmingham, *The Grandes Dames* (New York: Simon & Schuster, 1982).
12. Correspondence, Ernestine Thurman, Ph.D.

13. Ibid.; *Morning Advocate*, Nov. 30, 1979.

14. Donald M. Rawson, ''Caroline Dormon: A Renaissance Spirit of Twentieth Century Louisiana,'' *Louisiana History* 24 (Spring 1983); David Snell, ''The Green World of Carrie Dormon,'' *Smithsonian* 2 (Feb. 1972); brochure and correspondence, Louisiana Office of State Parks.

15. Brochure, Louisiana State Arboretum.

MISSISSIPPI

BILOXI

Dorsey, Sarah Anne Ellis, 1829–1879, Writer; NAW

Beauvoir, 200 W. Beach Boulevard (US 90); HABS, NHL

Sarah Anne Ellis Dorsey was a southern intellectual who taught her slaves to read and write, established a Sunday school for them, and wrote articles, signed "Filia," for magazines. But she is remembered less for her writing than for her generosity to ex-President Jefferson Davis, to whom she offered the use of her Biloxi estate, Beauvoir, when he wished a retreat in which to write his memoirs. She helped him work on the book and then offered to sell Beauvoir to him, secretly leaving him her entire estate. She died a few years after Davis made the first payment on the home.

Varina Ann Howell Davis (1826–1906, NAW), who had known Dorsey in girlhood, was abroad at the time Davis moved to Beauvoir, and on her return she was enraged by her husband's close association with another woman. She at first refused to come to Beauvoir. She was finally won over by Dorsey's goodwill and moved in, with their daughter Winnie, not long before her hostess died. She lived at Beauvoir until Davis's death in 1889, when she moved to New York. It served for many years as a Confederate Veterans Home but has now been restored as a shrine to the president of the Confederacy. It is open daily 8:30–5; adm.

CLINTON

Dickey, Sarah, 1838–1904, Educator; NAW

Monument at Grave, Site of Mount Hermon Female Seminary

Sarah Dickey, a graduate of Mount Holyoke Female Seminary, opened Mount Hermon Female Seminary in 1875 as a nonsectarian boarding school for black girls. It took considerable courage and faith to do so, for she was ostracized by townspeople and threatened by the Ku Klux Klan. Two months after she opened the school Charles Caldwell, a Negro leader who had given her lodging at his house, was killed by a mob. Pupils dared to come to the school, however, and she taught them basic academic subjects as well as practical skills. When the public school for blacks was closed, Dickey took in day pupils. She raised a daughter of Charles Caldwell and several other children who were left in her care. She won the love and respect of the black community and gradually all white prejudice against her disappeared. After her death the school went to the American Missionary Association and in 1924 it was closed.

The site of the school is about a mile north of Northside Drive. No buildings remain, but Dickey's grave is there, maintained by the Mississippi State Federation of Colored Women's Clubs. See Tougaloo, MS.

COLUMBUS

Peyton, Annie Coleman, 1852–1898, Crusader for Women's Education

Peyton Hall, Mississippi University for Women

Annie Coleman Peyton was the first woman whose portrait was placed in the Mississippi Hall of Fame. The honor was given in recognition of her efforts to initiate higher education for women in Mississippi. For some time she wrote newspaper articles and pamphlets signed "A Mississippi Woman," urging passage of a bill for a state-endowed college for women. Sallie Eola Reneau and Jennie Vaughn, among other women, joined her campaign, which resulted in 1884 in the establishment of the Industrial Institute and College, predecessor of the Mississippi University for Women. In answer to critics who feared that education would harm women, the school's defenders said it would fit women for "ways of modest usefulness, for works of true benevolence," and invest in its students "that character and those beautiful Christian graces that constitute her the charm of social life and queen of the home."[1]

HOLLY SPRINGS

Bonner, Katharine Sherwood (McDowell), 1849–1883, Writer; NAW (under McDowell)

Cedarhurst, 411 Salem Avenue (Private)

They thought she had taken leave of her senses when Katharine Sherwood Bonner left her husband, Edward McDowell, in Texas and her year-old daughter in Mississippi and went to Boston, Massachusetts, to seek a literary career. She found a friend in Henry Wadsworth Longfellow and was soon launched on her writing career, using the name of Sherwood Bonner. Her novel *Like Unto Like*

(1878) was dedicated to Longfellow and they remained lifelong friends. Her stories are rich in local color. She returned to Holly Springs, her birthplace and home, in 1878 to nurse her father and brother, both of whom died of yellow fever. Two years later, after taking up residence in Illinois to obtain a divorce, she ended her unhappy marriage. She died soon afterward of cancer and was buried in Hill Crest Cemetery. Cedarhurst, her birthplace, is open during the annual spring pilgrimage in April under the auspices of the Holly Springs Garden Club.[2]

Clark, Kate Freeman, 1876?–1957, Artist

Kate Freeman Clark Art Gallery, College Avenue

Kate Freeman Clark returned to Holly Springs after almost three decades of studying art in New York City. Her neighbors welcomed her. The family home had been empty too long. Holly Springs folk knew she had been a painter and had shown her paintings in galleries, but few had seen her work. Clark, a spinster nearing fifty and without close kin, settled quietly into her house. She restored it and added a studio, but for the next thirty-four years she never painted again. She was always going to paint "tomorrow."

Why did she not continue in the work she loved and did so well? She had studied at the Art Students League in New York City, where William Merritt Chase regarded her as one of his best pupils. Her biographer believes the deaths of her mother and grandmother—who had chaperoned her in New York, relieved her of all mundane duties, and given her constant encouragement—were psychological blows. She never sold any of her paintings, so changes in buyers' tastes following the advent of impressionist painting were of no moment. Her life is both a mystery and a tragedy.

Clark died and left Holly Springs part of her estate and all her paintings, with plans for a museum in which they could be shown. Her boxes of paintings, which had been stored in New York for more than forty years, were sent to Holly Springs and opened. The canvases were astonishing in their fresh, vibrant colors. There were too many to hang all at once. At last the town knew that "Freeman Clark" was a great artist.

The gallery, built and opened shortly after her death, is the pride of Holly Springs. It is open during Pilgrimage Week and at other times on request to the Bank of Holly Springs.[3]

JACKSON

Cook, Fannye A., d. 1964, Wildlife Conservationist

Fannye A. Cook Memorial, Mississippi Museum of Natural Science, 111 N. Jefferson

Frances A. Cook, better known as Fannye, majored in ornithology at the University of Colorado and at George Washington University. In 1926, observing the damage done to Mississippi, her home state, by two years of drought and fire, she dropped her studies at the Smithsonian Institution and began a campaign for conservation. For five years she traveled about the state, pointing out the need for a state agency to preserve the fast-vanishing wildlife. She helped organize the Mississippi Federation for the Conservation of Wildlife and served as its executive secretary. In time a state Game and Fish Commission was established and she was appointed a research assistant. No desk-bound researcher, she camped out in rugged terrain to conduct game censuses and waded Mississippi streams to collect specimens of freshwater fish. Many district wildlife museums were established, culminating in the opening of the Mississippi Wildlife Museum in 1939. She was its director and curator until 1958. In the year of her death the Mississippi Legislature recommended that the museum (now the Museum of Natural Science) be given her name.[4]

Wheatley, Phillis, c. 1753–1784, Poet; NAW

Statue, Jackson State University

Black women poets celebrated a festival here in 1973 on the two hundredth anniversary of the first publication by a black writer living in America. Phillis Wheatley's *Poems on Various Subjects, Religious and Moral* was published in London, England, in 1773. She was bought from a slave ship by the Wheatley family of Boston, Massachusetts, when she was about seven years old. The family educated her and treated her more like a daughter than a slave. She was sent to England with the two sons of the family, and because she was black and intelligent and could compose verse, Londoners made much of her (as did Americans). Her poems were published by the Countess of Huntingdon. Unfortunately, Wheatley's life took a turn for the worse when the members of the Wheatley family died or moved away without making provision for her, and she died in poverty. She lives on as a "first" in black history. The sculptor of the statue here is Elizabeth Catlett, one of America's leading Afro-American sculptors.

NATCHEZ

Davis, Varina Ann Howell, 1826–1906, Wife of Confederate President; NAW

The Briars, Briars' Lane (Off US 65–84 Bypass); HABS, NR

This mansion overlooking the Mississippi River was the scene of the marriage, on February 26, 1845, of Varina Ann Howell and Jefferson Davis. Varina spent her girlhood here, tutored by a New Englander before going for two terms to a female seminary in Philadelphia, Pennsylvania. Jefferson was a widower, eighteen years older than his bride. Two years after the marriage, he was elected to the U.S. Senate and later he became secretary of war. Varina enjoyed being a

Washington hostess. When Mississippi seceded and Davis became the president of the Confederate States, Varina continued to shine as the First Lady in a succession of Confederate capitals until the course of the war brought tragedy and unhappiness. For two years after the war she fought to gain her husband's freedom from a federal prison, and after he died she worked to defend his memory.

The Briars, restored and furnished with Georgian, English Regency, and French Victorian furniture, is open daily 9–5; closed some holidays; adm. See Biloxi, MS.

PICAYUNE

Nicholson, Eliza Poitevent Holbrook, 1849–1896, Publisher; NAW

Marker, City Hall

Because she was born near here on the Pearl River, Eliza Poitevent Holbrook Nicholson signed her early verses "Pearl Rivers" when she began sending them to newspapers and magazines. She had earned a small reputation for writing when she met Alva Holbrook, editor of the *New Orleans Times-Picayune*. He offered her a job on his paper and soon followed that with an offer of marriage. Although he was forty-one years her senior, Eliza consented. He died four years after the marriage, and Eliza took his place as publisher of the respected but failing newspaper. Later she married her business manager, George Nicholson, also considerably older than she. He remained in charge of the business end while she decided what should go into the paper and how it should be presented. She soon had the paper out of the red and with tripled circulation, not only proving that a woman could run a paper but that she had some innovative ideas about doing so.

When the town where she was born was incorporated in 1904 it was named in her honor, but with the name of the paper, not the woman. The marker speaks of her as a poet and a "pioneer in opening journalism to women."

TOUGALOO

Dickey, Sarah, 1838–1904, Educator; NAW

Dickey Infirmary, Tougaloo College

The building is named for Sarah Dickey, the woman who for twenty-eight years operated Mount Hermon Female Seminary at Clinton, Mississippi, q.v. It recognizes a lifetime of devotion to the cause of educating freedmen.

VICKSBURG

Davis, Eva Whitaker, 1892–1974, Preservationist

Eva W. Davis Memorial, Old Courthouse Museum, Cherry, Jackson, Monroe and Grove Streets; HABS, NHL

Eva Whitaker Davis, affectionately known as Miss Eva, began a one-woman campaign to save the old Warren County Courthouse, abandoned in 1939 when a new courthouse was built. The old building dated from 1858. Hating to see it demolished, she organized a historical society and with its help got permission from the Board of Supervisors to establish a museum. She personally assisted in cleaning and restoring the historical old building. The museum opened in 1946, with Davis as caretaker, guide, director, and maid of all work. It has grown from one to nine rooms, with displays of Confederate history, a restored courtroom, and a research library.

To gain public attention and support, Davis conducted a daily radio program, wrote weekly newspaper columns, and edited a cookbook. She also organized the Mississsippi Foundation for Historic Preservation, which saved several other historical sites from destruction. In 1966 the governing board of the museum added her name to the building. It is open Mon.-Sat. 8:30–4:30, Sun. 1:30–4:30; closed some holidays; adm.[5]

NOTES

In addition to the sources below, I have been given information from the Mississippi Agricultural and Industrial Board.

1. *Mothers of Achievement in American History, 1776–1976*, comp. American Mothers Committee (Rutland, Vt.: Charles E. Tuttle Co., 1976).
2. Correspondence, Marshall County Historical Society, Holly Springs.
3. Cynthia G. Tucker, *Kate Freeman Clark: A Painter Rediscovered* (Jackson: University Press of Mississippi, 1981); correspondence, Marshall County Historical Society and Bank of Holly Springs.
4. Correspondence and clippings, Mississippi Game and Fish Commission; brochures, Museum of Natural Science.
5. *Mothers of Achievement*.

MISSOURI

ANACONDA

Hearst, Phoebe Apperson, 1842–1919, Philanthropist; NAW

Phoebe Apperson Hearst Schoolhouse

Phoebe Apperson Hearst grew up on a farm near here and attended Salem school. She was teaching when a neighbor, George Hearst, came home from a mining expedition into Nevada. She and Hearst (twenty years her senior) were married and moved to San Francisco, California. George was a success in mining (gold and silver) and in business (oil, real estate, and newspaper publishing), and the couple took a leading place in San Francisco society. Phoebe took the responsibilities of wealth seriously and not only contributed generously to education and other causes but involved herself in such movements as the founding of the National Congress of Parents and Teachers. In 1963 a replica of the log cabin in which she had attended school was built on the original site (about two miles east of Anaconda), with funds donated by a niece. It was dedicated by the Franklin County Phoebe Apperson Hearst Memorial Association (now Historical Society).[1]

BELTON

Nation, Carry Amelia Moore, 1846–1911, Antisaloon Crusader; NAW

Monument, Belton Cemetery

The grave of Carry Amelia Moore Nation, who was noted for her aggressive tactics against the demon rum, went unmarked until 1924, when the Woman's Christian Temperance Union—which had once been embarrassed by her notoriety—erected a granite shaft inscribed: "Carry A. Nation, 1848–1911, Faithful to the Cause of Prohibition, 'She hath done what she could.' " See Eureka Springs, AR, and Lancaster, KY.

BOONVILLE

Cole, Hannah Allison, d. 1843, Pioneer

Monuments, Boonville High School and Briscoe Cemetery

In January 1810, Hannah Allison Cole, a widow with nine children, undertook a perilous journey from Central Missouri to what is now Boonville. She was accompanied by other family members. At one time they were separated from their provisions by the ice-packed, swiftly flowing river and for eleven days subsisted on slippery elm bark, acorns, and a single wild turkey. After their arrival, a fort was built at Cole's cabin. It became a community center and Cole a leading citizen of the settlement. The first court of Cooper County was held there in 1816. The first businesswoman in the territory, she operated a ferry over the Missouri River.[2]

BRANSON

O'Neill, Rose Cecil, 1874–1944, Illustrator and Writer; NAW

Memorabilia, Shepherd of the Hills Museum, Off State 76

Rose Cecil O'Neill is chiefly famous for the invention of the Kewpie doll. About 1909 she began drawing chubby angels with tiny wings, smiling faces, and tufts of hair on the tops of their heads. She called them Kewpies and wrote charming stories about their antics. Kewpies became a fad; they were used on greeting cards, soap, letter paper, and fabrics. In 1912 the first of thousands of Kewpie dolls were manufactured, O'Neill supervising their production and, with her sister, operating a Kewpie shop in New York City. Royalties from the tiny figures brought her some one and a half million dollars. She was able to live lavishly and to work at more solid writing and sculpture until the money was gone. She then returned to Bonnie Brook, a 350-acre farm her father had bought in the Ozarks, for her last years.

The Shepherd of the Hills Museum, seven miles west of town, is named for a novel by Harold Bell Wright. It is devoted to Ozark handicrafts and the work of Wright and O'Neill. Open early Apr.–Labor Day, daily 9–6; Labor Day–late Oct., daily 9–5; adm. The School of the Ozarks, on US 65 near Point Lookout, also has a museum displaying handicrafts and a gallery of famous persons from the Ozarks, including O'Neill. It is open Mar.-Nov., Mon.-Sat. 9–4:30, Sun. 1–4:30; closed holidays; adm.[3]

CAPE GIRARDEAU

Otahki, d. 1838, Cherokee Indian Victim

Monument at Grave, Trail of Tears State Park, State 177; NR

The monument and park symbolize the great blot on American history when in 1838 Georgia, with federal approval, forced the Cherokees to leave their tribal lands for Indian Territory (Oklahoma). The Cherokee Nation, spread over northwest Georgia into Alabama and Tennessee, had accepted the white man's civilization, invented an alphabet, and built roads, houses, and churches. They had a constitution and a legislature. Nevertheless, when gold was discovered on Cherokee lands in 1828, greedy miners decided that the Indians had to go. In spite of numerous treaties guaranteeing independence to the tribe, state and federal officials forced the Indians to leave. Rounded up and driven over the land by regular army troops, the Cherokee began their long march. A third of them died on the journey, and the route is called the Trail of Tears.

Otahki, daughter of Jesse Bushyhead, Cherokee leader, was buried here, many miles from home and many miles from the end of the trail. In 1962 the Otahki monument was dedicated to her.[4]

CARONDELET

Blow, Susan Elizabeth, 1843–1916, Kindergartner; NAW

Des Peres School, 6303 Michigan Avenue; NR

As a young woman, Susan Elizabeth Blow visited Germany, where she learned of the "children's gardens" where Friedrich Froebel's disciples taught young children in a new way, using large cylinders, cubes, and balls to introduce them to shapes and colors, and games and songs to stimulate their minds and bodies. When she came back home, she studied with a well-known kindergartner in New York and then offered to supervise a public kindergarten if the school board would provide a room and a teacher. The kindergarten opened in the Des Peres School in Carondelet in 1873, a forerunner of kindergartens throughout the school system and the nation. In 1935 the school was closed. After being used as a restaurant and bar, offices, and storage, the building was sold to the Susan Blow Foundation for use as a school museum. See Jefferson City, MO.[5]

CARTHAGE

Starr, Belle, 1848–1889, Bandit; NAW

Marker, Carthage Square

A stone in the sidewalk marks the site of the Shirleys' hotel, where Myra Belle Shirley was born. As Belle Starr, she became a legend in wild West stories, many far from true. During her short life she cut a swath of banditry throughout the Southwest, hanging out with Jesse James and the Younger brothers, holding up trains, and robbing banks. She lived with a succession of men, including Sam Starr, a Cherokee, whose name stuck to her, and she bore several children, none of whom seemed to come to any better end than did Belle, who was shot in the back by an unknown assailant. Her daughter, Pearl Starr, became a prostitute in Fort Smith, Arkansas, scene of many court appearances for Belle and her cohorts. Pearl, at least, had a soft spot in her heart for her mother, for she buried Belle at Younger's Bend, Oklahoma, and wrote the epitaph carved on the tombstone along with a carving of a bell, a star, and a horse: ''Shed not for her the bitter tear, Nor give the heart to vain regret; 'Tis but the casket that lies here, The gem that filled it sparkles yet.'' See Dallas, TX, and Bartlesville, OK.[6]

COLUMBIA

Gentry, Ann Hawkins, 1791–1870, Postmistress

Old Post Office, 1 S. 7th Street. Roadside Park

Gentry County was named for Richard Gentry, Ann Hawkins Gentry's husband, who was one of the pioneer settlers of Columbia in 1820. In 1837 Richard went off to fight in the Florida (Seminole) War and never returned. Ann was officially appointed the town's postmistress, taking her husband's place. She held this position from 1837 until five years before her death. The old post office (though not in use when Gentry was postmistress) was dedicated to her in 1977. The roadside park, three miles south of Stanberry, was dedicated as a memorial in 1960.[7]

St. Clair, Louella Wilcox (Moss), 1865–1947, College Administrator

St. Clair Hall, Columbia College

The board of Christian College knew they were shattering precedent when in 1893 they appointed a woman—Louella Wilcox St. Clair—to head the institution, but they felt she was ''eminently fitted to hold the office'' of president of a woman's college. She was the widow of Franklin Pierce St. Clair, who had been appointed president a few months earlier and had died of a heart attack with the term just begun. St. Clair submerged her grief in plans for the college. By the end of the year she had made a good many steps toward bringing the college into the twentieth century (before the century had begun). She launched a college magazine, installed electric lights, replaced old furniture and carpets with new. She organized an alumnae association, a Young Women's Christian Association branch, an orchestra—and she discarded bonnets for becoming hats.

St. Clair left the presidency twice, once because of ill health, again to accept a like position at Hamilton College in Kentucky, where she remained for six years. Her return to Christian College occurred in 1909. Two years later she married Woodson Moss, the college physician. St. Clair resigned in 1920, after twenty-five years of college service. Again a widow, she threw herself into public life and was the first Missouri woman ever nominated for a national office, running as a Democratic candidate for Congress. Her name was inscribed on a tablet in the Missouri state capitol. Christian College (renamed Columbia College) several years after her death dedicated a memorial organ in the chapel to Louella St. Clair Moss.[8]

Stanley, Louise, 1883–1954, Home Economist; NAWM

Stanley Building, University of Missouri-Columbia, Elm and Eighth Streets

Louise Stanley was the first woman to direct a bureau in the U.S. Department of Agriculture. By 1911, when she earned a Ph.D. in biochemistry from Yale University, she was teaching at the University of Missouri. She was head of the home economics department from 1917 to 1923. She worked ceaselessly for federal funds for the teaching of home economics and acquired a reputation in the field. When the Bureau of Home Economics was formed in the federal Department of Agriculture, she was selected as its chief.

During Stanley's tenure (1923–50), the department undertook studies that led to a number of changes now taken for granted: basic diet plans for families, widely used in government relief programs; time and motion studies, resulting in efficient housekeeping methods; studies of body measurements leading to standardized clothing sizes; establishment of the base-year prices for the cost-of-living index. Sometimes her goal of better family living conflicted with the department's goal of selling more wheat and sugar, but women's organizations and others interested in good nutrition backed her up. She remained a highly regarded professional in the field of home economics and was a mentor for young women entering it. The home economics building at the university was given her name in 1961.

HANNIBAL

Brown, Margaret Tobin, 1867–1932, Heroine

Molly Brown House, US 36 at Denkler Alley

The girl who became famous as "The Unsinkable Molly Brown" was born here. Margaret Tobin Brown migrated westward and in Leadville, Colorado, fell in love with and married James J. Brown, a miner. James struck it rich, but the young couple did not know the rules of society in Denver, Colorado, where they built a mansion, and Denverites snubbed them. Molly went to Europe, where she educated herself and studied dramatic techniques. She came home on the "unsinkable" *Titanic* in 1913, which sank and lost most of its passengers and crew. Molly helped to row a lifeboat and kept up the spirits of the shivering and terrified passengers by singing. Told about her bravery, reporters asked how she managed to survive. "Oh," she said, "I'm unsinkable." She returned to Denver an international heroine. The story, *The Unsinkable Mrs. Brown*, was made into a movie and a musical. Her early home has been restored to the period of about 1875. It details her early life in Hannibal and her heroism. It is open May 30–Sept. 10, daily 10–4.[9]

JEFFERSON CITY

Blow, Susan Elizabeth, 1843–1916, Kindergartner; NAW

Bust, State Capitol

The bust honoring Susan Elizabeth Blow, Missouri's pioneer kindergarten teacher, was unveiled in November 1983. See Carondelet, MO.

Dobbs, Ella Victoria, 1866–1952, Educator

Plaque, State Capitol

A bronze plaque in the capitol honors fifty-five women for their work in woman's suffrage. Included is the name of Ella Victoria Dobbs, a leader in childhood education and a professor of applied arts at the University of Missouri from 1911 until her retirement in 1936. She believed in teaching children, rather than subjects, and was one of the first to correlate art and handiwork with other school classes. She founded Pi Lambda Theta, an honor society for women, in 1911. The society presented her portrait to the university, where it hangs in the social room of Lathrop Hall. In 1940 the Women's Centennial Congress counted her as one of a hundred women successful in careers not open to the sex in 1840.[10]

LEE'S SUMMIT

Combs, Loula Long, 1881–1971, Horse Breeder

Longview Farm

Loula Long Combs, who grew up in Kansas City, Missouri, began riding at the age of four and at sixteen drove in the Royal Horse Show at Madison Square Garden, doing so well that the Barnum and Bailey Circus offered her a job. She declined. She was famed not only for her fast driving but for the extravagant hats she wore. In 1967 she became one of two representatives of the sport of horse racing in the Hall of Fame at Madison Square Garden. Her Kansas City home, 3218 Gladstone Boulevard, was given to the public and opened in 1940 as the Kansas City Museum of History and Science.[11]

Fillmore, Myrtle Page, 1845–1931, School Founder; NAW

Unity School of Christianity

Soon after Myrtle Page Fillmore and Charles Fillmore moved to Kansas City, Missouri, from Denver, Colorado, in 1884, they attended a lecture by E. B. Weeks, who subscribed to religious beliefs resembling those of Mary Baker Eddy. Myrtle's incipient tuberculosis cleared up after she began to follow Weeks' methods of faith healing and both the Fillmores went to Chicago, Illinois, to study with Emma Hopkins, founder of the Christian Science Theological Seminary. Eventually the Fillmores developed the Unity School of Christianity, teaching classes and writing literature to bring their message of "practical Christianity" to the public. Outgrowing their quarters in Kansas City, they purchased a large farm at Lee's Summit, now the headquarters of Unity. Myrtle wrote for the movement's publications and edited *Wee Wisdom*, a periodical for children.

MANSFIELD

Wilder, Laura Ingalls, 1867–1957, and Her Daughter, Rose Wilder Lane, 1886–1968, Writers; NAWM (under Wilder)

Laura Ingalls Wilder–Rose Wilder Lane Home and Museum, US 60 Business; NR

Laura Ingalls Wilder might be much surprised today to learn of her popularity, based on the Little House books and the television series "Little House on the Prairie." When she first lived here she was a farm wife, helping her husband on Rocky Ridge Farm and raising chickens. She was proud of her daughter, Rose Wilder Lane, who became a journalist. It was at Lane's suggestion that Wilder began, in her sixties, to write the stories of pioneer life as she herself experienced it and heard of it from her parents. She won fame, and unlike many authors whose fame faded with changing times, Wilder's popularity seems perennial. Her books deal with reality and humanity and are written with warmth and spirit. Her daughter became a nationally known journalist, a critic of the New Deal, conservative in outlook. The museum contains memorabilia of both mother and daughter. It is open May 1–Oct. 15, Mon.-Sat. and holidays, 9–4; adm.

NEVADA

Cottey, Virginia Alice (Stockard), 1848–1940, College Founder

Cottey College, W. Austin and S. Chestnut Streets

When Virginia Alice Cottey went to a school for girls in 1867 she was critical of the time spent on needlework and social graces at the expense of academic subjects. She and her sisters, Dora Cottey (1860–1956) and Kate Cottey (1862–1901), shared a dream of starting a different sort of school for women, one that would prepare students for active work in their communities and would develop their minds. In 1883, with the backing of businessmen in the community, Alice made a beginning. Land was chosen, a building erected, and Vernon Seminary opened its doors in 1884 with twenty-eight students. By the end of the year there were seventy-two. Two years later the school expanded in size, and since the townspeople always spoke of it as the Cottey sisters' school, it changed its name to Cottey College.

Alice married Samuel Stockard in 1890. She continued as head of the college and saw it grow in size and stature, but it was always a struggle to find enough money for the increasing number of applicants. In 1927 the P.E.O. Sisterhood agreed to accept Cottey College, thus making it probably the only women's college in the world owned and operated by a women's organization. Each member pays a dollar a year toward the college. The institution was accredited for membership in the North Central Association in 1940, just a few months before Alice's death. Cottey College celebrated its centennial in 1984.[12]

PRINCETON

Burk, Martha Cannary (Calamity Jane), 1852?–1903, Frontierswoman; NAW

Marker, at Site of Birthplace, near Ollen Owen Corner, State 36

Shifting fact from legend to discover the true role of Martha Cannary Burk, the woman who came to be called Calamity Jane, is not easy. She wrote an autobiography and a supposed series of letters to her daughter has been published, but neither is too exact as to what really happened in her life. Even the authenticity of the steel marker imbedded in the ground marking her birth site, as well as the date of her birth, is questionable. Suffice it to say that she was a colorful figure of western history, a sure shot, an expert horsewoman, had a liking for strong liquor and an awesome vocabulary when drunk. She teamed up with Wild Bill Hickok, claimed a marriage to Clinton Burk, and was companion to a number of other western characters. The heroine of a number of dime novels, she has been portrayed as the Florence Nightingale of the frontier, an Indian fighter, a bullwhacker, and an army scout. She seems to have achieved immortality by being her own strong, independent self in a tough male world.

ST. CHARLES

Sibley, Mary Easton, 1800–1878, College Founder; NAW

Sibley Hall, Lindenwood Colleges, Kingshighway and First Capitol Drive; NR

Mary Easton Sibley and her husband, George Champlin Sibley, settled in St. Charles, Missouri, after George had retired from his post as an agent of the Indian Bureau. Their early married life was spent at Fort Osage, to which the fifteen-year-old bride had traveled up the Missouri River from St. Louis by keelboat with her hope chest, her books, a piano, and household furnishings. The Sibleys were hospitable to travelers, who must have been surprised to find a home of such culture in that raw country. The Indians were delighted with her music. Mary began teaching the Indian girls, and this interest in education for young women inspired the couple to establish at their St. Charles home Lindenwood Female College, chartered in 1853 and soon affiliated with the Presbyterian church. During the early years of the college the students often saw "Aunt Mary" driving about the campus in her carriage, which they called the "Ship of Zion."

ST. LOUIS

Hahn, Nancy Coonsman, d. 1976, Sculptor

Memorial to Women of Upper Louisiana Territory, Jefferson Memorial. Kincaid Fountain and Reedy Memorial, St. Louis Art Museum. Daughters of American Colonists Fountain

Nancy Coonsman Hahn was born in St. Louis, where she attended Washington University and the St. Louis School of Fine Arts. She married Manuel Hahn in 1918. In addition to the public monuments she executed in St. Louis, her sculptures are in a number of museums and in other cities. She was the sculptor for the Missouri State Memorial in Cheppy-par-Varennes, France.

Hosmer, Harriet, 1830–1908, Sculptor; NAW

Thomas Hart Benton Statue, Lafayette Park

The Boston Medical School refused to admit Harriet Hosmer into its anatomy class, a prerequisite to the sculpture of a human body. Wayman Crow, the father of a school chum, got her into a class at the Medical College of St. Louis and arranged for her to live with his family. Hosmer was an athletic, outdoors person, and while in Missouri she climbed a peak which is named after her. Crow continued his interest in the young sculptor while she worked and studied in Rome, Italy, and he commissioned her first important commission in 1855, a kneeling figure of *Oenone*, which is now in the art gallery of Washington University. Another of her famous statues, *Beatrice Cenci*, is also in St. Louis, at the Mercantile Library. The statue of Missouri's Senator Thomas Hart Benton, draped in classical garments, was one of her major public commissions. It was unveiled in 1868 before a crowd of forty thousand, with Benton's daughter, Jessie Benton Frémont, in attendance.

Hosmer succeeded in a man's world, and she knew the cost. In a letter to Phebe Hanaford, one of the first American women to become a preacher, she wrote: "In a few years it will not be thought strange that women should be preachers and sculptors, and everyone who comes after us will have to bear fewer and fewer blows. Therefore I say, I honor all those who step boldly forward, and, in spite of ridicule and criticism, pave a broader way for the women of the next generation."[13]

Morgan, Mary Kimball, 1861–1948, Christian Science Educator; NAW

The Principia, 13201 Clayton Road

Mary Kimball Morgan and her husband developed the first Christian Science Church in St. Louis and she became, in 1896, an authorized Christian Science practitioner. Wishing to educate her sons in accordance with the principles of her faith, she taught them at home and was soon persuaded to include the children of some of her friends. From this grew a school, which expanded from elementary to include high school and then junior college. Christian Science families sent their children to the Principia for moral instruction as well as all the academic studies. Morgan then established, in Elsah, Illinois, a four-year college, also named Principia.

Turnbo-Malone, Annie Minerva, 1869–1957, Businesswoman and Philanthropist; NAWM

Annie Malone Children's Home, 2612 Goode Avenue

In 1900 Annie Minerva Turnbo-Malone manufactured a unique mixture for straightening the hair of Negro women and enhancing its sheen. Thirty years later when she moved her thriving business from St. Louis to Chicago, Illinois, she was one of the best-known and wealthiest Afro-American women in the country. She succeeded because of the great demand for her product, Poro, and also because she was a good businesswoman with a system of enfranchising agents. She built in St. Louis a factory employing a large number of workers and a school for training beauty operators, which she called Poro College. With its large campus, the school was a center for cultural, religious, and social life much appreciated by the black community, denied access to the city's restaurants and hotels. She lived simply, considering her wealth a trust to be used for the good of the community, and gave large sums to the local Young Men's Christian Association, Howard University, and local charities.

Turnbo-Malone left St. Louis in the late 1930s, but she retained a philanthropic interest in the city, continuing to serve on the executive board of the Colored Orphans' Home, for which she had donated the land in 1919. In 1946 her name was given to the home.[14]

NOTES

In addition to the correspondents mentioned below, I have had assistance from the following: the University of Missouri in Columbia; the Farmington Public Library; the Chamber of Commerce of Metropolitan St. Louis; the Missouri Division of Tourism; Missouri Valley College; the State Archives of Missouri; the Missouri Historical Society; Corinne B. Cott, superintendent of the Blosser Home in Marshall; the Independence Heritage Commission; and the Harry S Truman National Historic Site.

1. Correspondence and clippings, Phoebe Apperson Hearst Historical Society; Clarissa Start Davidson, "Women's Role in Missouri History," *The Missouri State Manual, 1971–72*.

2. *Mothers of Achievement in American History, 1776–1976*, comp. American Mothers Committee (Rutland, Vt.: Charles E. Tuttle Co., 1976).

3. Davidson, "Women's Role"; correspondence, Shepherd of the Hills Museum and the School of the Ozarks.

4. *Chronicles of Oklahoma* 40 (Autumn 1962), pp. 306–7.

5. Carondelet Historical Society Newsletter, Feb. 1984; correspondence, State Historical Society of Missouri.

6. *Legendary Ladies of Texas*, ed. Francis E. Abernethy (Texas Folklore Society in Cooperation with Texas Foundation for Women's Resources Women in History Project, Dallas, Tex.: E. Heart Press, 1981).

7. *Mothers of Achievement*; correspondence, State Historical Society of Missouri.

8. Allean Lemmon Hale, *Petticoat Pioneer: The Story of Christian College*, rev. ed. (St. Paul, Minn.: North Central Publishing Co., 1968); correspondence, Columbia College.

9. Correspondence, State Historical Society and Marion County Historical Society.

10. Agnes Snyder, *Dauntless Women in Childhood Education, 1856–1931* (Washington, D.C.: Association for Childhood Education International, 1972).

11. Correspondence and clippings, Longview Community College; *New York Times*, July 7, 1971; *Kansas City Star*, Aug. 20, 1967 and July 7, 1971; *Lee's Summit Journal*, Sept. 7, 1983.

12. Davidson, "Women's Role"; Cottey College Centennial Celebration (pamphlet).

13. Charlotte S. Rubinstein, *American Women Artists* (New York: Avon Books, 1982), quotation from Phebe Hanaford, *Daughters of America* (1882).

14. Correspondence, State Historical Society.

NORTH CAROLINA

ASHEVILLE

Vanderbilt, Edith Stuyvesant Dresser, 1873–1958, Philanthropist

Biltmore Industries, Grovewood Road; NR. Biltmore House and Gardens, US 25; NHL

Edith Stuyvesant Dresser, of Rhode Island, married George Washington Vanderbilt in 1898 and spent much of her time here at Biltmore House and Gardens, which her husband had established. A scientific farmer and a pioneer in forestry, George had a prize dairy farm, extensive gardens, and forests of rare trees. Edith enjoyed the country and took an interest in the crafts of the mountain people. In 1901 she established Biltmore Industries to preserve the Old World wool-manufacturing skills of the women. Biltmore House and Gardens can be visited daily 9–6; high adm. The shops on the grounds of Grove Park Inn are open Apr. 1–Oct. 31, Mon.-Sat. and holidays, 9–5:30, Sun. 1–6; tours of the workshops hourly Mon.-Fri. 9–4; rest of year open Mon.-Sat. 9–4:30.

BLOWING ROCK

Goodrich, Frances Louisa, 1856–1944, Teacher

Frances L. Goodrich Pioneer Museum, Pioneer Craft Center, Moses H. Cone Memorial Park, Milepost 294, Blue Ridge Parkway

Frances Louisa Goodrich, a teacher and missionary, began in the 1890s to encourage a revival among the mountain women of the old arts of spinning and weaving. She opened a shop in Asheville where the beautiful products could be sold. In 1930 she gave the shop to the Southern Highlands Handicraft Guild, recently organized by a number of men and women interested in mountain crafts. They included from North Carolina Lucy Morgan of Penland; Mary Martin Sloop of Crossnore; Clementine Douglas of the Spinning Wheel in Asheville; William J. Hutchins, president of Berea College; and a representative of Goodrich. The guild operates several shops in the Blue Ridge area. Goodrich wrote *Mountain Homespun* (1931) about her work with North Carolina native artisans. The shop is open May 1–Oct. 31, daily 9–5:30.[1]

BOONE

Cannon, Ruth Louise Coltrane, 1891–1965, Civic Leader

Cannon Music Camp, Appalachian State University

The daughter of a banker and wife of a Cannon Mills executive, Ruth Louise Coltrane Cannon had many interests outside of her home and was an enthusiastic worker in the community. She loved history and sought the preservation of North Carolina's heritage. She was one of the first members of the Roanoke Island Historical Association and was instrumental in the restoration of Tryon Palace and the creation of the Elizabethan Garden at Manteo. Her home on Lake Kannapolis, For Pity's Sake, was a horticultural showplace. She supported Lees-McRae College and Wingate College; a dormitory at the latter school was named in her honor. In recognition of her work in establishing the first music department in the Kannapolis schools, a building at A. L. Brown High School was dedicated to her. The Music Camp at Appalachian State, where high school students are given four weeks of intensive musical training and experience every summer, was given her name in 1969, and a residence hall at the school is named for Charles and Ruth Cannon.[2]

BRASSTOWN

Campbell, Olive Dame, 1882–1954, School Founder

John C. Campbell Folk School, Off US 64, Between Hayesville and Murphy; NR

A native of Massachusetts who moved South after marriage to John C. Campbell, Olive Dame Campbell began collecting traditional ballads and songs, many of them Elizabethan airs preserved by the highlanders. Such songs as "Black Is the Color of My True Love's Hair" and "Lord Randall" were brought to the attention of collectors, including the English musicologist Cecil J. Sharp. Some were published in a book coauthored by Campbell and Sharp in 1917, *English Folk Songs from the Southern Appalachians*. Campbell wrote many articles about the Appalachian people, their songs and crafts and heritage. She established the folk school in 1925, giving it the name of her husband, who died in 1919. Modeled after adult education programs she had studied in Scandinavia, the school offers courses in arts, crafts, music, and dancing, as well as agricultural, forestry, and management skills needed by community leaders. Campbell was instrumental in establishing the Southern Highlands Handicraft Guild to market Appalachian handcrafted items.[3]

CHAPEL HILL

Spencer, Cornelia Phillips, 1825–1908, Educator; NAW

Cornelia Phillips Spencer Dormitory, University of North Carolina

When her brothers entered the respected old University of North Carolina (established in 1795), Cornelia Phillips Spencer was left with only "crumbs from the college table," for women were not admitted. Up to that time she had studied with the boys and afterward she worked alone and was scholar enough to be able to teach Latin and Greek when she returned to Chapel Hill from Alabama as a widow with one child. After the Civil War, she began writing and working to improve educational facilities for southerners. During Reconstruction the university was forced to close, and Spencer, along with others, forced its reopening in 1875. As soon as she heard the news that it was to be reopened, she climbed the bell tower and rang the bell triumphantly. She then turned her efforts toward education for women and played a part in establishing the Normal and Industrial School for Women, later the Woman's College of the University of North Carolina at Greensboro, q.v.

The first women's dormitory at Chapel Hill was built in 1925—not without opposition from those who feared it would encourage women to attend—and given the name of Spencer. The stone at her grave in the old cemetery reads: "Historian, writer, teacher, friend of the university."[4]

CHARLOTTE

Dwelle, Mary Myers, 1891–1975, Preservationist

Mary Myers Dwelle Gallery, Mint Museum of Art, 501 Hempstead Place

The old Branch U.S. Mint coined dollars between 1837 and 1861 from gold mined in the Appalachians. In 1932 it was ordered demolished. Mary Myers Dwelle, who had long dreamed of an art museum for Charlotte, discussed the possibility of saving it, but it would cost fifteen hundred dollars just to buy the bricks and stones and have them moved to a new site. She was chairperson of the art department of the Charlotte Women's Club. Leila Mechlin, secretary of the American Federation of Art, came to speak at the club, and as Dwelle drove the speaker to the meeting she passed by the mint and told of her hope of saving it. Mechlin revised her speech, challenging the women to raise the money; almost a third of the needed sum was raised that same day. With this beginning, a group of concerned citizens purchased the materials and reconstructed on a new site the handsome old building, with its great gold eagle over the door. It opened as an art museum in 1936 with Dwelle as volunteer director. In 1968 the main gallery of the mint was renamed the Mary Myers Dwelle Gallery.

The museum, remodeled to include a museum of history, reopened in 1985. Call 704–337–2000 for hours of admission.[5]

CROSSNORE

Sloop, Mary Martin, 1873–1962, Missionary and Educator

Crossnore School

Mary Martin Sloop was the author of *Miracle in the Hills*, best-selling story of the founding of Crossnore School, but she didn't write a word of it. She was too busy. She and LeGette Blythe, who taped the story as Sloop told it, then typed and saw the book in print, were given the Mayflower Award in 1953 for the volume. It had been commissioned by McGraw-Hill at an earlier award ceremony when Sloop was named American Mother of the Year. She and her husband, Eustace Sloop, had come to the mountains as missionaries in 1908 and were appalled at the primitive living conditions: no roads, no schools, no access to medical care, poor nutrition. They started a Sunday school and sewing classes and sent a few girls to mission schools. They built a hospital and Crossnore School, raising funds by selling old clothes donated by their friends. It is said that when Sloop went to New York to receive the Mother of the Year Award she wore a hat bought at the school for two dollars, her only hat. She was too busy to read galley or page proof for her book, and by all reports had not taken the time to read it until the day of her death, yet it was selected by a book club, reprinted over and over, and went around the world in translation. It also brought into prominence the husband-wife team's long years of unselfish work in educating young people of the mountains for successful lives.

Crossnore is now a home for disadvantaged children, from first graders to high school seniors, who come from the mountain and piedmont areas of North Carolina. Funds are provided partially by the Weaving Room and Sales Store. Visitors are welcome.[6]

CULLOWHEE

Memorials, Western Carolina University

Western Carolina University has named several buildings for women who influenced the development of the institution. Dormitories were named for Ann Platt Albright (d. 1961), dean of women, 1935–50, and a teacher of history; and for Alice A. Benton, who joined the faculty in 1922 as professor of health and physical education, retiring in 1959. She instigated a chapter of Alpha Phi Sigma, national honorary scholastic society.

The Cordelia Camp Laboratory School, dedicated in 1965, honors Cordelia Camp (1884–1973), who was for twenty-three years director of student teachers at the college. The building serves as the Cullowhee Public School for grades one through twelve. A portrait of Camp hangs in the school. The Gertrude Dills McKee Building, a training school at the college, honors McKee, a member of the state senate, 1931–48, and a trustee of the university.

The little theater in the Stillwell Science Building was renamed for Josefina Niggli (1910–1983), poet, novelist, playwright, and educator. Born in Mexico, Niggli was several times rushed out of the country to escape revolutions, and got much of her education in San Antonio, Texas. She joined Western Carolina's faculty as drama teacher in 1956. Her *Mexican Village* (1945) is a collection of fine novelettes based on her Mexican experiences.

The Mary White Scott Residence Hall, dedicated in 1970, honors Scott (1897–1972), of Mebane, North Carolina. She lived a busy political life while her husband was state governor and then a U.S. senator, and she also kept active in education, church, 4-H clubs, and the Grange. Her childhood home in Mebane has been replaced by a home for the elderly, which includes the Mary Elizabeth White Scott Center.[7]

CURRIE

Slocumb, Mary Hooks, 1760–1836, Revolutionary War Heroine

Monument, Moores Creek National Military Park

The monument, erected in recent memory, memorializes not only Mary Hooks Slocumb but the other volunteer nurses of the lower Cape Fear River who went to the battleground on February 27, 1776, to nurse the wounded. Without supplies, they used torn bits of clothing and heartleaves to stop the flow of blood and bind the gaping wounds. According to legend, Slocumb dreamed of a bloody body wrapped in her husband's cloak. She dressed and rode through the forests all night seeking him. She stopped to help those who cried for water and suddenly her husband stood before her "as bloody as a butcher and as muddy as a ditcher." He told her that the North Carolina patriot band had defeated a group of Loyalists on their way to join the British. The battlefield is about twenty miles northwest of Wilmington and four miles west of US 421.[8]

DURHAM

Baldwin, Alice Mary, 1879–1960, Educator

Baldwin Auditorium, Woman's College, Duke University

Alice Mary Baldwin, born and educated in New England, interrupted her study for a Ph.D. in history at the University of Chicago to accept a temporary position in 1924 as dean of women of Trinity College in Durham. Two years after she joined the faculty Trinity became Duke University and Baldwin was named dean of the Woman's College. She remained at that post until she retired in 1947, and it was largely due to her influence that high standards of excellence were established at the very beginning. Her greatest efforts, both on the campus and in the world of scholarship, were directed toward promoting higher education for women. The class of 1943 of the Woman's College established a scholarship fund in her name, and in 1964 the auditorium was named for her.[9]

Biddle, Mary Duke, 1887–1960, Philanthropist

Mary Duke Biddle Music Building, Duke University. Duke Homestead State Historic Site, 2828 Duke Homestead Road. Sarah P. Duke Gardens, Duke University

Mary Duke Biddle was a granddaughter of the founder of the Duke tobacco fortune, and niece of James Duke, who established the Duke Foundation and changed Trinity College to Duke University. She married in 1915 Anthony J. Drexel Biddle, Jr., of Philadelphia, Pennsylvania (from whom she was divorced in 1931). Biddle had homes in New York City, Irvington-on-Hudson, New York, and Durham. With plenty of money and an interest in the arts and education, she was able to enrich a number of institutions, many of them in her native North Carolina. She made substantial gifts to her own college, Trinity, and in 1931 purchased the Washington Duke Homestead for the university (which gave it to the state of North Carolina). In 1938 she gave the school the Duke Gardens, which her mother had initiated. She also established the Mary Duke Biddle Foundation, half of its income to go to Duke, the rest to other philanthropies in which she had been interested. The homestead is a historical complex open Tues.-Sat., 9–5, Sun. 1–5. The gardens, on the west campus of Duke, are open daily 8–dusk.[10]

Williams, Mary Lou, 1910–1981, Musician

Mary Lou Williams Center for Black Culture, Duke University

Pianist, composer, and arranger of music, Mary Lou Williams was largely self-taught yet rose to a high position in the world of jazz. Her career spanned several jazz eras and styles. She wrote many popular songs and did arrangements for Benny Goodman, Duke Ellington, Louis Armstrong, and other band leaders. She wrote an ambitious *Zodiac Suite*, which was introduced at a town hall concert and was performed by the New York Philharmonic Symphony Orchestra. Following her conversion to Catholicism in 1957 she wrote mostly religious music, including several masses. She was artist in residence at Duke University in 1977, and in 1983 the center was dedicated in memory of the "great lady of jazz."[11]

EDENTON

Barker, Penelope Pagett, 1728–1796, Revolutionary War Heroine

Barker House, S. Broad Street; NR. Marker, US 17. Tea Party Memorial, Courthouse Green

On October 25, 1774, fifty-one Edenton women met, with Penelope Pagett Barker presiding, to protest the taxing of tea by the British and to support the resolutions drawn up by North Carolina's First Provincial Congress. They adopted and signed a resolution forswearing the drinking of East India tea and the importation of British manufactured goods. The meeting, which ended with the drinking of tea brewed from raspberry leaves, might have gone unnoticed except for a cruel caricature that appeared in a London paper in January 1775. It was entitled "A Society of Patriotic Ladies at Edenton in North Carolina" and shows a group of women around a table on which is spread a paper declaring that the ladies would not conform to the "pernicious custom of drinking tea" until the acts "which tend to enslave this our native country shall be repealed."

The Tea Party Memorial is a giant bronze teapot mounted on a cannon. The Barker House, with other buildings in Historic Edenton, is open Tues.-Sat. 10–4:30, Sun. 2–5; closed some holidays. At Cupola House, 408 S. Broad Street, a smiling portrait of Barker can be seen.[12]

FAYETTEVILLE

MacDonald, Flora, 1722–1790, Scottish Heroine

Monument, Cool Springs Street

Flora MacDonald was a Scottish heroine who is remembered for her attempt to smuggle Bonnie Prince Charlie to safety from Scotland to France, for which she was imprisoned for a year in 1746–47. In 1774 she and her husband, Allan MacDonald, moved from Scotland to North Carolina, where Allan enlisted as a Loyalist. Much of his success in recruiting Loyalists was due to Flora's influence. She wrote a friend, on her husband's departure for Cross Creek: "There are troublous times ahead I ween. . . . I hope all our ain are in the right." While he was away her house was looted, her servants ran away, her lands went back to nature, and she herself became ill and broke her arm in a fall from a horse. Allan was taken prisoner and when he was finally exchanged for a rebel the couple returned to Scotland. See Pekin and Red Springs, NC.[13]

GOLDSBORO

Weil, Sarah, 1856–1928, Social Worker

Plaque, Wayne County Community Building, E. Walnut and William Streets. Plaque, Public Library, 204 W. Chestnut Street; NR

The plaque on the Community Building reads: "In memory of Sarah Weil, 1856–1928, who for more than 30 years was president of the Bureau of Social Services and who cheerfully fostered community betterment. Erected by her friends 1929." When she founded the bureau it was called the Ladies Benevolent Society. The building itself was erected as a memorial to Wayne County World War I dead, and the Weil family, merchants of Goldsboro, were prime movers in the project. The public library is housed in the former home of Solomon and Sarah Weil, donated to the town for that use.[14]

GREENSBORO

Memorials, University of North Carolina, Greensboro

The University of North Carolina, which began as the State Normal and Industrial College, soon became the North Carolina College for Women, then the Woman's College of the University of North Carolina. It has long had the custom of naming residence halls and other buildings for men and women who have served the school in some way. The first woman honored in this way was Cornelia Phillips Spencer (1825–1908), of Chapel Hill, North Carolina, q.v., who was instrumental in getting the school established in 1891. Spencer Hall was built in 1904.

A hall was named for the great suffrage leader Anna Howard Shaw (1847–1919), president of the National American Woman's Suffrage Association. Her commencement address here in 1919 was one of her last appearances, and the following year International House was given her name.

Elliott Hall, the student union, was named for Harriet Wiseman Elliott (1884–1947), a leader in the suffrage movement and a teacher of history and political science at the college beginning in 1913. After it became the University of North Carolina, she was made dean of women.[15]

Bell, Martha McFarlane McGee, 1735–1820, Revolutionary War Heroine

Monument, Site of Battle of Guilford Courthouse, National Military Park

The marker, placed by a chapter of the Daughters of the American Revolution in 1929, honors Martha (Mattie) McFarlane McGee Bell's memory. It reads:

"Loyal Whig, Enthusiastic Patriot, Revolutionary Heroine." She was first married to Colonel John McGee, a commissioned officer in the British Army, who established a mill and ordinary on the trading path between the western settlements and the Virginia markets. When he died in 1773, Mattie was the richest widow in the region, with of course many suitors, but for some years she bided her time and continued to run the business. She then married William Bell, who shared her zeal for freedom from England. When General Charles Cornwallis visited the mill, hoping to get cornmeal to feed his troops, Mattie extracted a promise from him that he would not harm the home or the mill.[16]

Cone, Laura Weil, 1888–1970, Civic Leader

Residence Hall and Library, Bennett College

Laura Weil Cone was a courageous and tireless worker for the people of Greensboro. Her husband, Julius W. Cone, was president of a division of Cone Mills. She served on the board of Bennett College and made substantial contributions to it, including the money to furnish the library. She was also on the board of the Moses Cone Memorial Hospital. For many years she was on the board of trustees of the University of North Carolina, participating in the development of the Woman's College and the Consolidated University. A high-rise dormitory at the University of North Carolina at Greensboro is named for her and the student union, Elliott Hall, was in a measure made possible by gifts from the Cone family.[17]

Madison, Dolley Payne Todd, 1768–1849, Wife of U.S. President; NAW

Dolley Madison Room, Greensboro Historical Museum, 130 Summit Avenue. Plaque at Site of Birthplace, Guilford College, 5505 W. Friendly Avenue

Dolley Payne Todd Madison, destined to become one of the young nation's most popular and talked-about White House hostesses, lived in Greensboro for a very short time after her birth. The Paynes, a Quaker family, moved when she was an infant to Virginia and then Philadelphia, Pennsylvania. There she married John Todd, only to be left a widow three years later, with a child. Among her many suitors was James Madison, seventeen years older than Dolley and never considered a handsome man. But Dolley saw something she liked in him and they were married—happily, it turned out, for the union lasted until James's death forty-two years later. The museum, once the First Presbyterian church, has mementoes of Dolley; it is open Tues.-Sat. 10–5, Sun. 2–5. See Ashland and Orange, VA.

Turner, Kerenhappuck, fl. 1770s, Revolutionary War Heroine

Statue, Site of Battle of Guilford Courthouse, National Military Park

During the war Kerenhappuck Turner, in Maryland, received word that her son had been wounded in North Carolina. She saddled up her horse and rode three hundred miles hoping to save him. She found him suffering from a high fever induced by the wounds, and she invented an ingenious method of cooling his fever. As described by a descendant, "She secured tubs in which she bored holes. These tubs she suspended from the rafters and filled with cool water from the Bloody Run which flows nearby. The constant dripping of water on the ghastly wounds allayed the fever and saved her son's life."[18]

GREENVILLE

Cotten, Sallie Southall, 1846–1929, Clubwoman; NAW

Dormitory, East Carolina University

Sallie Southall Cotten was appointed in 1893 one of the lady managers of the Chicago World's Fair. She went about collecting books by North Carolina women to be exhibited with the International Library of women's books. She did so well that she served also for two later expositions. This brought her into touch with women all over the state, many of whom were discussing women's rights, and she helped them to organize clubs. She was instrumental in bringing them together in the North Carolina Federation of Women's Clubs in 1902 and remained active in the federation for twenty-five years. It was a force for progress in local civic reform, establishing libraries, improving education, enforcing child labor laws, and working for prison reform. It formed a loan fund for women's education, naming it the Sallie Southall Cotten Loan Fund. She wrote a history of the federation and was made an honorary life president. She is honored by the naming of a dormitory at the University of North Carolina at Greensboro as well as here. She spent her last years with a daughter in Massachusetts and at a meeting of women in Boston she was introduced as "the Julia Ward Howe of the South" and was given a standing ovation. In 1943 a Liberty ship was named for her.[19]

JUGTOWN

Busbee, Juliana Royster, 1876–1962, Artist

Jugtown Pottery

This area was settled by potters from Staffordshire, England, about 1740, but although their descendants still made pottery up to the twentieth century they had lost the original patterns and glazes. Juliana Royster Busbee and her husband, Jacques Busbee, both artists, knew there was an interest in well-made and well-designed pottery. They encouraged the local workers to produce such ware and, to overcome their resistance, established a potter's shop to be known as Jugtown. Juliana opened a tearoom in Greenwich Village, New York City, where the pottery and other handcrafted items were introduced to the public, while Jacques worked in Jugtown. By 1947, when Jacques died, the pottery enjoyed international acclaim. The pottery was closed for some time after the death of Juliana, but is now open, owned by Country Roads Incorporated, a nonprofit organization devoted to the preservation and development of American handicrafts.[20]

NEW BERN

Latham, Maude Moore, 1871–1951, and Her Daughter, May Gordon Latham Kellenberger, 1893–1978, Preservationists

Maude Moore Latham Memorial Garden and Kellenberger Gardens, Tryon Palace Restoration and Gardens Complex, George and Pollock Streets

Tryon Palace, a magnificent mansion built in 1770 as the home of Royal Governor William Tryon, burned to the ground in 1798, with the exception of one wing. As the seat of government had been moved to Raleigh, North Carolina, there was no attempt to reconstruct the palace. The land was divided and small homes built on it. But in 1939 the original plans for the building were discovered in the New-York Historical Society and this motivated Maude Moore Latham and her daughter, May Gordon Latham Kellenberger, both ardent preservationists, to attempt reconstruction of the historical site. After the war years some $4.5 million of the Latham and Kellenberger family wealth went toward the project. The state bought up the houses and cleared the grounds. The two women had collected art, antiques, and fine period pieces with which to furnish the restored building and two other restored homes. The complex is now a state historical site and a showplace ranking with Colonial Williamsburg, Virginia, a monument not only to the state but to the patriotic women who saved it. It is open for tours Tues.-Sat. 9:30–4, Sun. 1:30–4; closed some holidays; adm.[21]

PEKIN

MacDonald, Flora, 1722–1790, Scottish Heroine

Marker, State 731

A few miles north of the marker is the site of the home established by Flora and Allan MacDonald after 1775. Flora abandoned it after Allan was captured as a Tory prisoner at the battle of Moore's Creek Bridge. See Fayetteville and Red Springs, NC.

PENLAND

Morgan, Lucy Calista, 1890–1982, Craft School Founder

Penland School of Crafts

In 1920 Lucy Calista Morgan went to visit Appalachian School in Mitchell County, high in the Blue Ridge Mountains. Her brother, Rufus Morgan, an Episcopal minister, had founded the school. In addition to the school, the town had five houses, a post office, a general store, and a railroad station, but it was in the heart of a widespread community of cabins located on hillsides and beside creeks, connected only by steep, rough paths. The hill people were direct descendants of the earliest English-speaking settlers of America, "choice Americans," said Morgan. For two centuries they had been isolated, thus preserving Anglo-Saxon speech, music, and dances.

Morgan remained in that community for over forty years. After becoming acquainted with the mountaineers, she realized that the wonderful handicrafts, especially weaving, were not being preserved. At the same time, the women had few sources of income. Morgan studied weaving, brought looms to the mountains, taught the women the old skills, and thus was born Penland School, now recognized the world over as a center for all types of handicrafts, a magnet drawing people from many countries.

Morgan retired in 1962. Four years earlier her memories of the handicraft school, edited by LeGette Blythe, were published as *Gift from the Hills*. The school was then offering courses in over sixty crafts.[22]

RALEIGH

Memorials, North Carolina State University

Many women associated with North Carolina State University have been memorialized by having buildings named for them. Among them is Gertrude Mary Cox (1900–1978), the first woman on the regular teaching staff. From 1940 to 1960 she rose to professor, head of the department of experimental statistics, and director of the Institute of Statistics. She was instrumental in establishing the Research Triangle Institute. She found statistics not a dry and academic subject but a tool fraught with great consequences for the human race. In the course of her work she visited Egypt, South Africa, Thailand, and South American countries and served several of their governments as statistical advisor and program specialist. The seven-story physics and statistics building on the campus was given her name.[23]

The Extension Center was named for Jane Simpson McKimmon (1867–1957), in 1926 the first woman to graduate from the State College of Agriculture and Engineering, now North Carolina State University. She was one of the first to devote herself to a new field for women, one that grew directly out of their established roles as homemakers—home demonstration agents. She began by lecturing at the North Carolina Farmers Institutes in 1908 and organizing home demonstration clubs for rural women and 4-H clubs for girls. In 1911 she was appointed home demonstration agent for the state and in 1924 made assistant director of the state Extension Service. She organized over sixty thousand North Carolina women and girls to help each other toward a better rural life—more efficient homes, better nutrition, wholesome recreation. She herself returned to college late in life, earning a bachelor of science and then a master's degree when she was in her late fifties.[24]

Berry, Harriet Morehead, 1877–1940, Public Official; NAW

Memorial, Highway Commission Building, Salisbury Street

The memorial was erected in 1962 to honor "The Mother of Good Roads in North Carolina." Harriet Morehead Berry entered public administration as a stenographer with the North Carolina Geological and Economic Survey in 1901. She took an intelligent interest in its technical surveys and its promotion of good roads, with the result that three years later she was secretary to the survey. When her boss went into the army in 1917, Berry became acting head and began an intensive campaign for the establishment of a highway commission with authority and funds to create a system of hard-surfaced roads. In 1921 she was successful, universally credited with accomplishing "one of the most stupendous pieces of legislation in the history of the state," to quote the Raleigh *News and Observer*.[25]

Carroll, Delia Dixon, d. 1934, Physician

Carroll Infirmary, Meredith College

Delia Dixon Carroll graduated from the Women's Medical College in Philadelphia, Pennsylvania, in 1895 and five years later came to Meredith College as resident physician, where she remained until her death. In 1962 the infirmary was named for her, as the first woman doctor in Raleigh.

Cox, Gertrude Mary. See North Carolina State University in Raleigh.

Cruikshank, Margaret Mordecai Jones, 1878–1955, College President

Cruikshank Dormitory, St. Mary's College, 900 Hillsborough Street

Margaret Mordecai Jones Cruikshank graduated from St. Mary's School in 1896, then taught there for six years before her marriage to St. Mary's business manager, Ernest Cruikshank. In 1921 he was appointed president of Columbia Institute in Tennessee. He died the following year and she succeeded him as president. A decade later she returned to Raleigh as president of St. Mary's College, the first woman in this position. She remained as president until her retirement in 1946. Twenty years later the dormitory was given her name.[26]

Dix, Dorothea, 1802–1887, Crusader for the Mentally Ill; NAW

Dorothea Dix Hospital (State Hospital), Dix Hill, Boylan Drive

Hospitals in many states honor the name of Dorothea Dix, who spent much of her life changing conditions under which mentally ill patients were cared for. When she began her work, the gentle, compassionate woman from Maine had visited jails, almshouses, and other institutions to find that the insane were almost universally treated with less consideration than was given to animals. She petitioned the Massachusetts Legislature in 1843 to establish hospitals for those whose only "crime" was emotional incapacity. Successful there, she visited other states and persuaded them to do the same. This state institution was authorized in 1848 and opened in 1856. See Tuscaloosa, AL.

Douglas, Mary Peacock, 1903–1970, Librarian

Mary P. Douglas School, 600 Ortega Road

Mary Peacock Douglas was school library advisor in the state Department of Public Instruction from 1930 to 1947, promoting school libraries throughout the state by means of visits, writing, and demonstrations. In 1947 she became the first supervisor of libraries in the Raleigh public schools, remaining in this position until 1968. Her charismatic leadership made a lasting impression on the teachers, librarians, and school administrators who heard her talk and resulted in high standards for libraries and school librarians not only in the state but across the country. When she retired the North Carolina Association of School Librarians established an award named for her to honor outstanding contributions to school libraries.[27]

McKimmon, Jane Simpson. See North Carolina State University in Raleigh.

RED SPRINGS

MacDonald, Flora, 1722–1790, Scottish Heroine

Flora MacDonald College, 2nd Avenue, College, and Peachtree Streets; NR. Marker, State 71 and 211

Flora MacDonald College, founded in 1896 as Floral College by the Fayetteville Presbytery, was in 1914 given the name of Flora MacDonald, the Loyalist who visited America almost a century and a half earlier and got involved in the Revolution—on the losing side. The Robeson Country Day School now occupies the buildings. See Fayetteville and Pekin, NC.

ROANOKE ISLAND

Dare, Virginia, b. 1587, Colonist; NAW

Monument, Three Miles North of Manteo. Statue, Elizabethan Garden. Marker, US 64 and 264, Entrance to Fort Raleigh National Historic Site

The marker commemorates the first English colonies in the New World and the birthplace of Virginia Dare, born August 18, 1587, the first child born of English parents in America. Since all the first colonists disappeared, no one knows how long the child or any of the others survived. Paul Green's drama *The Lost Colony* is presented every summer, late June–early September. The Elizabethan Garden is open daily 9–8 when *The Lost Colony* is presented, 9–5 the rest of the year; adm.

Lander, Louisa, 1826–1923, Sculptor

Statue of Virginia Dare, Elizabethan Garden

Although Virginia Dare undoubtedly died an infant, the sculptor chose to portray her as she might have looked in young womanhood. Louisa Lander, a native of Salem, Massachusetts, was one of a group of American women sculptors who studied and worked in Rome, Italy, during the late nineteenth century.

The statue had an unfortunate career of its own. It was shipped to Boston, Massachusetts, but the ship was wrecked and Lander retrieved the statue after it had been at the bottom of the sea for two years. Repaired and exhibited in Boston, the statue came close to destruction again in a gallery fire. A collector bought it but died before paying for it, and Lander had it back again. She tried to sell it to the state of North Carolina but it was refused. In the end, the state got it as a gift through Lander's will. For some years it was on display in Raleigh, North Carolina, then shuffled from place to place, disregarded and vandalized. In the early 1950s it was rescued and placed on Roanoke Island, near the birthplace of Virginia Dare. Almost none of Lander's other sculptures have survived.[28]

SALISBURY

Tiernan, Frances Christine Fisher, 1846–1920, Writer; NAW

Monument, W. Innes Street. Marker, US 29 at Rowan County Line

Frances Christine Fisher Tiernan wrote genteel, romantic novels that were popular in her day. She herself was genteel and prim, used the pen name Christian Reid, and remained unmarried until she was in her forties. She is best remembered for her early books in which she used her native North Carolina as a background. After her books began bringing in money she traveled in Europe, and after her marriage she lived in Mexico, Haiti, and Santo Domingo, so that the later of her many novels had more exotic settings. She wrote rapidly, corrected little, and worked at her craft consistently. Her *Land of the Sky* gave this section of North Carolina its name. She was born in Salisbury and is buried near the marker, in Chestnut Hill Cemetery.

SEDALIA

Brown, Charlotte Hawkins, 1883?–1961, Educator; NAWM

Site of the Palmer Institute

Charlotte Hawkins Brown was born in North Carolina but moved with her family to Massachusetts, where she attended school while working in a hand laundry. She happened to meet Alice Freeman Palmer, president of Wellesley College, who was so impressed with the young black woman's intelligence that she saw to it that Brown attended normal school. She was then recruited by the American Missionary Association to teach at Bethany Institute in Sedalia. The school was in need of money, and Brown went North in 1902 to raise funds by giving concerts at resorts. On her return she renamed the school, which she now headed, the Palmer Memorial Institute in memory of her mentor, who died that year. In 1911 Brown married another teacher, Edward S. Brown, who served at Palmer Institute until they separated less than five years later. Charlotte built the school up from a rural grammar school emphasizing agricultural and mechanical arts to a liberal arts institution training young blacks through junior college, an institution highly respected throughout the country.

The school was always underfinanced and Brown had to spend much of her time raising funds. Some of her early supporters, such as the missionary association, disapproved of offering liberal arts education to blacks and withdrew their support. Brown then appealed to black southerners and tried to get the state to make Palmer a woman's department of the North Carolina College for Negroes in Durham. Instead the state offered to make Palmer a home for "delinquent colored girls." To this Brown replied: "After forty years of trying to help boys and girls with a desire to do something . . . to turn my whole attention to incorrigibles was more than I could do.''

Brown resigned as president of Palmer Memorial in 1952. The Institute continued until the fall of 1971. The Alice Freeman Palmer building was destroyed by fire, and some months later the school closed. The town of Sedalia, determined that the memory of the woman and the institution should not die, plans to establish in its place a center for Afro-American history and to turn the home and gravesite of Brown into a memorial in her honor.[29]

WASHINGTON

Dimock, Susan, 1847–1875, Physician; NAW

Marker, Site of Home, E. Main Street

Susan Dimock was born here and lived in Washington until after the Civil War, which closed the Washington Academy she attended and caused the family to lose most of its possessions. Her father died in 1864 and Dimock and her mother moved to Massachusetts. She had begun to study Latin, with a desire to become a doctor, and in 1866 she became a student at the New England Hospital for Women and Children. She spent three years at the University of Zurich in Switzerland, graduated with high honors, undertook more courses in Vienna, Austria, and Paris, France, and returned to New England Hospital as the best-trained woman physician in the country, with a promising future. In 1875 she took a leave of absence from her job as resident physician to visit England. The ship foundered off the Scilly Isles, almost all on board being lost. Dimock's body was recovered and returned to Boston for burial. In May 1872 the North Carolina Medical Society had made her an honorary member.

WILMINGTON

Eddy, Mary Baker Glover, 1821–1910, Church Founder; NAW

Marker, 3rd and Market Streets

Mary Baker Glover Eddy, the founder of the Christian Science Church, spent part of 1844 in Wilmington. She had not yet discovered the science of healing. In 1843 she married George Washington Glover, who brought her from New Hampshire to South Carolina and then to Wilmington, where he was a successful building contractor and a popular Mason. In June of 1844 George's business suffered losses and he contracted ''bilious fever'' and died. Mary, expecting a child, ill, grief-stricken, and without funds, was cared for by the local Masons, who took charge of the burial and sent an escort to accompany her back to her family in New England. During her short stay in Wilmington she became something of a celebrity because of her verses attacking the Whigs and Henry Clay.[30]

Greenhow, Rose O'Neal, c. 1815–1864, Confederate Spy; NAW

Monument, Oakdale Cemetery. Marker, 3rd and Dock Streets

The monument, a marble cross, is inscribed: ''Mrs. Rose O'N. Greenhow, a bearer of dispatches to the Confederate Government.'' At the outbreak of the Civil War Rose O'Neal Greenhow, a politically active widow, became involved in a Confederate espionage ring in Washington, D.C. She was arrested and imprisoned in 1862, first in her own home then in the Old Capitol Prison, where she waved a Confederate flag from the window and bedeviled the guards. To get rid of her, the War Department sent her South, where of course she was received with pleasure, her reputation having preceded her. In August 1863, she went abroad as an unofficial agent for the Confederacy, after publishing the journal of her imprisonment, which in turn assured her a warm welcome in England and France. A year later, the ship on which she was returning to America foundered off the coast near Wilmington while running a federal blockade. Fearing capture again, she insisted, against advice, on going ashore in a small boat. It overturned. Weighted down with the gold coins she had collected as royalties on her book, Greenhow drowned. Her body, washed ashore, was buried with full military honors.

Whistler, Anna Matilda McNeill, 1804–1881, "Whistler's Mother"

Marker, 3rd and Orange Streets

The mother of the eccentric artist James McNeill Whistler was born near this spot. She married Major George Whistler and when James was born they were living in Lowell, Massachusetts. Widowed in 1849, Anna Matilda McNeill Whistler's life centered around her son, then fourteen. In 1865 she joined him in London, England, where he was making a name for himself as one of the great painters. Anna was of a poetic, deeply religious nature. A small number of her letters, which had lain untouched for some eighty years, was found in the 1930s. In them she tells the story of her famous portrait. James had wanted to paint her standing, but as she was nearing seventy, she found it too difficult to stand for a long period, so he seated her in a chair. He exhibited the portrait in 1872 at the Royal Academy. Now his best-known work, it brought six hundred dollars when sold to the French government for the Louvre.[31]

NOTES

In addition to the sources mentioned below, I have had assistance from the Greensboro College Library; the Library of the University of North Carolina at Greensboro; the Public Library of Charlotte and Mecklenburg County; the New Hanover County Public Library; the Richard A. Thornton Library in Oxford; the Warren County Memorial Library in

Warrenton; the Cumberland County Public Library in Fayetteville; Montreat-Anderson College in Montreat; Penland School; North Carolina Department of Cultural Resources, Historical Publications Section, Division of Archives and History; Mary H. Kerr, of Warrenton; and Ruth Camblos of Asheville, whose *Round the Mountains* is a valuable travel guide.

1. Marguerite Schumann, *Tar Heel Sights: A Guide to North Carolina's Heritage* (Charlotte, N.C.: East Woods Press, 1983); Lucy Morgan and LeGette Blythe, *Gift from the Hills: Miss Lucy Morgan's Story of Her Unique Penland School* (Chapel Hill: University of North Carolina Press, 1971; first pub. 1958).

2. *Dictionary of North Carolina Biography*, ed. William S. Powell, vol. 1 (Chapel Hill: University of North Carolina Press, 1979), hereafter cited as Powell; correspondence and brochure, Appalachian State University.

3. Powell; correspondence and clippings, John C. Campbell Folk School.

4. Albert Coates, *By Her Own Bootstraps: A Saga of Women in North Carolina* (Chapel Hill, N.C.: thc Author, 1975).

5. Correspondence, clippings, and brochures, Mint Museum. Remodeling was in progress as this guide went to press.

6. *Mothers of Achievement in American History, 1776–1976*, comp. American Mothers Committee (Rutland, Vt.: Charles E. Tuttle Co., 1976); correspondence and clippings, Crossnore School, Inc.

7. Correspondence, West Carolina University.

8. Victor Robinson, *White Caps: The Story of Nursing* (Philadelphia, Pa.: J. B. Lippincott, 1946).

9. Powell.

10. Powell.

11. Duke University Bulletin; *Current Biography*, 1966.

12. Powell; *Women in the American Revolution*, comp. Mollie Somerville (n.p.: National Society Daughters of the American Revolution, 1974).

13. Sally Smith Booth, *The Women of '76* (New York: Hastings House, 1973).

14. Bernard Postal and Lionel Koppman, *A Jewish Tourist's Guide to the United States* (Philadelphia, Pa.: Jewish Publication Society of America, 1954).

15. Elisabeth A. Bowles, *A Good Beginning: The First Four Decades of the University of North Carolina at Greensboro* (Chapel Hill: University of North Carolina Press, 1967); Marguerite Schumann and Virginia T. Lathrop, *Bricks and People: A Walking Guide to the University of North Carolina at Greensboro* (Greensboro, N.C.: Alumni Association, 1973).

16. Powell.

17. Powell.

18. Robinson, *White Caps*.

19. Powell.

20. Powell; Ralph and Terry Kovel, *The Kovels' Collector's Guide to American Art Pottery* (New York: Crown Publishers, 1974).

21. Michael Olmert, "Great Collectors," *Historic Preservation* 34 (Nov.-Dec. 1982).

22. Morgan and Blythe, op. cit.

23. Correspondence and clippings, North Carolina State University at Raleigh.

24. Ibid.; Jane Simpson McKimmon, *When We're Green We Grow* (Chapel Hill: University of North Carolina Press, 1945).

25. Powell.

26. Powell; correspondence, St. Mary's College.

27. *Dictionary of American Library Biography*, ed. Bohdan S. Wynor (Littleton, Colo.: Libraries Unlimited, Inc., 1978).

28. Charlotte S. Rubinstein, *American Women Artists* (New York: Avon Books, 1982).

29. Terra Hunter, "The Correct Thing: Charlotte Hawkins Brown and the Palmer Institute," *Southern Exposure* 11 (Sept.-Oct. 1983).

30. Robert Peel, *Mary Baker Eddy: The Years of Discovery* (New York: Holt, Rinehart and Winston, 1966).

31. Anne Miller Downes, "A Portrait of Whistler by His Mother," *New York Times*, July 8, 1934, section 6; *New York Times*, May 5, 1934.

OKLAHOMA

ANADARKO

National Hall of Fame for Famous American Indians, US 62

The National Hall of Fame for Famous American Indians was organized in 1952 to recognize famous Native American leaders. Four women are represented: Alice Brown Davis, Roberta Campbell Lawson, Pocahontas, and Sacajawea. Susan Ryan Peters, a white woman adopted into the Kiowa tribe, was given special recognition in 1983.

Alice Brown Davis (1852–1935, NAW) was born in Indian country more than half a century before Oklahoma became a state. With her husband, George Rollin Davis, she established a trading post at Arbeka. When the youngest of their ten children was three, Davis was for some unexplained reason left to her own resources. She superintended the ranch, the store, and the post office, directing the activities of cowboys, farmers, and clerks and acting as legal representative of the Seminoles. When Oklahoma became a state in 1907 the Seminole Nation became a county and the tribal government was stripped of its power. Davis, as interpreter, advisor, and matriarch of her people, was virtually their leader. In 1922 she was briefly appointed chieftain of the Seminoles by President Warren G. Harding.

The bronze portrait bust of Davis, the work of Willard Stone, was dedicated in 1964 at the Oklahoma Pavilion of the New York World's Fair and then put in place in the outdoor museum of the American Indian Hall of Fame. The donors were members of Davis's family. Davis is also in the Oklahoma Hall of Fame (see Oklahoma City, OK).

Roberta Campbell Lawson (1878–1940, NAW) was the daughter of a Delaware, or Lenni-Lenape, Indian. She was a student of Indian music and culture. Her husband, Eugene Lawson, was a founder of the First National Bank of Nowata, Oklahoma, of which Roberta was a director. She began her interest in women's clubs in Nowata, organizing the town's first such club and serving as

Alice Brown Davis was the first woman chieftain of the Seminole Indians in Oklahoma. The bust, by Willard Stone, is in the National Hall of Fame for Famous American Indians, Anadarko, Oklahoma. Photography by Settle Studio.
Courtesy National Hall of Fame for Famous American Indians.

Roberta Campbell Lawson, Delaware Indian, was president of the National Federation of Women's Clubs. The bust, by Leonard McMurry, is in the National Hall of Fame for Famous American Indians, Anadarko, Oklahoma. Photography by Settle Studio. Courtesy National Hall of Fame for Famous American Indians.

its president. After she and her husband moved to Tulsa, Oklahoma, her club work expanded. She was an officer of the district, then the state Federation of Women's Clubs, and in 1935 was elected president of the General Federation for a three-year term. The state federation donated the bronze bust by Leonard McMurry in 1968.

Pocahontas (1595?–1617, NAW), the Virginian, is one of the most romantic figures in American history. The bust by Kenneth Campbell was unveiled in the Old Tower Church, Jamestown, Virginia, in 1965, before being placed in the Hall of Fame as a gift of the National Society of Colonial Dames.

Sacajawea (c. 1786–1812, NAW), a Shoshoni Indian, was famous for her role as guide and interpreter for the Lewis and Clark expedition to the Pacific in 1805–6. Her bust, by Leonard McMurry, was put in place in 1959.

Susan Ryan Peters (1873–1965) was a specialist in Indian art and artists. Her encouragement of the Native American culture brought her recognition from both Indians and whites. In 1954 the Kiowa tribe adopted her as a blood sister. A Susie Peters Art Scholarship is given each year to an outstanding art student.

The Hall of Fame is operated by the Oklahoma Department of Tourism and Recreation. Busts are displayed in a permanent outdoor memorial in a landscaped setting. It is open daily 9–5; closed holidays.[1]

BARTLESVILLE

Miller, Ellen Howard, 1862–1944, Farmer and Wildlife Protector

Ellen Howard Miller Game Preserve

A dove, said Ellen Howard Miller, can do as much work as a farm hand in destroying weed seeds, and one quail might gobble up as many as a thousand insects in a single day. Her interest in the birds of Oklahoma was not a sentimental one, for she ran a two-hundred-acre farm about twenty miles south of Bartlesville. For seven years she was chair of the State Federation of Women's Clubs' committee on birds, flowers, and wildlife, and during this period she went to the University of Oklahoma for two years to study ornithology. The "birdwoman of Oklahoma" lectured on wildlife. In 1926 the state fish and game commission made her farm the nucleus of the two-thousand-acre game preserve named for her.[2]

Starr, Belle, 1848–1889, Bandit; NAW

Statue, Woolaroc Museum, State 123

Belle Starr was born in Missouri and spent her life in various western states, settling in Oklahoma sometime around 1880 after she married Sam Starr, a Cherokee outlaw. Their home on the Canadian River was a hideout for Jesse James and other unsavory characters. See Carthage, MO, and Dallas, TX.

The Woolaroc Museum was established by Mr. and Mrs. Frank Phillips. It is open Tues.-Sun. 10–5.

CLINTON

Crawford, Isabel, 1865–1961, Missionary

Crawford House, 600 N. 13th Street (Private); NR

Isabel Crawford graduated from the Baptist Missionary Training School in Chicago, Illinois, in 1893 and was sent to work with the Kiowa, then "wild blanket Indians." She founded the Saddle Mountain Mission near present-day Hobart, Oklahoma, and ran it until 1906. She gained the trust and later the love of the Indians by standing up for their rights against exploitative whites. "There seems to be an organized effort to fleece them," she said. She had a lively pen and wrote several books about the mission, attributing her success to "splendid helpers, a cast-iron constitution, Scotch determination, Irish nonsense, the Divine call and the power of the Holy Spirit."

When the Kiowas wanted a church of their own they tried to raise the money for materials by contributions. Crawford suggested that they make quilts for sale. Both men and women went to work, and a third of the money raised for the church came from this source. It took six years. The first service in the "church built by quilts" was held in 1903. Three years later, when Crawford announced her resignation, one of the Indians rose and asked, "When you heap die, will you come back and be buried with us? We no speak English, when Jesus come you talk for us." She promised, and after her death her body was sent to Saddle Mountain. The pallbearers were six descendants of her first converts.

The Clinton house is now the only extant structure associated with Crawford. She owned it from 1916 until 1941, during a period when she was doing organization work for the American Baptist Home Mission Society and writing about her experiences.[3]

EDMOND

Canton, Ruby, 1885?–1928, Librarian

Memorial Window, Chapel of Song, Central State University

Ruby Canton was appointed librarian at Central State Normal School (now University) in 1908 and was on the faculty here for twenty years. It is said that when she became librarian she found records of over four thousand books never returned by their borrowers. She went about town with a wheelbarrow and collected all but one. She was the first person to teach library science in Oklahoma.[4]

FORT TOWSON

Orton, Dorothy Jane, 1915–1968, Army Officer and Preservationist

Fort Towson Historic Site, Off US 70; NR

Dorothy Jane Orton was the prime mover in the effort to restore the historical old army post, the place where the Confederate Indian forces under Stand Watie surrendered at the close of the Civil War. She was born in Fort Towson and attended school here before leaving for college. Early in World War II she enlisted in the Women's Army Corps, leaving after two and a half years with the rank of captain. In 1950 she was recalled to active duty and for the next three years she was commanding officer at Fort Lee, Virginia, and at Camp Breckenridge, Kentucky, and staff officer in Oklahoma City, Oklahoma. On her return to Fort Towson, she was appointed postmistress. She was active in the Fort Towson Commission's restoration of the military post. It is open Mon.-Fri. 8–5, Sat.-Sun. 1–5.[5]

LAWTON

Beal, Mattie (Payne), 1879–1931, Town Promoter

Mattie Beal House, 5th Street and Summit Avenue; NR

Mattie Beal drew Number 2 in the reservation land lottery of 1901 when the Kiowa-Comanche reservation of three million acres was opened. A man named Woods, who drew Number 1, chose a strip of land a mile long and a quarter of a mile wide, instead of the usual half mile square homestead, thus closing off Beal's access to the new town of Lawton. This ungallant act earned him the name of Hog and made him a first "male chauvinist pig."

Beal, a young and pretty telephone operator, got a lot of publicity, which brought her over five hundred letters proposing marriage from all over the United States and England. She chose Charles Warren Payne, co-owner of a lumberyard in the new town. She commuted her claim for townsite purposes, and more than three hundred new homes were built on Lawton's first subdivision, Beal Addition. Beal set aside lots for a park, a school, and a church (present Beal Heights Presbyterian). She and her husband remained town boosters all their lives. They built their colonial-style mansion in 1907; in 1971 when it was threatened with demolition, a committee was formed to restore the building for use as a museum. It is open only on the second Sun. of each month, 2–4, and by appointment (call Lawton Heritage Association); adm.[6]

MUSKOGEE

Foreman, Carolyn Thomas, 1872–1967, Historian

Thomas-Foreman Home, 1419 W. Okmulgee Street; NR

Carolyn Thomas Foreman came to Muskogee with her family in 1897 when her father, John R. Thomas, was appointed special judge of Indian Territory. He built this home the following year. Carolyn witnessed history being made as the town grew into a city, the territory became a state, and the Indians changed from tribal groups to state citizens. The Thomas home itself was a seedbed of change, for all visitors to the territory came to partake of its hospitality and discuss politics.

In 1905 Carolyn married Grant Foreman, who had come with the Dawes Commission to oversee the Indian allotments and then formed a law partnership with her father. The young couple shared an interest in history and writing and both loved travel. Carolyn's knowledge of French and Spanish were useful in her researches in foreign archives. In addition to her article writing she produced six scholarly books and coauthored another with her husband.

The Foremans lived in the family home for many years. After Carolyn died, it became the property of her niece, who deeded it to the Oklahoma Historical Society, with the many books and artifacts collected over the years by the Foremans. It is open to the public Tues.-Fri. 9–5, Sat.-Sun. 2–5.[7]

Francis, Milly, 1802?–1848, Creek Indian Heroine; NAW

Monument, Bacone College Campus

Milly Francis moved to Indian Territory along the "trail of tears" when the Creeks were forced to leave Georgia. In 1842 she was found living in poverty near Muskogee, then widowed with young children, and her case was reported to Washington, D.C. She had once saved the life of Captain Duncan McKrimmon of the Georgia militia, and the government voted her a pension of ninety-six dollars a year and a medal, but through the stupidity of the Indian service she died before she received any of the money. She had become a convert to Christianity. The monument was erected in 1933 by the faculty and students of Bacone College, a Baptist Indian college.

Journeycake, Sally, fl. 1830s, Delaware Indian

Memorial Building, Bacone State College

Sally Journeycake is memorialized chiefly because she was the first convert to Christianity among the Delaware (Lenni-Lenape) Indians. She moved from Ohio to Kansas when the whites broke their treaty with her people and was baptized there in 1853. Her son, Charles Journeycake, founded Bacone College. When the memorial was dedicated in 1937, the speaker was Sally's great granddaughter, Roberta Campbell Lawson (see Anadarko, OK).

Robertson, Alice Mary, 1854–1931, Teacher and Congresswoman; NAW

Alice Robertson Junior High School, S Street and Callahan Avenue

"I cannot be bought, I cannot be sold, I cannot be intimidated"—that was Alice Mary Robertson's slogan as she ran for Congress at the age of sixty-six. She had spent many of her years working for Indian education, teaching and farming. In 1920 she was elected to the House of Representatives, the second woman member of Congress.

The first Oklahoma congresswoman was a determined foe of woman's suffrage and had once been vice president of the state antisuffrage league. She began her congressional career by denouncing the League of Women Voters, though sometime later she changed her opinion. She fought the Sheppard-Towner bill, which funded clinics for mothers and children, because she felt it was an entering wedge to paternalistic legislation. She opposed the League of Nations because it would include people who believed in idols. She was against releasing Eugene Debs from prison. She was a foe of immigration: "Atheism, bigotry, fanaticism, defiance of American ideals—all are evils attendant upon the poison stream of immigration." She fought the bill to establish a federal Department of Education. She voted against the soldiers' bonus. By the time she ran for reelection in 1922 she had made so many enemies that she was soundly defeated.

She was a heroine, however, to many at home. Schools and university dormitories were named for her. Trees were planted in her honor. Portraits were painted and unveiled. In 1929 she was selected as Oklahoma's most famous woman. It was even proposed that she represent Oklahoma in Statuary Hall in Washington, D.C., but she lost out to Will Rogers. See Okmulgee, OK.[8]

NORMAN

Memorials, University of Oklahoma, University Boulevard and W. Boyd Street

The University of Oklahoma has four residential buildings in the women's quadrangle, with sixteen residential units. Each unit bears the name of an exceptional Oklahoma woman. Included are Alice Brown Davis (see Anadarko and Wewoka, OK), Roberta Campbell Lawson (see Anadarko, OK), Jane McCurtain, and Cynthia Ann Parker. The others are named for outstanding community women and faculty members.

Jane McCurtain (1842–1924) was born in Fort Towson, Oklahoma, the daughter of a Choctaw father and part-white mother. She married Jackson McCurtain in 1865 and when he was made chief of the Choctaw Nation she was his advisor and secretary. He died in 1885 and she slipped into his place and for thirty-nine years was leader of her people.[9]

Cynthia Ann Parker (1827–1864, NAW) was one of the few white women in American history who have been captured by Indians and found the Indian way of life a good one. Though returned to her relatives after many years with the Comanches, Parker felt that her life was no longer worth living apart from her Indian family and when hope was gone she died. Her son, Quanah, became one of the great chiefs of the Comanches, the last to surrender in 1875. A child when his mother was taken from him, he learned of her death only when grown. He then took her name for his family name and had her remains brought to Fort Sill for burial. He was buried beside her. Both bodies were moved in 1957 to the post cemetery in Lawton, Oklahoma. See Groesbeck and Poyner, TX.

Two residence halls for freshmen women are named for early Oklahoma missionaries and teachers: Elizabeth Jane Fulton Hester (1839–1929) and Ann Worcester Robertson (1826–1905, NAW). Hester taught at the Chickasaw Manual Labor Academy in the 1850s (see Tishomingo, OK). Robertson came from New England to Indian Territory with her missionary parents and became a linguist, translating religious works into the Creek language (see Park Hill, OK).

OKLAHOMA CITY

Oklahoma Hall of Fame, Oklahoma Heritage Center, 201 N.W. 14th Street

The Oklahoma Hall of Fame was started in 1928 by the Oklahoma Memorial Association to honor living persons who had rendered outstanding service to their fellow citizens. An annual banquet is held by the Oklahoma Historical Society to induct members into the Hall, and an "Hour of Remembrance" is held to honor those who have passed away. Portraits and photographs of honorees are displayed on the third floor of the Heritage Center.[10]

A few of the large number of women who have been inducted and who have not been noted elsewhere in this guide are the following: Maimee Lee Browne (1881–1963) came to Oklahoma City in 1923. She was born in Texas and had lived after her marriage in Texas and New Orleans, where she organized a State Congress of Parents and Teachers. She is credited with establishing parent education classes in the city schools. She was inducted into the Hall of Fame in 1938 and chosen Oklahoma Mother of the Year in 1951.[11]

Rachel Caroline Eaton (1869–1938), inducted into the Hall of Fame in 1936, was recognized as "the first woman of Indian descent to achieve distinction as an educator and writer of history." She was born in the Cherokee Nation, her mother a namesake and descendant of Nancy Ward, the "Beloved Woman" of the Cherokees. After teaching at the Cherokee Female Seminary in Tahlequah and in other schools, she was elected superintendent of schools in Rogers County.[12]

Lucia Loomis Ferguson (1886–1962) wrote ''The Woman's View,'' a column in the Scripps-Howard newspapers, for almost thirty years. She also wrote the ''Lucia Loomis'' column of advice to readers who sought help with problems. With her husband, Walter Ferguson, she had published, in the small town of Cherokee, the *Cherokee Republican*.[13]

Edith Johnson (1879–1961) was called Miss Edith by her faithful readers, who watched for her columns in the *Daily Oklahoman* for half a century.[14]

Anna Brosius Korn (1869?–1965) founded the Oklahoma Memorial Association and Hall of Fame and was its first president. She wrote the Oklahoma state song as well as the Missouri state song. She also wrote the legislation establishing November 16 as Oklahoma Day.[15]

Anna Lewis (1885–1961) was of Choctaw descent. She attended the Tuskahoma Female Institute before Oklahoma was a state. Later in life she built her own home on the site of the institute, using stone from the old building. She began her half century of teaching in Indian schools and at her retirement was head of the Department of History at the Oklahoma College for Women in Chickasaw. After she retired she lived in her beloved home in Tuskahoma.[16]

Jessie Elizabeth Randolph Moore (1871–1956) was born in the Chickasaw Nation after the tribe's removal to Indian Territory. She was admitted to the bar in 1923, was appointed assistant commissioner of charities and corrections the following year, and in 1942 was elected clerk of the state supreme court. She was a member of the Chickasaw Council and her last great honor was to serve as official representative of the Chickasaw Nation in 1954 at the dedication in Memphis of the Chickasaw Wing of the U.S. Air Force.[17]

Muriel Hazel Wright (1889–1975, NAWM) was a teacher, editor, historian, advocate of Indian rights, and civic worker. She was the one who, with George Shirk, initiated the historical marker program in Oklahoma. She was part Choctaw, proud of her Indian heritage, a member of the Choctaw Advisory Council. She was a contributor to the *Chronicles of Oklahoma*, published by the Oklahoma Historical Society, from 1922, associate editor 1943–55, and editor 1955–73. In 1971 the North American Indian Women's Association nominated her as the outstanding Indian woman of the twentieth century.[18]

Fraser, Laura Gardin, 1889–1966, Sculptor

Oklahoma Run, *Relief, Cowboy Hall of Fame and Western Heritage Center, 1700 N.E. 63rd Street*

Laura Gardin Fraser studied in Chicago, Illinois, with the noted sculptor James Earle Fraser, and then she married him. They formed one of the truly successful husband-wife teams in art history. The James Earle and Laura Fraser Studio Collection is housed in the Payne Kirkpatrick Memorial at the center.

Mesta, Perle Skirvin, 1889–1975, Politician and Diplomat; NAWM

Mesta Park Historic District; NR. Perle Mesta Room, Skirvin Plaza

Perle Skirvin Mesta was a young lady when her father, William Skirvin, invested some of his oil wealth in the fourteen-story Skirvin Hotel in Oklahoma City. It is still in business, one of the country's grand old hotels.

Perle married George Mesta in 1915, and they went to Washington, D.C., where Perle directed the Stage Door Canteen and developed talents as a political hostess. In the 1930s she joined the National Woman's Party and lobbied for passage of the Equal Rights Amendment. She worked within the Republican party until 1940, when she changed her allegiance to the Democratic party. During Harry S Truman's presidential campaign she gave an elaborate party in his honor at the Hotel Skirvin. After his election, when his daughter Margaret sang in Oklahoma City, Perle arranged another of her famous affairs at the hotel.

Although Mesta's appointment in 1949 to the post of U.S. minister to the Grand Duchy of Luxembourg was considered a return for her political help, it was an acknowledgment that she was a woman of common sense and a shrewd business woman, one who managed two large inheritances, her husband's and her father's. (George died in 1925, and she became a director in the Mesta Machine Company. Skirvin died in 1944.) Mesta was the third American woman to be given a diplomatic post. When asked how she wished to be addressed, she said, ''You can call me Madam Minister.'' Her remark was publicized and ''Call Me Madam,'' a musical about a woman ambassador, became a success on Broadway.

Mesta never forgot her Oklahoma roots, and she spent her last years here. Mesta Park is roughly bounded by N.W. 23rd Street, Walker Avenue, N.W. 16th Street, and Western Avenue. The house at 700 N.W. 16th Street was the Skirvin home.[19]

OKMULGEE

Robertson, Alice Mary, 1854–1931, Teacher and Congresswoman; NAW

Marker, State 56

The marker is near the site of the Nuyaka Mission, nine miles west of town, a mission to the Creek Nation founded in 1882 through the efforts of Alice Mary Robertson, later the first woman elected to Congress from Oklahoma (see Muskogee, OK). Her sister, Augusta Robertson Moore, was the first superintendent of the school. They were granddaughters of the Reverend Samuel A. Worcester and daughters of Ann Eliza Worcester and William S. Robertson of Park Hill, Oklahoma, q.v., the most influential white missionaries among the Creeks. The family gave much to the culture and education of the territory. Still remaining of the mission at Okmulgee is the ruin of a storm cellar.[20]

PARK HILL

Robertson, Ann Eliza Worcester, 1826–1905, Missionary and Linguist; NAW

Marker, North of Junction of US 62 and State 82

The marker indicates the site of the Park Hill Press, established in 1836 by Ann Eliza Worcester Robertson's parents, Samuel A. and Ann Orr Worcester, New England missionaries among the Cherokees. They brought with them from the Cherokee Nation in Georgia a printing press where they produced hundreds of Cherokee and English books and pamphlets. Robertson was ten when she accompanied the family on the long trek to the Cherokees' new homeland in Indian Territory. Her father, a scholar, wished her to have a classical education, so she was sent to an academy in Vermont, where she excelled in Greek and Latin. She returned to teach at Park Hill, then was appointed to a position at the Tullahassee Manual Labor School for the Creek Indians. She married the school principal, William S. Robertson. She learned the Creek language and with her husband prepared Creek texts for publication. Among her seven children was Alice Mary Robertson (see Muskogee and Okmulgee, OK).

The Civil War disrupted the Creek Nation. They joined the Confederacy, closed the schools, and ordered the missionaries to leave. After the war the Robertsons were invited to return; they rebuilt the school and reopened it, teaching faithfully for another twelve years, when the school burned down. William died in 1881 and Ann Eliza went to live with Alice Mary Robertson, where she completed the New Testament in Creek, an accomplishment she saw as "the crowning joy of my life." She spent her last twenty-five years translating into Creek the Psalms and Genesis and a hymnal, working from the Greek and Hebrew. She is buried in the Worcester cemetery at Park Hill beside her parents. The cemetery is maintained by the Oklahoma Historical Society.

TISHOMINGO

Hester, Elizabeth Jane Fulton, 1839–1929, Teacher

Betty Fulton Hall, Murray State College

Elizabeth Jane Fulton Hester was born in north Georgia where her father was a missionary to the Cherokees. In 1856 she felt called to go to the Indian Territory and began teaching at the Chickasaw Manual Labor Academy. Soon after her arrival she married George B. Hester, a merchant from Raleigh, North Carolina, who had come out with goods to sell. They lived in Tishomingo until 1861, she continuing to teach while he ran a store. After the schools disbanded because of the Civil War, they moved to Boggy Depot, Oklahoma. Throughout the war she cared for many sick and wounded soldiers and emigrants, turning the store into a hospital, while her husband was in the army.[21]

TULSA

Clubb, Laura A., 1873–1952, Art Collector

Clubb Collection, Philbrook Art Center, 2727 S. Rockford Road

Laura A. Clubb, a schoolteacher, married a cattleman, and after the family became wealthy from oil she began to buy paintings. She developed a discriminating taste, and when her collection grew she housed it first in the Clubb Hotel in Kaw City, Oklahoma, her hometown. It is now an important part of the art center in Tulsa. The center is the former residence of Mr. and Mrs. Waite Phillips, who gave it, with the grounds and funds for maintenance, to the city. Clubb was inducted into the Oklahoma Hall of Fame in 1931, as "one of the nation's foremost woman art collectors, pioneer teacher, one time oratory instructor at the Oklahoma Baptist University."

Another important collection at the Philbrook is the Indian Room, containing art and objects left by Roberta Campbell Lawson. It was given to the center by Lawson's son and his wife in 1947 as a tribute to her efforts to preserve the traditions of the Indians.

The center is open Tues.-Sat. 10–5, Sun. 1–5, and Tues. evenings; closed holidays; adm.[22]

Sacajawea, c. 1786–1812, Shoshoni Indian Guide; NAW

Statue, Gilcrease Institute of American History and Art, 2500 W. Newton Street

The statue of Sacajawea pointing the way for Lewis and Clark on their westward journey in 1805–6 is by Henry Lion, modeled after a sketch by Charles M. Russell. The romantic young Shoshoni woman who traveled across the country with the Corps of Discovery has many memorials. Another statue depicting her with Lewis and Clark, executed by Russell, is at the National Cowboy Hall of Fame and Western Heritage Center in Oklahoma City. See also Anadarko, OK.

The institute is a center for the study and exhibition of materials illustrating the development of the West from the pre-Columbian period through the nineteenth century. It is open Mon.-Sat. 9–5, Sun. and holidays (except Christmas) 1–5.

WAPANUCKA

Greenleaf, Mary Coombs, 1799–1857, Teacher

Marker, State 7 and 70

All that remains of the Wapanucka Academy, established by the Chickasaw Council for Chickasaw girls in 1852, are piles of stones and the grave of Mary Coombs Greenleaf, about a mile and a half northeast of the marker. The site is listed in the National Register, and the grave is maintained as a memorial by the Oklahoma Historical Society.

Greenleaf was a middle-aged woman living in Newburyport, Massachusetts, when she sent in her application for an appointment as a missionary to the Indians. She was sent to Indian Territory to teach at Wapanucka, warned that she might have to learn to ride a horse. She did and found it delightful. When school began she was kept busy, for in addition to teaching she had the care of thirty-three Indian girls while out of the classrooms. She had to cut and fit dresses for all of them and then supervise the girls' sewing. "But I did not come here to live at my ease," she wrote, "and I rejoice to labor with these red children, and train them up in the way they should go." They were trained to be good housekeepers and mothers, in accord with the general ideas of society at the time. Unfortunately, the little teacher was given just a year to labor among the Indians, for she died in 1857, a victim of dysentery, and was buried on the hillside near the school. A year later the Massachusetts Sabbath School Society published the *Life and Letters of Miss Mary C. Greenleaf, Missionary to the Chickasaw Indians*.[23]

WATONGA

Ferguson, Elva Shartle, 1867–1947, Newspaper Publisher

T. B. Ferguson Museum, 521 N. Weigel Street; NR

Elva Shartle Ferguson and her husband, Thompson Benton (T.B.) Ferguson, joined the rush to Oklahoma in 1892 when the Cheyenne-Arapaho country was opened for settlement. They chose a site in Watonga and established the *Watonga Republican*, a joint enterprise. When the new family arrived in town, Elva saw the saloons and heard the sounds of drunken revelry and vowed to return to Kansas the next day. "The homesickness of that night was enough to make any woman regret the thought of becoming a pioneer and the lofty ambition of wanting to be a state builder."

Morning brought brighter prospects, and the family remained, although, according to Elva, "it took about as much genius during that period to be a successful housewife and mother as it did to edit a paper. For the first year there were no meat markets, no home-grown vegetables, and although there were many cattle ranches, few milk cows." In 1901, T. B. was appointed territorial governor and Elva became a popular First Lady and politician. After T. B.'s death in 1921, Elva continued to edit the paper until 1930. Edna Ferber, whose heroines were almost always strong, ambitious women, lived with Elva for three weeks; the main character in her popular novel *Cimarron* is based on Elva.

The Ferguson house was saved from demolition by the Watonga Mothers' Self Culture Club in 1967. Ownership was transferred to the city and then to the state, which restored it as a museum. It is open Tues.-Sat. 9–5, Sun. 1–5.[24]

WEWOKA

Davis, Alice Brown, 1852–1935, Seminole Chief; NAW

Seminole Museum, 524 S. Wewoka. Marker, US 270

Part of the Seminole Museum is dedicated to Alice Brown Davis, who was the first woman chief of the Seminoles (see Anadarko, OK). She was superintendent of the Emahaka Mission here in 1908. The school was abandoned in 1914 and accidentally destroyed by fire in 1927. Wewoka is now the county seat of Seminole County, which comprises the former lands of the Seminoles. The museum, maintained by the Seminole Nation Historical Society, is open Feb.-Dec. daily 1–5, except Christmas Day.[25]

NOTES

In addition to the sources listed below, I have had assistance from Paul Lambert, Oklahoma Heritage Association; the library at East Central University; the libraries of the University of Oklahoma; Ponca City Chamber of Commerce; and the Oklahoma Tourism and Recreation Department.

1. Mrs. William S. Key, "Tribute to Alice Brown Davis," *Chronicles of Oklahoma* (cited hereafter as *Chronicles*) 43 (Spring 1965); correspondence and brochure, National Hall of Fame for Famous American Indians.
2. Lillian Dilly, "Ellen Howard Miller," *Chronicles* 26 (Summer 1948).
3. Hugh D. Corwin, "Saddle Mountain Mission and Church," *Chronicles* 36 (Summer 1958); Tully Morrison, "Isabel Crawford: Missionary to the Kiowa Indians," *Chronicles* 40 (Spring 1962); nomination form, National Register.
4. Muriel Wright, "Anna May Wilkerson Canton," *Chronicles* 26 (Winter 1948–49), a biography of Ruby Canton's mother; correspondence, Central State University.
5. Frances Imon, "Dorothy Jane Orton," *Chronicles* 46 (Winter 1968–69).
6. Correspondence, brochures, and National Register nomination form, Lawton Heritage Foundation.
7. J. Stanley Clark, "Carolyn Thomas Foreman," *Chronicles* 45 (Winter 1967–68); brochure.
8. Ruth Moore Stanley, "Alice M. Robertson, Oklahoma's First Congresswoman," *Chronicles* 45 (Autumn 1967).
9. Anna Lewis, "Jane McCurtain," *Chronicles* 11 (Dec. 1933).
10. Muriel Wright, "Origin of Oklahoma Day," *Chronicles* 23 (Autumn 1945); H.

Milt Phillips, "The Hour of Remembrance," *Chronicles* 41 (Winter 1963–64); vol. 23 has a list of honorees from 1928 to 1944.

11. Alice Browne Alspaugh, "Mrs. Virgil Browne," *Chronicles* 42 (Winter 1964–65).

12. Muriel Wright, "Rachel Caroline Eaton," *Chronicles* 16 (Dec. 1938).

13. Hope Holway, "Lucia Loomis Ferguson," *Chronicles* 41 (Winter 1963–64).

14. Naomi Taylor Casey, "Miss Edith Johnson, Pioneer Newspaper Woman," *Chronicles* 60 (Spring 1982).

15. Mark R. Everett, "In Memory of Anna Lee Brosius Korn," *Chronicles* 44 (Summer 1966).

16. Winnie Lewis Gravitt, "Anna Lewis: A Great Woman of Oklahoma," *Chronicles* 40 (Winter 1962–63).

17. Muriel Wright, "Jessie Elizabeth Randolph Moore," *Chronicles* 34 (Winter 1956–57).

18. *Chronicles* 52 (Spring 1974), pp. 3–21; *Chronicles* 53 (Fall 1975), pp. 397–99.

19. *Current Biography*, 1949; Perle Mesta and Robert Kahn, *My Story* (New York: McGraw-Hill, 1960).

20. Muriel H. Wright, George Shirk, and Kenny Franks, *Mark of Heritage* (Oklahoma City: Oklahoma Historical Society, 1976).

21. Joseph B. Thoburn, "Elizabeth Fulton Hester," *Chronicles* 6 (Winter 1928).

22. *Oklahoma: A Guide to the Sooner State*, comp. Kent Ruth (Norman: University of Oklahoma Press, 1957); David C. Hunt, *Guide to Oklahoma Museums* (Norman: University of Oklahoma Press, 1981); correspondence, Philbrook Art Center.

23. Carolyn T. Foreman, "Mary C. Greenleaf at Wapanucka Female Manual Labor School," *Chronicles* 24 (Spring 1946); Muriel Wright, *Mark of Heritage*.

24. Ferguson, "Picture of a Pioneer Town," in *Oklahoma Memories*, ed. Ann H. Morgan and Rennard Strickland (Norman: University of Oklahoma Press, 1981); correspondence, Watonga Public Library.

25. Correspondence, Seminole Nation Historical Society.

SOUTH CAROLINA

AIKEN

Schofield, Martha, 1839–1916, Educator; NAW

Martha Schofield School

After the Civil War many northern women volunteered to teach freed Negroes in the South. Among them was Martha Schofield, a Quaker from Pennsylvania. She was sent by the Freedmen's Relief Association to the Sea Islands of South Carolina, where she taught for several years. She then moved to Aiken to a dilapidated schoolhouse which she soon persuaded the Freedmen's Bureau to replace. In 1886 her school was incorporated as the Schofield Normal and Industrial School, having been supported through the years by funds from various groups, principally Quakers. Much of the money was raised by Schofield's lectures. By mid-century the school had become one of the South's most influential educational institutions for black students. Schofield believed that vocational training was the principal goal for Negro education, though she taught traditional subjects also. After her death the school continued as a public school.

BEAUFORT

Gleason, Kate, 1865–1933, Housing Developer; NAW

Kate Gleason Memorial Park

Kate Gleason was attracted to Beaufort late in her business career. She rejuvenated the town as a tourist resort by developing a beach, a golf course, and a clubhouse. The daughter of a machine-tool manufacturer of Rochester, New York, she worked with him and even went on the road selling machine tools. She developed her own business career in Rochester, went into the building of small houses, and acquired some wealth.

She visited France, where she took on the restoration of old houses and a twelfth-century castle tower in Septmonts. On one of her European visits she was accompanied by Libby Sanders. Every time Gleason became enthusiastic about the architecture and scenic beauty in Europe, Sanders replied, "You ought to see Beaufort, South Carolina." So when they returned to the United States, Gleason visited Beaufort. She bought property and began remodeling houses, some of which still exist in Beaufort. She built the Gold Eagle Tavern, for long a city landmark (demolished in the late 1960s). After her death, her sister Eleanor Gleason inherited much of the property. She gave land for the Beaufort Memorial Hospital and for the adjacent park as a memorial to Gleason.[1]

Mather, Rachel Crane, d. 1903, Educator

Marker, Site of Mather School, Ribaut Road

Shortly after the Civil War, Rachel Crane Mather, of Boston, Massachusetts, founded a school here. In 1882 the Women's American Baptist Home Mission Society assumed support of the venture, operating it as a normal school for Negro girls. With some changes, the school continued until 1968, when it was closed and sold to the state for the educational benefit of all races. The marker was erected in 1982, with some twenty members of the Mather School Alumnae Association present.[2]

Waterhouse, Mary Elizabeth, fl. 1891, and Other Clubwomen

Tablets, Beaufort County Library, 321 S. Harper Street

Mounted on the walls of the library are two tablets giving the history of the library. Mary Elizabeth Waterhouse is credited with establishing a literary society, the Clover Club, in 1891. In 1902 thirty club members established a circulating library and served as volunteer librarians until 1918, when a building was erected on land given by the city, with the aid of Carnegie funds. A new building was constructed in 1964.[3]

CHARLESTON

Butler, Susan Dart, 1888–1959, Educator

Dart Hall Branch, Charleston County Free Library

Susan Dart Butler grew up in a home where reading was encouraged, but she realized that other black children lacked not only books but access to schools in Charleston. Her parents erected on their own land a six-room building known as Dart Hall, where young Negroes were taught elementary subjects. Older girls learned sewing, and boys were introduced to such skills as blacksmithing and printing. Butler attended Atlanta University in Georgia and then, at her mother's insistence, went to a school in Boston, Massachusetts, to study millinery. Though successful in this field, she was more interested in the education of young people. Not until some years later, after marriage to Nathaniel Butler and the birth and death of a son, did she take up the work her father had begun at Dart Hall.

She opened up a library here, and traveled about the South to learn something about the organization and administration of a library. She succeeded in interesting the citizens of Charleston in donating books and funds to Dart Hall. When the Rosenwald Fund cooperated with the county to establish the Charleston County Free Public Library, Butler gave the use of Dart Hall. Later, after taking a course in library work, she became librarian of the Dart Hall Branch Library and served for twenty-six years in this position.[4]

Chapin, Sarah Moore, 1830?–1896, Temperance Worker; NAW

Drinking Fountain. Monument, Magnolia Cemetery

Sarah Moore Chapin discovered in herself a natural eloquence when she was unexpectedly called upon to speak at a temperance meeting in 1880. She organized the first Woman's Christian Temperance Union (WCTU) in South Carolina and gave the rest of her life to the organization. She traveled constantly, organizing unions for women and for girls and boys. Her ladylike appearance and ''masculine'' grasp of politics impressed audiences, who were carried away by her brilliant lectures. She was at first a bit afraid of advocating votes for women, fearing it would do the WCTU harm in the conservative South, but she came around to supporting suffrage. Her campaign for a state industrial school for girls resulted in the founding of Winthrop Normal College in Columbia, South Carolina. It later moved to Rock Hill and became the state college for women. The national WCTU erected a monument over her grave and in 1904 the southern members set up a memorial drinking fountain at a busy intersection in Charleston.

Gregorie, Anne King, 1887–1960, Historian

Anne King Gregorie Library, Fireproof Building, 100 Meeting Street; HABS, NHL

Anne King Gregorie played a role in the teaching, writing, and preservation of South Carolina's heritage. She wrote biographies of several public figures, including Thomas Sumter. She was a longtime member and curator of the South Carolina Historical Society and edited the *South Carolina Historical and Genealogical Magazine* from 1949 to 1958. She loved books, sacrificing much to build up a personal library, and it was her wish that the books be continuously used by students of history. The historical society now holds her collection and makes it available to researchers. Her gravestone in Christ Episcopal Churchyard, at Six Mile, Mt. Pleasant, South Carolina, reads "as teacher, author and editor, she helped to spread understanding of South Carolina's civilization."[5]

COLUMBIA

Chesnut, Mary Boykin, 1823–1886, Confederate Diarist; NAW

Chesnut Cottage, 1718 Hampton Street (Private); NR

"I was of necessity a rebel born," Mary Boykin Chesnut wrote, "Nobody could live in this state unless he were a fire-eater . . . . So I was a seceder." When the Civil War began, Chesnut was in the midst of it. Married to James Chesnut, who resigned his seat in the U.S. Senate to become a leader in the Confederate cause, she was smart enough to know she was living history. The diary she kept during those years is an exceedingly important historical record, as well as a revealing and emotional view of the war from the perspective of an intelligent woman. Against a background of dances, carriage rides, and almost hysterical partying, we see the structure of southern social and economic life crumbling into tragic loss and defeat. The *Diary from Dixie* was first published many years after her death and subsequent editions have kept it in print ever since.

Cunningham, Ann Pamela, 1816–1875, Clubwoman and Preservationist; NAW

Portrait, State Capitol

Ann Pamela Cunningham was born at Rosemont plantation on the Saluda, near Waterloo, South Carolina, q.v. The cause to which she devoted herself, the preservation of Mount Vernon, George Washington's home in Virginia, was suggested to her by her mother. Her mother had visited the shrine and was dismayed to see its rundown condition. Cunningham, writing as "A Southern Matron," sent a letter to the *Charleston Mercury* of December 2, 1853, addressed to the women of the South, suggesting that they purchase the historical site, restore it, and present it to the state of Virginia. Shortly afterward the two women and several others organized the Mount Vernon Ladies' Memorial Association of the Union. Women from northern states asked to join and several well-known people were recruited, including actress Anna Cora Mowatt and the lecturer Edward Everett.

In spite of the general interest aroused, it was a long and difficult project. Cunningham was crippled, as a result of an accident in her youth, and in later life suffered from rheumatism and loss of sight, yet she went about the work of organizing women from many parts of the country. It took years to persuade the owner of Mount Vernon to sell and to raise the money to purchase it. The Civil

War intervened and many refused to help because the project was run by women. At last, in 1867, Cunningham was able to move into Mount Vernon as resident director. She remained until shortly before her death. The Ladies' Memorial Association was one of the first patriotic organizations of American women and the preservation of Mount Vernon a demonstration of what women working together could accomplish. The Association is still the caretaker of Mount Vernon.

In addition to Cunningham, two other South Carolina women have been honored by memorials in the capitol—Emily Geiger (see Lexington, SC) and Wil Lou Gray (see West Columbia, SC).

Mann, Celia, 1799–1867, Midwife

Mann-Simons Cottage, 1403 Richland Street; NR

This white frame house belonged to Celia Mann, a black woman who bought her freedom from slavery in Charleston, South Carolina, and walked to Columbia to start a new life sometime in the early 1800s. The First Calvary Baptist Church was organized in the basement of the cottage after the Civil War, and services were held here until the congregation bought land. The church still stands across the street from the Mann house and Mann's descendants still hold membership there. Oddly, Mann is listed in the 1850 census as owning a slave. Since the slave was seventy, it was assumed she was an elderly relative, perhaps her mother. Mann's descendants (including a daughter named Simons) lived in the house for more than a hundred years. In 1968 the Columbia Housing Authority purchased the property. It has been restored to its original 1880 appearance by the Richland County Preservation Commission. It is open for tours Tues.-Sun. 10–2 by appointment (803–252–1450); adm.[6]

DENMARK

Wright, Elizabeth, 1876–1906, College Founder

Voorhees College; NR

In 1897 Elizabeth Wright, a graduate of Tuskegee Institute, began to teach black children on her back porch. Each paid ten cents a week to attend her classes. From that beginning grew the Denmark Industrial School. Wright walked miles through the country to speak before church groups to raise money for the school. Her dream was realized when Ralph Voorhees of New Jersey gave four hundred acres and money for buildings. Voorhees College is the result. Unfortunately, Wright, always delicate, had worn herself out and died at the age of thirty.

FORT MOTTE

Motte, Rebecca Brewton, 1738–1815, Revolutionary War Heroine

Fort Motte Battle Site, State 13; NR

Rebecca Brewton Motte was the widow of Jacob Motte and manager of the family estate on the Congaree River when in 1781 British invaders seized her mansion. She retired with her family to a farmhouse nearby. Francis Marion and Henry Lee laid siege to the British encampment, which they named Fort Motte, and deliberated whether to burn the mansion in order to dislodge the soldiers. They were reluctant to destroy the widow's property, but she took things into her own hands and offered them a bow and fire arrows with which to shoot flames onto the roof. The British, who were guarding a supply of gunpowder, hastily surrendered and both Whigs and Tories extinguished the flames. Then Motte graciously served dinner to the officers of both sides.

After the war was over Motte was almost bankrupt. She began to rebuild her fortune, paid off her husband's debts, and bought a tract of rice land on the Santee River.

The site of Fort Motte is marked by a large boulder which honors Motte's self-sacrificing act. John White's famous painting, depicting "Mrs. Motte directing Generals Marion and Lee to burn her mansion to dislodge the British," hangs in the Senate wing of the National Capitol in Washington, D.C.[7]

FROGMORE

Towne, Laura, 1825–1901 (NAW), and Other Educators

Penn Center Historic District, Land's End Road, St. Helena Island; NHL

Penn School, established here by Laura Towne and her friend Ellen Murray, was the first school for freed slaves in the South. Federal forces had taken possession of the sea islands and the white planters had fled, leaving behind hundreds of blacks without direction and short of food. Towne, who came from Philadelphia, Pennsylvania, and Murray, from Rhode Island, volunteered their services. The first arrived in Port Royal in April 1862, the second a few months later; Penn School began in a Baptist church in September. Towne, educated herself in academic subjects, taught the basic reading, writing, and arithmetic skills, not vocational skills. The school remained one of the important institutions of the postwar period, with Towne in charge for almost forty years. In 1870 it began training teachers.

A historical marker here gives a brief history of the school and includes a note that "the earliest known black teacher was Charlotte Forten, who traveled all the way from Massachusetts to help her people.'' Forten (later Grimké, 1837–1914, NAW) was here from 1862 to 1864. She wrote of her experiences in ''Life on the Sea Islands,'' published in the *Atlantic Monthly* in May and June 1864. Her struggle to induce the blacks to come to the school was the subject of a television drama.

After Towne's death and the retirement of Murray, the school was renamed the Penn Normal, Industrial and Agricultural School, with its emphasis changed to practical subjects: domestic skills for women, agriculture for men. After serving for some time as part of the state's segregated school system, it became a community center.[8]

GEORGETOWN

Baruch, Belle Wilcox, 1899–1964, Conservationist

Bellefield Nature Center, Off US 17

Belle Wilcox Baruch was the daughter of Bernard Baruch, who established his estate, the Hobcaw Barony, between Pawleys Island and Georgetown. She took over the 17,500 acres in 1958 and today the property is owned by the Belle W. Baruch Foundation. Baruch was a noted sportswoman—horsewoman, sailor, hunter, and pilot of her own plane. According to her father, she was ''a doer, not just a talker.'' She was a close friend of Edith Bolling Wilson, as her father was of President Woodrow Wilson. In addition to her interest in conservation, Baruch was known for many gifts to aid the handicapped.

A display area at the center features plants and animals of the region and the research activities of the Baruch Institutes. These provide field laboratory environments for Clemson University's Baruch Forest Science Institute and the University of South Carolina's Institute of Marine Biology and Coastal Research. Part of the mansion is used for offices and conference rooms. The nature center, which includes a videotape movie on the life of Baruch and a slide show on Hobcaw's history, is open Mon.-Fri. 10–5; Sat. 1–5. The estate and mansion are open for tours on Thurs., by appointment (803–546–4623).[9]

Pringle, Elizabeth Allston, 1845–1921, Rice Planter; NAW

Chicora Wood Plantation; NR

When she wrote about her experiences as a rice planter at White House and Chicora Wood plantations, Eliza Allston Pringle signed herself Patience Pennington. Patience was a quality she needed in dealing with the vagaries of labor, weather, and the economics of rice culture. She was not brought up to agriculture but was educated at a Charleston, South Carolina, school for young ladies. She was, however, the daughter of a man who cultivated many acres of rice lands and was named for an aunt who capably managed an inherited plantation, so when it was necessary for her to become a planter, she could and did.

She married John Pringle, of the White House on the Peedee River. The marriage was cut short by his death six years later, and Pringle moved back to her mother's house at nearby Chicora Wood. In 1880 she bought the Pringle plantation from her husband's heirs (since widows did not automatically inherit property), determined to manage it herself. She drove daily to the White House in a buggy, tucked up her skirts and walked about the muddy fields, overseeing her laborers and seeing that things were done properly. She was in her fifties when her mother died and she took over management of Chicora Wood, the one plantation her family saved after the disastrous war years. Again she had to purchase the land.

Rice was not the only product of her plantations. She raised other crops and livestock, including poultry and sheep. While resting from these labors, she read up on scientific farming, wrote stories, and kept a day-to-day account of her work. She gave up rice planting in 1906 when labor problems, storm damage, and the advent of mechanized rice cultivation brought her near bankruptcy. Her diary was published in 1913 as *A Woman Rice Planter*, and after her death *Chronicles of Chicora Wood* appeared. Both books are readable as well as historically valuable, and both give a picture of a capable, courageous, and observant woman who could laugh at her own disappointments and difficulties.

GRAY COURT

Gray, Wil Lou, 1883–1984, Educator

Marker, Young's Community, Off State 101

The marker reads: "Here at Young's School in 1915 Dr. Wil Lou Gray (1883–1984) initiated for her native county of Laurens a seven-school program of night education for adults which led to the adoption of a state-wide system and her national recognition as a tireless and effective opponent of illiteracy." Gray taught at Wallace Lodge School when it was housed in an abandoned lodge, almost falling down. Rough slab seats and painted boards for blackboards and a salary of thirty-five dollars a month failed to discourage her. She accepted it as a challenge and so interested the community that in 1906 it erected a new two-teacher school named Young's. By that time Gray was away studying at Vanderbilt University. She returned as principal of the school and then began the adult schools. Gray is in the South Carolina Hall of Fame at Myrtle Beach. See West Columbia, SC.[10]

LEXINGTON

Geiger, Emily, fl. 1780s, Revolutionary War Heroine

Tablet, Geiger Cemetery

In spite of the tablet erected here in 1974 and the plaque at the state capitol, the very existence of Emily Geiger has been disputed by historians. Tradition says that when General Nathanael Greene besieged the British at old Ninety-Six in 1781 he called for a courier to deliver a message to General Thomas Sumter. The country was so overrun with Tories that it was felt no man could get through, but young Geiger convinced the general she could deliver the message. On the second day she was intercepted and locked in a room while a woman was sent for to search her. She memorized the message and swallowed the paper. Since no evidence was found that she might be a spy, she was released and delivered the general's message orally.

McCLELLANVILLE

Pinckney, Eliza Lucas, 1722?–1793, Plantation Manager; NAW

Hampton Plantation State Park, Eight Miles North Off US 17; HABS, NHL

The Hampton rice plantation has been home to several distinguished persons, including Eliza Lucas Pinckney and her daughter, Harriott Horry, who was mistress of the plantation during the colonial period. A descendant, Harriott Horry Ravenel, wrote *Eliza Pinckney* (1896), telling the story of her ancestor's cultivation of indigo. Pinckney, born and educated in England, was a teenager when her father brought his family to Wappoo, a plantation near Charleston, South Carolina. When military duties called him back to Antigua, Pinckney, the oldest daughter, took over the management of three plantations. This, she wrote, "requires much writing and more business and fatigue of other sorts than you can imagine . . . . By rising very early I find I can go through with much business." Not content to depend on rice, she made efforts to adapt various foreign crops to South Carolina's climate and was successful in raising indigo from West Indian seeds. Others tried indigo and it was soon rivaling rice as the colony's major crop.

Eliza married Charles Pinckney in 1744 and for a time lived in England. The family was broken up with Charles's death in 1758 and Eliza again had to take over plantation management. Her lands were overrun during the Revolution and she suffered enormous losses. During her last years she spent much time here at Hampton with her daughter Harriott, widow of Daniel Horry, and a number of grandchildren. Here in 1791 she greeted President George Washington on his southern tour. She died two years later and Washington, by his own request, was a pallbearer.

The most recent owner of Hampton was Archibald Rutledge (1883–1973), poet laureate of South Carolina. He sold it in 1971 and it is now a state park. It is open Mar.-Sept., Sun., by appointment with the park superintendent (803–546–9361).[11]

MAYESVILLE

Bethune, Mary McLeod, 1875–1955, Educator and Civil Rights Leader; NAWM

Marker, Near Site of Birthplace

Not until twenty years after her death was notice taken that this small town was the birthplace of one of the most remarkable women of her time. Born of parents who had been slaves, Mary McLeod Bethune rose to become a leader in the civil rights movement, an advisor to President Franklin D. Roosevelt, and an observer for the United States at the founding of the United Nations. The child whose schooling began in a black mission school near Mayesville became herself an educator, the founder of Florida's Bethune-Cookman College (see Daytona Beach, FL). The memorial tablet here was dedicated in 1975. Bethune has been chosen for the South Carolina Hall of Fame at Myrtle Beach.

MT. PLEASANT

Hancock, Cornelia, 1840–1927, Educator and Civil War Nurse; NAW

Marker, Laing Middle School, US 17

In 1866 Cornelia Hancock was sent to South Carolina by a group of Philadelphia Quakers along with Laura Towne (see Frogmore, SC) to establish schools for freedmen. Hancock, who had been an outstanding nurse during the Civil War, set up her school in a small, bullet-riddled church in Mt. Pleasant. When enrollment grew to two hundred, she rented a large house. Later, federal funds made it possible to erect a proper school building, named for Henry Laing, one of the school's supporters. Hancock remained as principal for ten years. In the 1920s Laing became part of the public school system.

MURRELLS INLET

Huntington, Anna Hyatt, 1876–1973, Sculptor; NAWM

Brookgreen Gardens; NR

Anna Hyatt Huntington and her husband, Archer Huntington, of New England and New York, owned several old rice plantations in South Carolina, where they spent their winters. When Anna married Archer, a scholar and poet and founder of the Hispanic Society of America, she was herself an established artist. The couple created at Brookgreen a beautiful setting for Anna's sculpture, then added pieces from other artists to form an unrivaled collection of nineteenth- and early twentieth-century sculpture. Here in natural settings of groves, gardens, lakes, and streams are over four hundred pieces of sculpture. They range in size from the tremendous *Fighting Stallions* by Anna to the small fountain sculptures of Janet Scudder and Bessie Potter Vonnoh. Anna's sister Harriet Hyatt Mayor is also represented. The gardens were opened to the public in 1932 and may be visited daily 9–4:30; adm.

MYRTLE BEACH

South Carolina Hall of Fame, Myrtle Beach Convention Center, 21st Avenue N. and Oak Street

The South Carolina Hall of Fame is a nonprofit corporation conducted under a state charter and funded by the state, the city of Myrtle Beach, and the Myrtle Beach Area Chamber of Commerce. It was inaugurated in 1973, "to recognize and honor those contemporary and past citizens who have made outstanding contributions to South Carolina's heritage and progress." Almost all the inductees to date have been men, not women. Mary McLeod Bethune (1875–1955, NAWM), educator and civil rights leader of Mayesville, is an honoree. Wil Lou Gray (1883–1984), adult education specialist of Gray Court and West Columbia, is also honored.

The Hall of Fame is located in the civic alcove of the convention center and is open Mon.-Fri. 9–5.

ROCK HILL

Dacus, Ida Jane, 1873–1964, Librarian

Ida Jane Dacus Library, Winthrop College

In 1896 the library of Winthrop College was a study hall with a meager collection of books. Ida Jane Dacus was one of three students put in charge of it, and her experience there gave her a desire to go into library work. No other South Carolinian had yet entered a professional library school when she applied to Drexel Institute of Philadelphia, Pennsylvania. She returned to Winthrop in 1902 as librarian, and she retired in 1945. By that time the library had some sixty-three thousand volumes and many government documents. One of her hobbies was gardening, and "Miss Dacus's garden" behind the library keeps her memory fresh.[12]

Withers, Sarah, 1873–1955, Teacher and Writer

Withers Building, Winthrop College; NR

Sarah Withers was the first principal of Winthrop Training School, a model school built in 1912 where seniors could do their practice teaching for grades kindergarten through twelve. It was called Winthrop Training School until renamed in 1969 to honor Withers. She was the author of *Child World Primer*, one of the first series of beginning reading books for children. She edited other educational series and continued teaching in summer courses. For a time she was assistant to the state superintendent of public instruction.[13]

SPARTANBURG

Barry, Kate Moore, fl. 1770s, Revolutionary War Heroine

Walnut Grove Plantation, Off US 221; NR

Kate Moore Barry became famous for her part in the Battle of Cowpens, when she served as a scout for General John Hunt Morgan. Walnut Grove, her childhood home, has been restored and authentically furnished as the center of a complete plantation complex. To reach it, take US 221 off I–26 and follow the signs. It is open year-round, Sun. 2–5; and Apr.-Oct., Tues.-Sat. 11–5; closed holidays; adm.[14]

SUMTER

White, Elizabeth, 1883–1976, Artist

Sumter Gallery of Art, 421 N. Main Street; NR

The gift of some watercolor paints from her grandfather when she was four began Elizabeth White's artistic career. She graduated with a certificate in art from the College for Women in Columbia, South Carolina, and then studied at the Pennsylvania Academy of Fine Arts. During the 1930s she was invited to be a guest resident at Laurelton Hill, the Louis C. Tiffany mansion in Oyster Bay, New York, and she spent three summers at the MacDowell Colony in New Hampshire. She exhibited her work in many galleries. At home she was a member and founder of several cultural and art groups.

The White house, which now houses the gallery, had been in the artist's family since 1886. It was nominated for the National Register both because of its connection with a prominent family and for architectural distinction. White left the house to the Sumter Gallery of Art, which had been established in 1969. Restoration of the house was completed in 1977 and the art collection, originally housed in the old Carnegie Library, was moved to the new location. It is open Sept. 1–May 31, Mon.-Fri. 11–5, Sat.-Sun. 2–5; closed some holidays.[15]

WATERLOO

Cunningham, Ann Pamela, 1816–1875, Clubwoman and Preservationist; NAW

Marker, US 221

The Waterloo home of Ann Pamela Cunningham (see Columbia, SC) burned down in 1930. The marker here reads: "Rosemont. About 2 1/2 miles southwest, a granite monument stands at the site of Rosemont, birthplace and home of Ann Pamela Cunningham, founder and first regent of the Mount Vernon Ladies' Association of the Union. Through her efforts Mount Vernon was purchased by the association in 1858, and Washington's home was restored and maintained for posterity.''[16]

WEST COLUMBIA

Gray, Wil Lou, 1883–1984, Educator

Wil Lou Gray Opportunity School, W. Campus Road

When Wil Lou Gray first began teaching she was distressed to note the high rate of illiteracy in South Carolina, a deficiency brought glaringly to light during World War II when 67 percent of the state's draftees were rejected for educational reasons. Long before this, Gray had begun to establish night classes (see Gray Court, SC). She had written books needed to teach illiterate adults. The Wil Lou Gray Opportunity School, founded in 1921, was her greatest accomplishment. It started as a one-month elementary summer school for farm and mill girls over fourteen and women who had been unable to continue in school. After years of begging and borrowing facilities, Gray convinced the General Assembly to build a permanent year-round school for adults. She directed it until her retirement in 1957.

Retirement was not to be playtime for this dynamic woman. Her energies were channeled into the senior citizen movement and she soon saw the Federation of Older Americans and the South Carolina Commission on Aging set up to provide services to seniors. Gray richly deserved the honors bestowed on her, including election to the South Carolina Hall of Fame and the placing of her portrait in the state capitol.[17]

NOTES

In addition to the sources mentioned below, I have had assistance from the South Carolina Department of Parks, Recreation, and Tourism, which publishes a handsome brochure listing sites; South Carolina Historical Society; Myrtle Beach Chamber of Commerce; Abbeville-Greenwood Regional Library in Greenwood; Sumter County Library in Sumter; Charleston County Library in Charleston; and Cassie Nichols of Sumter.

1. *Beaufort Gazette*, Apr. 3, 1975; correspondence and clippings, County Council of Beaufort County.
2. Correspondence and clippings, County Council of Beaufort County.
3. Ibid.
4. *Dictionary of American Library Biography*, ed. Bohdan S. Wynor (Littleton, Colo.: Libraries Unlimited, Inc., 1978).
5. Flora Belle Surles, *Anne King Gregorie* (Columbia, S.C.: R. L. Bryan Co., 1968).
6. Correspondence, Mann-Simons Cottage.
7. Sally Smith Booth, *The Women of '76* (New York: Hastings House, 1973).

8. Correspondence, County Council of Beaufort County.

9. *New York Times*, Apr. 26 and May 28, 1964.

10. *South Carolina's Distinguished Women of Laurens County*, comp. Marguerite Tolbert and others (Columbia, S.C.: R. L. Bryan Co., 1972); correspondence, Laurens County Library.

11. Rita Stein, *A Literary Tour Guide to the United States: South and Southwest* (New York: William Morrow & Co., 1979).

12. Clippings and correspondence, Winthrop College.

13. Ibid.

14. Lonelle Aikman, ''Patriots in Petticoats,'' *National Geographic* 148 (Oct. 1975).

15. Brochure, Sumter Gallery of Art.

16. Correspondence, Laurens County Library.

17. Correspondence, Opportunity School.

TENNESSEE

BEERSHEBA SPRINGS

Murfree, Mary Noailles, 1850–1922, Writer; NAW

Marker, State 56

Mary Noailles Murfree, who wrote under the pen name Charles Egbert Craddock, spent summers here with her family. Here she listened to and talked with the mountain people who inhabit her novels and short stories. In 1857 the family moved from Murfreesboro to Nashville, Tennessee, and later to St. Louis, Missouri. She began to write essays and stories with a Tennessee mountain background, her first successful story appearing in the *Atlantic Monthly* in 1878.[1]

BENTON

Ward, Nancy, c. 1738–1822, Cherokee Leader; NAW

Tablet at Tomb, US 411; NR

The tablet, placed by the Nancy Ward Chapter, Daughters of the American Revolution, identifies Nancy Ward as "Princess and Prophetess of Tennessee, The Pocahontas of Tennessee, and the Constant Friend of the American Pioneer."

In 1755 during the Cherokee-Creek war, Ward's husband, Kingfisher, was killed and she took his place in the battle. She was then chosen "Beloved Woman" of the tribe, the head of the Woman's Council, and a member of the Council of Chiefs. She was friendly to the white settlers and twice warned them of impending attacks.

By 1817 Ward was too old to attend the Great Councils, but she spoke against giving up any more of the land to whites. Two years later, however, the matriarchal society of the Cherokee Nation was changed and Ward lost her status. The new governing group made a treaty by which much of the territory was lost, including Ward's home in Chota. She moved to a new location near Benton, Tennessee, where she ran a small inn until her death. In 1838 the Cherokees were forced to remove to Indian Territory. The gravesite and environs have been purchased by the state and plans are made to develop it as a park.

A statue of Ward made in the 1930s by James A. Walker and inscribed with her name was somehow placed over the grave of another near Norris in Grainger County. For years there have been unsuccessful attempts to move the statue to Benton, and it has now disappeared.[2]

CHATTANOOGA

Smith, Bessie, 1894–1937, Singer; NAW

Markers at Presumed Birth Site, 700 Block of Martin Luther King, Jr., Boulevard, and on 9th Street

According to one of Bessie Smith's biographers, ''If you were white in the years 1907 to 1937, chances are you never saw her and probably never even heard her name.'' Beginning in the early 1920s as a singer in carnivals and tent shows, Smith soon progressed to her own show, traveling from city to city and singing her unique style of the blues. Her themes—poverty, sex, joy, and grief—appealed to her black audiences, and it was among the black jazz musicians that her reputation was kept alive. She influenced a whole generation of musicians. Columbia Records erected a tombstone in her memory, with the epitaph ''The Greatest Blues Singer in the World Will Never Stop Singing.'' She is in the National Women's Hall of Fame.[3]

COVINGTON

Calhoun, Frances Boyd, 1867–1909, Writer

Marker, US 51

In 1908 a package was delivered to a publishing firm too busy to open it. Later a rhymed letter came from Frances Boyd Calhoun of Covington asking whether the manuscript of her book, *Miss Minerva and William Green Hill*, had been received, lost, shelved, or mayhap published under another name. ''If naught has befallen it,'' the verse ended, ''Please ship it at once C.O.D.'' The office at once opened the package, read the story, and passed it around to be enjoyed by others. It was published in February 1909, shortly after the publisher received a pen portrait of Calhoun. She was, she wrote, ''a Southerner of Southerners,'' and a widow (having been married only a year when her husband died).

Miss Minerva was the story of a boy's growing up in a particular world, which happened to be in East Tennessee, under the care of his spinster aunt, Miss Minerva. It delighted its readers and went on to over fifty printings. Calhoun never knew of its success. She died shortly after the book appeared. Later ''Miss

Minerva'' books—nearly a dozen—were written by Emma Speed-Sampson (1868–1947), of Richmond, Virginia.[4]

DEL RIO

Moore, Grace, 1898–1947, Singer; NAW

Marker, State 107

Two and a half miles from the town of Del Rio a marker indicates the birthplace of Grace Moore, the musical comedy and movie star and opera singer. Her family did not stay here long and Moore grew up in Jellico, Tennessee. Hearing the great Mary Garden sing inspired Moore to think about opera, and she had a chance to sing an aria from *Aida* with a concert artist in Washington, D.C. In 1928 she made her debut at the Metropolitan Opera. Both of Tennessee's senators and a Tennessee delegation were there to hear her sing, and she was given twenty-eight curtain calls. She succeeded on the stage, in Hollywood, and in opera. A movie based on her life, *So This Is Love*, was produced in 1953.

ELIZABETHTON

Patton, Mary McKeehan, 1751–1836, Powder Maker

Monument, Green Pine Community

Mary McKeehan Patton learned gunpowder making while still living in her native England. When she came to America she continued her trade in Pennsylvania before marrying a Revolutionary soldier, John Patton. Brigadier General Nathaniel Taylor persuaded the Pattons to move to the Watauga-Holston settlement where gunpowder was needed, and he built them a home and powdermill on Powder Branch. Patton turned out most of the powder used by Tennesseans in 1780 at the Battle of King's Mountain. Rocky Mount Historical Museum at Piney Flats has the huge iron kettle in which she made it. Her grave marker, erected 1932, is dedicated to ''one of that heroic band who established a civilization in the wilderness.''[5]

GERMANTOWN

Wright, Frances, 1795–1852, Abolitionist and Reformer; NAW

Nashoba Community Site

Flamboyant, impulsive, ambitious Frances Wright was one of the earliest feminists in America. She came from England to the United States when she was twenty-two, with her sister Camilla, twenty. They fell in love with America. Then they returned to England, where Wright wrote *Views of Society and Man-*

ners in America. She returned to the United States in 1824 and instituted, at Nashoba, an experiment in helping slaves to earn their freedom through labor. Because she was unable to remain in the community, it soon failed.

The Nashoba land stood idle for decades and was then sold by Wright's daughter. It was finally subdivided. A state historical marker outside of Memphis reads, "Here, in 1827, a Scottish spinster heiress named Frances Wright set up a colony whose aims were the enforcement of cooperative living and other advanced sociological experiments. It failed in 1830."[6]

KNOXVILLE

Greenwood, Marion, 1909–1970, Muralist

Mural, Student Center, University of Tennessee

In 1954 Marion Greenwood, who had won fame for her huge murals in Mexico, was a visiting professor at the University of Tennessee. She won a large commission for the mural, which deals with Tennessee music. The complex regionalist work depicts jazz and spirituals, folk dance, country and mountain music.[7]

Susong, Edith O'Keefe, 1890–1974, and Her Mother, Quincy Marshall O'Keefe, 1866–1958, Newspaperwomen

Tennessee Newspaper Hall of Fame, Communications and Extension Building, University of Tennessee

Of the twenty-seven persons honored in the Hall of Fame, only two are women. Edith O'Keefe Susong published the *Greeneville Sun* for over fifty years. The National Women's Press Club cited her as the outstanding newspaperwoman of the nation. When she took over the paper in 1916, it was named the *Democrat* and was printed on an old flatbed Country Campbell press powered by a gasoline engine. In 1920 she bought out the other two newspapers in Greeneville, Tennessee, and combined them as the *Democrat-Sun*. It became the *Greeneville Sun* in 1940. She was inducted into the Newspaper Hall of Fame in 1981. Her mother, Quincy Marshall O'Keefe, who served under her daughter as editor of the *Sun* for thirty-five years, had been inducted in 1979.[8]

LA GRANGE

Pickens, Lucy Holcombe, 1832–1899, Confederate Hostess; NAW

Marker, State 57 at Pine Street

Lucy Holcombe Pickens was born at La Grange on the cotton plantation of her parents, a distinguished Virginia family. They moved when she was young to

Marshall, Texas, q.v. She married the statesman Francis Pickens of South Carolina and went with him to Russia, where he was U.S. minister. There she was admired by the czar's imperial household, and there she bore her only daughter, Douschka. They returned to South Carolina, where Pickens managed to hold on to her property through and after the war, reigning there as a hostess and representative of southern womanhood.

LIVINGSTON

Sevier, Catherine Sherrill, c. 1754–1836, Pioneer

Marker, State 52

Catherine Sherrill Sevier (''Bonny Kate'') is reputed to have met John Sevier while he was fighting Indians before Tennessee became a state. In 1780, after his first wife died, John married Catherine, who thus became mother to his ten children. They had eight more. Meanwhile the settlers organized themselves into the State of Franklin and made John governor. In 1796 Tennessee joined the Union, and he was the first state governor. After John's death in 1815, Catherine came to live near Livingston, where she built log cabins to accommodate settlers she hoped would join her. Few came, but Catherine remained until shortly before her death. Her body was buried in Knoxville, Tennessee, beside that of her husband.[9]

MAXWELL

Crockett, Polly Finlay, 1788–1815, Pioneer

Marker, US 64

Polly Finlay Crockett, first wife of Davy Crockett, is buried in a graveyard near the marker. She married Crockett in 1806 and had three children. The marker was erected in her memory in 1956 by the Tennessee Historical Commission.

MURFREESBORO

Murfree, Mary Noailles, 1850–1922, Writer; NAW

Marker, at Lokey Avenue

Mary Noailles Murfree, who wrote under the pen name of Charles Egbert Craddock, was born at Grantlands, whose site is now marked by a large pine tree. She died in Murfreesboro. See Beersheba Springs, TN.

NASHVILLE

Bennett, Belle Harris, 1852–1922, Churchwoman; NAW

Belle H. Bennett Memorial, Scarritt College, 1008 19th Avenue S.

In 1889 Belle Harris Bennett attended a meeting of the Southern Methodist Woman's Board of Foreign Missions and timidly suggested that women missionaries needed more adequate training before they were sent into the field. She had learned of a school for this purpose established in Chicago, Illinois, but there was none in the South. As often happens, the person making the suggestion—Bennett—was appointed to collect funds to put her project into operation. She began traveling through the South speaking to church groups, and within a year Nathan Scarritt, of Kansas City, Missouri, had offered money and land for the proposed school. In 1892 the Scarritt Bible and Training School was dedicated in Kansas City.

Bennett lived for the rest of her life in Kentucky and was instrumental in establishing Sue Bennett College there (named for her sister). She continued her efforts to give women a voice in church councils, which succeeded in 1921. The following year she was appointed the first woman delegate to the Southern Methodist General Conference but was unable to attend because of failing health.

Scarritt College for Christian Workers was moved in 1924 to Nashville. A year later a clinic in Shanghai, China, was named for Bennett.

Cole, Anna Russell, 1846–1926, Philanthropist; NAW

Anna Russell Cole Auditorium, Tennessee Preparatory School Campus; NR

Anna Russell Cole was born in Augusta, Georgia, but most of her adult life was spent in Nashville. She married Edmund W. Cole, a banker, who established a foundation for a perpetual lectureship for the Biblical Department, now the Divinity School of Vanderbilt University. After her husband's death in 1899, Cole continued the lectureship and later endowed the university with a library, an office of dean of women, and a men's dormitory. Nashville considered her a grande dame who could always be counted on for contributions to the arts and to numerous charities. One of her interests was the Southern Sociological Congress, which studied social conditions in the South and sought to do away with illiteracy, child labor, and prostitution. She was a quiet advocate for peace, and at seventy she was a delegate to the International Peace Conference at Vienna, Austria.[10]

Fort, Cornelia Clark, 1919–1943, Aviator

Cornelia Fort Airpark, Briley Parkway

Cornelia Clark Fort was killed in a plane crash in 1943, the first woman pilot to die on active military duty in the history of the United States and the first

Tennessee woman casualty of World War II. She loved planes and flying, soloed in 1940, got a private pilot's license, then a commercial license, and became an instructor. On December 7, 1941, she was instructing in Hawaii. She almost collided with a bomber and to her horror saw that it was Japanese and was dropping bombs on Pearl Harbor. She returned to the mainland and went into the Ferrying Division of the Air Transport Command. She and the other women in the division delivered planes to army air bases in the United States, flying in open cockpit planes in freezing weather with none of the radio or safety aids that were later considered essential. In a letter written some time before her death she faced the fact that flying was dangerous but it was to her "a deeply personal possession of the soul . . . . I was happiest in the sky." Her memorial is a combined airpark, airport, and air harbor, built in 1945.[11]

Goodlet, Caroline Meriwether, fl. 1894, Clubwoman

Marker, Exchange Building

A wall marker on the front of the Exchange Building calls attention to the organization by Caroline Meriwether Goodlet of the National Daughters of the Confederacy—later the United Daughters of the Confederacy—on September 10, 1894.

Scholz, Belle Kinney, 1890–1959, Sculptor

Monument to Women of the Confederacy and Other Sculptures

Belle Kinney Scholz was born in Nashville. She was studying sculpture at the Chicago Art Institute at fifteen and two years later won her first commission. After her marriage to Leopold Scholz, also a sculptor, she often worked with him on sculptural commissions. A number of her works may be seen in Nashville. They include the Monument to the Women of the Confederacy, a replica of that in Jackson, Mississippi; the pediment of the Parthenon in Centennial Park; the Victory Statue at the War Memorial Building; a bust of Andrew Jackson in the state capitol; and busts of Admiral Albert Gleaves, Dean H. C. Tolman of Vanderbilt University, and Admiral David G. Farragut.[12]

NEW MARKET

Burnett, Frances Hodgson, 1849–1924, Writer; NAW

Markers at Site of Cabin, US 11E

One marker identifies the site of a cabin where Frances Hodgson Burnett lived in 1865. Here she met Swan Burnett, whom she married in 1873. Another marker mentions her most famous book, *Little Lord Fauntleroy*.

Burnett and her widowed mother and four siblings came to this sad little cabin from England. Her mother's brother, who had a business in Knoxville, Tennessee, had offered to help them find work, but when they arrived he was unable to fulfill his promise. The family, who had once been used to comfort, was reduced to poverty. Burnett tried to start a school, raised chickens, gave music lessons, and began to write stories. In 1868 *Godey's Lady's Book* bought one of her stories, and her career as a writer was off to a good start. After her marriage she and her husband left New Market, but she returned for occasional summers and some of her books were written here.

Aside from her writing, Burnett is remembered by British writers because she sued in the English courts for a pirated dramatization of *Little Lord Fauntleroy*. When she won, it established the dramatic rights of authors of novels published in Great Britain.

NUNNELLY

Whitson, Beth Slater, 1879–1930, Song Writer

Marker, West of State 48, at Nunnelly Road

The marker tells us that Goodrich, one mile west, was the birthplace of Beth Slater Whitson, "writer of poems, stories and songs. Her best-known song-lyrics were 'Meet me Tonight in Dreamland' and 'Let Me Call You Sweetheart.' She moved to Nashville in 1913 and is buried there in Spring Hill Cemetery."

NOTES

In addition to the correspondents noted below, I have had help from the Tennessee Historical Commission, the State Division for Tourist Development, the Clarksville-Montgomery County Public Library, and the Putnam County Library in Cookeville.

1. *Stories from Tennessee*, ed. Linda Burton (Knoxville: University of Tennessee Press, 1983).

2. *1975–1976 Tennessee Blue Book*, ed. Rita A. Whitfield (Nashville: State of Tennessee, 1976), p. 356; Marion E. Gridley, *American Indian Women* (New York: Hawthorne Books, 1974); correspondence, Marilou Awiakta, Memphis.

3. Carman Moore, "Blues and Bessie Smith," *New York Times*, Mar. 9, 1969, sec. 14.

4. Robert Drake, "Introduction" and "The Publishers' Story," in Frances Boyd Calhoun, *Miss Minerva and William Green Hill* (facsimile ed., Knoxville: University of Tennessee Press, 1976).

5. *Johnson City Press-Chronicle*, July 4, 1976; *Elizabethton Star*, July 14, 1976; correspondence, Elizabethton Public Library.

6. Peggy Robins, "Experiment at Nashoba Plantation," *American History Illustrated* 15 (Apr. 1980).

7. Charlotte S. Rubinstein, *American Women Artists* (New York: Avon Books, 1982).

8. "Notable Women in Tennessee History," *Tennessee Blue Book*, p. 359; correspondence, Ilene J. Cornwell, Southern Resources Unlimited, Nashville.

9. *Tennessee Blue Book*, p. 355; Mary Simmerson Logan, *The Part Taken by Women in American History* (New York: Perry-Nalle, 1972).

10. "Notable Women," p. 358.

11. Doris Brinker Tanner, "Cornelia Fort: A WASP in World War II," *Tennessee Historical Quarterly* 40 (Winter 1981); and 41 (Spring 1982).

12. "Notable Women," p. 359.

TEXAS

ACTON

Crockett, Elizabeth, 1788?–1860, Pioneer

Marker and Statue, Acton Cemetery

Elizabeth Crockett, born in Buncombe County, North Carolina, became in 1816 the second wife of Davy Crockett. She was the widow of a fellow soldier, with two children. Davy had three from his first marriage. The Crocketts moved from Tennessee to Texas in 1836, after he had served in the U.S. Congress. Shortly after their arrival in Texas Davy took part in the defense of the Alamo, where he was killed, leaving Elizabeth a widow once more. A statue surmounts a large pillar at her gravesite.[1]

AUSTIN

Driscoll, Clara (Sevier), 1881–1945, Preservationist; NAW

Laguna Gloria Art Museum, 3809 W. 35th Street; HABS, NR.
Marker, 2312 San Gabriel

Best remembered as the savior of the historical Alamo (see San Antonio, TX), Clara Driscoll lived in Austin from 1914 to 1933. She married Henry Sevier, a legislator and newspaper editor. They built Laguna Gloria, which she later gave to the Texas Fine Arts Association as an art gallery. Divorced in 1937, Clara took back her maiden name and was thereafter known as Mrs. Driscoll. She was a clubwoman, a writer, a strong Democratic party worker, and a businesswoman. Laguna Gloria is a showplace for regional and modern masters in many art forms. It is open Tues.-Sat. 10–5, Sun. 1–5, and Thurs. evenings until 9.

Ferguson, Miriam Amanda Wallace, 1875–1961, State Governor; NAWM

Executive Mansion, 1010 Colorado; NHL. Bust, State Capitol. Marker in Park Adjacent to Old Bakery, 1000 Block of Congress Street

Miriam Amanda Wallace Ferguson's political career began with her husband's downfall. Jim Ferguson was governor of the state from 1915 until 1917 when he was impeached and removed from office. Though he had been an active opponent of woman's suffrage, he helped his wife get elected to the governorship in 1924. Her initials, M. A., had been combined by a newspaperman and she was thereafter known as Ma Ferguson, a title she disliked. She was the second woman in the United States to take office as a state governor (inaugurated fifteen days after Nellie Tayloe Ross of Wyoming).

Ferguson remained in office for one term and after two successive losses returned for a second term in 1932. Though she shared the criticisms leveled at her husband, she nevertheless made a respectable record as governor. See Temple, TX.[2]

Hoblitzelle, Esther Thomas, 1894–1943, Singer

Esther Hoblitzelle Memorial Library, The Academic Center, University of Texas

Esther Thomas Hoblitzelle sang in New York City's Winter Garden as Esther Walker. She was said to have been one of America's finest delineators of southern tunes. In 1920 she married Karl Hoblitzelle and moved to his home in Dallas. She supported the Dallas Little Theater, sometimes performing there. Her husband's primary interest was drama—the theater and motion pictures. Ten years after his wife's death he gave the library to the University of Texas as a memorial to her.[3]

Ney, Elisabet, 1833–1907, Sculptor; NAW

Elisabet Ney Museum, 304 E. 44th Street; HABS, NR. Statues of Sam Houston and Stephen S. Austin, State Capitol. Memorial to Albert Sidney Johnston, State Cemetery

The first eminent Texas sculptor, Elisabet Ney was born in Germany and was already famous when she and her husband, Edmund Montgomery, emigrated to America. In 1873 they moved to Texas and established a home at Hempstead, q.v. The fact that she used her maiden name and even allowed it to be thought that she was unmarried though living with her ''dear friend'' made her subject to social criticism and some ostracism. But she soon won respect as an artist and was chosen to execute the statues of two of Texas's favorite sons for the state capitol and for Statuary Hall in the National Capitol. The studio, designed in 1892, is the property of the city of Austin. Newly restored and reopened as a museum, it is open Tues.-Fri. 11–4:30, Sat.-Sun. 2–4:30.[4]

Troutman, Joanna, 1818–1880, Flagmaker

Statue, State Cemetery

Joanna Troutman was never in Texas, but in 1913, long after her death, Texas claimed her as their adopted heroine and asked that her remains be sent from Knoxville, Georgia, to be interred in the Texas state cemetery. She won fame in 1833, when Texas was struggling to establish its rights as a state in the Mexican Republic. Troutman appealed to her native state for help and Georgia responded with a battalion (see Knoxville, GA). Troutman made the Lone Star Flag which they carried to Goliad. A statue by Pompeo Coppini surmounts the monument.[5]

BEAUMONT

Zaharias, Mildred Didrikson, 1911–1956, Athlete; NAWM

Babe Didrikson Zaharias Memorial Museum, Gulf Street Exit Off I–10. Marker, Forest Lawn Memorial Park

The Didrikson family moved to Beaumont in 1915, after a hurricane hit Port Arthur, Texas, q.v. Mildred (Babe) Didrikson Zaharias played on the high school basketball team. She was so outstanding an athlete that before she graduated she was chosen to play with the Employers Casualty Company's Golden Cyclones of Dallas, Texas. Women athletes found few competitive events open to them. In the 1932 Olympics only five events were open to women and no one could enter more than three. Babe won two gold and one silver medal and broke the world records in two of the events. In Dallas she was hailed as a heroine.

Opportunities for women to earn a living in sports were almost nonexistent. Babe appeared with the House of David baseball team and in vaudeville. In 1936 she tried golf. In a men's golf tournament she was paired with George Zaharias, and in 1938 they were married. George took over management of his wife's athletic career. She won many titles in golf, and after turning professional she joined other women to form the Ladies Professional Golf Association. She gave the game color and excitement. When she succumbed to cancer at the age of forty-five, the nation mourned the loss of one of the greatest women athletes in America. She had led the way in establishing a place for women in sports. She has been elected to many halls of fame, including the National Women's Hall of Fame in Seneca Falls, New York. The Texas Sports Hall of Fame in Grand Prairie has Zaharias memorabilia on display. The Beaumont museum also displays trophies and memorabilia. It is open daily 9–5.[6]

BROWNSVILLE

Porter, Gladys Sams, 1910–1980, Wildlife Conservationist

Gladys Porter Zoo, 500 Ringgold Street

Gladys Sams Porter was concerned about the vanishing wildlife of the world and felt that the best way to raise the public's consciousness of endangered species was to establish a first-class zoo. She chose Brownsville in south Texas, with its mild climate, as the ideal site. Construction of the zoo began in 1971. The entire project—building, stocking, equipping, and staffing the zoo—was done by one benevolent organization, the Sams Foundation, under the enthusiastic supervision of Porter. Her father, Earl C. Sams, had established the foundation and she succeeded him as head of it in 1950.

The zoo is one of the premier zoos in the world. It belongs to the city of Brownsville and is open every day of the year, 9 until an hour before dusk; adm. Children under 12 must be accompanied by an adult.[7]

CHICO

Babb, Bianca (Bell), 1855?–1950, Indian Captive

Marker, on FM 1810

Bianca Babb, aged about nine, and her thirteen-year-old brother, Dot Babb, were captured in 1865 by Comanches from their home, two miles south of the marker. Their mother was killed and another woman in the house was taken prisoner with the children. The woman escaped, but the children remained with different Indian groups for two years before their father was able to ransom them. Both spoke of the Indians without rancor and claimed to have been well treated. Bianca, later married to J. D. Bell, wrote of her experiences.[8]

CORPUS CHRISTI

Sidbury, Charlotte, 1830–1904, Businesswoman

Marker at Sidbury House, 1619 N. Chaparral

When Edward Sidbury died in 1881, his widow, Charlotte Sidbury, took over his lumber company and ran it successfully for years. She had previously managed her first husband's business between the time of his death in 1867 and her remarriage in 1875. She was also director of the Corpus Christi National Bank. While building her own fortune, she worked for many public improvements. Sidbury House was one of two houses she built about 1893. It is now the Junior League headquarters and is open to the public.[9]

DALLAS

Burson, Kalita Humphreys, 1918?–1954, Actress

Kalita Humphreys Theater, Dallas Theater Center

Kalita Humphreys Burson was the only child of Geraldine and Colonel R. W. Humphreys, of Liberty, Texas, q.v. She grew up in Texas—in Liberty, Dallas, and Galveston. Attracted by the legitimate stage, she spent years in New York City, where she performed in several Broadway productions. In Waco, Texas, where she was directing a play, she met Joe Burson, who had the leading role. They were married, moved to Liberty, and formed there the Valley Players, for whom they planned to build a theater. Both were killed in a tragic plane crash in 1954. In Liberty the Geraldine Humphreys Cultural Center includes the Humphreys-Burson Theater, now used by the Valley Players. The Dallas theater, designed by Frank Lloyd Wright, was financed in part by Geraldine Humphreys as a memorial to her daughter.[10]

Jones, Margo, 1912–1955, Theater Producer and Director; NAWM

Margo Jones Experimental Theater, Southern Methodist University

The theater in the round established and directed by Margo Jones in Dallas is no longer here, but her name is perpetuated at Southern Methodist University and in the Margo Jones award given annually to a producing manager. She knew early that presenting plays was to be her life work. After seeing a play performed in a hotel ballroom with the audience seated around the stage, she longed for a professional theater where the arena-type of staging could be used. With backing from the Rockefeller Foundation she was able to establish such a theater in Dallas. She was dedicated to the production of new plays and the work of new playwrights, and some of the famous American plays were first brought to the public in her theater. See Livingston, TX.

Starr, Belle, 1848–1889, Bandit; NAW

Markers, Site of Scyene Meeting Place, Belle Starr Lane and Scyene Road, and in City Park

Belle Starr lived in this vicinity at about age sixteen when she took a lover (probably Cole Younger) and gave birth to a daughter in 1868. William Quantrill's guerrillas often spent time at her father's house and she ran off with one of them and was married on horseback dressed in a black velvet riding habit. Younger was soon afterward sentenced to life in the state prison. Starr, ostracized, became a dance hall singer and professional gambler, leaving the child (whom she named Pearl Younger) with her parents. She soon took up with Jim Reed and in 1873 became a robber and outlaw. See Carthage, MO, and Bartlesville, OK.

FORT STOCKTON

Riggs, Annie Frazer Johnson, 1858–1931, Hotel Keeper

Annie Riggs Memorial Museum

In 1904 Annie Frazer Johnson Riggs, twice divorced and in need of support for her children, bought an adobe brick hotel in Fort Stockton for $4,750. She managed it until her death. The Riggs Hotel became famous as a meeting place for cowboys, drummers, travelers, and ranchers. In the dining room Riggs served her guests ample meals of fried chicken, potatoes, and cornbread for thirty-five cents. Overnight guests paid fifty cents per bed per night. In 1955 the Riggs family gave the building to the Fort Stockton Historical Society, which opened it as a local history museum. It displays cowboy gear, Indian artifacts, and early photographs, as well as the refurnished hotel lobby, parlor, dining room, kitchen, and a bedroom. It is open Sept.-May, Mon.-Sat. 10–12, 1–5, Sun. 1:30–5; June-Aug., Mon.-Sat. 10–8, Sun. 1:30–8; adm.[11]

GROESBECK

Parker, Cynthia Ann, 1827?–1864?, Indian Captive; NAW

Old Fort Parker State Historic Site, State 14. Statue, Parker Memorial Cemetery

Young Cynthia Ann Parker was carried away from this frontier fort in 1836 by Comanches who had killed five members of her family. She lived with the Indians, adopted their ways, married a warrior, and had several children. In 1860 the Texas Rangers recaptured Parker and her daughter, Prairie Flower, and reunited them with her white relatives. But she had forgotten her English and she mourned incessantly for her Indian home. Although she did recover the language and some of the white woman's housekeeping skills, she was bitterly lonely. After her little daughter died, Parker soon followed. She was buried in the Fosterville Cemetery in Poyner, Texas, q.v., but her remains were later removed to Oklahoma (see Norman, OK, under University of Oklahoma).

Old Fort Parker is a replica of the fort built by the Parker family. The Parker Memorial Statue, erected in 1932, has a column inscribed to Cynthia Ann. The park is open daily dawn to dusk; adm.

HAMILTON

Whitney, Ann, d. 1867, Heroic Teacher

Memorial, Courthouse Lawn. Marble Pillar, Graves-Gentry Cemetery

The memorial, in the form of granite blocks, commemorates the heroism of Ann Whitney, a schoolteacher who died in an attack by Comanches. After helping the pupils to escape through a back window of the log schoolhouse, she was shot and killed. Her grave was marked by schoolchildren.

HEMPSTEAD

Ney, Elisabet, 1833–1907, Sculptor; NAW

Liendo (Private); HABS, NR

Liendo was the home purchased by the artist Elisabet Ney and her husband, Edmund Montgomery, in 1873 after their arrival in Texas. The couple had one son, born a year before they moved to Liendo (their firstborn had died an infant). Montgomery gave up his medical practice and buried himself in philosophical writings, while Ney tried to bring up her son in her own image. She had been famous as a sculptor in her native Germany, and gradually she resumed this work. She soon won acceptance of her eccentricities and in 1890 was given commissions for statues (see Austin, TX). She is buried at Liendo under an oak tree.

HEREFORD

National Cowgirl Hall of Fame and Western Heritage Center, 515 Avenue B

The National Cowgirl Hall of Fame represents "women who have made a significant contribution to our Western heritage through their backgrounds as cowgirls, pioneers, educators, historians, missionaries, doctors, artists, or pace-setters." Many of the women honored by election are still living. Among honorees are women representing several western states. Sissy Thurman (d. 1968), of Texas, was one of the first three women inducted in 1975. Other Texas women chosen include Margaret Owens Montgomery (1922–1955), who organized and was first president of the Girls Rodeo Association; Sydna Woodyard (d. 1959), who performed in the 1940s and 1950s in Madison Square Garden and the Boston Garden; Mamie Burns, of the famous Pitchfork Ranch; Henrietta King, of the King Ranch (see Kingsville, TX); Sallie Reynolds Matthews (1861–1938), who spent almost all of her life on isolated western Texas ranches; and Reine Hafley

Shelton (d. 1979), who was brought up in the world of rodeo. She and her husband, Dick Shelton, starred in shows until the days of World War II, when the wild West era passed and most cowgirl events were abandoned.

Lucille Mulhall (1875?–1940) was an Oklahoma girl, star in the Wild West Show of her father, Zack Mulhall. Also from Oklahoma were Ann Lewis (d. 1968), who began barrel racing at the age of ten, and Augusta Metcalfe, a pioneer painter of the western scene. Washington State and the Northwest are represented by three women who are honored for the opening up of the West: Sacajawea, the Bird Woman; Narcissa Whitman, missionary, of Washington; and Mother Joseph (Esther Pariseau), also of Washington.

From Montana came Fannie Steele (1887–1983), chosen for the Cowgirl Hall of Fame as well as the National Cowboy Hall of Fame in Oklahoma City, Oklahoma. Louise Massey Mabie, "The Rhinestone Cowgirl" (d. 1983), from New Mexico, was honored not for her riding but her western music. Lilla Day Monroe (d. 1929) was a suffragist and humanitarian of Kansas. The 1984 honorees included the women of the Ingalls-Wilder family—Laura Ingalls Wilder, author of the Little House books; her mother, Caroline Ingalls; her sisters, Mary, Carrie, and Grace Ingalls; and her daughter, Rose Wilder Lane.[12]

HOUSTON

Blaffer, Sarah Campbell, 1884?–1975, Art Collector and Patron

Blaffer Gallery, University of Houston

Heir to two oil fortunes (her father's, of Texaco, and her husband's, Humble Oil), Sarah Campbell Blaffer had money to buy almost anything her heart desired. It was fortunate for Texas that she wished for such gems as Paul Cézanne's portrait of Madame Cézanne and Lucas Cranach's "Lucretia" and works by El Greco, Peter Paul Rubens, and Bartolomé Esteban Murillo. A collector whose tastes encompassed old masters and contemporary artists, Blaffer acquired more art than most Texans see in a lifetime. She endowed the Blaffer Foundation, which sponsors exhibitions to be shown throughout Texas. During her lifetime, Blaffer gave the University of Houston artworks dating from the fifteenth century to the modern day. Its art gallery was named in her honor. The gallery mounts eight to fifteen exhibits each year and schedules lectures, films, and tours.[13]

Hogg, Ima, 1882–1975, Philanthropist and Preservationist; NAWM

Bayou Bend, Houston Museum of Fine Arts, 1 Westcott Street

In presenting the distinguished alumnus award of the University of Texas to Ima Hogg in 1963, former Governor Allen Shrivers of Texas said of her: "Some persons create history. Some record it. Others restore and conserve it. She has done all three.'' Hogg was the daughter of James S. Hogg, politician, one-term governor, and booster of Texas. After his death in 1906 Hogg and her three brothers were left with what would become a large fortune in oil lands near West Columbia, Texas. Ima directed the expenditure of much of the money. She founded the Houston Symphony Orchestra, led in founding the Hogg Foundation for Mental Health, and for six years was on the Houston school board.

She preserved her family's estates at Quitman and West Columbia, q.v., and gave them to the state. Her own home, Bayou Bend, she gave to Houston's Museum of Fine Arts in 1966. It is filled with fine American furniture, collected over the years with taste and discrimination. It is open for tours by advance reservation only, Tues.-Fri. 10–11:45 and 12:45–2:30, and Sat. mornings. The second Sun. of every month, except Aug. and Mar., are Family Days, when no reservations are necessary and children under fourteen are admitted; closed holidays; flat-heeled shoes required.[14]

Ideson, Julia Bedford, 1880–1945, Librarian

Julia Ideson Building, Houston Public Library, 500 McKinney Avenue; NR

In 1903 Julia Bedford Ideson, a graduate of the University of Texas, was made librarian of the Houston Lyceum and Carnegie Library, a public library which had for fifty-five years existed as a subscription library. It had a staff of two full-time and one part-time, with a circulation of about sixty thousand. Ideson gave the next forty-two years to transforming it into the Houston Public Library. Two main library buildings were put up, the staff grew to forty-seven, and the circulation increased tenfold. Six branches and a bookmobile reached throughout the city. Ideson could not have accomplished this without energy, leadership, and executive ability—qualities she certainly possessed.

The Ideson Building houses the special collections, Texas and local history, and Houston materials. It is open Mon.-Sat. 9–6. The central library section is open Mon.-Sat. 9–9 and Sun. 2–6. Both have changing exhibits and programs.[15]

Moore, Edith Lotz, 1884–1975, Scientist and Conservationist

Edith L. Moore Sanctuary, Houston Audubon Society, 440 Wilchester

Edith Lotz Moore, a bacteriologist and pathologist for the U.S. Public Health Service, came to Houston's Camp Logan during the 1918 influenza epidemic. After the war she worked in government laboratories studying controls for malaria and bubonic plague. She married Jesse Moore, a milk inspector. Some twelve years later they moved out to the country and built a log cabin in the woods.

Houston expanded until it surrounded the pocket of wild country around the cabin. Moore hung on tenaciously to her land and when she died she left the Audubon Society twelve acres she had preserved as a sanctuary where others could walk in the woods and find the peace and happiness it had represented to her.[16]

KINGSVILLE

King, Henrietta Chamberlain, 1832–1925, and Her Granddaughter Henrietta Kleberg Armstrong, 1889–1969, Ranchers and Businesswomen

King Ranch; NHL. Henrietta M. King High School, Kleberg Avenue and 3rd Street; NR

When her husband died in 1885, Henrietta Chamberlain King inherited Santa Gertrudis, the biggest ranch in Texas, 500,000 acres, along with debts of $500,000. The great western cattle boom collapsed about this time and drought plagued the ranch almost continuously until 1893. She had an able ranch manager in Robert Kleberg, who married her daughter, Alice Gertrudis. For the next forty years King was boss of the ranch. When the town of Kingsville was founded King gave land for all the churches in town. She left an estate of over $5 million and a ranch double its original size.

After her death, the King Ranch Corporation was formed. Her granddaughter Henrietta Kleberg Armstrong was chairman of the board of the corporation from 1955 to 1968 and further developed the fabulous King Ranch into a vast scientific business. The ranch may be viewed from a loop tour around part of the premises.[17]

LIBERTY

Humphreys, Geraldine, 1876–1961, Philanthropist

Geraldine D. Humphreys Cultural Center

The center, financed in part by the Humphreys Foundation, occupies the site of Seven Pines, the home of Geraldine Humphreys. Rather late in life she married Colonel R. W. Humphreys. Their one daughter, Kalita, was killed in an airplane crash, along with her husband, Joe Burson. Desolated, Humphreys lived here, almost a recluse, until her own death in 1961. She gave a large contribution to Dallas for a theater named for Kalita Burson (see Dallas, TX). The cultural center includes the Humphreys-Burson Theatre, where plays are performed by the Valley Players, a group started by the Bursons.[18]

LIVINGSTON

Jones, Margo, 1912–1955, Theater Producer and Director; NAWM

Marker at Home, 517 S. Washington Avenue (Private)

Margo (christened Margaret) Jones used to enjoy sitting in the courtroom where her lawyer father was arguing cases. Naturally, she planned on becoming a lawyer too, until she realized that what she enjoyed was the drama in the courtroom, so she became a producer, the family barn her theater, her siblings the players and audience. She was fifteen before she saw her first professional play, *Cyrano* with Walter Hampden. She ultimately became a well-known producer and director, founder of a professional theater in Dallas, Texas, q.v.

MARSHALL

Pickens, Lucy Holcombe, 1832–1899, Confederate Hostess; NAW

Marker, US 80 and Bishop Street

Lucy Holcombe Pickens grew up here at Wyalucing, a mansion surrounded by cotton fields. At twenty-five she was still unmarried, though a beauty, with "titian hair, pansy eyes, and a graceful figure" and a reigning belle of the Deep South. Her mother took her to White Sulphur Springs in Virginia, where, if anywhere, she would certainly find a husband. She did. He was Francis W. Pickens of South Carolina. Though already twice married and twenty-seven years her senior, he was accepted by Lucy, and the couple were married at Wyalucing in the spring of 1858. They left at once for his post as U.S. minister to Russia. Lucy, with her beauty and her retinue of slaves, made a great impression on the court of the czar. The secession of southern states led to their return in 1860 to America, where Francis was elected governor of South Carolina. This gave Lucy a further chance to reign. Her likeness was engraved on the Confederate hundred dollar bill. See La Grange, TN.

MATAGORDA

McManus, Jane (Cazneau), 1807–1878, Publicist; NAW (Under Cazneau)

Marker at Site of Dream Colony, City Park

Jane McManus and her father and brother Robert McManus led a group of Germans to Texas in 1833 to form a colony. When the group refused to go farther than Matagorda, Jane and her father gave up the colonizing scheme and returned East, while Robert remained to become in time a successful and wealthy planter. This was not the end of Jane's dream of glory, for she wrote and lobbied for the annexation of Mexico, then of Cuba, and later for that of Santo Domingo and Nicaragua. Her career has been decribed as "a comedy of grandiose plans and bungled opportunities." She married William Leslie Cazneau, whom she had met in Matagorda. He was also a believer in Manifest Destiny, a schemer, and a dreamer.[19]

PORT ARTHUR

Zaharias, Mildred Didrikson, 1911–1956, Athlete; NAWM

Marker at Birthplace, 2232 7th Street (Private)

Mildred (Babe) Didrikson Zaharias, the first great American woman athlete, was born here into a large family. They moved to Beaumont, Texas, q.v., before she was of school age. The date of her birth does not seem to be recorded, but one of her sisters felt that it was 1911, and this is on her tombstone.

POYNOR

Parker, Cynthia Ann, 1827?–1864?, Indian Captive; NAW

Marker, Old Fosterville Cemetery

The first grave of Cynthia Ann Parker, who was captured as a child by Comanches and lived happily as an Indian for many years, was in this cemetery. Her son, Quanah, who never saw her again after she was rescued by Texas Rangers in 1861, became a leader of his people. When he learned of her death he mourned her, took her name, and eventually had her remains taken to his home near Fort Sill, Oklahoma, for burial. There are now numerous Parker descendants—Indian—some of whom were present at the dedication of the memorial to Parker here in 1969. See Groesbeck, TX, and the University of Oklahoma at Norman, OK.

QUITMAN

Hogg, Ima, 1882–1975, Philanthropist and Preservationist; NAWM

Miss Ima Hogg Museum, Governor Hogg Museum and State Park, 518 S. Main Street

Ima Hogg supervised and financed the restoration of her parents' first home here. They were Sarah Ann and James Stephen Hogg. James became governor of Texas when Ima was only nine and as her mother was in poor health Ima became a very important person in the governor's life. Her peculiar name, which never seemed to bother her in the least, came from a heroic poem written by an uncle. This is one of several historical properties restored and given the state by Ima (see Houston and West Columbia, TX). The shrine consists of three buildings: the Honeymoon Cottage (a replica of James's first home), the Stinson Home (Sarah Ann's family home), and the Ima Hogg Museum, constructed in 1969. The park is open daily. Tours of the three buildings are given Wed.-Sun. 9–12 and 1–4; adm. except to the museum.

REFUGIO

Scull, Sarah Jane Newman Robinson, 1817–post 1866, Rancher

Marker, Intersection of US 183 and State 202

Sarah Jane Newman Robinson Scull (or Skull) was a rancher and horse trader with a reputation of being a sure shot and a champion "cusser." She came to Texas around 1823, when Indian raids were frequent. By 1833 she was married to Jesse Robinson and had her own cattle brand. Two children were born to them before the couple was divorced. Sally then married George Scull, a gunsmith. She had several more husbands during her lifetime and became almost a legendary figure, "famed as a rough fighter . . . prudent men did not willingly provoke her in a row." During the Civil War her freight wagons took cotton to Mexico to swap for guns, ammunition, medicine, coffee, shoes, clothing, and other goods vital to the Confederacy. Dressed in trousers, with two pistols strapped to her waist, she bossed armed employees. After 1866 she disappears from history.[20]

RICHMOND

Long, Jane Wilkinson, 1798–1880, Pioneer Businesswoman

Markers, at Site of Home and at Boarding House, 200 Block of 4th Street

Jane Wilkinson Long has been called the Mother of Texas because she was probably the first woman of English descent to come to Texas and her daughter Mary the first child of English ancestry born here. She came with her husband, James Long, a physician and a professional soldier, when Texas was Spanish territory. He wanted to claim it for the United States. While he went off to fight for Texas independence, Jane insisted on remaining at Bolivar Point to await his return. All the others stationed there moved on until the pregnant Jane, her six-year-old daughter Ann, and a young servant girl were the only persons left. She waited and waited, feeding herself and the youngsters by catching fish and shooting birds. On December 21, 1821, she delivered the baby, Mary, alone during a snowstorm.

After being rescued she learned that she was a widow. James had been shot in Mexico. Bravely she went to work to support herself and to repay her husband's debts. He had invested and lost the whole family fortune in the ill-fated expedition. Jane got title to land near Fort Bend, the nucleus later for the town of Richmond. She opened a hotel in Brazoria in 1832 and five years later another in Richmond. She was well known to the colonizers and politicians of early Texas and she lived to see the country become a republic, then a territory of the United States, then a member of the Confederate states.[21]

SAN ANTONIO

De Zavala, Adina, 1861–1955, and Clara Driscoll (Sevier), 1881–1945, Preservationists; NAW (under Driscoll)

The Alamo; HABS, NHL. Spanish Governor's Palace, 105 Military Plaza; NHL

Adina De Zavala, author of the *History and Legends of the Alamo*, organized in 1893 a group of her friends as the De Zavala Chapter of the Daughters of the Republic of Texas. Their objective was the preservation of the old missions and landmarks of Texas. In 1899 she met Clara Driscoll (see Austin, TX) and interested her in saving the Alamo, the scene of the most famous battle of the 1863 Texas Revolution. The women bought one building, with Driscoll's money. Two years later the state repaid Driscoll and gave the entire site to the Daughters of the Republic of Texas. She contributed the money to buy the rest of the block containing the Alamo. A plaque in the old chapel honors Driscoll, and a marker has been placed at her grave in Alamo Masonic Cemetery.

De Zavala, who had become disenchanted with the Daughters, then formed the Texas Historical and Landmark Association to save from decay the old Spanish Governor's Palace, which had been used (or misused) as, among other things, a secondhand clothing store, a restaurant, and a schoolhouse.

The Alamo, properly titled Mission San Antonio de Valero, has two museums with displays on Texas history. Open Mon.-Sat. and holidays (except Christmas), 9–5:30. The Governor's Palace is open Mon.-Sat. 9–5, Sun. 10–5; closed some holidays; adm.[22]

McNay, Marion Koogler, 1883–1950, Art Collector and Philanthropist

Marion Koogler McNay Art Museum, N. New Braunfels Avenue

Marion Koogler McNay was "a discriminating collector, a generous patron, an earnest student of the fine arts, and a philanthropist of the first magnitude." She had an impressive collection of representative work by all the major figures in French art after 1875, a rich group of American watercolors, and many New Mexico crafts. They formed the nucleus of the present museum when she willed to the city her home, twenty-three acres surrounding it, and an endowment for its support. It was the first privately endowed museum in Texas.

Since its opening in 1954 as a public gallery, many other collectors have contributed notable paintings, sculpture, prints, and graphic arts to fill out the collections. The building has been expanded to house and display its magnificent holdings. The museum is open Tues.-Sat. 9–5, Sun. 2–5; closed some holidays; donation.[23]

Stinson, Katherine (Otero), 1891?–1977, and Her Sister Marjorie Stinson, 1896?–1975, Aviators

Stinson Field, San Antonio Municipal Airport

The Stinsons were a pioneer aviation family. Emma Beavers Stinson founded a flying school in San Antonio, where her daughters, Katherine and Marjorie Stinson, and her sons, Edward and Jack Stinson, all learned to fly. She and Katherine incorporated the Stinson Aircraft Company in 1913 and two years later opened Stinson Field. Katherine was the fourth woman to qualify for a pilot's license. Billed as "the flying schoolgirl," she performed at air shows across the country, thrilling crowds by diving, racing automobiles, and turning loops. She contracted tuberculosis in the 1920s and went to a sanitarium in New Mexico. There she met Miguel Otero, a World War I aviator and son of a territorial governor. They were married in 1928 and promised each other to give up flying.

Marjorie, who held pilot's license No. 9, issued when she was a teenager, had a less spectacular career. She taught more than a hundred student pilots while she herself was under twenty and was called the flying schoolmarm.[24]

SPUR

Elliot, Margaret A., 1899–1979, Teacher

Margaret A. Elliot Museum

In 1972 a group of former students of Spur schools began a search for means by which the dormant local museum might be revived and made into an appropriate memorial to Margaret A. Elliot, the woman for whom it was named. They hit upon an ingenious scheme to get support. They made copies of the weekly newspaper, *The Texas Spur*, cut up the individual news stories and mailed them to the children and grandchildren of the people about whom the stories were written, with a letter asking for support. With the contributions, they were able to get a curator, and today they are proud of their museum. The teacher who had inspired them left Spur to teach in a number of Texas schools, and when she returned she revitalized many of the town's institutions. Former students paid tribute to her memory when they visited the museum in 1984, the seventy-fifth anniversary of the founding of Spur.[25]

TEMPLE

Ferguson, Miriam Amanda Wallace, 1875–1961, State Governor; NAWM

Ferguson House, 518 N. 7th Street (Private); NR. Marker at Birthplace, Three Miles East of Sparks Baptist Church, Off State 95

Miriam Amanda Wallace Ferguson married James Ferguson, a cousin by marriage, in 1899. In 1915 he took office as governor of Texas, and in 1924 she became governor (see Austin, TX).

WEST COLUMBIA

Hogg, Ima, 1882–1975, Philanthropist and Preservationist; NAWM

Varner-Hogg Plantation Historical Park, Off State 35; HABS, NR

Ima Hogg, of Houston, Texas, q.v., preserved the country home of her father, James S. Hogg, the first native-born governor of Texas. It was originally a sugar and cotton plantation, with a Greek Revival house built in 1824. Martin Varner was the first Anglo-American owner of the land. Hogg furnished it with materials from the period 1830–50 and gave it to the state in 1958 as a park and museum. It is open Tues. and Thurs.-Sat. 10–11:30 and 1–4:30, Sun. 1–4:30; adm. The park is open Memorial Day–Labor Day daily, 1–5; in winter, 1–4:30. See Quitman, TX.

NOTES

In addition to the sources mentioned below, I have had assistance from the Texas State Library, Austin; Carnegie Library in Jefferson; the Marion County Historical Commission; the Texas Woman's University, Denton; Elisabet Ney Memorial Library, Austin; Mabel Davis Rose Garden, Austin; Rob and Bessie Welder Wildlife Federation, Sinton; A. M. and Alma Fiedler Memorial Museum, Seguin; and the Texas State Historical Association, Austin.

1. William M. Jones, *Texas History Carved in Stone* (Houston, Tex.: n.p., 1958).
2. Billy M. Jones, "Miriam Amanda Ferguson," in *Women of Texas*, ed. James M. Day and others (Waco, Tex.: Texian Press, 1972).
3. Correspondence, Harry Ranson Humanities Research Center, University of Texas, Austin.

4. Alice K. Scharfe, "Studio on the Frontier," *Americana* 11 (Mar.-Apr. 1983); Glenda S. Kachelmeier, "Elisabet Ney," *Texas Highways*, Mar. 1983; correspondence, Ney Museum.

5. William M. Jones, op. cit.

6. Mary Kay Knief, "The Babe," in *Legendary Ladies of Texas*, ed. Francis E. Abernathy (Dallas, Tex.: E. Heart Press, 1981).

7. Clippings and correspondence, Gladys Porter Zoo.

8. Correspondence, Texas Historical Commission. The Bell MS is in the University of Texas Archives.

9. Information from La Retama Public Library in Corpus Christi, and Texas Historical Commission.

10. Correspondence, Liberty Municipal Library.

11. Correspondence and clippings, Fort Stockton Historical Society.

12. Information from Cowgirl Hall of Fame.

13. Correspondence, Blaffer Gallery.

14. *New York Times*, Aug. 21, 1975; Michael R. Olmert, "The Great Collectors," *Historic Preservation* 34 (Nov.-Dec. 1982).

15. *Dictionary of American Library Biography*, ed. Bohdan S. Wynor (Littleton, Colo.: Libraries Unlimited, Inc., 1978).

16. Houston Audubon Society *Bulletin*, June 1975.

17. Tom Lea, *The King Ranch* (Boston, Mass.: Little, Brown & Co., 1957); *New York Times*, Oct. 24, 1969.

18. Correspondence and clippings, Liberty Municipal Library.

19. Robert E. May, "Lobbyists for Commercial Empire," *Pacific Historical Review* 48 (Aug. 1979).

20. Western Writers of America, *The Women Who Made the West* (Garden City, N.Y.: Doubleday & Co., 1980); Dan Kilgore, "Two Sixshooters and a Sunbonnet: The Story of Sally Skull," in *Legendary Ladies of Texas*.

21. Martha Ann Turner, "Jane Wilkinson Long," in *Women of Texas*.

22. Clifford Lord, *Keepers of the Past* (Chapel Hill: University of North Carolina Press, 1965).

23. Brochure and information from McNay Art Museum.

24. *New York Times*, Apr. 16, 1975 and July 11, 1977.

25. Information from the Margaret A. Elliot Museum.

VIRGINIA

ALEXANDRIA

Barrett, Kate Waller, 1857–1925, Social Worker; NAW

Kate Waller Barrett Memorial Building (Alexandria Library), 717 Queen Street. Plaque at Home, 404 Duke Street

One night a young unwed mother with her baby came to the door of Kate Waller Barrett, wife of a Richmond, Virginia, minister, asking for help. When Barrett talked to the mother she found that the woman was much like herself in background and held the same values. "It was all so different from what I had thought and imagined," she wrote. She began to take an interest in the unfortunate women referred to as fallen. When her husband, Robert Barrett, later became dean of St. Luke's Cathedral in Atlanta, Georgia, she opened a home for unmarried mothers. In search of funds, she wrote to Charles Crittenton, a millionaire who had founded a number of missions named for his daughter. Barrett's home thus became the fifth in a chain of Florence Crittenton Homes. (See Atlanta, GA.)

The Barretts settled in Alexandria in 1894 when Robert was appointed to an office in the Protestant Episcopal Church. He died two years later, leaving his wife and six children. To add to their limited income and to occupy her energies, Barrett gave much time to the Florence Crittenton missions. She became vice president and general superintendent of the national mission, with full responsibility for supervising its many homes across the country. In 1909 Charles Crittenton, president of the organization, died and she succeeded him, working in this capacity until her death. See Williamsburg, VA.

The building housing the public library was donated as a memorial to her by her son, Robert S. Barrett (who followed her as president of the mission) and his wife. The plaque at the old Barrett Home was erected in 1926 by the American Legion Department of Virginia to recognize her work with the legion's auxiliary in 1922 and 1923.[1]

ASHLAND

Madison, Dolley Payne Todd, 1768–1849, Washington Hostess; NAW

Scotchtown (Dolley Payne Home), State 685; HABS, NHL

Dolley Payne Todd Madison lived in this house from her seventh to her fifteenth year. It had formerly been the home of Patrick Henry, her mother's cousin. The family moved to Philadelphia, Pennsylvania, and there in 1790 Dolley married John Todd, Jr. Within three years Dolley was a widow with a young son. She chose for her second husband James Madison, a man much her senior and already recognized as one of the new nation's leading statesmen. When James was made secretary of state, Dolley became famous as a Washington hostess. During the War of 1812 when the British began to burn the public buildings, quick-witted Dolley salvaged many important documents and a Stuart portrait of George Washington before she fled to Virginia. See Orange, VA, and Greensboro, NC.

Scotchtown is open to the public Apr. 1–Oct. 31, Mon.-Sat. 10–4:30, Sun. 1:30–4:30; adm.

CHARLOTTESVILLE

Munford, Mary-Cooke Branch, 1865–1938, Educator; NAW

Munford Building, University of Virginia. Plaque, Alderman Library, University of Virginia

Mary-Cooke Branch Munford's great desire, as a young girl, was to go to college, but according to her mother's deepest beliefs, no well-brought up southern lady could be exposed to college life. Reluctantly, Munford gave up her dream. After she married Beverly Munford, whose ideas were more elastic than her mother's, she helped establish the first woman's club in Richmond, Virginia. When she launched a plan for a women's college coordinate with the University of Virginia, opponents were vehement. A college for women in Charlottesville, they said, "would destroy the spirit and character of the University." "There is no special need for highly educated women," claimed an editorial. Woman already has "all she needs to make herself agreeable to men." From 1910 until the outbreak of World War I bills were regularly sent to the legislature for the establishment of the coordinate college, all meeting defeat. But there were good results: the College of William and Mary opened its doors to women, and when the University of Virginia accepted women on the graduate level, Munford's name was given to the residence hall built for them. In the Alderman Library a tablet honors Munford, "Member of the Board of Visitors of this University, 1926–1938, who carried the devotion of a great mind and a flaming spirit into unselfish service to public education throughout Virginia. Her memorial is in numberless young lives set free."[2]

Sacajawea, c. 1786–1812, Shoshoni Indian Guide; NAW

Statue to Lewis and Clark, Ridge and Main Streets

Both Meriwether Lewis and William Clark, who in 1805–6 led the Corps of Discovery across the country to the Pacific Ocean, were born near here. Sacajawea, Indian wife of the French-Canadian guide who accompanied the party, was the only woman in the group. The bronze statue here, unveiled in 1919, shows Sacajawea crouched at the feet of Lewis and Clark. See Cloverport, KY.

CHOPAWAMSIC CREEK

Brent, Margaret, c. 1601–c. 1671 (NAW), and Her Sister Mary Brent, fl. 1600s, Catholic Pioneers

Memorial Cross

A large bronze crucifix, designed by George J. Lober, memorializes the first English Catholic settlers in Virginia, Margaret, Mary, and Giles Brent, who came here from Maryland about 1650 and established homes on Aquia Creek. The children of the Lord of Admington and Lark Stoke in Gloucester, England, they had arrived in Maryland in 1638 with a letter from Lord Baltimore recommending that they be granted land in the new colony. Margaret and Mary took up land at St. Mary's City. The family was influential in Maryland's early years, and Margaret is especially notable for managing her own affairs and for some years those of the proprietor and for asking for two votes in the colonial assembly. She was not given the vote, but she won respect from the assemblymen. Why the Brents left Maryland is not clear, but they established Virginia's first English-speaking Catholic colony. The site of their homes is some thirty-three miles from the District of Columbia on Chopawamsic Creek, a branch of the Potomac River.[3]

COBHAM

Rives, Amélie (Princess Troubetskoy), 1863–1945, Writer; NAW

Castle Hill, State 231

Amélie Rives (Princess Troubetskoy) spent her early years here at her family's estate, moving to Mobile, Alabama, when her father became head civil engineer of the Mobile and Birmingham Railroad. She began writing short stories and the *Atlantic Monthly* bought one in 1886, when she was twenty-three. Two years later a novel, *The Quick and the Dead?* shocked some of her readers but delighted many others. In 1896 she married Prince Pierre Troubetskoy, a painter and son of a Russian nobleman. In 1915 she published *Shadows of Flames*, one of the first realistic accounts of drug addiction. She had become an addict after doctors prescribed large doses of morphine. She regained her health at Castle Hill and retired here after Prince Troubetskoy died in 1936. Many of her novels use the estate as background, thinly disguised. The house, with its serene setting and carefully restored interior, is open Mar.-Nov., daily 10–5; adm.[4]

COVINGTON

Bailey, Anne Hennis (Mad Anne) Trotter, 1742–1825, Pioneer Soldier and Scout

Plaque, Near Falling Spring Waterfall, US 220

Anne Hennis (Mad Anne) Trotter Bailey, who came from England as an indentured servant, married Richard Trotter. After he was killed by Indians at Point Pleasant, West Virginia, q.v., she set out to avenge his death. Dressed in men's clothes and carrying an axe, rifle, and knife, she became an army scout. ''Mad Anne'' is credited with killing numerous Indians but escaped herself to live out her eighty-three years. In 1785 she married John Bailey. The plaque marks the site of the hut on Mad Anne Ridge where she spent some years.[5]

DANVILLE

Astor, Nancy Langhorne, Lady, 1879–1964, Member of British Parliament, and Her Sister, Irene Langhorne Gibson, 1873–1956, "The Gibson Girl"

Marker at Site of Home, Broad Street. Lady Astor Street

A post in front of a building marks the site of a frame dwelling, long since demolished, that was the birthplace of several beautiful women. Irene Langhorne Gibson married the artist Charles Dana Gibson in 1895 and was the first ''Gibson Girl,'' made famous by his drawings. Her sister Nancy Langhorne Astor married twice. The first marriage to Robert Shaw lasted only four years and ended in divorce. In 1906 she became the wife of Waldorf Astor, heir to one of the wealthiest men in the world. The couple lived in England, where Lady Astor ran for Parliament. She was elected in 1919 and held her seat for twenty-five years. The first woman to sit in the British Parliament, she fought for women's rights with the special fire and vigor that marked her style.

The Langhorne family lived at Mirador, in Greenwood, Virginia, while the girls were growing up. Lady Astor Street was so named in 1922.[6]

ELK CREEK

Sage, Caty, fl. 1787–1848, Indian Captive

Marker, US 21

The state marker, four miles south of the Wythe County line, tells us that James and Lovis Sage lived in this area, where their five-year-old daughter, Caty Sage, was captured by Indians in 1792. Fifty-six years later a brother found her living with Wyandot Indians in eastern Kansas.

FRONT ROYAL

Boyd, Belle, 1844–1900, Confederate Spy; NAW

Marker, US 340

After a brief period of incarceration in Baltimore, Maryland, when the federal forces caught on to her activities as a Confederate spy, Belle Boyd came to stay with an aunt in Front Royal. On May 24, 1862, General Stonewall Jackson prepared to recapture Front Royal from Union troops. Boyd had learned that the Union forces planned to destroy the bridges leading out of town and she raced on foot, dressed in a "dark blue dress and fancy white apron," across the battlefield to warn Jackson's troops. Somehow she got safely across with her message. The incident was widely reported, making Boyd famous in the South and notorious in the North and leading to her recapture and imprisonment in Washington, D.C. After the war was over Boyd lectured and wrote on her war experiences. The historical marker is about three miles southwest of town. See Martinsburg, WV.

GLENALLEN

Randolph, Virginia, 1874?–1958, Educator

Virginia Randolph Cottage; NHL

When she was eighteen, Virginia Randolph was put in charge of the Mountain Road School, a shabby little schoolhouse on a bare patch of ground in Henrico County. She begged gravel and had the ruts in the ground smoothed out. She got some good earth spread around, planted grass seed, and persuaded some of the parents of the children to plant trees. Inside the schoolroom she added curtains and plants to make the place more inviting. She begged leftover craft materials from white teachers so that her pupils could have the experience of sewing and weaving. The children in turn took their ideas home and the parents began to liven up their own homes.

The county superintendent of schools took note of this young teacher who "thought of her work in terms of the welfare of a whole community, and of the school as an agency to help people to live better." He wanted to have her teach other teachers to do likewise. He arranged for this by utilizing the services of Anna T. Jeanes.

Jeanes (1822–1907, NAW), a Philadelphia Quaker, had set up the Negro Rural School Fund, Anna T. Jeanes Foundation, which would pay the salaries of teachers such as Randolph. Randolph was appointed the first Jeanes Teacher, the forerunner of a host of dedicated teachers who would go into the rural schools throughout the South and inspire other teachers to give of their best. Randolph was supervisor of the Negro schools in her county for more than a quarter of a century. She saw the little school to which she had given her heart become the Virginia Randolph County Training School, with 235 pupils, some of them in the high school grades.[7]

GORE

Cather, Willa, 1873–1947, Writer; NAW

Willa Cather Birthplace, US 50 (Private); NR.
Marker, US 50

The old mill on Back Creek nearby is described in one of Willa Cather's novels, *Sapphira and the Slave Girl*. The writer was born in Gore and lived here in a house called Willowshade for the first ten years of her life. The children lived out-of-doors most of the time, enjoying the woods and fields and creeks. In 1883 the family moved with other Virginians to Nebraska, a far, far different world, a world of great spaces, isolation, and hard work. Some of Cather's best novels interpret that world, although she moved East again after her college years and lived in Pittsburgh, Pennsylvania, in Greenwich Village, New York City, and in New England.

HAMPTON

Pocahontas, 1595?–1617, Indian Princess; NAW

Memorial Window, St. John's Church, W. Queen and Court Streets

The story of the rescue of Captain John Smith by Pocahontas is known to every American schoolchild, although it may be pure fiction. The incident was recorded by Smith, a leader of the colony at Jamestown, in 1622, after Pocahontas died. He says he was captured by Indians under Chief Powhatan and was about to be killed when Powhatan's teenaged daughter interceded for him.

It is true that when Pocahontas was a few years older John Rolfe, one of the colonists—then a widower—courted her. She was taught the precepts of Christianity, baptized Rebecca, and in 1614 married to Rolfe. The couple visited England, where Pocahontas was presented to Queen Anne, attended a play by Ben Jonson, and was very popular in society. As they prepared to leave England, Pocahontas became ill and died, perhaps from exposure to cold and damp. She was buried at Gravesend. Through her son, Thomas Rolfe, she left a long line of descendants.

The memorial window was donated by Indian students at Hampton Institute. The parish museum is open Mon.-Fri. 9–3, Sat. 9–12. See Anadarko, OK.[8]

JAMESTOWN

Pocahontas, 1595?–1617, Indian Princess; NAW

Statue, Churchyard

The idealized statue of the young Pocahontas, by William Partridge, was erected in 1922 to honor the friend and protector of the fledgling colony. All of Jamestown, where the first permanent English colony was established in America in 1607, is a historical site, open daily, 8:30–5:30 in summer, shorter hours in winter. See Hampton, VA, and Anadarko, OK.

KILMARNOCK

Shuck, Henrietta Hall, 1817–1844, Missionary

Marker at Birthplace, State 3

Henrietta Hall Shuck, the daughter of a Baptist minister in Kilmarnock, went to China in 1835 as the bride of Jehu Lewis Shuck. She was the first American woman missionary to China. The couple began their labors in Macao, where Henrietta soon learned Chinese and her husband baptized the first Chinese converts. During her eight years in China she had five children, but that did not stop her from teaching twenty Chinese boys and six girls in a schoolhouse they erected in Hong Kong. She wrote of her life in *Scenes in China: or, Sketches of the Country, Religion, and Customs of the Chinese*, which was published in 1852. Henrietta never returned from China, dying there soon after the birth of her fifth baby.

LYNCHBURG

Spencer, Anne Scales, 1882–1975, Poet and Librarian

Anne Spencer House, 1313 Pierce Street; NR

Anne Scales Spencer came to Lynchburg in 1901 after marriage to Edward A. Spencer. She lived here for the rest of her life, making an impact on the community as organizer of the Lynchburg chapter of the National Association for the Advancement of Colored People; as librarian, 1924–46, at Dunbar High School (the first library in the city to serve blacks); and as a poet. Her home was a center of black culture in Lynchburg. Here she entertained James Weldon Johnson, a leading black poet of the Harlem Renaissance; Congressman Adam Clayton Powell; Paul Robeson, Roland Hayes, and Marian Anderson from the world of music; George Washington Carver, the great botanist; and a host of others.

Edward built for his wife a small studio in back of the main house, where she could write her poetry undisturbed. Her poems were published in magazines and many anthologies. She created a special garden which has been restored by the Hillside Garden Club. The house is under the jurisdiction of the Friends of Anne Spencer Memorial Foundation. The home is open six days a week 10–4:30, by appointment (804–846–0517).[9]

ORANGE

Madison, Dolley Payne Todd, 1768–1849, Washington Hostess; NAW

Montpelier, State 20 (Private); NHL

Montpelier was the estate of James Madison, who married Dolley Payne Todd Madison in 1794. They came to live here three years later, after he retired from the House of Representatives. In 1801, with his appointment as secretary of state, they moved to Washington, D.C., where Dolley was in her element as a hostess and unofficial First Lady for President Thomas Jefferson, a widower. Until 1817 the Madisons spent the late summer months at Montpelier to escape the Washington heat. Then, his second term of office at an end, they lived here until his death in 1836. They entertained constantly, for everyone wanted to visit James and enjoy Dolley's sparkle. She moved back to her beloved Washington for her last twelve years and died there. Her remains were brought to Montpelier about 1858 and buried under a gravestone inscribed "Wife of James Madison." The house is not open to the public, but the family cemetery is open in daylight hours. See Ashland, VA, and Greensboro, NC.

PEAKE

Barrett, Janie Porter, 1865–1948, Social Worker; NAW

Janie Porter Barrett School for Girls

As the first president of the Virginia State Federation of Colored Women's Clubs, Janie Porter Barrett led the organization in social service projects. She found an eight-year-old girl who had been thrown into jail for some minor infraction of the law, a discovery which highlighted the need for a rehabilitation center for black girls caught up in the justice system. The federation spent three years in fund-raising and bought a 147-acre farm in Peake (eighteen miles north of Richmond). There the Virginia Industrial School for Colored Girls was opened in 1915. Barrett moved to the school as resident superintendent and made the institution a model one, emphasizing the development of individual responsibility and training the inmates in elementary school subjects and domestic skills. She retired in 1940 and ten years later the name of the institution was changed to honor her.[10]

RADFORD

Inglis, Mary Draper, 1729–1813, Indian Captive

Monument, City Cemetery

The dramatic life of Mary Draper Inglis (Ingles) is celebrated annually here with a summer performance of *The Long Way Home*. She was captured by Indians at Draper's Meadows in 1755 and taken to Ohio, then to Kentucky (see Brent, KY). She managed to escape and after forty days of laborious travel through the wilderness, she reached home. Of the two sons taken with her, one was found seventeen years later, quite Indianized. The other died shortly after being taken captive. Inglis and her husband had four more children, and she lived to be eighty-three. The drama based on her life is performed at the site of her log cabin during June, July, and Aug.

RICHMOND

Glasgow, Ellen Gholson, 1873–1945, Writer; NAW

Glasgow Home, 1 W. Main Street; HABS, NHL

The first serious literature of the South was written by Ellen Gholson Glasgow, who was determined to portray in her novels the South as it really was and not as shown by romantic writers such as Mary Johnston and Amélie Rives. Glasgow wrote many novels, some (*Barren Ground, The Romantic Comedians*, and *The Sheltered Life*) regarded as significant in American letters.

The Glasgow house is leased to the Richmond school system for a humanities center and is owned by the Association for the Preservation of Virginia Antiquities.[11]

Valentine, Lila Meade, 1865–1921, Reformer; NAW

Plaque, House of Delegates, State Capitol

Lila Meade Valentine's concern for the well-being of her city impelled her to work for educational and health reforms. Noting the poor health of many schoolchildren, she supported a visiting nurses' group to instruct women in hygiene and nutrition. Out of this grew a dispensary, clinics, and a tuberculosis sanitarium. In 1900 she founded the Richmond Educational Association, composed of citizens who worked to improve the school system. On a visit to England in 1905 she was impressed by the suffragettes' fight for the vote and returned ready to work for suffrage. Political questions that affected women and children, she felt, required the woman's voice in decisions. The Equal Suffrage League of Virginia was organized in 1906 and Valentine was its president for eleven years.

Many of her papers are in the Valentine Museum, 1005 Clay Street. The museum was founded by the father of her husband Benjamin B. Valentine.

Van Lew, Elizabeth, 1818–1900, Union Agent; NAW

Monument, Shockoe Hill Cemetery

As the Union Army marched toward Richmond in 1864 Elizabeth Van Lew began to act and dress so oddly that she was thought to be crazy. But ''Crazy Bet'' was one of the Union's most successful agents, sending messages to the federal officers right under the noses of the Confederates. She had long been able to think for herself and act upon her principles. Hating slavery, she had freed all her slaves and purchased the freedom of their relatives from other owners. She was against secession and went frequently to Libby Prison to bring food and clothing to the federal officers there. She is said to have helped some of them escape, hiding them in her house on Grace Street. Naturally, she had few friends in the South, and she lived as a virtual outcast for many years. Financial help was given her by a Boston, Massachusetts, family whose son she had aided in Libby Prison, and General Ulysses S. Grant appointed her postmistress of Richmond. She was still a rebel, however, and a fighter for what she thought right; for years she paid taxes under protest on the grounds that as a woman she had no voice in the spending of them.

The monument over her grave, a Roxbury ''pudding stone'' from Boston's Capitol Hill, was erected by northern sympathizers.

Walker, Maggie Lena, 1867–1934, Banker; NAW

Home, 110A E. Leigh Street; NHL. Maggie Lena Walker High School, Lombardy Street

Maggie Lena Walker's mother was a freed slave, a cook in Elizabeth Van Lew's house. Walker grew up there, then went to normal school and taught for several years. In 1886 she married Armstead Walker, a contractor. Her career as an entrepreneur and woman bank president (the first in the country) began through volunteer work for a fraternal society, the Independent Order of St. Luke's. When she took over as secretary-treasurer, the order had $46.10 in cash and thousands of members who were potential claimants. She put its books in order, started new branches, and undertook a number of other programs to improve the financial status of her race. She sponsored a Penny Savings Bank which grew so big it lent money to the city of Richmond. Walker founded and presided over the Richmond Council of Colored Women, a group that raised thousands of dollars for Negro educational and health programs. In addition to her home, which is being restored by the National Park Service, the high school, a street, and a theater in Richmond were named for her.

Maggie Lena Walker, bank president of Richmond, Virginia. The 12 ½″ bronze bust, by P. Beneduce, was commissioned in 1934 when national black organizations set aside the month of October to recognize Walker's achievements. The original is in the Virginia Historical Society. Photography by Katherine Wetzel.
Courtesy Virginia Historical Society.

STAUNTON

Baldwin, Mary Julia, c. 1850–1897, Educator

Mary Baldwin College; NR

Mary Baldwin College started as Augusta Female Seminary in 1842. Mary Julia Baldwin was a student in 1844 and its principal from 1863 to 1897. During the Civil War when most schools closed their doors, the seminary remained open. Whenever they heard that the Yankees were coming, the girls hid the firewood and provisions in the dressing tables and desks. In 1895–96 the legislature changed the name of the school to Mary Baldwin Seminary in appreciation of her services as principal for thirty-four years. Baldwin controlled the academy for a full generation and at the time of her death was educating the daughters of her former pupils. In 1923 the school became a college.[12]

SWEET BRIAR

Guion, Connie Myers, 1882–1971, Physician

Guion Building, Sweet Briar College

Connie Myers Guion was born in North Carolina. She came to Sweet Briar as head of the chemistry department when the school was but two years old. She loved it and was sorry to leave after five years, but it was time to fulfill her dream of studying medicine. She earned her M.D. from Cornell Medical College in 1917 and was then associated with the New York Hospital for over fifty years, winning many awards as a distinguished physician and a woman of extraordinary achievements. Sweet Briar named its science building for her.[13]

TAZEWELL

Tynes, Mary Elizabeth, b. c. 1837, Civil War Heroine

Marker, US 61

The state marker tells us that "To the north was 'Rocky Dell,' the home of Samuel Tynes. From here on July 17, 1863, his daughter Molly rode across the mountains to Wytheville to warn the town of an attack by Federal Forces under Colonel J. T. Toland." Although some historians doubt the accuracy of the legend, it is popularly believed that Mary Elizabeth (Molly) Tynes took it upon herself to warn her neighbors of a federal raiding party meant to capture Wytheville. It might also cut the railway to eastern Tennessee and capture the lead mines on New River and the salt mines at Saltville. Molly rode over the Rich, Garden, and Walker Mountains, pausing at the cabins to rouse the inhabitants. There were few sturdy men left in the mountains, but the older men and boys seized their guns and forced the federal forces to withdraw. After the war Molly married her sweetheart, W. D. Davidson, and lived happily ever after—so far as is known.[14]

WILLIAMSBURG

Barrett, Kate Waller, 1857–1925, Social Worker; NAW

Barrett Hall, William and Mary College

Kate Waller Barrett, president of the National Florence Crittenton Mission (see Alexandria, VA), was also on the board of visitors of William and Mary College, which two years after her death gave her name to one of its buildings. See Atlanta, GA.

Rockefeller, Abby Aldrich, 1874–1948, Art Collector and Patron; NAW

Abby Aldrich Rockefeller Folk Art Center

When her husband, John D. Rockefeller, Jr., began the restoration of Colonial Williamsburg, Abby Aldrich Rockefeller partook of his enthusiasm. She had a home in Williamsburg and spent much of her time here with her seventeen grandchildren. Chief among her many interests was art. She and several other women were responsible for founding the Museum of Modern Art in New York City. She was one of the first to collect American folk art, and the museum she established here is perhaps the richest such collection in the country. It is open daily, 11–7.

NOTES

In addition to sources listed below, I have had help from the Virginia Historic Landmarks Commission, Richmond; the Commission on the Status of Women, University of Richmond; the Virginia Historical Society; the Richmond Public Library; the Lynchburg Public Library; the Virginia Museum of Fine Arts; the University Press of Virginia; and the Jones Memorial Library in Lynchburg.

1. Correspondence, Alexandria Library.
2. Walter Russell Bowie, *Women of Light* (New York: Harper & Row, 1963).
3. Correspondence, Alexandria Library.
4. Rita Stein, *A Literary Tour Guide to the United States: South and Southwest* (New York: William Morrow & Co., 1978).
5. Correspondence and clippings, West Virginia Department of Archives and History.
6. Christopher Sykes, *Nancy: The Life of Lady Astor* (Chicago, Ill.: Academy Chicago, 1980).
7. Bowie, op. cit.
8. Dixon Wecter, *The Hero in America* (Ann Arbor: University of Michigan Press, 1963).
9. *Southern Writers: A Biographical Dictionary*, ed. Robert Bain and others (Baton

Rouge: Louisiana State University Press, 1979); correspondence and brochures, the Friends of Anne Spencer Memorial Foundation.

10. Correspondence, Kym Rice, Virginia Women's Cultural History Project. This group in 1984 arranged an exhibit at the Virginia Museum of Fine Arts entitled "A Share of Honour," celebrating Virginia women, 1600–1945. See *"A Share of Honour"* (Richmond: Virginia Women's Cultural History Project, 1984), a rich and richly illustrated source of information on Virginia women.

11. Louis Auchincloss, *Pioneers and Caretakers: Nine American Women Novelists* (Minneapolis: University of Minnesota Press, 1965).

12. Isabella Blandin, *History of Higher Education of Women in the South* (Washington, D.C.: Zenger Publishing Co., 1975; repr. of 1908 ed.).

13. Nardi Campion and Rosamond W. Stanton, *Look to This Day: The Lively Education of a Great Woman Doctor* (Boston, Mass.: Little, Brown & Co., 1965); *New York Times,* Apr. 30, 1971.

14. David B. Sabine, "The Midnight Ride of Mollie Tynes," *Civil War Times Illustrated* 3 (Aug. 1964).

WEST VIRGINIA

ALDERSON

Willebrandt, Mabel Walker, 1889–1963, Lawyer and Public Official (NAWM) and Associates

Federal Industrial Institution for Women

Mabel Walker Willebrandt was the second woman to hold the post of assistant attorney general of the United States. When she was interviewed by President Warren G. Harding for the position he remarked that the only thing against her was her age (she was thirty-two). She noted that the condition would be solved by time. She was a controversial figure, due to her vigorous enforcement of prohibition laws and her involvement in national politics. Her prison work, however, was universally applauded. She led a campaign forcing federal officials to acknowledge that the incarceration of women criminals in county jails and state penitentiaries was a contributing factor to the increase in crime. The result was the establishment of the first federal prison for women, the Alderson prison, opened in 1928. The architect made the institution look like a women's college; there were no heavy walls, no armed guards. The inmates were taught garment making, gardening, dairying, and other vocations. A building here is named Willebrandt Hall.

The first administrator of the prison was Mary Belle Harris (1874–1957, NAWM), a graduate of Bucknell University in Lewisburg, Pennsylvania, where her father had been the university president. She became a prison administrator almost by chance. She returned from abroad in 1914 with no prospects and no job. Her friend Katherine Bement Davis offered her a position as superintendent of women and deputy warden of the workhouse on Blackwell Island, and she accepted. Harris initiated small reforms, a library, outdoor exercise space, and freedom from unnecessary and petty rules. From this position she went to the

State Reformatory for Women at Clinton, New Jersey, where she made similar changes for inmates. When the Alderson facility was opened, Willebrandt offered the superintendency to Harris, whose reputation was well established. She served here until 1941.

A hall is named for Katharine Bement Davis (1860–1935, NAW), another woman who made a career of prison administration. She was for thirteen years the head of the Bedford Hills, New York, Reformatory for Women, and later was Commissioner of Corrections for New York City. In this post she modernized the city's penal institutions in both concept and practice. Her studies of public health and hygiene resulted in *Factors in the Sex Life of Twenty-Two Hundred Women* (1929). She was widely recognized as a woman of common sense and efficiency. Among groups who honored her were the Woman's Board of the Panama-Pacific Exposition and the League of Women Voters.

GRAFTON

Jarvis, Anna, 1864–1948, Founder of Mother's Day

Mother's Day Shrine, Andrews Methodist Church, E. Main Street; NR

The first Mother's Day memorial sermon was preached in this church on May 10, 1908. It was the suggestion of Anna Jarvis, whose mother, Anna Reeves Jarvis, had died three years earlier. She sent five hundred carnations to decorate the church, and ever since then the carnation has represented the devotion of mothers. Jarvis, who never married herself, spent endless hours writing to officials in the hope of making the tribute to mothers universal (see Webster, WV). In 1910 the governor of West Virginia made the Mother's Day observance statewide; the following year every state in the union recognized the day; and in 1914 President Woodrow Wilson signed a congressional resolution declaring the second Sunday in May an annual Mother's Day. The idea has since spread to other countries.

West Virginia chartered a nonprofit corporation to acquire the church, improve its surroundings, and maintain it as a shrine to mothers. It is open daily 9–3.[1]

HILLSBORO

Buck, Pearl Sydenstricker, 1892–1973, Writer; NAWM

Pearl S. Buck Birthplace and Museum, US 219; NR

Pearl Sydenstricker Buck was born in the home of her grandparents, the Stultings. Her parents were missionaries to China and they had lost three of their four children there. So Carrie Stulting Sydenstricker came home to West Virginia to await the birth of this child. Buck was still an infant when her mother took her to China. There she spent her girlhood, learning Chinese as her first language. For a short time during the Boxer Rebellion she came back to West Virginia, but she lived in China, married there, taught school, and bore a daughter. She began her writing career with novels depicting Chinese life and the clash of cultures. *The Good Earth*, published in 1931, made her famous and wealthy and won the Pulitzer Prize. After a divorce from John Lossing Buck, she married Richard Walsh and lived in America. She brought up six adopted and two foster children, supervised their farm in Pennsylvania, and ran an apartment in New York City while maintaining a heavy writing schedule. In 1938 she became the first American woman to win the Nobel Prize in literature.

The Pearl S. Buck Foundation had begun restoration of the Hillsboro home before her death and in May 1974 it was officially dedicated as a museum and memorial to her. It is open May 15–Nov. 15, Mon.-Sat. 9–5, Sun. 1–5; adm.[2]

MARTINSBURG

Boyd, Belle, 1844–1900, Confederate Spy; NAW

Plaque, at Site of Boyd House, S. Queen Street

Belle Boyd, the famous Civil War spy, was born in this vicinity, where her father managed a tobacco plantation. She was given the usual educational advantages for a young woman of her class, four years at Mount Washington Female College in Baltimore, Maryland, then was introduced to Washington, D.C., society. She was a strong supporter of the Confederate cause, and she had a chance to prove it on July 3, 1861, when federal troops occupied Martinsburg. A Union soldier came into the house, insisted on raising the Stars and Stripes, and used abusive language. Boyd seized a pistol and shot him dead. She began carrying to Confederate officers information gleaned from listening to the occupying forces, and for the next three years she continued as a spy, her most daring exploit taking place at Front Royal, Virginia, q.v. She was imprisoned numerous times, banished to Canada, and at last sent to England with dispatches. She was only twenty when she ended her career of espionage by marrying a soldier—a Union officer.

MORGANTOWN

Moore, Elizabeth Irwin, 1832–1930, Educator

Elizabeth Moore Hall, West Virginia University

Elizabeth Irwin Moore was involved in West Virginia education for most of her long life. At fifteen she opened a school in her mother's dining room. After she married the Reverend John Moore, they supervised an academy for boys in Morgantown, then opened a second seminary for girls. He was superintendent; she was "lady principal" and teacher of mental and moral science and mathematics. She continued to head the school for two years after the death of her husband in 1864. Later the property bought by the Moores for the academy and the seminary was offered to the state for an agricultural college, now West Virginia University.

Moore left Morgantown for a few years, but she missed it so much that she came back and conducted Morgantown Seminary for girls for another twenty years. Afterward she became a grandmother to the women at the university, since her daughter, Susan Maxwell Moore, was the university's first dean of women. Moore was still living, still healthy and alert, when the hall named for her was dedicated in 1928.[3]

PHILIPPI

Reed, Ida L., 1865–1951, Hymn Writer

Marker Near Birthplace, US 119

The marker is about three and a half miles southwest of the poet Ida L. Reed's birthplace. It tells us that "she became famous for her religious writings, chiefly cantatas, poems and hymns, of which she wrote over 2000. Her hymns have been used in the services of eleven denominations in America. Many have been translated into foreign languages. Her most noted is 'I Belong to the King.' Miss Reed died July 8, 1951, and is buried here."

POINT PLEASANT

Bailey, Anne Hennis (Mad Anne) Trotter, 1742–1825, Pioneer Soldier and Scout

Monument, Point Pleasant Battlefield State Park; NR

A tall granite shaft in Tu-Endie-Wei Park marks the site of the Battle of Point Pleasant. On October 10, 1774, General Andrew Lewis and his Virginia frontiersmen were attacked by Shawnee warriors under Chief Cornstalk. In this, considered the first encounter of the Revolution, one Richard Trotter lost his life. His widow, Anne Hennis (Mad Anne) Trotter, swore eternal hostility to the Indians who had killed him. She began dressing in men's clothes and ranging the woods as a scout, warning frontier settlers of Indian movements. She carried an ax, a rifle, and a knife. So unfeminine was her behavior that her neighbors began calling her Mad Anne. She married John Bailey in 1785 but continued to range through the border country, sometimes called the White Squaw of the Kanawha. She spent some time in Covington, Virginia, q.v., and died in Ohio. She was buried near the site of Trotter's death. South of the battle monument is the stone marking her grave.

SUMMERSVILLE

Hart, Nancy, d. 1902, Confederate Spy

Nancy Hart Memorial, Courthouse Lawn

Unlike Belle Boyd (see Martinsburg, WV), Nancy Hart never capitalized on her adventures as a spy by lecturing or writing about it afterward, but West Virginians have made her a legend. (Another Nancy Hart, no relation, was a heroine of the Revolutionary War in Georgia.) The West Virginia Hart was a spitfire who joined in guerrilla forays in Calhoun County, an unlettered mountain girl who could ride and shoot with the best of the rangers. In 1861 federal guards picked up Hart, but as she seemed an innocent young girl they let her go. She carried back a headful of information about federal plans that proved useful to the guerrillas. Hart married Joshua Douglas, who enlisted with a regular Confederate cavalry company. In 1862 she was arrested again and put under guard in Summersville. There she charmed her young guard into letting her hold his gun, shot him with it, and made her escape on an officer's horse. She came back a week or so later accompanying some two hundred Confederates, who routed the Union men.[4]

SWEET SPRINGS

Royall, Anne Newport, 1769–1854, Journalist; NAW

Marker, State 3

The marker reads: "Anne Royall, America's first woman journalist, lived here. Widowed at 50, she became an author and prominent figure in national political life. In her newspaper, *Paul Pry*, at Washington, she set the style for modern columnists." Anne Newport Royall lived in Sweet Springs first as a servant then as the wife of Captain William Royall, whom she idolized. They read Voltaire together and she imbibed his views (ultraliberal at the time) of religion and society. William died in 1813 and Anne traveled in her coach with several servants to Alabama, seeking a warmer climate. Her life was shattered ten years later when William's relatives succeeded in breaking his will, leaving her penniless. She went to Washington, D.C., to ask for a widow's pension (William had fought in the Revolution), but things dragged on for years and meanwhile Anne turned to writing travel books. She went from town to town, covering many miles and writing about the country and its people with a realism unusual for the time. Between 1826 and 1831 she published ten volumes on her travels. She then moved permanently to Washington and began publishing *Paul Pry*, a weekly paper full of gossip and biting (some thought vitriolic) editorials. It lasted until 1836 and was succeeded by another, *The Huntress*, which she published until she was eighty-five. Her witty comments made for good reading but brought her numerous enemies and she was once tried as a "common scold." In her old age Congress finally awarded her $2,400. William's heirs took half of it; the rest went for legal fees and debts, leaving Anne $10.[5]

WEBSTER

Jarvis, Anna, 1864–1948, Founder of Mother's Day

Anna Jarvis House, US 119 (Private); NR

Anna Jarvis, whose devotion to her mother led to the founding of Mother's Day (see Grafton, WV) was born here. She and her mother both taught Sunday school in Grafton, and Jarvis attended Mary Baldwin College. She was living in Philadelphia, Pennsylvania, when she suggested that a special day be set aside annually in honor of all mothers. Others had had similar ideas (including Julia Ward Howe as early as 1872), but Jarvis's persistence in writing letters to state governors and legislators and to congressmen was effective. So heavy was her correspondence that she was forced to buy another house simply for storage. The commercialization of the day by florists, confectioners, and greeting card firms outraged her. In 1943, broken in health, she went to a sanitarium in West Chester, Pennsylvania, where she died.[6]

WHEELING

Cruger, Lydia Boggs Shepherd, d. 1867, Hostess

Monument Place (Shepherd Hall), Monument Place and Cruger Street (Private); HABS, NR

Lydia Boggs Shepherd Cruger entertained many distinguished visitors at her home here. She is chiefly remembered for persuading Senator Henry Clay to route the National Road past her house, thus bringing prosperity to the town. Her home is now the Osiris Temple and is open to tours by special permission.[7]

Davis, Rebecca Harding, 1831–1910, Writer; NAW

Plaque, Wheeling Civic Center Hall of Fame

Rebecca Harding Davis was the author of a strikingly realistic story, "Life in the Iron Mills," written in 1861 when stories of common people were a rarity. It was among her first literary efforts and was written out of her observations in a West Virginia steel town. It recorded, she said, "only the outline of a dull life, that long since, with thousands of dull lives like its own, was vainly lived and lost." The story was published in the *Atlantic Monthly*, and Rebecca, a thirty-year-old spinster, was invited by the publisher to go to Boston, Massachusetts, where she had the heady pleasure of meeting such literary giants as Nathaniel Hawthorne and Oliver Wendell Holmes. On her way back to Wheeling she stopped in Philadelphia, Pennsylvania, met and agreed to marry Lemuel Clarke Davis. They settled in Philadelphia and for the next years Rebecca was busy raising three children. One of them, Richard Harding Davis, was a romantic, colorful foreign correspondent and writer. Rebecca continued writing but never equalled the success of her earlier stories.[8]

Zane, Elizabeth (Clark), 1766?–1831?, Revolutionary War Heroine; NAW

Tablet, Site of Fort Henry Siege, 11th Street Mall

The tablet marks the site of the last battle of the American Revolution, fought in September 1782, before the fort had heard that the war was over. The defenders were led by the Zane brothers, who had founded the city, but the heroine of the battle was their sister Elizabeth Zane. She exposed herself to the fire of the besiegers by carrying gunpower from the Zane cabin, where it was stored, to the fort, where it was needed. Zane's exploit became a legend, and like many legends, there is some doubt about whether it actually happened, and if it did whether it was in 1777 or 1782. Lydia Cruger was at the fort in 1782 and she said the heroine was not Zane but Molly Scott. A fictional *Betty Zane* was written by a kinsman, novelist Zane Grey. A mural at the Wheeling Civic Center depicts the event. Zane married twice and continued to live in the area. Martin's Ferry, Ohio, just across the river, also claims Zane as its heroine.[9]

NOTES

In addition to the sources listed below, I have received help from the West Virginia Department of Commerce; West Virginia Wesleyan College; and the Harpers Ferry Center, National Park Service.

1. *Morgantown Dominion Post*, Mar. 2, 1969; *Family Weekly*, May 12, 1963.

2. *Republican Delta*, May 16, 1974; *Southern Living* 14 (Mar. 1979) and 16 (Oct. 1981).

3. Ethel Clark Lewis, "Interesting Daughters of West Virginia," *West Virginia Review*, Aug. 1929; correspondence, West Virginia University.

4. "Nancy Hart Story," *Nicholas* (West Virginia) *Chronicle*, July 31, 1969.

5. *Beckley* (West Virginia) *Post-Herald,* Nov. 2, 1964 and June 7, 1967.

6. *Liberty's Women*, ed. Robert McHenry (Springfield, Mass.: G. & C. Merriam Co., 1980).

7. Correspondence, Friends of Wheeling.

8. Tillie Olsen, "A Biographical Interpretation," in Rebecca Harding, *Life in the Iron Mills* (Old Westbury, N.Y.: Feminist Press, 1972); correspondence, Friends of Wheeling.

9. Clippings, West Virginia Department of Archives and History; correspondence, Friends of Wheeling.

REGION III

The Mid-Atlantic

The Mid-Atlantic region became, after the Revolution, the acknowledged political center of the nation. Groups from many northern European countries—English Quakers, the Dutch, Swedish, Danish—settled the region, but they never formed a cohesive whole until the struggle for independence brought them together. New York City, Philadelphia, Pennsylvania, Princeton, New Jersey, and Annapolis, Maryland, all served as the capital city of the new nation before the District of Columbia was formed.

New York City became the financial nerve center for the industrial nation that developed in the nineteenth century. The gateway to the country, it welcomed increasing tides of immigration. Some newcomers were channeled into the Midwest farmlands, some to cities already settled along the coast, and many remained to enrich the region as well as to present problems of assimilation.

Great industries grew up around the Chesapeake Bay and along the rivers of the eastern seaboard: chemicals, oil, steel, and coal to supply the needs of an expanding population. A class of entrepreneurs arose whose wealth was measured in princely proportions. An underclass of landless wage earners lived in near poverty. Between the two, a middle class profited from a technology that produced more and more goods.

There had always been, even in democratic America, some class division based on heritage, but in the industrial age and in the highly industrialized areas, the division became increasingly drawn along economic lines. Despite the efforts of social leaders like Caroline Schermerhorn Astor in New York to keep out those she considered unworthy, blood counted less than wealth as a determinant of social status.

These changes affected women and in a subtle way the image of womanhood. The upper-class woman, no longer needed as a goodwife presiding over an industrious household, became a consumer. She was still the guardian of the home, the moral center of society, but no longer a worker. As a lady, she reflected the success of her father or her husband by the way she spent his money.

She was not only a consumer but a conspicuous consumer, her status measured by material standards. In the process, she lost much. Supposed to be pure, she suppressed sexuality. Thought of as fragile, she gave up a healthy life for one of invalidism. She adopted extremes of dress that added to her physical problems. She was allowed no information on birth control, and she exchanged the services of a midwife for that of a male physician. Sigmund Freud diagnosed her as subject to hysterics.

Many women were quite happy to play the role of the lady. Other women rebelled, especially those who had the privilege of higher education. They saw the problems growing in the cities, the needs for educational and health reforms. Middle-class women, now with more leisure at their disposal, began to see their role as housekeepers expand to include the world at their gates. They worked first through their churches, then formed charitable organizations and women's clubs. Most did not understand poverty; they believed it could be remedied by training the poor in better habits or prohibiting alcohol or providing playgrounds. It was only when a few had closer contact with the poor in settlement houses and in helping organizations that they began to understand the dynamics of progress and poverty.

Remembered women of the Mid-Atlantic include representatives of the three different groups. There are the wealthy, with their great houses and lavish furnishings and their large philanthropic support of colleges, art galleries, hospitals, and centers for the performing arts. The role of wives and widows who had the disposal of great wealth acquired by their husbands cannot be overlooked. Second, there are the less well-to-do who displayed a growing awareness of social problems and worked together for change. And third, there are working-class women, members or organizers of labor unions, who fought for more than a bare subsistence wage. Beyond these are many women who reflect the energy and the stimulation of a growing country—women who were themselves entrepreneurs, artists, writers, educators, and politicians. Without the contributions of all of them, the Mid-Atlantic region would not have developed its present vitality.

DELAWARE

DOVER

Cannon, Annie Jump, 1863–1941, Astronomer; NAW, HFDW[1]

Cannon Building, Wesley Junior College, State and Cecil Streets

Annie Jump Cannon was a student at Wesley Junior College when it was called the Wilmington Conference Academy. She graduated at the age of sixteen and was sent to Wellesley College. From childhood she had been fascinated with the stars and had studied the constellations from her ''observatory'' in the attic of the family home, 34 S. State Street, using her mother's old astronomy book as a guide. At Wellesley she continued this study under Sarah H. Whiting. Her special interest was an investigation of the stellar spectra—the characteristics revealed when the light of a star is photographed through a prism. After graduating in 1884 she returned to Dover and spent the next ten years enjoying its social life, studying music, traveling, and perfecting photographic techniques. Following her mother's death, Cannon returned to her science studies at Wellesley, then at Radcliffe College. She was given a position at the Harvard College Observatory and remained there until a year before her death, having built a reputation as one of the world's great astronomers.

The state museum, 316 S. Governor's Avenue, has some of the medals and awards Cannon won through her lifetime. See the University of Delaware, Newark, DE.

O'Neill, Margaret Moffett, 1900–1975, Civic Leader

Margaret Moffett O'Neill Building, Federal and Court Streets

The Kent County Visitors Center was named for Margaret Moffett O'Neill, of Smyrna, Delaware, a prominent educator and administrator. She was a teacher in the Smyrna schools and very active in civic and church organizations. In 1950 she became the first woman elected to the Town Council of Smyrna. Later she was a state delegate to the White House Conference on Children and Youth, a member of the Commission on Human Rights, of the Kent County Planning Board, and of the Governor's Commission on Children and Youth. At the time of her death she had just been appointed to the state's Health Planning Council. Perhaps the honor she prized most was election as the Delaware Mother of the Year in 1964.[2]

Ridgely, Mabel Lloyd, 1872–1962, Preservationist and Civic Leader; HFDW

Ridgely House, the Green; NR

Almost single-handedly Mabel Lloyd Ridgely saved the historic old State House in Dover from neglect and mishandling. It was there that the Delaware Convention of 1787 ratified the federal Constitution and made Delaware the first state in the Union. Ridgely established the state archives in 1905 and remained on the State Archives Commission for the rest of her life. In the foreword of her book, *The Ridgelys of Delaware* (1949), she wrote: "I have decided on my epitaph. It is brief and I believe it is also truthful: 'She died of the Eighteenth Century.' "

Ridgely was, however, very much a woman of the twentieth century. She was president of the Delaware Women's Suffrage Association when the federal suffrage amendment was passed (though Delaware failed to ratify it), and when the Delaware League of Women Voters was formed she was its first president. Among other club and civic affiliations, she was a trustee of the University of Delaware. She took pride in the careful preservation of her home, the historical Ridgely House.[3]

Steele, Cecile Long, 1900–1940, Poultry Farmer; HFDW

First Broiler House, Delaware Agricultural Museum Complex, 866 N. Dupont Highway; NR

The only chicken house in the National Register of Historic Places, Cecile Long Steele's broiler house has been preserved because she started one of the state's thriving industries. At the Steele chicken farm in Ocean View, Delaware, she began marketing chickens when they reached two pounds. The delicious high-protein, low-calorie broiler meat was appreciated by consumers and the new venture spread to other farmers. Fifty years after Steele began selling her broilers, it was estimated that the industry accounted for over half of Delaware's agricultural income. It has spread, now, to other states. The state of the art has grown, too, since the ingenious poultry farmer fed and watered her chicks by hand and heated her brooder house with a coal stove.[4]

NEWARK

University of Delaware

Buildings at the University of Delaware are named for three women who were influential in its early days. As late as 1914 Delaware was the only state in the Union that offered no higher education for females. A number of concerned women began to promote a woman's college in 1910, and when they were successful they recruited Winifred Robinson (1867–1962) to be dean of the college. A graduate of the University of Michigan, she had taught in Michigan for a few years before going to Vassar College in 1900, where she taught biology and botany. She served as dean at the Woman's College from 1914 until 1938, a period when the school had a remarkable development, merging in 1921 with Delaware College to form the University of Delaware. Robinson Hall, erected in 1914, is used for classrooms and offices.[5]

Smyth Hall, a dormitory added in 1954, was named for Alice P. Smyth (1867–1957). She was one of the women who founded Delaware's first woman's club, the New Century Club, in 1889, and one of the founders of the Woman's College. She established its library and long continued to support its development. For members of the community she started the New Castle County Free Library, headquartered in the Wilmington Public Library. In 1927, to honor the memory of a friend, Mary Askew Mather, she began an experimental rural library service, with a bookmobile and stations in small communities. The American Association of University Women, of which she was a member, annually gives a Mather-Smyth scholarship to a Delaware woman student at the university.[6]

Warner Hall, one of the first buildings erected at the Woman's College, was named for Emalea Pusey Warner (1853–1948, HFDW), of Wilmington, Delaware, q.v., in recognition of her advocacy of the college's establishment and her efforts on behalf of education. In 1927 she was the first woman named to the board of trustees of the university.[7]

In 1952 a new dormitory was given the name of the famed astronomer, Annie Jump Cannon (see Dover, DE).

WILMINGTON

Hall of Fame of Delaware Women

The Delaware Commission for Women established the Hall of Fame of Delaware Women in 1981, choosing several women each year who have given "outstanding service to the home, the community, the State, and the Nation"—some still living, others chosen from history. The initials HFDW following the names of women elsewhere in this guide indicate election. Among others are Vera Gilbride Davis (1894–1974), of Dover, who began her public career in 1919 with involvement in the suffrage movement. She was the first woman to serve as bill clerk in the Delaware House of Representatives. She was also Delaware's first woman secretary of state, state senator, and in 1956 state treasurer.

Sallie Topkis Simms (1880–1976), of Wilmington, was considered the most important Jewish woman in Delaware history. She founded the Wilmington chapter of the National Council of Jewish Women and organized the Wilmington Young Women's Hebrew Association. She was treasurer of the National Woman's Party for eight years.[8]

Bissell, Emily Perkins, 1861–1948, Health Crusader; NAW

Emily P. Bissell Sanitorium, 3000 Newport Gap Pike

The first antituberculosis Christmas seals went on sale in 1907 in Wilmington. They were printed and sold by the organizer and secretary of the Delaware Chapter, American Red Cross, Emily Perkins Bissell. The idea came from the use of Christmas stamps by the Danish government to finance its fight against tuberculosis. Ever since that time the seals have been sold annually, first by the Red Cross and the National Tuberculosis Association, later by the Tuberculosis and Health Association, now the American Lung Association.

Bissell used part of the proceeds from sale of the seals to develop a home for consumptives, Hope Farm. This was taken over by the state of Delaware in 1925 and in 1953 was given her name.

Crowninshield, Louise du Pont, 1877–1958, Art Collector and Preservationist

Louise du Pont Crowninshield Research Building, Henry Francis du Pont Winterthur Museum. Eleutherian Mills, Hagley Museum, State 141; NHL

Louise du Pont Crowninshield, a daughter of Colonel Henry A. du Pont and a sister of Henry F. du Pont, grew up here near the powder mills along the Brandywine River that formed the basis of the great du Pont fortune. In 1900 she married a Bostonian, Francis Boardman Crowninshield, and moved to Massachusetts. Her chief interests were gardening, collecting antiques, and preserving historical buildings. She was a board member of the National Trust for Historic Preservation.

One of the buildings she preserved was Eleutherian Mills. It was the original home of E. I. du Pont, abandoned as a dwelling after the 1890 explosion of the nearby Brandywine powder mill. It was used for a time as a club for the workmen and later fell into disrepair. The garden plants were dug up and taken away to private gardens in Wilmington. Crowninshield had her father buy the old home, then she refurnished it and replanted the gardens. She has been described as "a born collector who had the added gift of being able to blend possessions into an harmonious and unobtrusive whole." In this house the Oriental rugs were "antiqued" by allowing a variety of pet dogs, Pekingese and poodles, to run about on them.

Winterthur Museum (six miles northwest of Wilmington on State 52) is open to the public. No reservations are needed to visit the eighteen rooms in the Washington wing or the gardens, sixty acres of natural plantings. Reservations are required for the main museum and may be obtained by writing the Reservations Office, Winterthur Museum, Winterthur, DE 19735. The Hagley Museum (three miles north on State 52, then half a mile east on State 141) is open Tues.-Sat. and Mon. holidays, 9:30–4:30, Sun. 1–5; adm. Eleutherian Mills is reached by jitney from the main museum.[9]

Shipley, Elizabeth Levis, c. 1690–1777, Minister and Pioneer

Shipley Street

Elizabeth Levis Shipley, a Quaker minister who first came here in the 1730s, was a founder of Wilmington. She had seen the place before that, in a dream. A guide had shown her this precise spot and told her, ''It is the design of Providence that the family of William Shipley settle here, where the blessing of Heaven shall descend upon you and your labors.'' Shipley persuaded her husband, William Shipley, to move to what was then Willingtown, a village of a few houses. He bought one lot on 2nd Street in the spring of 1735, then returned in the summer and bought all the town west of Market Street. Through the Shipleys' influence many Quaker families came from William Penn's colony to Delaware. They established markets, breweries, and shipping facilities and later intermarried with the Swedes, Dutch, and Finns who had settled Delaware. All prospered.

The story of Shipley's dream was related by Benjamin Ferris in *A History of the Original Settlements on the Delaware*, from which the English novelist, Charles Reade, adopted it for his *The Wandering Heir*. The Shipley house on 4th and Shipley Streets has disappeared, to be replaced by the Delaware Technical and Community College.[10]

Tubman, Harriet, 1820?–1913, Civil Rights Leader; NAW

Memorial Plaque, Civic Plaza

Harriet Tubman, the famous fugitive slave, led many of her race from the Delmarva Peninsula to freedom in the North. She was aided by the Quaker Thomas Garrett of Wilmington and by others associated with the underground railroad. Between 1849, when she made her break from a Maryland master, and the Civil War, she is thought to have brought out as many as three hundred slaves. See Baltimore, MD, and Auburn, NY.[11]

Warner, Emalea Pusey, 1853–1948, Clubwoman; HFDW

Warner Junior High School

Emalea Pusey Warner, who helped to establish the University of Delaware (see Newark, DE) was a suffrage leader. She was an organizer of the Wilmington New Century Club, which became a charter member of the General Federation of Women's Clubs. She was elected the first president of the Delaware Federation in 1898. Fifty years later she suggested that the affiliated clubs celebrate the anniversary by planting dogwood trees on the grounds of schools and public buildings. She did not live to see the trees, which stand as memorials to her as well as to the federation.[12]

NOTES

In addition to the correspondents mentioned below, I have had help from the Historical Society of Delaware and the State Division of History and Cultural Affairs.

1. The initials HFDW indicate that the individual was elected to the Hall of Fame of Delaware Women (see Wilmington, DE).

2. *Mothers of Achievement in American History*, comp. American Mothers Committee (Rutland, Vt.: Charles E. Tuttle Co., 1976); correspondence, Kent County Visitors Center.

3. *Wilmington Morning News*, Jan. 12, 1962; correspondence, Delaware Commission for Women.

4. National Register nomination form and correspondence, Delaware State Division of Cultural Affairs; Jane Vessels, "Delight-Sized Delaware," *National Geographic* 164 (Aug. 1983).

5. Correspondence, University of Delaware.

6. *Wilmington Journal—Every Evening*, Dec. 18, 1957.

7. *Wilmington Journal—Every Evening*, Apr. 13, 1948; correspondence, Delaware Commission for Women.

8. Correspondence, Delaware Commission for Women.

9. Walter Muir Whitehill, *Analecta Biographica: A Handful of New England Portraits* (Brattleboro, Vt.: Stephen Greene Press, 1969); Michael Olmert, "Great Collectors," *Historic Preservation* 34 (Nov.-Dec. 1982).

10. *Delaware: A Guide to the First State* (New York: Hastings House, 1955); Lynn Sherr and Jurate Kazickas, *The American Woman's Gazetteer* (New York: Bantam Books, 1976); correspondence, University of Delaware.

11. Correspondence, Carol Hoffecker, Chair, Department of History, University of Delaware.

12. See note 7.

DISTRICT OF COLUMBIA

WASHINGTON

Adams, Marion Hooper, 1843–1885, Photographer; NAW

Adams Memorial, Rock Creek Cemetery, Webster Street and Rock Creek Church Road, N.W.; NR

On the afternoon of December 6, 1885, Henry Adams went to his wife's room to see if she cared to see a caller and found her lying on the floor. She had killed herself by drinking a chemical from her photographic darkroom. She was only forty-two. Her friends mourned the small, amusing woman whom all called Clover.

Her husband, after saying, "Fate has smashed the life out of me," could not bring himself to speak of Marian Hooper Adams for many years. He arranged with his friend, Augustus St. Gaudens, to design a memorial. St. Gaudens designed a masterpiece, a large seated figure, the impassive face with closed eyes shaded by a cowl—not at all like Clover. Visitors to the memorial take away a feeling of universal sadness. It has been called "Nirvana," "Grief," or "Serenity." Henry Adams called it "The Peace of God," and St. Gaudens, "The Mystery of the Hereafter." Both Clover and Henry are buried here, but there is no inscription to tell us so.

The entrance to Rock Creek Cemetery (not near Rock Creek Park) is at Webster and 3rd Streets. The visitor should take the road west of St. Paul's Church and bear right to a gravel path. Along this path is the circular grove of evergreens and hollies surrounding the famed memorial. The cemetery is open daily 8–5.[1]

Anthony, Susan Brownell. See Johnson, Adelaide

Baldwin, Maria Louise, 1856–1922, Educator (NAW), and Others

Dormitories, Howard University, 4th and College Streets, N.W.

Howard University, Washington's predominantly black institution of higher learning, has named dormitories for several women who have contributed to the

This statue in Rock Creek Cemetery, Washington, D.C., is a memorial to Marian Hooper Adams. It is one of Augustus St. Gaudens' masterpieces of sculpture.
From the collection of the Library of Congress.

betterment of blacks in America. One is named for Maria Louise Baldwin, a resident of Massachusetts. She was the first black in New England to hold the position of master of a school. In 1916 she was appointed master of the Agassiz Grammar School in Cambridge, Massachusetts.

Prudence Crandall (1803–1890, NAW), a white woman who opened a school for girls in Canterbury, Connecticut, gave her name to one dormitory. The citizens of Canterbury harassed her when she admitted a black student and forced her to give up the school. She is considered a martyr to civil rights.

Truth Hall commemorates Sojourner Truth (c. 1797–1883, NAW). She named herself after she was freed from slavery and went about lecturing on religion and abolition. She spoke out for the cause of equal rights for women, at an 1851 convention in Akron, Ohio, where she delivered her famous speech, ''Ain't I a Woman?'' See New Paltz, NY, and Baltimore, MD.

Wheatley Hall is named for Phillis Wheatley (c. 1753–1784, NAW), the first Negro poet in America. She was purchased from a slave ship by a Massachusetts family that educated her along with their own children. In 1773 her *Poems on Various Subjects, Religious and Moral* was published in England. People were amazed that a black woman could write, and she enjoyed a brief period of fame, then was forgotten, except by her own race, for many years.

Another hall is named for Mary McLeod Bethune (1875–1955, NAWM), who has other memorials in Washington.

Barney, Alice Pike, 1859–1931, Artist and Art Patron

Barney Studio House, 2306 Massachusetts Avenue, N.W.

In 1902 Alice Pike Barney assessed Washington as a center of small talk with no art and little culture. She set about to change the climate by providing in her studio an intimate salon for artists and other geniuses. She filled the rooms with paintings, hers and those of her friends. She wrote, produced, and directed tableaux and plays, supported cultural and civic organizations, provided buildings for Barney Neighborhood House in southwest Washington, sponsored the creation of the Sylvan Theater on the grounds of the Washington Monument, and joined the suffragists. Her daughter Natalie Barney also became a talented artist.

After Barney's death Studio House was rented for many years, while her daughters donated most of her paintings and those of her friends to the National Museum of American Art. In 1960 they gave the studio to the Smithsonian Institution, which used it as an office. In 1979 it was renovated and opened to the public, ''evoking its original mood and intent as a setting for artistic enjoyment.'' It is open for informal guided visits on Wed. and Thurs. at 11 and on the 2nd and 4th Sun. of the month at 1; closed summers; reservations must be made in advance (202–357–3111). Concerts are also held at Studio House; write for information to Evenings at Barney Studio House, Department of Education, National Museum of American Art, Smithsonian Institution, Washington, DC 20560.[2]

Belmont, Alva Erskine Smith Vanderbilt, 1853–1933 (NAW), Lucy Burns, 1879–1966, and Alice Paul, 1885–1977 (NAWM), Suffrage Leaders

Sewall-Belmont House, 144 Constitution Avenue, N.E.; NHL

Alice Paul went to England in 1907 to study social work. There she was caught up in the militant suffrage movement led by the determined Pankhursts, who stopped at nothing in their attempts to draw the attention of Parliament to the cause of woman suffrage. Paul returned to the United States in 1912 eager to join the suffrage movement but found its leaders far from ready to follow their English sisters' aggressive tactics, preferring to win the franchise state by state rather than push for a federal constitutional amendment. With much difficulty Paul persuaded the National American Woman's Suffrage Association (NAWSA) to appoint a congressional committee to tackle Congress.

Lucy Burns had also come under the spell of the English suffragettes while studying at Oxford, and the experience changed her from scholar to activist. She took part in organizing, in street-corner speeches, and in prison hunger strikes. Returning to America in 1912, she joined Paul in organizing a spectacular women's parade in Washington on the eve of Woodrow Wilson's inaugural. Finding it difficult to work with the NAWSA, they formed the separate Congressional Union to work solely for the federal amendment. From that grew the National Woman's Party, which celebrated the victory for the enfranchisement of women in 1920 and at once introduced the Equal Rights Amendment, written by Paul "Equality of rights under the law shall not be denied or abridged by the United States or by any state on account of sex." Paul is in the National Women's Hall of Fame.

Alva Erskine Smith Vanderbilt Belmont, the wealthy widow of Oliver Belmont (and divorced wife of a Vanderbilt), was drawn into the suffrage cause after her husband's death in 1908. She opened the doors of her lavish home in Newport, Rhode Island, to suffrage meetings. In 1909, when the shirtwaist workers of New York City went on strike, Belmont hired the Hippodrome for a rally and persuaded Anna Howard Shaw, president of NAWSA, to speak. An audience of eight thousand came out in support of the strikers. Belmont also brought Christabel Pankhurst to America for a lecture tour. When the Congressional Union was formed, she joined and in 1921 contributed a large sum for the purchase of the historical mansion on Capitol Hill which has ever since been the Woman's Party Headquarters. The party now gives its support mainly to passage of the Equal Rights Amendment.

Busts of Belmont, Paul, and other woman's suffrage leaders are on view in the house. Now maintained by the National Park Service, it is open Tues.-Fri. 10–2, Sat., Sun., and some holidays 12–4.[3]

Bethune, Mary McLeod, 1875–1955, Educator and Civil Rights Leader; NAWM

Statue, Lincoln Park, E. Capitol at 12th Street, S.E. Bethune House, 1318 Vermont Avenue, N.W.

The seventeen-foot statue of Mary McLeod Bethune was erected in 1974 by the National Council of Negro Women, an organization she founded. Bethune stands with a small Negro boy and girl, handing them her legacy: "I leave you love. I leave you hope. . . . I leave you racial dignity." The statue is the work of Robert Berks. Bethune House, her last official residence, is the former headquarters of the National Council of Negro Women.

Bethune was the most influential Afro-American woman in the United States for over three decades. She was the founder of Bethune Cookman College in Daytona Beach, Florida. She educated Eleanor Roosevelt to the problems faced by blacks, and through Mrs. Roosevelt she was appointed, in 1935, to the National Youth Administration (NYA), a New Deal agency designed to help young people find employment. Bethune became director of the division of Negro affairs within the NYA and worked hard to integrate the defense industries. She was, with the exception of Walter White, the only person of her race who then had access to the White House. She is in the National Women's Hall of Fame.[4]

Bliss, Mildred Barnes, 1880–1969, Art Patron and Gardener

Dumbarton Oaks, 3101 R Street, N.W.

Mildred Barnes Bliss and her husband, diplomat Robert Woods Bliss, owned this Georgetown mansion from 1920 to 1940. Art collector, philanthropist, and horticulturist, Mildred formed a collection of books, manuscripts, paintings, drawings, and prints related to the history of gardens and landscape design. Robert was a collector of Byzantine and pre-Columbian art. To preserve their collections and make them available to scholars for research, the Blisses gave the property to Harvard University in 1940 and endowed the Dumbarton Oaks Research Library and Collection. In 1944 the estate became known worldwide as the scene of the Dumbarton Oaks Conferences, culminating in the first draft of the United Nations Charter.

Mildred was assisted in forming her collection of garden books by Beatrix Jones Farrand (1872–1959, NAWM), who designed the gardens at Dumbarton Oaks. They are considered the best work of Farrand, one of America's finest landscape architects. They also represent the one of all her designs that survives essentially unchanged. In addition to the formal gardens with their brick paths, a natural area was left, "the sort of place in which thrushes sing and dreams are dreamt." Farrand designed or acted as consultant for many other gardens, including those at Yale University, Princeton University, Vassar College, Oberlin

College, and Occidental College. In 1899 she and others founded the American Association of Landscape Architects.

Entrance to the gardens is at 31st and R Streets; open daily except during inclement weather, 2–5; adm. Entrance to the collections is on 32nd Street, between R and S Streets; open daily except Mon., 2–5; garden library rare book room weekends only. Entrance to the natural park is by Lover's Lane, off R Street between Avon Place and 31st Streets; open Apr. 1–Oct. 31, daily 8–sunset; pedestrians only.[5]

Boardman, Mabel Thorp, 1860–1946, Humanitarian; NAW

Memorial Plaque, Chapel of Joseph of Arimathea, Washington Cathedral, Wisconsin and Massachusetts Avenues, N.W.

Mabel Thorp Boardman was drawn into the American Red Cross when the organization was foundering under the leadership of the aging Clara Barton, whose highly individualistic management and informal financial arrangements were arousing criticism. In 1904 Barton resigned under pressure and a new board was chosen, under the leadership of Barton's sharpest critic, Boardman. In the next years she reorganized the Red Cross into state and local units, raised a permanent endowment fund of over $2 million, and erected a monumental headquarters in Washington as a memorial to the women of the Civil War. Although the acknowledged head of the organization, she gave her services voluntarily, insisting that a man be appointed the executive. After World War I she was chiefly concerned with organizing Special Services—Nurses Aides, Motor Corps, Home Service, and Gray Ladies—relying on well-to-do, socially prominent women as volunteers. Personally she resembled Queen Mary, so much so that it is claimed the duke of Windsor, visiting Washington, caught a glimpse of her and exclaimed, "Good Lord! There's Mother!"

Briggs, Emily Edson, 1830–1910, Journalist; NAW

Friendship House (The Maples), 619 D Street, S.E.; HABS, NR

Emily Edson Briggs arrived in Washington just after the Civil War broke out, when her husband, John R. Briggs, Jr., was appointed assistant clerk of the House of Representatives. After reading press reports critical of women clerks in government offices, Emily flew to their defense in an article for the *Washington Chronicle*. The owner of the paper, who as clerk of the House was also her husband's superior, was impressed with her style and engaged her to contribute a daily column, which he printed under the name "Olivia." With entrée to the White House, she was a friend and supporter to the troubled Mary Todd Lincoln. She became a full-fledged journalist, one of the first women admitted to the Press Gallery and the first president of the Woman's National Press Association. In 1892 she and her husband bought the Maples, a Capitol Hill mansion dating from 1795. He died six months after they moved in, and Emily lived there for another forty years, a popular Washington hostess. Since 1937 the house has been known as Friendship House and is used as a day nursery.

Burns, Lucy. See Belmont, Alva

Burroughs, Nannie Helen, 1878?–1961, Educator; NAWM

Nannie Helen Burroughs School, 5001 Grant Street, N.E.

The school Nannie Helen Burroughs founded as the National Training School for Women and Girls, and which took her name in 1964, was known as the school of the three B's: Bible, Bath, and Broom. Burroughs was educated in Washington, only to be turned down as a domestic science teacher in the public schools because she was too dark. She tried for a job as a government clerk, again failing because of her color. In Louisville, Kentucky, she found a position as secretary of the Foreign Mission Board of the National Baptist Convention. She was elected corresponding secretary of the National Baptist Woman's Convention, newly formed as an auxiliary to the men's convention; she became president in 1948.

For years she dreamed of establishing in Washington a school which would train black women and girls for respectable nonstereotypical careers and for expert homemaking. The Woman's Convention agreed to the purchase of a six-acre site she had chosen in northeast Washington and the school opened in 1909. It offered a wide range of subjects, academic and vocational. By the time it ceased regular operation in 1956, the school had educated thousands of black women from the United States, South Africa, Haiti, and Puerto Rico. One of Burroughs' students said of her that she considered "everybody God's golden nugget." Today the school serves the community by providing pre- and elementary school facilities for young children of working mothers.[6]

Caldwell, Mary, Marquise des Monstiers-Mérinville, 1863–1909, Philanthropist; NAW

Caldwell Hall, Catholic University of America, 620 Michigan Avenue, N.E.

Mary Caldwell's father died when she was eleven. A convert to Roman Catholicism, he made her and a sister wards of Catholic friends. He also left a legacy of several million dollars and provided in his will that Caldwell was to donate a third of her inheritance to the Catholic church to found a university. The Catholic hierarchy, in accepting her offer in 1884 to donate $300,000 for a national school of theology, stipulated that she was to be considered the founder of what became Catholic University of America. Later in life Caldwell, who had married François Jean Louis, Marquis des Monstiers-Mérinville, and lived abroad, renounced Roman Catholicism, saying that since living in Europe her "eyes have been opened to what that Church really is and to its anything but sanctity." Appalled, the university removed her portrait from its walls but retained her name on one of its buildings.

Cannon, Harriet, 1823–1896, Churchwoman; NAW

Memorial Window, Bishop's House, Washington Cathedral, Wisconsin and Massachusetts Avenues, N.W.

Harriet Cannon, a nursing sister in the Episcopal Sisterhood of the Holy Communion, longed for a more monastic religious life. Such a concept was opposed as "popish" by Episcopal leaders. No contemplative religious community had been officially countenanced in the Anglican church since the English monasteries were dissolved in the sixteenth century. Cannon and four other sisters, however, won the support of Bishop Horatio Potter when they took over management of the House of Mercy, a shelter for prostitutes in New York City. They brought some health and normalcy to the half-starved, ill-dressed young women in their charge. In 1865 the four sisters were allowed to establish the Community of St. Mary's, devoted to a life of prayer and devotion as well as an active life of labor. Sister Harriet, chosen their superior, retained the office for three decades. In addition to the House of Mercy, they managed for a time an orphanage, a home for women and children, St. Mary's School, and St. Mary's Hospital for Poor Children in New York. The memorial window commemorates Mother Harriet's place of honor in the history of the Episcopal church.

Cary, Mary Ann Shadd, 1823–1893, Reformer; NAW

Mary Ann Shadd Cary House, 1321 W Street, N.W. (Private); NHL

Mary Ann Shadd Cary was described by W. E. B. DuBois as "tall and slim, of that ravishing dream-born beauty—that twilight of the races that we call mulatto." She was the first Negro woman in North America to edit a newspaper. She was a lecturer, an army recruiter, a lawyer, a teacher. After the passage of the Fugitive Slave Act in 1850, this well-educated daughter of an outspoken Delaware abolitionist moved to Canada to help refugees from the South. With the assistance of the American Missionary Association, she started a school in Windsor, across the river from Detroit, Michigan. She founded and edited for four years a weekly newspaper, the *Provincial Freeman*, devoted to news of the Negroes in Canada. During this period she married Thomas Cary. She was teaching in Michigan by 1864 and got a special commission from the governor of Indiana to recruit a Negro regiment. She moved to Washington in 1869, then a widow, and enrolled in Howard University's law school. She dropped out, but returned ten years later to earn a law degree in 1883, when she was sixty.[7]

Cogswell, Alice, 1805–1831, Deaf Student, and Other Workers with the Deaf

Memorials at Gallaudet College, Kendall Green, Florida Avenue and 7th Street, N.E.

Alice Cogswell, for whom Cogswell Hall is named and who is shown in the Gallaudet Statue, lost her hearing at age two. Her father, Mason Cogswell, of Hartford, Connecticut, wondered how her mind could be developed when that avenue of communication was closed. When the child was seven, a group of Hartford citizens, led by Mason, sent Thomas Hopkins Gallaudet abroad to investigate methods of teaching the deaf; and on his return in 1817 they opened a school for the deaf in Hartford. Alice was its first pupil. In 1857 a national school for the deaf, now Gallaudet College, was founded, and Thomas Gallaudet's son Edward was its head. A statue of T. H. Gallaudet, with young Alice seated on his lap, stands at the college. The work of Daniel Chester French, it was unveiled in 1889.

The college has named other buildings and streets for men and women whose careers were meaningful to the deaf. Elizabeth Benson (1904–1972), for whom Benson Hall is named, was an authority on sign language and a faculty member for forty-odd years, except for three years when, as a member of the Woman's Army corps she taught lipreading to deafened soldiers.

Agatha Hanson Plaza is named for Agatha Tiegel Hanson (1873–1959). One of the first women students after the school became a college, she founded Phi Kappa Zeta Sorority. She went to teach in the Minnesota School for the Deaf.

Lowman Street commemorates Alto May Lowman (1865–1910), the first woman to complete a course of study at the college, earning a B.Ph. in 1892. She went on to become a teacher of the deaf in North Dakota and Maryland.

Switzer Drive is named for Mary E. Switzer (1900–1971, NAWM). Neither a student nor a teacher of the college, she contributed to the rehabilitation of the disabled as a director of the U.S. Office of Vocational Rehabilitation from 1950 to 1970. Her goal was nothing less than to have all disabled persons given help in finding satisfying work. The Vocational Rehabilitation Act of 1954, which provided for research, training of specialists, and building of centers for rehabilitation, came about as the result of her efforts.[8]

Coolidge, Elizabeth Sprague, 1864–1953, Music Patron; NAWM

Coolidge Auditorium, Library of Congress, Capitol Hill

Music lovers who move to Washington sooner or later discover the Coolidge chamber music concerts given on weekends in the Coolidge Auditorium. The hall and the concerts are Elizabeth Sprague Coolidge's gift to the country. She began sponsoring annual music festivals at South Mountain, near her home in

Pittsfield, Massachusetts. She not only endowed and managed these concerts but frequently performed in them, for she was an accomplished pianist. Very often they featured original compositions by living artists she sponsored. In order to commit the federal government to the support of music, she endowed the Elizabeth Sprague Coolidge Foundation at the Library of Congress. The auditorium was constructed at her expense and the chamber music concerts began in 1925. Often the instruments used are those donated by Gertrude Clark Whittall, q.v.[9]

Delano, Jane, 1862–1919, Nurse; NAW

Monument, National American Red Cross Building, D Street, Between 17th and 18th Streets, N.W.

The idealized figure of Jane Delano is a memorial to the organizer of the Red Cross nurses and to 296 other Red Cross nurses who died in World War I. Delano was called upon in 1908 to put together a reserve of trained nurses available for peacetime emergencies and possible wartime duties. The experience of the Red Cross during the Spanish-American War, with its improvised nursing and medical services, pointed up the need for such a reserve, but efforts had been unsuccessful because there was no coordination between the Red Cross and recognized nursing associations. Delano built up a roster of trained nurses who met her high qualifications for service. By the time the United States entered World War I, some eight thousand nurses were enrolled, and before the war ended Delano was able to supply two hundred thousand professional nurses, some for overseas duty and some for such domestic emergencies as the influenza epidemic in 1918. Delano died after the war while on an inspection tour in France. Her body was brought to Arlington National Cemetery for burial. The monument, by Robert Tait McKenzie, was unveiled in 1934. It is in the courtyard of the West Building, facing 18th Street.

Douglass, Helen Pitts, b. c. 1838, Civil Rights Worker

Cedar Hill (Frederick Douglass Home), 1411 W Street, S.E., Anacostia; HABS, NR

Helen Pitts Douglass was the second wife of Frederick Douglass, famed Negro spokesman for his race. His first wife, Anna Murray, whom he called "the post and center of my house," died in 1882. Eighteen months later he chose for his second wife the white, college-educated woman who had been his secretary. To her relatives who objected to the match, she said, "Love came to me and I was not afraid to marry the man I loved because of his color." Frederick, too, had to defend his choice. He wrote to Elizabeth Cady Stanton: "I could never have been at peace with my own soul or held up my head among men had I allowed the fear of popular clamor to deter me from following my convictions as to this marriage." They were happy and compatible, with goals in common.

Frederick died in 1895 and several years later Helen founded the Frederick Douglass Memorial and Historical Association to preserve Cedar Hill for posterity. The Victorian house is now part of the National Park Service. It has much of the original Douglass furniture, paintings, silver, glass, and books. It is open daily 9–5; in winter 9–4; hourly tours.[10]

Farrand, Beatrix Jones. See Bliss, Mildred

Folger, Emily Jordan, 1858–1936, Scholar; NAW

Folger Shakespeare Library, 201 E. Capitol Street, S.E.; NR

Henry Clay Folger retired from business—he was chairman of the board of Standard Oil of New York—in 1928. He was making plans for the Washington building that was to house his Shakespeare collection. He died two years later, and the completion of plans for the library fell on his wife, Emily Jordan Folger, also a student of Shakespeare's works. Construction had begun and administration of the institution was given over to Henry's alma mater, Amherst College, with a large endowment. Emily supervised completion of the building, assisted in selection of the staff, and oversaw the installation of furniture and antique works of art that were part of the collection.

The library's exhibition hall is open Mon.-Sat. 10–4; closed holidays. Plays, poetry readings, and concerts are held frequently, open to the public. The research library, unequaled in its collections of English and American history and literature, particularly in the Elizabethan period, is open to qualified scholars.

Giffin, Etta Josselyn, 1863–1932, Librarian for the Blind

Library of Congress Services to the Blind

For fifteen years Etta Josselyn Giffin was librarian of the Library of Congress Reading Room for the Blind, known to its clients as the Pavilion. During those years she won international prominence, but more important she won the affection and gratitude of the sightless who were transported from loneliness and monotony to companionship and adventure through the many activities she was able to provide. She later helped to found a new National Library for the Blind, unconnected with any other institution, and she directed it for the next twenty years. It served the needs of the blind in countless ways. They were employed to transcribe books into Braille and to print and bind the books for circulation throughout the country. When Giffin died, her loss was deeply felt and many wondered if the work could go on without her strong leadership. The National Library did continue for another nineteen years, when its services were merged with that of the Library of Congress, thus bringing full circle the work begun by Giffin.[11]

Gillett, Emma, 1852–1927, and Ellen Spencer Mussey, 1850–1936, Lawyers; NAW

Washington College of Law, American University, Nebraska and Massachusetts Avenues, N.W.

Inspired by news of Belva Lockwood's struggle to be admitted to the bar of the U.S. Supreme Court, Emma Gillett took her savings and left her dull teaching job in Pennsylvania for Washington. She enrolled in Howard University's law school, which was open to all without regard to sex or race, and graduated in 1883. She practiced in the District of Columbia and before the Supreme Court. Ellen Spencer Mussey, who had little formal training in the law, had worked with her husband, a teacher at Howard's law school, and she was admitted to the Washington bar by oral examination in 1893. She and Gillett began to give three young women lessons in law but found that the Columbian College refused to admit their students because "women did not have the mentality for law." They decided to form their own law school, and in 1898 the Washington College of Law was incorporated, with Mussey as its first dean. Both women were active in the District of Columbia and the National American Woman's Suffrage Association. Mussey joined in the Washington suffrage parade organized by Alice Paul on the eve of Woodrow Wilson's inaugural in 1912. Unruly and hostile crowds jostled and jeered at the marchers, and the police were unwilling or unable to protect them. Mussey suffered a stroke brought on by the occasion and the following year retired as dean of the college. Gillett succeeded her. Washington College is now affiliated with American University.

Grimké, Charlotte Forten, 1837–1914, Abolitionist; NAW

Charlotte Forten Grimké House, 1608 R Street, N.W. (Private); NHL

During the Civil War a call went out for volunteer teachers to go to the Sea Islands, off the South Carolina coast. The Union occupied some of the islands and the plantation owners had fled, leaving thousands of slaves and unworked cotton fields. Government officials took over the management of the plantations and began a program of educational and medical aid for the Negroes. Neither slave nor free, they were called contrabands—property taken during war. They were almost totally illiterate, for southern law forbade teaching slaves.

Among the northern women who offered themselves as teachers was Charlotte Forten Grimké, a black woman born into a Philadelphia, Pennsylvania, family of strong abolitionist sympathies. She had been teaching in Massachusetts and saw the Sea Islands project as an opportunity to do something for her race. The experiment was successful in that by the end of the war some two thousand children and many adults had received basic instruction and learned something about land management.

Some years later Grimké came to Washington, joined the Fifteenth Street Presbyterian Church, and in 1878 married its new pastor, Francis Grimké. He was the natural son of a slave woman and a South Carolina planter, Henry Grimké. Henry's white sisters, Sarah and Angelina Grimké, famous antislavery lecturers during the 1830s, were thus Francis Grimké's aunts. When they discovered the relationship, they assisted him in attending Princeton Theological Seminary.

Hayes, Lucy Webb, 1831–1889, Humanitarian, Wife of U.S. President; NAW

Hayes School of Nursing, American University, Nebraska and Massachusetts Avenues, N.W.

Of all the First Ladies up to her day, Lucy Webb Hayes, the wife of President Rutherford B. Hayes, was probably the best educated, the most representative of the new woman. She graduated from Wesleyan Female College in Cincinnati, Ohio, in 1850, two years before her marriage to Rutherford. Her strong antislavery views influenced him as he entered politics. While he served as an officer in the Union Army during the Civil War, she spent some time at his headquarters and became a favorite with the troops. After the war she helped found the Ohio Soldiers' and Sailors' Orphans' Home.

The Hayeses brought into the White House a new tone of family-centered, wholesome respectability. Lucy was well liked. Her modest dress was noted by the press, weary of extravagance and vulgar ostentation. For the first time liquor was banned in the executive mansion, even for state dinners, with the unhappy result that Lucy has gone down in popular history as Lemonade Lucy. After her death, philanthropists established in Washington the Lucy Hayes Deaconess Training School. The school of nursing was given her name when it was added to the university in 1956.[12]

Hearst, Phoebe Apperson, 1842–1919, Philanthropist; NAW

Hearst Hall, National Cathedral School for Girls, 3609 Woodley Road, N.W.

Phoebe Apperson Hearst was the wife of George Hearst, a mining engineer who made a fortune in gold and silver mining in the West. She was the mother of newspaper publisher William Randolph Hearst. Their fame cannot eclipse that of Phoebe, whose humanitarian philanthropies enriched every place she lived. She endowed libraries, kindergartens, and nurseries. Her wide interests included archeology, architecture, music, travel, and French. She came to Washington in 1886 when her husband was appointed to the Senate, and she continued to live in Washington after he died in 1891, dividing her time between Washington and California. Her contributions aided in the restoration of Mount Vernon, home of George Washington, and the building of the National (Washington) Cathedral. With Alice Birney she founded the National Congress of Mothers (later of Parents and Teachers). She is a founder of the National Cathedral School for Girls, which opened in Hearst Hall, its original building, in 1900. A portrait of her hangs in the school.

Johnson, Adelaide, 1859–1955, Sculptor; NAWM

The Woman Movement *(Busts of Susan B. Anthony, Lucretia Mott, and Elizabeth Cady Stanton), Crypt, U.S. Capitol*

Adelaide Johnson believed the woman's rights movement "the mightiest thing in the evolution of humanity." She did her first portrait bust of Susan B. Anthony (1820–1906, NAW) in 1886 for the annual woman's suffrage convention in Washington. She made another, which pleased her better, for display at the 1893 Columbian Exposition in Chicago, Illinois. She visited Anthony in her Rochester, New York, home to complete the work, and Anthony suggested that the new display should include her friend and coworker Elizabeth Cady Stanton (1815–1902, NAW) and between them "dear Lucretia Mott with her Quaker cap."

According to Stanton's memoirs, "I was summoned to Rochester by my friend Miss Anthony, to fill an appointment she had made for me with Miss Adelaide Johnson, the artist from Washington, who was to idealize Miss Anthony and myself in marble for the World's Fair." Lucretia Mott (1789–1880, NAW) was no longer living, so the sculptor had to work from photographs. She is shown with the Quaker bonnet, for she was a lifelong member of the Society of Friends, as had been her Nantucket forebears. Johnson added still another portrait, that of Caroline B. Winslow (1822–1896), Washington's pioneer homeopathic physician, president of the Moral Education Society of the District of Columbia, and a dedicated feminist.

The marble busts were placed in the center of the Gallery of Honor in the Woman's Building of the Exposition, where they were much admired. Johnson's dream of establishing a national monument to women was not realized until 1921, when the three marble busts, incorporated into the sculpture she called *The Woman Movement*, were placed in the Capitol, a gift of the National Woman's Party and the artist. The four busts made for the exposition are now in the Woman's Party headquarters, 144 Constitution Avenue, N.E. See, for Anthony, New York City (Hall of Fame), and Rochester, NY; for Stanton, Seneca Falls, NY, and Tenafly, NJ; for Mott, Philadelphia, PA.[13]

Johnston, Harriet Lane, 1830–1903, Philanthropist; NAW

National Museum of American Art, 9th and F Streets, N.W.
Lane-Johnston Building, St. Alban's School for Boys

A childless widow in her fifties, Harriet Lane Johnston came from Baltimore, Maryland, to Washington, where years before as Harriet Lane she had reigned over society as the hostess of the White House. She was the niece and ward of the bachelor President James Buchanan. The gay times had ended as the shadow of a civil war hung over the city and partisans of both sides withdrew from social diversions. Harriet married Henry Johnston and bore two sons, but by 1884 she had lost both children, her husband, and her beloved uncle. She sold the estate Buchanan had left her and moved to the capital to face life alone.

One thing that engaged her interest was the collection of art, another the support of St. Albans and the Washington Cathedral Choir School. She gave money to erect a statue of Buchanan, now in Meridian Hill Park, 16th and Euclid Streets, N.W. She gave the government her art collection and funds to establish a national gallery in Washington. The collection was scattered, stored, and ignored for years, then formed the nucleus of the National Museum of Fine Arts. Part of the Smithsonian Institution complex, it is open daily, except Christmas, 10–5:30. See Mercersburg and Lancaster, PA.

Keller, Helen, 1880–1968, Blind Worker for the Blind (NAWM) and Others

Effigies, Washington Cathedral, Wisconsin and Massachusetts Avenues, N.W.

The National Cathedral Association Bay is devoted to the role of women, with effigies, statues, and a stained-glass window featuring women. Among the adornments of the vaulted ceiling are effigies of Helen Keller, who overcame handicaps of blindness and deafness, and of Jane Addams (1860–1935, NAW), founder of Hull House in Chicago, Illinois, and winner of the Nobel Peace Prize. A statue of Isabella Thoburn (1840–1901, NAW), missionary to India and a leader in the Methodist deaconess movement, occupies a wall niche.[14]

King, Louisa Yeomans, 1863–1948, Gardener; NAW

Dogwood Grove, National Arboretum, 24th and R Streets, N.E.

No more fitting memorial could be designed for Louisa Yeomans King, a dedicated and influential gardener, than this grove. At her home in Alma, Michigan, she designed her own garden, corresponded with other horticulturists, and collected garden journals. In 1915 her first book on the subject appeared, *The Well-Considered Garden.* She favored a departure from the old-fashioned formal gardens with geometric plans and bright, precise patterns of color toward a more natural arrangement and massed colors. She was president of the Garden Club of Michigan and helped to found the Garden Club of America in 1913. The next year she was president of the Woman's National Farm and Garden Association. It was this group that established the dogwood grove in her memory. The arboretum is open Mon.-Fri. 8–5, Sat.-Sun. 10–5. The visitor's entrance is reached by following Bladensburg Road to R Street and turning right.[15]

Helen Keller, born in Alabama, became an internationally known speaker and writer, though blind and deaf. This effigy of her face is in the Washington Cathedral, Washington, D.C. The sculptor and carver was Constantine Seferlis. Photography by H. Byron Chambers. Courtesy Washington Cathedral.

Jane Addams, founder of Hull House in Chicago, Illinois, was a national figure, winner of the Nobel Peace Prize. This effigy of her face is in the Washington Cathedral, Washington, D.C. The sculptor and carver was Constantine Seferlis. Photography by H. Byron Chambers.
Courtesy Washington Cathedral.

Isabella Thoburn is remembered for her work in foreign missions and the Methodist deaconess movement. The statue, by Marion Brackenridge, carved by Roger Morigi, is in the Washington Cathedral, Washington, D.C. Photography by Morton Broffman. Courtesy Washington Cathedral.

Lockwood, Mary Smith, 1831–1922, and Other Clubwomen

Founders' Monument, Daughters of the American Revolution Building, C Street Between 17th and 18th Streets, N.W.

In 1890 the Sons of the American Revolution held a meeting at which a number of women were present. John Sherman of Ohio spoke, giving women credit for keeping the home fires burning during the Revolution; he said he was sorry women were ineligible to join the Sons. Mary Smith Lockwood at once prepared a protest, which filled three columns in the *Washington Post* of July 13. "Were there no mothers of the Revolution?" she asked: "Were these sires without dams? I trow not. I have heard of a man who had a dam by a mill site but who had no mill by a dam site, but I have yet to hear of a man who had a Revolutionary sire without a dam by the home site." She mentioned Molly Pitcher, Deborah Sampson, and Hannah Arnett as examples of women who served in the Revolution. Her column brought forth a letter from Mary Desha (1850–1911), a Kentucky schoolteacher then working for the government in Washington. She approved the idea of forming the Daughters of the American Revolution (DAR). They selected two other women who might join them: Eugenia Washington (d. 1900), a descendant of George Washington, and Ellen Hardin Walworth (1832–1915), who came from Saratoga Springs, New York, q.v. On October 11, 1890, these four and a number of other women met and organized the DAR. The event was commemorated in this monument by sculptor Gertrude Vanderbilt Whitney.[16]

McGroarty, Susan (Sister Julia), 1827–1901, Churchwoman; NAW

Trinity College, Michigan and Franklin Streets, N.W.

The Catholic University of America, founded in 1889 (by Mary Caldwell, q.v.), was for men only. Consequently, many Catholic women sought admission to non-Catholic colleges. When it was proposed to establish a woman's college near the university and use some of the same faculty, critics feared that it smacked of coeducation. Nevertheless, Sister Julia, provincial superior of the Sisters of Notre Dame de Namur, well known for her supervision of the order's many schools, undertook to plan for a woman's college. She modeled it on teacher training schools in Liverpool, England, and Glasgow, Scotland, but she also looked at Wellesley College and Vassar College. Trinity College, the first national Catholic college for women, enrolled its pioneer class in 1900, just a year before Sister Julia died.

Mears, Helen Farnsworth. See Willard, Frances

Meyer, Agnes Ernst, 1887–1970, Journalist and Reformer; NAWM

Eugene and Agnes Meyer School, 11th and Clifton Streets, N.W

Wife of Eugene Meyer and co-owner with him of the *Washington Post*, Agnes Ernst Meyer helped form the paper's policies and prepared significant investigative reports. Her first love was reporting and in 1942 she wrote firsthand accounts of "Britain's Home Front," the attempts by women of England to cope with food shortages and public health problems. Back home she toured American war industries and turned a spotlight on government waste, on the scandal of segregation in the army, and on the waste of human resources. After the war she revisited communities to find out how they planned a conversion to peacetime economy and found that few had any plans at all.

She campaigned for a federal department of health, education, and security, administered by a cabinet member. She encouraged women to become active not only in their own communities but in state and federal welfare measures. "Woman's place is in the home," she said—"but not just one home."[17]

Miner, Myrtilla, 1815–1864, Educator; NAW

District of Columbia Teachers College, 1100 Harvard Street, N.W.

Myrtilla Miner had much difficulty in finding a place to establish a school for black girls, but she persisted and opened her Colored Girls School in 1851. Harriot Hunt, feminist physician of Massachusetts, visited the school and wrote: "The establishment of a school for colored girls in a slaveholding district, is one of the triumphs of freedom. Miss Miner has exhibited an untiring zeal, energy, and benevolence, which is worthy of the cause of liberty; she met opposition with calm resolution, and carried her purpose by unflinching firmness." Among Miner's supporters was Harriet Beecher Stowe, who gave her one thousand dollars from the royalties of *Uncle Tom's Cabin*. The school began in a rented room and soon moved to a three-acre lot on the outskirts of town. Miner did a little practice shooting on the campus, which helped to discourage interference. The Civil War closed the school, but after the war it was continued irregularly as the Miner Normal School, then incorporated into the public school system and renamed Miner Teachers College. Later it merged with another school to form the District of Columbia Teachers College.[18]

Morris, Esther Hobart, 1814–1902, Suffragist; NAW

Statue, Statuary Hall, U.S. Capitol

The state of Wyoming chose Esther Hobart Morris in 1960 as one of its two foremost citizens to be represented in Statuary Hall. The bronze statue by Avard

Fairbanks is inscribed: ''Esther Hobart Morris, proponent of the legislative act in 1869 which gave distinction to the Territory of Wyoming as the 1st government in the world to grant women equal rights.'' On the right side of the pedestal: ''A grateful people honors this stalwart pioneer, who also became the 1st woman justice of the peace.'' Morris is credited with persuading members of the territorial legislature, over cups of tea in her living room, to include votes for women in the Organic Act creating the territory. Wyoming was just two months ahead of Utah in this respect, but Utah women lost their franchise by a federal law in 1887 and could not vote again until the state came into the union in 1896 with full suffrage. Wyoming refused to join the union in 1890 unless it could retain equal rights.[19]

Moten, Lucy Ella, 1851–1933, Educator; NAW

Moten Elementary School, Morris and Evans Roads, S.E.

In 1883 the principalship of the Teacher Training School for Colored Girls (the Miner School) was vacant. Frederick Douglass, a member of the Miner board, recommended Lucy Ella Moten, who had been teaching locally and was a graduate of the Normal School in Salem, Massachusetts. The board thought her well qualified except for being too youthful and ''far too fascinating'' for the position. Douglass asked her whether she was willing to give up the theater, card playing, and dancing. She agreed, tried to look less lovely, and got the appointment. She held the position for thirty-seven years. Believing that it demanded her very best, Moten continued to fill in what she conceived of as gaps in her own education. She went to the Spencerian Business College, took training in elocution and public speaking, and went through four years of medical training at Howard University. She studied education in New York University's graduate school and spent many summers in European travel. She expected from the students the same dedication, for she regarded teaching as ''a profession demanding the soundest culture and highest efficiency.'' By the time Moten resigned her position the school was nationally recognized as the best school of its kind in the country. It is now the District of Columbia Teachers College. The elementary school was given her name in 1954.[20]

Mott, Lucretia Coffin. See Johnson, Adelaide

Mussey, Ellen Spencer. See Gillett, Emma

Pariseau, Esther (Mother Joseph of the Sacred Heart), 1823–1902, Churchwoman and Architect

Statue, Statuary Hall, U.S. Capitol

At the time President Abraham Lincoln was signing the bill to establish a National Statuary Hall, a future candidate for representation was struggling to found, in the pioneer society of the Pacific Northwest, the elements of civilization—its first health care facilities, schools, and orphanages. She was Mother Joseph, born Esther Pariseau, who went to Washington Territory from Canada in 1856 and worked there for the next fifty years. At the time of her death she and her sister nuns had founded no less than fifteen hospitals and ten schools, as well as orphanages, homes for the aged, and shelters for the mentally ill. She was in addition architect, builder, carver in wood and wax, and fund-raiser for her numerous enterprises. Yet when this great and talented woman was nominated for a place in Statuary Hall, she was almost unknown. Her name does not appear in standard biographical works, and when her statue, representing the state of Washington, was added to the hall on May 1, 1980, the ceremony attracted very little press notice except in the Pacific Northwest. In 1952 the American Institute of Architects, amazed at the number of early buildings credited to her design, named her "The First Architect in the Northwest." The West Coast Lumbermen's Association, aware of her use of Douglas Fir for her carvings, recognized her as "the first white artisan to work with wood of the Pacific Northwest." The statue, by Felix de Weldon, shows the nun kneeling in prayer, at her feet the tools she used to design and build.[21]

Paul, Alice. See Belmont, Alva

Perkins, Frances, 1880–1965, Reformer and Public Official; NAWM

Frances Perkins Building (U.S. Department of Labor), 200 Constitution Avenue, N.W.

Frances Perkins was the first woman appointed to a cabinet post in the U.S. government. Her appointment as secretary of labor by President Franklin D. Roosevelt in 1932 surprised labor leaders. They were not ready to believe that a middle-aged woman identified with social reform could be an effective head of the department. They had not checked her record: two years with the New York Consumers' League; lobbying the state legislature for a shorter work week; a spell with the Committee on Safety of the city of New York, investigating the kind of conditions that led to the tragic Triangle Shirtwaist Company fire; years on the New York State Industrial Commission and the Council on Immigrant Education; and a post as industrial commissioner for the state of New York. She had worked for child health, protective legislation for women workers, factory safety, and a minimum wage law.

As the New Deal policies took shape, Perkins backed Roosevelt in his plans for emergency unemployment relief and long-range social security legislation. Feminists were dismayed when she suggested during the depression that married women workers should give the jobs to men; when, during the war, she opposed child care centers; and when she spoke against the Equal Rights Amendment, believing it would do away with women's hard-won protective laws. Overall, her record for creating a more equitable industrial society was a remarkable one. The Labor Building was given her name in 1980. She is in the National Women's Hall of Fame.

Post, Marjorie Merriweather, 1887–1973, Philanthropist and Art Collector; NAWM

Hillwood, 4155 Linnean Avenue, N.W.

With a fortune based on Postum, Grape Nuts, and Post Toasties, all concocted by her father, C. W. Post, Marjorie Merriweather Post never had to earn a living. She did, however, follow up her formal education with training in business, attendance at business meetings, and factory tours. After her father's death in 1914 she inherited the Postum Cereal Company, but she was represented on the board by her husbands, first Edward Close, then, after a divorce, E. F. Hutton. Post persuaded the company to expand into the frozen food market, after which it was named the General Foods Corporation. She was married twice more, once to Ambassador Joseph Davies, then to Herbert May, head of Westinghouse Corporation. Marjorie loved to build sumptuous homes and fill them with precious furnishings. The Washington residence, Hillwood, is a showplace for a collection of treasures of the czar unmatched outside of the Soviet Union, French eighteenth-century furniture, Royal Sèvres porcelain, and Beauvais tapestries. It is now a private museum, open to the public for guided tours by reservation (202–686–5807), Mon. and Wed.-Sat. at 9, 10:30, 12, and 1:30; stiff adm. Children under twelve not admitted. Gardens open Mon. and Wed.-Sat. 1–4; adm.[22]

Putnam, Brenda, 1890–1975, Sculptor

Puck Fountain, Folger Shakespeare Library, 201 E. Capitol Street, N.E.

Brenda Putnam, born in Minneapolis, Minnesota, studied under several American sculptors, including James Earle Fraser and Charles Grafly, and in Florence, Italy. Her work includes a mural for the U.S. Post Office in Caldwell, New Jersey, painted under the Works Progress Administration program, a bust of Susan B. Anthony for the Hall of Fame in New York City, and relief portraits (Maimonides, Solon, and Tribonian, lawgivers) in the House Chamber, U.S. Capitol.

Ream, Vinnie (Hoxie), 1847–1914, Sculptor; NAW

Statues of Abraham Lincoln, U.S. Capitol, Admiral Farragut, Farragut Square, K and 17th Streets, N.W., and Other Works

She was eighteen, charming, her eyes sparkling, her curls bouncing, and she wanted to make a statue of the president. When they told President Abraham

Lincoln about Vinnie Ream, and added that she was poor, he consented to sit for her. Shortly after the sittings were completed he was assassinated, which gave special appeal to her model of the weary, kindly man. In 1866 Congress granted her ten thousand dollars to make the marble statue. With this sum she went to Paris, France, and Rome, Italy, to work on it and study sculpture seriously. The statue, when placed in the Capitol's rotunda, did not please everyone, but it has stood the test of time. Ream married Lieutenant (later Brigadier General) Richard Hoxie in 1878 and a couple of years later the statue of Farragut, which was commissioned by the government, was unveiled. She had cast the figure from the propellor of Farragut's flagship. The Hoxies lived in Farragut Square and for some time Ream gave up sculpture to be a wife, mother, and hostess. In 1906 the state of Iowa commissioned a statue of Samuel J. Kirkwood for Statuary Hall. She completed the model for Sequoyah, Oklahoma's representative in the hall, shortly before her death, and it was cast in bronze by another sculptor, George Zolnay.[23]

Regan, Agnes Gertrude, 1869–1943, Churchwoman; NAW

Agnes Regan Hall, Catholic University of America, Michigan Avenue, N.E.

During World War I a school was established in Washington to train Catholic laywomen in social work. After the war it was desired to continue the school on a permanent basis and the suggestion was made that it be affiliated with Catholic University. Since the university did not enroll laywomen, the church turned to the National Council of Catholic Women, whose executive secretary was Agnes Gertrude Regan. Under the auspices of the council, the National Catholic Service School for Women opened its doors in 1921; the university agreed to grant a master's degree for the two-year postgraduate program. In 1922 Regan was appointed an instructor and three years later became assistant director. In addition to a heavy administrative load, which included much fund-raising, she remained an executive of the council. A few years after her death the school of social work was merged with Catholic University. Agnes Regan Hall was dedicated in 1950.

Rittenhouse, Sarah, 1845–1943, Preservationist

Armillary Sphere, Montrose Park, R Street Between 30th and 31st Streets, N.W.

Sarah Rittenhouse founded Montrose Park in Georgetown and is credited with saving it from a housing development in the early 1900s. The sphere, a memorial to her, was a gift in 1956 from the Georgetown Garden Club.

Royall, Anne Newport, 1769–1854, Journalist; NAW

Monument, Congressional Cemetery, 18th and E Streets, S.E.

Some sixty years after Anne Newport Royall died in poverty, a monument was erected at her grave "in appreciative recognition" by some men from Philadelphia, Pennsylvania, and Washington, D.C. The stone reads: "Anne Royall, Pioneer Woman Publicist, 1769–1854. 'I pray that the Union of these states may be eternal.' " Royall was not only a publicist but a tireless traveler. In the 1820s travel was not an easy matter, especially to a woman in her fifties, single and far from wealthy. She published a series of travel books, beginning with *Sketches of History, Life and Manners in the United States* (1826) and following it with books on Pennsylvania and the South. She was not always complimentary in her remarks about people and places, which probably added to the popularity of her books. In 1830 she settled down in Washington and began publication of a newspaper, *Paul Pry*, succeeded by *The Huntress*, in which she gave full vent to her views on politics and politicians. John Quincy Adams was one of her admirers, though he characterized her as "a virago errant in enchanted armor." She was once convicted of being "a common scold," and her fine was paid by John Eaton, then secretary of war. The monument in the cemetery is in Range 26, Site 194.

Sabin, Florence Rena, 1871–1953, Medical Researcher; NAWM

Statue, Statuary Hall, U.S. Capitol

Sculptor Joy Flinsch Buba chose to represent Florence Rena Sabin, Colorado's representative in Statuary Hall, seated on a laboratory stool, with a book and a microscope representing her work in medicine. The inscription reads: "Teacher, Scientist, Humanitarian. Johns Hopkins University 1902–1925. Rockefeller Institute 1925–1938. Colorado Public Health 1944–1953." Sabin had, indeed, three distinguished careers. One of the first women students to enter Johns Hopkins Medical School, she graduated in 1900 and returned as teacher for twenty-three years, the first woman appointed to its faculty. In 1925 she was offered a position as head of a section in the Rockefeller Institute in New York, where she spent the next part of her career studying the cellular aspects of immunity. When she reached the age of sixty-seven she was forced to retire, though still vitally interested in her work. She returned to Denver, Colorado, to live with her only sister. Appointed to a postwar planning committee to help assess the state's health needs, she found that the state had very serious problems: high infant mortality, poor milk controls, raw sewage in the streams, a high incidence of preventible disease, all compounded by an inefficient board of health and inadequate laws. She lobbied for passage of a series of health laws, working well past her eightieth birthday. She is in the National Women's Hall of Fame.

Sanford, Maria Louise, 1836–1920, Educator; NAW

Statue, Statuary Hall, U.S. Capitol

The full-length figure of Maria Louise Sanford shows a woman severely dressed, grim-faced, holding a book in her hand. The pedestal in inscribed: "The best known and best loved woman in Minnesota, Maria L. Sanford, Educator, Orator, Civic Leader. Sturdy and resilient Puritan, whose perceptive mind and reverence for classic truth and beauty quickened intellectual life within the pioneer state of Minnesota and beyond its frontiers." It is true that Sanford was of New England Puritan stock, a believer in honest work, thrift, self-help, and other strict virtues, but tributes from her students belie the impression of severity. She taught in Connecticut, at Swarthmore College in Pennsylvania, and at the University of Minnesota. An excellent and popular teacher, her classes in history, rhetoric, and English were always full, her subjects alive and intense. She loved poetry and art and often gave readings from her favorite poems. In 1899 she won a contest for "favorite teacher" and with the prize and contributions from students went to Europe to tour art centers. The sculptor of the figure was Evelyn Raymond.[24]

Scaravaglione, Concetta, 1900–1975, Sculptor

Bas-relief, Federal Trade Commission Building, Pennsylvania and Constitution Avenues, N.W.

Concetta Scaravaglione began studying art at the age of sixteen at the National Academy of Design and at twenty-five was showing her works and beginning a long teaching career. Some of her work was done during the depression under the Works Progress Administration art project. A versatile artist, she used wood, terra cotta, welded copper, bronze, and other materials. The bas-relief, *Agriculture,* is over the Constitution Avenue entrance of the Apex Federal Trade Commission Building. Her works are in the collections of many galleries, including the Museum of Modern Art and the Whitney Museum.[25]

Seward, Olive Risley, 1841–1908, Abolitionist

Statue, 601 N. Carolina Avenue, S.E.

Olive Risley Seward was a niece and ward of William H. Seward, President Abraham Lincoln's secretary of state. She edited *William H. Seward's Travels Around the World* (1873). The idealized portrait statue of her near Seward Square is the work of John Cavanaugh, erected in 1971.

Shaw, Anna Howard, 1847–1919, Minister and Suffrage Leader; NAW

Memorial Column, National American Red Cross Building, D Street between 17th and 18th Streets, N.W.

In 1929 the National Federation of Women's Clubs, along with three other national women's organizations, endowed one of the Ionic columns in the building in memory of Anna Howard Shaw and other clubwomen who served during World War I. Shaw's long leadership of the woman's suffrage movement ended just as the war was beginning. She was asked to chair the Woman's Committee of the U.S. Council of National Defense. Although seventy years old, she still had as much energy as ever and she threw herself enthusiastically into coordinating the work American women were doing to further the war effort. In the last year of her life she not only had the satisfaction of knowing that the suffrage amendment had passed both houses of Congress but was honored with the Distinguished Service Medal for her wartime services.[26]

Slowe, Lucy Diggs, 1885–1937, Educator; NAW

Memorial Window, Chapel, Howard University

As dean of women at Howard University, Lucy Diggs Slowe discovered that deans of women in Negro institutions were regarded as matrons rather than educators. She began courses in counseling and organized the deans and advisors in other schools to upgrade their skills and influence. She conducted studies of black college women in 1933 and found that less than half were being given opportunities for self-government. Many came from communities where they were denied active participation in civic life and from homes where religion preached an inferior status for women. They needed training in self-direction so that they could assist in directing others in the modern world. Her energies spilled over the edges of campus life and brought her into the National Council of Negro Women, as a founder and first secretary, and into the National Association of College Women, as its first president.[27]

Stanton, Elizabeth Cady. See Johnson, Adelaide

Terrell, Mary Church, 1863–1954, Civil Rights Lecturer; NAWM

Mary Church Terrell House, 326 U Street, N.W. (Private); NHL.
Mary Church Terrell Recreation Centers, 3301 Wheeler Road, S.E., and 1st and L Streets, N.E.

At eighty-nine, Mary Church Terrell was leading picket lines in Washington to desegregate lunchrooms. Several years earlier she had broken the color bar in the American Association of University Women. She was one of the first black women to secure a college degree (from Oberlin College, in 1884), but when she wanted to use her education to teach others, her father objected. "My father," she wrote, "felt that he was able to support me. He disinherited me, refusing to write to me for a year because I went to Wilberforce to teach. Further, I was ridiculed and told that no man would want to marry a woman who studied higher mathematics." She was one of the founders of the National Association of Colored Women, a charter member of the National Association for the Advancement of Colored People, a member of the Washington Board of Education. The only Afro-American delegate to the International Congress of Women in 1904 in Berlin, she addressed the convention in English, German, and French. Her *A Colored Woman in a White World* sums up her experiences in fighting second-class status for her race.[28]

Ward, Justine Bayard Cutting, 1879–1975, Musician

Ward Hall, Catholic University of America, Michigan Avenue, N.E.

Justine Bayard Cutting Ward's music books, written to introduce young children to music, have been translated into French, Dutch, and Italian, and are now begin used in schools in Europe, the United States, and the Philippines. She held that there is no amusical child. "They could be taught to communicate with each other in song, like young birds," she claimed. She taught very young children by reducing intricate musical forms into simple terms, using fingers and numerals to represent notes. A convert to Catholicism, she gave much of her life to promoting liturgical music for the church. She studied under Dom André Mocquereau at the Benedictine Abbey in Solesmes, France, and in 1928 formed a charitable corporation, named for him, for teaching and disseminating the Gregorian chant. In 1967 Catholic University named its music building in her honor.[29]

Whitney, Gertrude Vanderbilt, 1875–1942, Sculptor; NAW

Titanic *Memorial, 4th and P Streets, S.W., and Other Sculptures*

The founder of the Whitney Museum of American Art (see New York City), Gertrude Vanderbilt Whitney has several sculptures in the capital city. In addition to the memorial to victims of the *Titanic* sinking, she executed the *Spirit of the Red Cross* at the American Red Cross Building, a monument to the founders of the Daughters of the American Revolution (DAR) at the DAR Building, and a fountain at the Pan American Union.

Whittall, Gertrude Clark, 1867–1965, Music Patron

Whittall Pavilion, Library of Congress, Capitol Hill

In 1935 sprightly Gertrude Clark Whittall went to the Library of Congress and offered to donate two violins, a viola, and a cello, all made by Stradivarius, with bows for all crafted by François Tourte. A year later she added a third violin and a fifth bow to the collection, and in 1937 gave funds to construct a pavilion adjacent to the auditorium given by Elizabeth Sprague Coolidge, q.v. The pavilion, named for Whittall, exhibits the instruments when not in use. They are used often in the Coolidge concerts. When listeners cannot get into the auditorium, they may sit in the pavilion and listen to the music on speakers. Both the Whittall and Coolidge Foundations sponsor prizes for original compositions.[30]

Willard, Frances, 1839–1898, Temperance Leader; NAW

Statue, Statuary Hall, U.S. Capitol

Speaking at the dedication of the statue of Frances Willard, world-famous leader of the Woman's Christian Temperance Union, Senator Albert J. Beveridge displeased many feminists with his tribute: ''Willard sacrificed her own life to the happiness of her sisters. For, after all, she knew that, with all her gifts and all the halo of her God-sent mission, the humblest mother was yet greater far than she.'' Kentucky's Laura Clay, for one, remarked that Willard never saw herself in such a light.

The statue, erected in 1905 by the state of Illinois, is by Helen Farnsworth Mears (1872–1916, NAW), a sculptor from Oshkosh, Wisconsin. She was a student of Augustus St. Gaudens and winner of a competition for the Willard statue. Since Willard's was the first statue of a woman to be placed in Statuary Hall, it brought the artist a share of fame. Willard is also honored by a bust in the Hall of Fame, New York City. See Churchville, NY.[31]

Wilson, Edith Bolling Galt, 1872–1961, Politician, Wife of U.S. President; NAWM

Woodrow Wilson Home, 2340 S Street, N.W.; HABS, NHL

About a year after the death of his first wife, the lonely and depressed President Woodrow Wilson met Edith Bolling Galt, a forty-three-year-old childless widow, owner of a jewelry store in Washington. They were married in December 1915, and from that time on she was his best friend and trusted advisor. They discussed domestic and foreign problems, read together, and arrived at decisions together. The executive mansion was once again lively and homelike.

All changed when Woodrow suffered a massive stroke in October 1919. The White House was isolated, its gates padlocked and guarded. It was rumored that

Edith took over the presidency and made the decisions during this period, but she denied it. It was an extraordinarily crucial time, with the Treaty of Versailles under consideration. Believing that the president's resignation would prevent his recovery, she refused the advice of physicians that Woodrow should give up the office. At the end of his term, the Wilsons moved to the house on S Street, where Edith nursed her husband until his death in 1924. She spent the rest of her own life working on projects to perpetuate his memory. The house is open Mar. 1–Dec. 31, Tues.-Fri. 10–2, Sat.-Sun. and holidays 12–4; Feb., Sat.-Sun only, 12–4; closed Jan. and some holidays; adm.

NOTES

In addition to the correspondents listed below, I have had assistance from the following: the District of Columbia Public Library, thc Smithsonian Institution, thc National Council of Negro Women, and the Library of Congress.

1. Otto Friedrich, ''Clover and Henry Adams, A Most Unusual Love Story,'' *Smithsonian* 8 (Apr. 1977).

2. Charlotte S. Rubinstein, *American Women Artists* (New York: Avon Books, 1982); brochure, Barney Studio House.

3. Correspondence, Woman's Party Corporation.

4. Phillip Drotning, *A Guide to Negro History in America* (Garden City, N.Y.: Doubleday & Co., 1968).

5. *New York Times*, Jan. 19, 1969; brochures, Dumbarton Oaks.

6. *Library of Congress Quarterly Journal* 34 (Oct. 1977), pp. 356–60.

7. Harold B. Hancock, ''Mary Ann Shadd: Negro Editor, Educator, and Lawyer,'' *Delaware History* 15 (Apr. 1973).

8. *Gallaudet Today* 12 (Fall 1981); clippings and correspondence, Gallaudet College.

9. Patrick Hayes, ''My Monday Morning Country Store,'' *Library of Congress Quarterly Journal* 39 (Fall 1982).

10. Philip S. Foner, *The Life and Writings of Frederick Douglass* (New York: International Publishers, 1950).

11. Victoria Faber Stevenson, *Etta Josselyn Giffin, Pioneer Librarian for the Blind* (Washington, D.C.: National Library for the Blind, 1959).

12. Charles R. Williams, *The Life of Rutherford B. Hayes* (Boston, Mass.: Houghton Mifflin Co., 1914).

13. Jeanne M. Weimann, *The Fair Women: The Story of the Woman's Building* (Chicago, Ill.: Academy Chicago, 1981); Elizabeth C. Stanton, *Eighty Years and More* (New York: Schocken Books, 1971; repr. of 1898 ed.); correspondence, Woman's Party Corporation.

14. Robert B. Dickerson, Jr., *Final Placement: A Guide to Deaths, Funerals, and Burials of Famous Americans* (Algonac, Mich.: Reference Publications, 1982).

15. *American Gardens: A Traveler's Guide* (Brooklyn, N.Y.: Brooklyn Botanic Garden, 1977). This is an excellent handbook, revised and reprinted from *Plants and Gardens* 26, no. 3.

16. *New York Times*, July 11 and Oct. 10, 1915 and Nov. 11, 1922; Mary Simmerson Logan, *The Part Taken by Women in American History* (New York: Perry-Nalle, 1972; repr. of 1912 ed.).

17. *Current Biography,* 1949.

18. Harriot Hunt, *Glances and Glimpses; or, Fifty Years Social, Including Twenty Years Professional Life* (Boston, Mass.: John P. Jewett & Co., 1856; repr., Source Book Press, 1970).

19. T. A. Larson, "Woman Suffrage in Wyoming," *Pacific Northwest Quarterly* 56 (Apr. 1965).

20. Thomasine Corrothers, "Lucy Ellen [*sic*] Moten," *Journal of Negro History* 19 (Jan. 1934).

21. Sister Mary of the Blessed Sacrament McCrosson, *The Bell and the River* (Palo Alto, Calif.: Pacific Books, 1957); Mary McKernan, "Mother Joseph: Pioneer Nun in the Pacific Northwest," *American West* 18 (Sept.-Oct. 1981); correspondence, Sisters of Providence, Seattle, Wash.; National Register nomination form, Providence Academy, Vancouver, Washington.

22. See the *Architectural Digest*, Jan.-Feb. 1979 issue, for excellent color photographs of Hillwood.

23. Stephen W. Stathis and Lee Roderick, "Mallet, Chisel, and Curls," *American Heritage* 27 (Feb. 1976).

24. Gertrude B. Schofield and Susan M. Smith, "Maria Louise Sanford, Minnesota's Heroine," in *Women of Minnesota*, ed. Barbara Stuhler and Gretchen Kreuter (St. Paul: Minnesota Historical Society Press, 1977).

25. *New York Times*, Sept. 5, 1975.

26. Mildred Wells, *Unity in Diversity: The History of the General Federation of Women's Clubs* (Washington, D.C.: Federation, 1953).

27. Jeanne L. Noble, *The Negro Woman's College Education* (New York: Teachers College, Columbia University, 1956).

28. Noble; *Current Biography*, 1942.

29. *New York Times*, Nov. 19, 1975.

30. *Quarterly Journal of the Library of Congress* 33 (Apr. 1976).

31. Aileen Kraditor, *The Ideas of the Woman Suffrage Movement* (New York: Columbia University Press, 1965).

MARYLAND

ANTIETAM

Barton, Clara, 1821–1912, Red Cross Founder; NAW

Monument, Mansfield Avenue

At the beginning of the Civil War, Clara Barton was working at the Patent Office in Washington, D.C. She discovered how ill prepared the army was to care for sick and wounded soldiers, who were in need of food and medical supplies. With the help of a few friends she collected provisions and took them to the battlefields. In spite of opposition from army surgeons, she managed to commandeer army mules and wagons, to prepare food for the men, and go wherever help was needed. The soldiers remembered her as the Angel of the Battlefield.

The memorial is a rough marble slab with a cross of red bricks and a tablet commemorating her "act of love and mercy" which led to her eventual founding of the American Red Cross. The Dunkard church where she tended the wounded has been restored. See Glen Echo, MD, Bordentown, NJ, and Dansville and New York City, NY (Hall of Fame).

BALTIMORE

Bonaparte, Elisabeth Patterson, 1785–1879, Celebrity; NAW

Bonaparte Room, Maryland Historical Society, 201 W. Monument Street

In 1803, after a whirlwind courtship against opposition from both families, Napoleon Bonaparte's nineteen-year-old son Jerome married eighteen-year-old Elisabeth (Betsy) Patterson, daughter of one of Baltimore's wealthiest men. Napoleon refused to consider the marriage valid and ordered Jerome to return to France. When they sailed in 1805, Napoleon had so arranged matters that no port on the coast would allow Betsy to disembark. She went alone to England, where she bore a son to the husband who had by now been persuaded to abandon her. After Napoleon's downfall in 1815 she traveled about European capitals as Madame Bonaparte. Legends about Betsy continue to flourish in Maryland. The Bonaparte Room has some of her furniture and other belongings. It is open Tues.-Sat. 11–4, Sun. 1–5.

Cone, Claribel, 1864–1929, and Her Sister Etta Cone, 1870–1949, Art Collectors and Patrons; NAW (under Claribel Cone)

Cone Collection, Baltimore Museum of Art, Art Museum Drive, Wyman Park

Claribel and Etta Cone were daughters of a German-Jewish immigrant who began as a peddler, earned enough to open a grocery store, and financed his sons' Cone Mills in North Carolina which brought the family a fortune. The sisters used their share of the wealth to form what became an internationally famous collection of modern French painting and sculpture. Claribel had a flair for entertaining and this brought the sisters into contact with Gertrude Stein and her brother Leo, who were living in Baltimore in the 1890s. When the Cones went to Europe they were frequent visitors at the Stein apartment in Paris, France, and Leo guided them about the art museums and studios. Soon the two sisters were enthusiastically buying Picassos, Matisses, Cézannes, and Manets. In Baltimore they were familiar sights at concerts and exhibitions, Claribel's portly figure adorned with exotic jewelry and scarves, Etta less flamboyant.

Claribel died first, leaving her collection to Etta, suggesting that "if the spirit of appreciation of modern art in Baltimore becomes improved," it might go to the Baltimore Museum. Etta left both collections to the museum, along with enough money to finance a wing for their display. It is open Tues.-Fri. 10–4, Sat.-Sun. 11–6, and Thurs. 6–10 P.M.; closed holidays; adm.

Coppin, Fanny Jackson, 1837–1913, Educator; NAW

Coppin State College, 2500 W. North Avenue

Fanny Jackson Coppin was born into slavery. When she was a young girl an aunt purchased her freedom and then made it possible for her to go to Oberlin College, one of the few colleges then open to blacks. She graduated in 1865, with the dream of sharing her educational advantages with others of her race. She went to teach at the Institute for Colored Youth in Philadelphia, Pennsylvania, eventually becoming principal of the school. She was there for thirty-seven years, leaving in 1902 to go to South Africa with her missionary husband, Levi Coppin. Two years after she left, the institute moved to Cheyney, Pennsylvania, q.v., where it is now Cheyney University. Coppin State College evolved from a similar training school established in 1900. It was given her name in 1926 in recognition of her contributions to Negro education.

Harper, Frances Ellen Watkins, 1825–1911, Lecturer and Poet; NAW

Frances Ellen Harper School, W. Carrolton Avenue and Riggs Road; NR

Frances Ellen Watkins Harper, the child of free Negro parents, was orphaned before she was three and was brought up by an uncle who ran a school for free blacks in Baltimore. She imbibed from him not only his strong antislavery ideals but his love of learning. In 1850 she left Baltimore to teach sewing in Ohio and then in Pennsylvania (see Philadelphia, PA). While she was there Maryland passed a law making free Negroes entering the state from the North liable to be sold as slaves. She never returned to her native state but spent the subsequent years lecturing on abolition and pleading for the education of blacks. She married Fenton Harper in 1860 but the marriage ended with his death four years later. She is considered one of the pioneer Afro-American writers. The school named for her is now a residence for the elderly.[1]

Jackson, Lillie May Carroll, 1889–1975, Civil Rights Activist

Lillie Carroll Jackson Museum, 1320 Eutaw Place. Lillie M. Jackson Elementary School, 1501 Ashburton Street

Lillie May Carroll Jackson was for thirty-five years the dynamic leader of the Baltimore branch of the National Association for the Advancement of Colored People (NAACP). When she was first elected the NAACP president, Baltimore was thoroughly segregated. A black woman could enter most of the big department stores, but she could not try on a hat or dress. Black policemen could not wear uniforms. Public schools were segregated; blacks were barred from the University of Maryland; Jim Crow regulations were enforced in housing and transportation. By the time Jackson died, legal restrictions of this sort were all part of the past. One by one, the goals for which she and the NAACP had fought were won: the Civil Rights Bill (1957), the Public Accommodations Law (1964), the Voting Rights Act (1965), and the Fair Housing Act (1968), followed by amendments establishing equal employment opportunities.

Jackson's home is now a "museum for the masses," a permanent tribute to humanity's search for freedom. It is open Tues. and Thurs. 1:30–5; other days by appointment. The nonprofit museum corporation plans to erect a bronze sculpture in Eutaw Place Square as a further monument to Jackson and all the freedom fighters who worked with her.[2]

Knipp, Anna Heubeck, 1870–1966, Clubwoman

Anna Heubeck Hall, Goucher College

Goucher College opened in 1888 as the Woman's College of Baltimore. One of its first students was Anna Heubeck Knipp, who with four other young women made up the first graduating class in 1892. Most of her life thereafter, especially after her marriage in 1905 to George W. Knipp, was spent in church work in Baltimore. About 1930 she began writing the histories of the various organizations to which she had belonged. She initiated the Goucher Alumnae Association, was a college trustee for twenty years, and wrote a history of the school. In 1937 the college named its newest building for her.[3]

Pickersgill, Mary Young, fl. 1813, Flagmaker

Star-Spangled Banner House, 844 E. Pratt Street; NHL

Mary Young Pickersgill was a maker of ships' banners and flags, with skills in spinning, weaving, and sewing taught her by her mother, Rebecca Young, who made the Grand Union flag in 1775. In 1813, Pickersgill got the biggest order of her career, to make an American flag "so large that the British will have no difficulty in seeing it." The flag, 36 by 42 feet, with 15 stars and 15 stripes, was too large to be finished in this small house, so part of the work was done in a nearby brewery. She received $405.90 for her work.

The flag was flown over Fort McHenry during the British bombardment in 1814, and the sight of it inspired Francis Scott Key to compose "The Star-Spangled Banner." The Flag House is allowed to fly both the 1814 banner and the present U.S. flag twenty-four hours a day. The original flag sewn by Pickersgill is in the Smithsonian Institution. The house is furnished as it might have appeared in 1814, with mementoes of the family and of Francis Scott Key and a replica of the famous banner. The house and adjacent museum are open Mon.-Sat. 10–4, Sun. and holidays 1–4; adm.

Ponselle, Rosa Melba, 1897–1981, Opera Singer

Villa Pace and Rosa Ponselle's Museum, 1526 Greenspring Valley Road

Rosa Melba Ponselle's first Metropolitan Opera role was that of Leonora in Verdi's *La Forza del Destino*, sung on November 15, 1918. She was only twenty-one and had had very little formal voice training. It is said that Enrico Caruso, who sang with her in that performance, had encouraged the Met to offer her the role. She did so well in this demanding part that she remained with the opera company for nineteen seasons. Her voice has been described as a "big, pure, colorful" soprano. Her beauty and ability to infuse the roles with emotion made her long the reigning star of the Met.

She left the opera in 1937, following a marriage to Carle A. Jackson of Baltimore. She moved here and in 1950 became the artistic director of the Baltimore Opera. Villa Pace, a mansion designed to resemble a villa in Tuscany and named after an aria she had sung in the Verdi opera, was built in the 1940s. Although severely damaged by fire in 1979, it has been restored and opened as a museum with funds left by Ponselle. It is open for guided tours Wed., Sat., and Sun. 1–4; adm.[4]

Reese, Lizette Woodworth, 1856–1935, Poet; NAW

Monument, Western Senior High School, 4600 Falls Road.
Shrine, Eastern High School, 33rd Street at Loch Raven Road

Lizette Woodworth Reese's seventy-fifth birthday was the occasion of a large gathering in the poet's honor, presided over by H. L. Mencken, who considered her one of the greatest poets of her time. She wrote several books of poetry and prose works while teaching in the Baltimore schools for forty-eight years. The memorial at Western High is a bronze tablet on which one of her poems, ''Tears,'' is inscribed. It was dedicated in 1923, while Reese was still living. The shrine at Eastern, near her home, is a pink marble monument sculptured by her friend Grace Turnbull, set in a grove of trees. It was erected in 1939 by the city of Baltimore and the Women's Literary Club of Baltimore, to which Reese had long belonged. In 1963 the Maryland Poetry Society dedicated six white pines to her memory, planted at her graveside. Still another tribute to her is a bas-relief made by Beatrice Fenton, erected in 1943 on the second floor of the Enoch Pratt Free Library.[5]

Grace Turnbull (1880–1976) was not only an artist but also a student of religion and philosophy. She exhibited her works of art often, won prizes, and sold to leading galleries. In addition to the Reese monument, she was the sculptor of the Naiad Fountain at Mt. Vernon Place, East Square.[6]

Richmond, Sarah E., 1843–1921, and Lida Lee Tall, 1873–1942, Educators

Memorials, Towson State University

Richmond Hall memorializes Sarah E. Richmond, a woman who attended Towson State University when it opened in the Old Red Man's Hall on Paca Street as the Maryland State Normal School. She graduated in 1866, after six months of training. She remained as a teacher, rose to principal, and then to dean of women. She inspired students with a genuine interest in teaching, and she persuaded legislators to supply more and better facilities. The college grew from a small teacher-training institute to an accredited teachers' college, with several changes in name; in 1976 it became Towson State University.[7]

The Lida Lee Tall Learning Resources Center is named for Lida Lee Tall, who succeeded as principal of the school in 1920. She was a graduate of Columbia University's Teachers College and had been working as teacher, school administrator, and educational editor for sixteen years before her appointment by the State Board of Education. During her administration the school changed from a two-year normal school to a four-year college and her title changed to president. She did not confine her talents and interests to Towson alone but spread her influence in ever-widening circles through the city, state, and nation. During the Herbert Hoover administration she was on the National Education Commission.[8]

Rogers, Julia Rebecca, 1854–1944, Feminist

Julia R. Rogers Library, Goucher College

In the late 1870s and early 1880s five close friends and early feminists often met at Julia Rebecca Rogers' house to talk over their aspirations, read books, and support each other. M. Carey Thomas, future president of Bryn Mawr College; Mary Garrett, (1854–1915, NAW), wealthy activist; Mamie Gwinn, later a teacher at Bryn Mawr; and Elizabeth King, founder of the Arundell Good Government Club were the other four. Rogers was the quietest and most genuinely intellectual. Together they founded the Bryn Mawr School for Girls, opened in 1885, to give girls an education equal to that of their brothers. Garrett contributed a building and was president of the board of trustees. The group was also behind the organization of the College Club, welcoming young women coming to Baltimore as teachers. It became a branch of the National Association of University Women, now the American Association of University Women.

Rogers and Garrett offered to raise funds for the Johns Hopkins Medical School, on condition that the school admit women on the same terms as men. The trustees accepted their conditions, Garrett provided most of the $500,000 needed, and the school opened its doors to women in 1893. They also tried to force the university to admit women to its graduate school. When it refused, Rogers wrote that she had intended to leave money to the school but had decided against it. At her death it was revealed that Goucher College was the recipient of her estate—$900,000. She bequeathed her house on Charles Street to the College Club.[9]

Seton, Saint Elizabeth Ann, 1774–1821, Religious Founder; NAW

Seton House, 600 N. Paca Street; NHL

Elizabeth Ann Seton, widowed mother of five children, came to Baltimore from New York City in 1808 to start a school for Catholic girls. A convert to the Roman Catholic church, Seton soon took vows as a religious. The following year she accepted an offer of land at Emmitsburg, Maryland, q.v., where she was to realize her deepest wish, to found a religious order. She and her three daughters and a small band of sisters arrived at their new home on June 24, 1809, and there founded the first American sisterhood, the Sisters of Charity of St. Joseph. Mother Seton was beatified in 1963 and canonized in 1975, the first American-born saint of the Roman Catholic church. The Seton House is open by appointment. Seton is in the National Women's Hall of Fame. See New York City and Yonkers, NY.

Szold, Henrietta, 1860–1945, Zionist Leader; NAW

Plaque at Playground, Baltimore and Aisquith Streets

Henrietta Szold was told that a visit to Palestine would disenchant her with the idea of founding a Jewish state. When she first went there in 1909 the country was under corrupt Turkish rule; a few struggling Jewish colonies had been established on land bought from Arab farmers; they were miserably poor. But she fell in love with the country and felt an overpowering need to help the people, particularly the children. She returned to her Baltimore home a dedicated Zionist and threw herself into raising funds to send to Palestine. On February 24, 1912, a new women's organization, Hadassah, was organized "to promote Jewish institutions and enterprises in Palestine, and to foster Zionist ideals in America." Szold was its founding president. World War I prevented her immediate return to Palestine, which was made a British mandate, but in 1920 she reached the country where she was to spend much of her life and on which she would have an unforgettable impact.

She believed that a Jewish state would restore the ideals of Judaism. She believed, too, that the Jews could not find spiritual homes in Palestine unless they could work and live in peace with their Arab neighbors. She hoped for a binational state and an agreement between the two peoples which would reconcile their national aspirations and ensure the free development of both. Unhappily, the politicians—British, Arab, and Jewish—did not see it that way. Israel became a state three years after her death. She was buried on the Mount of Olives, but it is now in Jordan territory and it is said that her grave can no longer be located.

The plaque here marks the site of the first night school started by Szold for European Jews fleeing pogroms. Many of them came to Baltimore, where her father was a rabbi. In addition to memorials to her in Jerusalem, there are monuments in New York City and Pittsburgh, PA.[10]

Tall, Lida. See Richmond, Sarah

Truth, Sojourner, c. 1797–1883, Reformer; NAW

Sojourner-Douglass College, 500 N. Caroline Street

In 1980 Antioch University's Homestead-Montebello Center in Baltimore became an independent institution and adopted the name Sojourner-Douglass to honor significant historical contributions of two black Americans: Sojourner

Truth (see Washington, D.C., and New Paltz, NY) and Frederick Douglass. It is now an accredited adult evening college, providing opportunities for education linking the world of work with the academic community. Students are admitted without regard to race, sex, religion, nationality, or handicap. Had Sojourner, the freed slave and fighter for civil rights, dreamed of such an institution, she would have given it her full blessing.[11]

Tubman, Harriet, 1820?–1913, Civil Rights Leader; NAW

Harriet Tubman Hall, Morgan State University, Hillen Road and Cold Spring Lane

Harriet Tubman, famed as the Moses of her people, was born in Bucktown, on Maryland's Eastern Shore, to a slave family whose parents on both sides had come from Africa in chains. She married John Tubman, a free black, but did not thereby gain her own freedom. In 1849, fearing to be sold again, she escaped to Philadelphia, Pennsylvania. In the following years she returned South many times, leading others to freedom. Rewards offered for her capture reached forty thousand dollars. She became well known and respected among blacks and whites alike, went about speaking on abolition, and during the Civil War worked as a Union spy. Despite her work for the army, the government never paid for her services. When she was in her eighties Congress took account of public opinion and granted her a small pension, but it was given her as the widow of Nelson Davis, a man she married after John's death. She settled in Auburn, New York, q.v. In 1978 her story was brought to the television screen in "A Woman Called Moses," with Cicely Tyson playing Tubman. See Wilmington, DE.[12]

Turnbull, Grace. See Reese, Lizette

CHESTERTOWN

Kerr, Sophie (Underwood), 1880–1965, Author

Sophie Kerr Rare Book Room, Library, Washington College, State 213

Sophie Kerr was born in Denton, on the Eastern Shore of Maryland. She early made up her mind to be a writer and began with short stories, accepted and published in popular magazines. Eventually she went to work on the *Woman's Home Companion*, where she rose to managing editor. After her move to New York she wrote novels, stories, articles, plays, even cookbooks (for she loved cooking). "I write only to entertain," she said, "I certainly have no message for the world. It is just light fiction." Of her twenty-two published novels, no single title stands out as memorable. Her stories dealt with the emotional lives of women, but in the slick, happy-ending manner of the women's magazines for which she wrote them. In some she used the setting of the Eastern Shore, which she always loved. "If you were not born there," she wrote, "you will not truly know the people." Her legacy to Washington College—which had given her an honorary D.Litt.—amounted to $573,000. The income from half of this is used for the Sophie Kerr Prize, awarded annually to a graduating senior who shows promise as a writer. Fourteen times the value, in dollars, of the Pulitzer Prize, it is a much sought-after award.[13]

CLINTON

Surratt, Mary Jenkins, 1820?–1865, Convicted Conspirator; NAW

Surratt House, 9110 Brandywine Road; NHL

Clinton was once called Surrattsville and the chief structure in it was the Surratt House, tavern, store, polling place, post office, and home of a respectable family, that of John Surratt and Mary Jenkins Surratt. They owned a twelve-hundred-acre farm. The Civil War ruined the family. One son went to fight with the Confederates. The slaves who worked the land ran away. Union troops pillaged the farm. In 1862 John died, and Mary moved to Washington, D.C., to run a boarding house.

It was there that John Wilkes Booth plotted the assassination of President Abraham Lincoln. One of his associates turned state's evidence and implicated Mary in the conspiracy. A wave of terror, fear, and confusion had followed the assassination, and the military court that tried the conspirators accepted the testimony. Mary was convicted and hanged.

The town of Surrattsville believed she was innocent, as do most historians. They continued to give the schools the Surratt name. In 1965 the owner of the Surratt house gave it to the Maryland–National Capital Park and Planning Commission. It was restored and ten years later formally dedicated as a historical monument. At the ceremony, the chairman of the Restoration Committee explained that they were present "to remove this blot, this blemish, this cloud from the name of one of our local residents." The house is open Mar. 1–Dec. 15, Thurs.-Fri. 11–3, Sat.-Sun. 12–4; adm.[14]

COLLEGE PARK

Porter, Katherine Anne, 1890–1980, Writer

Katherine Anne Porter Room, McKeldin Library, University of Maryland

A collection of short stories, *Flowering Judas*, published in 1930, established Katherine Anne Porter as one of the leading American short-story writers. Although critics lauded her works as they appeared over the years, none were bestsellers until her first novel, *The Ship of Fools*, appeared in 1962. She had been working on the novel for many years while she subsisted on hack work, taught, lectured, lived on a Guggenheim Fellowship, and wrote scripts in Hollywood. "I could not make a living writing," she said, "because I would not write the kind of books editors wanted me to write." When the long-expected novel was published, it was a major publishing event. It was a Book of the Month Club selection. In 1965 it was made into a major motion picture. Her *Collected Short Stories* won a National Book Award and a Pulitzer Prize.

The room at the library, a replica of her own library, with her papers and memorabilia, may be visited by appointment (301–454–2853).[15]

EMMITSBURG

Seton, Saint Elizabeth Ann, 1774–1821, Religious Founder; NAW

The Shrines of Elizabeth Ann Seton; NR

Elizabeth Ann Seton established here the first American sisterhood, the Sisters of Charity of St. Joseph (see Baltimore, MD). The order spread to Philadelphia, Pennsylvania, and New York and is still active in schools, orphanages, and hospitals. Mother Seton was regarded as saintly in her lifetime, and in 1907 the first steps were taken leading to her beatification and finally her canonization in 1975. The shrines are open for visits daily but these are not permitted without a guide. Tours must be arranged well in advance by calling the Pilgrimage Office (301–447–2321). See New York City and Yonkers, NY.

FREDERICK

Fritchie, Barbara, 1766–1862, Legendary Heroine; NAW

Barbara Fritchie House, 156 W. Patrick Street

John Greenleaf Whittier's poem immortalized Barbara Fritchie as a heroine of the Civil War. Whether or not the legend is based on fact, it is one beloved by Americans. According to the story, Confederate troops passed the house of the ninety-six-year-old woman. In patriotic defiance she had hung the Union flag from an upper window. General Thomas (Stonewall) Jackson ordered his men to fire on the flag, which they did, breaking the flagstaff. Fritchie caught the flag.

> "Shoot, if you must, this old gray head,
> But spare your country's flag," she said.

Jackson gallantly stopped the firing.

"Who touches a hair of yon gray head
Dies like a dog! March on!" he said.

Whittier's poem, published in the *Atlantic Monthly* in October 1863, stirred immediate controversy. Did it really happen? Fritchie was dead, so she could not tell. The dispute seemed settled in her favor by 1913, when her grave was moved to Mount Olivet Cemetery and marked by a memorial on which the poem is inscribed. Her house, which had been demolished in 1869, was rebuilt in replica in 1926 and has become almost a national shrine. Winston Churchill, visiting the United States in 1942, came by the house with President Franklin D. Roosevelt. The president had only a vague idea of Fritchie's role in history, but Winston endeared himself to the bystanders by reciting the whole poem by heart. The museum is open Mon. and Wed.-Sat. 9–5, Sun. 1–5; adm.

FROSTBURG

Simpson, I. Jewell, 1882–1969, Educator

Simpson Hall, Frostburg State College

I. Jewell Simpson grew up on the campus of Western Maryland College in Westminster, where her father was a science instructor. She chose the field of education for her own career. In 1920 she began work at the State Department of Education and five years later became assistant state superintendent of schools, the first woman to rise this high in Maryland's educational system. She conducted teachers' workshops and prepared study guides and courses of study for the schools. She was well liked and effective throughout her career. After retirement in 1942, she fulfilled her own dream by traveling all over the world, to South America, Europe, the Middle East, Africa, and the Far East.

Frostburg State College, which opened in 1902 as a normal school, is now a four-year college. A dormitory was named for Simpson in recognition of her work in teacher training.[16]

GEORGETOWN

Knight, Kitty, 1775–1855, Legendary Heroine

Kitty Knight House, State 213

The British Navy, in the War of 1812, was trying to subdue the former colonies by burning small settlements along the coast. They landed at Georgetown and set most of the houses afire, but two brick houses were left, one of them occupied by an old lady, sick and almost destitute. Kitty Knight, a spinster of thirty-eight, caught the soldiers just as they set fire to the house and warned them that they were about to burn a human being. She persuaded Admiral Sir George Cockburn, not noted for his manners or humanity, to put out the fire and leave town.

The story has been romanticized over the years and some make out Knight to be a young and beautiful woman whose appeal touched the hearts of the British and saved the town from total destruction. The old lady's house did become Knight's after the war, when she bought it. It has been restored and is now an inn. A tablet by the door adds to the legend: "In honor of Mistress Kitty Knight, Revolutionary Belle and Beauty, a friend of General George Washington. When the British burned Georgetown in 1813 her heroic efforts saved this house which later became her home." Knight's grave in St. Francis Xavier's, the old Bohemia churchyard, is also handsomely marked. The inn is open daily 5–9; Fri. and Sat. until 10:30 P.M.; Sun. 1–9.[17]

GLEN ECHO

Barton, Clara, 1821–1912, Red Cross Founder; NAW

Clara Barton National Historic Site, 5801 Oxford Road

Clara Barton, the Angel of the Civil War Battlefield, founder of the American Red Cross, and savior of victims of disaster, built this house when she was in her late seventies and still as active as ever. The house was built partially from lumber salvaged after the Johnstown, Pennsylvania, flood of 1889. Barton had rushed there, as she did to each new scene of disaster where the Red Cross might be of help. Temporary buildings were erected to shelter the homeless, and afterward Barton proposed to sell the lumber. When local dealers protested, she thriftily shipped it to Maryland. This house was the headquarters of the Red Cross until 1904 and her home until she died. It is furnished with her personal belongings and period furniture and is open daily 10–5. See Antietam, MD, Bordentown, NJ, and Dansville and New York City, NY (Hall of Fame).[18]

KINGSTON

Carroll, Anna, 1815–1893, Military Strategist; NAW

Kingston Hall, West Side of State 667 (Private); HABS, NR

Anna Carroll has been called the Great Lady of the Civil War, an unrecognized military genius, and President Abraham Lincoln's secret weapon. Feminists like to claim that she was responsible for planning the strategy that resulted in a victory for the Union by having troops move up the Tennessee River rather than up the Mississippi. She herself made this claim, but not until some years after the war ended. She presented a petition to Congress for payment for her wartime services and continued to submit it over the next fourteen years. Her cause was taken up by leading suffragists, and by the time she died she and others were convinced that she had been a major factor in winning the Civil War and unjustly deprived of the credit and compensation due her. Historians, on the whole, doubt her claims. It must be said that she was no crank. She was an intelligent, verbal, and powerful woman, involved in the Know Nothing movement, approving of

William Walker's filibustering expeditions in Central America, and, while pro-Union, opposed to the abolitionists in Congress.

Kingston Hall, her birthplace, was built by her father, Thomas King Carroll, who was in 1830–31 governor of Maryland. Anna is buried in the Trinity church graveyard in Cambridge, Maryland, her marble monument inscribed, "Maryland's most distinguished lady. A great humanitarian and a close friend of Abraham Lincoln." The old Grand Army of the Republic soldiers kept a flag flying over her grave as long as any of them lived. The flag is still placed there by veterans in the American Legion.[19]

LILYPONS

Pons, Lily, 1904–1976, Singer

Lilypons Water Gardens, 21717 Lilypons Road

The town of Lilypons was named in 1932 for the opera singer Lily Pons, a friend of G. L. Thomas, who developed here a three-hundred-acre tract of water lilies and other aquatic plants—and who must have enjoyed the play on words. The ponds are the country's largest breeding center for ornamental fish.

Pons, a French-born singer, was the leading coloratura soprano at the Metropolitan Opera for twenty-five years. In addition to an exquisite voice, she possessed a charming personality and a high degree of showmanship. She traveled in the lavish tradition of movie and opera stars on concert tours with André Kostelanetz, to whom she was married from 1938 to 1958. In 1940, on becoming an American citizen, she said, "I owe everything to this country." One of her most moving performances, however, took place in liberated Paris, France, in 1944 when she sang "La Marseillaise" to a crowd of 250,000 in the Place de l'Opéra.

The gardens at Lilypons are open daily 9–3, Sun. 1–3.[20]

SAINT MARY'S CITY

Brent, Margaret, c. 1601–1671, Businesswoman; NAW

Painting, Old State House, Saint Mary's City Historic District

Margaret Brent is credited with being the first woman in America to demand the vote. A Catholic spinster, she left England for Maryland in 1638 with a sister and two brothers, bringing in servants and establishing plantations. As manager for herself and others she acquired a reputation as a clever businesswoman. She so impressed Governor Leonard Calvert that he made her his executrix. His death in 1647 occurred at a critical time for the colony. He had imported soldiers from Virginia to quell a rebellion, but due to a severe corn shortage and lack of money in the estate fund to pay the men, mutiny and civil disaster threatened. He had pledged his fortune and that of his brother, Lord

Baltimore, the colony's proprietor in England, to pay the soldiers. Brent had herself declared attorney for Lord Baltimore, then sold some of his cattle and paid the men.

On January 21, 1648, she appeared before the Maryland Assembly requesting to be allowed two votes, one for herself as a freeholder and one as a representative of the Calvert interests. Meanwhile, Lord Baltimore, unaware that she had saved the colony from an embarrassing if not dangerous position, angrily denounced her for meddling in his affairs. The assembly set him straight. Brent, they wrote, "deserved favour and thanks . . . for her so much concurring to the public safety." But they refused to give her even one vote. The painting in the State House shows her appealing for suffrage. The building, a replica of the original one, is open May-Oct., daily 10–5; Nov.-Apr., Tues.-Sun. 10–4.[21]

SALISBURY

Parkhurst, Marion Veasey, 1879–1958, Civic Leader

Memorial Tree, City Park

When Marion Veasey Parkhurst began to introduce the Congress of Mothers into the Baltimore, Maryland, schools, the school board resisted the whole idea of meddling mothers. The goals of the women were simply to open communication between parents and teachers and thus support the public school system, an extension of the parents' concern for their own families. They persisted and were finally successful in overcoming the school administrators' distrust. The Congress perceived needs the school boards had never considered: hot lunches, clothes closets, housing for single teachers, student aid, dental clinics, and immunizations. When necessary, members invaded the legislative halls to lobby for such measures as mothers' pensions and equalization of school support from state funds.

Parkhurst, state president of the Congress of Parents and Teachers from 1917 to 1929, was honored in 1965 at the Golden Anniversary Convention of the Maryland Congress by the establishment of a "Mrs. Harry Elkins Parkhurst Scholarship." The oak tree was planted in her memory by the Wicomico Council of Parents and Teachers.[22]

NOTES

In addition to the correspondents mentioned below, I have had assistance from the Maryland Historical Society, the Maryland Bicentennial Commission, and the Enoch Pratt Free Library.

1. Correspondence, Maryland Historical Trust.

2. Langston Hughes, *Fight for Freedom* (New York: Norton, 1962), pp. 176–79; *Notable Maryland Women*, ed. Winifred G. Holmes (Cambridge, Md.: Tidewater Publishers, 1977); brochure, Jackson Museum.

3. Elaine G. Breslau, in *Notable Maryland Women*.

4. *New York Times*, May 26, 1981; *Liberty's Women*, ed. Robert McHenry (Springfield, Mass.: G. & C. Merriam Co., 1980).

5. Frances Fleming, in *Notable Maryland Women.*

6. Beverly Berghaus Chico, in *Notable Maryland Women.*

7. Jean R. Moser, in *Notable Maryland Women.*

8. Ibid.

9. Kathryn Allamong Jacob, in *Notable Maryland Women*; *The Making of a Feminist: Early Journals and Letters of M. Carey Thomas*, ed. Marjorie Housepian Dobkin (Kent, Ohio: Kent State University Press, 1979).

10. Irving Fineman, *Woman of Valor* (New York: Simon & Schuster, 1961); correspondence, Maryland Historical Trust.

11. Brochure, Sojourner-Douglass College.

12. Phyllis Hathaway, in *Notable Maryland Women; Newsweek*, Dec. 11, 1978.

13. Mary Gay Calcott, in *Notable Maryland Women*; James Lardner, ''Sophie Kerr's Choice Prize,'' *Washington Post*, May 16, 1983; correspondence, Maryland Historical Trust.

14. ''The Case for Mary Surratt,'' *Southern Living* 14 (May 1979); *Time* 106 (Oct. 13, 1975); brochure, Surratt House.

15. *Current Biography*, 1963; *Liberty's Women.*

16. Jean R. Moser, in *Notable Maryland Women.*

17. Mary-Carter Roberts, ''Kitty Knight,'' mimeographed, Tourist Division, Maryland Department of Economic Development.

18. Foster Rhea Dulles, *The American Red Cross* (New York: Harper & Bros., 1950).

19. Mary-Carter Roberts, ''Anna Ella Carroll,'' mimeographed, Tourist Division, Maryland Department of Economic Development.

20. *Newsweek*, Feb. 23, 1976.

21. Julia C. Spruill, *Women's Life and Work in the Southern Colonies* (New York: Norton, 1972).

22. Nancy Revelle Johnson, in *Notable Maryland Women.*

NEW JERSEY

BELLEVILLE

Maass, Clara Louise, 1876–1901, Nurse

Clara Maass Memorial Hospital, 1A Franklin Avenue

Early in the twentieth century American doctors in Cuba were working on the theory that yellow fever, a serious and often fatal disease, was transmitted by the mosquito. To find out, they had to allow humans to be bitten by mosquitoes that had fed on a patient. Among those who offered to participate in the experiment was a young nurse, Clara Louise Maass, who had nursed victims of the disease in Cuba and the Philippines. She and two others in the experiment died; she was the only American, and the only woman, to be sacrificed. With the knowledge gained from this fatal experiment, Major William Gorgas, who was in charge of the research, wrote that "large sums of money and many lives have been saved, and will yearly be saved, by this discovery of the manner of propagation of yellow fever."

In 1952 the Newark German Hospital, in which Maass had received her nursing training, changed its name to honor her memory. See East Orange, Newark, and Wayne, NJ.[1]

BORDENTOWN

Barton, Clara, 1821–1912, Red Cross Founder; NAW

Clara Barton School, Crosswicks and Burlington Streets

A tablet at the entrance to the little brick schoolhouse bears the following inscription: "In this building, from 1852 until 1854, Clara Barton, the founder of the American Red Cross, taught school. Here she established one of the first free public schools of New Jersey in 1853. The building was restored by the school children of the state and dedicated on June 11, 1921.'' Barton was in her early thirties when she came here from her Massachusetts home to teach. She persuaded the school board to make the school free. Up to this time parents had had to pay to send their children to school, and of course poor children were rarely sent. After the fees were dropped, enrollment increased so rapidly that a new school had to be built, and when it was opened a man was appointed to oversee its operation.

Barton resigned, and perhaps it was fortunate that her teaching career soon came to an end. When the Civil War broke out she turned her attention to the plight of sick, wounded, and hungry soldiers. After the war she went to Europe, learned about the International Committee of the Red Cross, and came home to organize an American branch. The rest of her life was spent in work with the Red Cross.

The little schoolhouse had been used as a school for many years, possibly before the Revolution, and was in shabby condition when Barton came here to teach. It is open by appointment. See Antietam and Glen Echo, MD, and Dansville and New York City, NY (Hall of Fame).

Wright, Patience Lovell, 1725–1786, Artist; NAW

Plaque on House, 100 Farnsworth Avenue (Private)

Patience Lovell Wright modeled figures as a hobby when her children were young, and, after her husband died, she began to make wax sculptures as a means of income to support herself and three children. Choosing well-known living figures, she made a traveling exhibition of waxworks that excited much interest, as it was the first of its kind. In 1772 she went to England, where she modeled many important persons, including the king and queen, whom she addressed familiarly as George and Charlotte. Her outgoing personality and skill at making lifelike images made her the rage of London.

She enjoyed intrigue and was in a good position to carry gossip between her English and colonial friends during the Revolution. At any rate, she was supposed to have been a spy for the Americans. It is so charged on the memorial plaque. Although the house here is old enough to have been lived in by Wright, as reputed, there is no sure evidence that it ever was.

EAST ORANGE

Maass, Clara Louise, 1876–1901, Nurse

Memorial Tree, at Corner of North Arlington Avenue and New Street

Clara Louise Maass, the nurse who died during research on yellow fever in Cuba (see Belleville, NJ), was born in East Orange, the eldest of nine children in a poor family. Among memorials to her are a postage stamp issued by Cuba and one issued by the United States. The tree was dedicated on November 23, 1963, during the New Jersey Tercentenary observances. See Newark and Wayne, NJ.

ELIZABETH

Arnett, Hannah White, 1733–1823, Revolutionary War Heroine

Marker, Cemetery of First Presbyterian Church, Near Broad Street

Hannah White Arnett is remembered for speaking her mind in a roomful of men. In 1776 the British offered "protection of life and property" to all colonists proclaiming loyalty to the Crown. Many of the Elizabethtown (now Elizabeth) merchants were inclined to accept the offer, for some had little source of income while the war cut off trade. When Arnett heard a group of them discussing the prospects in her home, she broke into the meeting to declare them traitors and cowards if they deserted the Revolutionary cause. The men capitulated to her zeal and voted to hold out against the British.

In 1909 the Boudinot Chapter of the Daughters of the American Revolution erected this plaque, reading: "Near here rests Hannah White Arnett. . . . Her patriotic words, uttered in the dark days of 1776, summoned discouraged men to keep Elizabethtown loyal to the cause of American independence."[2]

FREEHOLD

Pitcher, Molly (Mary Ludwig Hays McCauley), 1754?–1832, Revolutionary War Heroine; NAW (under McCauley)

Monmouth Battle Monument, Monmouth Battlefield National Historic Landmark, State 522

Mary Ludwig Hays McCauley was the wife of John Hays, a gunner in the Pennsylvania State Regiment, and served with him through his seven years of service in the Revolutionary cause. During the Battle of Monmouth, June 28, 1778, she carried water from a spring to the parched soldiers, who called her Molly Pitcher. The source of the water, near Throckmorton, has recently been marked the Molly Pitcher Spring. When Hays fell at his battery, overcome by heat, his wife stepped into his place and loaded the cannon for the rest of the engagement. A soldier who was at the battle wrote in his journal that as Molly was reaching for a cartridge a cannon shot from the enemy passed close enough to tear her petticoats. She coolly went on loading. After Hays died, Molly married John McCauley. In 1822 Pennsylvania voted her a forty dollar annuity for her services. The battle monument has a bas-relief of Molly. See Carlisle, PA.[3]

HADDONFIELD

Estaugh, Elizabeth Haddon, 1680–1762, Town Founder; NAW

Plaque on a Tree on Hancock Avenue. Tablet, Friends' Burying Ground

Elizabeth Haddon Estaugh founded Haddonfield. In 1701 she was sent from England to manage property her father had bought, intending to emigrate with his family. Only twenty-one, the Quaker woman was an excellent property manager. She has been endeared to generations of readers through the story of her proposal to a Quaker minister: "I have received from the Lord a charge to love thee, John Estaugh." The story was first told by Lydia Maria Child and then by Henry Wadsworth Longfellow in his "Theologian's Tale." Elizabeth and John married in 1702 and founded "New Haddonfield" in 1713. Her father gave the land for the first Friends Meeting House here. After his death Elizabeth and John inherited most of his New Jersey lands.

When the town celebrated its bicentennial in 1913, the tablet was placed near her grave, honoring her as "founder and proprietor." The Hip Roof House, on King's Highway, East, was once her home. Another home, burned down in 1842, has been replaced, but it has in the backyard the original still house she built to brew medicinal whiskey, much appreciated by the Indians. Greenfield Hall, next door to the Hip Roof House, is the headquarters of the Haddonfield Historical Society. It has many Estaugh possessions and is open Tues. and Thurs. 2–4:30, except July, Aug., and holidays.

HANCOCK'S BRIDGE

Hancock, Cornelia, 1840–1927, Civil War Nurse; NAW

Commemorative Flagstone, Alloways Creek Friends' Meeting House

Cornelia Hancock was born at Hancock's Bridge, once the scene of a bloody Revolutionary War battle. In a later day, the Battle of Gettysburg brought the Civil War close to Hancock and she volunteered to serve as a nurse. Dorothea Dix, superintendent of army nurses, would not have her; she was too young and too pretty. Undaunted, Hancock began to work wherever she saw the need and proved so resourceful and competent that she soon had charge of eight tents of amputees. Throughout the war she served in one battlefield after another, supported by the surgeon general, who ordered that she be allowed to work wherever she chose and was needed. When the war was over, she kept on serving her fellow citizens, first in a school for blacks in South Carolina, then in Philadelphia, Pennsylvania, organizing charities, and then at Wrightville, a south Philadelphia settlement which she helped change from a slum to a model neighborhood.

MONTCLAIR

Lang, Florence Osgood Rand, 1861–1943, Artist and Art Patron

Rand Wing, Montclair Art Museum, Bloomfield and S. Mountain Avenues

Florence Osgood Rand Lang was a native of Westfield, Massachusetts, and an early resident of Montclair. Both cities have benefited from her support of the arts, as have Nantucket, Massachusetts, where she spent summers, and Pasadena and Claremont, California, where she was a frequent visitor. Her parents had given Rand Park to Montclair, and most of her benefactions perpetuated the Rand name (rather than that of her husband, Henry Lang). She gave the Montclair Art Museum funds for a new building in 1913–14, an addition in 1924, and an Indian wing in 1929. In 1931 the Rand Wing was completed. Ten years later the Arts Council of New Jersey awarded her its first medal of honor for her many gifts to the museum. Noted for its fine collection of American paintings, many by New Jersey artists, the museum is open year-round except during July and Aug., Tues.-Sat. 10–5, and Sun. 1–5:30.[4]

MORRISTOWN

Eustis, Dorothy Harrison Wood, 1886–1946, Seeing Eye Founder; NAW

The Seeing Eye, Washington Valley Road

The Seeing Eye, which trains dogs to guide blind persons and then trains the owners to become mobile, was developed by Dorothy Harrison Wood Eustis, a native of Philadelphia, Pennsylvania. While living in Vevey, Switzerland, she began breeding dogs, hoping to develop the qualities of intelligence and faithfulness she saw in her own German shepherd. Her first dogs were successfully used for police and army duty in Switzerland. She learned of a school in Potsdam, Germany, that taught dogs to lead blind war veterans and wrote an article about it for the *Saturday Evening Post.* Morris Frank, a young blind man in Nashville, Tennessee, wrote and asked where he might obtain such a dog. Her first guide dog was trained for him.

The public attention given to Frank and his dog brought more requests, and soon afterward Eustis returned to the United States to recruit sponsors for a guide-dog training school. The school was first established in Nashville, then moved to New Jersey. Thousands of dogs, German shepherds and other breeds, have now been trained and placed with owners. Casual visitors are not admitted to the buildings except on special occasions.

NATIONAL PARK

Whitall, Ann Cooper, 1716–1797, Patriot

Whitall House, Red Bank Battlefield, 100 Hessian Avenue; HABS, NR

When British bullets whistled through the upstairs room where Ann Cooper Whitall was spinning, she did what women had been doing right along; she kept the wheels spinning and after the battle nursed the casualties. First she moved herself and the spinning wheel to the basement and finished the day's tasks. Then she bandaged wounds, meanwhile scolding the Hessians for coming to America to fight for the British.

Her stubborn adherence to principle under trying conditions was a trait inherited by her great-great-granddaughter, M. Carey Thomas, who became president of Bryn Mawr College (see Bryn Mawr, PA). The furnishings in this house include Whitall's spinning wheel. National Park is a small community named for the twenty-acre park near Camden, New Jersey, commemorating the Battle of Red Bank, October 22, 1777. The house is maintained by the Daughters of the American Revolution and guided tours are given daily; adm.[5]

NEW BRUNSWICK

Douglass, Mabel Smith, 1877–1933, College Founder; NAW

Douglass College, Rutgers University

Before 1918, New Jersey women in search of a high-quality college education had to leave the state. The State Federation of Women's Clubs sought to change this. It enlisted the talents of Mabel Smith Douglass, then president of the College Women's Club in Jersey City, in an attempt to persuade venerable Rutgers University to accept female students. The university was shy of coeducation but gladly accepted affiliation with a separate women's college. Douglass worked for several years to raise funds and gain support for the New Jersey College for Women, which opened its doors in 1918. Douglass was its first dean, and during her fourteen years there she gave the growing college her own personal stamp. The emphasis was on liberal arts, although vocational courses were also offered. In a speech she gave in 1927 she urged college women to get involved in politics.

A bust of Douglass, executed by Archimedes Giacomantonio, was donated to the college by a friend in 1938, and in 1955 the name of the college was changed to honor her memory. It is now part of Rutgers.[6]

NEWARK

Maass, Clara Louise, 1876–1901, Nurse

Monument, Fairmount Cemetery, Central Avenue and 11th Street

The monument bears a likeness of Clara Louise Maass, the young army nurse who succumbed to yellow fever in Cuba during the investigation of the causes of the disease. It has an inscription describing her career and death. See Belleville, East Orange, and Wayne, NJ.

PRINCETON

Stockton, Annis Boudinot, 1736–1801, Estate Manager and Poet

Morven, 55 Stockton Street; HABS, NHL

Annis Boudinot Stockton was bound to be overlooked by historians. Her father, Elias Boudinot, was president of the Continental Congress; her husband, Richard Stockton, was a signer of the Declaration of Independence; she might be dismissed as merely a daughter and a wife. But Stockton deserves notice. She managed a large household and brought up six children at Morven, a name she gave the home her husband built. She was hostess there to George Washington and other Revolutionary leaders. After her husband's death she managed the estate for years and continued to entertain, especially when the U.S. Congress met at Princeton. Above all, she read widely and wrote elegiac poetry.

Morven remained in the family for many years, then was leased to several governors of New Jersey and at last given to the state to be used as the official mansion of the state's chief executive. It may be visited by appointment.[7]

SHORT HILLS

Terry, Julia Lawrence, 1868?–1947, Philanthropist

New Eyes for the Needy, 549 Millburn Avenue

New Eyes for the Needy exists "to provide new prescription eyeglasses for individuals in the United States to whom no other funds, public or private, are available." Discarded eyeglasses and frames are solicited from all over the country, and are tested, graded, and reusable ones distributed to overseas missions and hospital clinics on request. Julia Lawrence Terry began the project during the Great Depression when she met many unemployed persons at New York City welfare food stations who needed glasses and had no means of obtaining them. Using her own funds, she sent them to the Knapp Memorial Hospital for free eye care and new glasses and then began requesting donations of glasses from the public throughout the world. From her home in Short Hills and later an office on Park Avenue in New York City, she operated the project with "no overhead, no red tape or paid helpers, no committee meetings or organizations." To this day, there is but one paid staff member; all the work is done by volunteers. "Old-age" magnifying glasses were sent to the Frontier Nursing Service in Kentucky. One of Terry's beneficiaries wrote: "I have received something much beyond the good helpful glasses, something like renewed faith in the practical goodness of folks."[8]

TENAFLY

Stanton, Elizabeth Cady, 1815–1902, Woman's Rights Leader; NAW

Grindelwald, 135 Highwood Avenue (Private); NR

Twenty years after Elizabeth Cady Stanton wrote the Declaration of Principles presented at the 1848 woman's rights convention in Seneca Falls, New York, she and her growing family moved from New York City to this house. In those twenty years she had become, with Susan B. Anthony, the recognized leader of the American campaign for woman's rights. She had traveled back and forth across the country speaking for the cause, had written reams of tracts and newspaper articles, had withstood verbal and physical attacks for her liberal views, had managed a household with seven active youngsters, and had survived it all with an unfailing sense of humor and balance.

She lived in Tenafly from 1868 until 1887. In her memoirs, *Eighty Years and More*, she speaks nostalgically of the happy days her family shared with their neighbors under the old oaks and majestic chestnut trees. Her husband, Henry Stanton, and her neighbor, Isaac England, were both connected with "that dignified journal, the New York *Sun*," but were not too dignified to join the frolics on the blue hills of New Jersey. In those years, however, Stanton was one of the busiest women in America. To help pay for the education of her children, she became in 1869 a lecturer for the Lyceum Bureau and for twelve seasons filled speaking engagements under its management. She and Anthony spent many hours writing the first volumes of the *History of Woman Suffrage*. She was president of the National Woman's Suffrage Association.

In her last year in Tenafly, Stanton attempted to vote. She and Anthony went to the polling place, in the same room where Stanton usually went to pay taxes, for she was owner of the house. The inspectors refused to accept her ballot and were treated to a lecture on the rights of taxpaying citizens, whereupon one said, "I know nothing about the Constitutions, State or national. I never read either; but I do know that in New Jersey, women have not voted in my day, and I cannot accept your ballot."

The Victorian house in Tenafly has been much altered in appearance since the Stantons lived there. It is now privately owned and occupied. See Washington, DC (under Adelaide Johnson), and Seneca Falls, NY.[9]

TRENTON

Katzenbach, Marie Hillson, d. 1970, Educator of the Deaf

Marie H. Katzenbach School for the Deaf, Sullivan Way

Marie Hillson Katzenbach was prominent in New Jersey's educational system, serving for forty-three years on the State Board of Education. Her work for the education of deaf children, which brought her international recognition, began with her appointment to the board of the state school for the deaf in 1923. In 1948 she was given an honorary degree by Douglass College (then New Jersey College for Women) for her educational work. The school for the deaf, which was given her name in 1965, is part of the public school system, a day and boarding school for hearing-impaired young people between the ages of four and twenty-one. It offers numerous vocational courses and prepares students for further education at Gallaudet College in Washington, D.C.[10]

UNION

Caldwell, Hannah, d. 1780, Patriot

Tablet, Caldwell Parsonage, 886 Caldwell Avenue

Hannah Caldwell, wife of James Caldwell, Presbyterian minister, was alone here with her children, one an infant, during a Revolutionary battle. A British soldier's bullet tore through the house and killed Hannah. Her body and the children who survived were taken out of the house, which was then set afire. The townspeople were outraged. Her husband, known as ''the fighting parson,'' was himself shot to death by the British a year later. The orphaned children were taken in by Deacon Ephraim Sayre, whose homestead still survives in Madison, New Jersey. The rebuilt parsonage is now occupied by the Union County Historical Society. Its museum is open the 2nd and 4th Sun. of the month, 2–4, or by appointment.[11]

Livingston, Susan, b. 1748, Revolutionary War Heroine

Liberty Hall, Kean College Campus; HABS, NHL

Susan Livingston was the daughter of William Livingston, rebel governor of New Jersey. During the Revolution, he seldom spent the night in their home, Liberty Hall, because the British were eager to catch all leading patriots. One night British officers came to the house intending to arrest him and seize his papers. Susan assumed command and foisted on the officers, with a disarming smile, some old legal papers instead of valuable notes regarding the militia. The house was occupied by descendants of the Livingstons until it was purchased by Newark State College. The college changed its name to that of the Kean family, then owners of the 120-acre historical estate.[12]

WAYNE

Askew, Sarah B., 1877–1942, Library Administrator; NAW

Sarah B. Askew Library, William Paterson College

In 1905 the New Jersey Public Library Commission could count only sixty-six public libraries in the state. They hired a young Pratt Institute graduate, Sarah B. Askew, to expand the system. Accepting the challenge to be "organizer and missionary" for libraries, Askew drove a horse and buggy over sandy roads and down mountain trails visiting small towns that needed information and inspiration to start or enhance local libraries. She worked with the commission for most of her subsequent years, aided by the State Teachers' Association, the Federation of Women's Clubs, and other women's organizations. She established a county library system that was a model for others across the country. She fostered school libraries. She sent book trucks to carry books to communities too poor and isolated to have a library. During World War I she gathered books from all over the state for military camps and troop ships and sent books into military hospitals, and at the beginning of World War II she helped organize the Victory Book Campaign to provide reading matter for soldiers. At the time of her death, New Jersey had 12 county libraries and 316 local libraries. The college named their new library building for her in 1956.

Maass, Clara Louise, 1876–1901, Nurse

Memorial Window, United Methodist Church, 99 Parish Drive

The window was presented to the church by Emma Maass, older sister of Clara Louise Maass, who died in Cuba of yellow fever, a martyr to medical research (see Belleville, NJ). The inscription says she "made the supreme sacrifice for science, that others might live." See East Orange and Newark, NJ.

WEST TRENTON

Dix, Dorothea, 1802–1887, Humanitarian; NAW

Dorothea Dix Memorabilia Room, Trenton Psychiatric Hospital

Dorothea Dix, a slim, dignified Maine spinster, came to New Jersey in 1844 and visited almost every jail and almshouse in the state. She was looking for mentally deranged persons, who were confined in such places because New Jersey had no public asylum for them. The luckier ones had been sent to New

York or Pennsylvania institutions or left to their own resources. Others she found confined to unheated sheds, in dark, unventilated jail cells, some chained, most half starved, none receiving more than minimal care. On January 23, 1845, she presented "A Memorial to the Senate and General Assembly Relative to the Care of Idiots, Epileptics and the Insane Poor of the State." She had made similar surveys and written similar memorials in other states and had moved their legislatures to give hospital care to the mentally ill. She followed up her memorial with meetings with New Jersey legislators, converting those who were opposed to her view. An act to establish a state lunatic asylum was passed unanimously just two months and two days after her memorial was read.

Dix always regarded the Trenton Hospital as her own creation. She chose its location, overlooking the Delaware River, and in her travels she often stopped to visit. When she was almost eighty she became ill while in the neighborhood and a quiet apartment was offered her under the eaves of the classic pediment facing the Delaware. Here she spent the last six years of her life, lovingly cared for by the staff. The apartment was destroyed by fire in 1964, but some of her possessions are in the room maintained in her memory. It is on the fifth floor of the Stratton (Administration) Building.[13]

NOTES

In addition to correspondents mentioned below, I have been helped by the Montclair Public Library's New Jersey Women's Information and Referral Service and Alma White College (now closed) in Zarephath.

1. New Jersey Historical Sites Evaluation, provided by the New Jersey Department of Environmental Protection, Trenton.
2. Summit College Club, American Association of University Women, "Women of New Jersey: 1976 Bicentennial History of Women" and "Eminent Women of New Jersey" (pamphlets, 1976).
3. Elizabeth Evans, *Weathering the Storm: Women of the American Revolution* (New York: Charles Scribner's Sons, 1975).
4. *New York Times*, June 10, 1923.
5. Sibyl Groff, *New Jersey's Historic Houses: A Guide to Homes Open to the Public* (New York: A. S. Barnes, 1971); M. Carey Thomas, *The Making of a Feminist*, ed. Marjorie Housepian Dobkin (Kent, Ohio: Kent State University Press, 1979).
6. *New York Times*, Apr. 24, 1927, June 3, 1938, and Sept. 27, 1963.
7. Alfred Hoyt Bill, *A House Called Morven: Its Role in American History* (Princeton, N.J.: Princeton University Press, 1978; first printed 1954).
8. *New York Times*, June 16, 1934, and Nov. 10, 1947.
9. Elizabeth Cady Stanton, *Eighty Years and More* (New York: Schocken Books, 1971; repr. of 1898 ed.).
10. *New York Times*, Feb. 8, 1965, and Feb. 5, 1970.
11. Summit College Club, op. cit.
12. Summit College Club, op. cit.; Margaret Truman, *Women of Courage* (New York: William Morrow & Co., 1976).
13. Clippings and correspondence, Trenton Psychiatric Hospital.

NEW YORK

ALBANY

Spencer, Elmina R., fl. 1860s, Civil War Nurse

Relief Portrait, Western Staircase, State Capitol

As the "million-dollar" staircase was built in the capitol, it was embellished with portraits, carved in stone, of great men. Late in the operation it was found that among all the greats no females were included. Six women were chosen to represent the sex: Susan B. Anthony, suffrage leader; Clara Barton, founder of the American Red Cross; Captain Molly Pitcher, Revolutionary War heroine; Harriet Beecher Stowe, writer; Frances E. Willard, temperance leader; and Elmina R. Spencer, the least known of all.

Spencer was a teacher in Oswego, New York, as was her husband, R. H. Spencer. At the outbreak of the Civil War, both enlisted. She spent almost three years after Antietam working in army hospitals in Washington, D.C. and other places close to the fighting. She carried with her tea, coffee, beef tea, and other provisions to refresh the wounded men and at times foraged the countryside on horseback for more substantial provisions. It is hard to credit the account that she was once saved from being wounded when a bullet hit the "elastic steel wires of her crinoline."[1]

AUBURN

Tubman, Harriet, 1820?–1913, Civil Rights Leader; NAW

Harriet Tubman Home, 180–182 South Street; NHL. Plaque at County Courthouse, Genesee Street. Monument, Fort Hill Cemetery, Fitch Street off Parker

The cemetery monument is inscribed: "Heroine of the Underground Railroad. Nurse and Scout in Civil War." Harriet Tubman was famous throughout the

Northeast as the fugitive slave who returned again and again to the South, despite a price on her head, to lead her people to freedom (see Wilmington, DE, and Baltimore, MD). A few years before the Civil War she bought a farm in Auburn from her friend William H. Seward. There she took in elderly blacks who had no way to make a living. The Home for Indigent Aged Negroes continued for a few years after her death. Now restored, the building is maintained as a museum by the Auburn A.M.E. Zion Church. It is open occasionally and can be seen by appointment (315–253–2621). The plaque at the courthouse was erected by the people of Auburn. Tubman is in the National Women's Hall of Fame.

AURIESVILLE

Tekakwitha, Kateri, 1656–1680, Mohawk Catholic Heroine; NAW

Statue, Entrance to the Shrine of North American Martyrs, State 5S

In 1980, in an impressive ceremony at Vatican City, Italy, an American Indian maiden whose vow of virginity earned her the name of Lily of the Mohawks was beatified by Pope John Paul II. She thus became the first North American Indian candidate for sainthood. Kateri Tekakwitha, the daughter of an Algonquin mother and a Mohawk chief, was born in what is now Auriesville, the site where the Algonquins tortured and killed several French missionaries. She survived a smallpox epidemic that killed her parents and left her face badly scarred. In 1676, despite objections from others of her tribe, she converted to Catholicism, choosing the name of Kateri, or Catherine. Harassed because of her faith, she fled to Canada to live in a Christian Indian village. There she took a vow of chastity and lived an exemplary life of prayer and labor until she died at the age of twenty-four. According to witnesses, upon her death her pockmarked face was transformed into flawless beauty. The heroic stone statue, by Adrienne Bouvier, was erected in 1923. See Fonda, NY. [2]

AUSTERLITZ

Millay, Edna St. Vincent, 1892–1950, Poet; NAW

Steepletop, East Hill Road (off State 22); NHL. Marker, Taconic State Parkway near Harlemville, Northbound

Edna St. Vincent Millay's lyric poetry had special appeal to the liberated women of the 1920s and 1930s. She lived and worked for some years in Greenwich Village, New York City, in a close group of freedom-loving writers and artists. Her *Ballad of the Harp-Weaver* won a Pulitzer Prize in 1923. Besides being a serious artist, she was caught up in social protest, demonstrating against the execution of Sacco and Vanzetti, crusading for women's rights, and writing a radio play about Lidice, the town deliberately wiped out by the Nazis. Steepletop was the home of Millay and her husband, Eugen Jan Boissevain. It is now the Millay Colony for the Arts, Inc., a place where writers, composers, and visual artists may work undisturbed. It will eventually have a museum of Millay memorabilia.

BEACON

Brett, Cathryna Rombout, d. 1764, Farmer and Miller

Madam Brett Homestead, 50 Van Nydeck Avenue; NR

Cathryna Rombout Brett (Madam Brett) and her husband, Roger Brett, built this homestead in 1709 on land along the Hudson River inherited from her father, a New York City merchant. After Roger died, Madam Brett ran the farm (some eighty-five thousand acres) and built a mill on Fishkill Creek. The gristmill was of such great use to the settlers that it was said ''all roads lead to Madam Brett's mill.'' Seven generations of the same family lived here until it was purchased in 1954 by the Daughters of the American Revolution. The house, with period furnishings and a formal garden, may be visited May 1–Oct. 31, Fri.-Sun. 1–4; adm.[3]

BOLTON LANDING

Sembrich, Marcella (Stengel), 1858–1935, Singer; NAW

Marcella Sembrich Memorial Studio, State 9N, Lake George

The Polish-born singer Marcella Sembrich made an American appearance at the Metropolitan Opera House in 1883, the Met's first season. She was an operatic star in Europe, and she returned there, but from 1897 to 1908 she sang in America, one of the Metropolitan's great attractions. After her retirement from opera, she continued to sing in concerts for another decade. She had a prima donna temperament, enjoyed gowns by Paquin of Paris, France, and had a famous collection of jewels. She kept silence for long periods to protect her voice. She took long walks, watched her diet, and lived a quiet and somewhat lonely life. She never became an American citizen. Her husband, Wilhelm Stengel, had been her piano teacher and became her manager and secretary. Some time after his death she built her summer retreat here on Lake George. It is now a museum displaying mementoes of her career and is open July–early Sept., daily 10–12:30 and 2–5:30.

BUFFALO

Bethune, Louise Blanchard, 1856–1913, Architect; NAW

Lafayette Hotel, 391 Washington Street, Lafayette Square

The Lafayette Hotel, built in 1904, is the chief building and the only surviving public building in the Buffalo area designed by Louise Blanchard Bethune. After serving an apprenticeship in drafting with an architect, Bethune opened her own architectural firm in 1881 and three months later married her partner, Robert Bethune. They designed all manner of buildings, from chapels to banks and schools. When elected to the American Institute of Architects in 1888, Louise was its first woman member, and she did not hesitate to express her feminist point of view on such matters as equal pay and equal recognition for women architects. In a speech given to the Women's Educational and Industrial Union in 1891 she cited instances of a woman architect receiving a tenth of the salary received by a male for the same type of work.

She refused to enter the competition for a design for the Woman's Building at the World's Columbian Exposition of 1893. "The idea of a separate Woman's Board," she wrote, "expresses a sense of inferiority that business women are far from feeling." She did not approve of competitions and thought it unfortunate that the practice should be revived "by women and for women."[4]

Cornell, Katharine (McClintic), 1893–1974, Actress; NAWM

Katharine Cornell Theater, State University of New York at Buffalo

Katharine Cornell decided on a stage career while in her teens when she saw Maude Adams in *Peter Pan*. It was some years, however, before her dream began to take shape. She joined a stock company in 1918 and had the pleasure of returning to Buffalo for a run of several weeks at the Star, a theater owned by her father. In 1921 she married Guthrie McClintic, director of the Garrick Theater in New York City. Through the next three decades she was a reigning actress on the New York stage, starring in such roles as Candida in George Bernard Shaw's play, Elizabeth Barrett Browning in *The Barretts of Wimpole Street*, and Shakespeare's Juliet. Shaw described her as "a gorgeous dark lady from the cradle of the human race," and audiences raved about her statuesque beauty and mellifluous voice.[5]

CARMEL

Ludington, Sibyl, 1761–1839, Patriot

Statue, State 52, at Lake Gleneida. Marker, State 22, North of Pawling

On the night of April 26, 1777, word came to the Ludington house that the British were burning Danbury, Connecticut, just across the state line and twenty-five miles from the hamlet of Fredricksburg, where the Ludingtons lived (now renamed Ludington). Danbury was a supply center and its loss would be a vital blow. The volunteers in Colonel Henry Ludington's militia were urgently needed, but as the messenger was exhausted and could ride no further, sixteen-year-old Sibyl Ludington offered to spread the alarm. Mounting her horse, she galloped through the night, knocking at doors to awaken the men. They reached Ridgefield in time to help drive the British back to their ships in Long Island Sound.

One hundred and fifty years later a chapter of the Daughters of the American Revolution placed markers along Sibyl's route in Putnam County, and in 1961 the statue of the female Paul Revere was erected at Carmel. It was a gift of the sculptor, Anna Hyatt Huntington. A U.S. postage stamp commemorates Sibyl's ride.[6]

CASTILE

Greene, Cordelia Agnes, 1831–1905, Physician

Cordelia A. Greene Library, 11 S. Main Street

While still in her teens Cordelia Agnes Greene was helping her physician father in his Water Cure Sanitarium. Hearing that a woman, Elizabeth Blackwell, had been granted a medical degree, she decided to become a doctor too. In 1855 she received an M.D. from Western Reserve University. She bought the sanitarium after her father's death and operated it for many years as the Castile Sanitarium, treating women patients with medicine, hydrotherapy, Swedish exercise, diet, prayer, and love. She was universally trusted by her patients, who included Frances E. Willard of the Woman's Christian Temperance Union. Suffragists Susan B. Anthony, Anna Howard Shaw, and Mary Livermore were friends. Castile's Political Equality Club was organized at the sanitarium. Greene, as its president, went before the Town Board to tell them that "taxation without representation is tyranny." The public library, for which she gave the grounds and a fund for maintenance, was dedicated in her honor in 1897. The sanitarium building, still standing, serves as housing for the elderly.

Another young woman from Castile, Clara A. Swain (1834–1910), began her study of medicine at Greene's sanitarium. She received her M.D. in 1869 from the Woman's Medical College of Pennsylvania, and a few months later, with another missionary, Isabella Thoburn, sailed for India. She was the first woman physician to go to India. After twenty-seven years of missionary labor, she came home to Castile, where she wrote *A Glimpse of India* (1905). Her last years were spent in the home of Greene's niece and successor at the sanitarium. A Clara Swain Hospital was built at Bareilly, India, and a monument was erected at her grave in Castile Cemetery.[7]

Jemison, Mary, 1743–1833, Indian Captive; NAW

Statue and Log Cabin, South End Letchworth State Park.
Markers on Thruway, Eastbound, at Scottsville Service Area and on State 408 and 63, Near Mt. Morris

Most white women whose captivity by Indians is recorded took the first opportunity to escape, but not Mary Jemison. She was taken from her Pennsylvania home by a raiding band in 1758 when she was fourteen. Her whole family was wiped out. Jemison was adopted by a Seneca family, who took her to the banks of the Ohio River and treated her well. About 1762 she returned to the ancestral home of the Senecas, the Genesee Valley, where she acquired land, ran cattle, grew crops, and lived as the Indians did. She was married twice, to Indian men, and had eight children who, according to Indian custom, took her name. She was known as the White Woman of the Genesee.

Letchworth Park occupies land that once belonged to her and the cabin is one she built with her own hands for a daughter. It has been moved from its original site to the park. The statue, depicting Jemison as she arrived in the Genesee Valley with a child on her back, was erected in 1910. The sculptor was Henry Kirke Brown. The Castile entrance to the park, open all year, is off County Highway 38. See Caledonia and Orrtanna, PA.[8]

CHURCHVILLE

Willard, Frances, 1839–1898, Temperance Leader; NAW

Marker at Site of Birthplace, 24 S. Main Street

A hardware store and apartments occupy the site of Frances Willard's first home. She moved westward with her family when only two years old and after some years on the Wisconsin frontier moved to Evanston, Illinois, which became her permanent home. Her life was devoted, after 1874, to the Woman's Christian Temperance Union. See Washington, DC, and New York City (Hall of Fame).

COLONIE

Lee, Ann, 1736–1784, Religious Founder; NAW

Watervliet Shaker Historic District, Watervliet-Shaker Road; NR.
Marker, Albany Airport

"As Father, God is the infinite Fountain of intelligence, and the Source of all power. . . . But, as Mother, 'God is Love' and tenderness." That was the creed of Mother Ann Lee, who came to America from England in 1774 with eight followers. They bought property at Niskayuna, near Albany, New York, and established the United Society of Believers in Christ's Second Appearing, commonly called the Shakers (see New Lebanon, NY).

Lee came to America after being persecuted in England, but she found no warmer welcome here. When the group settled at Niskayuna in 1776, a writer reported, "We are just informed of a new order of fanatics . . . pretending to be a religious sect . . . a disgrace to both religion and to human nature." The site of Niskayuna is on the Albany-Shaker Road. A rest home named for Lee is on part of the colony's lands. The Shaker Cemetery, near Albany Airport, has graves of early Shakers, including Mother Ann.[9]

COOPERSTOWN

Bassett, Mary Imogene, 1856–1922, Physician

Mary Imogene Bassett Hospital, Atwell Road

The daughter of two physicians, Mary Imogene Bassett was bound to follow the family profession, in spite of prejudice against women doctors. She graduated from the Woman's Medical College in Philadelphia, Pennsylvania, in 1887, joined in her father's rural practice until his death and then carried on the work, devoting almost every hour to her profession, gradually overcoming the prejudice and hostility first experienced. Edward Severin Clark, a patient and admirer, heard her say that she and other practitioners could do better if they had a local laboratory. He built her a hospital. Almost completed in 1918, it was turned over to the army as a convalescent hospital. Early in 1922 it opened to the public as the Mary Imogene Bassett Hospital, with Bassett herself in charge. Less than four months later the town was mourning her sudden death from a stroke.[10]

Cooper, Susan Fenimore, 1813–1894, Writer; NAW

Memorial Window, Christ Church, 69 Fair Street

Susan Fenimore Cooper, eldest child of the novelist James Fenimore Cooper, was herself a writer, a botanist, and a humanitarian who left her mark on Cooperstown. After her father's death in 1851 she prepared introductions to collections of his work and wrote her own memoirs. She was the prime mover in the establishment of Thanksgiving Hospital after the Civil War (now replaced by the Bassett Hospital). In 1870 she established the Orphan House of the Holy Saviour, where unusual opportunities for vocational training were given orphaned boys and girls. The home went under more than one name (including the Susan Fenimore Cooper Foundation) over the years, closing in 1942. A Cooperstown writer described Cooper: "A sweet face framed in dangling curls, a manner somewhat prim, but always gentle and placid, a figure slight and spare, with a bonnet and Paisley shawl that are all but essential to the resemblance."[11]

CORNWALL-ON-HUDSON

Barr, Amelia Huddleston, 1831–1919, Novelist; NAW

Amelia Barr House, Mountain Road (Private); NR

Amelia Huddleston Barr wrote some eighty-one books, most of them painstakingly researched historical novels. In addition, she produced a stream of articles and poems. For almost three decades she was able to earn a good living from her writing. In 1885 she moved from New York City to Cornwall and later bought the cottage she called Cherry Croft. Her autobiography, *All the Days of My Life* (1913), will probably outlive all her other writings.

DANSVILLE

Barton, Clara, 1821–1912, American Red Cross Founder; NAW

Clara Barton Street. Marker, State 15, South of Cohocton

The marker points out that Dansville was a health resort and "in 1881 Clara Barton, a patient at the sanitarium, founded the American Red Cross." Barton went to Dansville in 1873, living first in the water-cure establishment and then in a house of her own (razed in 1960). In 1877 she began the five-year campaign to organize an American Red Cross and win the United States's adherence to the Geneva Treaty. The first local Red Cross chapter met in Dansville. See Antietam and Glen Echo, MD, Bordentown, NJ, and New York City (Hall of Fame).

ELIZABETHTOWN

Boissevain, Inez Milholland, 1886–1916, Suffragist; NAW

Mount Inez, Adirondack Mountains

Inez Milholland Boissevain lived a brief thirty years but she crammed into those years a great deal of enthusiastic work for the causes in which she believed passionately: suffrage, socialism, pacifism, the rights of labor, and human rights. While a student at Vassar College she led her class in a votes-for-women movement. The authorities considered the subject too hot to handle and prohibited all meetings about it, so Boissevain conducted lively rallies in a graveyard just off the campus. She graduated from law school and was then able to give legal counsel to strikers. She lived a bohemian life in Greenwich Village, New York City, among its radicals and artists. Although she espoused a "natural observance of the mating instinct" unfettered by legal ties, she herself married the romantic businessman, Eugen Jan Boissevain. After her death Boissevain married the poet Edna St. Vincent Millay, who had been one of Inez's admirers (see Austerlitz,

NY). Inez's friends gave her a memorial service in Statuary Hall at the National Capitol, and the citizens of Elizabethtown renamed Mt. Discovery for her.

FONDA

Tekakwitha, Kateri, 1656–1680, Mohawk Catholic Heroine; NAW

Tekakwitha Shrine, State 5

The shrine to Kateri Tekakwitha, the first North American Indian to be beatified by the Roman Catholic church, is near the Iroquois village, Caughnawaga, where she lived when she was converted to Catholicism (see Auriesville, NY). She was baptized here on Easter Day, 1676. The village has been excavated and the site of the Indian longhouse marked. A bronze plaque is on a hilltop near the shrine.

GENEVA

Blackwell, Elizabeth, 1821–1910, Physician; NAW

Blackwell Hall, Hobart College

The authorities of Geneva College, predecessor of Hobart College, were astonished to receive in 1847 an application from a woman for admission to the medical school. In modern times no female had taken a medical degree. The administration decided to let the students make the decision, and the students, believing the whole thing a spoof, voted to admit Elizabeth Blackwell. Of course they did not know that she had already read medicine in the libraries of physicians and studied anatomy in a private school, nor that she had been turned down by every medical school in Philadelphia, Pennsylvania, and New York, as well as Harvard University, Yale University, and Bowdoin College. Nor did she know, until later, that the students had only voted for her admission as a joke.

She arrived in November, and although she met with some rudeness from the students and faculty and stares from the townspeople, her poise, intelligence, and dedication to study soon won their respect. She graduated with an M.D. in 1849, thus opening the door for other women to medical training. Today Hobart and William Smith Colleges give an annual Elizabeth Blackwell Award. Blackwell is in the National Women's Hall of Fame. See New York City.

GROSSINGER

Grossinger, Jennie, 1892–1972, Hotel Executive; NAWM

Grossinger's, State 17, Catskill Mountains

At first it had no heat, no electricity, no indoor plumbing, but Jennie Grossinger's mountain boardinghouse was inexpensive and served plentiful kosher meals, so

Germans and Jews from New York City found it a great place for a vacation. Jennie and her husband, Harry Grossinger (she married a cousin with the same last name), assisted her parents in running the modest hostelry. They gradually took it over and expanded it so that by the time Jennie died it had not only the plumbing but all the other amenities of a luxury resort—twelve hundred acres of space, thirty-five buildings, tennis courts, a children's camp, and resident professional entertainers. The ''everything'' in the slogan, ''Grossinger's has everything,'' included Jennie's warm personality and increasingly her fame as an executive and philanthropist. It is now a year-round resort, and it continues to be family-run.

HARRISON

Earhart, Amelia (Putnam), 1897–1937, Aviator; NAW

Monument, Harrison Railroad Station

At an unlikely spot, the railroad station, is a monument to America's favorite female flyer. It consists of a bronze plaque and propeller mounted on a boulder. Amelia Earhart lived at nearby Rye with her husband, publisher George Putnam. She learned to fly in 1921. In 1928 she was the first woman to fly the Atlantic (as a passenger) and in 1932 the first woman to fly it alone. She made the first solo flight from Honolulu to the American mainland and flew nonstop from Mexico City to Newark, New Jersey. In 1937, while attempting an around-the-world flight, she disappeared. She had captured the imagination of the world with her boyish charm and devil-may-care attitude. She was known as Lady Lindy and the First Lady of the Air. In 1963 the United States remembered her by issuing a commemorative airmail stamp. She has been elected to the National Woman's Hall of Fame.

HYDE PARK

Roosevelt, (Anna) Eleanor, 1884–1962, Humanitarian; NAWM

Val-Kill (Eleanor Roosevelt National Historic Site)

Anna Eleanor Roosevelt was much more than the wife of President Franklin D. Roosevelt. Before her marriage she had worked in settlement houses, visited factories and sweatshops, and formed some opinions of her own about American society and its problems. Once married, she was dominated by her mother-in-law, and only as her children began to mature did she feel free to throw herself into the role of political aide to her polio-stricken husband. She joined the League of Women Voters, mobilized Democratic women in New York State, and walked picket lines with the Women's Trade Union League. By the time Franklin became president, Eleanor had formed a network of dynamic women leaders in Washington, D.C., who were working on women's issues. As the president's wife, she toured coal fields, relief projects, and factories, reporting to him and making straightforward suggestions on ways to deal with the problems that beset the depression-torn country. By the time of her death she had become a national heroine and the recognized first lady of the world.

Never very comfortable in the Roosevelt family home at Hyde Park because of the pervading presence of Franklin's mother, Sara Delano Roosevelt, Eleanor had a fieldstone vacation cottage built for her at Val-Kill, a mile and a half to the east. She and two friends, Nancy Cook and Marion Dickerman, built a furniture factory behind the cottage, where they made colonial-style bedsteads and trestle tables. When it went out of business, she remodeled the factory and moved into it. There she spent most of her remaining years, enjoying its peace and informality, entertaining her many friends as well as visiting statesmen. In 1984, on the anniversary of her birth, October 11, Val-Kill was officially opened to the public. Roosevelt is an electee to the National Women's Hall of Fame. See New York City.[12]

IRVINGTON

Walker, Sarah Breedlove, 1867–1919, Cosmetician and Businesswoman; NAW

Villa Lewaro, N. Broadway, US 9; NR

Before black became beautiful and Afros were stylish, Negro women wanted only to straighten their hair. Various methods were devised to accomplish this, and in 1905 Sarah Breedlove Walker concocted a formula which transformed tight curls into shining smoothness. Beginning in St. Louis, Missouri, she moved her growing business to Denver, Colorado, where she married Charles J. Walker. At first she went from door to door selling her product, then gave public demonstrations of the Walker Method. She was so successful that she built a large plant in Indianapolis, Indiana. She eventually employed some three thousand workers. Known as Madame C. J. Walker, she was one of the outstanding black business tycoons in the country.

She built a townhouse in New York City and in 1917 built Villa Lewaro, a mansion designed by a Negro architect. She was to enjoy it for only two years. Her will provided for many bequests to educational and social institutions, but the bulk of her million-dollar estate went to her daughter A'Lelia, who was eventually forced to sell Villa Lewaro and its lavish furnishings. The house was then used as a home for the elderly.

ITHACA

Donlon, Mary Honor, 1894–1977, Politician and Judge

Donlon Hall, Cornell University

When named to the U.S. Customs Court in 1955, Mary Honor Donlon became the first woman from New York to hold a life appointment to a federal bench. A graduate of Cornell University's law school in 1921, Donlon believed that women should involve themselves in politics, which, she held, "is really only the housekeeping processes of government." She ran as a Republican candidate for Congress in 1940. She helped draft the legislation which created New York State's Workmen's Compensation Board and in 1945 was appointed its chair. Several years later she began administering the state's first compulsory nonoccupational disability benefits law, which she had a hand in drafting. A Cornell University trustee for almost three decades, she was honored by the naming of a dormitory for her in 1961. She also established at the university the Mary Donlon Professorship, to be filled by a woman.[13]

Van Rensselaer, Martha, 1864–1932, Home Economist; NAW

Van Rensselaer Hall, Cornell University

First it was called an extension program for farm wives, then homemaking, then home economics, and now it is human ecology. Martha Van Rensselaer's work in the field began in 1900, when at a salary of $350 a year she organized an extension program for Cornell University's College of Agriculture. She issued useful pamphlets, beginning with "Saving Steps," something rural women could appreciate, and following that with advice on sanitation, interior decorating, nutrition, dressmaking, and child care. All were eagerly snapped up by some twenty thousand women and used in local study clubs, not all rural. Soon she was cochair with her close friend Flora Rose of a department of home economics, which, after a series of changes, became the New York State College of Home Economics, coordinate with other colleges at Cornell. Van Rensselaer's contribution, during a time when family patterns were shifting, was to emphasize and retain the social values of the home. A new home economics building, being erected as she died, was named in her honor.[14]

JOHNSTOWN

Knox, Rose Markward, 1857–1950, Businesswoman; NAW

Knox Athletic Field, Between 1st and 4th Avenues and S. Perry and Glebe Streets. Knox Junior High School

When Rose Markward Knox and Charles Knox bought a gelatine business in 1890, they decided it had a much wider potential market than as an invalid food.

Rose experimented with it and published a book of recipes using unflavored gelatine, *Dainty Desserts*. Charles died in 1908 and fifty-one-year-old Rose decided to run the business until her sons were old enough to take it over. She ran it a woman's way, preparing ads directed to women, concocting recipes with eye appeal, writing booklets and a newspaper column on uses for gelatine. She kept the factory sparkling clean and ran it efficiently. She treated her employees well, closing the back door and inviting everyone to enter by the front, like "ladies and gentlemen." Long before most factories cut the work week, her employees worked a five-day week and received vacation and sick leave.

Rose was called the First Lady of Johnstown. She contributed much to the city besides the athletic field. Of the sons who were to run the business, one died early and the other was not allowed to take the presidency from her until she was ninety. The factory in Johnstown closed in 1975.[15]

MALONE

Wilder, Laura Ingalls, 1867–1957, Writer; NAW

Marker, near Wilder Home, Stacy Road (Private)

Laura Ingalls Wilder, who started writing when in her sixties and became phenomenally successful, used every place she had lived as a background for her children's stories. She never lived in Malone; it was the home of her husband's parents. The Ingalls family had moved to Minnesota before Wilder met and married Almanzo Wilder. The Little House stories are so popular and the places she wrote of so real that folks still like to go and look at the home, though it is not open to the public. They visit the Fairground, the Three-Cornered Park, the graves of Almanzo's grandparents, and the site of the Academy, all described in Wilder's *Farmer Boy*. Her stories—pure Americana—have been used in a popular television series. There is a permanent display of Wilder family material in the Franklin County House of History, 51 Milwaukee Street.[16]

NEW LEBANON

Lee, Ann, 1736–1784, Religious Founder; NAW

Mount Lebanon Shaker Community, US 20; HABS, NHL

A private school is now housed in the Shaker community founded by followers of Mother Ann Lee about 1780. A New Light Baptist revival in this area left many of its converts disillusioned, and when they heard of the Shakers who had settled in Niskayuna, near Albany (see Colonie, NY), they went to find out what kind of religion this dynamic woman preached. Essentially, they discovered, it was deeply religious, democratic, advocating equal rights and responsibilities for men and women and celibacy for all. In nearby Old Chatham there is a private Shaker Museum with a fine collection of Shaker handmade objects.[17]

NEW PALTZ

Truth, Sojourner, c. 1797–1883, Reformer; NAW

Sojourner Truth Library, State University of New York, College at New Paltz

"My name is Sojourner Truth. The Lord named me Sojourner because I am to travel up and down the land showing the people their sins and being a sign unto them." From 1810 to 1827 the slave named Isabella lived in New Paltz, where she had at least five children by a fellow slave. Two of her girls were taken from her and sold. In 1827 she fled the household of her owners and was taken in by Isaac and Maria Van Wagener. Shortly afterward New York emancipated its slaves, and Isabella went to New York City, taking the name Van Wagener. About 1843 she heard the voice commanding her to change her name and take up a career of religious lecturing. Leading abolitionists recognized her gifts of eloquence and helped her to find audiences. Her reputation grew until she was one of the best-known antislavery speakers. She also contributed greatly to the cause of women's rights when she appeared at suffrage meetings. She is in the Women's Hall of Fame. See Washington, DC (under Maria Baldwin), and Baltimore, MD.

NEW YORK

Hall of Fame for Great Americans, W. 181st Street and University Avenue

New York University established in 1901 a Hall of Fame to honor leaders of the nation. The hall, designed by Stanford White, has an open-air colonnade displaying bronze busts of the chosen great Americans. When New York University moved from University Heights, the Hall of Fame was left behind at what is now Bronx Community College. Due to lack of funds, nominations have not been made since 1976.

Eleven women have been elected, beginning in 1905 with New England's Mary Lyon, Maria Mitchell, and Emma Willard.

Jane Addams (1860–1935, NAW) established Hull House in Chicago, Illinois, where a generation of social workers developed their skills. They went into other cities to start similar projects. Working through education, health care, and advocacy before legislative bodies, they brought about needed social changes, for the study of conditions led straight to the political, legal, and economic causes of poverty. In 1931 Addams shared the Nobel Peace Prize with Nicholas Murray Butler. She was elected to the Hall of Fame in 1965. She is also in the Women's Hall of Fame in Seneca Falls, New York. See Allentown, PA.

Susan Brownell Anthony (1820–1906, NAW) was elected in 1950, and the bust was unveiled in 1952 as a gift of the National Federation of Business and

Professional Women's Clubs. It is the work of sculptor Brenda Putnam, who also executed the bust of Harriet Beecher Stowe. Anthony was, of course, one of the chief advocates of equality for women, particularly of their right to vote. She is in the Women's Hall of Fame in Seneca Falls. See Rochester, NY, and Washington, DC (under Adelaide Johnson).

Clara Barton (1821–1912, NAW) has about as many memorials as any other American woman, and her election to the Hall of Fame in 1976 was a crowning honor. She is remembered for her work in founding free public schools in New Jersey, for her Civil War role as a nursing administrator, and for her founding of the American Red Cross. She is in the Women's Hall of Fame. See Antietam and Glen Echo, MD, Bordentown, NJ, and Dansville, NY.

Charlotte Saunders Cushman (1816–1876, NAW) was America's leading actress in the mid-nineteenth century. She was elected in 1915, and ten years later the bust was unveiled, with a dedicatory address by Otis Skinner. It was a gift of the men and women of the stage and admirers and relatives of the actress. The sculptor was Frances Grimes (1869–1963), who had been an assistant to Augustus St. Gaudens. She was the sculptor also of the bust of Emma Willard.

Mary Lyon (1797–1849, NAW) started Mount Holyoke Female Seminary in Massachusetts in 1837. In 1893 the school became Mount Holyoke College. Her bust was unveiled in 1927, a gift of the college's alumnae. The sculptor was Laura Gardin Fraser (1889–1966), an artist whose public sculptures can be seen in many American cities.

Maria Mitchell (1818–1889, NAW), of Nantucket, Massachusetts, was America's first great woman astronomer. She was appointed to the faculty of Vassar College when it first opened its doors in 1865. The bust, by Emma F. Brigham, was a gift of William Mitchell Kendall. It was unveiled in 1922.

Alice Freeman Palmer (1855–1902, NAW) was a great educator. She served Wellesley College as teacher, vice president, acting president, and president between 1879 and 1888. She also spent some time as dean of women at the University of Chicago. The Hall of Fame bust, the gift of Wellesley College, was unveiled in 1924 by her former husband, George Herbert Palmer. It was the work of sculptor Evelyn Beatrice Longman.

Harriet Beecher Stowe (1811–1896, NAW) wrote *Uncle Tom's Cabin*, which touched the hearts and minds of Americans and made them feel "what a cursed thing slavery is." She was elected to the Hall of Fame in 1910. The bust, by Brenda Putnam, was the gift of the New York City Colony of the National Society of New England Women. It was unveiled in 1925.

Lillian Wald (1867–1940, NAW), founder of the Henry Street Settlement, was nominated in 1970. When the campaign for her election was begun, Commissioner Robert Moses said: "She bridged the gap between the haves and have nots. She fired the young with ambition and patriotism. She lived with the other half, shared their lot and improved it. She helped to get women to vote."

The name of Emma Hart Willard (1787–1870, NAW) ranks high in the history of women's education. Her Troy Female Seminary, now the Emma Willard

School (see Troy, NY), was established in 1821. Willard was elected in 1905 and the bust, unveiled in 1929, was a gift of the Emma Willard School alumnae. The sculptor was Frances Grimes.

Frances Willard (1839–1898, NAW) was elected in 1910. The National Woman's Christian Temperance Union (WCTU), which Willard had led through its founding years and for the rest of her life, donated the bust. It is the work of Lorado Taft. It was unveiled in 1923, with an address by Anna A. Gordon, then president of the WCTU and the longtime friend and idolizing biographer of Willard. See Churchville, NY, and Washington, DC.[18]

Addams, Jane. See Hall of Fame

Anthony, Susan Brownell. See Hall of Fame

Austen, Elizabeth Alice, 1866–1952, Photographer

Elizabeth Alice Austen House, 2 Hylan Boulevard, Rosebank, Staten Island; Landmark of New York, HABS, NHL

Elizabeth Alice Austen was a skilled photographer. Working with heavy equipment and doing all her own developing, she made some seven thousand glass slides showing her world between 1880 and 1930. She photographed immigrants at Ellis Island, crowds in New York's East Side, and picnics on Staten Island. She made no money from her photography, and after the deaths of her grandfather and mother she had no means of support. She was rescued from the City Farm Colony by friends who belatedly realized her situation and the value of her work. An illustrated story of her career appeared in *Life Magazine* in September 1951, and the proceeds enabled her to spend her last few months in a private nursing home. Her slides went to the Staten Island Historical Society. The city acquired the house, made a park around it, and is making efforts to establish in it a photographic museum as a memorial to Austen.[19]

Barton, Clara. See Hall of Fame

Birch, Louise, 1879?–1976, Educator

Birch-Wathen School, 9 E. 71st Street

In partnership with Edith Wathen (d. 1950), Louise Birch opened the Birch-Wathen School in 1921, with classes from kindergarten through high school. She had once lived in the White House as tutor for President Theodore Roosevelt's grandchildren and had worked at a settlement house before teaching for some years. Many famous persons are alumni of the school, including Barbara Walters and Robert Heilbroner. Birch was headmistress of the school until 1966 and a trustee until her death.[20]

Blackwell, Elizabeth, 1821–1910, and Her Sister Emily Blackwell, 1826–1910, Physicians and Hospital Administrators; NAW

New York Infirmary, 308 E. 15th Street, at Stuyvesant Square East

Elizabeth Blackwell was the first woman in the United States to get a medical degree from a regularly established college (see Geneva, NY). After she graduated in 1849 she went abroad for further training. She then set up a practice in New York City, only to find that a woman doctor was looked upon as nothing but an abortionist. She was barred from practice in city hospitals, insulted by medical colleagues, discriminated against by landlords. She opened a one-room dispensary for treating poor women and children and began accumulating funds to found a hospital where women could be treated by female doctors.

She was joined by her sister Emily Blackwell, who had earned her M.D. at Western Reserve University in 1854, and by Marie Zakrzewska, an 1856 graduate of Western Reserve. They opened the New York Infirmary for Women and Children at 64 Bleecker Street on Florence Nightingale's birthday in 1857. "Dr. Zak" soon went to Boston, Massachusetts, to found another women's hospital, still flourishing in Roxbury, Massachusetts.

In 1868 the Blackwells added to the infirmary a women's medical college. The following year Elizabeth left America for her native England and remained there for the rest of her life. Emily continued to operate both the hospital and the medical school for the next thirty years. When Cornell University Medical School in New York opened its doors to women, Emily saw no need for a separate women's college and closed hers. She had seen 364 physicians graduate there.

Bliss, Lizzie Plummer. See Rockefeller, Abby

Braslau, Sophie, 1888–1935, Singer; NAW

Plaque, Godmother's League, 255 W. 71st Street

Godmother's League, a shelter for babies, is supported by the Braslau Memorial Fund. The inscription on the bronze plaque reads: "An everlasting tribute from friends and admirers to Sophie Braslau, the great and beloved singer, in remembrance of her love for little children." It was unveiled in 1939, four years after the death of the concert singer. Braslau sang for the Metropolitan Opera and was much in demand as a soloist with the principal orchestras until cancer cut short her career.

Breckinridge, Aida de Acosta, 1884–1962, Organization Official

Eye Bank for Sight Restoration, Manhattan Eye, Ear, and Throat Hospital, 210 E. 64th Street

Aida de Acosta Breckinridge lost the sight of one eye from glaucoma. In honor of her ophthalmologist, William H. Wilmer, she founded the Wilmer Opthalmological Institute at Johns Hopkins Medical School in 1929. One of his students suggested that an eye bank to supply corneal tissue would be valuable. Although some fifteen thousand Americans, it was thought, could have sight through corneal transplants, the acquisition of an eye was a matter of luck. Breckinridge followed the suggestion and founded the Eye Bank. She was its director from 1945 to 1955. Eye banks have since been established in many cities.

Breckinridge has another claim to fame. In 1903 she made a solo flight over Paris, France, in a balloon. When she landed she was greeted, "Mademoiselle, you are the world's first woman pilot." Her society parents were not pleased. In fact, they were shocked and kept the whole thing a secret until 1932, when the feat was made public.[21]

Burnett, Frances Hodgson, 1849–1924, Writer; NAW

Fountain, Conservatory Gardens, 5th Avenue and 105th Street

The sculpture fountain by Bessie Potter Vonnoh was erected in Central Park in 1937 in memory of Frances Hodgson Burnett, the popular author of *Little Lord Fauntleroy, The Secret Garden*, and other treasures dear to the hearts of children around the turn of the century.

Cabrini, Saint Frances Xavier, 1850–1917, Churchwoman; NAW

Plaque, Statue of Liberty, Liberty Island. Cabrini Health Care Center, Columbus Hospital, 227 E. 19th Street

The plaque at the Statue of Liberty honors famous immigrants to the United States who have enriched the American way of life by contributing creative ideas. The first name on the list is that of Mother (now Saint) Frances Xavier Cabrini. She was born in Italy and sent to America by the pope in 1889 to work with New York's immigrants. She became a naturalized citizen of the United States in 1909 and the following year was made superior general of the order she had founded, the Missionary Sisters of the Sacred Heart. In 1946 she became the first American citizen to achieve sainthood. Several church and school buildings in New York bear her name.

Callery, Mary, 1903–1977, Sculptor

Untitled Sculpture, Top of Metropolitan Opera House, Lincoln Center, and Other Sculptures

Known for her spaghetti-thin figures with seeming India-rubber flexibility, Mary Callery won both praise and derogation for the sculpture at the Metropolitan Opera House. The controversial sculptor was influenced by Pablo Picasso and Fernand Léger. Critics praised her developing talent in show after show. ''I would like the spectator,'' she said, ''to have a special pleasure in each object I make, a fresh vision.'' Other works by Callery in New York include *The Fables*, a frieze on the facade of Public School 34, 30 E. 12th Street, and *Acrobats, Monument* at Wingate Public School in Brooklyn. See Pittsburgh, PA.[22]

Churchill, Jennie Jerome, 1854–1921, Society Leader; NAW

Tablet, 426 Henry Street, Brooklyn

The bronze tablet on the wall of the Brooklyn house was dedicated in 1952 to mark the approximate birthplace of Jennie Jerome Churchill, wife of Lord Randolph Churchill and mother of Sir Winston Churchill. Jennie was not to be lost in the male shadows of her distinguished relatives. After her marriage to the son of the duke of Marlborough, she founded and edited the quarterly *Anglo-Saxon Review* to foster better understanding between England and America. She also wrote memoirs, essays, and plays. She joined with other American women in Britain to equip a hospital ship during the Boer War. When Winston's political career was in the balance, his mother, in his own words, ''left no wire unpulled, no stone unturned, no cutlet uncooked'' in helping him toward the goal of prime minister of England.[23]

Colden, Jane, 1724–1766, Botanist; NAW

Cadwallader Colden House, Cedar Grove Cemetery, Queens

Jane Colden and her father, Cadwallader Colden, lived in the house here preserved. He was a noted physician and naturalist, and she roamed the fields with him collecting the plants of the new world. A family visitor wrote of her: ''Jennie is a Florist and Botanist, she has discovered a great number of Plants never before described and has given their Properties and Virtues, many of which are found useful in Medicine, and she draws and colours them with great beauty.''

Jennie's portfolio of four hundred drawings, ink impressions of leaves, and descriptions of American flowers and trees is now in the British Library. A portion was published for the first time in 1963.[24]

Cook, Alice Rice, 1900?–1973, Educator and Management Consultant

Alice Rice Cook Lecture Hall, New School for Social Research, 66 W. 12th Street

Alice Rice Cook founded the New School for Social Research in 1951 to bring about changes in attitudes of women who had been secluded at home, so that they could take a significant part in community activities and prepare for worthy employment. She offered courses to women on subjects ranging from self-discovery to art. She also counseled business organizations in human relations and coauthored with Lillian M. Gilbreth a book on the management of employees. From 1927 to 1946 she was president of a flourishing brick company. In 1970 former students and colleagues named the lecture hall for her.[25]

Corbin, Margaret Cochran, 1751–c. 1800, Revolutionary War Heroine, NAW

Monument, Fort Tryon Road, 192nd Street and Broadway, and Other Markers

Margaret Cochran Corbin ("Captain Molly"), who was born on the Pennsylvania frontier, won fame during the Battle of Fort Washington on November 16, 1776. (Fort Washington was later named Fort Tyron.) Called "the first American woman to take a soldier's part in the War for Liberty," she took over her husband's job, after he was fatally wounded, and loaded his gun until she herself was felled by a shot. She lost the use of one arm. Her war service was recognized in 1779 when she was given a soldier's half pay and enrolled in the Invalid Regiment at West Point, New York, q.v. Tablets in her memory are at 190th Street and Fort Washington Avenue and at Holyrood Church, 179th Street and Fort Washington Avenue. See Chambersburg, PA.

Cushman, Charlotte. See Hall of Fame

Diller, Angela, 1877–1968, and Elizabeth Quaile, 1874–1951, Music Educators; NAWM (under Diller)

Diller-Quaile School of Music, 24 E. 95th Street

"I don't teach a method," Angela Diller said. "I try to open people to music. Music is something that flows eternally." She played the piano by ear before she started formal training, then studied and taught while experimenting with musical methods. She and Elizabeth Quaile met while teaching at the Music School Settlement on East 3rd Street. They formulated theories of music education which they further developed at the David Mannes School. In 1921 they founded their own school to teach music theory and techniques to children, adults, and especially teachers. Their materials have been used to teach thousands of musicians. Quaile, unlike Diller, was largely self-taught, but she was equally dedicated to music.[26]

Dock, Lavinia. See Wald, Lillian

Dodge, Grace, 1856–1914, Social Worker; NAW

Grace Dodge Hall, Teachers College, Columbia University.
Greyston Conference Center, 690 W. 247th Street, Riverdale; Landmark of New York

The cornerstone of Grace Dodge's humanitarian service was dedication to helping young women born into circumstances less fortunate than her own. One of her first voluntary positions was chair of the New York Charities Aid Association's Committee on the Elevation of the Poor in their Homes. An informal club of working girls grew into the Industrial Education Association. Finding that well-trained teachers were in short supply, she helped to organize a teacher training school which eventually became Teachers College. In 1907 the household arts building was named for her. She was reserved, yet commanding, and always warmly interested in people. Greyston, the family home, was given to Teachers College in 1961 by Dodge's nephew as a memorial to her.[27]

Dreier, Mary. See Wald, Lillian

Force, Juliana Rieser. See Whitney, Gertrude

Freeman, Mary Wilkins, 1852–1930, Writer; NAW

Bronze Doors, American Academy of Arts and Letters, 633 W. 155th Street

The doors are "dedicated to the memory of Mary E. Wilkins Freeman and the Women Writers of America." Freeman's short stories and novels, published between 1880 and 1923, were popular. They also won critical praise from Henry James, Sarah Orne Jewett, and others. Yet after her death they fell into obscurity, dismissed as ephemeral local color. In the 1970s they were rediscovered and some republished by feminists who appreciate the realism with which Freeman saw the plain and poverty-hardened women of northern New England. She grew up in New England and later lived in Metuchen, New Jersey, as the wife of Charles M. Freeman, whom she married when she was forty-nine. So real is her portrayal of the late nineteenth-century New England that critics speak of a fictional country, Wilkinston, inhabited by her characters.[28]

Green, Gretchen, d. 1971, Humanitarian

Memorial Rainbow Roof, Institute of Rehabilitation Medicine, New York University Medical Center, 400 E. 34th Street

The small sky-park atop the Institute of Rehabilitation Medicine was dedicated to Gretchen Green "for her many years of faithful volunteer work" as an honorary member of the auxiliary board. She was a woman of wide interests, always ready to enrich her own life and that of others. She studied social work, became a Big Sister to the poor, a policewoman, and welfare director in Boise, Idaho. In New York she worked with the immigrants at Ellis Island then went abroad, visiting Morocco, Tagore, India, and Venice, Italy. During World War II she operated a Camel Corps Canteen in Africa. She was made a member of the Order of the British Empire for her work in helping the British rebuild their country after the war. She was also one of the founders of the school for Seeing Eye dogs.[29]

Guion, Connie Myers, 1882–1971, Physician

Dr. Connie Guion Building, New York Hospital–Cornell Medical Center, 525 E. 68th Street

"If that's a clinic and that's the way poor people get treated, then something has got to be done about clinics. . . . Back home we treat cows and chickens better than you treat people." This was Connie Myers Guion's indignant reaction when, as a Wellesley College student, she visited an eye clinic in Boston, Massachusetts. Years later, Guion's name was given to this building, housing more than eighty well-run outpatient clinics. It was dedicated to her on May 8, 1963, while she was still living. She was associated with the New York Hospital for over fifty years and won many awards as a distinguished physician and a woman of notable achievements. She was never one to keep silent when she saw something that needed correcting. As a Bellevue intern she rebelled against the twenty-four-hour ambulance shift. She was told that it had been a twenty-four-hour stint for a hundred years. "Well," she said, "the century's up." Soon after, twelve-hour shifts were instituted.[30]

Harkness, Rebekah West, 1915–1982, Dance Patron and Philanthropist

Harkness Ballet Foundation, 4 E. 75th Street

Rebekah West Harkness, widow of William Hale Harkness, was a sculptor, a composer, a traveler, and, above all, a patron of the dance. When she founded the Harkness Ballet in 1964, she said, "What I have in mind to do for the ballet will take not only a fortune but the almost total dedication of the rest of my life.'' She was artistic director of the Harkness Ballet, the creator of Harkness House, a ballet school and home for the company, and owner of a theater presenting dance companies to New Yorkers.[31]

Havemeyer, Louisine Elder, 1855–1929, Art Collector and Suffrage Worker; NAW

H. O. Havemeyer Collection, Metropolitan Museum of Art, 5th Avenue and 82nd Street

Louisine Elder Havemeyer, while a student in Paris, France, met the expatriate American artist Mary Cassatt, who introduced her to avant-garde French painters. From her pocket money Havemeyer bought a painting by Edgar Degas and became his first American patron. Later, she joined her husband, H. O. Havemeyer, in filling their luxurious mansion with art, great masters as well as modern French paintings. After he died, she turned her attention to women's rights. She assisted Alice Paul in her efforts to force the federal government's attention to equal suffrage. She went so far as to try to burn President Woodrow Wilson in effigy on the White House lawn. Arrested, she was taken to the disgraceful Occoquan workhouse, where she spent three days, in company with other women protesters. Afterward she joined the others on the ''Prison Special,'' a train that toured the country for a month arousing public opinion on behalf of suffrage. Havemeyer left most of her art collection to the Metropolitan Museum of Art, under the name of her husband.

Heck, Barbara Ruckle, 1734–1804, Churchwoman; NAW

Plaque, John Street Methodist Church, 44 John Street; Landmark of New York, NR

Methodism was brought to America by Barbara Ruckle Heck. She came from Ireland in 1760 just after her marriage to Paul Heck and settled in New York City with a group of coreligionists. Though they had been Methodists at home, they found no church for their faith in New York. When she discovered some of the group playing cards, she felt they were losing their religion and insisted that one of them, Philip Embury, begin preaching. In 1767 the group rented a loft in which to hold services and the following year built the Wesley Chapel on John Street. The Hecks themselves moved soon afterward to the upper Hudson Valley, then to Canada, but the church on John Street, now in the city's financial district, has continued as a center of Methodism. The structure has been replaced three times. A plaque commemorates Embury and Heck: ''Their works do follow them.''

Holt, Winifred (Mather), 1870–1945, Worker for the Blind; NAW

The Lighthouse, 111 E. 59th Street

While studying sculpture in Italy, Winifred Holt saw blind students at a concert obviously enthralled with the music. This motivated her to give up sculpture and devote herself to making theater and music available to the blind. Later, in New York, she began to work toward her goal, first through a special ticket bureau, then through an association which eventually became the National Society for the Prevention of Blindness.

Holt began a survey of the sightless in New York State and found that they needed a good deal more than cultural pleasure. Many could be rehabilitated, and much could be done to prevent blindness. Holt's main interest became the training of those with sight impairment to become self-supporting. The association rented a loft where such persons could be trained to produce saleable articles, and this grew into the first Lighthouse, opened in 1913. Other Lighthouses, centers for training and recreation, opened in other cities and countries. In 1922, when Holt married Rufus Mather, they requested donations to the Lighthouse movement in lieu of wedding gifts, raising over $500,000.

Horney, Karen Danielsen, 1885–1952, Psychoanalyst; NAWM

Karen Horney Clinic, American Institute for Psychoanalysis, 329 E. 62nd Street

Karen Danielsen Horney's studies in psychoanalysis centered on feminine psychology and women's emotional life. She rebelled against Sigmund Freud's view of woman's psychological development. "The view that women are infantile and emotional creatures, incapable of responsibility and independence, is the work of the masculine tendency to lower women's self respect," she said. She left Germany in 1923 for a teaching position in Chicago, Illinois, and two years later she came to New York. Here she built up a practice and organized the Association for the Advancement of Psychoanalysis and its teaching arm, the American Institute. She founded its *American Journal of Psychoanalysis* and was its editor until her death. Many of her ideas, heretical when promulgated, have been accepted into the mainstream of psychology, and her followers have extended still further her theories on the female mind. The clinic named in her honor was opened in 1955—on Freud's birthday.[32]

Huntington, Anna Hyatt, 1876–1973, Sculptor; NAWM

Sculptures, Hispanic Society of America, Broadway at 155th Street, and Others

Anna Hyatt Huntington's husband, Archer Huntington, founded the Hispanic Society, and many of her sculptures grace its outer court. The *Cid Compeador* is a copy of the original erected in Seville, Spain, in 1927. Four seated bronze warriors complete the composition. Four marble animal groups are on the terraces. On the walls are Don Quixote and Boabdil, carved in limestone. At Riverside Drive at W. 93rd Street is her equestrian statue of Joan of Arc, erected in 1915. A small Joan of Arc relief is at the Cathedral Church of St. John the Divine, Amsterdam Avenue at 113th Street. A statue of José Marti is at Central Park South and Avenue of the Americas. Many of her works are in Brookgreen Gardens in South Carolina, a garden established by the Huntingtons as a showcase for American sculpture.

Hutchinson, Anne, 1591–1643, Dissenter; NAW

Hutchinson River Parkway, Pelham Bay Park

Hounded out of Massachusetts by the clergy for unorthodox views, Anne Hutchinson came to New York in 1642. The crime for which she had been expelled from Massachusetts was confronting the clergy, expressing opinions, and speaking out when it was firmly believed that women should keep silent on matters of religion. From Boston she went to Narragansett Bay, where she and her husband established what is now Portsmouth, Rhode Island. After her husband died, Anne decided that she and her six children could live by farming in New Netherland (New York). She believed the Dutch who sold her the land had bought it from the Indians. The Indians thought she had stolen it from them, and a year after her arrival they massacred her and all but the youngest of the children. Her name was long afterward given to the parkway which passes near the site of the massacre.

Isaacs, Edith Rich, 1878–1956, Theatrical Editor and Critic; NAWM

Theatre Arts Center, James Weldon Johnson Community Center, 120 E. 110th Street

The Theatre Arts Center was established in Harlem in 1959 and dedicated to Edith Rich Isaacs' memory because of her theater work. She believed theater was an educational medium, an important form of recreation, and a social force. As editor of *Theatre Arts* magazine for many years, her editorial support widened the field to include community, regional, and college groups. She worked with Hallie Flanagan on the Federal Theatre Project (see Poughkeepsie, NY). Her interest in black culture led to an exhibition of the Blondiau–Theatre Arts collection of primitive African art, and after the show—the first of its kind in New York—she bought the collection to prevent its dispersal. Eventually it was divided between Howard University in Washington, D.C., and the Schomburg Center in New York City. Even after she was bedridden with crippling arthritis,

Isaacs continued writing on the theater. Her *The Negro in the American Theatre* was published in 1947.

Keller, Helen, 1880–1968, Blind Worker for the Blind; NAWM

Helen Keller Room, American Foundation for the Blind, 15 W. 16th Street. Helen Keller National Center for Deaf-Blind Youths and Adults, 111 Middle Neck Road, Sands Point

Helen Keller lost sight and hearing at the age of eighteen months. Through the skill and devotion of Anne Sullivan, who had been trained at the Perkins Institute in Massachusetts, she was taught to communicate by finger language, then to read, and finally to speak. Her life, beginning so disastrously and rising to such great heights, is a continuing inspiration to all handicapped persons, and she is one American heroine known to all school children. The story of her life and that of Anne Sullivan (later Macy), whom she called Teacher, has been told in books, films, and most recently in the play and film *The Miracle Worker*. Keller began working with the American Foundation for the Blind after World War I, raising funds, lecturing, and lobbying for passage of legislation on behalf of the handicapped. The memorial room is open to visitors during weekdays by appointment (212–924–0420). See Washington, DC.

Kelley, Florence. See Wald, Lillian

Kellor, Frances. See Wald, Lillian

Lazarus, Emma, 1849–1887, Poet; NAW

Plaques, at the Statue of Liberty, Liberty Island, and at International Arrival Building, Kennedy Airport

Ask anyone what America's immigration policy is and he or she is likely to quote:

> Give me your tired, your poor,
> Your huddled masses yearning to breathe free,
> The wretched refuse of your teeming shore.
> Send these, the homeless, tempest-tost to me,
> I lift my lamp beside the golden door!

The poet who wrote these lines was no poor immigrant. Emma Lazarus was a well-to-do, well-educated woman, descended from Sephardic Jews who had been in the New World since the seventeenth century. She was a cousin of Benjamin Cardozo, Supreme Court justice. Her heartfelt sympathy with European emigrants was stirred by the persecution of Jews that broke out in 1881–82 after the assassination of Czar Alexander II of Russia. In 1883 she wrote the sonnet "The New Colossus" to be sold at a literary auction to aid the Statue of Liberty fund. The verses were inscribed on the base of the statue and have ever since been accepted by the American people as unquestioned public policy. The American Museum of Immigration History at the base of the Statue of Liberty is open daily 9–5; open until 6 in summer.

L'Esperance, Elise Strang, 1878?–1959, Physician; NAWM

Strang Clinics, New York Infirmary, 320 E. 15th Street, and Preventive Medicine Institute, 55 E. 34th Street

It is largely due to Elise Strang L'Esperance that women today regularly have physical examinations, including a Pap smear, to check on the possibility of cancer. She was one of the last to graduate from the Woman's Medical College founded by the Blackwells before Cornell's medical college opened its doors to women. She worked with a pathologist at Cornell whose specialty was cancer, and this led to her greatest contribution to medicine, the establishment of the Strang clinics. They were named for her mother, Kate Depew Strang, who died of cancer.

Lewisohn, Irene, 1892–1944, Theater Worker; NAW

Irene Lewisohn Library, Neighborhood Playhouse School of the Theatre, 340 E. 54th Street. Irene Lewisohn Costume Reference Library, Metropolitan Museum of Art, 5th Avenue and 82nd Street

The Neighborhood Playhouse grew out of Irene and Alice Lewisohn's early work with theatrical presentations for the Henry Street Settlement. Together the sisters built and presented to the settlement one of the earliest "little theaters" in the country. It was a major center for the production of experimental and exotic plays. Performances included Japanese Noh plays, Chinese fantasies, miracle plays, Yiddish drama and dance, and works by Sholem Asch, James Joyce, and George Bernard Shaw. Alice, after her marriage, spent much of her time abroad. Irene devoted herself increasingly to a museum of costume art, which after her death went to the Metropolitan Museum. The costume library is open to those with special interest, by appointment.

Loeb, Sophie Simon, 1876–1929, Journalist and Child Welfare Worker; NAW

Memorial Fountain, Central Park

The marble children's fountain, donated by August Heckscher in Sophie Simon Loeb's memory, was dedicated in 1936. Loeb's interest in legislative action on behalf of children began when, as a feature writer for the *Evening World*, she interviewed poor widows who had been forced to send their children to orphan asylums. Herself fatherless, she had worked in a shop while her brother sold newspapers so that her mother might keep the family together. She was appalled that New York's assistance program gave mothers no help in keeping their children at home, thus breaking up families. A few citizens, like Hannah Bachman Einstein (1862–1929), founder of the Widowed Mothers' Fund Association, had proposed public aid to widowed mothers. Loeb publicized their efforts. In 1913 she and Einstein were appointed to a state commission to study the problem. The bill they wrote was opposed by state-supported orphanages and private organizations that Einstein called "bureaucrats of philanthropy" and was defeated by one vote. But after a strong newspaper campaign they were successful in getting passage of the Child Welfare Act in 1915, years before the social security system of the 1930s.

Loehmann, Frieda, 1874?–1962, Fashion Merchandiser

Loehmann's, Inc., 2500 Halsey Street, Bronx

Frieda Loehmann was the grande dame of cut-rate fashion merchandising. Her career began in 1920 when she came to New York with her husband, Charles Loehmann. He had been forced by paralysis to retire from his position as flutist with the Cincinnati Symphony. She had been a coat buyer, and it occurred to her that the coats the Fifth Avenue stores could not sell were still worth buying if the price was right. She went to the Seventh Avenue merchants and offered them cash for what was to them unsaleable merchandise, took the garments to her Brooklyn store, and sold them to eager buyers. In the next decades, her flair for forecasting style trends and business sagacity, combined with hard work, built up a $3 million business.

Frieda, who is described as vivid and flamboyant, with silver hair pulled taut from a pale face, lived in a four-room penthouse above the store in Brooklyn. After her death the store was closed, but her son Charles, who had opened his own store in the Bronx, took over the business and expanded it. At the time of his death in 1977 there were thirty-eight Loehmann stores across the nation. The Halsey Street address is the executive office of the business.[33]

Longman, Evelyn Beatrice (Batchelder), 1875–1954, Sculptor

The Genius of the Telegraph, *American Telephone and Telegraph Company Building, Broadway and Fulton Street*

Evelyn Beatrice Longman was chosen to design the crowning gilt statue for the American Telephone and Telegraph Building at 195 Broadway in 1917. Variously entitled the *Spirit of Communication* or the *Genius of Electricity*, it became a corporate symbol and appears on telephone book covers across the nation. The twenty-foot statue was later moved to the lobby of the company's present building.[34]

Lowell, Josephine Shaw, 1843–1905, Charitable Worker; NAW

Memorial Fountain, Bryant Park, Avenue of the Americas, Between W. 40th and 42nd Streets

In 1876 Josephine Shaw Lowell was appointed the first woman member of the State Board of Charities. She inspected orphanages, hospitals, jails, and poorhouses, finding most of them far from satisfactory and the system riddled with political intrigue. Her reports brought about some improvement in conditions. Later she turned her critical eye on privately funded charities in the city, which were uncoordinated and inefficient. This resulted in the founding of the Charity Organization Society. She worked out her own philosophy of public aid, stressing reformation and rehabilitation, rather than simply relief of poverty, and insisting that charities be professionally administered and free of political interference. The granite fountain honoring Lowell, which dominates the western end of the park, was designed by Charles A. Platt and presented to the city in 1912.[35]

Lozier, Clemence Harned, 1813–1888, Physician and Reformer; NAW

New York Medical College, 5th Avenue and 106th Street

Graduating from the Syracuse Medical College in 1853, not long after Elizabeth Blackwell had opened the door of medical training to women, Clemence Harned Lozier was Blackwell's predecessor in establishing the first woman's school of medicine in the state. Her New York Medical College and Hospital for Women opened in 1863, with seven students and eight faculty members, Lozier at the head. Over the following years she funneled a large part of her time and the income from a lucrative private practice into this school and its hospital, where women could be treated by female doctors. Lozier was a reformer in many fields: antislavery, suffrage, sanitation, sensible dress, higher education for women, Indian rights, prison improvement, temperance, and peace. In 1918 the widely recognized medical school she founded was absorbed into the New York Medical College of the Flower and Fifth Avenue Hospital.

Lyon, Mary. See Hall of Fame

McCormick, Katharine Dexter, 1875–1967, Birth-control Advocate and Philanthropist; NAWM

McCormick Library, Planned Parenthood Federation of America, 810 7th Avenue

The birth-control pill might have been developed without Katharine Dexter McCormick's help, but she hastened its development by her generous support of research at the Worcester Foundation for Experimental Biology. The experiments resulted in the synthetic progesterone and estrogen named Enovid in 1960. McCormick had long been interested in endocrinology as she thought it might be able to cure the mental illness of her husband, Stanley McCormick, comptroller of International Harvester. She established a research foundation at Harvard Medical School to study the subject, but it did not help her husband, who died insane in 1947. McCormick had been an ally of Margaret Sanger from the time the latter was arrested for distributing birth-control leaflets. She was one of those who smuggled diaphragms into the country from Europe, and she hoped some more effective birth-control method, such as an oral contraceptive, could be found. She left the Planned Parenthood Federation a $5 million endowment as a memorial to Stanley McCormick.

Mannes, Clara Damrosch, 1869–1948, Musician; NAW

Mannes College of Music, 157 E. 74th Street

Clara Damrosch Mannes came from a distinguished musical family, married a musician, and brought up children who also reached distinction in the world of music. She and her husband, David Mannes, had successful musical careers, he as concertmaster of the New York Symphony Society, she as pianist and singer, both as recitalists. In 1916 they founded the David Mannes Music School, which offered amateur music lovers as well as future professionals training in music. They directed the school together. They compiled a collection of children's songs designed to give young people joy in music.

Marchais, Jacques, d. 1948, Dealer and Specialist in Tibetan Art

Jacques Marchais Center of Tibetan Art, 338 Lighthouse Avenue, Staten Island

If one wished to visit a Lama temple and could not get to Tibet, one could at least visit this unique and authentic center of Tibetan art. Its founder used the professional name of Jacques Marchais while a dealer for ten years in Oriental art. The center's opening in 1945 realized a twenty-year dream of Madame Marchais. Her husband, Harry Klauber, was in the chemical industry and well able to support her undertaking. She designed and built the center, which occupies a site on top of Lighthouse Hill overlooking the lakes and woodlands of Staten Island. Klauber outlived her only eight months. He provided for the museum to be continued under a board of trustees as a memorial to his wife. It consists of the temple with its lamasery altar, a library for the study of Tibetan culture, and a tranquil landscaped garden with lotus pool, Buddhas, stone sculptures, and a birdhouse. It is on a shady street, marked only by a small sign at the entrance, "Tibetan Art." It is open Apr.-May and Oct.-Nov., Sat. and Sun. 1–5; June-Sept., Fri.-Sun. 1–5; closed Dec. 1–Apr. 1; adm.[36]

Matthews, Victoria Earle, 1861–1907, Social Worker; NAW

Plaque, White Rose Mission, 262 W. 136th Street

Victoria Earle Matthews, daughter of a black slave and a white master, was being brought up as a white child in her father's house when her mother, who had escaped to the North, found that the Civil War had freed her. She returned to Georgia to regain custody of Matthews and another daughter, Anna, both light-skinned. Matthews joined with other Negro women in several organizations, predecessors of the National Association of Colored Women. She was concerned about black girls enticed into prostitution by spurious employment agencies. In 1897 she opened the White Rose Industrial Association's home for Negro girls newly arrived in New York. There women were trained for jobs; then mothers' clubs were added, plus a kindergarten and recreational clubs. Matthews was the leader of the settlement until failing health forced her to give it up.

Maxwell, Anna Caroline, 1851–1929, Nursing Educator; NAW

Anna C. Maxwell Hall, Columbia-Presbyterian Medical Center, 179 Fort Washington Avenue

Anna Caroline Maxwell was buried in Arlington National Cemetery with full military honors because of her services during the Spanish-American War in 1898 and during World War I. Her chief contribution, however, was in peacetime nurses' training. Beginning in 1892 she was for almost three decades head of the nurses' training school at the Presbyterian Hospital, and during those years she raised immeasurably the standards of performance and training of nurses. She changed the course from two to three years and later affiliated with Teachers College to allow nurses to earn a bachelor of science degree along with that of Registered Nurse. She spent the available money on top-notch instructors and charged tuition instead of paying the nurses allowances, thus shifting the emphasis from hospital service to education. After her retirement in 1921, she was made honorary chairman of a committee to raise funds for a nurses' residence at the medical center, which was then named for her.

Mead, Margaret, 1901–1978, Anthropologist

Margaret Mead Hall of Pacific Peoples, American Museum of Natural History, Central Park West at 79th Street

Margaret Mead, who made the American Museum of Natural History her professional home for fifty-two years, had begun the design of the Hall of Pacific Peoples before she died. It contains many of the items she collected on her numerous trips to the Pacific. Her first book, *Coming of Age in Samoa* (1928), chronicled the primitive tribal ways of Polynesian islanders. She continued the study of the peoples of the Pacific throughout her lifetime and was considered the world's foremost interpreter of their culture. Her fearless journeys alone into societies westerners called primitive inspired a generation of younger researchers. No closet scholar, Mead constantly related the past to the problems of modern society, other cultures to those of America. She was not afraid to draw large conclusions and to popularize her discoveries. She was an early feminist as well as a believer in the value of the multigenerational family. Her outspoken views about legalizing contraceptives, marijuana, and abortions; about extending Social Security to housewives; and about the rights of the young were all voiced long before they became commonplace. Mead was elected to the National Women's Hall of Fame.[37]

Meyer, Annie Nathan, 1867–1951, Publicist; NAWM

Annie Nathan Meyer Drama Library, Barnard Hall, Barnard College, Broadway at 118th Street

Annie Nathan Meyer is credited with having originated the idea of a woman's college associated with Columbia University. She proposed it in an article in the January 26, 1888, issue of *The Nation*, and she and her husband contributed time and money to have Barnard College established. Once the college opened, she was concerned that Jewish and black women be given equal opportunities with white, Gentile students. She was an antisuffragist, and after women won the vote she was fond of reminding them that the franchise had not begun a new era in politics. Her portrait in the college parlor is inscribed "Author of the Original Plea for the Establishment of Barnard College."

Mills, Florence, 1895–1927, Entertainer; NAW

Florence Mills House, 220 W. 155th Street (Private); NHL

Florence Mills took part in the Harlem Renaissance of the 1920s when Afro-American artists were attracting the favorable attention of whites. With little formal training, she had perfected her blues singing and developed her unique style of dancing on the vaudeville stage and in Harlem nightclubs. Born Florence Winfrey in Virginia, she took the name of Mills when, at the age of eight, she appeared with two sisters as "the Mills Trio." In 1921 she was propelled into a starring role when one of the leads of *Shuffle Along* fell ill. She made a hit and earned leading roles on the New York and London, England, stages. Her promising career was cut short by an early death.

Mitchell, Lucy Spraque, 1878–1967, College Founder; NAWM

Bank Street College of Education, 610 W. 112th Street

When Lucy Sprague Mitchell came to Manhattan in 1913 she decided she did not like the educational system in the city's public schools. The superintendent of public schools was reported to have said, "I like to pause at 11 o'clock and reflect that all over New York thousands of pupils are reading the same page of the same book." Regimentation was the order of the day. School desks were screwed to the floor. Mitchell felt impelled to change this old-fashioned system. She had taught school, had been dean of women at the University of California, and was taking courses at Teachers College from the innovative educator John Dewey. In 1916 she and her husband, with funds from her cousin, Elizabeth Sprague Coolidge (see Washington, DC), established a private educational institution to teach and study progressive education. First called the Bureau of Educational Experiments, it grew into the Bank Street College of Education, guided by Mitchell for four decades.

Mitchell, Maria. See Hall of Fame

Moody, Lady Deborah Dunch, c. 1600–1659?, Town Developer; NAW

Lady Deborah Moody House, 27 Gravesend Neck Road (Private). Tablets, Entrance to Gravesend Cemetery and Hall of Long Island Historical Society, 128 Pierrepont Street, Brooklyn

Deborah Dunch Moody, the daughter of a British member of Parliament, married Henry Moody, created a baronet by King James I. She was also a granddaughter of a bishop, but in spite of these high connections, Lady Moody found after her husband died in 1629 that she was not allowed to travel freely about the realm. Taking gold coins sewed into her clothes and those of her thirteen-year-old son, she fled to the New World. She found Boston, Massachusetts, as full of government regulation as England and moved on to New Amsterdam. The polyglot population, religious freedom, and cheap land here suited her. She bought land in what is now Brooklyn and founded the town of Gravesend. It was enclosed by palisades to keep out the Long Island Indians. She bought Coney Island from the Indians. She insisted on social, political, and religious freedom in Gravesend and wished it to be receptive to culture. Its charter declared that "We the People shall make our own laws for our quiet and peaceful existence."

Murray, Mary Lindley, 1726–1782, Patriot

Tablet, Park Avenue, Near 37th Street

The tablet reads: "For services rendered her country during the American Revolution, entertaining at her home, on this site, Gen. Howe and his officers, until the American troops under Gen. Putnam escaped. September 15, 1776." It was erected by the Daughters of the American Revolution in 1903. The story of Mary Lindley Murray's part in the Revolution is based on the memoirs of James Thacher, an American army surgeon. "Most fortunately," he wrote, "the British generals, seeing no prospect of engaging our troops, halted their own, and repaired to the house of a Robert Murray, a quaker and a friend of our cause; Mrs. Murray treated them with cake and wine, and they were induced to tarry two hours or more. . . . By this happy incident General Putnam, by continuing his march, escaped a rencounter with a greatly superior force, which must have proved fatal to his whole party. One half hour, it is said, would have been sufficient for the enemy to have secured the road at a turn, and entirely cut off Putnam's retreat. It has since become almost a common saying, among our officers, that Mrs. Murray saved this part of the American army." A well-known painting by E. P. Moran depicts "Mrs. Murray's Strategy."[38]

O'Reilly, Leonora. See Wald, Lillian

Ottendorfer, Anna Sartorius Uhl, 1815–1884, Newspaper Publisher; NAW

Ottendorfer Branch, New York Public Library, 135 2nd Avenue, and Stuyvesant Polyclinic Hospital, 137 2nd Avenue; Landmarks of New York, NR

Anna Sartorius Uhl Ottendorfer emigrated to the United States from Bavaria in 1836 with her husband, Jacob Uhl, a printer. They settled in New York City, bought the German language weekly the *Staats-Zeitung* and built it up into a daily newspaper with a large circulation. Anna combined the care of a large family with work on the paper, her duties including business management and sometimes typesetting and printing. After Uhl died she married Oswald Ottendorfer, who had been her editor. The paper was of enormous influence in spreading liberal ideas among the German community in New York as well as in cities, such as Milwaukee, Wisconsin, with large German populations.

The Ottendorfers were as generous as they were prosperous. Among her benefactions were the Herman Uhl Memorial Fund, in memory of a son who died in 1881; a woman's pavilion at New York's German Hospital; and the Isabella Home for aged German-American women, a memorial to a daughter who died in 1873. The Freie Bibliothek, built through Anna's generosity in 1884, is now a part of the public library system and the German Dispensary, another of her gifts, is a clinic.

Packer, Harriet Putnam, 1820–1892, School Founder

Packer Collegiate Institute, 170 Joralemon Street, Brooklyn Heights

Two days after the Brooklyn Female Academy was destroyed by fire in January 1853 the trustees met, with long faces. Where could they find funds to rebuild? At that moment a letter was delivered from Harriet Putnam Packer, whose late husband had been a member of the board. She proposed "to apply sixty-five thousand dollars of his property to the erection of an Institution for the education of my own sex, in the higher branches of Literature in lieu of that now known as the Brooklyn Female Academy." The trustees accepted, the new institution was built on the site of the old, and it was given a more appropriate name. A bronze tablet at the right of the entrance of the institute credits Packer with founding the school. A marble portrait bust by Charles Calverly is in the chapel. Two other women are honored here: philanthropist Emma Wilson Schoonmaker (1859–1937) by a bronze tablet and Clara R. Talcott (1834–1870) by a marble bas-relief "in token of the loving memory of her friends and pupils." The poet Marianne Moore, who lived in Brooklyn, had this to say of Packer Institute: "Search the world over, you could not find a saner elegance, teaching more initiate, equipment more modern, together with a deep reverence for bequeathed value."[39]

Palmer, Alice Freeman. See Hall of Fame

Palmer, Sophia French, 1853–1920, Nursing Educator; NAW

Palmer Library, American Journal of Nursing, 555 W. 57th Street

The *American Journal of Nursing* was begun in 1900 as the official journal of the Nurses' Associated Alumnae, with Sophia French Palmer as its editor. For more than ten years she used her own home as its office, not only editing the magazine but managing its business as well. Professional nurses felt that the publication was a necessary force to upgrade the training and practice of nursing, and in Palmer they had an editor who was well fitted to establish communication between nurses, keep them informed on vital social issues, and promote reforms in nursing education. She had previously been involved in training nurses at several hospitals, and for two years edited an earlier journal, *Trained Nurse and Hospital Review*. Many legislative reforms in the field resulted from her outspoken and informed editorials. She has been honored also by the naming of a library in her memory at Massachusetts General Hospital School of Nursing in Boston.

Quaile, Elizabeth. See Diller, Angela

Reid, Helen Rogers, 1882–1970, Newspaper Publisher; NAWM

Helen Reid Hall, Barnard College, Broadway at 188th Street

Helen Rogers Reid worked her way through Barnard College by tutoring, clerking, and housekeeping. Her first job after graduation was as social secretary to Elizabeth Mills Reid. Since the Reids' Madison Avenue mansion was the scene of many social gatherings, Helen came into contact with leaders of society. She spent some time in London, England, where Whitelaw Reid was ambassador to the Court of St. James. In 1911 she married the Reids' only son, Ogden Mills Reid. When her husband inherited the family paper, the *New York Tribune*, it was doing dismally, and Helen began to bring it back to life by working as an advertising solicitor. In 1924 she promoted its merger with the *Herald*. As vice president and then president of the *Herald Tribune*, she made the paper a powerful force in Republican politics. She had been committed to women's rights since her college days and she hired many women for the paper, including Clementine Paddleford as food writer, Irita Van Doren as literary editor, and Marie Mattingly Melonie to direct a forum on current problems. Dorothy Thompson was a columnist. Helen was a trustee of Barnard from 1914 to 1956. Helen Reid Hall, a dormitory, was opened in 1961.

Rice, Julia Barnett, 1860–1929, Antinoise Campaigner

Isaac L. Rice Mansion (Villa Julia), 346 W. 89th Street (Private); Landmark of New York, NR

Disturbed by the constant whistle blowing, bell ringing, and horn tootling of the boats on the nearby Hudson River, Julia Barnett Rice began a campaign against such unnecessary noise. She hired Columbia University students to count the whistles and discovered that in one place during an eight-hour stretch almost three thousand blasts were heard. The sounds were uncoordinated as to tone, duration, or meaning.

Rice, the wife of Isaac L. Rice, a well-to-do attorney, thought of moving from their elegant and distinguished home, but she found that the patients in hospitals on the East River suffered from the noise as much as she did. A physician herself (an 1885 graduate of the Woman's Medical College of the New York Infirmary), she felt that noise was not only troublesome but unhealthy. She appealed to municipal and state authorities. They were powerless. The Hudson River was a federal waterway and the steamboats, tugs, and other craft were not subject to local regulation. Julia wrote to her congressman, and he saw to it that a law was passed giving authority to the Board of Supervising Inspectors to punish unnecessary boat whistling. Rice then investigated other bothersome city noises and organized a national Antinoise Society, aided by some of the most distinguished men in the country, including Mark Twain and William Dean Howells. One of the society's triumphs was the marking of quiet zones around hospitals.[40]

Richman, Julia, 1855–1912, Educator; NAW

Julia Richman High School, 2nd Avenue and 67th Street

On her appointment as district superintendent of schools in 1903, Julia Richman was given her choice of districts. She chose the Jewish ghetto because of her sympathy for immigrant children who needed help with the difficult adjustment to life in the New World. She took up residence in the district. Her principals met in the "Teachers House" for conferences; some of the teachers, as well as three social workers, lived there. Richman had been a principal for nineteen years and was associated with the Educational Alliance, founded in 1889 to aid the Americanization of Jewish immigrants. As school superintendent she supervised fourteen day and night schools. She established a special school for delinquent children and separate classes for retarded and "defective" children. Seeing all about her a "life of degradation" that threatened the youth, she undertook neighborhood improvement programs, sometimes arousing opposition in the community because of her zeal for moral as well as social change. As one project, she set up an outdoor home for consumptives on unused ferry boats.[41]

Rockefeller, Abby Aldrich, 1874–1948, Lizzie Plummer Bliss, 1864–1931, and Mary Quinn Sullivan, 1877–1939, Art Patrons and Museum Founders; NAW

Museum of Modern Art, 11 W. 53rd Street

Abby Aldrich Rockefeller, Lizzie Plummer Bliss, and Mary Quinn Sullivan met at a now historic luncheon to talk about establishing a museum of modern art. All were collectors of paintings that others, including their own families, thought too outrageous to be hung on the walls of their homes, let alone a public gallery—such paintings as were being produced by Pierre-Auguste Renoir, Edgar Degas, Pablo Picasso, Paul Cézanne, and Vincent van Gogh.

Rockefeller was the wife of John D. Rockefeller, Jr., who hated modern art. She was careful to use her own money when she began collecting American paintings by such young artists as Winslow Homer and John Marin. She used her children's nursery (after they grew out of it) to display her collections. She added paintings of the modern French school, and soon she outgrew the space in her home. Bliss (named Lizzie but called Lillie) had been collecting the paintings of Arthur Bowen Davies, who helped form her taste. She owned in time twenty-seven Cézannes, many Georges Seurats, and the largest private collection of Arthur Davies. Sullivan, an artist and teacher of art, moved from her Indianapolis, Indiana, home to New York early in the twentieth century and became acquainted in art circles. She married Cornelius Sullivan in 1917 and in their home on Long Island they began to collect modern French paintings and sculpture.

The three women invited A. Conger Goodyear, a founder of the Albright Gallery of Buffalo, New York, to head their effort to launch the Museum of Modern Art. They opened the museum first in an office building in the year of the stock market collapse, 1929. Bliss died two years later, leaving the museum over one hundred pieces from her collection, with the condition that it be on a sound financial basis within three years. Six hundred thousand dollars were raised—in the midst of a depression—and the future of the museum was assured. In 1939 it moved to its present building. The sculpture garden occupies the site of Rockefeller's former home. Many of her paintings and drawings were left to the museum. Her collection of folk art is in another museum, one named for her, in Williamsburg, Virginia. Sullivan was one of the first trustees of the Museum of Modern Art. She opened her own gallery, after her husband's death, to exhibit paintings by talented young Americans. She sold his collection in 1937 and was preparing to put her own on the auction block but died before the sale. Rockefeller bought two of her paintings and donated them to the museum in memory of her friend.

The museum is open Mon., Tues., Fri., and Sat. 11–6, Thurs. 11–9, and Sun. 12–6; adm.

Roebling, Emily Warren, 1843–1903, Engineer, Lawyer, and Writer

Plaque, Northern Tower, Brooklyn Bridge

John Roebling, designer of the Brooklyn Bridge, died while in the early stages of its planning. His son, Washington Roebling, succeeded him as engineer, only to become bedridden as the result of "the bends" from spending too much time in the underwater caissons. Washington's wife, Emily Warren Roebling, watched the progress of construction through a telescope from their Brooklyn Heights home and described what she saw so accurately that Washington could continue to direct the work. She acted as his secretary and messenger and "smoothed over all friction between the municipal authorities, rival engineers, and ambitious men." She wrote articles for the Brooklyn papers defending her husband's controversial methods. Her knowledge of engineering impressed those who came to visit Washington.

Though Emily never bragged, she was not the self-effacing wife she has been called. She was one of the first women lawyers in New York, receiving a certificate of law from New York University. Her graduation essay was on "The Wife's Disabilities." She traveled widely, wrote articles and books, and was active in the Daughters of the American Revolution and a host of other patriotic associations. A resident of Trenton, New Jersey, she represented the women of New Jersey on the Board of Lady Managers of the World's Columbian Exposition in 1893. As for Washington, he recovered from his disability and survived Emily by more than twenty years.

The tablet on the bridge honors Washington and Emily Roebling. It was erected by the Brooklyn Engineers Club in 1951. The inscription ends, "Back of every great work we can find the self-sacrificing devotion of a woman." During the centennial observance of the Brooklyn Bridge in 1983, Emily's part in the construction was rediscovered. Citicorp, in conjunction with the National Women's Hall of Fame, established an annual national award, to be called an "Emily," for women who have excelled in business, science, or technology. Winner of the first Emily Award, 1984, was Muriel Siebert, president of her own financial firm. Citicorp also nominated Emily for the National Women's Hall of Fame.[42]

Roosevelt, (Anna) Eleanor, 1884–1962, Humanitarian; NAWM

Roosevelt Home (Sara Delano Roosevelt Memorial House), 47–49 E. 65th Street, at Park Avenue; Landmark of New York, NR

Anna Eleanor Roosevelt, one of the best-loved and best-known American women of the twentieth century, called this her home during one of the most frustrating periods of her life. Her mother-in-law, Sara Delano Roosevelt (1855–1941), had the double house built to share with her son, Franklin D. Roosevelt. Franklin and Eleanor moved into one side of the house in 1908, and Sara lived in the other until she died. Doors connected the interiors of the houses and were always open. Sara considered the Roosevelt children her own and tried to control every aspect of their upbringing. Eleanor bore it more or less patiently, partly because she truly felt inadequate as a wife and mother and partly because she feared losing her husband's affection if she put her foot down. She found satisfaction in activities outside her home. After women won the vote she took part in the League of Women Voters. She joined the Women's Trade Union League, developing friendships with labor leaders and social leaders who supported them. After Sara's death the Roosevelts left this house and it was bought for use by Hunter College students. Sara Delano Roosevelt is memorialized by a park between Chrystie and Forsyth, Canal and Houston, made in the 1930s by razing a line of buildings. See Hyde Park, NY.[43]

Sanger, Margaret Higgins, 1879–1966, Birth-control Pioneer, NAWM

Margaret Sanger Center, Planned Parenthood of New York City, Abraham Stone Memorial Library, 380 2nd Avenue. House, 17 W. 16th Street (Private); Landmark of New York

"When the history of our civilization is written," said H. G. Wells, "it will be a biological history and Margaret Sanger will be its heroine." While working as a nurse in the Lower East Side, Margaret Higgins Sanger was shocked by the suffering of tenement women. Many were forced into too-frequent pregnancies, all were worn out by caring for too-large families on too-small incomes, and some died from self-induced abortions. Although middle-class women seemed able to control family size by the few known methods of contraception, birth-control information was withheld from poor women and even physicians were ill informed about methods.

Sanger went abroad to find out what was known about contraceptives in Europe. On her return she began publication of an outspoken magazine, *The Woman Rebel*, but the post office would not accept it for mailing; it was labeled obscene. She wrote *Family Limitation*, with detailed discussion of birth-control techniques, but she was not allowed to distribute it. In 1916 she opened a clinic at 46 Amboy Street in Brownsville. It was closed by the police.

Sanger had enemies, but she also had many allies. Her sister Ethel Byrne was convicted and sent to the workhouse in 1917 for giving contraceptive advice. Juliet Rublee organized a Committee of One Hundred to free Byrne, and she helped to found the American Birth Control League in 1921. Hannah Stone supervised the Sanger birth-control clinic, after it was allowed to operate, and kept such careful records and statistics that many physicians were brought to approve birth control. After Stone's death in 1939 her husband, Abraham Stone, took her place as director of the clinic.

The house where Sanger lived in 1923 housed her famed clinic from 1930 to 1973. It is now a private residence. Sanger is a member of the National Women's Hall of Fame.

Schneiderman, Rose, 1892–1972, Labor Leader; NAWM

Plaque, Brown Building, Washington Place and Greene Street

Women jumped to their deaths from ninth-story windows; others, trapped behind closed doors, perished in the flames. Some fell from twisted and buckled fire escapes. In all, 146 workers died in the fire that broke out on March 25, 1911, at the Triangle Shirtwaist Factory, occupying the top stories of the Brown Building. The world was shocked by the tragedy, but it was outraged when the contributory causes to so much loss of life became known. There was no sprinkler system. Some doors were locked to keep workers in and union organizers out;

others opened inward and the press of frightened women kept them closed. The fire ladders reached only to the sixth floor; the fire was on the ninth.

At a memorial meeting for the victims, held by the New York Women's Trade Union League (WTUL), workers, officials, and well-meaning citizens listened to speakers calling for better factory inspections. A resolution called for a state agency to work on fire prevention. But union leaders wanted more than a resolution and charitable contributions. Rose Schneiderman, a tiny red-headed woman, rose to speak. A low-paid worker from the age of thirteen, she had gone into a cap factory as a sewing machine operator, joined a union, and begun to organize other workers. In a soft voice that somehow carried to the gallery, she spoke of the many workers who were maimed every year in unsafe factories, of starvation wages, and of police power used to put down the workers when they used the only means they had to protest, the strike. "I know from my experience," she finished, "it is up to the working people to save themselves. The only way they can save themselves is by a strong working-class movement."

A factory investigation commission was appointed, and a "golden age" of social legislation followed. The work week was cut down, child labor was outlawed, safety laws were enacted. Schneiderman went on organizing for the WTUL and then for the International Ladies' Garment Workers' Union, leading them in strike after strike to force better conditions for wage earners. Her activities brought her into association with Eleanor Roosevelt and with Frances Perkins, who had witnessed the Triangle Fire and worked with the factory commission before becoming U.S. secretary of labor. Schneiderman was appointed by President Franklin D. Roosevelt to the National Recovery Administration, and from 1937 to 1943 she was secretary of the New York State Department of Labor.

On the fiftieth anniversary of the Triangle Fire, March 25, 1961, the plaque was erected on a corner of the building. It was, in fact, a fireproof building, still standing, restored and used by New York University. Present at the dedication ceremony were elderly women survivors of the fire and Eleanor Roosevelt, Perkins, and Schneiderman. The plaque honors the dead women: "Out of their martyrdom came new concepts of social responsibility and labor legislation that have helped make American working conditions the finest in the world."[44]

Seton, Saint Elizabeth Ann, 1774–1821, Churchwoman; NAW

Shrine of Elizabeth Ann Seton, 7 State Street; Landmark of New York, NR. Elizabeth Seton Library, College of Mount St. Vincent, W. 261st Street and Palisade Avenue, Riverdale. Convent and Girls' School, 32 Prince Street, at Mott; Landmark of New York, NR

As the widow of a wealthy New York merchant, Elizabeth Ann Seton lived from 1801 to 1804 in a house where the shrine now stands, known as the James

Watson house. The fragile socialite then converted to the Catholic faith and moved with her five children to Maryland. There she took the vows of a nun and, as Mother Seton, founded the American branch of the Sisters of Charity. In 1975 she was canonized, America's first native-born saint.

A statue of her stands over the doorway of the church and a stained-glass window over the altar commemorates her life. The convent and school were founded by the Sisters of Charity and built in 1826 near old St. Patrick's, New York's first Roman Catholic cathedral. In 1856 the Sisters of Charity purchased Fonthill, a castle built for the actor Edwin Forrest, and used it as a library, named for Mother Seton, for the College of Mount St. Vincent. It is now an administration building. See Baltimore and Emmitsburg, MD, and Yonkers, NY.

Shaver, Dorothy, 1897–1959, Business Executive; NAWM

Dorothy Shaver Designer Rooms, Costume Institute, Metropolitan Museum of Art, 5th Avenue and 82nd Street

As director of interior decoration and fashion for Lord and Taylor, Dorothy Shaver worked directly with fashion designers and producers and formed a bureau of fashion advisors. She emphasized American fashions by designers Claire McCardell, Lilly Daché, and Rose Marie Reid. In 1945 she was made president of Lord and Taylor, remaining in office until her death fourteen years later. When she started as president, her annual salary was $110,000, and she was well worth it; profits soared. When she died, the city of New York, as a salute to her, planted trees along fifteen blocks of Fifth Avenue (42nd to 57th Streets). She was instrumental in forming the Costume Institute for the Metropolitan Museum. The Shaver Designer Rooms are open to those with special interest, by appointment.

Simkhovitch, Mary Kingsbury, 1867–1951, Social Worker; NAWM

Greenwich House, 27 Barrow Street

Greenwich House was founded by Mary Kingsbury Simkhovitch in 1902 as a cooperative social settlement. The Massachusetts-born wife of a Russian-born professor at Columbia University, Simkhovitch had served her apprenticeship in working with the poor. In Boston, Massachusetts, she was organist for a black church, where she learned that the primitive and unsanitary dwellings in the slums were owned by upstanding white members of exclusive churches. She had visited Denison House in Boston, and in New York she was head resident of the College Settlement House on Rivington Street in the Lower East Side. For three years she worked in a house supported by the Unitarian church, where she found its approach the direct opposite of her own beliefs. It emphasized religious and moral uplift rather than her concept of cooperation with neighborhood residents and openness to new, even radical, social theories.

In establishing Greenwich House she wanted to work closely with the people of the neighborhood so that when there was opportunity for change there would be real understanding of what was desirable and achievable. Her work supported a theater, a music school, neighborhood parks, and low-cost housing. She retired as director of the house in 1946 but continued to serve on the City Housing Authority.[45]

Stebbins, Emma, 1815–1882, Sculptor; NAW

Angel of the Waters, *Bethesda Fountain, Central Park, 5th Avenue and 72nd Street. Columbus Statue, Brooklyn Civic Center*

Emma Stebbins began studying sculpture in Italy at the age of forty-two. The *Angel of the Waters*, her most famous work, was made in her Rome studio and cast in Munich, Germany. When unveiled in 1873 it was hailed as a masterpiece. In Rome she met the actress Charlotte Cushman and they became lifelong friends. After Cushman's death, Stebbins spent several years writing a biography of her friend.

Stowe, Harriet Beecher. See Hall of Fame

Sullivan, Mary Quinn. See Rockefeller, Abby

Szold, Henrietta, 1860–1945, Zionist and Humanitarian; NAW

Tablet and Tree, Prospect Park, Brooklyn

The tablet marks an oak tree planted in 1936 in honor of Henrietta Szold. It is near the Payne monument on a hill east of the Long Meadow. Szold, of Baltimore, Maryland, was the organizer of the Jewish women's Hadassah. Her greatest accomplishment was the saving of thousands of children brought to Palestine from Germany and Poland through the Youth Aliyah during Hitler's rise to power. Many of them were the sole survivors of their families. A street in the Lower East Side is named for Szold. See Baltimore, MD, and Pittsburgh, PA.

Towle, Charlotte, 1896–1966, Social Worker; NAWM

Charlotte Towle Memorial Library, Spence-Chapin Services to Family and Children, 6 E. 94th Street

In naming their library for Charlotte Towle, the social work agency recognized her as a leader and innovator in her field. From the time of her graduation from

Goucher College in 1919 until her retirement from the School of Social Service Administration of the University of Chicago after thirty years there, she was working on solutions to the problem of man's relationship with himself and the world. Her *Common Human Needs* has been used as a textbook of social work since its publication.

Valle, Marta, d. 1975, Youth Leader

Marta Valle Junior High School, 145 Stanton Street

A tiny, dynamic woman with auburn hair and a sparkling sense of humor, Marta Valle grew up in Spanish Harlem, which she remembered as a small-townish place with friendly neighbors. She earned a master's degree in social work. In 1967, the city, which had hitherto planned services to Puerto Ricans with the government of Puerto Rico, made Valle their liaison between the city and the Puerto Rican community. It created the Youth Services Agency and appointed her its commissioner. After four years she left the post to direct continuing education at Columbia University's School of Social Work. She established Valle Consultants, a human relations research and advisory organization. She also founded the Puerto Rican Institute for Social Research and was at the time of her death its executive director.[46]

Wald, Lillian, 1867–1940, Nurse and Settlement House Founder; NAW

Henry Street Settlement, 263–267 Henry Street; Landmark of New York, NHL. Lillian D. Wald Playground, Monroe Street, East of Montgomery

Lillian Wald, trained as a nurse, felt impelled to do something to improve living conditions in the Lower East Side. She persuaded some friends to finance a small center for a volunteer nursing service, and the Henry Street Settlement opened in 1893. From that time until the present the settlement has grown into one of the great urban centers of social service. The original building on Henry Street developed into a complex of social and cultural institutions, including the Neighborhood Playhouse founded by the Lewisohn sisters and a music school founded by Grace Harriet Spofford (1887–1974, NAWM). The public health nurses, the first visiting nurses, lived at the house, forming a close circle of friendships, and from time to time the house had distinguished guests and residents. Jane Addams visited the settlement on trips from her pioneer Hull House in Chicago, Illinois.

Florence Kelley (1859–1932, NAW), who had lived at Hull House, came to Henry Street with her children in 1899 as head of the newly formed National Consumers' League, which prevailed on the public to buy only goods manufactured and sold under decent working conditions. She lived at Henry Street for more than twenty-five years. She would read the papers at breakfast and comment with biting wit about meaningless news reports while stories of human need were ignored.

In a flat next door to the settlement lived Leonora O'Reilly (1870–1927, NAW), who had begun life as a poor factory worker and rose to power as a trade union organizer. She and Wald in 1903 became executive council members of the new Women's Trade Union League, and O'Reilly became a spokesperson for the rights of labor.

Florence Kellor (1873–1952, NAWM) worked with Wald on problems of immigrants and promotion of naturalization, later becoming an expert in the field of industrial and international arbitration. She lived for years with another friend of the settlement, Mary Dreier (1875–1963, NAWM), who began her lifelong involvement in labor reform when she first met O'Reilly in 1899.

For some twenty years Lavinia Dock (1858–1956, NAWM) lived at the settlement. She had trained as a nurse at Bellevue Hospital, graduating in 1886, and wrote the standard nursing school text, *Materia Medica for Nurses* (1890). She superintended nurses' training at Johns Hopkins Medical School and at the Illinois Training School. In 1907 she and Adelaide Nutting published *A History of Nursing*, which for the first time gave women credit for their contributions to health care. From 1896, when she moved to Henry Street, until long after she left, Dock was increasingly involved in feminist causes.

These are only a few of the many women, some from the working class, others from wealthy families, who came to Henry Street as volunteers and formed a women's network of shared friendships, concerns, and activities. At the center of this vitality was Lillian Wald. She was elected in 1970 to the Hall of Fame for Great Americans, q.v.[47]

Wallace, Lila Acheson, 1889–1984, Publisher and Philanthropist

Lila Acheson Wallace Library, Juilliard School, Lincoln Center

Of her ninety-four years, Lila Acheson Wallace gave most of them to the creation of beauty. She helped save the ancient temple of Abu Simbel from the rising waters of the Nile. At the Bronx Zoo her World of Birds delights visitors. She made vast contributions to the Metropolitan Museum of Art and to the Juilliard School of Music. She was the main benefactor of the Monet gardens restoration in Giverny, France, and nearer home, in Garrison, New York, she restored the historical Boscobel to its early splendor. With her husband, DeWitt Wallace, she founded the *Readers' Digest*. She designed its headquarters in Pleasantville, New York, from its well-chosen paintings to its magnificent grounds.[48]

Warburg, Frieda Schiff, 1876–1958, Philanthropist

Sculpture Garden, Jewish Museum, 1109 5th Avenue, at 92nd Street

Frieda Schiff Warburg served on the board of the Jewish Theological Seminary of America and gave its gates in memory of her parents, Jacob and Therese Schiff. Her six-story mansion was given to the seminary for a Jewish museum in affirmation of her faith in "the fundamental traditions of Judaism and the contribution they can make to the solution of present-day problems." She and her husband, Felix M. Warburg, gave their Hartsdale, New York, estate, Woodlands, to a school district; it is called the Warburg Campus. Also with him she founded the Felix M. and Frieda Schiff Warburg Foundation.

The Jewish Museum, the world's largest repository of Jewish ceremonial art, is open Sun. 11–6, Mon.-Thurs. 12–5; closed some holidays; adm.[49]

Webb, Aileen Osborn, 1892–1979, Craft Organization Official

American Craft Museum, 44 W. 53rd Street

Aileen Osborn Webb was a guiding force in developing a national craft program which affects thousands of professional and avocational craftsmen. She founded the American Craftsmen's Council in the 1940s to provide education in handicrafts and to stimulate public interest in the work produced. The Craft Museum, opened in 1953 by the Council, serves as headquarters, exhibition space, a library, and the home of its publication, *American Crafts*. The museum is open Tues.-Sat. 10–5, Sun. 11–5; adm. The library is open Tues.-Fri. 12–4:30.[50]

Whitney, Gertrude Vanderbilt, 1875–1942, Sculptor, Art Patron, and Museum Founder, and Juliana Rieser Force, 1876–1948, Museum Director; NAW

Whitney Museum of American Art, 945 Madison Avenue, at 75th Street

Gertrude Vanderbilt Whitney was a sculptor of distinction. Among her sculptures in New York City are panels for the Victory Arch, the Washington Heights Memorial, and a statue of Peter Stuyvesant in Stuyvesant Square. She generously sponsored other American artists, buying and exhibiting their work, until she had built up a sizeable collection of contemporary art. She offered it in 1929 to the Metropolitan Museum of Art, which rejected it. She then founded and endowed the Whitney Museum.

The nucleus of the museum was an organization formed by Whitney and Juliana Rieser Force, first called the Friends of the Young Artists, then the Whitney Studio Club. Its four hundred members, active sponsors of liberal art, threw their support behind the new museum, which opened in Greenwich Village. Force, as its first director, stressed art research and a publication program to acquaint the public with what was new in the American art world. Such artists as John Sloan, Edward Hopper, and Reginald Marsh were thus given publicity. During the depression, Juliana helped organize the Public Works of Art program and encouraged state acquisition of works of art for public buildings.

The museum moved in 1966 to its present magnificent new structure. It is open Tues. 11–8, Wed.-Sat. 11–6, Sun. and holidays 12–6; adm.

Willard, Emma Hart. See Hall of Fame

Willard, Frances. See Hall of Fame

Wise, Louise Waterman, 1874–1947, Charitable Worker; NAW

Louise Wise Services, 12 E. 94th Street

Louise Waterman Wise was the wife of Rabbi Stephen S. Wise of the Free Synagogue, a leader in the crusade for clean government and social justice, and she shared his goals. Concerned for orphaned Jewish children who were placed in asylums because no agency handled adoptions by Jewish families, she established and headed for twenty-five years the Child Adoption Committee of the Free Synagogue. When Hitler began his persecution of German Jews, Wise founded and headed the women's division of the American Jewish Congress to alert the public to the dangers he posed. She opened refugee houses in New York where from 1933 to 1939 free food and shelter was given to some three thousand refugees from central and eastern Europe. After the war she worked with Jews who had survived the Holocaust. She was so offended by the British denial of immigration to Palestine that when the Foreign Office offered her a decoration in 1946 for her wartime services she refused it. Louise Wise Services continues the work of the Child Adoption Committee, adapted to present-day needs.

Zenger, Anna Catharine Maul, 1704–1751, Publisher

Zenger Room, Federal Hall National Memorial, 28 Wall Street, at Nassau Street; Landmark of New York, NHL

The Zenger Room is a memorial to freedom of the press. As publisher of the *New York Journal*, Peter Zenger exposed government corruption, so incensing the colonial governor and council that in 1734 he was arrested for libel. Without money for bail, he was in jail for ten months before the trial. His wife, Anna Catharine Maul Zenger, saw that the paper came out and earned enough income to support their six children. Peter was defended by lawyer Alexander Hamilton and acquitted, the first great American victory for a free press. He died in 1746 and Anna continued to publish the weekly paper and a number of books. When one of the sons was old enough to take her place, she continued to run a shop, selling books and miscellaneous items. Federal Hall is open Memorial Day–Labor Day, daily 9–4:30, rest of year closed weekends.[51]

OGDENSBURG

Farnham, Sally James, 1876–1943, Sculptor

Soldiers and Sailors Monument, Library Park

Sally James Farnham was born in Ogdensburg. She taught herself sculpture, and her talent led to encouragement from Frederic Remington and other artists. She executed a number of statues in public places, including an equestrian statue of Simón Bolívar in New York City's Central Park, a Civil War memorial in Rochester, New York, and another Soldiers and Sailors Monument in Bloomfield, New Jersey. The Ogdensburg monument, honoring soldiers and sailors of the Town of Oswegatchie who served in the Civil War, was erected in 1905.[52]

PENN YAN

Wilkinson, Jemima, 1752–1819, Religious Leader; NAW

Markers, State 54, Nine Miles South of Penn Yan, and State 14, Five Miles South of Dresden

Penn Yan is in Jerusalem Township, which was home to Jemima Wilkinson after 1794. At the age of twenty-three, at her home in Rhode Island, Wilkinson fell into a deep trance. Thirty-six hours later she revived, told people she had been taken to heaven, had spoken to God, and was now a spirit named Public Universal Friend. For the next twelve years she traveled about New England preaching her gospel, which derived from Quaker belief in simple living and celibacy as the highest standard of life. In 1790 she joined a group of her disciples near Seneca Lake in New York, where almost three hundred believers were clearing land and building homes. Wilkinson herself moved farther west a few years later to Keuka Lake to establish New Jerusalem. As with all such religious leaders, a certain amount of derogatory folklore grew up around her name, but she is remembered around Yates County as a good woman, a leader of her people, a friend to the Indians, and a significant factor in settling western New York. After her death the group of believers gradually disintegrated.

POUGHKEEPSIE

Flanagan, Hallie Ferguson (Davis), 1890–1969, Theater Educator; NAWM

Flanagan Theater, Vassar College

Hallie Ferguson Flanagan taught at Vassar College from 1925 until 1935, when she left to head up the Federal Theater Project under the Works Progress Administration, and again from 1939, when Congress terminated the project, until 1942. The project, established to provide jobs for theater people during the depression, became under Flanagan a daring network of regional theaters fostering the best work of native playwrights and contributing immeasurably to the vitality of the American theater. At Vassar, Flanagan established the Experimental Theater. She married Vassar's Professor Philip H. Davis. Both Vassar and Smith College (where she taught from 1942 until 1955) have named theaters for her.

PRATTSBURG

Whitman, Narcissa Prentiss, 1808–1847, Missionary; NAW

Narcissa Prentiss Home, Mill Pond Road. Plaque, Franklin Academy. Hall, Prattsburg Presbyterian Church

Narcissa Prentiss Whitman, born here on a March day in 1808, was destined to travel far from home, to help open the West to immigration, and to die a martyr to her religion. In 1836 Narcissa married Marcus Whitman, a physician who had just returned from a trip to the Pacific Northwest and was fired with enthusiasm for establishing a mission among the Oregon Indians. Whitman, deeply religious, was eager to accompany her new husband to the West, although no white women, and few white men, had ever attempted the journey. For most of the route, there were no roads and no maps. The trip would have to be made on horseback or on foot, through country inhabited by Indians.

Another couple accompanied the Whitmans, Henry and Eliza Spalding (1807–1851, NAW). The two women made history on their journey across the plains and Rocky Mountains. Both kept journals and wrote vivid letters home which have been preserved as a remarkable record of the six-month trip. On arrival in the Oregon country they went to separate missions, Narcissa to Waiilatpu (now in Washington State) and Eliza to Lapwai (now Idaho). They built homes, cultivated the land, and set up schools. Marcus treated the Indians who were ill or injured. In 1843, largely due to Marcus's influence, the great westward migration of Americans began. An epidemic of measles brought to the Whitman mission by immigrants killed many of the Indian children, who had no immunity to the disease. The Indians believed Marcus's medicines were causing the deaths. In 1847 a band of Cayuse fell upon the Whitman household, brutally killing Marcus and Narcissa and twelve others.

In 1936 Narcissa's childhood home was restored as a shrine to the martyred pioneer. It is now the property of the Presbyterian Board of National Missions. The road from Prattsburg to Naples (State 53) has been named the Narcissa Prentiss Highway, and from Prattsburg to Kanona it is the Spalding-Whitman Highway. A memorial garden at the house is planted with shrubs sent by a group of Cayuse Indians, descendants of those the Whitmans had converted to Christianity. The home is open during the summer months, Fri.-Sun. 1–5.[53]

ROCHESTER

Anthony, Susan Brownell, 1820–1906, Suffrage Leader (NAW), and Her Sister Mary Anthony, 1827–1907, School Administrator

Susan B. Anthony Memorial, 17 Madison Street; NHL. Anthony Memorial, University of Rochester. Marker, Thruway, Westbound, at Seneca Service Station

Susan Brownell Anthony never owned a home of her own. The family home on Madison Street was left to Mary Anthony, her younger sister, friend, and supporter. Mary attended the Seneca Falls convention in 1848, and when she returned home she spoke enthusiastically of Elizabeth Cady Stanton and the other leaders in the new woman's movement. From that time on she was an activist, though overshadowed by her sister's fame. For many years she was principal of a school in Rochester. She held positions in the city and state suffrage organizations, wrote for newspapers, and spoke for the cause. From 1897 until 1907 she paid taxes on the house under protest, because she was "taxed without representation."

In 1850 Susan met Stanton, beginning a lifelong friendship and a dedication, for both, to the cause of women's equality. They appeared before legislative committees to persuade them to give women the same voting rights men had. Stanton, married and with children, did much of the writing, while Susan, single and free, arranged meetings, secured speakers, raised money, and organized women around the country.

Susan spent her last years, when not traveling, in the Rochester home with Mary. Both campaigned to have women accepted at the University of Rochester. Here Ida B. Harper came to write the *Life of Susan B. Anthony*. Here also came Adelaide Johnson, the sculptor, to do portrait busts of Susan and Stanton. In 1905 the aging sisters traveled to Oregon and California. Susan died in the Rochester home the following year, and Mary did not live long after that.

Rochester has many memorials to Susan. The building at the University of Rochester was named for her in 1914. A tree and plaque in Seneca Park bear her name. A window in the A.M.E. Zion Church commemorates her. Every year the city celebrates her birthday. The old home is open Wed.-Sat. 1–4, except holidays; adm. See New York City (Hall of Fame) and Washington, DC (under Adelaide Johnson).

SARATOGA SPRINGS

Scribner, Lucy Skidmore, 1853–1931, College Founder

Scribner Library, Skidmore College

Skidmore College, founded by Lucy Skidmore Scribner, widow of John Blair Scribner, began as a club for working women. In 1904 she built a clubhouse where they could study and socialize, with classes in music, domestic science, literature, stenography, and physical culture—a nice mix of practical and mind-stretching courses. Needing more space, she bought the former Temple Grove Seminary, which then became the Skidmore School of the Arts, a memorial to her parents. The school was accredited as a college in 1916 and gave its first degrees in 1919. Three years later its name was changed to Skidmore College.

Trask, Kate Nichols, 1853–1922, Author; NAW

Yaddo, Union Avenue

Each year a select group of serious artists, writers, and composers comes to the fifty-five room Gothic mansion at Yaddo to work without cost or disturbance. The woman who created this retreat was Kate Nichols Trask. Kate adopted the name of Katrina when she began writing poetry and novels. She and her husband, Spencer Trask (chairman of the *New York Times* publishing company), knew many of the literary figures of the day and entertained them at their three-hundred-acre estate in Saratoga Springs. Spencer was accidentally killed in 1909 and Katrina continued plans they had begun together to make their home an artists' colony. She was married in 1921 to George Foster Peabody, who agreed with her plans for Yaddo. Four years after her death Yaddo began receiving its first resident guests.

The colony's first executive director was Elizabeth Ames (d. 1977). It was due to her sensitivity and giftedness that the colony is "magical," in the words of John Cheever, one of its guests. Ames did not like to call it a colony or retreat. She thought of it as "a splendid private home, where a small 'house party' of friends may feel wholly at ease to work or play, as the mood suggests." She started the annual music festivals at Yaddo and made the institution an integral part of the Saratoga Springs community. Rose gardens only are open to visitors, daily, dawn to dusk.[54]

Walworth, Ellen Hardin, 1832–1915, Clubwoman; NAW

Walworth Museum, The Casino, Congress Park

Ellen Hardin Walworth's life was one of public leadership and private tragedy. After freeing herself from an abusive and unstable husband, she supported herself and eight children by operating the family homestead, Pine Grove, as a girls' boarding school and summer hotel. Her elder son, intercepting threatening letters from his father to Ellen, shot and killed his father, for which he was sentenced to life imprisonment. After years of effort, during which she studied law, Ellen was able to secure his release.

In spite of this personal turmoil and heavy responsibility, Walworth was involved in much public activity. As a member of the Saratoga Monument Association she helped to identify and mark sites of the Battle of Saratoga. In the 1880s she moved to Washington, D.C., where she secured a government job. A founder of the Daughters of the American Revolution, she served as its first secretary general and editor of its magazine. She was one of the first to urge the establishment of a national archives.

Pine Grove, which had been in the family for four generations, was demolished in 1955. A number of the rooms and their furnishings were removed to the Casino, where they form the Walworth Museum. Operated by the Saratoga Springs Historical Society, it is open July-Aug., daily 9:30–4:30, Sept.-Oct., Mon.-Sat. 10–4, Sun. 1–4; Nov.–Memorial Day, Wed.-Sun. 1–4; adm.[55]

SENECA FALLS

The National Women's Hall of Fame, 76 Fall Street

The National Women's Hall of Fame was established "to honor in perpetuity those women, citizens of the United States of America, whose contributions to the arts, athletics, business, education, government, the humanities, philanthropy and science, have been of greatest value for the development of their country." It was founded in Seneca Falls, considered the cradle of feminism in the United States because it was here that the first woman's rights convention was held. The first honors ceremony of the Hall of Fame was held in 1973, with twenty women chosen for permanent honor. Fifteen others had been added by 1985. Almost all are noted elsewhere in this guide.

Humanitarianism: Clara Barton, Dorothea Dix, Mary Harris (Mother) Jones, Lucretia Mott, Margaret Sanger, Sojourner Truth, Harriet Tubman

Government: Abigail Adams, Susan B. Anthony, Carrie Chapman Catt, Belva Lockwood, Alice Paul, Frances Perkins, Eleanor Roosevelt, Margaret Chase Smith, Elizabeth Cady Stanton

Athletics: Mildred (Babe) Zaharias

Education: Jane Addams, Mary McLeod Bethune, Helen Keller, Juliette Gordon Low, Elizabeth Bayley Seton

Science: Elizabeth Blackwell, Rachel Carson, Amelia Earhart, Alice Hamilton, Margaret Mead, Florence Sabin, Helen Brooke Taussig

Arts: Marian Anderson, Pearl Buck, Mary Cassatt, Emily Dickinson, Helen Hayes, Bessie Smith

The hall occupies a remodeled bank building and has educational exhibits pertaining to the feminist world. It is open May-Oct., Mon.-Fri. 10–4, Sat.-Sun. 12–4; Nov.-Apr., Mon.-Fri. 10–4, Sat. 12–4; closed some holidays; adm.[56]

Bloomer, Amelia Jenks, 1818–1894, Journalist and Women's Rights Leader; NAW

Amelia Bloomer House, 53 E. Bayard Street, in Women's Rights National Historical Park; NR

Dexter Bloomer, postmaster of Seneca Falls, appointed his wife, Amelia Jenks Bloomer, a deputy postmaster. She was a leader of a temperance group and publisher of its paper, the *Lily*. In addition to temperance news she published feminist articles, some written by her neighbor Elizabeth Cady Stanton. Early in 1851 Stanton and her cousin Elizabeth Smith Miller dropped into the deputy postmaster's office, also the publishing office of the *Lily*, both wearing a strange costume, a short skirt over ankle-length pantalettes. They were enthusiastic about the comfort of the dress, and Amelia described it in the next issue of her paper. Newspapers copied her article, subscribers wrote for patterns, and the dress, dubbed the Bloomer, became a fad. It was adopted by most of the leading advocates of women's rights, including Amelia, and some continued to wear the bloomers for several years, despite ridicule, not only for comfort but as a symbol of freedom from society's restrictions on women.

Amelia and Dexter moved West in 1853, settling finally in Council Bluffs, Iowa. The Seneca Falls house is part of the Women's Rights National Historical Park.

Stanton, Elizabeth Cady, 1815–1902, Women's Rights Leader; NAW

Stanton House, 32 Washington Street, in Women's Rights National Historical Park; NHL

Elizabeth Cady Stanton had rebelled against the role assigned to women since girlhood, and when she married Henry Stanton she insisted on leaving out the word "obey" from her marriage vows. Immediately after their wedding the Stantons attended an antislavery convention in London, England, where, much to their surprise and indignation, women were not allowed to take part. She discussed this outrage with another attendant, Lucretia Mott, a Quaker minister from Pennsylvania. "We resolved," she wrote, "to hold a convention as soon as we returned home, and form a society to advocate the rights of women." Eight years passed without their being able to follow up on this resolve, eight years of housekeeping and babies for Stanton. Then Mott came to nearby Waterloo, New York, to visit a cousin, Martha C. Wright. Jane Hunt, also of Waterloo, invited Stanton to spend the day with her, Mott, Wright, and another neighbor, Mary Ann McClintock.

In the company of these warm, intelligent Quaker women, Stanton was moved to express her feelings. "I poured out," she wrote, "the torrent of my long-accumulating discontent, with such vehemence and indignation that I stirred myself, as well as the rest of the party, to do and dare anything." Forthwith, the five women decided to call a woman's rights convention. They wrote a notice and published it the next day, July 14, 1848, in the *Seneca County Courier*, calling a convention at the Wesleyan Chapel in Seneca Falls for July 19 and 20.

The next step was to prepare a declaration to be presented to the convention, provided anyone came. While they discussed it, Stanton began to read aloud the Declaration of Independence. Why not adapt this listing of the wrongs of the American colonists to the wrongs of American women and call it a Declaration of Principles? Stanton was elected to formulate the document.

Three hundred men and women came to the meeting. After two days of speeches, sixty-eight women and thirty-two men signed their names to the Declaration of Principles. The woman's rights movement was on its way.

Nobody thought to preserve or commemorate the scene of this historical event. The Wesleyan Chapel, 126 Fall Street, became an opera house, a movie theater, a car dealership, and a laundromat. At last the Seneca Falls Historical Society erected a bronze tablet commemorating the convention. The State Department of Education erected a plaque in front of the Stanton house. In 1978 a couple from Seattle, Washington, came to visit Seneca Falls and saw a "For Sale" sign on the house. "We couldn't believe a national landmark could just be sold," they said. They bought it and installed a caretaker while they planned a museum. The following year the Elizabeth Cady Stanton Foundation was formed to preserve the home, the chapel, and the nearby houses of Amelia Bloomer and, in Waterloo, the homes of Jane Hunt and Mary Ann McClintock.

Legislation establishing the Women's Rights National Historical Park was signed December 28, 1980. The Park Service acquired the Stanton house and the Wesleyan chapel. The Bloomer, Hunt, and McClintock houses (see Waterloo, NY) are included in the park. As they are restored, they will be open for visits. The visitor center, on Fall Street, is open Mon.-Fri. 9–5, Sat. 10–4, Sun. 12–4. During June, July, and Aug., park rangers conduct tours of the park sites that are open. In addition, the Seneca Falls Historical Society, 55 Cayuga Street, maintains a museum with memorabilia of the woman's rights leaders. See (for Stanton), Tenafly, NJ, and Washington, DC (under Adelaide Johnson). Stanton is in the National Women's Hall of Fame.[57]

SHERWOOD

Howland, Emily, 1827–1929, Educator and Reformer; NAW

Emily Howland Elementary School, Southern Cayuga Central School

At the age of twenty-nine, Quaker abolitionist Emily Howland declared her independence. She had dutifully attended female academies, performed female chores, and accompanied her father to antislavery meetings. Her mother, who was in poor health, was unapproachable, but a dutiful daughter could not be independent without permission, not in 1857. So Howland wrote to her mother. "May I," she asked, "give a little of my life to degraded humanity?... May I try if I really can to make the world a little better for having lived in it?... [I]f all my life is to go on as have the last ten years, I know I shall feel at the end of it as tho' I had lived in vain." The opportunity that had come to her was to take ailing Myrtilla Miner's place as principal of the Miner school for Negro girls in Washington (see Washington, DC). Howland won her way, ran the school for two years, then came home until 1863. She then went again to Washington to help with the black refugees from the South, crowded into squalid camps under government supervision. Before she left there she persuaded her father to buy four hundred acres on the Potomac River to settle black families. She came home again in 1865, nursed her mother through her last illness, and remained to keep house for her father. He died when she was in her forties, leaving her a wealthy mistress of the family estate. She donated land and built a new school for the Quaker Sherwood School, then served as its director and chief support for forty-two years. It later became part of the public school system and was then given her name. She wrote her own epitaph: "I strove to realize myself and to serve." A niece added these words on the grave marker: "Purposes nobly fulfilled."[58]

SYRACUSE

Greenwood, Marion, 1909–1970, Muralist

Mural, Slocum Hall Lobby, Syracuse University

Marion Greenwood is best known for her great murals in Morelia and Mexico City, Mexico. She first went across the border into Mexico in the 1930s and met Pablo O'Higgins, an expatriate American artist, who introduced her to fresco painting. She loved the Mexican people and studied the history of the country in the course of her work. Revolutionary in spirit and influenced by the Mexican muralists Orozco and Diego Rivera, she was commissioned by the Mexican government to do several murals. When she returned to the United States she painted some of the New Deal art projects; most of them have, sadly, been painted over or changed in design by bureaucrats. The wall painting at Syracuse, executed in 1965, was dedicated to women of the world.[59]

TROY

Sage, Margaret Olivia Slocum, 1828–1918, Philanthropist NAW

Russell Sage College, College Street

On her way from her home in Syracuse, New York, to Mount Holyoke Seminary, Margaret Olivia Slocum Sage fell ill at Troy and when she recovered was persuaded to enroll instead in the Troy Female Seminary. She graduated in 1847. Twenty-two years later she married Russell Sage, whose first wife had been a classmate at the seminary, and who had recently moved to New York City, where he was a highly successful businessman. Olivia was interested in supporting many charities, but she had a hard time getting Russell to part with money for any of them. He did give a dormitory to Emma Willard's seminary. In 1906, when he died, Olivia found herself one of the wealthiest women in the country. Her first use of the money was to endow the Russell Sage Foundation for the improvement of living conditions in the United States. She purchased Constitution Island, in the Hudson River off West Point, to give to the military academy, preserving the home of writers Susan and Anna Warner (see West Point, NY). In 1910 she provided a new campus to Troy Seminary—now the Emma Willard School—and several years later used the old campus for Russell Sage College. By the time of her death her benefactions equaled those of the great spenders Andrew Carnegie, John D. Rockefeller, and J. P. Morgan.

Willard, Emma Hart, 1787–1870, Educator; NAW

Emma Willard School, Pawling and Elm Grove Avenues; NR.
Willard Library, 2nd Street

When she opened her school in 1821, Emma Hart Willard called it the Troy Female Seminary, and she assured the New York legislature that she wished to produce "no college bred females" and that "public speaking forms no part of female education." She came to New York from Vermont hoping to get state support for a school for women. No such support was forthcoming, but her *Plan for Improving Female Education*, which she presented to the legislature, is a classic document in the history of women's education in America. Despite her disclaimers about the kind of training her school would offer, Willard did in fact provide a serious course of study that could match that available to many college men. It included science, mathematics, history, languages, and literature, as well as the womanly arts of household management and moral behavior. Its chief product was teachers, who carried Willard's respect for learning throughout the United States. A distinguished alumna (class of 1832) was Elizabeth Cady Stanton. She described Willard as a splendid-looking woman who "fully realized my idea of a queen." In 1895 the seminary was renamed the Emma Willard School. It moved to its present location in 1910. Willard was nominated to the Hall of Fame in New York City in 1905.

WATERLOO

Hunt, Jane, fl. 1840s, Feminist

Hunt House, 401 E. Main Street, in Women's Rights National Historical Park; NR

The home of Jane Hunt was the site of the meeting in July 1848 at which five Quaker women reformers met and decided to call a convention to discuss the inequities and indignities suffered by the sex. The call to the Seneca Falls convention was drafted here. The mahogany table around which the women sat is now one of the treasures in the Smithsonian Institution.

McClintock, Mary Ann, fl. 1830–1870s, Feminist

McClintock House, 16 E. Williams Street, in Women's Rights National Historical Park; NR

A second meeting of the five women who called the Seneca Falls convention is thought to have been held at the McClintock house. Elizabeth Cady Stanton read her Declaration of Principles which was to be presented at the convention: "We hold these truths to be self-evident: . . . The history of mankind is a history of repeated injuries and usurpations on the part of man toward woman, having in direct object the establishment of an absolute tyranny over her." It went on to present facts ranging over every aspect of woman's status. Mary Ann McClintock was later a resident of Philadelphia, Pennsylvania, where in 1873 her son-in-law helped open to women students the Pennsylvania College of Dental Surgery.[60]

WEST POINT

Corbin, Margaret Cochran, 1751–c. 1800, Revolutionary War Heroine; NAW

Monument, West Point Cemetery

On November 16, 1776, Margaret (Molly) Cochran Corbin was by the side of her husband, an artilleryman, during the Hessian assault on Fort Washington (see New York City). When he was fatally wounded, she stepped into his place and served his gun until she, too, was shot. In 1779 she was awarded a soldier's half pay and enrolled in the Invalid Regiment, created for those injured in the service. She lived for some years in West Point, where the regiment was garrisoned. She was a familiar sight here, treated with affection and respect. She reserved the right to receive the customary ration of rum or whiskey from the commissary. The Invalid Regiment was disbanded in 1783 and Corbin's later years are undocumented. According to one story, she went back to Pennsylvania, where she was born, and died there in 1800. Her story has been confused with that of another Pennsylvania heroine, Molly Pitcher (see Chambersburg, PA). It is more likely that Corbin remained near West Point and died in Highland Falls. In 1926 the Daughters of the American Revolution arranged for the removal of her remains from Highland Falls to West Point and marked her grave with a monument.[61]

Warner, Susan Bogert, 1819–1885, Author, and Her Sister Anna Bartlett Warner, 1824–1915, Gardener and Author

Warner House and Anna B. Warner Memorial Garden, Constitution Island, East Bank of Hudson River, Opposite West Point; NHL

Susan Bogert Warner sent the manuscript of her first book to a number of publishers. A reader at Carter's wrote on it, ''Fudge.'' Putnam's took a chance on it. Entitled *The Wide Wide World*, it came out in 1851, and more than one generation of little girls read and reread it. It was the first book by an American to sell a million copies. Critics called it ''a swamp of lachrymosita,'' ''a malarial book,'' and other unkind names, but it appealed to its readers, and its writer sent out more books like it, one or more every year, for thirty years. She sometimes used the pen name of Elizabeth Wetherell. Her sister Anna Bartlett Warner tended her garden, wrote *Gardening by Myself*, and composed the well-known hymns ''Jesus Loves Me, This I Know'' and ''Jesus Bids Us Shine.'' Her pen name was Amy Lothrop.

For all their activity, the sisters never grew rich. Anna outlived Susan by thirty years, refusing to sell Constitution Island, for they had always planned that it would become part of the West Point military reservation. Margaret Olivia Slocum Sage (see Troy, NY) bought the island and gave it to the government in 1908, reserving Anna's right to live in the home. The fifteen-room house, with the family possessions, Anna's garden, and the Revolutionary War monuments on the island may be visited from mid-June to Oct. Guided tours leave the West Point South Dock on Wed. and Thurs. at 1 and 2 P.M. for two-hour visits. Reservations are required. Call 914–446–8676, Mon.-Fri. 10–11:30 or write Constitution Island Association, Box 41, West Point, NY 10996.[62]

YONKERS

Seton, Saint Elizabeth Ann, 1774–1821, Churchwoman; NAW

Elizabeth Seton College, 1061 Broadway

When Elizabeth Seton College, a small Catholic college, was founded in 1961, it chose the name of Mother Seton, founder of the first American sisterhood, the Sisters of Charity. She was beatified in 1963 and in 1975 was canonized. See Baltimore and Emmitsburg, MD, and New York City.

NOTES

In addition to the sources listed below, I have had help from the Storm King Art Center, Mountainsville; the Manhattanville College Library; Upstate Medical Center, State University of New York, Syracuse; the New York State Historic Trust, Department of Parks and Recreation; Wayne County Historical Society; Schoharie County Historical Society; Oswego County Historical Society; the Finger Lakes Library System, Ithaca. In New York City, I had help from the Schomburg Center for Research in Black Culture; Park Avenue Christian Church; the New York Convention and Visitors Bureau; Greensward Foundation; New York University Hall of Fame; New York Landmarks Conservancy; and the New York City Landmarks Preservation Commission. I am grateful to the New-York Historical Society for the use of its collections.

1. Cecil R. Roseberry, *The Capitol Story* (Albany, N.Y.: State of New York, 1964); L. P. Brockett, *Woman's Work in the Civil War* (Philadelphia, Pa.: Zeigler, McCurdy & Co., 1867).
2. Marion E. Gridley, *America's Indian Statues* (Chicago, Ill.: Amerindian, 1966); correspondence and brochures, Shrine of North American Martyrs.
3. Brochure, Madam Brett Homestead.
4. Jeanne M. Weimann, *The Fair Women* (Chicago, Ill.: Academy Chicago, 1981); correspondence, Lockwood Memorial Library, State University of New York at Buffalo.
5. Correspondence, Lockwood Memorial Library.
6. *Women and the American Revolution*, comp. Mollie Somerville (National Society, Daughters of the American Revolution, 1974); *Liberty's Women*, ed. Robert McHenry (Springfield, Mass.: G. & C. Merriam Co., 1980).
7. Elizabeth P. Gordon, *The Story of the Life and Work of Cordelia A. Greene* (Castile, N.Y.: Castilian, 1925); correspondence, Greene Library.
8. Jeanne L. Gardner, *Mary Jemison, Seneca Captive* (New York: Harcourt Brace & World, 1966); brochure, Letchworth State Park.
9. *Life and Gospel Experience of Mother Ann Lee*, quoted in Robert Peel, *Mary Baker Eddy: The Years of Discovery* (New York: Holt, Rinehart & Winston, 1966).
10. Clinton Van Zandt Hawn, "The Mary Imogene Bassett Hospital," in Louis C. Jones, *Cooperstown* (Cooperstown, N.Y.: New York State Historical Association, 1982); correspondence and clippings, New York State Historical Association.
11. Ralph Birdsall, *The Story of Cooperstown* (Cooperstown, N.Y.: Augur's Bookstore, 1948); correspondence, New York State Historical Association.
12. Geoffrey C. Ward, "Eleanor Roosevelt at Val-Kill," *Smithsonian* 15 (Oct. 1984).

13. *New York Times*, Mar. 8, 1977; *Current Biography*, 1949 and 1977.

14. "Martha Van Rensselaer," *Journal of Home Economics* 24 (Sept. 1932).

15. Correspondence, Johnstown Public Library.

16. Donald Zochert, *Laura: The Life of Laura Ingalls Wilder* (Chicago, Ill.: Henry Regnery Co., 1976).

17. Jane H. Kay, "Last of the Shakers," *Historic Preservation* 34 (Mar.-Apr. 1982).

18. *The Hall of Fame for Great Americans at New York University*, rev. ed., ed. Theodore Mello (New York: New York University Press, 1967).

19. Harmon H. Goldstone and Martha Dalrymple, *History Preserved: A Guide to New York City Landmarks and Historic Districts* (New York: Simon & Schuster, 1974); correspondence, Staten Island Historical Society Library.

20. *New York Times*, Sept. 29, 1976.

21. *New York Times*, May 29, 1962; *Current Biography*, 1962.

22. *New York Times*, Feb. 14, 1977; *Current Biography*, 1955.

23. Edna Huntington, *Historical Markers and Monuments in Brooklyn* (New York: Long Island Historical Society, 1952). Historians now say the house at 197 Amity Street, not 426 Henry, was Jennie's birthplace.

24. Virginia S. Eifert, *Tall Trees and Far Horizons* (New York: Dodd, Mead & Co., 1965); Arthur E. Peterson, *Historic Queens* (New York: 1924).

25. *New York Times*, May 1, 1973.

26. *New Yorker*, Sept. 20, 1958, pp. 33–34.

27. Goldstone and Dalrymple, op. cit.

28. Michele Clark, "Afterword," in Mary Wilkins Freeman, *The Revolt of Mother and Other Stories* (Old Westbury, N.Y.: Feminist Press, 1974).

29. *New York Times*, Nov. 16, 1971.

30. Nardi R. Campion and Rosamond W. Stanton, *Look to This Day! The Lively Education of a Great Woman Doctor: Connie Guion, M.D.* (Boston, Mass.: Little, Brown & Co., 1964); *New York Times*, Apr. 30, 1971.

31. *New York Times*, June 19, 1982; *Current Biography*, 1974 and 1982.

32. *New York Times*, Aug. 26, 1973.

33. *New York Times*, Sept. 24, 1962 and Nov. 19, 1977.

34. Charlotte S. Rubinstein, *American Women Artists* (New York: Avon Books, 1982).

35. Gerard R. Wolfe, *New York: A Guide to the Metropolis* (New York: New York University Press, 1975).

36. Fred W. McDarrah, *Museums in New York*, 4th ed. (New York: A Frommer Book, Simon & Schuster, 1983); *New York Times*, Feb. 16, 1948.

37. Margaret Mead, *Blackberry Winter: My Earlier Years* (New York: Simon & Schuster, 1972); clippings and correspondence, American Museum of Natural History.

38. Sally Smith Booth, *The Women of '76* (New York: Hastings House, 1973).

39. Marjorie Nickerson, *A Long Way Forward: The First Hundred Years of the Packer Collegiate Institute* (New York: Packer Collegiate Institute, 1945); *A Marianne Moore Reader* (New York: Viking Press, 1961); correspondence, Packer Collegiate Institute.

40. Mary S. Logan, *The Part Taken by Women in American History* (New York: Perry-Nalle, 1912; repr. 1972).

41. *Julia Richman: Two Biographical Appreciations of the Great Educator, by Her Sisters*, 1961, repr. in *Lives to Remember*, ed. Leo Stein (New York: Arno Press, 1974).

42. Logan, op. cit.; Richard Stengel, "A Birthday Portfolio for the Brooklyn Bridge,"

Smithsonian 14 (Apr. 1983); Edna Huntington, op. cit.; correspondence, National Women's Hall of Fame and Josephine Haggerty, Brooklyn Bridge Centennial Commission.

43. Ronald Sanders and Edmund V. Gillon, Jr., *The Lower East Side* (New York: Dover Publications, 1979).

44. Ibid.; Schneiderman, *All for One* (New York: Paul S. Eriksson, Inc., 1967); Barbara M. Wertheimer, *We Were There: The Story of Working Women in America* (New York: Pantheon Books, 1977); *New York Times*, Mar. 25 and 26, 1961; correspondence, International Ladies Garment Workers Union.

45. *Current Biography*, 1943.

46. *New York Times*, Nov. 21, 1975.

47. Beatrice Siegel, " 'Family' of Nurses Fight for Justice," *New Directions for Women*, Mar.-Apr. 1983; *New York Times*, Sept. 7, Oct. 30, and Nov. 8, 1970.

48. Rita Reif, "Lila N. A. Wallace, Portrait of a Great Patron," *New York Times*, May 12, 1977; *Reader's Digest* 125 (July 1984).

49. Stephen Birmingham, *"Our Crowd": The Great Jewish Families of New York* (New York: Harper & Row, 1967); *New York Times*, Sept. 15, 1958.

50. McDarrah, *Museums; Current Biography*, 1958.

51. Ellen M. Oldham, "Early Women Printers of America," *Boston Public Library Quarterly*, Jan., Apr., and July 1958, repr. in *Lives to Remember*, op. cit.

52. Correspondence and clippings, Ogdensburg Public Library.

53. Clifford M. Drury, *First White Women Over the Rockies* (Glendale, Calif.: Arthur H. Clark Co., 1963–66); clippings, brochure, correspondence from Valentine C. Pratt, Corning, New York, and Elfrieda Kraege, United Presbyterian Church in the U.S.A.

54. *New York Times*, Mar. 30, 1977.

55. Brochure, Historical Society of Saratoga.

56. Correspondence, National Women's Hall of Fame.

57. Eleanor Flexner, *Century of Struggle: The Woman's Rights Movement in the United States*, rev. ed. (Cambridge, Mass.: Belknap Press, 1975); Elizabeth Cady Stanton, *Eighty Years and More* (New York: Schocken Books, 1971; repr. of 1898 ed.); *History of Woman Suffrage*, vol. 3 ed. Elizabeth C. Stanton and others (Rochester, N.Y.: Susan B. Anthony, 1886); correspondence, National Women's Hall of Fame; Sarah A. Lytle, Charleston, S.C.; The Mynderse Yonkers, Mynderse Academy, Seneca Falls; and the U.S. Department of Interior, Women's Rights National Historical Park.

58. Judith C. Breault, *The World of Emily Howland: Odyssey of a Humanitarian* (Millbrae, Calif.: Les Femmes, 1974); *Liberty's Women*, op. cit.; correspondence, Edward Kabelac, historian, Town of Ledyard, Aurora, New York.

59. Rubinstein, op. cit.

60. Correspondence, Women's Rights National Historical Park.

61. Elizabeth Evans, *Weathering the Storm: Women of the American Revolution* (New York: Charles Scribner's Sons, 1975); Fairfax Downey, "The Girls Behind the Guns," *American Heritage* 8 (Dec. 1956).

62. Van Wyck Brooks, *The Flowering of New England* (New York: E. P. Dutton, 1936); Dorothy H. Sanderson, *They Wrote for a Living: A Bibliography of the Works of Susan Bogert Warner and Anna Bartlett Warner* (West Point, N.Y.: Constitution Island Association, 1976); Mabel Baker, *Light in the Morning: Memories of Susan and Anna Warner* (West Point, N.Y.: Constitution Island Association, 1978); correspondence, Constitution Island Association. The birthdate of Anna is given as 1827 in *NAW*, but 1824 as given by Baker is correct; her mother died in 1826.

PENNSYLVANIA

ALIQUIPPA

Aliquippa, Queen, d. 1754, Indian Chief

Aliquippa is named for Queen Aliquippa, who lived in the village in the 1740s and was head of her tribe. There seems to be some question as to which tribe it was, whether Iroquois, Conestoga, Mohawk, or Seneca. She was well known to the settlers and traders here, including George Washington, who once presented her with a bottle of rum. When she died the Indian agent George Croghan wrote the colonial authorities, "Alequeapy, the old quine, is dead."[1]

ALLENTOWN

Addams, Jane, 1860–1935, Social Worker (NAW) and Others

Memorial Windows, Lees Memorial Chapel, Alumnae Hall, Cedar Crest College

Jane Addams, the founder of Hull House in Chicago, is one of three American women represented by stained-glass windows in the college chapel at Cedar Crest College. The other two are Mary Lyon (1797–1849, NAW), founder of Mt. Holyoke College, and Clara Barton (1821–1912, NAW), Civil War nurse and founder of the American Red Cross.

The windows, dedicated in 1954, were the gift of Fortunetta Lees of Chicago, Illinois, a graduate of Cedar Crest (1897) and a member of the board of trustees.[2]

AMBLER

Haines, Jane Bowne, 1869–1937, Horticulturist

Haines House, Ambler Campus, Temple University

The Ambler campus of Temple University is a continuation of the Pennsylvania School of Horticulture for Women, founded by Jane Bowne Haines in 1911 and operated by her until her death. Haines House, once known as McAlanon's Farm and used as the school director's residence, was renamed in her honor in the 1970s. She got her early training and interest in horticulture as a child, following her father about in his Cheltenham nurseries. After attending Bryn Mawr College, however, she felt that the field of scientific agriculture offered little to women and decided on a career in library work. The death of her father drew her back to Cheltenham to operate the nursery. She changed her mind about the attraction agriculture offered women and decided to open a school where they could specialize in raising flowers, shrubs, and trees. The present campus provides for men and women a full four-year college curriculum and includes a department of horticulture.[3]

BETHLEHEM

Doolittle, Hilda, 1886–1961, Writer; NAWM

Marker, 10 E. Church Street

Hilda Doolittle, who signed her poems H.D., was born on this site, now City Center Plaza. The state historical marker, dedicated in 1982, tells us that "H.D. sought the Hellenic spirit and a classic beauty of expression." A major American artist, she drew on mythology, astrology, and psychology for self-understanding and inspiration. After 1911 she lived abroad almost all her life, studying and writing. Her personal search for identity as a woman and an artist make her especially appealing to the modern woman.[4]

Watteville, Henrietta Benigna Zinzendorf von, 1725–1789, Educator; NAW

Moravian College, W. Church Street

Henrietta Benigna Zinzendorf von Watteville came from Saxony to America with her father, Count Zinzendorf, in 1841. The following year a school was organized in Germantown for the daughters of the settlers, with sixteen-year-old Benigna as head mistress. Later the school moved to Bethlehem. She returned to Europe in 1743 and married Baron John von Watteville, who was sent to America as a Moravian church bishop. They remained only a short time, but she made a third visit in 1784–85. Each time she was in Bethlehem she took a hand in reorganizing the school's curriculum. It bore a series of names, and in 1953 became part of four-year coeducational Moravian College.[5]

BRYN MAWR

Thomas, Martha Carey, 1857–1935, College Administrator; NAW

M. Carey Thomas Library Building, Bryn Mawr College

When Bryn Mawr College was about to open its doors, Martha Carey Thomas, a graduate of Cornell University and the University of Zurich, offered herself as its first president. She also set forth her ideas as to how the school should be run—with the highest standards. She was not appointed president, but she was made dean when the college opened in 1885. She became president in 1894 and remained so until 1922, shaping, with her strong personality and firmly held feminist ideals, the college's destiny. She insisted that it offer an education equal to or better than the best men's colleges, with stiff entrance examinations, a broad curriculum, and demanding language requirements. She held to her goals, and Bryn Mawr has from the first been one of the finest American colleges. The magnificent library building named for her exemplifies her urge for perfection and elegance.[6]

Woerishoffer, Emma Carola, 1885–1911, Social Worker and Philanthropist; NAW

Carola Woerishoffer Graduate Department of Social Economy and Social Research, Bryn Mawr College

Emma Carola Woerishoffer graduated from Bryn Mawr College in 1907. She had a great deal of money in her own right, but she felt that giving money to worthy causes was no substitute for an understanding of the roots of poverty and misery. It was a time of bitter labor strife, the great corporations fighting the militant trade unions, with labor legislation lagging behind. Woerishoffer took a job in a laundry so that she could see for herself the working conditions and how they affected the workers. Her outspoken and heartfelt criticisms led to her appointment as an official factory inspector for New York State, but her capacity for good came to an end when she was killed in an automobile accident in 1911. She had left Bryn Mawr $750,000, with no strings attached, a godsend to the struggling college. Carey Thomas had been planning a new department to prepare women for paid and unpaid positions in social service, and when the department materialized it was given Woerishoffer's name. It was one of the few professional schools at that time devoted to preparation for sociological and industrial economics.

CALEDONIA

Jemison, Mary, 1743–1833, Indian Captive

Marker, US 30 at State 234

The state historical marker gives the information that Mary Jemison, the "White Woman of the Genessee," lived here before her capture by the French and Indians in 1758. Her story stands out in the history of Indian captivities because she remained with the Indians for the rest of her life, marrying into the Seneca culture. There are numerous memorials to Jemison. See Orrtanna, PA, and Castile, NY.

CARLISLE

Pitcher, Molly (Mary Ludwig Hays McCauley), 1754?–1832, Revolutionary War Heroine; NAW (under McCauley)

Monument, Hanover Street, Between South and Walnut Streets.
Gravestone Markers, Old Graveyard, E. South Street

Pennsylvania shares with New Jersey (see Freehold, NJ) the honors given to Molly Pitcher as a battlefield heroine. She was a resident of Carlisle and the wife of John Hays, a soldier in the Pennsylvania Regiment. On June 28, 1778, at the Battle of Monmouth (New Jersey), she carried water to the fighting men, who dubbed her Molly Pitcher. When her husband was overcome and fell at his post, she stepped into his place and loaded cannon. After the war Hays died and she married John McCauley. In 1822 the state of Pennsylvania gave her a pension for her war services. A monument was placed at her tomb as part of the 1876 centennial observance, and later a cannon, flag, and flagstaff were added. The imposing life-size statue was erected in 1916. Molly's exploits are sometimes confused with those of another Pennsylvania heroine, Molly Corbin of Chambersburg, q.v. New York State has also chosen to honor Molly Pitcher; she was one of six notable women to be honored with stone relief portraits in its capitol at Albany.

CHAMBERSBURG

Corbin, Margaret Cochran, 1751–c. 1800, Revolutionary War Heroine; NAW

Marker, US 11

The state historical marker is near Rocky Spring (a mile and a half north of Chambersburg), birthplace of Margaret (Molly) Cochran. Molly married John Corbin and when he enlisted in the Continental Army she followed him into the battlefield. At Fort Washington, in New York, John was fatally shot in battle

Molly Pitcher is commemorated by this statue in Carlisle, Pennsylvania, for her heroism during the Battle of Monmouth, June 28, 1778. The statue was erected in 1916. Photography by Steinmetz Photo Workshop.
Courtesy Commonwealth of Pennsylvania, Department of Commerce.

on November 16, 1776. Molly took his place as a gunner until she herself was hit. She lost the use of one arm. She returned to Pennsylvania after the war and in 1779 the state awarded her relief and recommended her for a general pension. Assigned to an Invalid Regiment, she went to West Point, New York. It is believed that she next went to Highland Falls, New York, where she died and was buried. The Daughters of the American Revolution had her remains removed in 1926 for interment in the military cemetery at West Point. See West Point and New York City, NY.

Wilson, Sarah, 1795–1871, Philanthropist

Wilson College

Sarah Wilson had little, if anything, to do with the planning of a college for women at Chambersburg. But at the crucial moment she dug into her pocket and came up with the thirty thousand dollars the Presbyterians needed to put the project into operation. Her wealth came from several thousand acres in farm- and timberland that her father and brothers had developed and which she had managed successfully after it became hers. The college was given her name when it was incorporated in January 1869, and her portrait was hung in one of its buildings.[7]

CHEYNEY

Coppin, Fanny Jackson, 1837–1913, Educator; NAW

Coppin Hall, Cheyney University

Fanny Jackson Coppin, an ex-slave and a graduate of Oberlin College, taught at the Institute for Colored Youth in Philadelphia, Pennsylvania. She introduced into the curriculum industrial arts, giving Afro-American youth their first opportunity to acquire industrial skills that would prepare them for urban life. She married Levi Coppin in 1881 and in 1902 she joined him in missionary work and lectured on her favorite topic, the right of all to an education. When the days of slavery were over, she said, people asked what the blacks would do with an education, just as they had earlier asked what woman would do with an education. ''Rather ask, what will she do without it?'' The Institute moved in 1904 to Cheyney and in 1951 was renamed Cheyney State College, with a building named for Coppin. See Baltimore, MD.

COATESVILLE

Lukens, Rebecca Pennock, 1794–1854, Iron Manufacturer; NAW

Lukens Steel Company, Main Office Building, 50 S. 1st Avenue; NR

Rebecca Pennock Lukens made a name for herself at a time when women were not known for running businesses and in a field, heavy manufacturing, where women are still rare. Her father and her husband were both ironmasters. When her husband, Charles Lukens, died in 1825 he left no will, a murky title to the Brandywine Mill, heavy debts, and a half-finished contract to make iron plates for the steamship *Codorus*. Although Lukens had several children, one newly born, she was determined to carry on the business in accordance with her husband's wishes. She finished the *Codorus* contract and got further contracts for plates for the locomotives, steamboats, and machinery vital to the economy of a growing America. After her death the Brandywine Iron works was renamed for her; it survives as the Lukens Steel Company.

COLUMBIA

Wright, Susanna, 1697–1784, Pioneer and Poet; NAW

Wright's Ferry Mansion, 2nd and Cherry Streets; NR

At the time Susanna Wright lived here, growing mulberry trees, making silk, and writing poetry, it was at the very edge of white settlement in Pennsylvania. Her father ran a ferry, consisting of two canoes lashed together, across the Susquehanna River. She never married, but she ran her father's household after her mother died and later cared for her brother's family. Though seemingly isolated on the frontier, the home was the resort of fur traders and travelers bound for the western country, and Wright was noted for her hospitality and witty conversation. To her neighbors she became a legal and medical advisor. To the Indians she was a sympathetic friend. Literary folks in Philadelphia, Pennsylvania, kept her supplied with books and appreciated her verses, few of which have survived. Her English-style stone house remained in the family until early in the twentieth century; it was bought and restored in 1974 by the Louise Steinman Van Hess Foundation. It is open May 1–Oct. 31, Tues., Wed., Fri., and Sat. 10–3; adm.[8]

DUBLIN

Buck, Pearl Sydenstricker, 1892–1973, Writer and Humanitarian; NAWM

Green Hills Farm, 520 Dublin Road; NHL

The Good Earth, Pearl Sydenstricker Buck's novel about a Chinese peasant family, was the first sympathetic, realistic portrayal of Chinese life in Western literature. Published in 1931, it was an immediate best-seller, was translated into many languages, became a play and a film, won a Pulitzer Prize, and made Buck's name a household word. She was the daughter of American missionaries to China and had spent most of her life in that country, except during their furloughs in America and her college years at Randolph Macon.

After her second marriage, to Richard Walsh, she lived here on the farm and sometimes in a New York apartment, where she brought up a large family of adopted and foster children, writing one to five books a year. She is remembered for her interpretation of Asian culture, for her adoption agency for Asian-Americans, for her feminism, for her assistance to the handicapped, and for her generosity to humankind. She was the first American woman to win a Nobel Prize for literature, for *The Exile*, a biography of her mother. She has been elected to the National Women's Hall of Fame.

Green Hills is reached by State 313 from Doylestown and is a mile from the main route, near Perkasie. It is open Mon.-Fri. 9–5; tours at 10:30 and 2; closed holidays; adm.

ECKVILLE

Edge, Mabel Rosalie Barrow, 1877–1962, Conservationist

Hawk Mountain Sanctuary, Hawk Mountain Road

Mabel Rosalie Barrow Edge used to bird-watch in New York City's Central Park around 1915. One day she happened to meet Willard G. Van Name, a celebrated zoologist of the Museum of Natural History who was concerned about vanishing species of native birds. He imbued her with his concern and she founded the Emergency Conservation Committee, which consisted, most of the time, of one member, herself. From her office she launched letters to foes of conservation—lumbermen, sportsmen, and even the Audubon Society—and to newspapers, legislators, and anyone she considered misinformed or mischievous. Her interest spread from birds to all wildlife, including snakes, skunks, and bats. She bought Hawk Mountain, with its three peaks in the Kittanniny range, in 1934, and made it a sanctuary for birds, especially hawks and other migrating birds of prey. In a *New Yorker* profile, Van Name is quoted as having called Edge "the only honest, unselfish, indomitable hellcat in the history of conservation." The sanctuary is open daily, 8–5; adm. The hawk and eagle migrations occur late Aug. to late Nov.[9]

GETTYSBURG

Wade, Jennie, 1845–1863, Civil War Casualty

Jennie Wade House, Baltimore Street (US 140)

On June 26, 1863, the Confederate Army invaded Pennsylvania and on July 1 the great Battle of Gettysburg commenced. Young Jennie Wade, whose home was between the lines, stayed in her kitchen, baking the bread so much needed by the fighters. She was the first civilian fatality of the battle when a bullet tore into the house. Her home has been preserved as a Civil War museum, open May 1–Sept. 1, daily 9–9; rest of year, 9–5; adm.

GLADWYNE

Henry, Mary Gibson, 1884–1967, Botanist and Plant Explorer

Henry Foundation for Botanical Research, 801 Stony Lane

The Henry Foundation, dedicated to the collection and preservation of choice rare and endangered American native plants, was founded in 1948 by Mary Gibson Henry. Since the 1920s she had been traveling about the country seeking native plants that she could not obtain from commercial sources. She went up and down the Atlantic coast, fought briars, waded in swamps, and sometimes had to be pulled out of the mud, all in search of elusive plants. In 1931 she picked out a ''blank spot on the maps'' of Canada and set off to explore a valley near the Peace River. She and her daughter traveled a thousand miles by horse and foot, taking carrier pigeons along so they could send messages out to her husband. They shot game for food, once shot a bear, and again ''faced a pack of wolves and had a perfectly marvelous time.'' Mt. Mary Henry in northern British Columbia is named for her.

The forty-acre garden is open to visitors Apr.-Oct., Tues. and Thurs. 10–4, or by appointment. Call for directions to the foundation (215–525–2037).[10]

HARRISBURG

Oakley, Violet, 1874–1961, Artist

Murals, Senate Chamber, Supreme Court Room, and Governor's Reception Room, State Capitol

In 1889 when Violet Oakley was commissioned to decorate the walls of the governor's reception room in the capitol, it was believed to be the first commission of the kind given to a woman. A series of decorative panels, entitled ''The Founding of the State of Liberty Spiritual,'' depicts events in the life of William Penn. Later, Oakley was chosen to complete the mural decorations for the other rooms that had been planned and begun by Edwin A. Abbey. She was awarded a medal of honor from the Architectural League of New York because of her workmanship and success in the decorative treatment of historical subjects. Reproductions of the murals in full color were published in a portfolio, *The Holy Experiment—A Message to the World from Pennsylvania* (1922). See Philadelphia, PA.[11]

HORSHAM

Ferguson, Elizabeth Graeme, 1737–1801, Writer; NAW

Graeme Park, Keith Valley Road, West of State 611 (Private); HABS, NHL

Elizabeth Graeme Ferguson lived at this estate near Philadelphia, Pennsylvania. It was built by Governor Keith, bought by her father, and inherited by Elizabeth in 1772. In the fall of 1777 her husband, Henry Ferguson, joined the British, while Elizabeth was friendly to the Revolutionary cause. She became involved in a scandal when she naively delivered to George Washington a letter from a well-known clergyman advising the rebels to surrender. After that she developed another peace plan concerned with a bribe to a Continental Congress delegate, Joseph Reed. He was to be persuaded to use his influence to put an end to the war on terms advantageous to Britain. Reed's reply was that he was not worth purchasing, but that if he were, the king of England was not rich enough to buy him. Because of Elizabeth's misguided activities and her husband's loyalism, her whole estate was confiscated. She managed through friends to get part of it back and lived there quietly writing poetry until forced to sell in 1791.[12]

KENNETT SQUARE

Freeman, Hannah, 1730–1802, Lenni-Lenape Survivor

Marker, East Side of State 52 (West Chester Road)

According to the plaque, Hannah Freeman, "the last of the Indians in Chester County, was born in the vale about 300 yards to the east on the land of the protector of her people, the Quaker Assemblyman William Webb. Her mother was Indian Sarah and her grandmother Indian Jane of the Unami Group, their totem the tortoise, of the Lenni-Lenape or Delaware Indians." In spite of Webb's protection, Freeman's life ended in the county almshouse, where she was sent when too old to peddle her baskets and brooms from house to house. The original plaque, on the estate of Pierre S. du Pont, near Longwood, was dedicated in 1925 by descendants of Webb. It was subsequently stolen and in 1976 replaced by Longwood Gardens. It is a mile north of US 1 (Baltimore Pike).

LANCASTER

Johnston, Harriet Lane, 1830–1903, Hostess and Art Collector; NAW

Wheatland, 1120 Marietta Avenue; NHL

Harriet Lane Johnston was the niece of bachelor James Buchanan, and she chose him, her favorite uncle, as her guardian when both parents died. She was just turning twenty when Buchanan bought Wheatland, and her vivacious good spirits attracted other young people to the staid old mansion. When Buchanan was elected president of the United States she accompanied him to Washington and reigned as White House hostess. After his term ended, she returned with him to Wheatland, living here until her marriage in 1866 to Henry Johnston. She inherited the estate when Buchanan died and she spent summers here until 1884 when she sold it and moved to Washington, D.C. Wheatland is open for tours Apr. 1–Nov. 30, daily 10–4:15; adm. See Mercersburg, PA, and Washington, DC.

Nevin, Blanche, 1841–1925, Sculptor

Fountains, 300 Block E. King Street and at Intersection of King and W. Orange Streets

Blanche Nevin lived in Lancaster while her father was president of Franklin and Marshall College. She studied art in Philadelphia, Pennsylvania, and then went abroad to study and work in England. One biographer remarked that she loved travel and only settled down to work when the spirit moved her. She exhibited a statue of Maud Muller (from a poem by John Greenleaf Whittier) in the Woman's Pavilion at the Centennial Exposition of 1876 in Philadelphia. For the World's Columbian Exposition of 1893 she competed with much younger sculptors, submitting models illustrating woman evolving from ancient bondage to the advanced ideas of the nineteenth century. As a Pennsylvania artist she was selected to execute the statue of General Peter Muhlenberg, one of the state's representatives in Statuary Hall in Washington, D.C.

In her fifties she bought Windsor Forges, near Churchtown, which had been the home of her grandparents, and settled there. She was remembered as an interesting, if slightly eccentric, hostess. The two fountains, one surmounted by a life-size bronze lion, the other in the form of a marble cross ornamented with flowers, were her gifts to Lancaster in memory of her mother.[13]

LIVERPOOL

Reifsnyder, Elizabeth, 1858–1922, Medical Missionary

Marker, US 15 and 11

Elizabeth Reifsnyder graduated from the Woman's Medical College of Pennsylvania in 1881 and two years later was sent to Shanghai, where she opened the Woman's Union Mission Hospital. She spent more than thirty years in China and during her few years in America she lived in Liverpool. She was the first American woman surgeon to remove an ovarian cyst from a Chinese woman, and all the eyes of the woman's relatives and neighbors were on her; success established the doctor's skill in treatment. The state historical marker is near

Reifsnyder's home, which still stands on the northwest corner of the square, privately owned and not open to the public.[14]

MERCERSBURG

Johnston, Harriet Lane, 1830–1903, Hostess and Art Collector; NAW

Marker, Lane House, 16 N. Main Street (Private); NR

Harriet Lane Johnston, later White House hostess for her uncle, President James Buchanan, was born here. Her mother died when she was nine, and she was sent to a boarding school in Lancaster. When her father also died, the young woman was made Buchanan's ward (see Lancaster, PA, and Washington, DC).

MONTOURSVILLE

Montour, Madam, c. 1684–c. 1752, Iroquois Chief; NAW

Montoursville, originally Otstonwakin, was named for Madam Montour, a chief of the Iroquois Nation. A county and a mountain in Pennsylvania are also named for her. Part French, she was educated in Canada before she joined the Iroquois, either by captivity or marriage. Her first name is not recorded. She won the respect and trust of Pennsylvania and New York colonial leaders for whom she served, between 1711 and 1744, as interpreter and Indian agent. She was described as of a good family, handsome, and genteel. A supposed daughter, Margaret, also had a town named for her: ''Margaret's Town'' was the original name of Williamsport, Pennsylvania. Queen Esther, who lived near Athens, Pennsylvania, was probably a granddaughter, and Montour Falls, New York, was named for another granddaughter, Catherine.

MORRISVILLE

Penn, Hannah Callowhill, 1671–1726, Administrator; NAW

Pennsbury Manor, on the Delaware River South of Bordentown Road, Near US 1 and 13; NR

In 1699 William Penn returned to Pennsylvania after a seventeen-year absence, bringing with him his second wife, Hannah Callowhill Penn. Their stay was brief, for they were forced by business matters to return to England in 1701, but Hannah won the esteem of William's associates by her common sense and ability in managing Pennsbury, their forty-acre farm, while he was in Philadelphia. For some time after they went back to England William was in such poor health that much of the administration of Pennsylvania affairs was in Hannah's capable hands. William trusted her business sense so completely that he made her executrix of his will. She had eight children, one born in Pennsylvania, but only five lived beyond childhood. Pennsylvania remained in the possession of Hannah's children and grandchildren until the Revolution.

The manor house at Morrisville has been reconstructed and furnished in early period furnishings. With its many outbuildings and formal gardens, it is open from late Apr. to late Oct., Tues.-Sat. 9–5, Sun. 12–5; rest of year, Tues.-Sat. 10–4, Sun. 12–4:30; closed some holidays; adm.

NEW BRIGHTON

Lippincott, Sara Clarke (Grace Greenwood), 1823–1904, Writer; NAW

Marker, Clarke Home, 1221 3rd Avenue (Private)

Sara Clarke Lippincott moved to White Cottage in New Brighton with her family when she was a young woman. She wrote a series of letters, signed them Grace Greenwood, and sent them to the *Home Journal*. Readers began to look forward to the flowery epistles signed Greenwood. Lippincott soon moved on to brighter pastures in New York, toured the continent, wrote travel pieces, joined the suffragists, and in 1853, with her husband, Leander Lippincott, founded a children's magazine, *Little Pilgrim*. It survived until 1875. Sara was a popular writer and lecturer whose ideas and their expression mirrored the concerns of the day. The marker was erected by the state.

ORRTANNA

Jemison, Mary, 1743–1833, Indian Captive

Statue, Church of St. Ignatius Loyola, Near State 234

It was near this spot that Mary Jemison, a fourteen-year-old white girl, was taken from her home in 1758 by Indians who destroyed her homestead and killed most of her family. Despite this traumatic experience, Jemison never returned to the white world but chose to remain with the Indians and adopt their way of life. The first description of her captivity appeared while she was still living: James Everett Seaver's *A Narrative of the Life of Mrs. Mary Jemison* (1824). The statue here was set up in 1923. See Caledonia, PA, and Castile, NY.

PHILADELPHIA

Medical College of Pennsylvania and Hospital, 3300 Henry Street

The medical college, established in 1850 as the Female Medical College of Pennsylvania, was the first medical school for women in the country. When its first class graduated the following year, police had to be present to guard the women against violent male medical students, a foretaste of the prejudice the young women M.D.'s were to meet. Over the years the attitude changed; objection to women treating the ill virtually disappeared. The school itself went through many changes. Its name became the Woman's Medical College. A hospital was added. It moved its quarters several times. During the Civil War it was forced to close for a while. Its course, originally a four-month term in each of two years, was expanded, its curriculum widened. Women physicians became available as teachers and administrators. And of course tremendous advances in medicine itself were taking place. In all of its development, some remarkable women took the lead.

Portraits of many of those associated with the college and hospital have been donated to the school. There is one of Hannah Longshore (1819–1901, NAW), whose brother-in-law, Joseph Longshore, was one of the group of Quakers who established the school. Hannah enrolled in the first session. She taught for a time, but she soon had so large a private practice that she gave up teaching. Women too embarrassed to take their health problems to a male doctor were eager to put themselves into the care of a warm and understanding woman.

There is a portrait of Ann Preston (1813–1872, NAW), whose search for medical training inspired the establishment of the school. She was one of its first graduates and one of its first teachers. In 1858 the Philadelphia Medical Society ostracized the college, making it impossible for women to be admitted to public teaching clinics or enter medical societies. In order to provide clinical experience, Preston established a small woman's hospital in connection with the college. Both closed during the Civil War but in 1861 the hospital was reopened with Emeline Cleveland as first resident. Cleveland (1829–1878, NAW) had been given the opportunity to take postgraduate training at La Maternité in Paris, France. She remained as resident and professor until her death, while carrying a private practice, supporting an invalid husband, and bringing up a son, who also became a physician.

Rachel Bodley (1831–1888, NAW), chemist and botanist, succeeded Cleveland as dean of the medical college in 1874. During her fourteen years as dean she expanded the course to three years and improved opportunities for clinical training. Her place was taken by Clara Marshall (1847–1931, NAW), who taught materia medica and therapeutics. She served for three decades, years in which research resulted in great medical advances. Louis Pasteur and others had shown the role of bacteria in disease, and the need for bacteriology and laboratory techniques was apparent.

Martha Tracy (1876–1942, NAW) was the next dean. During her administration the school went through a series of crises. The old hospital and college buildings were abandoned for new structures. The depression was severely felt until the state Federation of Women's Clubs came to the rescue and spearheaded a funding drive.

A large part of American medical history, as well as the history of the medical college, is embodied in the lives of these and other alumnae and administrators. See also Philadelphia's Catharine Macfarlane.[15]

Carnell, Laura H., 1867–1929, Educator

Carnell Hall, Temple University, Broad Street and Montgomery Avenue. Laura H. Carnell School, Frontenac and Devereaux Streets

When Temple University opened, its founder, Russell H. Conwell, cast about for someone to help design its courses. He had noticed Laura H. Carnell among the volunteers teaching classes for adults at a Baptist evening school, where she demonstrated much concern for the students. She had studied at Cornell University, the University of Chicago, and Cambridge University. He offered her a job at the university and she remained here for thirty-four years. She began as principal of the Women's Department in 1893, held various positions, and finally, in 1925, became associate president. She kept in close touch with the students, attending football games and many of the undergraduate functions. In 1930 the building adjoining Conwell Hall was named for her and the Temple University Women's Club placed a memorial plaque on the building. The public school which was given her name also has a scholarship fund in her memory.[16]

Cohen, Katherine Myrtilla, 1859–1914, and Bessie Potter Vonnoh, 1872–1955, Sculptors

Busts, Smith Memorial, Gateway to West Fairmount Park

Richard Smith left $500,000 for a monument to Pennsylvania's naval and military heroes of the Civil War. Two women were among those selected to execute busts: Katherine Myrtilla Cohen and Bessie Potter Vonnoh. Cohen, who executed the bust of General James A. Beaver, studied first in Philadelphia, her native city, then went to Paris, France, and worked with first-rate artists.

Vonnoh, who did the bust of Major General S. W. Crawford, was a student of Lorado Taft in Chicago, Illinois. He wrote of her that she got her start at the Columbian Exposition in 1893; it "brought new revelations and new enthusiasms. From that time her pathway was clear." Her small Tanagra-like figurines and her pieces with the central theme of mother and child became familiar as she took part in exhibitions and sold to galleries. Many of her groups of children form the central themes of fountains such as the memorial to Frances H. Burnett in Central Park, New York City. She married the painter Robert Vonnoh.[17]

Drexel, Mother Mary Katharine, 1858–1955, Religious Founder; NAWM

Katharine Drexel Branch, Free Library of Philadelphia, Knights and Fairdale Roads

Mother Mary Katharine Drexel, "the richest nun in the world," was born in Philadelphia. She and her two sisters inherited an estate of $14 million, with which they resolved to continue the charitable activities of their parents, the socially elite Francis Anthony Drexels. Katharine took a sympathetic interest in western American Indians and in southern blacks. Advised to become a missionary to the Indians, she entered a convent in 1889 and two years later founded a new order, the Sisters of the Blessed Sacrament for Indians and Colored People. The order, backed by Mother Katharine's wealth, founded a large number of missions and schools throughout the South and the West, as well as in urban centers of the North. The cause of Mother Katharine's beatification was opened in 1964 and steps have been taken toward her canonization by the Roman Catholic church.

Foley, Margaret, c. 1827–1877, Sculptor

Fountain, Horticulture Center, West Fairmount Park

Few works survive by this talented self-taught sculptor. Margaret Foley grew up in Vergennes, Vermont, beginning to carve as a youngster. In 1860 she joined other American sculptors in Rome, Italy, attracted by the availability of marble and skilled marble cutters. She attained a reputation for finely modeled portrait medallions and busts. The fountain, a marble basin surmounted by lacy acanthus leaves, the trunk supported by three children, was made for the 1876 Philadelphia Centennial Exposition. The following year the artist died while vacationing abroad.[18]

Frishmuth, Harriet Whitney, 1880–1980, Sculptor

Berwind Tomb, Aspiration, *Laurel Hill Cemetery*

Harriet Whitney Frishmuth, a native of Philadelphia, studied art in Paris, France, and Berlin, Germany. She was known as a sculptor of "lithe feminine figures," and especially liked to work with dancers who could hold a pose. Many of her sculptures can be seen in parks and gardens throughout the eastern states, among them *Joy of the Waters*, a fountain at the Museum of Fine Arts in Dayton, Ohio; a memorial sundial in Englewood, New Jersey; the Morton Memorial in Windsorville, Connecticut; and a bust of Woodrow Wilson at the state capitol in Richmond, Virginia. The monument at Laurel Hill, a large granite figure carved from a single block, was commissioned by Mrs. Harry A. Berwind in 1933.[19]

Harper, Frances Ellen Watkins, 1825–1911, Lecturer and Poet; NAW

Harper House, 1006 Bainbridge Street (Private); NHL

Before the Civil War Frances Ellen Watkins Harper was giving antislavery lectures throughout the North. The tall, light-skinned black woman impressed her audiences not only for her message, given in a clear, melodious voice, but also for her poetry. She was the best-known black poet since Phillis Wheatley. Many of her verses reflect her concern for the needs of Afro-Americans and her criticism of intolerance. She settled in Philadelphia in 1871, the widow of Fenton Harper and mother of a daughter. She helped to organize the National Association of Colored Women in 1896. See Baltimore, MD.

Macfarlane, Catharine, 1877?–1969, Physician

Macfarlane Cancer Detection Clinic, Medical College of Pennsylvania and Hospital, 3300 Henry Avenue

Catharine Macfarlane graduated from the Woman's Medical College in 1898 and for almost all the years between then and 1966 was on the staff of the college hospital. She became known for her pioneer use of radium for cancer treatment, which she began in 1903 after hearing of the substance from Marie Curie. She advocated regular checkups for women to detect breast and uterine cancer and opened a clinic for breast self-examination. She won the Lasker Award in Public Health and the Elizabeth Blackwell Award from the New York Infirmary. Macfarlane lived to be ninety-two years old, dying in the hospital where she had spent her long productive life. The volunteers of the cancer clinic presented a portrait of her to the medical college in 1947.[20]

Madison, Dolley Payne Todd, 1768–1849, White House Hostess; NAW

Todd House, 4th and Walnut Streets

Dolley Payne Todd Madison, who was born in North Carolina and brought up in Virginia, moved with her family to Philadelphia when she was in the bloom of her youth. Here she met and married John Todd, Jr., a Quaker lawyer. Three years later Dolley was a widow. Yellow fever had killed her husband and a two-month-old son, leaving her with one boy a year old. Dolley's youth and natural high spirits saw her quickly through her bereavement. Philadelphia, thc capital of the new nation, was the liveliest city in America and she had a number of suitors. Among all she might have chosen, she decided on the congressional leader, James Madison, seventeen years her senior, a brilliant and hard-working scholar. The difference in their temperaments seems to have created exactly the right mix. Throughout their forty-two years of marriage they remained devoted to each other.

Dolley began a long and successful career as a Washington hostess when President Thomas Jefferson, a widower, chose her to preside over White House functions. James was his secretary of state. After James became president, Dolley continued to be the arbiter of fashion and the determiner of manners for the new capital. When British troops in 1814 set fire to the executive mansion, quick-witted Dolley rescued important documents and the famous Gilbert Stuart portrait of George Washington before fleeing to Virginia.

The Todd House, in which she lived so briefly, is open daily 9–5; closed some holidays; tickets may be obtained at the visitor center.

Moore, Marianne, 1887–1972, Poet; NAWM

Marianne Moore Room, Rosenbach Foundation Museum, 2010 Delancey Place

Marianne Moore grew up in a magic family circle of three—she, her widowed mother, and her brother—who took private names for each other from *The Wind in the Willows* and shared their joys and enthusiasms. She was always open to experience, whether it was the mundane teaching at Carlisle Indian School, the boring revision of the Dewey Decimal System, or the thrilling trips to literary shrines of England. She lived in Greenwich Village, New York City, after World War I and in Brooklyn, New York, from 1929 to 1966. She loved Brooklyn. It gave her, she said, "the kind of tame excitement on which I thrive." She rode the subway, visited the zoo, explored the botanical gardens, and rooted for the Brooklyn Dodgers. All of these impressions she transmuted into a rich mosaic of poetic images. She was acknowledged on both sides of the Atlantic as one of the great modern poets and was awarded a shower of literary prizes. After her death the Rosenbach brothers, her admirers, had her Greenwich Village apartment removed and reassembled in Philadelphia, with her furnishings, books, photographs, and literary papers. The museum is open Tues.-Sun. 11–4; closed holidays; adm.[21]

Mott, Lucretia Coffin, 1793–1880, Abolitionist and Women's Rights Leader; NAW

Marker, State 611, North of Cheltenham Avenue, Elkins Park

"When the true history of the anti-slavery cause shall be written," said Frederick Douglass, "women will occupy a large space in its pages. . . . Foremost among those noble American women, in point of clearness of vision, breadth of understanding, weight of character, and widespread influence was Lucretia Mott." Lucretia Coffin Mott, the quiet, restrained Quaker minister, with her Nantucket, Massachusetts, background, was a moving spirit in the Seneca Falls, New York, convention of 1848 and one of the dedicated workers throughout her life in the fight for women's emancipation. She and her husband, James Mott, lived at Roadside, Old York Road and Township Line Road, in Montgomery County. Her house no longer exists but the community is named LaMott in her memory. The state historical marker tells us that "her most notable work was in connection with antislavery, women's rights, temperance and peace." She is in the National Women's Hall of Fame. The Germantown Historical Society, 5214 Germantown Avenue, has historical Mott items. It is open Tues. and Thur. 11–5, Sun. 1–5; adm. See Washington, DC (under Adelaide Johnson).[22]

Oakley, Violet, 1874–1961, Artist

Studio, 627 St. George's Road (Private); NR

Violet Oakley was a muralist, illustrator, and worker in stained glass, who won acclaim for her murals in the state capitol in Harrisburg, Pennsylvania, q.v. She worked with Jessie Willcox Smith on illustrations for *Evangeline* in 1897, and for some years Oakley, Jessie Smith, and Elizabeth Shippen Green shared a succession of studio-homes in and around Philadelphia. Oakley made stained-glass windows for the Church of All Saints in New York City; the Convent of the Holy Child in Sharon Hill, Pennsylvania; and the Church of the Epiphany, in Boston, Massachusetts.[23]

Peter, Sarah Worthington King, 1800–1877, Charitable Worker; NAW

Moore College of Art, 20th Street and Parkway

The first school of industrial art for women in America was established not through love of art but to train women left without means of support to earn a decent living. The charitable American wife of the British consul in Philadelphia, Sarah Worthington King Peter sympathized with such women and believed they could be taught industrial arts—wood engraving, lithography, and designing household necessities such as wallpaper and carpets, at that time mainly imported from Europe. She opened classes in 1848 in her own home. It became the Philadelphia School of Design and became affiliated with the Franklin Institute two years later. It gave the first art instruction to generations of women artists, including Jessie Willcox Smith and Emily Sartain (its principal from 1866 to 1920). It merged in 1932 into the Moore Institute of Art, Science, and Industry, now the Moore College of Art. Not long after establishing the school, Peter was widowed and went back to her former home, Cincinnati, Ohio, where she turned her attention to the work of the Catholic church.

Pratt, Anna Beach, 1867–1932, Social Worker; NAW

Anna B. Pratt School, 22nd and Susquehanna Avenue

Anna Beach Pratt graduated from Elmira College in New York, later decided to enter social work, and in 1906 became overseer of the poor in Elmira. There she introduced charity organization methods, as opposed to the Lady Bountiful approach to poverty. She came to Philadelphia to take a course at the University of Pennsylvania in 1916 and remained for the rest of her life. She was convinced that social workers were needed in schools, beginning in the lowest grades. She believed that the roots of maladjustment, unhappiness, and poverty lay in the child's development. In order to understand the child, it was necessary to take account not only of the child's educational development but also of his or her health, home, social environment, and emotional growth. She was successful in convincing educators to include casework and counseling services in the Philadelphia public school system. The Pratt School was named for her in 1955.

Ross, Elizabeth Griscom, 1752–1836, Seamstress; NAW

Betsy Ross House, 239 Arch Street

Thousands of Americans believe that the American flag was born in this house, designed and stitched by Elizabeth (Betsy) Griscom Ross. The story is that she was visited by a committee of the Continental Congress—George Washington, George Ross (her late husband's uncle), and Robert Morris—who asked her to make a flag for the nation, which in 1777 existed only in their hopes for a Revolutionary victory. The contract was given to her. The story went down within her family until 1870, when a grandson told it and attempted to confirm it by documents. No hard evidence has been found, and it is too late now; the story of Betsy Ross has become enshrined in legend, children's stories, and paintings—and in the hearts of her countrymen. The Flag House, Ross's birthplace, was set aside as a national shrine in the late nineteenth century, paid for by ten-cent subscriptions from school children and patriotic societies. It is open daily, 9–5; closed some holidays.

Stevenson, Christine Wetherill, 1878–1922, Actress and Art Patron

Philadelphia Art Alliance, 251 S. 18th Street

The Art Alliance, recognized as a significant and unique Philadelphia institution, was founded by Christine Wetherill Stevenson, wife of William Yorke Stevenson. In 1915 she brought together a group of Philadelphians interested in the arts. She had studied art, music, and history in Europe and on her return to her home founded the Plays and Players Club to present theatrical performances, in many of which she took leading parts. She felt it important to popularize the

The Betsy Ross House in Philadelphia, Pennsylvania, is the ''Birthplace of Old Glory,'' where Ross stitched the first American flag.
Courtesy Commonwealth of Pennsylvania, Department of Commerce.

best in all the arts, though her first love was the stage. ''We should create our own standards,'' she said, ''not in imitation of those in Europe, but chiseled boldly out of our different experiences, traditions, and ideals.''

Shortly after founding the art center she went to California, where she presented religious plays in outdoor amphitheaters in Hollywood under the auspices of the Theosophical Society. The alliance was given the family home by her father's will. A memorial to Christine, a terra cotta bas-relief by R. Tait McKenzie, is displayed over the dining room entrance. The eight galleries of paintings, sculpture, and applied arts are open Mon.-Sat. 10:30–5; closed holidays. Concerts, lectures, and special events are scheduled.[24]

Vonnoh, Bessie Potter. See Cohen, Katherine

Zimbalist, Mary Curtis Bok, 1876–1970, Music Patron; NAWM

Curtis Institute of Music, 1726 Locust Street

Mary Curtis Bok Zimbalist was the daughter of Cyrus Curtis, publisher of the *Ladies' Home Journal*, and Louisa Curtis, its editor. She married Edward Bok, the second editor of the *Journal*. Mary's life revolved not around publishing but around music. Her father played the organ, her mother sang, and she studied piano. Bok, too, was part of the musical world, spearheading a campaign to endow the Philadelphia Orchestra. After her mother's death, Mary gave funds to the Settlement Music School as a memorial. In 1924 she founded the Curtis Institute of Music, which has been called the musical United Nations. It had close ties to the Philadelphia Orchestra and numbered among its students many of the century's leading composers and performers, including George Antheil, with whom Mary formed a long-lasting friendship. Bok died in 1930, and in 1943 Mary married Efrem Zimbalist, concert pianist and director of the Curtis Institute.

PITTSBURGH

Callery, Mary, 1903–1977, Sculptor

Constellation I, Constellation II, *and* Three Birds in Flight, *Sculptures, Aluminum Company of America Headquarters, 1 Allegheny Square*

Mary Callery grew up in Pittsburgh in a wealthy family. Her study of art, which began when she was twelve, included four years at the Art Students League in New York. In Paris, France, from 1930 to 1940, she was one of Pablo Picasso's devoted admirers. On her return to the United States she developed her own style, thin metal sculptures that have been called ''ballet in bronze.'' Her twelve-foot aluminum sculpture above the glass entrance space of the Alcoa building is only one of many architectural pieces which mark her as an accomplished artist. See New York City.[25]

Lampkin, Daisy E. Adams, 1883?–1965, Civil Rights Leader; NAWM

Marker, Daisy E. Lampkin Apartments, 2519 Webster Avenue

The state historical marker, dedicated in 1983, pays tribute to Daisy E. Adams Lampkin for leadership in the Afro-American struggle for civil rights, particularly in the National Association for the Advancement of Colored People (NAACP). "Outstanding as an NAACP organizer, Mrs. Lampkin was its National Field Secretary 1935–47. President, Lucy Stone Civic League, 1915–65. A charter member, National Council of Negro Women, and Vice President, The Pittsburgh Courier." Lampkin lived here until her death.[26]

Schenley, Mary Croghan, 1827–1903, Romantic Heroine and Philanthropist

Mary Croghan Schenley Memorial Fountain, Schenley Plaza. Schenley Park, Forbes Street and Bigelow Road

The Croghan-Schenley story is one of romance and pathos. Mary Croghan Schenley was the granddaughter of General James O'Hara, an early Pittsburgh landowner, and daughter of wealthy William Croghan. At fifteen, she eloped from a Staten Island girls' school with Edward Schenley, a dashing Englishman three times her age and twice widowed. As she was expected to inherit a large fortune, Edward was thought to be a scoundrel and a fortune hunter. However, the marriage was not unhappy, nor did Edward ever control the estate his wife eventually inherited. The couple went to live in England. Her father, a widower, doted on his only child and built for her near his home Picnic, an English mansion. For a few years the couple, with three of their eventual nine children, lived here, but Edward longed for his native land and they returned to England.

Mary never again lived in America but she always considered Pittsburgh her home. She gave much of her land (valued at her death at $50 million) to the city, including the three-hundred-acre Schenley Park. The Fort Pitt Blockhouse, at Pennsylvania Avenue between Water and Barbeau Streets, was part of her inheritance; she gave it to the Daughters of the American Revolution. The mansion, Picnic, stood empty from the time William Croghan died in 1872 until 1945, when it was demolished. One room, too beautiful to be lost, has been preserved in Pittsburgh's Cathedral of Learning.[27]

Stein, Gertrude, 1874–1946, Writer; NAW

Marker at Birthplace, 850 Beech Avenue (Private)

Not long after Gertrude Stein was born here to a German-Jewish couple her father took her to Austria. She lived in Paris, France, then in California, and not until 1892 did she return to live in Pennsylvania. Stein spent four years studying at Johns Hopkins Medical School (after graduating cum laude from Radcliffe College). Without finishing the medical course, she went abroad and for almost all of her life thereafter lived in France. A famous and controversial writer with a style all her own, her impact on American letters and the English language was tremendous, and her friendship with the early French impressionists was a significant factor in their acceptance. Her birthplace has recently been restored and a marker dedicated by the Allegheny West Civic Association. It is not open to the public.[28]

Swisshelm, Jane Cannon, 1815–1884, Journalist and Reformer; NAW

Marker, Braddock Avenue Near Penn Lincoln Parkway

The site of Jane Cannon Swisshelm's home, Swissvale, is near the state historical marker to the ''Renowned editor, abolitionist, Civil War nurse, advocate of women's rights and temperance.'' Another marker is at the Saks Fifth Avenue entrance to Gimbel's Department Store, 6th Avenue.

Swisshelm was a woman, in Amelia Bloomer's words, of ''dare-devil independence.'' She had impressed on her the legal plight of married women when, after she had nursed her mother through her last illness, her husband proposed to sue the mother's estate for her services; the money, of course, would be his. Indeed, Jane found life with James Swisshelm very difficult. After 1842 they lived on his family's farm, which she named Swissvale. She began writing for the newspapers and started one of her own, *The Saturday Visiter* (she insisted on this spelling). It was a lively and outspoken publication with a national circulation of six thousand. In 1851 Jane left her husband and moved with her only child to St. Cloud, Minnesota, where she published *The St. Cloud Visiter* and stirred up more controversy.

She returned to Swissvale after the Civil War, having sued her ex-husband's estate for the property, and remained here until her death.[29]

Szold, Henrietta, 1860–1945, Religious Leader; NAW

Memorial Window, Tree of Life Synagogue, Wilkins and Shady Avenue

The window memorializes Jews in public life in America, including Henrietta Szold. She was a Baltimore, Maryland, native, a founder of Hadassah, the Jewish women's organization formed to foster Zionism. She went to Palestine first in 1909 and returned again and again during its years of settlement, helping young Jews escape from the Hitler regime in Europe, organizing social services, and establishing vocational schools and hospitals. Israel became a state three years after her death. She is buried there on the Mount of Olives. See Baltimore, MD, and New York City.[30]

SCRANTON

Slocum, Frances, 1773–1847, Indian Captive; NAW

Memorial Stone, Everhart Museum of Natural History, Nay Aug Park

In 1835 a fur trader among the Miami Indians near what is now Peoria, Indiana, noticed that one of the women had white skin. She was Frances Slocum, the widow of a war chief, owner of many horses and cattle. When he questioned her, he learned that she came from the Wyoming Valley near Scranton, that her family had survived the Wyoming massacre of 1778, but that shortly after that she had been captured by Delaware Indians. From the age of five she lived with them, married twice, first a Delaware, then a Miami. She never tried to reach her family and had now no wish to give up her Indian life. In fact, she had learned to distrust whites.

Her family in the meantime had never ceased their search for the missing little sister. The trader tried to reach them through the postmaster at Lancaster, Pennsylvania, and several years later her brother in Wilkes-Barre, Pennsylvania, learned of the discovery. He, a sister, and another brother went to visit Slocum, then sixty-four years old. Though she was glad to see them, she refused to go home with them; she wanted to die where "the Great Spirit will know where to find me." Several books were written about the "lost sister of Wyoming," and her story is a favorite in Indiana, where a forest is named for her. See Wilkes-Barre, PA.

SPRINGDALE

Carson, Rachel, 1907–1964, Ecologist; NAWM

Rachel Carson House, 611 Marion Avenue; NR

Rachel Carson's book, *Silent Spring*, shocked the country in 1962 with its warnings that the pesticides used in agriculture were so dangerous that the day might soon come when no birds would sing, fish would die in the streams, and human life would be grievously affected. The manufacturers said she was wrong, and farmers claimed they could not grow crops without the pesticides, but others believed her. Her book had far-reaching consequences in regulations protecting the environment. It was indeed a landmark book.

Carson was born in this house, originally part of her father's sixty-three-acre farm. She lived here until she left to study at Johns Hopkins University. She was for most of her life a biologist and writer for the U.S. Fish and Wildlife Service. Among her books are *Under the Sea-Wind* (1942), *The Sea Around Us* (1951), *The Sense of Wonder* (1965), and *The Edge of the Sea* (1971). All combine literary style with a love of nature and the ecologist's concern for environmental preservation. Carson is in the National Women's Hall of Fame. The Carson House is being restored as a monument to her and a library of ecology.[31]

TITUSVILLE

Tarbell, Ida, 1857–1944, Journalist; NAW

Marker, Tarbell Home, 324 E. Main Street (State 27) (Private)

The state has marked the home where Ida Tarbell lived during her school years. Titusville was the original oil town, and when in 1902 *McClure's Magazine* wished to publish articles on the development of the Standard Oil Trust, Tarbell was given the writing assignment—partly because she was a good investigator and partly because she had lived here. She had heard much from the independent oil men in town about the hated tactics of Standard Oil. Her father blamed the failure of his business and the suicide of his partner on the corporation. When her *History of the Standard Oil Company* was published in 1904, it created a sensation. She had tried to be objective, but she could not conceal her moral outrage at the company's manipulations. President Theodore Roosevelt called her a "muckraker," given to digging up the dirt about American society. The term was soon applied to other journalists who investigated sore spots in the economy. When Tarbell wrote a similarly critical book on the tariff, President Woodrow Wilson called it "good plain common sense." See Wattsburg, PA.

WATTSBURG

Tarbell, Ida, 1857–1944, Journalist; NAW

Marker, State 8, Southwest of Town

The state historical marker points out that the celebrated writer was born in her grandfather's log house at nearby Hatch Hollow. After the publication of her book on Standard Oil, Ida Tarbell kept on writing and also lectured on the Chautauqua circuit, speaking on ethics in American business, the League of Nations, and disarmament.

WHITE DEER

Smith, Catherine, 1740–1800, Mill Operator

Marker, Old US 15, South of Junction with New Highway

Catherine Smith was left by the death of her husband in 1773 with ten children to support and no estate except for a location of three hundred acres. According to a local historian, she was "of the type that did not sit idly by and let her neighbors support her family, but realizing that a grist and sawmill were both much wanted in that new country at that time, she set about the task." She built a stone house on this site and operated the sawmill and gristmill, then in 1776 completed a boring mill where many gun barrels for the Continental Army were manufactured. Unfortunately, the mills were burned by Indians in 1779 after the Wyoming massacre. She rebuilt them but was ejected from the land. Despite repeated petitions to the legislature she could not regain her property. Pennsylvania at long last recognized her contribution by naming a mountain for her and erecting a marker.[32]

WILKES-BARRE

Palmer, Ellen Webster, 1840–1918, Humanitarian

Statue, Wilkes-Barre Municipal Conservatory, Near Union Street

Ellen Webster Palmer came to Wilkes-Barre after her marriage to a socially prominent attorney. To her the beauty of the town was marred by the presence of grimy, poorly dressed boys who worked in the coal mines as breaker-boys, door-boys, and mule-boys. Their faces showed no joy of childhood. They swore and swaggered like men. There was little she could do in the 1890s to offer them health care or to cut down their hours of labor or to provide for mine safety, but she could try to bring smiles to their faces. She set up a night boys' club, with books, a melodeon, and workbenches for hobbies. She read to them, sang to them, and gave them love and warmth. The group took on the name of the Boys' Industrial Association, and the town remembered her fondly.[33]

Slocum, Frances, 1773–1847, Indian Captive; NAW

Frances Slocum State Park. Frances Slocum Playground, N. Pennsylvania Avenue and Scott Street

In 1842, John Todd's *The Lost Sister of Wyoming* brought to the attention of Pennsylvanians the strange tale of Frances Slocum, a child captured by Indians in the Wyoming Valley in 1778, carried off to western Pennsylvania and then to Indiana, where she was found years later living as an Indian among the Miamis (see Scranton, PA). Her story, first published by Todd and later by John F.

Meginness (1891), was choice reading both in Pennsylvania and Indiana. The Slocum Park is ten miles northwest of town.

WYOMING

Swetland, Hannah Tiffany, 1749–1809, Pioneer

Swetland Homestead, 885 Wyoming Avenue; NR

Hannah Tiffany Swetland and her husband, Luke Swetland, came to the Wyoming Valley when it was claimed by Connecticut. At the time of the Revolution they had been married fourteen years and had four sons. On July 3, 1778, Indians attacked the settlement and massacred many of the inhabitants. Hannah and her family escaped, but a month later Luke was captured by Senecas. Supposing him dead, she trudged with her boys through the woods to her home in Kent, Connecticut. Luke, meanwhile, had been kept by the Indians, then held by Americans as a suspected Tory spy, then detached to duty as a scout for the army, and some years passed before he was able to find his family. They returned to Wyoming when Luke was seventy-one, cleared land, built this homestead, planted orchards, and helped to establish a church. Their descendants owned the property until recently. The house, furnished in the 1800–1860 period, is open June 1–Labor Day, Fri.-Sun. 12–5; rest of year by appointment; adm.[34]

NOTES

In addition to the sources mentioned below, I have had assistance from the Department of Commerce, Commonwealth of Pennsylvania; the Historical Society of Dauphin County; and the State Library of Pennsylvania, Genealogy and Local History Collection.

1. *Notable Women of Pennsylvania*, ed. Gertrude B. Biddle and Sarah D. Lawrie (Philadelphia: University of Pennsylvania Press, 1942), cited hereafter as Biddle; Dixon Wecter, *The Hero in America* (Ann Arbor: University of Michigan Press, 1963).
2. Correspondence and dedication pamphlet, Cedar Crest College.
3. Biddle; correspondence, Temple University.
4. Correspondence, Pennsylvania Historical and Museum Commission.
5. Biddle.
6. M.Carey Thomas, *The Making of a Feminist: Early Letters and Journals*, ed. Marjorie Housepian Dobkin (Kent, Ohio: Kent State University Press, 1979).
7. Biddle.
8. Elizabeth Meg Schaefer, "Wright's Ferry Mansion," *Antiques* 122 (Dec. 1982).
9. Robert L. Taylor, "Oh, Hawk of Mercy!" *New Yorker*, Apr. 17, 1948; *New York Times*, Dec. 1, 1962.
10. Mary Gibson Henry, "An Autobiography," *Plant Life* 6 (1950), pp. 11–30; *New York Times*, May 29, 1963, p. 40; brochure, Henry Foundation.
11. "The Vision of William Penn: Murals by Violet Oakley," *American History Illustrated* 14 (Jan. 1980), with fine illustrations.
12. Biddle.

13. Biddle; Jeanne M. Weimann, *The Fair Women* (Chicago, Ill.: Academy Chicago, 1981); clippings and correspondence, Lancaster County Library.

14. Guglielma Fell Alsop, *History of the Woman's Medical College* (Philadelphia, Pa.: J. B. Lippincott, 1950); correspondence, Pennsylvania Historical and Museum Commission.

15. Alsop, op. cit.

16. Biddle; correspondence, Temple University.

17. Fairmount Park Art Association, *Sculpture of a City: Philadelphia's Treasures in Bronze and Stone* (New York: Walker Publishing Co., 1974); Biddle.

18. Charlotte S. Rubinstein, *American Women Artists* (New York: Avon Books, 1982).

19. Fairmount Park Art Association, op. cit., p. 302; *New York Times*, Jan. 4, 1980.

20. Alsop, op. cit.; *New York Times*, May 29, 1969.

21. *A Marianne Moore Reader* (New York: Viking Press, 1961).

22. Dorothy Sterling, *Lucretia Mott* (Garden City, N.Y.: Doubleday & Co., 1964); correspondence, Pennsylvania Historical and Museum Commission.

23. Rubinstein, op. cit.

24. Biddle; Theo B. White, *The Philadelphia Art Alliance, Fifty Years, 1915–1965* (Philadelphia: University of Pennsylvania Press, 1965).

25. Rubinstein, op. cit.; *New York Times*, Feb. 14, 1977; *Current Biography*, 1955.

26. Correspondence, Pennsylvania Historical and Museum Commission.

27. Clippings and correspondence, Pittsburgh History and Landmarks Foundation.

28. Ibid.

29. Correspondence, Pennsylvania Historical and Museum Commission.

30. Correspondence, Tree of Life Congregation.

31. Clippings, correspondence, and National Register nomination forms, Pittsburgh History and Landmarks Foundation.

32. Biddle.

33. Biddle.

34. Biddle.

REGION IV

The Midwest

In 1763 the British tried to confine settlements in America to the area east of the Appalachian Mountains. In part this was an attempt to keep peace with the country's original inhabitants, the Indians. But trappers and hunters penetrated the wilderness, followed by land speculators and hardy settlers. In 1775 Daniel Boone and others cut the Wilderness Road through the Cumberland Gap. The Ohio Company of Virginia had been formed in 1747 to colonize the Ohio River Valley, and by the time the Revolution was over the United States was claiming a good part of the Midwest and settlers were moving in. Good soil, abundant water and rainfall, and plenty of fish and game attracted those from eastern states and many immigrants from European countries. Over the years the Spanish in the South and Southwest, the French in the North and in Louisiana gave up their claims by treaty or through purchase by the United States. By the close of the War of 1812 settlement had reached the Mississippi, and by the end of the Civil War, it had spread to the Pacific Coast and even to Alaska and Hawaii.

Women were very much a part of this westward movement, as pioneers, as missionaries, and as teachers in the new settlements. In addition, almost a new breed of woman emerged. Army wives learned to cope with life on frontier posts. Women took up homesteads and were farmers, cattle raisers, miners, hunters, and explorers. Cowgirls rode the range and performed in rodeos. Sharpshooters like Annie Oakley joined wild West shows. There were female bandits, gamblers, and prostitutes who gave color to the western scene.

Perhaps most striking is the emergence of educated Native American leaders and professional women. Some became spokespersons for their race and changed American attitudes toward the Indians. Women who visited the Southwest gained a respect for the Hispanic and Indian cultures.

By the time the midwestern states were being settled, American women were beginning to achieve some of their goals. Educational opportunities were opening up. Two great midwestern schools pioneered in accepting women and minorities:

Oberlin College in 1833 and Antioch College in 1852. Harriet Beecher Stowe got her inspiration for *Uncle Tom's Cabin* while living in Ohio.

During the Civil War midwestern women joined their northern sisters in caring for the wounded. The Sanitary Commission, predecessor of relief organizations, collected food and medical supplies for the army hospitals. One of the triumphs of the commission was the 1863 Sanitary Fair organized by Mary Livermore and Jane Hoge in Chicago, Illinois. Conceived, planned, and directed entirely by women, the fair raised over seventy thousand dollars. Other cities in the Midwest and East raised similar amounts. The success of such endeavors gave women a new appreciation of their own abilities. At the end of the war, when women found themselves still barred from the polls while the Fourteenth Amendment gave black males the vote, the suffrage movement gained new impetus.

Equal suffrage took on an almost symbolic meaning to women, who realized that to fight such evils as poverty, drunkenness, and prostitution they needed political power; the key to such power was the vote. Women who had the advantages of education were beginning to see the need for sweeping social changes. Hull House, established in Chicago in 1889, became a prototype for community work, from which the social work concepts of the twentieth century evolved. The first women to hold positions in federal offices established on behalf of women and children were midwesterners.

The participation of women in the 1893 World's Columbian Exposition held in Chicago was another great triumph for the sex, not only in demonstrating the products of women all over the world but in showing that they could successfully organize and carry out a woman's program. The women of every state were brought into the planning as "lady managers," and many of them returned home to organize civic clubs in their own towns.

The Midwest today is regarded as the heartland of America, its small towns and great stretches of land typically American. Its cities boast fine art galleries, symphony orchestras, universities, and libraries, many initiated, supported, and managed by women.

ILLINOIS

BENTON

Logan, Mary Simmerson Cunningham, 1838–1923, Patriot and Writer; NAW

Marker at Home, 204 S. Main Street (Private)

Mary Simmerson Cunningham Logan lived in Benton from the time of her marriage to John Alexander Logan in 1855 until he was elected to Congress. Washington, D.C., then became their principal home. It was Mary who suggested that a day be set aside to decorate the graves of Union heroes and John, as senator, who sponsored the legislation setting aside Memorial Day as a national holiday. After John died, her civic role expanded. She was on the Board of Lady Managers of the World's Columbian Exposition in 1893 and accompanied Bertha Honoré Palmer to Europe to solicit participation by foreign governments. Logan's *Thirty Years in Washington* (1901) and her volume of biographical sketches of notable women, *The Part Taken by Women in American History* (1912) are useful to this day.[1]

BLOOMINGTON

Von Elsner, Marie Eugenia (Marie Litta), 1856–1883, Concert Singer

Monument, Evergreen Cemetery

During her concert career Marie Eugenia Von Elsner, a native of Bloomington, was called "the second Jenny Lind." She adopted the stage name Marie Litta. Although she first sang at Steinway Hall in New York City at age nine, it was not until she had studied in Cleveland, Ohio, and in Paris, France, that she was ready to make her operatic debut. She appeared with Colonel James Mapleson's company at Drury Lane, London, in 1876, and made her first American appearance three years later in Boston, Massachusetts. A promising career was cut short when she died at the age of twenty-seven of spinal meningitis. At the base of the column that rises above her grave are inscribed memorials, including the words: "This monument was erected by the citizens of Bloomington to the memory of her who won fame for herself and reflected it upon the city of her birth."[2]

CEDARVILLE

Addams, Jane, 1860–1935, Settlement House Founder and Pacifist; NAW

John H. Addams Homestead, 425 N. Mill Street (Private); NR. Monument, in Family Burial Plot. Marker, State 26

Jane Addams, destined to become Illinois' most illustrious woman, was born into a prosperous family in Cedarville. She went from here to nearby Rockford Female Seminary. After she graduated, she spent several years rather aimlessly. Often ill and depressed, she was drawn toward helping the poor but unable to fix on a method. She saw herself as typical of many young women, well educated according to the standards of the time and well intentioned, sympathetic to need but lacking real understanding of the problems that beset society and divided it into warring groups.

Her solution was a simple and pragmatic one: "I gradually became convinced," she wrote, "that it would be a good thing to rent a house in a part of the city where many primitive and actual needs were found, in which young women . . . might restore a balance of activity along traditional lines and learn of life from life itself; where they might try out some of the things they had been taught." A visit to Toynbee Hall in London's East End, a settlement formed for the very purpose she herself envisioned, convinced her to make the attempt in Chicago. Thus Hull House was begun, and Addams left Cedarville to live at the settlement for the rest of her life (see Chicago, IL). At her death her remains came back to Cedarville for burial. A shaft over the grave is inscribed: "Jane Addams of Hull House and the Women's International League for Peace and Freedom." Historical items from the house may be seen at the Stephenson County Historical Society at 1440 S. Carroll Avenue in Freeport. It is open Fri.-Sun. 1:30–5.

CHICAGO

Addams, Jane, 1860–1935, and Ellen Gates Starr, 1859–1940, Settlement House Founders; NAW

Hull House, 800 S. Halsted Street; Chicago Landmark, HABS, NHL.[3] *Jane Addams School, 10810 S. Avenue H. Jane Addams School of Social Work, University of Illinois at Chicago. Jane Addams Housing Project, Roosevelt and Racine Streets*

In 1889 Jane Addams and Ellen Gates Starr came to Chicago to settle among the poorest and most miserable inhabitants of the city to study the causes of poverty and ways of ameliorating misery. They were able to rent part of the Hull mansion, once the country estate of a businessman, then surrounded by the homes of Chicago's working class, mainly European immigrants. Addams was to live there for the rest of her life, offering her neighbors practical help of all kinds along with friendship and love. Other young women who, like her, felt a desire to give of themselves, came to help at Hull House, and some went elsewhere to found similar settlements. Wealthy women gave money for the many projects—children's centers, gymnasiums, classes, and dormitories—that grew up around the settlement.

Their efforts were welcomed by all as laudable charities, but when they began to campaign for changes in social conditions such as the abolition of sweatshops and child labor, shorter working hours, labor unions, and industrial safety, Addams began to be viewed as a dangerous radical. While her international reputation grew and she was welcomed as a lecturer on social problems, she was a thorn in the flesh to Chicago's politicians. In World War I she was an outspoken pacifist, and it is difficult today to believe how widely she was mistrusted. By the time of her death, however, the wartime unpopularity was forgotten, her winning of the Nobel Peace Prize was lauded, and she was universally mourned as one of America's greatest women. She is represented in the Hall of Fame in New York City and in the National Women's Hall of Fame in Seneca Falls, New York.

Starr was a devout believer in the efficacy of classical art and literature to improve the lives of the workers. She realized, however, that low wages and long hours successfully conspired against her goals and this led her to espouse socialism as the only means of removing the economic repression dominating the lives of the poor. "For the children of the degraded poor," she said, "and the degraded rich as well, in our present mode of life, there is no artistic hope outside of [a] miracle." An impassioned partisan of working women, she was a charter member of the National Woman's Trade Union League and active in labor protests. At one point she was arrested for interfering with a police officer, but, according to her biographer, her "delicate, one hundred pound frame, pince-nez, and impeccable speech persuaded the jury of the implausibility of the charge."

Hull House has continued its work, and although the complex of buildings that grew up around it was demolished when the University of Illinois built its Chicago Circle campus in 1963, the services are still offered in neighborhood settings. Hull House itself was saved and restored. Somewhat dwarfed by the surrounding college buildings, it serves as a museum dedicated to the memory of Addams and other settlement workers. It is open Mon.-Fri. 10–4 and also, in summer, Sun. noon–5; closed holidays.

Bartelme, Mary Margaret, 1866–1954, Judge; NAWM

Mary Bartelme Homes, 542 S. Dearborn Street and 2737 W. Peterson Avenue

A protegée of Myra Bradwell, q.v., Mary Margaret Bartelme graduated from Northwestern University Law School in 1894, practiced for several years, and was then appointed public guardian for Cook County, one of her duties being the placement of orphans. She was concerned about young girls in trouble and established a separate court in which cases of teenaged girls accused of immoral behavior were heard in private. Her recommendations to the judge were generally followed. From 1927 to 1933 she was presiding judge of the Cook County Juvenile Court. Her philosophy was that there are no bad children; only confused, neglected, love-starved, and resentful children. She persuaded women's clubs to finance halfway houses for dependent girls, beginning in her own home. When a young woman was ready to leave the residence she was given a suitcase full of clothes with which to make a new start. Bartelme's women supporters called her Suitcase Mary, but they continued to fund homes named for her long after she retired.[4]

Bauer, Sybil, 1903–1927, Athlete

Tablet, Carl Schurz High School, 3601 N. Milwaukee Avenue

The tablet honors Sybil Bauer, an Olympic swimming champion who died of an illness while at the height of her fame and on the eve of marriage to a beloved fiancé. She began her swimming career while in high school, where she also played basketball, indoor baseball, and field hockey. She was a student at Northwestern University and president of the Women's Athletic Association at the time of her death. Northwestern has also erected a memorial to her (see Evanston, IL).[5]

Bond, Carrie Jacobs, 1862–1945, Song Writer; NAW

Carrie Jacobs Bond School, 7050 S. May Street

Carrie Jacobs Bond, a poor widow in her thirties with a son to support, ran a boardinghouse in Chicago and painted china to eke out a living. Somehow from this bleak background she wrote beautiful songs which she performed at social gatherings. One of her friends lent her money to publish a book, *Seven Songs as Unpretentious as a Wild Rose* (1901). "I Love You Truly" and "Just a-Wearyin' for You" were among the seven. They touched the hearts of America, as they do still. In 1910 she moved to California, which inspired her masterpiece, "A Perfect Day." See Janesville, WI.

Bradwell, Myra, 1831–1894, Lawyer; NAW

Myra Bradwell School, 7736 S. Burnham Street

Myra Bradwell tried to get admitted to the practice of law in Illinois in 1869. She had studied under her husband, a judge, and published a successful and influential legal paper, the *Chicago Daily News*. Her application to the Illinois bar, however, was denied by the state supreme court. Justice Bradley, who rendered the opinion, had his own ideas about the proper role of a wife. "The harmony of interests and views which belong to the family institution is repugnant to the idea of a woman adopting a distinct and independent career from that of her husband. . . . A married woman is incapable, without her husband's consent, of making contracts which shall be binding on her or him . . . [which renders] a married woman incompetent fully to perform the duties and trusts that belong to the office of an attorney and counselor." He cited as his authority "the law of the Creator." The U.S. Supreme Court upheld the decision in 1873, on the grounds that it was a matter for state jurisdiction. Not until 1890 did Illinois allow her to practice law, although she had long been recognized as America's leading female lawyer.[6]

Buckingham, Kate Sturges, 1858–1937, Philanthropist

Buckingham Fountain, Grant Park. Kate Buckingham School, 9207 S. Phillips Avenue

Kate Sturges Buckingham's father left several million dollars to his three children. Her brother and sister both died before she did, leaving their shares to her, which made her one of the wealthiest women in Chicago. She donated the Buckingham Fountain to the city in 1928 as a memorial to her brother. She and her sister had given many splendid art collections to the Art Institute of Chicago, and Buckingham added more. The Field Museum of Natural History was also the recipient of generous gifts. Buckingham explained that when she was young Chicagoans had to travel far to see things of beauty. "I am glad I have lived to see the day when people come from far and wide to see beautiful things in Chicago."[7]

Doggett, Kate Newell, 1827–1884, Clubwoman

Fortnightly Club (Lathrop House), 120 E. Bellevue Street (Private); Chicago Landmark, HABS, NR

"My dear Mrs. Hitchcock," she wrote, "will you meet a half-dozen friends here at 3 P.M. *precisely* next Friday for an hour's talk of a project that greatly interests me, has no connection with flannel for the Fiji-islanders." Who could resist? Not Hitchcock, nor any of the other invited friends of Kate Newell Doggett. The little meeting resulted in the formation in 1873 of Chicago's first long-lived woman's club, the Fortnightly. It is still active, and its history parallels the changes in women's lives over a century.

Doggett was not looking for publicity or fame. Well-bred women kept their affairs out of the papers, which may account for the fact that little has been recorded of her life, not even her maiden name. She was well educated, spoke several languages, was a reputable botanist—a member of the Academy of Science—and held ''bluestocking'' parties in her home. She lost her beloved husband in 1876 and never recovered from her grief. Some years later she moved to Cuba and died there.

In addition to the small founding group, other women were invited to join the Fortnightly. Some who would have liked to do so were not allowed to because their husbands or fathers disapproved, but over the years many of Chicago's outstanding women became members. Musicians and physicians, reformers and actresses, cat lovers and art collectors, travelers and stay-at-homes gathered every two weeks to hear the reading of literary papers and learned lectures by eminent men and women. Though the club was said to represent women of ''brain, blood, and bullion,'' it did channel into social change a large source of civic energy. The club met first in rented quarters; then in 1922 it acquired the Bryan Lathrop residence as its permanent home.[8]

Flower, Lucy Coues, 1837–1921, Social Reformer; NAW

Lucy Flower Vocational High School, 3545 W. Fulton Boulevard

Lucy Coues Flower spent thirty years attempting to make the city a better place for children. She was on the board of a number of institutions whose very names have an archaic ring: the Half Orphan Asylum (now Chapin Hall), the Home for the Friendless, the Lake Geneva Fresh Air Association (providing vacations for slum children), and the Protective Agency for Women and Children. She promoted school bathtubs for children whose tenement homes had no such amenities. She sponsored sewing and manual training classes in elementary grades.

She once became annoyed with the Cook County commissioners because they were not adequately caring for abandoned children. Borrowing a baby, she sat it on the conference table around which the commissioners were meeting and walked away. After a few moments of consternation they sent after her and begged her to take the child back. Then they discussed the problem.

When it came to her attention that many of the nurses in the county hospital were unqualified political appointees, she helped to found the Illinois Training School for Nurses, the first one in the city. She had many friends, but she also made a few enemies among politicians on whose toes she stepped. Of one, who lost his job through her influence, she said he had realized that ''not every Flower is born to blush unseen.''[9]

Hansberry, Lorraine, 1930–1965, Playwright; NAWM

Lorraine Hansberry Branch, Chicago Public Library, 4314 S. Cottage Grove Avenue

One night when Lorraine Hansberry was eight her house was surrounded by a mob; a brick thrown through the window just missed her. Her father, a believer in American justice, had deliberately moved his black family into a white area of Chicago. The family won a decision from the U.S. Supreme Court that should have, but in practice did not, open up white neighborhoods to anyone who wished to live in them. Her father became disillusioned, and Hansberry never made peace with the system that relegated her, because of her color, to half-day sessions in a segregated school. At the University of Wisconsin she found classes dull until she saw a play and began writing for the stage.

Her first play, *A Raisin in the Sun*, about a black family struggling for survival, opened in 1959. The first play by a black woman ever to appear on Broadway, it was a tremendous success. As her second successful play, *The Sign in Sidney Brustein's Window*, was enjoying a long run in New York City, Hansberry lay dying of cancer. In her short life she had contributed greatly to American drama and, even more, had spoken out forcefully and effectively against racism.

Hoffman, Malvina, 1885–1966, Sculptor; NAWM

Figures in Hall of Man, Field Museum of Natural History, S. Lake Shore Drive at 12th Street

Malvina Hoffman was commissioned by the Field Museum of Natural History in 1930 to produce figures illustrative of racial types from all over the world. In preparation, she traveled for two years in remote countries, bringing back models from which, during three more years, she sculptured over a hundred heads and figures of men and women. Intended as studies in anthropology rather than art, the work nevertheless earned her international recognition as a sculptor.

She was brought up in a musical family, where she learned to incorporate in her art musical structure, balance, and rhythm. She was further influenced by her regard for Anna Pavlova and the Russian ballet. She studied with Auguste Rodin; learned bronze casting, chasing and finishing; and studied anatomy and dissection—all skills necessary, she felt, to her work as a sculptor.

Jackson, Mahalia, 1911–1972, Gospel Singer; NAWM

Mahalia Jackson School, 917 W. 88th Street

''Making a joyful noise unto the Lord'' was what Mahalia Jackson called her singing. It was not exactly jazz or blues of the kind heard in her Louisiana home, nor was it just like the hymns she sang in the Greater Salem Baptist church in Chicago. It was gospel singing—songs originally composed by black musicians for black churches—with Jackson's own strong syncopated rhythms, delivered in a deep contralto voice. Her first big hit was "Move on Up a Little Higher," recorded in 1945, when she was living in Chicago. It brought her acclaim from music critics and devotion from fans. She made other recordings and sang in concerts, on television, and on radio. She would not appear in nightclubs or theaters: "It's not the place for my kind of singing."[10]

Keller, Annie Louise, 1901–1927, Teacher Heroine

Annie Keller School, 3807 W. 111th Street

The school is named for Annie Louise Keller, a heroic teacher who died while saving the children in her charge from the devastation of a tornado. See White Hall, IL.[11]

Lathrop, Julia Clifford, 1858–1932, Settlement House Worker; NAW

Julia Lathrop Public Housing Project, 2905 N. Leavit Street.
Julia C. Lathrop School, 1440 S. Christiana Avenue

Julia Clifford Lathrop was one of the first residents at Hull House, where she lived for twenty years. During the 1893 depression she was a volunteer investigator of applicants for relief, and she was appalled at conditions prevailing in the county charity agencies. Governor John Peter Altgeld appointed her to the State Board of Charities, which involved visits to poorhouses. This resulted in the writing of a book objecting to the mixing of young and old, sick and insane, delinquents and unfortunates in the almshouses and county farms. Lathrop said the inmates were not getting the specialized treatment they needed and that poorly trained staff, some of them political appointees, added to the problems.

Lathrop's work in pushing for a juvenile court system and her study of public schools led to her appointment in 1912 as the first head of the federal Children's Bureau. Its landmark studies of maternal mortality, juvenile delinquency, mental illness, child labor, and mothers' pensions led to legislation vastly improving life for many helpless people who needed a champion in the federal establishment.

Lewis, Julia Deal, d. 1966, Clubwoman and Philanthropist

Julia Deal Lewis Library, Loyola University, 820 N. Michigan Avenue

Julia Deal Lewis founded the Illinois Club for Catholic Women in 1920 and headed it from that time until her death. While directing three art shops of her own, she taught singing and dramatics to young women at the House of the

Good Shepherd. She and her prosperous husband, Frank Lewis, considered themselves ''partners of the Lord'' in spending their wealth for the good of others. They established the Lewis Foundation, which was the chief benefactor of Loyola University, and donated millions to the Stritch School of Medicine. Honored by many lay and religious organizations, Julia Lewis prized especially the ''Pro Papa et Ecclesia Medal'' of Pope Pius XII.[12]

Longman, Evelyn Beatrice (Batchelder), 1875–1954, Sculptor

Illinois Centennial Monument Reliefs, Logan Square, Logan and Kedzie Boulevards

Evelyn Beatrice Longman had been a student of Lorado Taft at the Chicago Art Institute before going to New York City to work with Daniel Chester French. She became one of America's best-known women sculptors and is represented in parks and gardens throughout the country. In private life she was the wife of Nathaniel Horton Batchelder. Her most outstanding work in Chicago is the seven-foot-high relief sculpture on the base of the Centennial Monument. The tall marble column was dedicated in 1918 to commemorate Illinois' one hundredth year of statehood.[13]

McCormick, Nettie Fowler, 1835–1923, Philanthropist; NAW

Fowler Hall, McCormick Theological Seminary, 5555 S. Woodlawn Avenue

After her marriage to Cyrus H. McCormick, Nettie Fowler McCormick took a real interest in Cyrus's business, the manufacture of the mechanical reaper he had invented. In 1871 when his factory was destroyed in the great fire Nettie encouraged him to rebuild it at once. She remained his close business associate and advisor, and after he died (1884) she took over virtual management of the business. She was influential in organizing the International Harvester Company. She gradually withdrew from business life and spent much of her time in disposing of her wealth. The chief of her many philanthropies in the United States and foreign countries was the McCormick Theological Seminary, which her husband had supported from the first. She took part in the design of the buildings, the development of doctrine, and the selection of faculty. When one prospect hesitated to join the faculty because of its inadequate library, she donated a new one. Fowler Hall was named for her. The gymnasium, built after her death, was largely paid for by her gift. Of the over $4 million donated to the institution by the McCormicks, the last million was a memorial to Nettie.[14]

McDowell, Mary Eliza, 1854–1936, Settlement House Worker; NAW

Mary McDowell Settlement of Chicago Commons Association, 1335 W. 51st Street. Mary McDowell School, 1419 E. 89th Street

When Mary Eliza McDowell, daughter of a well-to-do Chicago family, first came to the area "back of the yards," its most striking characteristic was its odor. Added to the rotting refuse of the meat-packing plants was the stench of uncollected garbage and open sewers. A stagnant backwater of the Chicago River emitted foul-smelling waste carbonic gas, which earned it the name of Bubbly Creek. Workers from the stockyards lived in drab houses on treeless streets. Wages were low, hours long, working conditions miserable. This area was chosen by the Philanthropic Committee of the Christian Union of the University of Chicago as the site for its settlement house in 1894. McDowell, who had set up a kindergarten at Hull House, was its first director. A violent and bloody strike in the packing houses had just been settled, leaving the workers bitter, "without courage and self-confidence."

McDowell did what she could to change conditions, beginning with protests to City Hall and the Health Department that earned her the name of "the garbage lady." The results were not encouraging. The lawyer for the city told her delegation that "in every great city there must be a place segregated for unpleasant things. Of course the people living there are not sensitive." McDowell was there to tell him that the people were indeed sensitive. She rallied the neighborhood women, the members of the Chicago Woman's Club, and her friends from Hull House, but it was not until the women were given the municipal vote in 1913 that they got the results they wanted—a bureau of city waste under a qualified engineer.

McDowell remained as director of the settlement until 1929. She was also for some years the city's commissioner of public welfare. The house, originally the University of Chicago Settlement, officially changed its name in 1956, but it was always—at least to its neighbors—McDowell's settlement.[15]

Newbury, Mollie Alpiner Netcher, 1867–1954, Retail Merchant

State-Madison Building (Former Boston Store), 22 W. Madison Avenue; Chicago Landmark

Mollie Alpiner Netcher Newbury loved her work. She rose from clerk to buyer at the Boston Store, and learned how to buy, display, and sell merchandise. Charles Netcher, the store's president, noticed the young buyer and courted her. After they were married it would have been unseemly, of course, for her to go back to work, so she stayed at home, ran his household, and cared for their four children. In the evenings she and Netcher discussed every detail of the store's management. "We talked business just as other people talk love," she said. "He entrusted things to me from the first."

When in 1904 Charles died suddenly, Mollie simply stepped into his place. The *Chicago Tribune* expressed surprise that a woman "whose role for fourteen years has been the all-engrossing one of wife, mother and the active head of her own large establishment, can . . . take over the management of a business involving millions, with absolute confidence in her ability to succeed." Over the next half century she expanded sales volume five times, replaced the building with a handsome larger one, and at the same time made a second fortune in downtown real estate. Her second husband, Solomon Newbury, went to the store with her every day but took no part in the business. She was universally regarded as a brilliant, if old-fashioned, business woman, Chicago's Merchant Princess. In 1946 she sold the store, and two years later it closed. The building, considered an architectural treasure, was converted into office space.[16]

Palmer, Bertha Honoré, 1849–1918, Society Leader; NAW

Jackson Park Historic Landscape District and Midway Plaisance, Jackson and Washington Parks and Midway Plaisance Roadway; NR

The World's Columbian Exposition, held at this spot in 1893, was a great event in Chicago's history. That it was also an important part of women's history is due in large part to Bertha Honoré Palmer, wife of Potter Palmer; she was appointed chairperson of the Board of Lady Managers for the fair. She recruited women from all over the country and many foreign countries to make the Woman's Building truly representative of the best in women's art, craft, literature, and history. The building itself was designed by a woman architect, Sophia Hayden. Murals were commissioned to women artists, including expatriate Mary Cassatt. Books by and about women were collected for display. Sculptures and fountains by women graced the courtyards and halls. Residences and child care centers were provided for women who visited the fair. Not since the great sanitary fairs of the Civil War had women demonstrated their ability to plan and execute such a vast and successful undertaking.

Palmer was a leader of Chicago society. She lived in a palace which included an art gallery full of modern French paintings; she owned jewelry comparable to that belonging to crowned heads. A beautiful, intelligent, and vivacious woman, she was adored by her husband, builder of the Palmer House hotel. When he drew up a will leaving his fortune to her, his lawyer suggested that she might marry again and the millions would go to another man. "If she does," said Potter, "he'll need the money." She was not, however, just a social butterfly. She joined the Chicago Woman's Club in its campaigns for civic improvement, and sometimes she showed up at Hull House to lend her support to whatever the settlement workers needed.

The Midway Plaisance, a mile-long plaza, is now an integral part of the campus of the University of Chicago.[17]

Patterson, Eleanor Medill, 1881–1948, Publisher; NAW

Cissy Patterson Mansion (Later Cyrus McCormick Mansion), 20 E. Burton Way; Chicago Landmark

Redheaded, hot-tempered Eleanor (Cissy) Medill Patterson was the granddaughter of Joseph Medill, who published the *Chicago Tribune*, and daughter of Robert Patterson, who succeeded to the editorship of the paper. In spite of this newspaper connection, Patterson's sally into journalism did not begin until she was almost fifty, after two marriages—one ended by divorce, the other by death—and following the fast-moving, free-spending life of a wealthy society matron. Nor did she have to begin at the bottom: although she knew nothing about running a paper, she was hired in 1930 as editor and publisher of the Washington (D.C.) *Herald*. Less than ten years later she owned the paper and its evening counterpart, the *Times*, which had been losing money under the management of William Randolph Hearst. Her capable and imaginative leadership of the combined *Times-Herald* brought up its circulation until it topped all others in the city. Patterson, called the most powerful woman in America—also "the most hated"—had found her niche.

She lived only a short time in the Chicago mansion, which her father had built for her and which was designed by Stanford White. It later belonged to the Cyrus McCormicks, cousins on her mother's side.

Porter, Eliza Chappel, 1807–1888, Teacher and Civil War Worker; NAW

Eliza Chappel School, 5145 N. Leavit Street

Eliza Chappel Porter opened the first school in Chicago in 1833. The tiny frontier settlement adjoining Fort Dearborn apparently had enough children in need of schooling to justify her efforts. The schoolhouse was a log cabin. By the following year her school qualified for money from the legislature, and it moved into a new Presbyterian church built by Eliza's friend Jeremiah Porter.

Eliza at twenty-six had already been teaching for ten years, first in her own "infant school" in Rochester, New York, then in Mackinac Island, where her pupils included the children of American Fur Company employees and Indian boys and girls. Although forced to interrupt her teaching several times by illness, she was dedicated to the goals of spreading her religious beliefs in schools for the young and of training teachers for such schools. In 1835 she married Jeremiah Porter and left Chicago.

Twenty-three years later she and her husband returned to Chicago. They were here during the Civil War, when Eliza worked with the Chicago Sanitary Commission. She spent most of the war years in the field, assisting wounded soldiers, recruiting nurses, running a diet kitchen, at times shoulder-to-shoulder with Mother Bickerdyke (see Galesburg, IL).

Price, Florence Beatrice Smith, 1888–1953, Composer; NAWM

Florence B. Price School, 4351 S. Drexel Boulevard

The first black woman to win recognition for symphonic composition, Florence Beatrice Smith Price came from Little Rock, Arkansas, to Chicago in 1927. She was a graduate of the New England Conservatory in Boston, Massachusetts, an accomplished pianist, organist, and composer. She came to the attention of Frederick Stock, conductor of the Chicago Symphony, when she won first prize in 1932 for a composition. The following year the orchestra presented her Symphony in E Minor at the Century of Progress Exposition. She appeared that same year with the Chicago Women's Symphony playing her Piano Concerto in F Minor. For the next twenty years Price continued writing symphonies, songs, short choral works and teaching pieces.

Solomon, Hannah Greenebaum, 1858–1942, Clubwoman and Philanthropist; NAW

Hannah G. Solomon School, 6206 N. Hamlin Avenue

In 1910 Hannah Greenebaum Solomon found herself walking about the city dump, clutching the hem of her long lace dress in one white-gloved hand, a dainty parasol in the other. She was on her club's committee to investigate the city's wholly inadequate waste disposal system. She told the story afterward to illustrate how ready, though ill prepared, she and the other clubwomen were to take on civic problems.

Concerned about Jewish immigrants in Chicago and the conditions under which many lived, she had in 1897 established a Bureau of Personal Service to help newcomers. She was involved in the founding of the juvenile courts and the Illinois Industrial School for Girls, later the Park Ridge School. She was asked to form a congress of Jewish women for the Parliament of Religions at the World's Columbian Exposition. Out of this came the first nationwide organization of Jewish women, the National Council of Jewish Women, of which she was the first president.[18]

Starr, Ellen Gates. See Addams, Jane

Thompson, Mary, 1829–1895, Physician; NAW

Mary Thompson Hospital, 140 N. Ashland Avenue

Referred to by the *Chicago Medical Journal* as "Miss Doctoress Thompson," Mary Thompson faced male hostility when she began practicing medicine in

Chicago near the end of the Civil War, but some years later she was elected to an office in the Chicago Medical Society. She had won a place as one of the most highly respected women members of the profession and was regularly published in the medical journals. Soon after she began to practice she could not get a child into a hospital because females were barred. At once she organized backing for a hospital for women and children. It was built in 1865, with Thompson as head of staff. The hospital burned in the 1871 fire, but twenty-four hours later Thompson was treating victims in rented quarters.

Thompson had also set up a woman's medical college in connection with the hospital, so that women could get advanced degrees in the city. Both buildings were rebuilt after the fire. The hospital was renamed for her after her death and was later relocated to Ashland Avenue; the college became part of the McGraw Medical Center at Northwestern University.[19]

Wells-Barnett, Ida Bell, 1862–1931, Civil Rights Leader; NAW

Wells-Barnett Home, 3624 S. Martin Luther King, Jr., Drive (Private); NHL. Ida B. Wells Housing Project, 454 E. Pershing Street

Ida Bell Wells-Barnett made an early bid for Negro rights when, hardly out of her teens, she sued the Chesapeake and Ohio Railroad because the conductor tried to force her to move from a "white" to a "colored" coach. She learned of the decision in her favor when she saw the headline "Darkey Damsel Gets Damages." Three years later the decision was overturned by the Tennessee Supreme Court.

At a time when she owned half of a Memphis newspaper, three of her friends were lynched. Her fiery denunciation of the crime and the society that condoned it resulted in the destruction of her office by a mob, who might have lynched her too had she not been away from the city. She then began a one-woman crusade against lynching and other crimes against her race. In 1893 she was in Chicago protesting against the virtual exclusion from the World's Exposition of blacks and black culture. She married a Chicago lawyer, F. L. Barnett, and Chicago was her home for the rest of her life. The first federal housing project in Chicago was named for the courageous crusader.[20]

Willard, Frances, 1839–1898, Temperance Leader; NAW

Memorial Fountain, Lincoln Park

The fountain honoring Frances Willard, president of the Woman's Christian Temperance Union, is called "The Little Water Girl." See Evanston, IL, and Janesville, WI.

Young, Ella Flagg, 1845–1918, Educator; NAW

Ella Flagg Young School, 1424 N. Parkside Avenue

Ella Flagg Young was appointed superintendent of Chicago schools in 1909. The following year she was the first woman elected president of the National Education Association. Women had been the nation's teachers for many years, had founded schools and colleges, had trained generations of other teachers, and had contributed in many ways to education in the United States. Yet the public school system was still dominated by male boards of education (elected by male voters), by male school administrators, and by an educational philosophy Young found sadly lacking in an understanding of the needs of school children. She was a follower of John Dewey and worked closely with him for some years at the University of Chicago. While constantly hampered in her efforts to upgrade teacher training, to broaden the curriculum (even to include sex education), and to give teachers a voice in school administration, she was nevertheless one of the most effective educators of her time, one whose name adds luster to the history of Chicago's schools.

DECATUR

Boyd, Anne Morris, 1884–1974, Librarian and Educator

Anne M. Boyd Room, Decatur Public Library, 247 E. North Street

While teaching in a small Illinois school and seeing how strongly books influenced children's lives, Anne Morris Boyd decided she wanted to be a children's librarian. She took library training at James Millikin University in Decatur, then went to work at the Kansas State Agricultural College. Here it was one of her duties to sort, classify, and catalog a basement full of government documents. She became enamored of them and though it was far removed from her original interest—children's literature—much of her subsequent career was devoted to making documents intelligible and available to scholars.

Following stints at the St. Louis Public Library and the Decatur Public Library, she went to the University of Illinois Library School, which became her home for thirty-two years. Her courses in working with government documents and in book selection were well attended. The Anne M. Boyd Room was dedicated in 1959, the same year in which she received an Alumni Award from Millikin University. The Anne M. Boyd Award is given annually to a graduate library student.[21]

DEERFIELD

Castle, Irene Foote (McLaughlin), 1893–1969, Dancer and Animal Rescue Worker; NAWM

Orphans of the Storm Animal Shelter, 2200 Riverwoods Road

Many remember the Tango, the Maxixe, and the Castle Walk, popularized by the dance team of Irene Foote Castle and Vernon Castle. The two were married in 1911 and began a joint career in show business and dancing. Young, clean, happily married, and well mannered, they made a hit. Irene's fashions—bobbed hair, headband, light floating dresses—were copied across the nation. Vernon joined the Royal Flying Corps in 1916 and two years later died in a plane crash. Irene married a wealthy Chicago, Illinois, sportsman, Frederic McLaughlin, and settled down to raise a family. She also began animal rescue work, giving "Pooch Balls" to raise funds for stray animals, and in 1928 she established the shelter in Deerfield. She helped on the 1939 movie *The Story of Irene and Vernon Castle*, in which the leads were taken by another famous dance team, Fred Astaire and Ginger Rogers.[22]

ELSAH

Morgan, Mary Kimball, 1861–1948, College Founder; NAW

Principia College

Mary Kimball Morgan and her husband, William Morgan, were founders of the Christian Science Church in St. Louis, Missouri. In 1896 she became a practitioner and also began to educate her children at home according to the principles of the church. Other families sent their children to her. A year after she founded her school, known as the Principia, it was endorsed by Mary Baker Eddy. Not much later the school owned an entire block in St. Louis. She added a high school class and a two-year college course. In 1932 the four-year college was established at Elsah. Morgan herself moved to Elsah to live and continued as president of Principia College until 1938, when she was succeeded by a son. The town that grew up around the college has been declared a National Historic District.

EVANSTON

Baker, Edna Dean. See Harrison, Elizabeth

Bauer, Sybil, 1903–1927, Athlete

Memorial, Patten Gymnasium, Northwestern University

Sybil Bauer was the first woman to break an athletic record set by a man when she broke the world record in the one-hundred-meter backstroke at the 1924

Olympic Games. During the years 1922 to 1927 she was one of the most successful women in athletic competition. She shunned publicity, never exploiting her victories. Following her early death from illness, her fellow students at Northwestern set up the memorial for her. See Chicago, IL.[23]

Garrett, Eliza Clark, 1805–1855, Philanthropist

Garrett Evangelical Theological Seminary, 2121 Sheridan Road

Eliza Clark Garrett was widowed in 1848, inheriting a sizeable estate which she decided to use for the benefit of her denomination, the Methodist church. In her will, executed in 1853, she set aside more than one-third of her estate, some $250,000, for the erection and endowment of a theological institution to be called the Garrett Biblical Institute. About this time a site had been selected for Northwestern University, and it was decided to locate the biblical school nearby. The institute in time became a graduate school of theology.[24]

Merged with the institute some years later was the pioneering Chicago Training School for City, Home, and Foreign Missions established in 1855 by Lucy Rider Meyer (1849–1922, NAW) and her husband, Josiah Meyer. It offered a two-year course for women entering religious and missionary careers. During the Meyers' involvement with the school, which lasted until 1917, it was a forceful center of a religious-oriented social work for Chicago Methodists. As many as forty philanthropic enterprises were traceable to the Meyers and their students. They included Wesley Memorial Hospital, the Chicago Old People's Home, and the Lake Bluff Orphanage. Lucy's primary interest was the deaconess movement which was just opening up in Protestant denominations. She wrote a history of the movement and edited its newspaper.

Gordon, Anna. See Willard, Frances

Harrison, Elizabeth, 1849–1927 (NAW), and Edna Dean Baker, 1883–1956, Educators

National College of Education, 2840 Sheridan Road

In 1887 when Elizabeth Harrison founded the Chicago Kindergarten Training School, girls with an eighth-grade education could learn a smattering of Friedrich Froebel's kindergarten methods and go to work as teachers of young children. Harrison's school required high school graduation for entrance and gave a thorough three-year course in the humanities, science, and social science in addition to kindergarten philosophy and techniques. Her graduates were ready to give preschoolers a wealth of creative stimulation. Harrison herself had studied with the most renowned teachers in the United States and abroad since she first visited a kindergarten and discovered a "world of glorious thought and inspiring activity." During its early years the training school's students and faculty were all women.

Edna Dean Baker was Harrison's assistant from 1915 until 1920, when she succeeded as president. It was during her term, which lasted until 1949, that the school became the National College of Education and moved to Evanston, expanding its program. The students used the Mary Crane Nursery at Hull House as well as its own laboratory school, the Children's School, as training centers. The latter was founded and directed for thirty-four years by Baker's sister, Clara Belle Baker (1885–1961).[25]

Hill, Elizabeth Webb, 1898–1978, Physician

Elizabeth W. Hill Pavilion, Evanston Hospital, 2040 Brown Avenue

Elizabeth Webb Hill received her M.D. from the University of Illinois Medical School in 1929 and after interning at Chicago's Provident Hospital opened up her own practice. The only place that accepted black patients in Evanston was the Community Hospital, first consisting of a few beds in the home of a Negro doctor. Hill got together twenty women and organized the Women's Auxiliary of Community Hospital, which raised money to buy sheets, blankets, and equipment.

After she had been chief of the hospital's staff for some years, she decided it was time to erect a real hospital building for black doctors and patients. Some of the Negro groups opposed it, fearing it would only perpetuate segregation in medical care. "We can't wait fifteen years for integration," Hill said, "the people are ill now." The new building was dedicated in 1952. Many awards and honors came to the doctor. The Community Hospital gave her a plaque after thirty-five years as its chief medical officer. She was in 1975 appointed to the medical staff of the Northwestern University Medical School and the same year was named senior attending physician in internal medicine at Evanston Hospital. Shortly after her death the Evanston Hospital Corporation acquired Community Hospital and renamed it for Hill. A multipurpose center for elderly residents of Evanston, recently opened near the site of her office, has been named Hilltoppers.[26]

Meyer, Lucy Rider. See Garrett, Eliza

Willard, Frances, 1839–1898, and Anna Gordon, 1853–1931, Temperance Leaders; NAW

Frances Willard House, 1730 Chicago Avenue; HABS, NHL

In December 1873 a spontaneous antisaloon campaign sprang up in the Midwest. Groups of women went to saloons, knelt in the streets, and prayed for the liquor merchants and their customers. The movement spread like wildfire. A woman's temperance union was organized in New York State and another in California. It is said that within six months some three thousand saloons closed their doors.

Women in Chicago, Illinois, joined the crusade and the next year met at Bloomington, Illinois, to form a statewide woman's temperance union. They chose as their leader Frances Willard, who had been dean of women at Northwestern University. From that time until her death Willard's career was the Woman's Christian Temperance Union (WCTU).

It was due to Willard that the organization stood during her lifetime for much broader principles than the mere closing of saloons. She persuaded women who were reluctant to join the suffragists that they needed the vote to protect their homes from the evils of strong drink, and she led them into many social reforms. The movement became international after Willard visited San Francisco, California, and saw the young girl prostitutes in Chinatown. She realized that women the world over needed to band together for protection. Willard has been honored by inclusion in the Hall of Fame in New York City and representation in Statuary Hall in the National Capitol. See Chicago, IL, and Janesville, WI.

Anna Gordon met Willard in 1877. A strong friendship developed between the two women and Gordon became Willard's live-in private secretary, working with her until the latter's death. Gordon continued in the home for the next thirty-three years. The leadership of the WCTU had devolved on Lillian M. N. Stevens, and Gordon continued her role as second in command, while devoting much of her energy to the perpetuation of Willard's memory. After Stevens died in 1914, Gordon herself succeeded to the presidency. Her flair for getting public attention by such acts as pouring three hundred bottles of illegal whiskey into the sewer while reporters watched helped raise large sums for the union. The WCTU joined the Anti-Saloon League in its fight for a federal prohibition amendment. Gordon then directed the energies of the organization toward world prohibition and was elected president of the world's WCTU.

The building at the rear of the Evanston home is the national headquarters of the WCTU. It can be visited Mon.-Fri. 9–12 and 1–4, by reservation only (312–864–1397).

FOREST PARK

Goldman, Emma, 1869–1940, Anarchist Lecturer and Writer (NAW), and Other Radicals

Monuments, Forest Home Cemetery, 863 S. Desplaines Avenue

The Haymarket riot of 1886 and its aftermath in the execution of four radical leaders and the imprisonment of four others is one of the landmarks of labor history. On May 4 the police broke up a peaceable meeting in Haymarket Square, Chicago, Illinois, protesting police brutality. Someone threw a bomb and the police began shooting. At least seven demonstrators were killed by gunshot. Eight leaders of the meeting were brought to trial, and although the defendants neither threw the bomb nor knew who threw it, their speeches and writings "might have inspired" its throwing; this made them accessories and all were

Frances Willard, leader of the Woman's Christian Temperance Union, was chosen by the state of Illinois as one of its representatives in Statuary Hall in the National Capitol, Washington, D.C. The sculptor of the statue was Helen Farnsworth Mears, of Oshkosh, Wisconsin.
Courtesy Architect of the Capitol, Washington, D.C.

convicted. Four were hanged. Labor leaders formed an association to raise money for a monument to the martyrs, which was finally erected at Forest Home Cemetery (then called Waldheim). The monument has always meant a great deal to the more radical members of the labor movement, and many socialists, labor activists, and civil rights leaders chose to be buried near it in Dissenters Row, some in unmarked graves, others with monuments.

The best known was Emma Goldman. A Russian Jew, she came to America in 1885 and for fifty years was a firebrand in American society. She became an avowed anarchist after the Haymarket affair, believing in the replacement of a political and authoritarian social structure by free association of strong, independent individuals. Her radicalism led her to espouse acts of violence, such as the attempted murder of Henry Clay Frick during the Homestead Steel Strike in 1892, for which Goldman's lover, Alexander Berkman, spent fourteen years in the penitentiary. Goldman herself was incarcerated at Blackwell's Island, where she served her fellow prisoners as nurse and counselor. When President William McKinley was shot, Goldman was blamed, though she could not be convicted of complicity. She edited a radical monthly, *Mother Earth*; she lectured on a variety of subjects; she wrote pamphlets; she fought for free speech, civil rights, and the rights of women.

During the postwar Red scare in 1919 Goldman and Berkman were deported to Russia. She stayed only two years, then, disillusioned, she left to reside in Europe and Canada. In 1934 she was given permission to return for ninety days to America, where she made political speeches. "You are still free in America," she said, "you are free to come here and listen to me, with no army of police descending upon you. No spies enter your homes for incriminating documents. No legalized assassins shoot you down in the streets."

After Goldman's death authorities allowed her body to be brought back to Illinois to be buried near her Haymarket idols. Her monument bears a bas-relief of her face by Jo Davidson, the dates of her birth and death (curiously, it reads 1939 instead of the correct year, 1940) and a quotation: "Liberty will not descend to a people, a people must raise themselves to liberty."

Voltairine de Cleyre (1866–1912), also radicalized by the Haymarket events, is buried at this spot, by her choice. She met Goldman while teaching English to Jewish factory workers in Philadelphia, Pennsylvania, and she began contributing articles to *Mother Earth*. After McKinley's assassination Senator Joseph Hawley offered a thousand dollars to "get a good shot at an anarchist." De Cleyre offered herself as a target if he would first agree to let her explain to him the principles of anarchism. An ascetic, she wore ragged clothes, welcomed poverty, and shunned marriage.[27]

Lucy Parsons (1853?–1942), widow of Albert Parsons, one of the hanged men, had been a radical even before her marriage and the Haymarket incident that ended it, and she continued speaking against wage slavery for another fifty years. She was a light-skinned Negro, probably a slave in childhood, although she never admitted it. She was tall and strikingly beautiful, with a powerful and musical speaking voice. Considered dangerous by the establishment, she was supported by Chicago liberals, including Jane Addams, who once posted bail for her. She felt that only socialism would free women from economic, political, and religious constraints and allow them to be in charge of their own lives. Although her biographer believes Parsons was born in 1853, her grave marker gives her birthdate as 1859.[28]

Elizabeth Gurly Flynn (1890–1964, NAWM) met Parsons at a convention of the Industrial Workers of the World (IWW) in 1907. Then only seventeen and a high school student, Flynn admired Parsons. "I remember Mrs. Parsons speaking warmly to the young people, warning us of the seriousness of the struggles ahead that could lead to jail and death before victory was won." Flynn became an organizer for the IWW and took part in many of the bloodiest strikes in the history of labor. Joe Hill, "the Troubadour of the IWW," dedicated to her his song "The Rebel Girl." She was a founder of the American Civil Liberties Union (ACLU), but when she joined the Communist party the ACLU expelled her from its executive board. She was sent to prison for three years for advocating the overthrow of the government by force and violence. She visited Moscow several times; unlike Goldman, she continued to believe in the Revolution. She died in the Soviet Union and was given a state funeral in Red Square. The marker in the cemetery reads: "Elizabeth G. Flynn, 1890–1964, 'The Rebel Girl,' Fighter for Working Class Emancipation."[29]

GALESBURG

Bickerdyke, Mary Ann Ball, 1817–1901, Civil War Nurse; NAW

Statue, Courthouse Square

Mary Ann Ball Bickerdyke was the best loved of the many untrained but skilled and kindhearted women who volunteered to nurse sick and wounded soldiers of the Civil War. She ran her operations—laundries, diet kitchens, a dairy, and a henyard—with or without government sanction and was known to ride roughshod over regulations that got in the way of her giving the best possible care to "her boys." She worked in hospitals and on battlefields, on ships and on troop trains. Newspaper reporters dramatized her work and the soldiers idolized her. When she was not nursing, she lectured to raise money for the Sanitary Commission. Many stories of her ingenuity and audacity have been told, including her retort when a surgeon asked on whose authority she was acting: "On the authority of Lord God Almighty."

Two years after Bickerdyke's death the state of Illinois appropriated money for a statue, which was unveiled in 1906. It shows Mother Bickerdyke giving a wounded man a drink. At the base are inscribed words attributed to General William Tecumseh Sherman when an officer complained about her: "She outranks me."[30]

The sculptor was Theo Alice Ruggles Kitson (1871–1932), a Massachusetts woman whose powerful war memorials stand in over fifty sites across the country.[31]

JACKSONVILLE

Walworth, Ellen Hardin, 1832–1915, Clubwoman; NAW

Marker, S. Main and College Streets

The marker, where the Philip Morris Building now stands, is at the site of Ellen Hardin Walworth's birthplace. She was the daughter of John and Sarah Hardin, who built the first brick house in Jacksonville. She went to school here and moved away in 1851 when her widowed mother married Reuben Hyde Walworth, the last chancellor of New York State. The following year Ellen married her stepbrother, Mansfield Walworth. She is chiefly remembered as one of the founders of the Daughters of the American Revolution. There are memorials to her in Saratoga Springs, New York, and in Washington, D.C.

LEMONT

Dudzik, Josephine (Mother Mary Theresa), 1860–1918, Religious Founder

Shrine, Grounds of the Motherhouse of the Franciscan Sisters of Chicago, The League of the Servant of God Mother Mary Theresa, 1220 Main Street

Josephine Dudzik and her family arrived in Chicago, Illinois, in 1881 from their native Poland. A devout Catholic family, they sought in America not only a better life but religious freedom. As she worked in her parish church, the miseries of the unemployed and the bitter labor struggles she witnessed in Chicago touched her. She began taking in homeless elderly women; the house was soon filled with such unfortunates.

The severe unemployment and distress following the World's Columbian Exposition of 1893 impelled Dudzik to open a house of refuge. Under the auspices of St. Stanislaus Kostka parish, a group of young women of the Third Order of St. Francis formed a sisterhood in 1894 and elected Dudzik their superior. She took the name of Mary Theresa. At first in a rented apartment, later in a home built through the earnings of the sisters, the new congregation began taking in the destitute and handicapped. St. Joseph's Home in Avondale opened in 1898. The following year an orphanage was built adjacent to the home, where the sisters cared for many infants and young children. A statue of Mother Mary Theresa at the shrine shows her holding in her arms one of her first young charges, a crippled child.[32]

MOLINE

Brooks, Marguerite, 1896–1982, Hospital Administrator

Marguerite N. Brooks Learning Resource Center and Laboratory, Moline Public Hospital

Marguerite (christened Margret) Brooks graduated from St. Joseph's Hospital School of Nursing in Chicago, Illinois, and did postgraduate work at Cook County Hospital. Some years later when she was made administrator of the Public Hospital in Moline, her hometown, some grumbled that it was no job for a woman. She proved them wrong. She worked to make the hospital support itself instead of burdening the taxpayers. She extended the school of nursing, established a school of X-ray technology, worked with Black Hawk College students in a practical nursing course, and made the hospital a center for innovative health care programs. She retired in 1977 and shortly afterward the new learning resource center and laboratory was named for her.[33]

MT. OLIVE

Jones, Mary Harris, 1830–1930, Labor Agitator; NAW

Monument, Union Miners Cemetery; NR

The only union-owned cemetery in the country is dominated by the memorial to Mary Harris Jones (Mother Jones), beloved by laboring men. She joined the cause of working men's rights after the Chicago, Illinois, fire of 1871 which burned down her home. Finding refuge with the Knights of Labor, she began to attend their meetings and listen to the problems of the workers. Afterward she went from one industrial area to another, helping to organize, to educate, and to do what she could in strikes, especially in the coal miners' struggles.

She was able to dramatize strikes by such tactics as leading miners' wives with brooms and mops to attack strikebreakers. Once she led a caravan of strikers' children from the textile mills of Kensington, Pennsylvania, to the home of President Theodore Roosevelt in Oyster Bay, New York.

She often visited the Union Miners Cemetery after it was established in 1899 to receive the bodies of workers killed in a strike, and she asked to be buried there beside them. Her funeral was attended by thousands, including prominent union leaders and miners who came from all parts of Illinois. In 1934 the Progressive Mine Workers of America began soliciting funds for an appropriate monument to the "Joan of Arc of the coal fields." When it was dedicated in 1936, every newspaper in the country covered the ceremony. Each year Mt. Olive celebrates October 12 not as Columbus Day but as Miners Day, and throngs visit the monument to Mother Jones and the martyrs of labor wars. Mary Harris Jones was elected in 1985 to the National Women's Hall of Fame.[34]

MURPHYSBORO

Logan, Sallie Oliver, 1851–1936, Businesswoman

Sallie Logan Library

A strong, high-spirited woman of Irish ancestry, Sallie Olive Logan, wife of Thomas Logan, was an enthusiastic partner in her husband's business of breeding and racing horses, and after he died she continued it. She also took his place as a director of the Murphysboro Electric Railway, Light, Heat, and Power Company and of the Murphysboro Telephone Company. She had already served as secretary and treasurer of the latter business. In her will she left her house and four lots at 18th and Walnut Streets to the city to be used as a free public library and community center. The house has since been razed and replaced by a modern building. In 1976 a plaque memorializing Sallie and other members of the Logan family was erected at a corner of the property.[35]

NAUVOO

Smith, Emma Hale, 1804–1879, Mormon Leader; NAW

Joseph Smith Homestead and the Mansion House; NR

''The wife of my youth and the choice of my heart,'' said Joseph Smith, ''undaunted, firm, and unwavering—unchangeable, affectionate Emma.'' Joseph was the prophet who translated the Book of Mormon from golden plates and founded the Church of Latter Day Saints. After he was murdered by a mob at the Carthage jail in 1844, Emma Hale Smith chose to remain in Nauvoo while most of the Mormons began their long trek to find a new home in Utah. Her life had never been an easy one, and toward the end she had to face the fact that she was not Joseph Smith's only wife. He had received revelations concerning plural marriage and had begun to practice it some time before his death.

Emma married a non-Mormon in 1847, but remained true to the faith herself and brought up Joseph's sons as believers. Emma died in Nauvoo and was buried here, along with Joseph and Hyrum Smith. The Homestead, a log cabin which served as the first Nauvoo home of the family, and the Mansion House, the permanent home, are part of the Joseph Smith Historic Center, maintained by the Reorganized church. They are open Memorial Day–Labor Day, 8–8; rest of year 8:30–5; closed some holidays.

PEORIA

Bradley, Lydia Moss, 1816–1908, Philanthropist

Bradley University, Bradley Avenue

Lydia Moss Bradley came from Indiana to Peoria after marriage to Tobias Bradley. They prospered here—Tobias eventually became president of the First

National Bank—but their family life was tragic, for all six of their children died young. They planned to found an educational institution to commemorate the children, but Tobias died before the plan could be effected. Lydia increased her wealth fourfold, mainly by ventures in real estate. In addition to generous gifts to the city, including a hospital site, a home for aged women, and a park named for her daughter Laura, she donated $250,000 for a site for Bradley Polytechnic Institute and $2 million for an endowment. She had always had an interest in watchmaking and she brought a school of horology from Indiana to Peoria. Bradley Hall and Horology Hall were erected in 1897. The school was coeducational from the start, with special emphasis on domestic science for women students. It became Bradley University in 1946.[36]

SAVANNA

Hay, Helen Scott, 1869–1932, Red Cross Nurse

Marker, American Legion Post 148, Chicago Avenue and 4th Street

Helen Scott Hay was chief nurse of the American Red Cross in Europe from 1919 until 1922. From her headquarters in Paris she directed nursing work in the Balkans and projects for nursing schools in Poland, Czechoslovakia, Greece, and Bulgaria. She faced the League of Red Cross Societies to urge basic nurse training for all public health nurses and for high educational standards for nurses throughout Europe. She was born near Lanark, Illinois, and attended Savanna High School before going to the Illinois Training School for Nurses in Chicago.[37]

SPRINGFIELD

O'Neill, Lottie Holman, 1876–1967, Legislator

Statue, Rotunda, State Capitol, 2nd Street

Lottie Holman O'Neill was elected to the Illinois General Assembly in 1922, the first woman elected to this body. A feminist and prohibitionist, she was returned to the House thirteen times, then elected to the Senate three times. Her only defeat came in 1930 when she resigned to run unsuccessfully for the U.S. Senate. In her early years she gained a reputation as a free-swinging liberal but later became more conservative, supporting Senator Joe McCarthy and Senator Barry Goldwater. In the 1940s she proposed that the United States withdraw from the war. At the time of her retirement in 1963, she was the dean of all women legislators in the United States.[38]

Wendt, Julia Bracken, 1871–1942, Sculptor

Illinois Welcoming the Nations, *Sculpture, and Statue of James Monroe, State Capitol*

Julia Bracken Wendt, born in Apple River, Illinois, was one of a group of young women—all students of Lorado Taft in Chicago, Illinois—who helped execute pieces for the World's Columbian Exposition of 1893. Her large sculpture now in the capitol was cast in bronze after it was exhibited at the Illinois pavilion. She married the painter William Wendt and they moved to California, where they often exhibited together.[39]

URBANA

Bevier, Isabel, 1860–1942, Home Economist; NAW

Bevier Building, University of Illinois

The University of Illinois called Isabel Bevier to its faculty in 1900 as a home economist. Domestic science at that time was becoming less domestic and more scientific. Bevier was trained in agricultural chemistry and chemical sanitation. For a time she ran into trouble with the State Farmers' Institute, which wanted the household science department to include sewing and dressmaking and which, incidentally, influenced legislative appropriations for the College of Agriculture. Bevier's views emphasizing science prevailed, and she remained with the university until 1921, gaining a widespread reputation through her writings and her participation in the American Home Economics Association.

WAUKEGAN

Bowen, Louise de Koven, 1859–1953, Social Reformer; NAWM

Bowen Park, 1917 N. Sheridan Road; NR

Louise de Koven Bowen was an early resident of Chicago, Illinois, a well-to-do member of the power elite, a stockholder in the Pullman Company and International Harvester, a friend of the Cyrus McCormicks, but that did not stop her from fighting oppression and injustice within the corporate system. "Stockholders," she said, "are partners in a business in which they own shares; if they are indifferent to the conditions under which their employees work they are as culpable as if they were the actual employer, and . . . it is always possible to acquire this knowledge and to protest or approve at the annual meeting of the company." She first became aware of the conditions under which many Chicagoans lived when teaching a boys' Sunday school class. She established a club for boys and helped them find jobs, then became involved in the Kitchen Garden movement, which had nothing to do with either kitchens or gardens but was a system of teaching little girls the elements of housekeeping. She wished to build model tenements to replace the wooden shanties which had been erected after the 1871 fire. She worked in hospitals and helped form a visiting nurse agency and get school nurses. She was an early supporter of Hull House and was its treasurer for many years.

In 1911 Bowen's husband, Joseph Tilton Bowen, died. She bought the Waukegan estate and as a memorial to him established there a country club for the use of Hull House and its neighbors, to "extend a constant hospitality to those most sorely in need of rest, of health, and of recreation." The property remained a part of the Hull House complex until it was purchased by the Waukegan Park District in 1963. The farmhouse on the property is now a museum maintained by the Waukegan Historical Society. It is open Wed. and Fri. 10–2:30, and the first and third Sun. of the month 1–3.[40]

Shimer, Frances Wood, 1826–1901, College Founder

Shimer College, 438 N. Sheridan Road

Frances Wood Shimer was an early teacher, a graduate of a normal school in Albany, New York. She and a classmate, Cindarella Gregory, founded Mount Carroll Seminary in 1853. A few years later Frances married Henry Shimer. The school began as a coeducational school but during the Civil War became a women's institution. Known for its experimental curriculum, it was long associated with the University of Chicago. In 1896 the school was transferred to a board of trustees and it was then renamed the Frances Shimer School. It is now Shimer College, a four-year liberal arts, coeducational college. A marker was erected in 1968 at Shimer Campus Drive, off State 78 near Mt. Carroll, giving a short history of the school, a pioneer in the junior college movement.[41]

WHITE HALL

Keller, Annie Louise, 1901–1927, Heroic Teacher

Monument, Whiteside Park, Facing Main Street

April 19, 1927, was a day White Hall will never forget. At noon a cyclone struck Centerville district, near Carrollton, where Annie Louise Keller was teaching school in a brick building. Hastily she did what she could to protect her young students, who huddled under their desks while she attempted to brace the doorway with her body. The news spread fast, "The schoolhouse has been struck!" Parents and rescuers ran to the scene, among them Howard Hobson, a young farmer who was engaged to marry the attractive teacher. He helped to free Keller's crushed body from the fallen bricks and timber and then went to White Hall to tell the distraught family—her mother and sister—of the tragedy. All of the pupils in the school survived, and the community erected the monument, by sculptor Lorado Taft, to commemorate the teacher who gave her life to protect those of the children. A school in Chicago, Illinois, is named for Keller.[42]

NOTES

In addition to the correspondents noted below, I have had assistance from the following: the University of Illinois at Chicago Circle; Hinsdale Public Library; Oak Park Public Library; the Bryan-Bennett Library in Salem; Lake Forest Library; Starved Rock Library System in Ottawa; the State Department of Conservation; the Illinois Department of Tourism in Chicago; Jean Pomerance, of the Commission on Chicago Historical and Architectural Landmarks; the Illinois State Historical Library; the Landmarks Preservation Council in Chicago; the Latter-Day Saints Visitor Center in Nauvoo; the Chicago Public Library; and the Chicago Historical Society.

1. ''Women in Illinois History,'' mimeographed, prepared by Illinois Division of Tourism, Department of Business and Economic Development, 1975; Jeanne M. Weimann, *The Fair Women: The Story of the Woman's Building* (Chicago, Ill.: Academy Chicago, 1981).

2. Charles Claghorn, *Biographical Dictionary of American Music* (West Nyack, N.Y.: Parker Publishing Co., 1973); James Henry Mapleson, *The Mapleson Memoirs* (New York: Appleton-Century, 1966); Georgia L. Osborne, *Brief Biographies of the Figurines on Display in the Illinois State Historical Library* (Springfield, Ill.: State of Illinois, 1932 [the figurines are no longer on display, but the biographies are useful]); correspondence and clippings, McLean County Historical Society, Bloomington.

3. The designation ''Chicago Landmark'' is given by the Landmarks Preservation Council and Service; see *Chicago Landmark Structures: An Inventory* (Chicago, Ill.: the Council, 1975).

4. Herman Kogan, *The First Century: The Chicago Bar Association* (Chicago, Ill.: Rand McNally, 1974).

5. Osborne, *Brief Biographies; New York Times*, various dates, 1922–27.

6. ''Women in Illinois History''; *The History of Woman Suffrage*, vol. 2, ed. Elizabeth C. Stanton, Susan B. Anthony, and Matilda J. Gage (New York: Fowler and Wells, 1882).

7. James L. Reidy, *Chicago Sculpture* (Urbana: University of Illinois Press, 1981); *Chicago Tribune*, Dec. 15, 1937; *Townsfolk*, May 1939.

8. Muriel Beadle, *The Fortnightly of Chicago: The City and Its Women, 1873–1973* (Chicago, Ill.: Henry Regnery Co., 1973).

9. Graham Taylor, *Pioneering on Social Frontiers* (Chicago, Ill.: University of Chicago Press, 1930); Beadle, in *The Fortnightly*, tells the story of the abandoned baby but thought it was a device of Mary Wilmarth, first president of the Hull House board.

10. *Current Biography*, 1957.

11. White Hall *Register Republican*, July 1927; correspondence, White Hall Township Library and Naomi Keller.

12. Correspondence and clippings, Loyola University.

13. Reidy, *Chicago Sculpture*.

14. Stella V. Roderick, *Nettie Fowler McCormick* (Rindge, N.H.: R. Smith, 1956); *Guide to the McCormick Collection of the State Historical Society of Wisconsin*, ed. Margaret R. Hafstad (Madison: State Historical Society of Wisconsin, 1973).

15. Allen F. Davis, *Spearheads for Reform: The Social Settlements and the Progressive Movement, 1890–1914* (New York: Oxford University Press, 1967); Mary E. McDowell, "The Significance to the City of Its Local Community Life," *Proceedings of the Conference of Charities and Correction* (Pittsburgh, Pa.: Conference of Charities and Corrections, 1917).

16. Margaret Corwin, "Mollie Netcher Newbury: The Merchant Princess," *Chicago History* 6 (Spring 1977).

17. Beadle, *The Fortnightly*; Weimann, *The Fair Women.*

18. Jacob Rader Marcus, *The American Jewish Woman* (New York: Ktav, and Cincinnati, Ohio: American Jewish Archives, 1981).

19. Correspondence and clippings, Mary Thompson Hospital.

20. Ida B. Wells-Barnett, *Crusade for Justice: The Autobiography of Ida B. Wells*, ed. Alfreda M. Duster (Chicago, Ill.: University of Chicago Press, 1970); Dale Spender, *Women of Ideas and What Men Have Done to Them* (London: Routledge and Kegan Paul, 1982).

21. *Dictionary of American Library Biography*, ed. Bohdan S. Wynor (Littleton, Colo.: Libraries Unlimited, Inc., 1978).

22. *New York Times*, Jan. 26, 1969; correspondence, Deerfield Public Library.

23. Osborne, *Brief Biographies.*

24. Mary Simmerson Logan, *The Part Taken by Women in American History* (New York: Perry-Nalle, 1972; first printed 1912); Edith Deen, *Great Women of the Christian Faith* (New York: Harper & Bros., 1959).

25. *Women's History Sources: A Guide to Archives and Manuscript Collections in the United States*, ed. Andrea Hinding and others (New York: R. R. Bowker Co., 1979).

26. Clippings and correspondence, Evanston Public Library; Lila Fraizer, of Orangevale, California.

27. Emma Goldman, *Voltairine de Cleyre* (Berkeley Heights, N.J.: Oriole Press, 1932); Terry Perlin, "Anarchism and Idealism: Voltairine de Cleyre," *Labor History* 14 (Fall 1973).

28. Carolyn Ashbaugh, *Lucy Parsons, American Revolutionary* (Chicago, Ill.: Charles H. Kerr, 1976).

29. Elizabeth G. Flynn, *The Rebel Girl, An Autobiography* (New York: International Publishers, 1973; first published in 1955 as *I Speak My Own Piece*).

30. Victor Robinson, *White Caps: The Story of Nursing* (Philadelphia, Pa.: J. B. Lippincott, 1946); David R. Collins and Evelyn Witter, *Notable Illinois Women* (Rock Island, Ill.: Quest Publishing, 1982)—written for young people, this book has useful short biographies.

31. Charlotte S. Rubinstein, *American Women Artists* (New York: Avon Books, 1982); Collins and Witter, *Notable Illinois Women.*

32. Henry Maria Malak, *Servant of God Mother Mary Theresa of Chicago* (Lemont, Ill.: League of the Servant of God Mother Mary Theresa, 1982); *The Apostle of Mercy from Chicago* (newsletter) 20 (Dec. 1977); correspondence, League of the Servant of God.

33. Collins and Witter, *Notable Illinois Women.*

34. John N. Keiser, "The Union Miners Cemetery at Mt. Olive, Illinois, A Spirit-Thread of Labor History," *Journal of the Illinois State Historical Society* 62 (Autumn 1969).

35. Helen W. Linsenmeyer, " 'Aunt Sallie' Logan Held Her Own in a Famous Family,"

Southern Illinoisian, Nov. 24, 1982 (Logan was a sister-in-law of General John A. Logan); correspondence, Jackson County Historical Society, Murphysboro.

36. *Liberty's Women*, ed. Robert McHenry (Springfield, Mass.: G. & C. Merriam Co., 1980).

37. Meta R. Pennock, *Makers of Nursing History* (New York: Lakeside, 1928).

38. "Women in Illinois History"; *New York Times* Feb. 18, 1967.

39. Rubinstein, *American Women Artists*.

40. Louise de Koven Bowen, *Growing Up with a City* (New York: Macmillan, 1926); Jane Addams, *The Excellent Becomes the Permanent* (New York: Macmillan, 1932); brochure, Waukegan Historical Society.

41. Osborne, *Brief Biographies*.

42. Osborne, op. cit.; White Hall *Register Republican*, July 1927; correspondence, White Hall Township Library and Naomi Keller.

INDIANA

DECATUR

Stratton-Porter, Gene, 1863–1924, Naturalist and Writer; NAW

Monument, Adams County Courthouse

Now thought of principally as a writer for children (*A Girl of the Limberlost* and *Freckles*), Gene Stratton-Porter was one of the first conservationists, one who cared about the preservation of the wilderness and its creatures. When she submitted *Freckles* to her publisher he wanted her to cut out "all that nature stuff" so that the book would sell. It was not cut out and the book did sell; twenty years after publication (1904) it had sold nearly two million copies. The story is based on Stratton-Porter's own experiences while studying the life history of vultures. From childhood she had been fascinated with birds and, encouraged by her father, had spent hours wandering the woods, learning to know its inhabitants.

Her wildlife photographs are remarkable, especially when one realizes that she carried forty pounds of camera equipment into swamps and briar patches, climbed trees and ladders (up for each shot, down to change plates for the next shot), and carefully courted the birds for days beforehand so that they would accept her presence.

She married Charles Porter in 1886 and for the first few years of their marriage they lived in Decatur, later moving to Geneva, Indiana, q.v. The monument was erected by the schoolchildren of Adams County. See Lagro and Rome City, IN.[1]

EVANSVILLE

Barton, Clara, 1821–1912, Nurse and Red Cross Founder; NAW

Memorial, Iowa and Edgar Streets. Clara Barton Hall, Deaconess Hospital, 600 Mary Street

One of Clara Barton's greatest contributions to the Red Cross when she organized the American association was to include, in addition to responsibility for war relief, emergency assistance in case of disaster. Much of her life after 1881 was spent in going about the country providing for victims of fires, floods, and similar catastrophes. In 1884, when the Ohio River flooded, she came here to help. The memorial commemorates that event. The Clara Barton Hall is a residence for student nurses.[2]

FOUNTAIN CITY

Coffin, Catharine White, 1803–1881, Antislavery Worker

Levi Coffin House National Historic Landmark, 115 N. Main Street (US 27)

For twenty years the Quakers Levi Coffin and Catharine White Coffin operated the Grand Central station of the underground railroad from this house. (The town was then known as Newport.) They sheltered some two thousand slaves on the escape route from nearby Kentucky to Canada, putting themselves in jeopardy of prosecution for breaking the Fugitive Slave Law. Harriet Beecher Stowe based the character of Eliza in *Uncle Tom's Cabin* on the story of a slave woman Catharine described to her. The Coffins are also in the story, as Rachel and Simeon Halliday. In her *Key to Uncle Tom's Cabin* Stowe wrote, "The character of Rachel Halliday was a real one, . . . Simeon Halliday, calmly risking fine and imprisonment for his love to God and man, has had in this country many counterparts among the [Quaker] sect."

Levi and Catharine, both of North Carolina (though he was descended from the Coffins of Nantucket, Massachusetts), were married in 1826. He described her as "an amiable and attractive young woman of lively, buoyant spirits. Her heart has ever been quick to respond to the cry of distress." They moved to Indiana in 1827.

The real Eliza Harris did reach safety in Canada. Levi tells in his *Reminiscences* of meeting her there in later years. Her escape route on State Route 1, north of Pennville, has been marked by a stone cairn and bronze plaque placed by the Pennville Historical Society. The Coffin House, owned by the state and operated by the Wayne County Historical Society, is open June 1–Sept. 15, Tues.-Sun. 1–4:30; Sept. 15–Oct. 31, weekends; adm. See Jean Rankin, in Ripley, OH.[3]

GENEVA

Stratton-Porter, Gene, 1863–1924, Naturalist and Writer; NAW

Limberlost State Memorial, 200 E. 6th Street; NR

After her marriage to Charles Porter, Gene Stratton-Porter moved from Decatur, Indiana, q.v., to Geneva, where her husband was a pharmacist. Oil discovered on farmland he owned enabled them to build the fourteen-room cabin, which she named for the Limberlost swamplands. It was while living here that she began her career as a photographer and writer. In 1913 the swamp was filled in and the Porters moved to Rome City, Indiana, q.v. The Limberlost Cabin, presented to the state in 1947, along with Stratton-Porter's moth and butterfly collection, is open July-Oct., daily 9-noon, 1–5; Nov.-June, Tues.-Sun. 9-noon, 1–5. See Lagro, IN.

GREENCASTLE

Mansfield, Arabella Babb, 1846–1911, Lawyer; NAW

Dormitory, DePauw University

Arabella Babb Mansfield was the first American woman to be admitted to the bar. Given the popular ideas of 1869 regarding women's abilities, one might have expected the press to take a good deal of notice when Judge Francis Springer of Iowa ruled that she had passed her examinations with honor and admitted her to practice in the state. A few scattered notices in newspapers resulted and Susan B. Anthony's paper, the *Revolution*, hailed the event as a landmark, but otherwise it passed without comment. Mansfield never practiced law but went quietly back to her teaching at Iowa Wesleyan University, where her husband also taught. In 1879 they both moved to DePauw University, where she taught until her death. See Mt. Pleasant, IA.

INDIANAPOLIS

Bolton, Sarah Tittle Barrett, 1814–1893, Poet; NAW

Sarah T. Bolton Memorial Park, S. 13th Avenue. Plaque, Rotunda, State Capitol, Washington Street and Capitol Avenue

The park, five miles southeast of the city, was Beech-Bank, the final home of the poet who wrote "Paddle Your Own Canoe." Sarah Tittle Barrett Bolton conceived this famous poem of courage while sewing up strips of carpeting for the state house and senate chambers. One of the first literary women of the Mississippi Valley, she was unofficial poet laureate of the Hoosier State. In 1896 she was among the Indiana writers who formed the American Writers' Association, later the Western Association of Writers. This group, the first such organization in the United States, had sixty-four charter members, of whom thirty-nine were women.[4]

Walker, Sarah Breedlove, 1867–1919, Cosmetician and Businesswoman; NAW

The Madame C. J. Walker Manufacturing Company, 1036 N. Capitol. Madame Walker Urban Life Center, Inc., 617 Indiana Avenue; NR

One day as Sarah Breedlove Walker, a black sharecropper's daughter, was carrying a load of laundry balanced on her head, an idea formed in her mind. Her problem was to support her daughter and herself (a widow, aged thirty-four) in a less toilsome and better paid occupation than washerwoman. Why not make salves and soaps for hair care specifically designed for Negro women? She spent the next few years devising her secret formulas, including an oil, Glossine, that would straighten hair. She moved from St. Louis, Missouri, to Denver, Colorado, to begin the manufacture of the products, married C. J. Walker, and began her business as Madame C. J. Walker. The factory and headquarters of the business were established in Indianapolis in 1910, less than five years after she had begun the enterprise.

The company employed some three thousand persons, many of them female "Walker agents" who went about the country dressed in black skirts and white shirtwaists demonstrating the products. Josephine Baker, the black singer who made a great hit in France, fascinated Parisians with her "Walker Coiffure"; they copied it under the name of "Baker-Fix." Madame Walker soon had competition, but it did not seem to cut into her profits. She was the first black woman millionaire, owned a townhouse in New York City, and built a palace on the Hudson River. She was noted not only for her business success but also for many philanthropies, some to institutions in Indianapolis, many to Negro schools. Her former plant on Indiana Avenue has been renovated and restored by the Urban Life Center for cultural, charitable, and historical purposes. It is to include a ballroom, office and commercial space, the Walker Theater, and a visual arts center.[5]

LAGRO

Stratton-Porter, Gene, 1863–1924, Naturalist and Writer; NAW

Memorial, Across from Hopewell Church

The Hopewell Memorial Association erected this memorial to Gene Stratton-Porter on August 17, 1975, marking the birthplace and birthday of Indiana's famous and beloved writer. The family moved to Wabash, Indiana, when she was eleven. See Decatur, Geneva, and Rome City, IN.

NEW HARMONY

Fauntleroy, Constance Owen (Runcie), 1836–1911, Clubwoman

Fauntleroy Home, 411 West Street, New Harmony State Memorial

New Harmony was founded by Father George Rapp in 1815, a utopian community for some three hundred German immigrants. After ten years, during which the farming community prospered, the Rappites moved to Pennsylvania and sold New Harmony to another visionary, Robert Dale Owen. Owen's progressive colony had a kindergarten, a trade school, and a free public school system. Constance Owen Fauntleroy, Owen's granddaughter, was brought up in the company of scholars and thinkers. She had studied music in Stuttgart, Germany, for five years before coming to New Harmony. Here she organized, on September 20, 1859, the Minerva Club, said to be the first woman's club in the country. It went out of existence in 1863 but the Fauntleroy home and club records were preserved until purchased by the Indiana Federation of Women's Clubs as a shrine to the woman's club movement. When New Harmony became a historical memorial, the home was turned over to the state. It is open daily, 9–5, except Nov.-Apr., when it is closed Mon.; adm.

Fauntleroy married James Runcie and moved to Madison, Wisconsin, where she formed another club called the Brontë. Later, in St. Joseph, Missouri, she formed the Runcie Club.[6]

Wright, Frances (D'Arusmont), 1795–1852, Reformer; NAW

Plaque, Rappite Rooming House, New Harmony State Memorial

Frances Wright came to New Harmony in 1825 for a brief visit before going to Nashoba, Tennessee, to found her own community, one in which slaves could live and raise produce with which to purchase their freedom. Her colony was a disaster and by 1828 she had left it to return to New Harmony. She helped Robert Dale Owen edit the *New Harmony Gazette*, and after Owen's commune began to crumble, she moved to New York and continued working with him on the *Gazette* and its successor, the *Free Enquirer*. She had meanwhile found a better place to promulgate her views—the lecture platform. She lectured on freedom of thought, for rationality, for free universal education of children from the age of two. She asked that women be given control over their children and their property. She said there was no necessary connection between morality and religion. All her ideas, naturally, were highly controversial, which only meant that her audiences were large and that some of the ideas met with acceptance. In 1831 she married Phiquepal D'Arusmont, whom she had met at New Harmony.[7]

PERU

Slocum, Frances, 1773–1847, Indian Captive; NAW

Frances Slocum State Recreation Area

Frances Slocum was a white child, captured in 1778 from her Pennsylvania home by Delaware Indians. She was traded to the Miamis and gradually adopted their ways. She lived with the Indians all her life; was married twice, both times to Indians; and had four children. She was known as the White Rose of the Miamis. In 1835 a visiting fur trader noticed her white skin and learned who she was. He eventually got in touch with her family in Pennsylvania, who had sought her for years, but she refused to give up her Indian life. Several memorials to her exist in Pennsylvania. The Miami County Historical Museum in the Courthouse in Peru has Slocum mementoes. See Wabash, IN.

RICHMOND

Gaar, Julia Meek, 1859–1944, Traveler and Museum Founder

Julia Meek Gaar–Wayne County Historical Museum, 1150 N. A Street

In 1929 Julia Meek Gaar bought an Egyptian mummy which had been on display in a Cairo shop for forty years. The Egyptian government refused to allow it to leave the country, and the purchaser had to appeal to the U.S. State Department to get it released. It is now a star attraction in the Wayne County Museum, along with many other historical rarities collected by the intrepid traveler, Gaar. She made one trip around the world, as well as seven to Europe and three to Egypt, where she traveled two thousand miles across the Sahara. In 1930 the County Historical Society acquired a building and Gaar's collections, along with those of other residents. In 1940 the museum was given Gaar's name. It is open Tues.-Sun. 1–5.[8]

Gurney, Eliza Kirkbride, 1801–1881, College Founder; NAW

Earlham College

Earlham College was founded as a boarding school in 1847 by a group of Quakers, including Eliza Kirkbride Gurney and her husband, Joseph Gurney.

Its name came from Earlham Hall in Norwich, England, the Gurney ancestral home. One of the family was the celebrated prison reformer, Elizabeth Gurney Fry. Both Eliza and Joseph were Quaker ministers. Before her marriage she had spent several years traveling about the United States and Canada with another celebrated Quaker minister, Hannah Backhouse, and after Joseph's death, late in 1847, she returned to the life of a traveling preacher. She visited President Abraham Lincoln in 1862, telling him she spoke for many thousands who approved of his efforts on behalf of the slaves. Earlham was coeducational from the start and remains a fine liberal arts college.

ROCKVILLE

Strauss, Juliet, 1863–1918, Journalist

Strauss Memorial Fountain, Turkey Run State Park

''Ideas of a Plain Country Woman,'' the department in the *Ladies Home Journal* edited by Juliet Strauss after 1906, helped to make the *Journal* the most widely circulated woman's paper in the world. She began her career in journalism when in her teens, with contributions to the Rockville paper and a regular column in an Indianapolis paper. When she married Isaac Rice Strouse, editor of the Rockville paper, she used his name but her own spelling, Strauss.

At the time of the state centennial in 1915, Strauss wrote the governor pleading for legislation to save Turkey Run, originally Bloomingdale Glens, from devastation by the lumber industry. She had spent part of her childhood in this ''paradise of rocky gorges, glens, bathing beaches, and waterfalls.'' Governor Samuel Ralston appointed her to a commission to save the area and the park came into being. In 1922 the Women's Press Club of Indiana unveiled the fountain, a sculpture by Myra Reynolds, to her memory. The park is north of Rockville via US 41 and State 47.[9]

ROME CITY

Stratton-Porter, Gene, 1863–1924, Naturalist and Writer; NAW

Gene Stratton Porter State Memorial; NR

After Limberlost Swamp was drained in 1913, Gene Stratton-Porter moved from Geneva, Indiana, to this spot near Rome City (one mile south on State 9, then one mile east). She designed and built the twenty-room cabin, named it Wildflower Woods, and lived here for several years. In 1919, however, she moved permanently to California, where she formed her own motion picture company to produce movies based on her stories. By the time of her death her books had sold millions of copies. The memorial is open Mar. 1–Oct. 31, daily 9–12 and

1–5; rest of year, Tues.-Sat. 9–12 and 1–5, Sun. 1–5; adm. See Decatur, Geneva, and Lagro, IN.

ST. MARY'S-OF-THE-WOODS

Guerin, Anne Therese (Mother Theodore), 1798–1856, College Founder

Anne Therese Guerin Hall, St. Mary's-of-the-Woods College

Anne Therese Guerin (Mother Theodore) was a French Sister of Providence. She was sent to America with other nuns in 1840 to assist the bishop of Vincennes with educational work in his diocese. Mother Theodore, who had had years of educational work in France, might well have been dismayed when she arrived at her destination, an untamed wilderness, the only accommodation a rough log cabin. The nuns set to work to build a school, even helping roll logs, while they struggled to learn English. "If it is God's work," she said, "we cannot fail." In 1841 St. Mary's, the first academy for young women in Indiana, was ready for pupils. In 1846 it was chartered, with powers to grant degrees. When Mother Theodore died she left behind her a secure institution, as well as a growing community and a number of flourishing schools in other parts of the state. The hall named for her at the college is a residence hall and administration office.[10]

WABASH

Slocum, Frances, 1773–1847, Indian Captive; NAW

Frances Slocum Cemetery and Monument, Mississinewa Road

Frances Slocum is buried here with her husband, Osage, and two sons. The grave and monument were relocated here in 1965, when a reservoir flooded the original site. See Peru, IN.

WEST LAFAYETTE

Earhart, Amelia, 1897–1937, Aviator; NAW

Earhart Hall, Purdue University

Amelia Earhart, "Lady Lindy," was America's charismatic woman aviator. In June 1935 she was invited to come to Purdue University as a counselor to its women students and a special advisor in aeronautics. The university purchased a Lockheed Electra for her to use as a flying laboratory. She had already proved that women were capable flyers. She had flown the Atlantic alone, made the first solo flight from Honolulu to the mainland, and made a nonstop flight from Mexico City, Mexico, to Newark, New Jersey. Now she wanted to expand the world's knowledge of human and mechanical response to high altitudes and high temperatures and planned ''just one more flight'' to prove her theories. That one flight, an attempt to circle the globe, began in March 1937 and ended in a tragedy and a mystery. Earhart simply disappeared. The date of her death is supposedly July 2, 1937. See Atchison, KS.

NOTES

In addition to the correspondents mentioned below, I have had assistance from Barbara E. Rhinehart of Purdue University, Pamela Bennett of the Indiana Historical Bureau in Indianapolis, the Historic Landmarks Foundation, and the Indiana Historical Society Library.

1. Deborah Dahlke-Scott and Michael Prewitt, ''A Writer's Crusade to Portray Spirit of the Limberlost,'' *Smithsonian* 7 (April 1976).
2. Correspondence, Deaconess Hospital.
3. Harriet B. Stowe, *The Key to Uncle Tom's Cabin* (Boston, Mass.: John P. Jewett & Co., 1854); John A. Scott, *Woman Against Slavery, The Story of Harriet Beecher Stowe* (New York: Thomas Y. Crowell Co., 1978); *Reminiscences of Levi Coffin* (Cincinnati, Ohio: Western Tract Society, 1876); correspondence and brochure, Levi Coffin House.
4. Eva Draegert, ''Cultural History of Indianapolis: Literature, 1875–1890,'' *Indiana Magazine of History* 52 (Sept. and Dec. 1956).
5. Jill Nelson, ''The Fortune that Madame Built,'' *Essence*, June 1983; Tom Rumer, ''Rebirth on the Avenue,'' *Indianapolis Monthly*, n.d.; *Indianapolis News*, Dec. 20, 1982; correspondence, Madame Walker Urban Life Center.
6. Mildred Wells, *Unity in Diversity: The History of the General Federation of Women's Clubs* (Washington, D.C.: the Federation, 1953); Charity Dye, *Some Torch Bearers in Indiana* (Indianapolis, Ind.: Hollenbeck Press, 1917); Michael de Courcy Hinds, ''New Harmony: A Heritage Restored,'' *House and Garden* 149 (Aug. 1977); correspondence, brochures, and clippings, New Harmony.
7. Correspondence, Indiana State Library.
8. Clippings, Julia Meek Gaar–Wayne County Museum.
9. Suellen M. Hay, ''Governor Samuel M. Ralston and Indiana's Centennial Commission,'' *Indiana Magazine of History* 71 (Sept. 1975).
10. Dye, *Some Torch Bearers*.

IOWA

AMES

Opel, Anna Christensen, 1884–1978, Gardener

Plaque, Iowa Arboretum and Botanical Garden

In 1970 the Federation of Garden Clubs dedicated an acre in the arboretum to Anna Christensen Opel, a recognized authority on wildflowers. She had attended almost every meeting of the Garden Club for eighteen years, had served on its board, and was conservation chair. She lectured on wildflowers and for twenty years had a popular weekly radio program. A lover of nature almost from birth, she taught herself the botanical names of plants and made and identified a large collection of leaves and ferns. She served on the Greenwood Cemetery Board in Muscatine, Iowa, her hometown, and a portion of the cemetery there is named for her.[1]

ARNOLD'S PARK

Gardner, Abbie (Sharp), c. 1844–1921, Indian Captive

Spirit Lake Massacre Log Cabin (Gardner Cabin), Monument Drive; NR

This restored cabin was the home of the Gardner family, victims of the massacre of 1857 when renegade Sioux Indians killed all its members except fourteen-year-old Abbie Gardner, who was taken captive. She was ransomed after two and a half months and soon after married Cassville Sharp. She returned to the Gardner home, the only one remaining in the settlement. The story of the captivity was told by Lorenzo Lee in 1857 and in 1885 by Gardner herself in the popular *History of the Spirit Lake Massacre and Captivity of Miss Abbie Gardner*. The cabin was still in her possession at her death and has been preserved as a museum.

Operated by the State Historical Society, it is open Memorial Day–Labor Day, daily (except Tues.) 11–5.[2]

BOONE

Eisenhower, Mamie Doud, 1896–1979, Wife of U.S. President

Mamie Doud Eisenhower Birthplace, 709 Carroll Street

Mamie Doud Eisenhower was born here on November 14, 1896, the daughter of John Doud, a meat packer. She did not live long in Boone; by 1906 she was living in Denver, Colorado, with her parents and sisters. She met Dwight D. (Ike) Eisenhower in San Antonio, Texas, and they were married in 1916. For the next decades she lived the way military wives do, moving from place to place, often left alone to run the household while Ike served his country, rising from second lieutenant to five-star general and supreme commander of all the allied forces. When he was elected the thirty-fourth U.S. president, Mamie was a popular First Lady, content to leave politics to her husband. The five-room house where Mamie was born has been restored and furnished in Victorian style, with a museum and library illustrating her life. It is open Apr.-Dec., Tues.-Sun. 1–5; other times by appointment (515–432–1896); adm.[3]

Shelley, Kate, 1865–1912, Railway Heroine

Kate Shelley High Bridge. Memorial, Sacred Heart Cemetery.
Kate Shelley Trail

On the night of July 6, 1881, Kate Shelley noticed from her home that a track-inspection train crossing Honey Creek had plunged into the creek. The bridge was out, and she knew a passenger train was due to follow in a short time and that the inspection team could not stop it. In a drenching rain and in darkness, the fifteen-year-old Irish lass made her way across the wooden trestle bridge over the Des Moines River, reaching the Moingona station in time to stop the approaching train. She became one of the few heroines of railroad history. A Chicago, Illinois, newspaper raised money to pay off the mortgage on her widowed mother's home. Frances Willard gave her a scholarship. The state of Iowa and the city of Dubuque gave her medals. The old bridge she crossed was given her name, and the bridge which replaced it in 1901 now bears her name. The monument at her grave in Sacred Heart Cemetery gives a brief history of her heroism. It was erected in 1956 by the Order of Railway Conductors and Brakemen, "with enduring gratitude to the women of railroading." The hiking trail, which leads through twenty-five miles of Boone County, passing several historic spots, was a project of the Boy Scouts in 1972. See Moingona, IA.[4]

Mamie Doud Eisenhower's birthplace in Boone, Iowa, is lovingly preserved in memory of the wife of Dwight D. Eisenhower, president of the United States. Photography by Stokka Photographers.

Courtesy Boone County Historical Society.

BURLINGTON

Darwin, Mary Platt, 1821–1886, Suffragist

Mary Darwin House, 537 Summer Street (Private); NR

Mary Platt Darwin attended Oberlin College, graduating in 1845, and returned to Burlington, where for a time she ran a school in this house. She was an officer in the Iowa suffrage organization and became a popular and forceful speaker on women's rights. Her liberal ideas on the relations of the sexes (she herself was divorced) offended some members of the local suffrage society and for some time she was shut out of the movement. She then became active in the temperance cause and advocated suffrage as the best way women could achieve reform goals.[5]

BURR OAK

Wilder, Laura Ingalls, 1867–1957, Writer; NAWM

Laura Ingalls Wilder Park and Museum, US 52

Laura Ingalls Wilder, the popular author of the Little House books, wrote about Burr Oak, where Ma and Pa came with the girls to run the Burr Oak House or old Masters' Hotel. The hotel is being restored. So well known and well loved are Wilder's stories that every place about which she wrote becomes a mecca to her fans. The park is ten miles north of Decorah and three miles south of the Minnesota state line. See Independence, KS, Walnut Grove, MN, and Pepin, WI.[6]

CHARLES CITY

Catt, Carrie Lane Chapman, 1859–1947, Suffrage Leader; NAW, IWHF[7]

Marker at Girlhood Home (Private)

Carrie Lane Chapman Catt was born in the West, where women could vote in state and local elections before they could in the East. She had to work her way through Iowa State College, however, when her father opposed her going to college. She attended the first convention of the National American Woman's Suffrage Association (NAWSA), which joined the two wings of the suffrage movement after twenty years of separation. Catt was a brilliant tactician, a magnetic speaker, and the obvious choice for a successor to the aging Susan B. Anthony. She was chosen president of the association in 1900 but resigned four years later because of her husband's health. He died in 1905, leaving her financially independent.

In 1915 she was again drafted to replace Anna Howard Shaw in the NAWSA presidency. The organization had lost much of its energy by then and was being challenged by Alice Paul's Woman's Party, which was committed to winning the vote by a federal amendment and to using militant tactics to do so. Catt wished to work for equal suffrage state by state. Nevertheless, much of the credit for passage of the Nineteenth Amendment in 1920 goes to her. The marker at her girlhood home, three miles south, off US 218, was placed in 1938 by the Floyd County Federation of Women's Clubs. In 1983 she was elected to the National Women's Hall of Fame.

CLARINDA

Shambaugh, Jessie Field, 1881–1971, Rural Educator; NAWM, IWHF

Goldenrod Schoolhouse, Page County Fairgrounds; NR

The one-room schoolhouse was where Jessie Field Shambaugh began her work in 1901 with rural boys and girls in agriculture, the beginning of the 4-H clubs. She was elected Page County superintendent of schools, wrote a book on farm arithmetic, and got farm institutes and colleges to participate in bringing to schoolchildren information about modern farming techniques and methods. National attention was drawn to her innovative plans to make education relevant to the children attending rural schools. The 4-H clubs were eventually sponsored by the U.S. Department of Education. The 1873 schoolhouse has been made a 4-H museum.

DAVENPORT

French, Alice (Octave Thanet), 1850–1934, Writer; NAW

Alice French House, 321 E. 10th Street (Private); NR

The *Davenport Gazette* published Alice French's first short story in 1871, under the pen name Frances Essex. She had lived here from the age of six, the daughter of one of the city's leading citizens. Her first serious story appeared in *Lippincott's* in 1878. Entitled "Communists and Capitalists," it was signed Octave Thanet to conceal the fact that she was a woman. Since she wrote on social and economic problems, she felt that she would get more attention from editors and readers as a male writer. She was, however, encouraged to turn to fiction and began writing stories of life in the rural South, becoming by the end of the century one of the most popular and well-paid American authors. The house, a rather undistinguished Queen Anne revival, is preserved for its literary association rather than for its architectural value. It has been converted into apartments.[8]

Sudlow, Phoebe W., 1831–1922, Educator

Sudlow Junior High School, 1414 E. Locust Street

In 1874 when Phoebe W. Sudlow was named superintendent of the Davenport public schools, she was believed to be the first woman to serve as a city school superintendent in the United States. The school board offered her less money than her male predecessor. "Gentlemen," she said, "if you are cutting the salary because of my inexperience, I have nothing to say; but if you are doing this because I am a woman, I'll have nothing more to do with it." The board capitulated. Two years later she was elected the first woman president of the Iowa State Teachers Association. A vigorous exponent of women's rights, she continued to campaign for equal pay for men and women teachers, not only in Davenport but throughout the Midwest. When she was nearing ninety the school district voted to name a school for her, and in 1936 the Daughters of the American Revolution dedicated to her a bronze marker at the school.[9]

Wittenmyer, Annie Turner, 1827–1900, Civil War Worker; NAW, IWHF

Annie Wittenmyer Home, 2800 Eastern Avenue

While she cared for sick and wounded soldiers of the Civil War, Annie Turner Wittenmyer heard many of them worry about what would happen to their children if they should not survive. She promised to see that provision was made for soldiers' orphans, and on a trip to Washington in 1865 she got the government to donate new barracks at Davenport to the Iowa Orphans' Home Association. Here she set up the home which was in 1949 renamed in her honor.

During the war she had been disgusted at the poor food served the wounded. The standard breakfast consisted of strong coffee; fried fat bacon, swimming in grease; and bread. She persuaded the army to let her establish diet kitchens, supervised by women, to ensure that patients had proper food and clean water. After the war she continued her humanitarian work, wrote books and hymns, edited a women's newspaper, and worked to establish in Ohio a Woman's Relief Corps home for ex-nurses and the widows and mothers of veterans.

DES MOINES

Iowa Women's Hall of Fame, Iowa Commission on the Status of Women, 507 10th Street

One of the accomplishments of the new feminist movement was the establishment in almost every state of a commission on the status of women. The Iowa legislature established such a commission in 1972 to assure equality for all the women of the state. One of its projects is the Women's Hall of Fame, which began in 1975 to honor women—living or dead—who have had a significant impact on the state and particularly on Iowa women. (Honorees listed elsewhere in this state are identified by the initials IWHF.)

Among others are Mary Newbury Adams (1837–1901), of Dubuque, a pioneer in organizing women's clubs; Amelia Bloomer (1818–1894, NAW), a leader in the Seneca Falls, New York, women's rights movement, popularizer of the reform dress named for her, and, after her move to Council Bluffs, a noted speaker on suffrage; Susan Glaspell (1876?–1948), of Davenport, author; Pearl Hogrefe (1889–1977), English professor for forty-six years at Iowa State University; Dorothy Houghton (1890–1972), appointed in 1953 director of the Federal Office of Refugees, Migratory and Voluntary Assistance; Ola Miller (1872–1937), Iowa's secretary of state and founder of the Iowa State Patrol; Caroline Pendray (1881–1958), of Maquoketa, the first woman to serve in the Iowa legislature and later the first woman in the state senate; Ruth Sayre (1896–1980), appointed to the National Agricultural Advisory Commission, a founder of the Associated Country Women of the World; Ida B. Wise Smith (1871–1952), president of the National Woman's Christian Temperance Union (WCTU) for eleven years and of the state WCTU for twenty years; and Virginia P. Bedell (1896–1975), a county attorney and for nineteen years a member of the State Board of Parole.[10]

Meredith, Anna Kauffman, 1907–1981, Art Patron

Meredith Gallery, Des Moines Art Center, Grand Avenue at 45th Street

Anna Kauffman Meredith served for nineteen years on the Des Moines Art Center's board of directors, from 1962 until her death. She attended the famed Emma Willard School in Troy, New York, graduated from Vassar College, and married E. T. Meredith, Jr. (son of the Meredith Publishing Company's founder). Anna endowed the gallery in the Pei wing in 1968 and also established an art scholarship. The art center, designed by Eli Saarinen, is an outstanding example of museum planning. It is open Tues.-Sat. 11–5, Sun. 12–5.[11]

Samuelson, Agnes, 1887–1963, Educator; IWHF

Samuelson Elementary School, 3929 Bel-Aire Road

For twelve years Agnes Samuelson was state superintendent of public instruction. Her reputation was based on her insistence that children in rural schools be given adequate educational services. She succeeded in consolidating districts and in getting adoption of the equal-school-aid formula to provide equal education for all schoolchildren, regardless of the wealth of the property owners in their districts. The elementary school was named for her after her death in recognition of her contribution to education in the state.[12]

Savery, Annie Nowlin, 1831–1891, Lawyer, Suffragist, and Hotel Keeper

New Savery Hotel and Spa, 4th and Locust Streets

Annie Nowlin Savery helped found the first Des Moines Public Library, led a funding campaign for a public hospital, and fought to correct horrible conditions in the county jail. In 1870 she and her friend Amelia Bloomer went to the Iowa legislature to lobby for woman's suffrage. Her interest in the property rights of married women led her to study law, and in 1875 she was one of the first three women to get a law degree from the University of Iowa Law School. She and her husband, James Savery, went into the hotel business and built a Savery Hotel on 4th Street. A second Savery House, built in 1865, was later removed and replaced by the present hotel.[13]

Walker, Nellie Verne, 1874–1973, Sculptor

Suffrage Memorial, Iowa State Capitol

Nellie Verne Walker was born in Red Oak, Iowa. A student of Lorado Taft in Chicago, Illinois, she exhibited a bust of President Abraham Lincoln at the Chicago Exposition in 1893. She had fashioned it from a block of marble given her by her father, a stonecutter. Among her works is the statue of Chief Keokuk at Keokuk, Iowa, and the bust of James Harlan, Iowa's representative in Statuary Hall in the National Capitol. She lived for some time at Eagles Nest Camp, a retreat for artists near Oregon, Illinois. Dainty and diminutive, she surprised those who saw her working on her large monuments. The suffrage memorial honors pioneer women campaigners for equality.[14]

EARLVILLE

Suckow, Ruth, 1892–1960, Writer; NAWM, IWHF

Ruth Suckow Park, S. Radcliffe and 5th Street. Ruth Suckow Memorial Library

For some years Ruth Suckow raised honey in her apiary here while writing the short stories and novels that earned her a reputation as one of America's finest realistic writers. Iowa readers were shocked when her first novel, *Country People*, appeared in 1924. They felt that it depicted Iowa as a dreary waste. But she was considered by H. L. Mencken as one of the best writers to come out of the Midwest. Her stories, many dealing with the poverty, drabness, and helplessness of rural women dominated by Old World traditions, were published by leading periodicals such as *Smart Set*. She sold the apiary and moved to New York in 1926.[15]

FAIRFIELD

Woods, Mehitable Ellis, 1813–1891, Civil War Worker

Monument, City Cemetery, North B and Stone Streets

Mehitable Ellis Woods (Auntie Woods) served as an agent of the Ladies Aid Society among the Iowa troops during the Civil War, traveling with a commissary wagon under soldier escorts. She was given an honorary commission of major by Governor Samuel J. Kirkwood, which enabled her to make her trips close to the battlefields carrying provisions and hospital supplies to the men. After the war was over she continued serving as a one-woman disaster relief organizer, helping out when grasshoppers destroyed crops, when cyclones struck, and whenever fires burned out family homes. This ten-foot-high granite monument was erected by friends to commemorate her charitable works.[16]

IOWA CITY

Hillis, Cora Bussey, 1858–1924, Child Welfare Worker; IWHF

Institute of Child Behavior and Development, University of Iowa

Concern for children led Cora Bussey Hillis to organize a number of groups to work for their welfare: the Iowa Congress of Mothers, the Des Moines City Union of Mothers Clubs, the Save the Babies Fresh Air Camps, and the Iowa Child Welfare Association. As she began to realize that scientific standards of quality existed for almost everything but children, she conceived the idea of a center devoted to the scientific study of the normal child—the nation's most valuable asset—and she established in 1917 the Child Welfare Research Station. It eventually became a part of the University of Iowa. An elementary school in Des Moines, Iowa, is named for her.[17]

Ream, Vinnie (Hoxie), 1847–1914, Sculptor; NAW

Samuel Kirkwood Statue, First State Capitol

Vinnie Ream was born in Madison, Wisconsin. While in her teens she won a commission for a statue of President Abraham Lincoln to be placed in the U.S. Capitol. Because of her youth and inexperience, many objected to her winning and criticized the statue when it was finished and put on display. It survived the objections and is considered today a creditable representation of the Civil War president. Ream went to Rome, Italy, to study and to have the statue put in marble. On her return she won further commissions, one for the statue of Governor Samuel Kirkwood for Statuary Hall, of which this is a replica. She married Brigadier General Richard Hoxie.[18]

MARSHALLTOWN

Binford, Jessie, 1876–1966, Social Worker; IWHF

Binford House, 110 N. 2nd Avenue; NR

Jessie Binford was born in Marshalltown and made her reputation as ''the conscience of Chicago,'' working with Jane Addams at Hull House. For sixty years she served there as an advocate for the poor, opposing child labor in the garment industry, founding and directing the Juvenile Protective Association. When she was over eighty she fought to save Hull House from demolition. After it was closed, Binford came back to Marshalltown and organized a club for underprivileged boys. Her family home was donated to the City Federation of Women's Clubs.[19]

MOINGONA

Shelley, Kate, 1865–1912, Railway Heroine

Kate Shelley Memorial Park and Railroad Museum

A hundred years after Kate Shelley's heroic act which averted a railroad tragedy, the railroad museum and park were dedicated to her memory. See Boone, IA.[20]

MT. PLEASANT

Mansfield, Arabella Babb, 1846–1911, Lawyer and Educator; NAW, IWHF

Mansfield Room, J. Raymond Chadwick Library, Iowa Wesleyan College

The large seminar room in the library was dedicated to one of Iowa Wesleyan College's most distinguished alumnae in 1968, ninety-nine years after she became the first woman regularly admitted to the practice of law in the United States. Arabella Babb Mansfield had studied law with her brother and with her husband, John Mansfield. Husband and wife applied for admission to the bar at the same time, and the judge, ruling that ''men'' and ''male'' in the law included women, admitted them both in June 1869—in contrast to other judges who had excluded women, especially married women, from legal practice. Neither of the Mansfields ever practiced law. John taught natural history at Iowa Wesleyan and Arabella taught English and history. Arabella later taught at DePauw University in Indiana (see Greencastle, IN).[21]

MUSCATINE

Holley, Susan Clark, 1855–1925, Civil Rights Figure

Clark Home, 200 Block of W. 3rd Street (Private); NR

Susan Clark Holley's father, Alexander Clark, was a prominent businessman of Muscatine. When Susan was denied admission to a public school because she was black, he sued the school board and took the case all the way to the Iowa Supreme Court. It ruled in 1868 that no child could be denied access to a public school in Iowa because of color, nationality, religion, dress, or economic status. Clark was later appointed consul general to Liberia. Susan graduated from high school in Muscatine and married Richard Holley, a minister of the A.M.E. church. For some years she ran a successful dressmaking shop in Cedar Rapids, Iowa. In the 1970s her girlhood home was moved a block west from its original location and remodeled into apartments.[22]

WEBSTER CITY

Eberle, Mary Abastenia St. Leger, 1878–1942, Sculptor; NAW

Statuettes, Kendall Young Library, 1201 Wilson Avenue

Webster City was the birthplace of Mary Abastenia St. Leger Eberle, although she left here when quite young. For a time she lived in Puerto Rico, where she began making figures of the people she saw on city streets. When she studied in New York City and in Italy she again found her inspiration in the people. She went to New York City's East Side to study the faces and figures of its women and children, its Polish, Greek, Russian, and Jewish immigrants. Through her friendship with Charlotte Crosley, librarian of the Kendall Young Library, Eberle gave the library the original plaster models of twenty-two of her statuettes: a child with downcast face and shyly lifted eyes, a grandmother cradling a child, a ragpicker, a child making mud pies, and buoyant dancing children. Many of the bronze figures are in the great art museums of the country. The plaster models are fully as valuable and are highly prized by the library, where they are on permanent display.[23]

NOTES

In addition to the sources mentioned below, I have had assistance from the Park Historian, Herbert Hoover National Historic Site in West Bend; the Muscatine Art Center; the State Historical Society of Iowa; and the State Historical Department of Iowa, Division of Historic Preservation.

1. Ethel W. Hanft, *Remarkable Iowa Women* (Muscatine, Iowa: River Bend Publishing, 1983).

2. Herbert V. Hake, *Iowa Inside Out* (Ames: Iowa State University Press, 1968).

3. Ibid.; brochures and correspondence, Boone County Historical Society.

4. Western Writers of America, *Women Who Made the West* (Garden City, N.Y.: Doubleday & Co., 1980); brochures and correspondence, Boone County Historical Society.

5. Correspondence and National Register nomination form, Iowa State Historical Department.

6. William T. Anderson, "A Visit to Laura Ingalls Wilder Country," *Americana* 11 (Sept.-Oct. 1983).

7. The initials IWHF indicate an electee to the Iowa Women's Hall of Fame (see Des Moines, IA).

8. National Register nomination form, Iowa State Historical Department.

9. Ethel W. Hanft and Paula Manley, *Outstanding Iowa Women, Past and Present* (Muscatine, Iowa: River Bend Publishing, 1980); LeRoy G. Pratt, *Discovering Historic Iowa* (Des Moines: Iowa Department of Public Instruction, 1975).

10. Correspondence and information sheets, Iowa State Commission on the Status of Women.

11. Hanft, *Remarkable Iowa Women.*

12. Iowa Women's Hall of Fame.

13. Hanft, op. cit.; Louise R. Noun, *Strong-Minded Women: The Emergence of the Woman Suffrage Movement in Iowa* (Ames: Iowa State University Press, 1970).

14. Winona Reeves, *The Blue Book of Iowa Women* (Keokuk, Iowa: the Author, 1914); *Art and Architecture* 12 (Nov. 1921).

15. Elizabeth Hardwick, "Introduction," in Ruth Suckow, *Country People* (New York: Arno Press, 1977); Margaret M. Kiesel, "Iowans in the Arts: Ruth Suckow in the Twenties," *Annals of Iowa* 45 (Spring 1980); correspondence, Iowa State Historical Department.

16. Correspondence, Jefferson County Historical Society, Fairfield.

17. *Iowa Journal of History and Politics* 31 (Oct. 1933).

18. Charlotte S. Rubinstein, *American Women Artists* (New York: Avon Books, 1982).

19. Iowa Women's Hall of Fame; correspondence, Marshalltown Public Library.

20. Brochures and correspondence, Boone County Historical Society.

21. Correspondence, Iowa Wesleyan College.

22. Hanft and Manley, op. cit.; correspondence, Ethel Hanft.

23. Correspondence, Kendall Young Library.

KANSAS

ARGONIA

Salter, Susanna Madora, b. 1860, Mayor

Salter House, 220 W. Garfield Street; NR. Plaque, Public Square

In 1887 Kansas gave women a vote in municipal elections. The Woman's Christian Temperance Union made prohibition a campaign issue, and a caucus of members headed by Susanna Madora Salter selected a ticket. The "wets" drew up their own ticket and as a joke put Salter down for mayor. To the surprise of all, and the annoyance of Salter, she was elected on April 4, 1887. When the council of five men met she said, "You are the duly elected officials of this town, I am merely your presiding officer." With a population of five hundred, there was little official business, but as the nation's first woman mayor of a city, Salter got a lot of public attention. The Salters moved to Oklahoma in 1893, with their six children. She lived well into her nineties.

The citizens of Argonia remember their one-term mayor by maintaining the home in which she lived as a museum commemorating one of the milestones in the history of women's achievement. The museum is being refurbished by the Western Sumner County Historical Society and is at present open for tours by appointment (316–435–6733). The plaque was erected in 1933 by the Woman's Kansas Day Club.[1]

ATCHISON

Earhart, Amelia (Putnam), 1897–1937, Aviator; NAW

Amelia Earhart Birthplace, 223 N. Terrace (Private); NR. Plaque, City Hall. Amelia Earhart Memorial Airport. International Forest of Friendship at Warnock Lake

Amelia Earhart was born here in her grandparents' home. She became a world-famous flyer, the first woman to cross the Atlantic by air, the first woman to fly the Atlantic alone, and the first person to fly nonstop across the continental United States. On an attempted round-the-world flight in 1937 she and her copilot disappeared. What happened to them has remained a mystery.

She began flying while living in California, bought her first plane when she was twenty-five, and from that day on flying was her life. She was an inspiration to other women, especially so to other aviators.

The Ninety-Nines, an international women pilots group, established near her place of birth the International Forest of Friendship, where trees from all fifty states, and from territories and countries around the world, are planted. Granite plaques embedded in Memory Lane honor those who make contributions to aviation. The City Hall plaque was unveiled in 1982 on the fiftieth anniversary of Earhart's solo transatlantic flight. The forest is open daily and maps of the walking paths are available at the Chamber of Commerce, 104 N. 6th Street. Exhibits of Earhart memorabilia may be seen at the Atchison County Museum, 1440 N. 6th Street, open Memorial Day–Labor Day, Sun. 1–5. See West Lafayette, IN.[2]

CHANUTE

Johnson, Osa Leighty, 1894–1953, Explorer, Writer, and Film Maker

Martin and Osa Johnson Safari Museum, 16 S. Grant Avenue

I Married Adventure was the title of Osa Leighty Johnson's book about her years with Martin Johnson. She was sixteen when she married the photographer, who had just returned from a voyage with Jack London to the South Seas. The young bride had no idea of the adventures into which her husband was to lead her. Their first trip was to the Solomon Islands and New Hebrides. There Osa was captured by cannibals and only saved by the appearance of a British gunboat in the harbor. She was frightened, but she never doubted Martin's ability to get her out of trouble. This was only one of many exciting adventures in the twenty-seven years of their marriage. In 1921 they made the first of many expeditions to Africa, where they photographed wild animals for the American Museum of Natural History. In America they lectured, showed their films, and wrote books and articles about their exciting life, becoming the most famous, most talked-about adventurers in America.

In 1937 Martin was killed in a plane crash but Osa returned to Africa, where she supervised the Twentieth-Century Fox expedition in filming *Stanley and Livingstone*. Osa was a petite five feet two inches, weighed 112 pounds, and was one of the best-dressed women in America. One interviewer described her as "having the face and form of a movie star, the heart of a home-loving woman, and the courage of a lion." She died in New York as she was preparing to return to Africa, which she considered her home. She felt lost in civilization. "Everything in the city is so artificial," she said, "I can hardly wait to get back to the jungle. I prefer it out there . . . I am Queen of the Jungle.'' She was buried in Chanute, where her mother still lived. The Safari Museum, with its African exhibits, is open Mon.-Sat. 10–5, Sun. 1–5; closed holidays; adm.[3]

EMPORIA

Massee, May, 1881–1966, Publisher; NAWM

Massee Collection, Emporia State University Library

May Massee was the most prestigious publisher of children's books during the mid-twentieth century. Her New York office was transferred intact to the library here in 1972. The collection includes the books published under her direction during her twenty-seven years at the Viking Press. Four are books that won the Caldecott Medal for distinguished picture books for children, and more than twenty won Caldecott citations. Ten won the Newbery Award for excellence in literature for children, and thirty more were cited for honors.

In the dedication ceremony of the Massee Collection, her career was summed up by Annis Dunn, who said her ''forceful influence brought children's books to a peak of excellence never before achieved in this or any other country.''

INDEPENDENCE

Wilder, Laura Ingalls, 1867–1957, Writer; NAWM

Little House on the Prairie, Off US 75. Memorial Plaque, Courthouse

The log cabin made famous by Laura Ingalls Wilder as the ''little house on the prairie'' in her series of books for children has been reconstructed on its former site. Since the Wilder books, so dear to children, were brought to the television screen, readers and viewers are eager to see the places about which Wilder wrote. She lived here in 1870, when her father was so poor that they lived as squatters on Indian land. The cabin is thirteen miles southwest of town; highway signs direct the traveler to the house, which is open May 15–Sept. 1, Mon.-Sat. and holidays 10–5, Sun. 1–5. See Burr Oak, IA, Walnut Grove, MN, and Pepin, WI.[4]

LAWRENCE

Spencer, Helen Foresman, d. 1982, Art Collector and Philanthropist

Helen Foresman Spencer Museum of Art, University of Kansas, 1301 Mississippi Street

The museum was dedicated in 1977, named for its principal benefactor, Helen Foresman Spencer. The University of Kansas had long had an art museum, established by Sallie Casey Thayer (1856–1925). Thayer was not only an avid art collector but sponsor of cultural activities in Kansas City, Kansas. Her collection of old masters and objects of art were donated to the university and exhibited in Spooner Hall, originally the university library.

Spencer, widow of industrialist Thomas Aldred Spencer and a philanthropist of wide tastes and large means, gave not only the money but time and creative ideas to the institutions she chose to support. Her will left a million-dollar fund to purchase paintings and other art works for the Spencer Museum. The Thayer Memorial was incorporated in the new museum, retaining its name in identifying credit lines. The museum is open Tues.-Sat. 9:30–4:30, Sun. and holidays 1–4:30.[5]

Taylor, Lucy Hobbs, 1833–1910, Dentist; NAW

Lucy Hobbs Taylor Building, 809 Vermont Street; NR

Lucy Hobbs Taylor tried to enter medical school in 1859 but was turned down. She studied privately with a doctor who suggested that dentistry might be more suitable for a woman. But when she sought an apprenticeship with a dentist, that calling, too, was deemed unsuitable. She did manage to learn the basic techniques and then applied to the Ohio College of Dental Surgery, which would not accept women. Since a degree was not then a prerequisite to practice, Taylor opened an office and was finally accepted into the state dental association and allowed to get a degree, with four months' of study, from the Ohio College. In 1867 she and her husband, James Taylor, who became a dentist under her instruction, moved to Lawrence, where they built up one of the largest dental practices in the state. The Italianate-style building used as home and office by the Taylors was recently placed on the National Register of Historic Places. It is occupied by a hairstyling business owned and operated by a woman.[6]

Watkins, Elizabeth Miller, 1861–1939, Benefactor

Elizabeth M. Watkins Community Museum, 1047 Massachusetts Street

Elizabeth Miller Watkins gave up school at fifteen in order to help out her family, whose fortunes suffered in 1874, the year of the great grasshopper invasion. She took an office job with the J. B. Watkins Land and Mortgage Company, where she rose to be assistant secretary to the company. She gave up her job in 1909 to marry J. B. Watkins. When he died in 1921, she was left an extremely wealthy woman. Her next eighteen years were spent carrying out plans they had made together for the investment of that wealth to enhance life in Lawrence. The Watkinses lived in a big white house adjoining the campus of the University of Kansas. Many of their gifts built Watkins Memorial Hospital; Watkins Hall, a scholarship hall for women students; and Miller Hall, named for her family. The

J. B. Watkins Building was deeded to the city for use as a city hall. Later it was acquired by the Douglas County Historical Society and opened in 1975 as a museum named for Elizabeth. It is open Tues.-Sat. 10–4, Sun. 1:30–4.[7]

Watson, Carrie M., 1858–1943, Librarian

Watson Library, University of Kansas

After Carrie M. Watson graduated from the University of Kansas, she visited the college. There she saw the registrar writing down the names of new students. She volunteered to help and was immediately made his secretary and assistant librarian. She was twenty. She became head librarian less than ten years later, and did not retire until she was sixty-three, retaining the title of librarian emerita until her death. In spite of a reputation for sternness, Watson was loved as well as respected. She was ''Aunt Carrie'' to generations of students. The library was named for her in 1931, while she was still alive to appreciate the honor.[8]

LINDSBORG

Swensson, Alma Lind, 1859–1939, Musician

Alma Swensson Hall, Bethany College

Alma Lind Swensson and her husband, the Reverend Carl Swensson, were instrumental in establishing Bethany College and the Bethany College Oratorio Society, later known as the Lindsborg Messiah Chorus. Their first performance of Handel's *Messiah* was given in 1882, with Alma singing the soprano solos. She sang in the *Messiah* until the end of her life. The Messiah Festival is still held annually during Easter Week in Presser Auditorium on the college campus, and the Oratorio Society still flourishes. In 1949 a new dormitory at the college was named for Alma.[9]

MEDICINE LODGE

Nation, Carry Amelia Moore, 1846–1911, Antisaloon Crusader; NAW

Carry A. Nation House, 211 W. Fowler Avenue; NHL

At the time Carry Amelia Moore Nation and her second husband, David Nation, moved to Medicine Lodge, Kansas was legally dry. But those who wished to imbibe could get all the liquor they wanted at a so-called pharmacy or joint. Nation's first husband had been an alcoholic, and she attributed all the ills of society to strong drink. In the summer of 1889 she went to one of the joints and sang a temperance song, gathering a crowd and closing up the establishment. From this mild beginning she went on to more and more violent attacks on places that sold liquor, smashing bottles, glasses, and furniture with the hatchet that became her trademark. For some time, since the places she attacked were illegal, she escaped being arrested, but during her lifetime she was jailed, beaten, and mobbed. One judge is said to have sentenced her to ''ninety days for disturbing the peace and destroying private property and God forgive me for not strangling her with my bare hands.'' The home where she lived from 1889 until about 1902 is now a museum operated by the Woman's Christian Temperance Union, open daily 8–5; adm. See Wichita, KS.

ST. PAUL

Hayden, Margaret (Mother Mary Bridget), 1814–1890, Churchwoman; NAW

Marker, Roadside Park

St. Paul was originally Osage Mission, where the Jesuits founded the Osage Manual Labor School to teach Indian boys industrial skills. In 1847 the superintendent invited the Sisters of Loretto to head up a girls' department and four of the nuns responded, traveling from St. Louis, Missouri, by boat and then by rough lumber wagon. Among them was Margaret Hayden (Sister Bridget), who emigrated from her home in Ireland to Missouri when she was six and joined the order at Cape Girardeau in 1841. Under the sisters the school developed rapidly, and by the time Sister Bridget became mother superior in 1859, it had seventy-three girls enrolled and was considered the best school in the Indian country. After the Civil War, with most of the Indians removed to Indian Territory, the school taught daughters of white settlers. Osage Mission suspended business during Mother Bridget's funeral, as a mark of respect to the woman who had become an important and much-loved figure in the community. Five years later the buildings burned to the ground.

TOPEKA

Monroe, Lilla Day, d. 1929, Suffragist and Historian

Pioneer Woman Statue, State House Grounds

The Kansas Pioneer Women's Memorial Association was organized with the purpose of having a statue commemorating the pioneer women of Kansas erected on the grounds of the state capitol. The chief mover in the association was Lilla Day Monroe, herself an important Kansas figure, dynamic and influential. She was the first woman admitted to practice before the Kansas Supreme Court (1895). In Topeka she led the struggle for woman suffrage, founded a Good Government Club, and edited a magazine, the *Club Member*. After women won the vote she started a second paper, the *Kansas Woman's Journal*. During the 1920s she began collecting the stories of other pioneer Kansas women. Her work in the memorial association ended when the statue, by Robert Merrill Gage, was dedicated in 1928. But the collection of the memoirs, with its task of soliciting and editing the letters that poured in, went on. "It has been my most satisfying piece of public service," she wrote, "I have discovered some of the finest spirits in the whole world."

Yet the world was not to share these pioneer memoirs for many years. Monroe died before the task was completed. Her daughter, Lenore Monroe Stratton, took over the project, carefully typing, indexing, and annotating each of the eight hundred stories. Eventually she had to abandon the task and the files were stored in the attic of Monroe's old home. There they remained until 1975 when a great-granddaughter, Joanna Stratton, during a semester break from Harvard University, visited the house and explored the cabinets in the attic. "A human pageantry came alive before my eyes," she wrote. In 1981 Stratton published *Pioneer Women: Voices from the Kansas Frontier*, based on the memoirs. It is a remarkable contribution not only to the history of Kansas but to the story of the women who civilized the frontier.

The courage and strength of these women are epitomized by the statue, a watchful woman with a rifle across her lap, guarding an infant and a kneeling child. Betty Wollman (d. 1927), one of the original free soil leaders in Leavenworth, Kansas, is believed to have been the inspiration for the statue.[10]

WALKER

Custer, Elizabeth Bacon, 1842–1933, Army Wife and Writer

Monument, Near Site of Old Fort Hays

A local rancher erected the monument in 1931 to commemorate Elizabeth Bacon Custer, the wife of General George Custer. For the twelve years of their marriage, Elizabeth traveled with George from army camp to army camp. When he was killed she was left with no home and a pension of thirty dollars a month. She devoted the fifty-seven years of widowhood to memorializing her beloved "Autie," writing a series of books that not only supported her nicely but gives us a vivid picture of what it meant to be an army wife, living in makeshift dwellings, always a second-class citizen even when married to an officer.

WICHITA

Murdock, Louise Caldwell, 1858–1915, Interior Designer; NAW

Murdock Collection, Wichita Art Museum, 619 Stackman Drive

Although Louise Caldwell Murdock spent most of her life in Wichita, she made frequent trips to New York City and Chicago, Illinois, with her husband and

The Kansas Pioneer Women's Memorial Association had this statue by Merrill Gage erected on the Statehouse Grounds in Topeka, Kansas. The association was organized by Lilla Day Monroe, a woman's suffrage leader and historian of Kansas women pioneers. Courtesy Kansas State Historical Society, Topeka.

there took the opportunity to visit the great art collections. Aware of the narrow horizons of the women of her own town and the lack of climate for creative effort, she conceived the idea of forming a woman's club. She was the first president of the Wichita Twentieth Century Club, formed in 1896.

Murdock became interested in domestic architecture, and with her father's help she designed the first fireproof building in Wichita, the Caldwell-Murdock Building. Following her husband's death, Murdock went to New York City to study interior design. On her return she went into business as the first interior decorator in Kansas. Her first clients were, naturally, friends who wished help in selecting rugs and furniture. Then came the public buildings, the Wichita Club, the Crawford Theater, the Wichita Country Club, and the Carnegie Library. She left the city a bequest for the buying of an art collection. The Roland P. Murdock Collection of American Art, named for her husband, became part of the Wichita Art Museum twenty-three years later—after her survivors, a son, sister, and mother, had passed away. It is considered one of the great collections of American art in the country.[11]

Nation, Carry Amelia Moore, 1846–1911, Antisaloon Crusader; NAW

Fountain, Cowtown

The fountain commemorating the famous temperance reformer (see Medicine Lodge, KS) was erected by the Woman's Christian Temperance Union at another location in 1918. It was knocked over by a beer truck in 1945 and only recently has money been found to move and restore it. One of the first bars attacked by Nation was the Hotel Carey, later the Hotel Eaton, East Douglas Street, which has a portrait of her, hatchet in hand, in its lobby.

NOTES

In addition to the sources mentioned below, I have had help from the following: the Mayor's Commission on the Status of Women, Topeka; Highland Community College, Highland; Farrell Library, Kansas State University, Manhattan; Kansas State Historical Society, Topeka; Kansas Travel Division; Hillsboro Public Library; Ellsworth County Historical Society, Ellsworth.

1. Monroe Billington, "Susanna Madora Salter—First Woman Mayor," *Kansas Historical Quarterly* 21 (Autumn 1954); correspondence and clippings, Dixon Township Library, Argonia.
2. Correspondence and clippings, Atchison County Historical Society.
3. *Current Biography*, 1940; *New York Times*, Jan. 8, 1953; Osa Johnson, *I Married Adventure* (Philadelphia, Pa.: J. B. Lippincott, 1940); correspondence, Safari Museum.
4. William T. Anderson, "A Visit to Laura Ingalls Wilder Country," *Americana* 11 (Sept.-Oct. 1983).
5. "Helen Foresman Spencer Museum of Art," brochure, n.d.; Carol Shankel, *Sallie*

Casey Thayer and Her Collection (Lawrence: University of Kansas Museum of Art, 1976); correspondence, Carol Shankel, Spencer Museum.

6. Correspondence and National Register nomination form, Douglas County Historical Society, Lawrence.

7. Correspondence, Douglas County Historical Society.

8. Clippings and manuscripts, Carrie Watson Library, University of Kansas.

9. Correspondence, Bethany College.

10. Joanna L. Stratton, *Pioneer Women* (New York: Simon & Schuster, 1981).

11. Bess Innes Galland, ''Some Recollections of Louise Caldwell Murdock,'' pamphlet, Wichita Art Museum, 1963.

MICHIGAN

ADRIAN

Haviland, Laura Smith, 1808–1898, Abolitionist and Humanitarian; NAW, MWHF[1]

Statue, City Hall

Laura Smith Haviland's statue was erected by popular subscription to honor a woman who did much for the state's children and for blacks throughout the South and Midwest. She first came to Michigan Territory in 1829, a few years after her marriage to Charles Haviland. They farmed in Raisin Township and formed with other Quakers the first antislavery society in the territory. When conservative Quakers objected to their activities in the underground railroad, they left the Society of Friends. They opened at their farm a school for orphans and indigent children, which grew into the Raisin River Institute, a preparatory school open to children without regard to sex or color. The institute was converted into an orphan's home, the forerunner of a Michigan home for dependent and neglected children. At the base of the monument, a seated figure holding Haviland's book, *A Woman's Life Work*, is the inscription "I was thirsty and ye gave me to drink."

ASHTON

Shaw, Anna Howard, 1847–1919, Minister, Physician, and Suffrage Leader; NAW, MWHF

Monument, Frayer Halladay Park

"Like most men, my dear father should never have married," wrote Anna Howard Shaw. "Thus when he took up his claim of three hundred and sixty acres of land in the wilderness of northern Michigan, and sent my mother and five young children to live there alone until he could join us eighteen months later, he gave no thought to the manner in which we were to make the struggle and survive the hardships before us. He had furnished us the land and the four walls of a log cabin.''

Shaw's mother took one look at the cabin, with no floor, no door, no windows, and sank to the ground, overwhelmed and unable to take charge. The oldest child, a son, became ill after a few months and left to join his father. Shaw, at twelve, and her young brother struggled to clear land, plant crops, cut wood, haul water, and build furniture. Their father sent them money from time to time and boxes of books to fill their ''leisure time.'' When the Civil War broke out he and the older boys enlisted. Shaw's opinion of men and the world of men was understandably low. She longed to return to school and to pursue an ambition to become a minister.

Her first sermon was preached in Ashton, when she was twenty-three and had not yet been able to go to college. It was a shock to her family. They offered to send her to college if she would give up preaching. She chose the ministry, at the cost of isolation from the family. She graduated from Boston University's divinity school in 1878 and in 1880 was ordained by the Methodist Protestant church, the denomination's first woman minister. She next enrolled in medical school, earning an M.D. in 1886. Her great talents were also given to the suffrage cause. She was the dynamic and beloved president of the National American Woman's Suffrage Association from 1904 to 1915.[2]

BATTLE CREEK

Truth, Sojourner, c. 1797–1883, Civil Rights Lecturer; NAW, MWHF

Marker, Oak Hill Cemetery, South Avenue and Oak Hill Drive.
Truth Street

The ex-slave who gave herself the name of Sojourner Truth when she began a career of lecturing on religion and, later, women's rights, came to Battle Creek to live in 1858, occupying a house at 10 College Street. She had won the hearts of suffragists when she rose to speak at a meeting in Akron, Ohio, in 1851. Refuting the opinion of a man who was present, she pointed out that nobody opened doors for her, nobody helped her over puddles, ''And ain't I a woman? . . . I have plowed and planted and gathered in the barns and no man could help me! And ain't I a woman? . . . If the first woman God ever made was strong enough to turn the world upside down all alone, these women together ought to be able to turn it back and get it right side up again!'' Her eloquence and logic were persuasive and her speech has taken its place as one of the primary documents of women's history.

Battle Creek, which was an abolitionist stronghold and a station on the underground railroad, still honors Sojourner Truth. The marker was placed on her grave in 1929. The Kimball House Historical Museum, 196 Capitol Avenue, N.E., has Sojourner Truth memorabilia on display.

White, Ellen Harmon, 1827–1915, Church Founder; NAW

White House, 63–65 Wood Street

A Maine woman, Ellen Harmon White was living in Battle Creek when she received a vision in right living. She was told that man should eat no meat; drink no alcohol, tea, or coffee; use no tobacco, but live on nuts, grains, and vegetables. It was not the first vision she had had. Since the 1840s she had been preaching that the second coming of Christ was imminent, advocating observance of the seventh-day Sabbath, and writing about her religious experiences. She and her husband, James White, moved to Battle Creek in 1855 and five years later their followers chose the name Seventh-Day Adventists for their new denomination.

The dietary rules White had received in her vision were adopted by the church, which formed the Health Reform Institute. One of their patients was Charles W. Post, who came with "chronic appendicitis." He was cured, not by the Adventists but by a Christian Science healer. He took up the health diet, however, and established his own sanitarium, inventing Postum and Grape Nuts. Others joined the movement, including Harvey Kellogg, under whose superintendency the Health Reform Institute became the Battle Creek Sanitarium. He invented flaked cereal (Granose) and toasted corn flakes to accommodate patients who had false teeth. Thus White might be regarded as the person responsible for making Battle Creek the breakfast food center of the world, as well as for establishing a religious denomination that makes physical purity a tenet of faith.

The White house is open for Sat. afternoon tours and by appointment.[3]

BLOOMFIELD HILLS

Booth, Ellen Warren Scripps, 1863–1948, Educator; NAW

Cranbrook Academy of Art and Cranbrook Institute of Science, 500 Lone Pine Road; NR

About 1908 Ellen Warren Scripps Booth and her husband, George Booth, purchased several hundred acres northwest of Detroit, Michigan, where they built Cranbrook, named for an English estate. Needing a school for their five children, they established an elementary school, Brookside, following this with a number of other educational and cultural institutions.

The Cranbrook Foundation, to which the Booths gave liberally, formed the financial basis of the various schools, the art gallery, and the science institute. Ellen, shy and retiring, left most of the business arrangements to her husband but took a great interest in the schools. Following her death and that of her husband soon afterward, the estate passed to the Cranbrook Foundation. The art museum is open Tues.-Sun. 1–5; closed holidays; adm. The institute is open Mon.-Fri. 10–5, Sat. 1–9, Sun. 1–5.[4]

COLDWATER

Eddy, Mary A., c. 1855–1940, Librarian

Plaque, Coldwater Public Library, 12 E. Chicago Street

Mary A. Eddy was appointed the first librarian of the Coldwater Free Public Library in 1881. The collection of thirty-five hundred books, some from the school district library, were then kept in a little brown house that had been used since 1874 by the Ladies' Library Association. A new building was dedicated a few years after the consolidation of the two libraries into a public institution. Eddy, whose starting salary was three hundred dollars a year, is remembered as a rather prim and precise woman, watching over the reading room with an eagle eye and rapping for quiet with her letter opener. She is also remembered as a fine librarian, helping readers solve a variety of problems and encouraging the studious. She was chiefly responsible for founding the first Michigan State Library Association in 1891, and it is for this accomplishment that the library board honored her with the memorial plaque, placed in 1966.[5]

DETROIT

Bonstelle, Jessie, 1871–1932, Actress and Theater Manager; NAW

Bonstelle Theater, 3424 Woodward Avenue

Jessie Bonstelle began reciting temperance verses at a tender age and was thoroughly stagestruck by the time she was in her teens. She went on the stage in 1866 and continued acting, somewhere along the way changing her name from Laura Justine Bonesteele to Jessie Bonstelle. She graduated to theater management in Buffalo, New York, and Detroit. She lived for the theater. She hired and fired actors, chose the plays, directed and staged the productions, and often appeared herself in the plays. In 1925 she got the backing of Detroit businessmen and opened her own Bonstelle Playhouse. A few years later it became the Detroit Civic Theater, supported by public subscription. Since 1915 the theater she founded has been a part of Wayne State University's drama department.

Fox, Emma Augusta Stowell, 1847–1945, Clubwoman and Parliamentarian

Emma A. Fox Primary School, 17300 Fargo. Tablet at Auto Club Building, 131 Bagley Street

Emma Augusta Stowell Fox was chosen a candidate for president of the United States in 1940. It was a mock Republican Convention, staged entirely by women but witnessed by Henry Ford and a hundred other men of note. Fox made parliamentary usage her special interest. She founded the Detroit Parliamentary Law Club in 1899 and directed it for the next forty-five years. She instructed hundreds of women in the art of organizing clubs and conducting meetings. Her *Parliamentary Usage for Women's Clubs* (1902) served as a guide to many club presidents through the maze of motions, seconds, and tablings. She was the second woman to serve on the Detroit Board of Education, and in recognition of her two-year term (1893–95), the school was named for her in 1962. The plaque on the Auto Club building, erected on the site of her early home, was placed by the Detroit Federation of Women's Clubs.[6]

Hackley, Emma Azalia Smith, 1867–1922, Singer; NAW

E. Azalia Hackley Memorial Collection of Negro Music, Dance, and Drama, Detroit Public Library, 5201 Woodward Avenue

Emma Azalia Smith Hackley was a musical genius, able to play the piano by ear from the age of three. She went through normal school and then taught at Clinton School for several years, but music was so important to her that she continued to study voice, violin, and French and to sing in a choral group. After her marriage to Edwin Hackley she moved to Denver, Colorado, with him and there earned a bachelor of music degree from the University of Denver. There, and later in Philadelphia, Pennsylvania, she used her musical entrée to gain for other Negro artists paid positions on the concert stage and in orchestras. She lectured to groups of black young people, encouraging them to develop racial pride and presenting the idea of a classical type of Negro beauty. A selection of her talks was published in 1916 as *The Colored Girl Beautiful.*

Leslie, Annie Brown, 1869–1948, Journalist; NAW

Nancy Brown Peace Carillon, Belle Isle

For twenty-three years the *Detroit News* carried a column on the women's page in which letters, chiefly from women, were answered with sage, sincere, and simple advice. Not a Lonely Hearts column, it ranged from wedding advice to career counseling, from business advice to public policy. Other columns followed, some for young people. Signed at first simply "Experience," then "Nancy Brown," the columns were eagerly read and the writer, Annie Brown Leslie, won a devoted following. Civic groups found in her an ally in raising money for charity and cultural causes.

In 1930 one of her admirers suggested a get-acquainted party for her readers. It was attended by more than thirty thousand people, including a small white-haired Mrs. J. E. Leslie. But where was Nancy Brown? Only the office knew that Mrs. Leslie was the columnist. At a 1940 Sunday sunrise service, attended by her "column" family, the Nancy Brown Peace Carillon (a hundred-foot tower of limestone) was dedicated, and her identity was at last disclosed.

Palmer, Lizzie Merrill, 1838–1916, Philanthropist; NAW

Palmer Park

Lizzie Merrill Palmer and her husband, Thomas Palmer, gave the city of Detroit their former estate as a park. One of its attractions is a log cabin which Thomas built for his wife and which she furnished with pioneer family heirlooms. She had been a resident of Michigan as early as the 1850s. Her considerable estate was left to found in Detroit "a school to be known as the Merrill-Palmer Motherhood and Home Training School." She said in her will: "I hold profoundly the conviction that the welfare of any community is divinely, and hence inseparably, dependent upon the quality of its motherhood." The school opened its doors in 1922, offering to college-level women training in infant development and in homemaking.

The Merrill-Palmer Institute, as such, has been discontinued, its buildings, name, and some of its programs having been absorbed by Wayne State University.[7]

Stansbury, Margaret, 1866–1908, Settlement House Worker

Franklin-Wright Settlements, 3360 Charlevoix

Margaret Stansbury was chiefly responsible for the development of social settlement activity in Detroit. She came to the city to study music in 1894 but soon went to Hull House in Chicago, Illinois, to work with Jane Addams, returning to Detroit in 1897 to take a position at the Franklin Street Day Nursery. For eleven years she worked for better housing, clinics, public baths, evening school, and playgrounds. One of the many tributes paid to her was: "Through such souls alone, God, stooping, shows sufficient of his light for us in the dark to rise by." In 1967 the settlement merged with the Sophie Wright settlement, named for an equally loved New Orleans woman who had given her life to education. The latter settlement is now called the Sophie Wright Settlement Program Center, 4141 Mitchell Street.[8]

Stratton, Mary Chase Perry, 1867–1961, Ceramicist

Pewabic Pottery, 10125 E. Jefferson Avenue; NR

A self-taught ceramicist, Mary Chase Perry Stratton specialized in colorful architectural tiles. She began to study glazes as a young girl and made many discoveries of secrets in firing processes that had been lost for centuries. She founded the pottery in 1904 in collaboration with a neighbor, Horace J. Caulkins, who had a kiln for making dental enamel. In 1907 they built a studio and she named it for the nearby Pewabic River, not realizing at the time that it was an Indian name for "copper color in clay." She developed a special iridescent glaze and continued making tiles. In 1918 she married the architect of the studio building, William B. Stratton.

Among her most demanding commissions was the tiling for the crypt and stations of the cross in the Shrine of the Immaculate Conception in Washington, D.C. The tiles for the floor of the sanctuary at St. Paul's Cathedral, 4800 Woodward Avenue, Detroit, were also produced at the pottery. Examples of Stratton's work may be found in many other buildings in Detroit and elsewhere. Pewabic Pottery is now owned by Michigan State University and is used for studios and galleries.[9]

KALAMAZOO

Stone, Lucinda Hinsdale, 1814–1900, Clubwoman; NAW, MWHF

Monument, Bronson Park, Park and South Streets. Wall Marker, Ladies Library Association of Kalamazoo (Private), 333 S. Park Street; NR

Lucinda Hinsdale Stone, wife of a Baptist minister, was principal of the "female department" of Kalamazoo College. She had progressed as far as she could go in her own education, attending female seminaries, and she advocated higher education for women. In 1852, responding to requests to include women of the community in what had been informal gatherings in her home, she established the Ladies Library Association. She and her husband, James Stone, helped persuade the University of Michigan to admit women, then to appoint women to the faculty. In 1890 the university awarded her an honorary Ph.D. The monument, a boulder with a bronze tablet, was placed in the park by the Daughters of the American Revolution in 1914.

LANSING

Michigan Women's Hall of Fame (MWHF), Michigan Women's Studies Association, Inc.

On October 20, 1983, the Michigan Women's Hall of Fame held its first annual awards dinner. Organized by the Michigan Women's Studies Association to honor distinguished women, it elected ten living and seven historical women. Four of these have monuments at other Michigan sites: Sojourner Truth of Battle Creek, Laura Smith Haviland of Adrian, Anna Howard Shaw of Ashton, and Lucinda Hinsdale Stone of Kalamazoo. The others represent three different fields of activity.

Elizabeth Chandler (1807–1834, NAW), who spent only her last four years in Michigan Territory, was a Quaker from Philadelphia, Pennsylvania. She organized the first antislavery society in Michigan on a farm near Adrian. Many of her antislavery poems were set to music and sung by abolitionists across the country.

Josephine Gomon (1892–1975), of Detroit, was executive secretary to Mayor Frank Murphy during the Great Depression. She helped organize the New Deal for Detroit and afterward continued as a civil rights activist and public welfare reformer.

Pearl Kendrick (1890–1980), of Grand Rapids, was an internationally known bacteriologist whose research, with that of Grace Eldering, resulted in the first successful vaccine against whooping cough.

The 1984 historical honorees included Madame La Framboise (see Mackinac Island, MI), and the following:

Caroline Bartlett Crane (1858–1935, NAW) was a minister and reformer. She was ordained and installed at the Unitarian church in Kalamazoo, Michigan, in 1889 and for almost a decade she worked to make the church a seven-day community center of practical Christianity. After her marriage to Augustus Crane in 1896 she turned her energies to improving the city's health and sanitation. She was responsible for legislation requiring meat inspection, for city street cleaning services, and for a central charity referral agency. She was called America's public housekeeper.

Martha Longstreet (1870–1953) was a physician who gave over forty-five years of service to the Saginaw, Michigan, community. She was a staff doctor there at the Children's Hospital and consulting physician to other hospitals. She founded a community center, a preschool children's clinic, a home for the aged, and a home for girls.

Mary Spencer (1842–1923), for many years head of the Michigan State Library, built the library up from a collection of sixty thousand volumes to a quarter of a million and established a number of special departments and collections that made the library one of the finest in the country.

Bertha Van Hoosen (1863–1952, NAWM), a surgeon, was founder and first president of the American Medical Women's Association (AMWA). She earned her M.D. from the University of Michigan in 1888, when there was still great opposition to women in medicine, but she gradually established a paying practice in Chicago, Illinois, where she taught gynecology and obstetrics. In 1913 she was named chief of the gynecological staff at Cook County Hospital in Chicago. In spite of her acknowledged ability, the medical societies refused to admit her and other qualified women physicians, so she organized the AMWA. Her autobiographical *Petticoat Surgeon* was published in 1949.[10]

LITCHFIELD

Thorpe, Rose Hartwick, 1850–1939, Poet; NAW

Monument, State 60

Fifteen-year-old Rose Hartwick Thorpe read a story set in the English Civil War in which a young Cavalier, sentenced by the Puritans to be shot as a spy when the evening curfew bell was rung, was saved by a young woman who ran to the belfry and wrapped herself around the bell clapper. The man was reprieved, then pardoned by Oliver Cromwell. Rose turned the story into a verse, "Curfew Must Not Ring Tonight," and the poem became a favorite for dramatic readings in churches, schools, and Chautauquas. Thousands of copies were printed and it was translated into several languages, all without financial benefit to Thorpe, who knew nothing of copyrights. She went on writing, however, and edited several moralistic monthly papers. She and her family moved from Litchfield to San Antonio, Texas, where she was inspired to produce another perennial favorite, "Remember the Alamo." The monument, a fieldstone base topped by a cast-iron bell, was erected in 1934 at the time of the centennial celebration of the town's founding.[11]

MACKINAC ISLAND

La Framboise, Madeline Marcotte, 1780–1846, Fur Trader; MWHF

St. Anne's Church, Huron Avenue

Madeline Marcotte La Framboise is buried here, as is her daughter, on land she once owned and donated to the church. Half French and half Ottawa Indian, she was held in high esteem by the garrison of Fort Mackinac and its residents and other traders. She was raised in an Indian village and grew up unable to read or write, yet she managed to converse in Ottawa and Chippewa dialects as well as French and English and as an adult she taught herself to read and write French. The handsome, graceful, and refined woman married Joseph La Framboise, a well-known French trader, and accompanied him on his fur-trading missions among the Indians. On one of his trips he was shot by an Indian, and Madeline, after burying his body, continued his work. For fifteen years she wintered in the Grand River Valley, buying furs, and returned to Mackinac Island for the summers. She was one of the most successful traders, powerful enough to put some fear into the established fur companies, who were happy when she retired in 1821.[12]

Woolson, Constance Fenimore, 1840–1894, Writer; NAW

Anne's Tablet, Woolson Rampart, Sinclair Grove, East Bluff

The monument honoring Constance Fenimore Woolson is named for the heroine of her first novel, *Anne*, published in 1882, expressing the author's own love for the island. Woolson, who numbered among her forebears the writer James Fenimore Cooper, began her career with travel and descriptive sketches and most of her work was identified with regions in which she had lived or traveled. She is credited with being one of the first writers not from the South who treated the postwar South sympathetically. For the last fourteen years of her life she lived abroad, where she produced a number of novels and formed a long-lasting friendship with Henry James, who valued her as a woman and a writer. The memorial here was established in the early 1900s. In addition to the tablet, bearing a quotation from Woolson's novel, stone benches at the site have titles of her works chiseled on them.[13]

PORT HURON

Miller, Bina West, 1867–1954, Insurance Executive

North American Benefit Association, 1338 Military Street

Bina West Miller in 1891 conceived the idea of founding a society of women to provide low-cost life insurance for its members. Because no mortality tables existed for women, insurance companies were unwilling to insure their lives. Miller believed the death of a wife and mother was a serious loss to a family and insurance was necessary to help make up the financial loss. She borrowed money to establish the Woman's Benefit Association of the Maccabees. She was supreme record keeper, then supreme president from 1911 to 1948. Her job involved traveling about organizing local chapters and counseling women on finances. At the time of her death the society had nearly $125 million in insurance and had paid out in excess of $94 billion. In 1917 it erected its own building in Port Huron. Among its activities were health centers, a summer camp, a junior department, and an official magazine. She married George Miller in 1929. The Benefit Association now insures men as well as women.[14]

ROCHESTER

Jones, Sarah Van Hoosen, 1892–1972, Farmer

Oakland University

Sarah Van Hoosen Jones was the beloved niece of Bertha Van Hoosen (see Lansing, MI, in Michigan Women's Hall of Fame). She graduated from the University of Michigan in 1921, the first woman to earn there a Ph.D. in genetics. After graduation, she managed the family farm in Rochester, where she raised purebred Holsteins. She belonged to the Michigan Master Farmers Club, was a member of the Michigan State Board of Agriculture, and from 1943 to 1955 was on the governing board of the University of Michigan. She was influential in establishing the campus in Rochester that became Oakland University. Upon retirement, she donated her property to her alma mater.[15]

Wilson, Matilda Rausch, 1883–1967, Farmer and Philanthropist

Oakland University

For many years Matilda Rausch Wilson and her husband, Alfred Wilson, operated Meadow Brook Farms, raising and breeding cattle, horses, swine, and poultry. In 1957 they presented the farm, 1,600 acres, with its 125-room Tudor house and a 25-room home and other buildings to the University of Michigan. It established a new campus there which became Oakland University, opened in 1959. Wilson (formerly married to auto manufacturer John Dodge) wore several hats: a businesswoman (chairman of the board of directors of a bank), a politician (State Board of Agriculture, 1932–38, and state lieutenant governor, 1940), a national officer in the Salvation Army, and an authority on roses. She continued to live on the campus of the university and take part in its functions. The Annual Homecoming Weekend, which fell on her birthday, was popularly known as Mrs. Wilson's Weekend.[16]

NOTES

In addition to the correspondents mentioned below, I have had help from the following: the Bentley Historical Library, University of Michigan, Ann Arbor; the Library of Michigan, Lansing; the Grand Rapids Public Library; the Alma Public Library; the Lansing Public Library; and the Michigan Department of Education.

1. The initials MWHF indicate an electee to the Michigan Women's Hall of Fame. See Lansing, MI.

2. Anna Howard Shaw, *The Story of a Pioneer* (New York: Harper & Bros., 1915).

3. Kathleen A. Smallzried, *The Everlasting Pleasure: Influences on America's Kitchens, Cooks and Cookery* (New York: Appleton-Century-Crofts, 1956); brochure and correspondence, Adventist Historic Properties, Battle Creek.

4. Martha M. Roberts, *Public Gardens and Arboretums of the United States* (New York: Holt, Rinehart and Winston, 1962).

5. Phyllis Holbrook, "Early Library Days in Coldwater," *Michigan Librarian* 32 (Oct. 1966); *Coldwater Daily Reporter*, June 23, 1982; correspondence and clippings, Branch County Library, Coldwater.

6. *Mothers of Achievement in American History, 1776–1976*, comp. American Mothers Committee (Rutland, Vt.: Charles E. Tuttle Co., 1976).

7. Correspondence, Detroit Public Library.

8. Alice T. Crathern, *In Detroit . . . Courage Was the Fashion: The Contribution of Women to the Development of Detroit from 1701 to 1951* (Detroit, Mich.: Wayne State University Press, 1953).

9. Ralph and Terry Kovel, "Pewabic Pottery," in *The Kovels' Collector's Guide to American Art Pottery* (New York: Crown Publishers, 1974); Crathern, *In Detroit*.

10. Brochure and correspondence, Michigan Women's Hall of Fame, Michigan Women's Studies Association, Inc., Lansing.

11. Correspondence, Litchfield District Library.

12. John E. McDowell, "Madame La Framboise," *Michigan History* 56 (Winter

1972); Edwin O. Woods, *Historic Mackinac* (New York: Macmillan, 1918); correspondence, Mackinac Island Public Library.

13. Correspondence and clippings, Mackinac Island Public Library.

14. *National Cyclopedia of American Biography*, vol. 44.

15. *Women's History Sources: A Guide to Archives and Manuscript Collections in the United States*, ed. Andrea Hinding and others (New York: R. R. Bowker Co., 1973).

16. *Mothers of Achievement*; *National Cyclopedia of American Biography*, vol. 59.

MINNESOTA

FAIRFAX

Muller, Eliza, 1831–1876, Relief Worker

Monument, Fort Ridgely State Memorial Park Cemetery

Eliza Muller, wife of the Fort Ridgely doctor, went through the horror of the Sioux Indian uprising in 1862, in which many Indians were killed and a dozen or so whites were wounded. She pitched in to nurse the survivors, and the year after her death the monument was erected memorializing her "valor and devotion to the care of the sick and wounded soldiers and refugees." The site is some seven miles south of Fairfax, accessible from State 4.[1]

GLENWOOD

Helbing, Cleora Caroline, 1892–1966, Indian Agent

Helbing Art Collection, Pope County Historical Society, Lake Shore Drive

During twenty-four years with the Department of the Interior, Cleora Caroline Helbing traveled to every U.S. Indian school. She had been trained in home economics and served as supervisor of women's work in Georgia and in Louisiana before joining the Indian Service as a home economics supervisor. She helped young women to find new and more efficient ways of homemaking, then extended her practical programs to meet the needs of Indian boys. She did much to raise the standard of living for Indians, for which she was honored by the Department of the Interior's distinguished service award in 1956. Following retirement she began to raise funds for a new Pope County Historical Society building. Over the years she had been given and had purchased an outstanding collection of American Indian crafts, and these she offered to the museum. A gallery displaying textiles, baskets, and pottery from her collection was dedicated in 1969, four years after her death. It is open May 1–Sept. 1, Mon.-Fri. 9–12 and 1–4:30, Sat., Sun. 1–5; rest of year, Mon.-Fri. only; closed holidays; adm.[2]

MINNEAPOLIS

Comstock, Ada Louise (Notestein), 1876–1973, College Administrator; NAWM

Comstock Hall, University of Minnesota

Comstock, who was born and brought up in Moorhead, Minnesota, q.v., was so well and favorably known as a teacher and scholar that she was chosen the first dean of women at the University of Minnesota. After five years here, the only woman administrator in a male-dominated faculty, she was asked to go to Smith College in Massachusetts as dean. Believing strongly in education for women, she was pleased to move to a woman's college. But there, too, the trustees were male. During 1917–18, in the absence of the president, she ran the college, but the trustees refused to give her the title of acting president. The insult to her and to womanhood was assuaged when Radcliffe College offered her the presidency in 1923. Her task there was no easy one, for Radcliffe was still not much more than an annex to Harvard University, and Comstock had to work hard to establish it as a strong woman's college. In 1943, the year Harvard was persuaded to accept classroom coeducation, Comstock resigned to become the wife of an old friend, Wallace Notestein. Smith, Radcliffe, and the University of Minnesota have all named dormitories for her. She also served with distinction on many educational and governmental commissions, including the National Commission on Law Observance and Enforcement, of which she was the sole woman member.[3]

Countryman, Gratia Alta, 1866–1953, Librarian

Minneapolis Public Library

"A public library is the one great civic institution supported by the people which is designed for the instruction and pleasure of all the people, young and old, without age limit, rich and poor . . . educated and uneducated. . . . It should be 'all things to all men' in the world of thought." This was the philosophy of Gratia Alta Countryman, whose entire working life was spent at the Minneapolis Public Library. She began to work here right out of college. She was happiest when she found another group who needed books to read. The bedridden, the factory worker, the fireman, the woman in a shelter, as well as the scholar and the student were served by the library during her forty-six years here.

When she was made librarian, the first woman to head a public library in so large a city, her friends were distressed because the trustees paid her two-thirds of the salary they had paid a man and expected her to do the work she had done as assistant librarian as well as that of the chief administrator. She accepted graciously and proceeded to expand the library's facilities and services. In 1904, when she took charge, the library had 43 persons on the staff and the circulation was 500,000. When she retired in 1936 there were 250 persons working here and circulation was over 3.5 million volumes. Highly respected and visible in her chosen profession, Countryman was also the hub of a warm family, including an adopted son, and the center of a wide circle of friends.[4]

Gilman, Catheryne Cooke, 1880–1954, Settlement Worker

North East Neighborhood House, 1929 Northeast 2nd Street

Minneapolis at the turn of the century had to absorb a tide of immigration from eastern Europe. In 1913 80 percent of the population of eastern Minneapolis was of foreign birth or descent. There was a great need for educational, health, and recreational services on a nonpartisan and nondenominational basis. To fill this need, North East Neighborhood House was established in 1915 with Robbins Gilman as head resident. Catheryne Cooke Gilman, who married him that same year, helped to establish classes teaching job skills, English, cooking, and hygiene. The Gilmans realized that immigrants had much to give Americans from their cultural backgrounds. Rather than trying to make all conform to a preconceived American standard, they made a conscious effort to emphasize ethnicity while maintaining neighborhood unity.[5]

Morris, Lucy Wilder, 1864–1935, Clubwoman and Preservationist

Lucy Wilder Morris Park, Falls of St. Anthony, 6th Avenue, S.E.

St. Anthony Falls, named by Father Louis Hennepin in 1680, was in 1921 just a riverbank dump. The Daughters of the American Colonists bought the property, made a tablet memorializing Father Hennepin, and built a park with a stairway down to the river. When finished, it was named Lucy Wilder Morris Park, in honor of the woman who had inspired it. Morris came to Minneapolis after her marriage to James T. Morris in 1890. She organized a chapter of the Daughters of the American Revolution in 1913 and began to record oral histories of pioneers, which she published in *Old Rail Fence Corners* (1914). She was responsible for the planting of over one thousand elm trees in the city on Arbor Day 1916 to honor Charles M. Loring, father of the city's park system. She also turned her attention to the preservation of Yorktown, Virginia, as a national military park. She went to Congress herself and "with a willing heart but often most unwilling legs" walked the halls of the Capitol. She was successful in persuading enough legislators to pass the bill in 1923, and then she became the first woman appointed to a commission for a military park.[6]

Sanford, Maria, 1836–1920, Educator; NAW

Sanford Hall, University of Minnesota. Memorial Marker, Loring Park. Sanford Junior High School, 3524 42nd Avenue, S.

In 1958 Minnesota chose Maria Sanford as one of two citizens to represent the state in Statuary Hall at the Capitol in Washington, D.C. She was not a native of Minnesota but was recruited to teach at the University of Minnesota in 1880. A Connecticut teacher, later a school principal and college professor in Pennsylvania, she met the president of the fledgling Minnesota University at Chautauqua, and he invited her to come to Minneapolis. Later he said, "The greatest thing I ever did for the university was to bring Maria Sanford here." She taught rhetoric and elocution and passed on to her students a love of poetry and art. She became known throughout the city and the state as a lecturer on the arts, public affairs, and woman suffrage. She retired in 1909 and the following year the university named the first women's dormitory for her.[7]

MOORHEAD

Comstock, Ada Louise (Notestein), 1876–1973, College Administrator; NAWM

Comstock House, 5th Avenue and 8th Street, S.; NR

Ada Louise Comstock was born in Moorhead, the daughter of Solomon G. Comstock, a banker who served in the state and national governments, a supporter of Moorhead College. Her mother was Sarah Comstock, founder of the local women's club. Ada attended high school here before going on to the University of Minnesota in 1892. She went then to Smith College, Columbia University, and Paris, France, for an education that was to make her one of America's famed college administrators. She was dean of women at the University of Minnesota and then at Smith College and president of Radcliffe College, 1923–43 (see Minneapolis, MN).

The house built by her father in 1883 has been restored and is open to the public from Memorial Day to Labor Day, Sat., Sun. 1–4:30; adm.[8]

NEW ULM

Gág, Wanda, 1893–1946, Artist and Writer; NAW

Wanda Gág Childhood Home, 226 N. Washington Street (Private); NR

Wanda Gág was born in New Ulm, a town settled by immigrants from Germany, Hungary, and Bohemia. She herself was Bohemian, one of seven children, and never spoke English until she went to school. When her father died, leaving the family a tiny insurance and their house, everyone expected fifteen-year-old Gág,

Maria L. Sanford, professor at the University of Minnesota, Minneapolis, was chosen to represent her state in Statuary Hall in the National Capitol, Washington, D.C. The sculptor was Evelyn Raymond.
Courtesy Architect of the Capitol, Washington, D.C.

the eldest child, to quit school and help support the family. But Gág was determined that she and all her sisters and her one brother should at least finish high school. She earned money by her art, drawing for newspapers, making place cards, valentines, and postcards. While contributing thus to the family finances, she won scholarships to the Minneapolis School of Art and later the Art Students' League in New York City. She developed her own style in drawings, woodcuts, and lithographs, but recognition as a serious artist came slowly.

Some of her work caught the attention of a publisher of children's books and she was launched on a successful career as illustrator and writer of such books as *Millions of Cats* (1928). Her stories, with their folktale quality, have become classics of children's literature. With her royalties she was able to buy a farm in New Jersey, which she named All Creation. When she died of cancer, at fifty-three, her ashes were scattered there.

NORTHFIELD

Baker, Laura, 1859?–1960, School Founder

Laura Baker School, 211 Oak Street; NR

In 1897 Laura Baker, who was working in the Minnesota State School, decided that custodial care was not enough for the developmentally handicapped individuals there. She was certain that methods could be devised to train and educate many of them for independent and even productive lives. She opened a private boarding school in Minneapolis, Minnesota, for "nervous and backward" children. The terms morons, imbeciles, and feeble-minded were never used, as Baker thought them degrading. Many parents tried to conceal retarded children and it was necessary for Baker to seek them out and convince the parents that there was hope for them. By the end of the year, with eight pupils enrolled, Baker moved her school to Northfield, where she was able to get a large house with spacious grounds. The school grew in size and reputation and soon townspeople as well as parents were attending performances of music and dance and craft shows put on by the pupils.

During the forty-five years Baker was the active head of the school, many of the pupils became self-supporting and several were able to graduate from college. The school became a nonprofit, tax-exempt corporation. Her niece and then a grandniece and great-grandnephew succeeded to its management. In 1985 it was still the only private residential school for the mentally retarded in Minnesota.[9]

Larson, Agnes, 1892–1967, Historian, and Others

Memorials, St. Olaf College

Agnes Larson was one of four Larson sisters, three of whom attained the distinction of listing in *Who's Who of American Women*, Agnes in history, Henrietta in business history, and Nora in bacteriology. They came from a stable Norwegian-American family of the Lutheran faith. They moved to Northfield in 1911 and between then and 1923 all attended St. Olaf College. By 1926 Agnes was teaching history here, where she was to remain for the rest of her professional life, although she spent some years in study off the campus. She worked for eighteen years researching the Minnesota white pine industry, resulting in publication of a landmark book on the subject in 1949.

In 1951 the name of Gertrude Hilleboe (1888–1976) was given to a hall at the college. She graduated here in 1912 and joined the faculty as dean of women. She served through two world wars, the 1917 influenza epidemic, and the Great Depression, retiring in 1958. She was hostess to such famous campus visitors as Crown Prince Olav and Princess Martha of Norway.

The name of Agnes Kittlesby (d. 1926) was given to a new dormitory in 1957. She had been the third woman graduate of St. Olaf when she took her diploma in 1900. She then returned to teach here for a decade before going to China, where she set up schools for the children of American missionaries.

A dormitory was named in 1938 for Agnes Theodora Mellby (d. 1918), the first woman to receive the B.A. from St. Olaf (1893). She was for the next sixteen years preceptress of the college, as well as teaching several subjects.[10]

RED WING

Densmore, Frances, 1867–1957, Specialist in American Indian Music; NAWM

Densmore Collection, Goodhue County Historical Society, 1166 Oak Street

In 1907 Frances Densmore began recording the songs of Big Bear, a Sioux living on the White Earth Reservation in northern Minnesota. She continued to study the traditional music of the Native Americans until she had nearly three thousand phonograph recordings. Without her interest and unremitting effort, this vital part of a vanishing culture would have been lost. Her interest in Indian music was awakened by reading Alice Cunningham Fletcher's *A Study of Omaha Music*. Encouraged by Fletcher, Densmore traveled many miles through wild country, sometimes by boat or birchbark canoe, carrying heavy field equipment and converting any accessible place into a recording studio. The Smithsonian's Bureau of American Ethnology sponsored her work and published her many articles and books. The Library of Congress owns most of the original recordings. While not off in the wilds, Densmore lived in Red Wing, at 729 W. 3rd Street, now in a historic district listed in the National Register. The Historical Society has many of Densmore's papers and a permanent display of photographs. It is open year-round, Tues.-Sun. 1–5; closed weekends in Jan.-Feb.[11]

Nelson, Julia Bullard, 1842–1914, Humanitarian

Julia B. Nelson House, 219 5th Street (Private); NR

For twenty years after the Civil War Julia Bullard Nelson labored in Texas and Tennessee, teaching freedmen. This was a job that took much courage, for the Ku Klux Klan was a threat and most whites refused to associate with those who worked with ex-slaves. During her first year in Columbus, Texas, only two white women ever spoke to her. At Warner Institute in Jonesboro, Tennessee, where she taught for nine years, she found less prejudice. The school was a community center, and the white residents were interested in the school's success.

In Red Wing she was a paid organizer for the state Woman's Christian Temperance Union, held office in the union, and edited its paper, the *White Ribbon*. She was president of the state Woman's Suffrage Association between 1890 and 1896. Once, while lecturing on suffrage, one of her listeners said women should not vote because they could not bear arms. ''Women don't bear arms,'' she said, ''they bear armies.'' An individualist who did what her conscience and common sense dictated no matter what people might say, Nelson was considered a radical; for a time she met almost as much prejudice in Red Wing as she had in the South, and for some years after her death Red Wing all but forgot her. The state suffrage association placed a memorial tablet in the Woman Citizen Building on the state fair grounds in St. Paul, Minnesota. Today she is given her due as one of the town's illustrious citizens: the home where she spent her last fifteen years is a historic landmark, and her efforts on behalf of humanity are recognized.[12]

ROCHESTER

Dempsey, Julia (Sister Mary Joseph), 1856–1939, Churchwoman; NAW

Mayo Clinic

A tornado that hit Rochester in 1883 changed Sister Mary Joseph's life from that of teacher to nurse. Mother Alfred, of the Convent of the Congregation of Our Lady of Lourdes, decided that the town needed a hospital. She persuaded William W. Mayo to staff the hospital, called Julia Dempsey (Sister Mary Joseph) back from a teaching job in Kentucky to be trained for nursing, and by 1889 the hospital built by the sisters was open, with Sister Mary Joseph as head nurse. Later she became Mayo's first surgical assistant, and in 1892 superintendent of St. Mary's Hospital, predecessor of the now world-famous Mayo Clinic. When the hospital outgrew the capacity of the sisterhood to furnish nurses, Sister Mary Joseph established the St. Mary's Hospital School for Nurses to train laywomen. In 1922, when a new surgical pavilion was opened at the hospital, she was given a standing ovation. ''I do not deserve the plaudits given me tonight,'' she said, ''but will take them and distribute them among the sisters with whom I have worked so many years trying to make St. Mary's Hospital a House of God and the Gateway of Heaven for suffering humanity.''

ST. CLOUD

Swisshelm, Jane Grey Cannon, 1815–1884, Newspaper Publisher and Women's Rights Activist; NAW

Marker, Lawn of Shoemaker Hall, St. Cloud State College

The marker identifies the site of the editorial offices where Jane Grey Cannon Swisshelm published her *St. Cloud Visiter*—she insisted on the spelling—between 1857 and 1863. She had published the *Saturday Visiter* in Pennsylvania before moving to St. Cloud. The move was made when her marriage to James Swisshelm became intolerable. She brought with her their only child. Later James divorced her for desertion. She blamed him less than she did society for his attitudes. ''Was it any fault of his,'' she wrote, ''that all that [the wife] can acquire by her labor-service or act during coverture, belongs to her husband?'' Her crusades for married women's property rights were influential in getting the law changed in Minnesota.

Her paper, which expressed freely her own views of women's rights, abolition, and politics, ran counter to the opinions of the boss of the Democratic party in central Minnesota. He and his cohorts sued her for libel and went so far as to destroy her press. She at once started another paper, the *St. Cloud Democrat*, and continued her jibes at conditions and persons she disliked and of which she disapproved. During the Civil War she did some nursing and wrote angry letters to the paper about the conditions she found in military hospitals. Those who liked her were her staunch friends; those who did not were implacable enemies. She eventually sued for part of her husband's estate, Swissvale, in Pennsylvania, won it, and went there to live out her days.[13]

ST. PAUL

Bishop, Harriet E., 1817–1883, Missionary and Teacher; NAW

Harriet Island, Mississippi River

St. Paul was a primitive village on the edge of civilization when Harriet E. Bishop responded to a request for teachers in the West. In 1847 she opened the first permanent citizen day school in the area. The school attracted only a handful of students at first, but it grew and won the acclaim of Catharine Beecher's Board of National Popular Education, under which she had trained. The Sunday schools she started grew into the first Protestant churches in St. Paul. She took part in the early temperance movement. She was herself the victim of abuse from a drunken husband, whom she divorced in 1867 after a marriage of less than ten years. She was also a pioneer in the movement for women's rights, serving as an officer for the American Equal Rights Association in 1869. Harriet Island was named for her in recognition of her pioneer work in education.[14]

Brown, Hallie Quinn, 1850–1949, Teacher; NAW

Hallie Q. Brown Community Center, 270 Kent Street

The center is named for Hallie Quinn Brown, a black woman whose parents had been slaves, though both were of mixed blood. One of Brown's grandmothers was white, as was one of her great-grandfathers. Her father, who had purchased his freedom, was a successful man, owner of property, and able to educate his children. Hallie graduated from Wilberforce University in Ohio in 1873 and went to Mississippi as a teacher. Later, after graduating from the Chautauqua Lecture School, she traveled extensively in America and Europe, speaking on Negro life, songs, and folklore. She also gave talks on temperance. In 1899 she was a representative at the International Congress of Women. Her contributions to raising the status of women of her race included organizing clubs for Afro-American women and the writing of *Homespun Heroines*, a collection of biographies of Negro women. See Wilberforce, OH.

McHugh, Anne (Sister Antonia), 1873–1944, College President

College of St. Catherine

Anne McHugh (Sister Antonia) was associated with the College of St. Catherine during its years of struggle and growth and is considered its founder-builder. It was founded in 1905 but graduated its first group of women in 1913. It achieved regional accreditation three years later. Sister Antonia, of the Sisters of St. Joseph of Carondelet, was dean from 1914 to 1929, then president until 1937. During her presidency she received the Pope Pius XI *Pro Ecclesia et Pontifice* medal, an LL.D. from the University of Minnesota, and an alumni award from the University of Chicago.

Working with her was Ellen Ireland (Mother Seraphine, 1843–1930). She served as superior of the sisters' St. Paul Province for thirty-nine years. During those years they opened more than thirty new schools, five hospitals, and the college. She visited all her convents once a year.[15]

Meyers, Sister Anna Marie, 1891–1975, Educator

Christ Child School, 2078 Summit Avenue

Paralyzed from the waist down and confined to a wheelchair as the result of an automobile accident that occurred while she was a teacher at the College of St.

Catherine, Sister Anna Marie Meyers refused to be dominated by a physical handicap. She decided to devote herself to the education and rehabilitation of retarded children and young adults. Two rooms of the Christ Child Community Center were provided for her use, and so successful were her classes that Richard C. Lilly, president of the First National Bank in St. Paul, led others in contributing to her project. In 1950 an old house on Summit Avenue was purchased for her school, and five years later work was begun on a new building at the site. An extension school was added to assist employed retarded workers by offering day and evening classes. Many of Minnesota's handicapped persons and their families have benefited from Sister Anna Maria's determination to make something of a shattered life.[16]

Ripley, Martha Rogers, 1843–1912, Physician; NAW

Memorial Plaque, State Capitol Rotunda, University Avenue

Martha Rogers Ripley was inspired to become a doctor because of the illness she saw in the New England mill towns where she lived with her husband, a paper mill operator. She got her M.D. from Boston University Medical School in 1883. Shortly afterward her husband was injured in a mill accident and Ripley was forced to undertake the support of her family. She moved to Minneapolis with her husband and three daughters and began a medical practice, specializing in obstetrics and pediatrics. In 1886 she established the Maternity Hospital, open to women, wed or unwed, rich or poor. Social services as well as medical care were offered. The hospital was renamed for her in 1955 but went out of existence two years later. In addition to her medical career, Ripley was a strong suffragist, a member of the Woman's Christian Temperance Union, a fighter for public hygiene, well known and respected far beyond her own city and state. The memorial plaque, installed in 1939, speaks of her as a ''champion of righteousness and justice'' serving ''with farsighted vision and sympathy.''[17]

Sawyer, Ruth, 1880–1970, Writer; NAWM

Rare Book Collection, College of St. Catherine

The children's books written by Ruth Sawyer over many years delighted the children to whom they were read and won the author numerous honors. She began by telling stories to children in the New York Public Library and by collecting and retelling folktales from Ireland and Spain. Her first book to win wide recognition was *Roller Skates*, based on her own early life in New York. It won the Newbery Award in 1937. The collection of rare works of children's literature made by the College of St. Catherine was named for her.

Ueland, Clara Hampson, 1860–1927, Suffragist and Reformer; NAW

Memorial Plaque, State Capitol Rotunda

Clara Hampson Ueland, wife of a prominent judge in Minneapolis and mother of seven children, was an early student of Friedrich Froebel's kindergarten methods and had a kindergarten in her home, a rambling house on the outskirts of Minneapolis. She and the other mothers formed a Kindergarten Association and sponsored several free kindergartens in Minneapolis as well as a training school for teachers. She also helped a small art school to develop into the Minneapolis Institute of Arts. She was the president of the Minnesota Woman's Suffrage Association from 1914 until the vote was won five years later and was given much of the credit for the victory. After the Nineteenth Amendment was ratified she became the president of the state League of Women Voters, and for the next years, until her death from an auto accident, she was an active lobbyist for women's concerns. In addition to the plaque honoring her, a fellowship fund was established in her name for women graduate students in government and citizenship at the University of Minnesota.[18]

STILLWATER

Palmer, Nelle Obrecht, 1893–1970, Innkeeper

Lowell Inn, 102 N. 2nd Street

The Lowell Inn, a prize-winning hotel and restaurant that has been called the Mount Vernon of the West, has been run by the Palmer family ever since Nelle Obrecht Palmer and Arthur Palmer took over its management in 1930. Nelle was born in Madison, Minnesota, into a family whose ten children were all taught to play musical instruments. They formed a family band and toured the Midwest giving concerts. In 1927 Nelle married Arthur, musical director of the company, and they formed a stock company. After a few years on the road, the couple was hired to manage the Lowell Inn. Their years of travel gave them many ideas about how a hotel should be run, and gradually they put them into effect. By 1945 they were owners of the inn. Arthur ran the kitchen, with Nelle out in front. While he tried to keep up with the bills, Nelle bought hand-blocked Belgian and Irish table linens and Wedgwood and Spode dinner service. Colored crystal goblets and silver candelabra graced the dining room. Arthur died in 1951, and Nelle continued to preside over the hostelry, giving it the style and hospitality that kept customers coming back. A portrait of Nelle hangs in the lobby.[19]

WALNUT GROVE

Wilder, Laura Ingalls, 1867–1957, Writer; NAWM

Plaque, Plum Creek (on a Private Farm). Wilder Museum

If anything testifies to the interest Americans take in their country roots, it is the affection they show for Laura Ingalls Wilder, the author of the Little House books. No less than eight sites, in seven states, have been set aside in memory of the writer and the places she mentioned in her series of books. Walnut Grove is the scene of her *On the Banks of Plum Creek*. The museum here is open daily, in the summer 10–7, in the winter 11–4. The Ingalls dugout, a mile north, and a plaque on the farm of Harold and Della Gordon, can be seen only in season. An outdoor pageant is given in July. See Burr Oak, IA, Independence, KS, and Ripon, WI. There are also marked sites in Missouri, South Dakota, and New York.[20]

WINONA

Molloy, Mary (Sister Mary Aloysius), 1880–1954, Churchwoman

College of St. Teresa

At the age of twenty-seven Mary Molloy had a Ph.D. from Cornell University and the world before her. She elected to respond to a request to initiate college courses for a Catholic religious community in the remote town of Winona. The school, Winona Seminary, soon became the College of St. Teresa. Molloy, as dean and later president, established high academic standards for the college, and then used her prestige to plead for such standards in other Catholic colleges for women. There were too many ''small, struggling, inefficient and useless so-called colleges,'' she said, that could offer nothing better than high school courses and ought to be closed.

In 1922 Molloy exchanged lay for religious status, taking the name Sister Mary Aloysius. She spent two years in Rochester, Minnesota, as a novitiate of the Sisters of St. Francis. Not until 1946 did she retire from the presidency of St. Teresa. It was then a first-class college offering women an education equal to any offered men students.[21]

NOTES

In addition to the sources mentioned below, I have had help from the Minnesota Historical Society, St. Paul.

1. Gretchen Kreuter, ''Women's Historic Sites in Minnesota,'' mimeographed, c. 1976.

2. Ibid.

3. Ibid.; Susan Margot Smith, in *Women of Minnesota: Selected Biographical Essays*, ed. Barbara Stuhler and Gretchen Kreuter (St. Paul: Minnesota Historical Society Press, 1977), cited below as *WOM*.

4. Nancy Freeman Rohde, in *WOM*.

5. Winifred W. Bolin, ''Heating Up the Melting Pot,'' *Minnesota History* 45 (Summer 1976); Elizabeth Gilman in *WOM*; *Women's History Sources*, ed. Andrea Hinding and others (New York: R. R. Bowker Co., 1979).

6. Marjorie Kreidberg, ''An Unembarrassed Patriot: Lucy Wilder Morris,'' *Minnesota History* 47 (Summer 1981).

7. Geraldine S. Schofield and Susan M. Smith, in *WOM*.

8. Kreuter, op. cit.

9. Correspondence and clippings, Northfield Historical Society and Laura Baker School, Northfield.

10. Carol Jenson, ''The Larson Sisters,'' in *WOM*; correspondence and clippings, St. Olaf College.

11. Nina M. Archabal, in *WOM*; Nancy L. Woolworth, ''Miss Densmore Meets the Ojibwe,'' *Minnesota Archaeologist* 38 (Aug. 1979); correspondence and clippings, Goodhue County Historical Society, Red Wing.

12. Julia Wiech Lief, ''A Woman of Purpose: Julia B. Nelson,'' *Minnesota History* 47 (Winter 1981); correspondence, Goodhue County Historical Society; nomination form, National Register.

13. Abigail McCarthy, in *WOM*; Jane Swisshelm, *Half a Century* (Chicago, Ill., 1880), quoted in Eleanor Flexner, *Century of Struggle*, rev. ed. (Cambridge, Mass.: Belknap Press, 1975).

14. Winifred D. W. Bolin, in *WOM*; Kreuter, op. cit.

15. *WOM*, pp. 335–36; Patricia Condon Johnston, ''Reflected Glory: The Story of Ellen Ireland,'' *Minnesota History* 48 (Spring 1982).

16. *WOM*, p. 336; Kreuter, op. cit.

17. Winton U. Solberg, ''Martha G. Ripley,'' *Minnesota History* 39 (Spring 1964); *WOM*, p. 340.

18. *WOM*, p. 342.

19. Patricia Condon Johnston, ''Nelle Palmer of Stillwater,'' *Minnesota History* 48 (Spring 1983).

20. William T. Anderson, ''A Visit to Laura Ingalls Wilder Country,'' *Americana* 11 (Sept.-Oct. 1983).

21. Sister Karen Kennelly, in *WOM*.

OHIO

CHILLICOTHE

Peter, Sarah Worthington King, 1800–1877, Charitable and Church Worker; NAW

Adena, W. Allen Avenue, Extended, Off State 104; HABS, NR

Sarah Worthington King Peter, who was to become an influence for good in Cincinnati, Ohio, in Cambridge, Massachusetts, and in Philadelphia, Pennsylvania, spent her youth here, in the home built by her father. It is a great Georgian mansion designed by Benjamin Latrobe.

As the wife of Edward King, Sarah lived in Cincinnati, where she helped to found the Cincinnati Protestant Orphan Asylum in 1833. Following King's death, she moved to Cambridge, where her sons attended Harvard University. On a visit to Philadelphia she met the widowed British consul, William Peter, who became her husband in 1844. She established the Philadelphia School of Design, later the Moore Institute of Art, Science, and Industry. Widowed for the second time in 1853, she returned to Cincinnati, became a Catholic convert, and gave much of her time and effort to the church. She left her home there to the Franciscans, along with a collection of art and Georgian furniture.

Adena is now a state memorial and is open Apr. 1-Oct. 31, daily except Mon. 9:30–4:30; adm.

CINCINNATI

Beecher, Catharine. See Stowe, Harriet

Braun, Emma Lucy, 1889–1971, Botanist; NAWM

Buzzardroost Rock, Lynx Prairie

Lynx Prairie is one of several prairies, isolated grasslands with an entirely different plant life from the surrounding forests, found in the hills of Adams

County near Cincinnati. The Department of the Interior has declared Buzzardroost Rock Lynx Prairie a Registered Natural Landmark, possessing "exceptional value in illustrating the natural history of the United States."

The woman who discovered and studied the small prairies and dedicated herself to saving them was Emma Lucy Braun, a longtime botany teacher at the University of Cincinnati. She was founder, editor, and writer for *Wildflower*, in which she early voiced her concern for the preservation of habitats. She encouraged and advised the Ohio Chapter of the Nature Conservancy in plans to combine the prairies into a national park to be called "Edge of Appalachia."

Braun often took her students on field trips through this region. She retired from teaching early (at fifty-nine) to work on her great *The Deciduous Forests of Eastern North America*, a valuable reference on forest ecology. She discovered several new plant species, one of which is now called *Eupatorium luciae brauniae*.[1]

Cary, Alice, 1820–1871, and Her Sister Phoebe Cary, 1824–1871, Poets; NAW (under Alice Cary)

Cary Cottage, 7000 Hamilton Avenue; NR

When Robert Cary married a second wife, friction developed between Alice and Phoebe Cary, his poetic daughters, who read constantly, and their stepmother, who thought reading a waste of time. He built a new house, leaving the old cottage to Alice and Phoebe, still in their teens, and their younger brothers and sister. The girls wrote verses which were published in newspapers and gained critical acclaim from such literary figures as John Greenleaf Whittier and Edgar Allan Poe. In addition to poetry, Alice wrote short stories, one of them, *Clovernook*, dealing with their life in Cincinnati.

Years after the Cary sisters had left here to take up residence in New York City, the cottage was acquired by Georgia and Florence Trader, q.v., who established Clovernook Home and School for the Blind. When the school outgrew the cottage, it was used only occasionally. It was recently restored to its original character and is operated by the school as a historical landmark, open to the public the first Sun. of each month, 1–4.[2]

Segale, Rose Maria (Sister Blandina), 1850–1941, Churchwoman

Santa Maria Community Services, 2104 St. Michael Street

One of the city's most colorful figures, Rose Maria Segale (Sister Blandina) contributed much to Cincinnati in the early twentieth century, and her influence is still strong here. She came to Cincinnati when she was a child, later took her vows at the Sisters of Charity motherhouse, and almost immediately was sent on missions to Ohio, then to Colorado, and Santa Fe and Albuquerque, New Mexico. For some twenty years she helped build civilization in the Southwest, founding schools and orphanages. She had to be both tough and wise to survive in that time and place. In 1897 she returned to Cincinnati to work with Italian immigrants in the Basin area. With Sister Justina and the help of sponsors, she founded the Santa Maria Italian Educational and Industrial Home. Santa Maria has changed to meet new needs of the city, with neighborhood centers, youth service projects, a child care center, and a community house.[3]

Storer, Maria Longworth Nichols, 1849–1932, Ceramicist; NAW

Rookwood Pottery, Celestial and Rookwood Place; NR

Maria Longworth Nichols Storer's interest in pottery was aroused by a visit to the Philadelphia Centennial Exposition in 1876, where both she and her husband were fascinated by the Japanese pottery exhibit. On her return to Cincinnati she began taking classes in china painting and worked in a small studio, experimenting with clay, glaze, and color. In 1880 she built a studio with a kiln, named it Rookwood for the family estate, and began serious production of art pottery. It was not at first a commercial success, but it soon began receiving high awards and the pieces were collected by museums. Maria lost her first husband, George W. Nichols, and then married Bellamy Storer.

Rookwood Pottery went out of production in the 1960s, but the Tudor-style building on Mt. Adams, which Maria designed and built in 1892 as its final home, still exists. The kiln room is now an unusual restaurant, with the original kiln an integral part of the dining room design. Prized pieces of Rookwood art pottery are on display.[4]

Stowe, Harriet Beecher, 1811–1896, Writer, and Her Sister Catharine Beecher, 1800–1878, Educator; NAW

Harriet Beecher Stowe House, 2950 Gilbert Avenue; NR

In 1833 a remarkable family moved to Cincinnati from New England. The Reverend Lyman Beecher, with his second wife and children from both marriages, came on invitation from Lane Seminary. Several of the older children had already left home for careers of their own, but two of the daughters who were to become famous were still at home: Catharine Beecher (thirty-seven) and Harriet Beecher Stowe (twenty-two).

Almost at once Catharine started the Western Female Seminary, and Harriet taught there. Catharine's goal was to educate the benighted westerners, especially the immigrants flocking to the cities of the Midwest. Her *Treatise on Domestic Economy*, published in 1841, added to the fame she had already achieved for her sponsorship of education for women. Feminists, even of her day, were not in accord with her philosophy that "Heaven has appointed to one sex the superior, and to the other the subordinate station."

As for Harriet, she married Calvin Stowe in 1836 and in the first seven years of marriage bore five children. "I am but a mere drudge," she wrote, "with few ideas beyond babies and housekeeping." She managed to do some writing, however, encouraged by her husband, and sold enough of her tales to hire a housekeeper. Not until the Stowes moved back to New England did she find time to write seriously, but the seeds of her famous *Uncle Tom's Cabin* were planted while she lived here. A visit to Kentucky gave her a glimpse of slavery, and she visited the Quaker John Rankin, whose home was a station on the underground railroad, and heard the story of Eliza Harris's escape from slavery by crossing the river on blocks of ice.

The Stowe House, which might better be called the Beecher House, was for a time a museum devoted to Negro history. It is now a community center managed, under an agreement with the Ohio Historical Society, by the Citizens Committee on Youth. It is open for tours Tues., Wed., and Fri. 10–4.

Taft, Anna Sinton, 1852–1931, Art Collector

Taft Museum, 216 Pike Street; HABS, NHL

Anna Sinton Taft was the only child of David Sinton, who had amassed a considerable fortune selling iron for cannonballs to both North and South during the Civil War. She married Charles Phelps Taft, of another wealthy and powerful Cincinnati family. He was half brother to U.S. President William Howard Taft. Anna took her place in Cincinnati as one of the grandes dames, a supporter of art, culture, and civic projects. She long presided over the symphony orchestra, then the opera. When her father died in 1900, Anna and Charles inherited the Pike Street mansion, which they filled with art treasures. They entertained lavishly, the guests including royalty, artists, and patrons of the arts. In 1927 they gave the house, the land, and the art collection, along with a million dollars, to the newly formed Cincinnati Institute of Fine Arts for the citizens of Cincinnati. After they passed away, Charles in 1930, Anna the following year, the home was transformed into an art gallery of unique importance. It is open weekdays 10–5, Sun. and holidays (except Thanksgiving and Christmas) 2–5.[5]

Trader, Georgia, 1876–1944, and Her Sister Florence Trader, 1878–1964, Workers for the Blind

Clovernook Home and School for the Blind, 7000 Hamilton Avenue; NR

The cottage home of Alice and Phoebe Cary, q.v., came on the market in 1903. Georgia and Florence Trader wanted to purchase it for a school and home for the blind. They approached William A. Procter, president of the Procter and Gamble Company, with their plans. He purchased the eight-room farmhouse and its grounds, and the Trader sisters renovated the building and took in their first three residents. Georgia was herself blind and had worked to establish classes for the visually impaired in the Cincinnati public schools. The cottage was soon outgrown and the first unit of Trader House was opened in 1913. With the continued help of Procter, the sisters expanded the training and employment program for both men and women with impaired vision. It is now a flourishing complex where many books and magazines are printed in Braille and where workers produce fine weaving and other handicrafts for sale.[6]

CLEVELAND

Bolton, Frances Payne, 1885–1977, Congresswoman

Frances Payne Bolton School of Nursing, Case Western Reserve University, 2121 Abington Street

As a member of the board of Lakeside Hospital, wealthy Frances Payne Bolton was distressed to learn that nurses were treated as domestic servants and required to live in attic rooms. Her first public speeches brought these facts to the attention of the public. She gave $1.5 million to Western Reserve to establish a school of nursing. When she was elected to Congress in 1940 she continued her efforts to advance the nursing profession. She had already persuaded the secretary of war to establish an Army School of Nursing. She now pushed through an act creating a Cadet Nurse Corps.

During her thirty years as Ohio's representative in Congress she specialized in African affairs, sponsored bills affecting minors and women, worked for international peace agreements, and was universally acknowledged one of the finest members of Congress. The Lakeside Hospital School of Nursing, established in 1898, was the predecessor of the school now named for Bolton.[7]

Eastman, Linda Ann, 1867–1963, Librarian; NAWM

Eastman Branch, Cleveland Public Library, 11602 Lorain Avenue. Eastman Reading Garden

As librarian of the Cleveland Public Library from 1918 to 1938, Linda Ann Eastman worked to make books available to all segments of the city's population. Before her appointment she had been on the staff for twenty-five years. She had helped to establish the Ohio Library Association and organized a full-time School of Library Science at Western Reserve University. She had added a Braille collection and set up a children's Library League. When librarian William Brett was killed in 1918 the trustees had no hesitation in appointing Eastman to the position, though no woman had yet headed a library in so large a city as Cleveland.[8]

Rogers, Grace Rainey, 1867–1943, Art Patron and Philanthropist; NAW

Rousseau de Rottière Room, Cleveland Museum of Art, 11150 East Boulevard

A shy, retiring woman best known for her benefactions, Grace Rainey Rogers was a native of Cleveland and grew up somewhat overshadowed by other members of her family. Her mother was Eleanor Mitchell Rainey, founder of a handicraft school and social settlement that was given her name and a trustee of the Cleveland Museum of Art. Her father made a fortune in the coke industry. Her cousin was first president of the University of Chicago. Her brother, Paul J. Rainey, was a noted big-game hunter and explorer. Rogers lived in New York City after her marriage to Henry Welsh Rogers and began her own career of art collecting and patronage.

The room she gave to the art museum in 1942 was considered one of the most important acquisitions the museum ever received. The doors, wall panels, rugs, and art objects had been designed for Louis XV's comptroller and had earlier been installed in Rogers' New York City apartment.

DAYTON

Doren, Electra Collins, 1861–1927, Librarian

Electra C. Doren Branch, Dayton Public Library, 701 Troy Street

When Electra Collins Doren was eighteen she was made assistant librarian of the Dayton Public Library. For almost all her adult years she was on its staff, serving as head librarian from 1913. She was not one to guard books possessively. Her one aim was to make them accessible, first through a good card catalog, then by opening the shelves, and throughout her career by sending books to places where they would be used—military posts, schools, factories, and remote areas where no branches were located. In her last years she was busy planning a branch library in north Dayton, and after her death the library board gave it her name. It was dedicated in 1928, and her friend Linda Anne Eastman (see Cleveland, OH) paid tribute to Doren, who "felt very strongly that books are one of the greatest blessings in life."[9]

GREENVILLE

Oakley, Annie, 1860–1926, Sharpshooter; NAW

Annie Oakley Park, State 127

When Annie Moses was quite young, her father died, leaving her mother with fifteen children. The family faced stark poverty and Annie's childhood was one of misery. For a time she was placed in a foster home. As a teenager she was able to help out by shooting rabbit, squirrel, and quail for sale, and it is claimed that she earned enough to pay off the mortgage on her mother's farm. At fifteen she was such a good shot that she competed with a champion, Frank Butler. She won, and a year later married Butler. The couple put on demonstrations of their skills, Annie changing her name to Annie Oakley. They joined the Buffalo Bill Wild West Show in 1884 and remained with it for seventeen years, traveling throughout the United States and visiting Europe. It was a hard life, but it made Annie famous as Little Miss Sure Shot and the Girl of the Western Plains.

The Butlers returned to Greenville in 1926, both ill. Frank died just eighteen days after his beloved companion, and they were buried in the Moses plot in Brock Cemetery, near Annie's birthplace. The Garst Museum, 105 N. Broadway, has an Oakley Room, with memorabilia. It is open Tues.-Sun. 1–5.[10]

HILLSBORO

Thompson, Eliza Trimble, 1816–1905, Temperance Reformer; NAW

Mother Thompson House, 133 Willow Street (Private); NR.
Markers at Entrances to Town

Eliza Trimble Thompson became a patron saint of the Woman's Christian Temperance Union, which had its beginnings in the women's crusade that started in Hillsboro and Springfield, Ohio, in December 1873. Inspired by a lecture from Dio Lewis, a band of women led by Thompson made an appeal to druggists who sold liquor. Then they gathered courage to visit a saloon, where Thompson knelt on the floor and led the ladies in prayer.

In Springfield the women were led by Eliza Daniel Stewart (1816–1908, NAW). Stewart's book, *Memories of the Crusade*, is subtitled "a thrilling account of the great uprising of the women of Ohio in 1873, against the liquor crime. By Mother Stewart, the leader."

For about three months the praying bands continued, with varying degrees of success, until they were stopped by a court injunction. But stories of their efforts were carried by the newspapers and the movement spread like wildfire. In places as far apart as Grass Valley, California, and Fredonia, New York, women's temperance unions sprang up, and in 1874 the Woman's National Christian Temperance Union was organized at Cleveland, Ohio. It was to unite women across the country and to become one of the most important agents of change in American life.

MARTINS FERRY

Zane, Elizabeth, 1766?–1831?, Revolutionary War Heroine; NAW

Betty Zane Memorial, Walnut Grove Cemetery, End of 4th Street

On September 11, 1782, Indians under the authority of the British attacked Fort Henry. Colonel Ebenezer Zane had fortified a house nearby with a powder magazine, but so swift was the attack that most of the powder was still in the house when it was urgently needed at the fort. His teenaged sister, Elizabeth Zane, was in the fort at the time and she volunteered to fetch more powder. She dashed to the house, grabbed a tablecloth, filled it with powder, and then made the return trip to the fort, the Indians firing at her while she ran. The story of her bravery made its way into history, although the details are misty. The statue commemorating the event was erected in 1928. The Betty Zane Frontier Days Festival is held annually in Martins Ferry. Wheeling, West Virginia, also claims her as a heroine.

MASSILLON

Jenkins, Mary Owens, fl. 1840s–1880s, Civil War Soldier

Marker, West Brookfield Cemetery

According to the inscription, ''Mary Owens Jenkins served in the Civil War 1861–1865 in Co. K, 9th Penn. Vol. Cav. under the name of John Evans.'' The stone was placed in 1937 by the Daniel Ritter Camp 93, Sons of Union Veterans of the Civil War, over a previously unmarked grave. Two members of the group had investigated the legend about Jenkins. They found three surviving Jenkins children living in Ohio and Pennsylvania who told their mother's story. She did indeed serve in the Union Army, for the best of motives: she wanted to be near her lover, William Evans, and, dressed as a man, enlisted with him. Both were in the battle of Gettysburg, where William was killed and Mary wounded. Her identity was discovered and she returned to her home in Danville, Pennsylvania, later to marry William Jenkins, with whom she came to the North Lawrence–Massillon area.[11]

Rotch, Charity, 1765–1824, Philanthropist

Marker, Intersection of Oxford and 11th Streets, N.E.

Charity Rotch and her husband, Thomas Rotch, were Quakers who came from New England to Ohio early in the nineteenth century. Their home, Spring Hill, was a station on the underground railroad. Thomas died in 1823, having planned that a sum of money should go to the establishment of a Quaker school for children. Charity outlived him less than a year. She left much of her estate to found "a benevolent institution for the education of destitute orphan and indigent children, more particularly those whose parents are of depraved morals, that they may be trained up in the habits of industry and economy." Two years later the Charity School opened. It was in existence, though not under the same name, and not with the same moralistic approach, until 1924. A boulder inscribed with information about the school was put in place in 1927.[12]

RIPLEY

Rankin, Jean Lowry, d. 1878, Abolitionist

Rankin House State Memorial, Liberty Hill, Off US 52; HABS, NR

Jean Lowry Rankin and John Rankin lived here before the Civil War and ran one of the stations of the underground railroad. One of their friends was the Reverend Lyman Beecher, of Cincinnati, Ohio, whose daughter Harriet Beecher Stowe heard from Rankin the exciting story of Eliza Harris's escape from slavery by crossing the icy Ohio River. Years later Stowe embodied the story in *Uncle Tom's Cabin*, the book that brought the horrors of slavery home to thousands of readers. Both the Rankins are buried in Ripley Cemetery, with a monument reading "Freedom's Heroes." The Rankin home was purchased by the state in 1938 and has been restored and dedicated as a state memorial, under the supervision of the Ohio Historical Society. It is open Apr.-Oct., daily except Mon., 9:30–5; adm.[13]

SALEM

Cowles, Betsey Mix, 1810–1876, Abolitionist and Reformer; NAW

Marker, Entrance to Town

The historical marker reads: "Salem founded 1806. First Woman's Rights Convention Held in 1850." Betsey Mix Cowles was president of the convention, which was held on April 19 and 20. She was one of Oberlin College's first graduates, a schoolteacher and a strong abolitionist. At the Akron, Ohio, woman's rights convention in 1851 she presented a report on labor, containing the radical suggestion that women should be paid the same as men for their work. In 1852 she was instrumental in founding the Ohio Woman's Rights Association.[14]

WILBERFORCE

Brown, Hallie Quinn, 1849–1949, Teacher and Lecturer; NAW

Hallie Q. Brown Memorial Library, Central State University

The Brown family moved to Wilberforce about 1870 so that Hallie Quinn Brown and her brother could attend Wilberforce University, a school primarily for blacks. She graduated in 1873 and went into teaching and lecturing. From 1893 until about 1903 she taught elocution at Wilberforce, but much of her time was spent on speaking tours in America and England. She had heard Susan B. Anthony speak while a student and at once espoused the cause of woman suffrage. Her lectures covered a wide range, including temperance and church work, her main interest being the interpretation of Negro life. She was one of the first Afro-American women to organize others of her race in women's clubs. See St. Paul, MN.

YELLOW SPRINGS

Memorial Buildings, Antioch College

Antioch College opened in 1853 as a coeducational college, with a distinguished New England educator, Horace Mann, as president. Mann had a fine educational philosophy, stressing the development of the whole personality, including the individual's social conscience. He was, however, not quite prepared by the society in which he lived for some of the ideas of the young women attracted to the school, one of the very few of collegiate grade open to females, and sometimes he had doubts about coeducation, "the great experiment."

Antioch has named a number of its buildings for women who were associated with the college. Pennell Hall commemorates Rebecca Pennell (1821–1890), Antioch's first female professor. She was listed as "Miss R. M. Pennell, Professor of Physical Geography, Drawing, Natural History, Civil History and Didactics." She was Mann's niece and had been teaching in New England for fifteen years when appointed to her college post. In 1855 she married Austin Dean.[15]

Susan Way Dodds (1830–1911) was one of the individualists who made life difficult for Mann. When her name was called as a graduate in the 1866 commencement, she rose in her place and declined the diploma. Although she had scrimped and saved to get an education, she rose on a point of honor. She had some time earlier adopted the reform dress, a tunic over bloomers. Mann was ready to accept the costume, but the trustees insisted on more conventional attire at graduation. She refused. Although many of her fellow students and townspeople applauded her stand, the trustees were firm and she left without a diploma. She went to medical school, earned an M.D., established a sanitarium for women in St. Louis, and wrote books on hygiene. Antioch made amends by giving Dodds a diploma and an honorary M.A. in 1884, and now there is a dormitory named for her.

Rice Hall bears the name of Rebecca Rice, who graduated in 1860, founded a successful girls' school in Chicago, Illinois, served as a trustee of Antioch, and left her personal library to the college. She was a classmate of Olympia Brown, who related in her memoirs a conversation between Rice and Mann. He asked if she thought the education of women would lead to their wishing to enter the professions. She said she believed it would. He replied that if he believed that, "he was doing very wrong in remaining at the head of a coeducational school."[16]

NOTES

In addition to the sources mentioned below, I have had assistance from the State of Ohio, Department of Economic and Community Development and the Office of the Governor; the Martha Kinney Cooper Ohioana Library Association, Columbus; the Rutherford B. Hayes Presidential Center, Fremont; the Harding House and Museum, Marion; the Stark County Convention and Visitors Bureau and the McKinley Museum, Canton; the Harrison Tomb State Memorial, North Bend; Cleveland Public Library; Roscoe Village; the Ohio State University Center for Women's Studies; Alda Vitz, Cincinnati; and Helen Patterson, Geneva.

1. Perry A. Peskin, "A Walk through Lucy Braun's Prairie," *Explorer* 20 (Winter 1978).
2. Correspondence, Clovernook School.
3. Clippings from Zimmerman Library, University of New Mexico; *Cincinnati Enquirer*, Aug. 3, 1975.
4. Herbert Peck, *The Book of Rookwood Pottery* (New York: Bonanza Books, 1969); Ralph and Terry Kovel, *The Kovels' Collector's Guide to American Art Pottery* (New York: Crown Publishers, 1974); correspondence, Adams, Gaffney & Associates, Inc., Cincinnati.
5. Stephen Birmingham, *The Grandes Dames* (New York: Simon & Schuster, 1982); Pudy Lame, "The Tafts of Pike Street," MS, and correspondence from Taft Museum.
6. Correspondence, Clovernook School.
7. Hope Chamberlin, *A Minority of Members: Women in the U.S. Congress* (New York: New American Library, 1974).
8. *Dictionary of American Library Biography*, ed. Bohdan S. Wynor (Littleton, Colo.: Libraries Unlimited, Inc., 1978).
9. Ibid.
10. Brochure and clippings, Garst Museum.
11. Clippings and correspondence, Massillon Museum.
12. Ibid.
13. Brochure, Rankin House State Memorial.
14. *The Salem, Ohio 1850 Women's Rights Convention Proceedings*, comp. and ed. Robert W. Audretsch (Salem, Ohio: Salem Area Bicentennial Committee and Salem Public Library, 1976).
15. Madeleine B. Stern, *We the Women: Career Firsts of Nineteenth Century America* (New York: Schulte Publishing Co., 1963).
16. Olympia Brown, *Acquaintances, Old and New, Among Reformers* (Milwaukee, Wis.: S. E. Tate Printing Co., 1911); correspondence and clippings, Antioch College.

WISCONSIN

GREEN BAY

Tank, Mrs. Niels Otto, d. 1891, Missionary and Benefactor

Tank Cottage, in Heritage Hill State Park (State 57 and 172); NR

The oldest standing house in Wisconsin was built in 1776 for fur trader Joseph Roi, and sold later to Niels Otto Tank and his wife. They were wealthy Norwegian missionaries who arrived in 1805 to establish a Moravian colony for Norwegians. Otto died in 1865 and Madame Tank remained here until her death, devoting her wealth and life to missionary work. She presented Tank Park to the city in 1880 in memory of her husband. The house has been moved from its original site on the Fox River to the park. It is furnished with original Tank furniture, much of it of Dutch origin. Heritage Hill State Park is a complex of furnished historical buildings, open June1–Labor Day, daily 10–5, May 1–31 and Labor Day–Oct. 31, Sat. and Sun.

GREENBUSH

Kohler, Ruth, 1906–1953, Preservationist

Plaque, Sylvanus Wade House, Old Wade House State Park, Junction of State 23 and Kettle Moraine Drive; HABS, NR

The Wade House, built in 1851, was a stagecoach inn, a stopping place between Sheboygan and Fond du Lac, run by the Wade family from the time when the road was made of planks until a few years ago. The inn was purchased by the Kohler Foundation of Kohler, Wisconsin, carrying out the wishes of several members of the Kohler family. Ruth Kohler oversaw the work of restoration.

As chairman of the Committee on Wisconsin Women, she was responsible for preparing historical exhibits for the 1948 centennial, and she wrote *The Story of Wisconsin Women*. She organized the Women's Auxiliary of the Wisconsin Historical Society and was vice president of the society.

Wade Park includes many other buildings, serving as a museum of Wisconsin's pioneer days. It is operated by the Wisconsin State Historical Society. Tours are led by costumed interpreters in July and Aug., Mon.-Fri. 10–5; in May, June, Sept., and Oct., weekdays 9–4, Sat. and Sun. 10–5; adm.

JANESVILLE

Bond, Carrie Jacobs, 1862–1946, Song Writer; NAW

Monument, at Site of Birthplace, 1806 W. Court Street (Private)

Carrie Jacobs Bond, the woman who was to win hearts with her songs, spent a happy childhood in Janesville. Her family was musical, and as she practiced the piano she dreamt of being a song writer. She moved to Chicago, Illinois, after being widowed. It was there that she began writing the songs that made her famous, including "I Love You Truly" and "Just a Wearyin' for You." See Chicago, IL.

Willard, Frances, 1839–1898, Temperance Leader; NAW

Frances Willard Schoolhouse, 1401 E. Craig Avenue; NR

Frances Willard came to Janesville, then in Wisconsin Territory, in 1846, riding in a covered wagon with her New England family. There was a church here, but only occasionally was there a preacher. There were no schools. Both her mother and father were educated and both attended Oberlin College briefly after traveling West. Willard lived a tomboy life, wanted to be called Frank, and got her early education from her mother. The family moved later to Evanston, Illinois, which was to be her home and heaquarters during her long career as leader of the Woman's Christian Temperance Union.

The original site of the family home, Forest Home, 1720 S. River Road, is marked. The house itself has been relocated and is private. The schoolhouse where she taught is owned by the Frances Willard–Rock County Historical Society. See Chicago and Evanston, IL.

JOHNSTOWN CENTER

Wilcox, Ella Wheeler, 1850–1919, Writer; NAW

Plaque, Home on Scharine Road (Private)

"Laugh and the world laughs with you; Weep, and you weep alone." Of the many who read and quote these lines, few can tell who wrote them. The author was Ella Wheeler Wilcox, born in Johnstown Center; she lived here and in Windsor, Wisconsin, during her youth. Her mother, who loved to read romantic novels and memorize poetry, undoubtedly contributed to Wilcox's dream of escaping poverty by becoming a successful author. She began writing while young and, surprisingly, it was a rejection that gave her career a start. Some love poems she sent to a Chicago, Illinois, publisher were turned down as too revealing to print, especially as they were entitled "Poems of Passion." The rejection, and the reason for it, became known. The book was snapped up by another publisher, and in its first two years it sold sixty thousand copies. Not really sensational, the poems tended toward the sentimental and moralistic. After Wilcox married Robert Wilcox, they moved to New York and then to Connecticut.

KENOSHA

Bradford, Mary Davison, 1856–1943, Teacher and School Administrator

Bradford Senior High School, 3700 Wash Road. Bradford Building (Reuther Alternative High School), 913 57th Avenue

Mary Davison Bradford served in the Kenosha public schools for forty-three years. In 1910 she was made superintendent of schools for the city of Kenosha, a post she held until 1921. Her memoirs, published in the *Wisconsin Magazine of History* (1930–32) and later in a separate volume, detail the development of educational theory and practice in the city over almost half a century. A part of the memoirs describing the early days of her family in Wisconsin was published as *Pioneers! O Pioneers* (1937), "to give children a picture of pioneer life and pioneer schools in Wisconsin."[1]

Harvey, Cordelia Adelaid Perrine, 1824–1895, Civil War Nurse

Cordelia Harvey School, 2012 19th Avenue

Cordelia Adelaid Perrine Harvey was the wife of Louis Powell Harvey, governor of Wisconsin. Soon after his inauguration, while leading an expedition to relieve Wisconsin troops that had suffered severe losses in the Battle of Shiloh, he fell from a steamboat and drowned. His widow decided to honor his memory by carrying on the relief work he had begun. She was appointed Sanitary Agent in St. Louis, with responsibility for collecting medical supplies and inspecting army hospitals. Alarmed by what she considered an unnecessary rate of mortality in the field hospitals, she fought to have the wounded sent to their homes or to real hospitals to be cared for. She went to Washington, D.C., to plead with President Abraham Lincoln. He and his commanders believed that a furloughed soldier would never willingly return to the fight. Harvey pointed out that dead soldiers never returned either. As a result of her efforts, three army hospitals were established in Madison, Wisconsin. Lincoln proposed that one should be named for her, but she asked that it be named for her husband.[2]

MADISON

Mears, Helen Farnsworth, 1872–1916, Sculptor; NAW

The Genius of Wisconsin, *State Capitol*

Helen Farnsworth Mears was born in Oshkosh, Wisconsin, into a family poor in material wealth but rich in ambition and mutual support. Her mother, Elizabeth Mears, was Wisconsin's earliest poet, publishing under the name of Nellie Wildwood. Her father, who had studied medicine, taught Helen anatomy and set up a workshop for her. She and her sister Mary Mears, a writer, were lifelong companions. Helen's first artistic success was *The Genius of Wisconsin*, submitted to the World's Columbian Exposition in 1893. This led to help from a wealthy philanthropist of Milwaukee, Wisconsin, and a prize from the Milwaukee Women's Club, enabling her to study in New York. There the well-known sculptor Augustus St. Gaudens took her into his studio as an assistant. She enjoyed a period of prosperity and fame but was never able to earn more than enough for a bare living. Many of her best works have disappeared because she could not afford to put them into marble. Her early death is said to have been brought on by the stress of overwork and poverty. Her most memorable public work is the statue of Frances Willard, leader of the Woman's Christian Temperance Union, for Statuary Hall in the National Capitol. The Paine Art Center in her home town has many of her surviving works.[3]

Peck, Roseline Willard, 1808–1899, Pioneer Farmer

Marker, 125 S. Webster Street

Roseline Willard Peck was the first white woman in Madison. She came here in 1837 from Vermont, the wife of Eben Peck. Eben had come first, to look over the land, and a few years after they arrived he disappeared. It was reported that he had set off for the Oregon country, but Roseline believed he was in Texas, with a wife and six children and that he "probably had her picked out" when he first came west. Their daughter, the first child born in Madison, was named Wisconsiana Victoria Peck. The deserted Roseline moved to Baraboo and farmed her land there until her death. An English visitor who availed himself of her hospitality had the temerity to publish an account of the visit, describing her as "a bustling little woman, about as high as the door," which was five feet, and painting an unflattering picture of her abode. Peck wrote to the Wisconsin Historical Society, indignantly setting the record straight. A picture of her shows a sour-faced woman, perhaps understandably embittered by what life had given her.

The log house in Madison was occupied next by Robert L. Ream, and here his daughter Vinnie Ream (1847–1914), later to win fame as a sculptor, was born. The cabin was torn down in 1857.[4]

White, Helen Constance, 1896–1967, Educator and Writer; NAWM

Helen C. White Hall, University of Wisconsin, 600 N. Park Street

Helen Constance White came to the University of Wisconsin in 1919 from a New England home and a woman's college (Radcliffe College). She settled comfortably into the midwestern coeducational scene. She earned her Ph.D. at Wisconsin and taught English here until almost the end of her days, retiring in 1965 as head of the English department. She combined teaching with the writing of scholarly books and articles on medieval and Renaissance literature and wrote a series of historical novels dealing with periods when great changes were taking place in the world of ideas. She served as president of the American Association of University Women, the Modern Humanities Research Association, and the American Association of University Professors. Needing to be able to pack and be off to meetings at short notice, she once asked a dressmaker for advice and was told to wear a color-coordinated wardrobe. To White this meant one color, so she chose purple. She was thereafter known as the Purple Princess, easily recognized wherever she went.[5]

MILWAUKEE

Jacobs, Mary Belle Austin, 1867–1929, Social Worker

Memorial, Kosciusko Park, 9th and Lincoln Streets

Mary Belle Austin Jacobs was known as the Jane Addams of Milwaukee. She was the wife of Herbert Jacobs, warden of the Wisconsin University Settlement Association. The settlement house where they lived was in the old Fourteenth Ward, a section with the poorest housing and the greatest degree of dependency, plagued by sweatshops, child labor, crime, tuberculosis, and smallpox, with the highest death rate in the city. Jacobs, practical as well as idealistic, was active in all the club work. She visited the homes of the community to discover problems and needs, and she founded a woman's club. The settlement has now gone out of existence, but the monument in the children's section of Kosciusko Park commemorates Jacobs. It is a statue of a young girl, the work of sculptor Sylvia Shaw Judson (1897–1978), unveiled in 1931. On its base is written, "Within this garden dwells a lovely spirit—the spirit of joy and beauty."[6]

Kander, Lizzie Black, 1858–1940, Social Worker; NAW

Kander Auditorium, Milwaukee Girls' Trade and Technical High School, 813 N. 19th Street

Lizzie Black Kander, a member of a Reformed Jewish congregation, was concerned about the problems facing Jewish immigrant families around the turn of the century. "The immigrant poor," she said "are a direct result of tyranny and oppression, of the persecutions that have been heaped upon them from generation to generation." She and other women founded Milwaukee's first settlement house, called simply the Settlement. She was president of the Settlement from 1900 to 1918. To earn money for its programs she and four others wrote and published *The Settlement House Cook Book: The Way to a Man's Heart.* Well over a million copies were sold from the time of its first appearance in 1901, with Kander constantly revising it. It became the Settlement's chief source of funds, and it is still being published.

Kander, a member of the Board of School Directors of Milwaukee, was the main force behind the establishment of a girls' vocational high school.[7]

Meir, Golda (Meyerson), 1898–1978, Israeli Prime Minister

Golda Meir Library, University of Wisconsin at Milwaukee.
Golda Meir School, 1542 N. 4th Street

Golda Meir's years in Milwaukee were not entirely happy ones. But her first eight years as an abjectly poor Jew in Russia were so miserable that when her family emigrated to America she thought Milwaukee wonderful. "Everything looked so colorful and fresh, as though it had just been created . . . It was all completely strange and unlike anything I had seen or known before, and I spent the first days in Milwaukee in a kind of trance." The two-room apartment into which the family of five moved seemed to her the height of luxury. She picked up English quickly at the Fourth Street School, made friends, and was reasonably happy until she was fourteen. Her parents opposed her attending high school to prepare for teaching and wanted her to marry young—and a man of their choice. Meir ran away to live with her sister in Denver, where she met the man she was later to marry, Morris Meyerson.

Returning to Milwaukee at the age of eighteen a dedicated Socialist, Meir finished high school and registered at the Milwaukee Normal School. As she and her family learned of the movement of the Jewish people from countries of persecution to Palestine, Meir wished with all her heart to go to the Jewish homeland. She married Meyerson in 1917 but the war prevented their leaving for Palestine until 1921. From the time of their arrival until her death, Meir was committed to the establishment of a Jewish state. The settlement years were extremely difficult, and life was never easy for her or the children. She took increasingly responsible roles in the Israeli government, was minister of labor, then foreign minister, and finally prime minister.[8]

Mortimer, Mary, 1816–1877, Teacher; NAW

Mortimer Hall, University of Wisconsin at Milwaukee

Mary Mortimer was the first principal of Milwaukee Female College. A plump little Englishwoman, she first came to Milwaukee in 1848 with the intention of starting a girls' school, but a cholera epidemic forced her return to the East. However, she met the famous Catharine Beecher, who was interested in training women to teach frontier schools (see Cincinnati, OH). She spent some time with Beecher and her sister, Harriet Beecher Stowe, planning a curriculum for such a training institution. The Milwaukee Female Institute was founded in 1851 and for the next fifteen years, with some interruptions, Mortimer was its principal and often the buffer between its trustees and the sometimes difficult Beecher. The college merged with Downer College to form Milwaukee-Downer College in 1895, and in 1964 this became part of Lawrence University. The building named for Mortimer is now a treasured part of the University of Wisconsin campus.[9]

Sabin, Ellen, 1850–1949, School Administrator; NAW

Sabin Hall, University of Wisconsin at Milwaukee

Ellen Sabin established a reputation as an outstanding teacher in the state of Oregon, where she was in 1887 made Portland's superintendent of schools. She was offered the presidency of Downer College, a girls' school at Fox Lake, Wisconsin, in 1891, at half the salary she was making but with a free hand to develop the school. Her first years convinced her that the community was too small and too remote for a first-class school, and arrangements were made to merge it with the Milwaukee College for Women. A new campus for Milwaukee-Downer College was established on the north edge of Milwaukee in 1897. Under Sabin's aggressive leadership the college offered practical courses in homemaking, which she considered women's chief vocation, as well as nursing and occupational therapy, gymnastics, art, and biblical literature. Sabin retired in 1921. Although the college no longer exists, having been absorbed by Lawrence University, the campus is part of the University of Wisconsin at Milwaukee, and the building named for Sabin still stands.[10]

ONEIDA

Minoka-Hill, Lillie Rosa, 1876–1952, Physician; NAWM

Memorial, Outside of Town

The plaque reads: "Physician, good samaritan, and friend to all religions in this community, erected to her memory by Indians and white people. 'I was sick and you visited me.' " Lillie Rosa Minoka-Hill was a Mohawk Indian. When her parents died, the five-year-old girl was taken into the home of a Quaker physician in Philadelphia, Pennsylvania. She earned her M.D. in 1899 from the Woman's Medical College of Pennsylvania. She began a practice in Philadelphia, but when she married Charles Hill, an Oneida Indian, and moved to Oneida with him in 1905, she knew he wanted a wife who would stay at home, bear children, and care for the family. She had six children in nine years and learned to live in a small house without running water and to cook on a wood stove. But she talked to the Oneida medicine men and women on the reservation and began to use their herbal remedies to treat her neighbors.

Hill, who had proudly begun to accept his wife's status as a healer, died in 1915, leaving little to support his family, the youngest of them twins only five months old. Minoka-Hill continued to use her medical knowledge, although she had no medical license in Wisconsin and thus could not charge fees or get patients admitted to a hospital. She was generally paid in kind: food, wood, services; she never got rich in worldly goods. In time she was the only doctor in the community. In 1934, thirty-five years after she got her medical degree, she borrowed one hundred dollars from other physicians and got her state license.

In 1947 the Indian Council Fire gave her the Indian Achievement Award for her philanthropy, and she was adopted into the Oneida tribe. The Oneida community erected the monument in her honor. Her son and grandson founded in 1981 the Dr. Rosa Minoka-Hill Foundation, headquartered in Boulder, Colorado, to support educational programs among Native Americans.[11]

OSHKOSH

Hooper, Jessie Jack, 1865–1935, Suffragist and Pacifist; NAW

Jessie Jack Hooper House, 1149 Algoma Boulevard (Private); NR

After several years of civic and club work in Oshkosh, Jessie Jack Hooper heard Susan B. Anthony speak and decided that the key to social change lay in woman suffrage. She felt that clubwomen had been trying "to dig a hole with a teaspoon" when a steam shovel was needed. First in the state suffrage organization and then on a national level, she lectured and lobbied for equal voting rights for women. After the Nineteenth Amendment was ratified in 1920, she became the first president of the Wisconsin League of Women Voters. In 1922 she quit the office to run for the U.S. Senate on the Democratic ticket. She lost to the invincible Robert La Follette, though she did carry the city of Milwaukee.

In 1924 she invited women representing a number of national women's associations to band together in the cause of world peace. Out of this grew the Conference on the Cause and Cure of War, headed by Carrie Chapman Catt. One of the most tireless workers, Hooper got thousands of signatures to a disarmament petition, and in 1932 she and women from all over the world presented petitions bearing over eight million names to the League of Nations disarmament conference in Geneva, Switzerland.[12]

PEPIN

Wilder, Laura Ingalls, 1867–1957, Writer; NAWM

Reconstructed Little House, State 183. Pepin Park, State 35

Laura Ingalls Wilder was born in Pepin in a log cabin, which she called the "Little House in the Big Woods" when she began her saga of an American pioneer family. The Little House books are so popular, particularly since the television program based on them appeared, that visitors flock to sites she brought to life for them. She was sixty-five when she began her series with *The Little House in the Big Woods*. The replica of the cabin, seven miles north of town, is open all year. See Burr Oak, IA, Independence, KS, and Walnut Grove, MN.[13]

PORTAGE

Gale, Zona (Breese), 1874–1938, Writer; NAW

Zona Gale Breese Memorial Library, 804 Macfarlane Road

Zona Gale was born in Portage and lived here, the only child of a close family, until she went away to the University of Wisconsin. She moved to New York City in 1901, supporting herself by reporting for newspapers and free-lancing for magazines, but often returned to her hometown. Finally she settled in Portage, where she was involved in liberal politics, woman suffrage, and pacifism. In her 1920 novel, *Miss Lulu Bett*, she portrays the narrowness of a middle-class, small-town family, against which the heroine rebels. Gale dramatized the best-selling book and the drama won the Pulitzer Prize in 1921. When she was fifty-three she married a Portage businessman, William Breese. Her Portage home, Edgewater Place, 506 W. Edgewater Street, was given to the Civic League and is open to the public by appointment.[14]

Kinzie, Juliette Magill, 1806–1870, Pioneer Writer; NAW

Old Indian Agency House; HABS, NR

Juliette Magill Kinzie was born in Connecticut and received a good education, so it must have been something of a culture shock to travel through the primitive wilderness and to live among the Indians in Wisconsin. She came after her marriage to John Kinzie, agent to the Winnebago Indians, and their first home was in the officers' quarters. Two years later the government built the present house for its agent. Kinzie wrote about the wedding journey and the brief time she spent here in *Wau-bun: The "Early Day" in the North-west*. It was published in 1856, after the Kinzies moved to Chicago, Illinois, and serves as a primary source of early Northwest history.

Agency House was restored and refurnished in 1932 as a centennial project of the National Society of Colonial Dames of America in the State of Wisconsin. It is a mile and a quarter east on State 33, then half a mile north along the canal. It is open May 1–Oct. 31, daily 10–4; rest of year by appointment; adm.[15]

RACINE

Brown, Olympia, 1835–1926, Minister and Suffrage Leader; NAW

Olympia Brown Hall, Universalist Church of the Good Shepherd, 7th Street and College Avenue. Olympia Brown School, 5915 Erie Street

As a student at Antioch College, Olympia Brown decided to become a minister. It was not easy to find a theological school that would admit a woman, but she was allowed to register at Saint Lawrence University in New York, where she met much prejudice and dire predictions of failure. She completed the course, was ordained, and found a pastorate in Massachusetts.

She married John Henry Willis, who consented to her keeping her own name (she was a follower of Lucy Stone), and in 1878 he moved with her to Racine, where she had been called to be pastor of the Universalist Church of the Good Shepherd. Brown resigned her pastorate in 1887 to devote herself to an even more absorbing work—women's rights. Her greatest efforts in the movement were in Wisconsin, where she was president of the state suffrage association from 1884 until 1912. She maintained vigorous support for women's rights well into her eighties. More militant than many of her contemporaries, she distributed suffrage literature in front of the White House during President Woodrow Wilson's administration. Her life spanned the struggle from its early days until victory was achieved in 1920.[16]

STEVENS POINT

Halsted, Gertie Hanson, 1890–1982, Radio Broadcaster

Radio Station WWSP-FM, University of Wisconsin at Stevens Point

A pioneer in radio broadcasting when very few women were in the industry, Gertie Hanson Halsted taught at the University of Wisconsin at Stevens Point (then Stevens Point Normal School) from 1920 to 1953. She first became involved in radio when a station established by the department of agriculture at Stevens Point encouraged students and faculty to participate. She studied broadcasting and in 1940 helped to establish the campus radio workshop and guided students in preparing educational programs. She was a member of the National Association of Educational Broadcasters. After her retirement she married Harry Halsted and moved to Florida. The campus radio station was dedicated to her in 1974 and a plaque citing her contributions to broadcasting was prepared for display at the studio.[17]

Parkhurst, Helen, 1887–1973, Educator; NAWM

Lecture Hall, University of Wisconsin at Stevens Point

As a teacher in a rural school, Helen Parkhurst was faced with the problem of teaching forty farm boys of all ages in a one-room school. She hit upon the idea of dividing them into four groups, each corner of the room given to a particular subject, the older students helping to teach the younger ones. Later she realized how valuable the plan had been and she perfected what she called the Laboratory Plan of instruction. A student was free to move from one subject laboratory to another, following his own interest and working at his own pace. Because it was first used in a school in Dalton, Massachusetts, it was known as the Dalton Plan.

Parkhurst studied with Madame Montessori, who had educational ideas similar to her own. She started the Dalton School in New York City about 1920 and published a book describing the plan. Her ideas spread to other countries, several of which honored her with awards. The lecture hall here at the University was named for her in recognition of her work in progressive education. Near the beginning of her career, in 1913–15, she had taught here.

Schumann-Heink, Ernestine Roessler, 1861–1936, Opera Singer; NAW

Monument, Pioneer Park

Ernestine Roessler Schumann-Heink won the hearts of Americans as a star with the Metropolitan Opera, with which she spent five seasons, and then as a concert singer. Born in Bohemia, she became an American citizen in 1905 and was a dedicated American. She was deeply affected by World War I. Her oldest son joined the German Navy and was lost at sea; her other sons fought in the American forces. She devoted her talents to the war effort, giving concerts for the Red Cross, touring army camps, and entertaining service men. After the war she continued her warm and motherly relationship with veterans. In 1933 she declared herself an exile from Nazi Germany. She had relatives and friends in Stevens Point and was popular with the people here, who dedicated to her the memorial, a stone monument surmounted by a bell.[18]

VIROQUA

Stone, Lucy (Blackwell), 1818–1893, Women's Rights Leader; NAW

Memorial Tablet, 400 Block of N. Rock Avenue

The tablet calls attention to the "first Woman's Rights address and anti-slavery speech ever by a woman in the great Northwest." Lucy Stone's name ranks beside that of Susan B. Anthony and Elizabeth Cady Stanton as a pioneer in the feminist movement of the nineteenth century. She lectured throughout the country pleading for the two causes close to her heart, the abolition of slavery and equality under the law for women. While she was speaking here, on July 4, 1856, the platform suddenly collapsed. As they pulled her from the wreckage, the indomitable Stone remarked, "So shall this nation fall unless slavery is abolished." When Stone married Henry Blackwell, she insisted on retaining her own name and her own bank account. Women who followed her practice were called Lucy Stoners. The plaque was erected here by her daughter, Alice Stone Blackwell, born a little more than a year after the event it commemorates.[19]

WATERTOWN

Schurz, Margarethe Meyer, 1833–1876, Kindergartner; NAW

Tablet, N. 2nd and Jones Streets. School Building, on Grounds of Octagon House, Watertown Historical Society Museum, 919 Charles Street; NR

At the north side of the entrance to town is a sign welcoming the visitor to Watertown, "Home of America's First Kindergarten." The tablet is inscribed to the memory of Margarethe Meyer Schurz, "who established on this site the first kindergarten in America, 1856." The school building was moved to the museum grounds in 1956. Its interior represents the school as managed by Schurz in accordance with the ideas and beliefs of Friedrich Froebel, with whom she had studied in her native Germany. She married Carl Schurz, a refugee from Germany after the 1848 revolution, and in 1856 they established a home in Watertown. Although the kindergarten here did not last long, and the principal student was Schurz's own daughter, Agathe, it was the first school in America taught on Froebelian principles. In a reversal of the general policy, the town has chosen to honor as its greatest citizen the educator rather than her husband, who was a Civil War general, a senator from Missouri, and minister to Spain under President Abraham Lincoln. The tablet to her memory was erected by the Saturday Club Women in 1929. The schoolhouse is open May-Oct., daily 10–5; adm.[20]

WOODRUFF

Newcomb, Kate Pelham, 1886–1956, Physician

Lakeland Memorial Hospital, Arbor-Woodruff Area

The Lakeland Memorial Hospital was built here in 1953, three years before the death of Kate Pelham Newcomb, whose persistency led to its establishment. She practiced medicine first in Detroit, Michigan, and gave it up for a short time after arriving in Wisconsin in the 1920s. But the need for physicians was so great that she began her practice again, traveling in wintertime through the countryside in a car fitted with skis on the front wheels and tractor treads on the rear. In the most inaccessible areas she traveled on foot, wearing snowshoes, and won the name of the Angel on Snowshoes.

She became a celebrity when a mathematics teacher, to impress on her students how much a million really was, suggested that a million pennies be donated to the hospital Newcomb wanted. The pennies flowed in, and the story was made the subject of a "This Is Your Life" episode on television. The problems of the rural practitioner were dramatized for a nationwide audience, resulting in the flooding of the tiny Woodruff post office with letters, checks, and money orders until there was more than $100,000.[21]

NOTES

In addition to the sources mentioned below, I have had assistance from the State Historical Society of Wisconsin, Madison; Outagamie County Historical Society, Appleton; Brewer Public Library, Richland Center; and the Alverno College Research Center on Women.

1. "Memoirs of Mary D. Bradford," *Wisconsin Magazine of History* (cited hereafter as *Wis. Mag.*) 14 (1930) to 16 (Sept. 1932); correspondence, Simmons Library, Kenosha.
2. Cordelia P. Harvey, "A Wisconsin Woman's Picture of President Lincoln," *Wis. Mag.* 1 (March 1918); correspondence, Simmons Library.
3. Charlotte S. Rubinstein, *American Women Artists* (New York: Avon Books, 1982); correspondence, Oshkosh Public Library.
4. "Reminiscences of the First House and First Resident Family of Madison," *Wisconsin Historical Collections* 6 (1869–72).
5. *Ms Magazine*, Jan. 1982.
6. Ruth Harman and Charlotte Lekachman, "The Jacobs' House," *Wis. Mag.* 16 (1932–33).
7. Victoria Brown, *Uncommon Lives of Common Women: The Missing Half of Wisconsin History* (Madison: Wisconsin Feminists Project Fund, Inc., 1975).
8. Golda Meir, *My Life* (New York: G. P. Putnam's Sons, 1975); *New York Times* Dec. 9, 1978.
9. Correspondence, Lawrence University, Appleton.
10. Ibid.
11. Victoria Brown, op. cit.; "Dr. Rosa Minoka-Hill Foundation," pamphlet, and other material from Richard G. Hill, Oneida Tribe of Indians of Wisconsin.

12. Lawrence L. Graves, "Two Noteworthy Wisconsin Women: Mrs. Ben Hooper and Ada James," *Wis. Mag*. 41 (Spring 1958).

13. William T. Anderson, "A Visit to Laura Ingalls Wilder Country," *Americana* 11 (Sept.-Oct. 1983).

14. Correspondence, Portage Free Library.

15. *Some Historic Houses*, ed. John C. Fitzpatrick (New York: Macmillan, 1939).

16. Brown, *Acquaintances, Old and New, Among Reformers* (Milwaukee, Wis.: S. E. Tate Printing Co., 1911).

17. University of Wisconsin at Stevens Point, *Pointer Alumnus*, Winter 1982; correspondence, Portage County Historical Society.

18. Correspondence, Portage County Historical Society.

19. Stewart H. Holbrook, *Dreamers of the American Dream* (Garden City, N.Y.: Doubleday & Co., 1957); correspondence, Rhoda S. White, Vernon County Historical Society, Viroqua.

20. Alice Snyder, *Dauntless Women in Childhood Education* (Washington, D.C.: Association for Childhood Education International, 1972).

21. Adele Comandini, *Dr. Kate, Angel on Snowshoes: The Story of Kate Pelham Newcomb* (New York: Rinehart, 1956).

REGION V

The West

The American West, comprising most of the states west of the Mississippi River, is as big as all the rest of the states together. When first settled by whites, the states were only vaguely defined areas and later were designated territories with shifting boundaries before joining the Union, one after another, as states. The first to become a state, California, joined the Union in 1850, and only three others had attained statehood as late as the first U.S. centennial in 1876.

In 1803 the Louisiana Territory was purchased by the United States from France, thus annexing the vast lands between the Mississippi and the Continental Divide. Territory west of the Divide—the present states of California, Colorado, Nevada, Utah, and parts of Wyoming, New Mexico, and Arizona—was acquired from Mexico under the 1848 Treaty of Guadalupe Hidalgo, which also recognized Texas as part of the United States. In 1863 the Gadsden Purchase added more territory to Arizona and New Mexico. The latter joined the Union in 1912 as the forty-seventh and forty-eighth states, respectively. Alaska was acquired by purchase from the Russians in 1869; Hawaii was annexed and given territorial status in 1898; both joined the Union in 1959. Politically, therefore, the West is new territory. It was settled too late to participate in the founding of the nation or to prevent its dissolution in the Civil War. Compared to the rest of the country, it has little history.

After negotiating the Louisiana Purchase, President Thomas Jefferson sent out a Corps of Discovery to find the "northwest passage," for it was generally believed that by following the Missouri River to its source, then crossing a divide to the Columbia River, the ocean could be reached. Accompanying the corps was one woman, the Indian wife of its guide and interpreter. The second known overland expedition was one sent by John Jacob Astor in 1811 to establish a fur-trading station on the Pacific. That party, too, had one woman, the wife of its guide. Thus Sacajawea and Marie Dorion were the first historical women to cross overland from the Midwest to the Pacific Coast. These women were not instant heroines. Although their stories appeared in reports of the expeditions, not until many years later were their journeys recognized as remarkable.

The first white women to cross the Rocky Mountains westward were two missionary wives, Narcissa Whitman and Eliza Spalding, who arrived in the Oregon country in 1836. Four other missionary couples followed two years later. Their presence was in part responsible for the beginning of what has been called the greatest mass migration in modern times. Between 1841 and 1845 over 11,000 emigrants walked or rode across the desert and over the mountains. Gold discoveries later increased the numbers; over 85,000 came in 1849–50, and by the time the transcontinental railroad was completed in 1869, an estimated 350,000 pioneers had traveled the Oregon Trail. It is no wonder that in some parts of the desert the ruts cut by their wagon wheels are still visible.

Motives for joining the migration were varied. Free, fertile land, a slave-free society, and independence from debts were chief inducements, but some critics think it was a type of mass madness that drove men to move families 2,500 miles. Considering the hardships of travel without roads and adequate maps, with known shortages of water and feed for livestock, and with unknown dangers of attack by wild animals and Indians, it must have taken the very highest degree of hope and a strong sense of adventure for men and women to set out on such a journey.

The story of the West was dramatic enough to be popularized in novels and movie "westerns," where stereotypes replaced real characters. Desperadoes, cowboys, and Indian fighters became heroes. Women such as Calamity Jane, Poker Alice, and Klondike Kate—the prostitute with the heart of gold—became heroines. These stereotypes were later replaced by others: sunbonnetted pioneer mothers, madonnas of the trail, reluctant pioneers, gentle tamers. Women were variously depicted as martyrs to their husbands' and fathers' ambitions, as independent adventurers pushing their little families onward, or as fragile vessels carrying with them the tokens of the civilizations in which they were nurtured. Historians are still trying to answer questions and form generalizations about the early western woman. Did she represent a more aggressive and independent type of womanhood, or did she remain conservative, subscribing to the conventional view of women's role as primarily domestic? Women's diaries and journals, even their fiction, are scrutinized in search of enlightenment.

It would appear that the pioneers' problems in settling an untamed country, coping with the isolation and heavy labor of plains farming, and retaining the amenities of family life might well produce a new type of woman, and that society would respond by giving her more responsibility, more freedom, and more honor than was accorded to women elsewhere. It is true that when western institutions of learning were established, most were coeducational. It is also true that western women gained the vote much sooner than their eastern sisters. They were especially fortunate in many states in inheriting not the English common law but the Hispanic law which recognized community property.

As one reads their stories, however, it is clear that the old, conventional view of women's sphere died hard. In 1870, when Oregon was ready for statehood, its constitutional convention discussed giving married women rights to property they had owned at the time of marriage. One delegate objected: ''In this age of woman's rights and insane theories, our legislation should be such as to unite the family circle, and make husband and wife what they should be—bone of one bone, and flesh of one flesh.'' In 1878 women had to go to the state supreme court to force the University of California to open up its law school to their sex. The first women who tried to practice medicine in the West met with the same discrimination as their counterparts in the East. Working women were as shamefully exploited as in the sweatshops of eastern cities. Teachers had to fight for equal pay. The women who worked for suffrage were vilified in the press just as viciously as those in the rest of the country. The freedoms they won were earned by hard campaigning against entrenched male views of a woman's place.

ALASKA

ANCHORAGE

Clark, Orah Dee, 1875?–1965, Teacher

Orah Dee Clark Junior High School

Orah Dee Clark came to Alaska in 1906 and taught for twenty-five years in rural, mission, and Alaska Native Service schools, retiring in 1945. She organized Anchorage's first school in 1915 and was its first superintendent. The school building served later as Pioneer Lodge and was moved in the 1960s to Ben Crawford Memorial Park. Clark earned the love and respect of her pupils. One said she made even dull subjects interesting by her own enthusiasm. As a tribute to her years of dedication, the school administration gave her name to the school in 1959.[1]

Mears, Jane Pound Wainwright, d. 1953, Pioneer

Jane Mears High School

Jane Pound Wainwright Mears organized the Anchorage Woman's Club in 1915 and was its first president. She first came to Alaska when Anchorage was still known as "Skip Creek Tent City." She and her husband, Frederick Mears, superintendent of construction for the Alaska Railroad, lived in a large house on Government Hill. Most of the social functions of the town were held there.[2]

BIG DELTA

Wallen, Erika, 1875–1969, Roadhouse Operator

Rika's State Historical Park

Located at the junction of the Tanana and Delta Rivers, the roadhouse known as Rika's was a stopping place for travelers along the old Richardson Highway.

At this spot they had to take a ferry to cross the Delta River en route to the Alaskan interior. When the highway was replacing the old Valdez Trail, between 1909 and the 1940s, roadhouses were built some twenty-five miles apart along the way to offer food and shelter to those using the trail. For many years this one was operated by a Swedish immigrant, Erika Wallen, known as Rika. She arrived in the United States as a child and was in Alaska as early as 1918. How she met John Hadjukovich, who first ran the roadhouse, has not been established, nor what their relationship was. She acquired the property in the 1920s, either by sale or as a gift from him, and in 1925 she was naturalized and homesteaded it. From that date until 1947 she was postmistress, as well as proprietor of the roadhouse.

Rika served good meals, although she never made her mark as a cook. Such luxuries as fresh milk and domestic fowls were always available, as well as wild meats, berries, and fish. She gardened; raised sheep, goats, and chickens; kept honey bees; and made cheese. She even processed and wove the wool from her sheep.

After World War II a bridge was built over the river, and the road was realigned, bypassing Rika's place. It was accepted as a National Historic Site, and for a time it belonged to the Alyeska Pipeline Service Company, which gave it to the state as a historical park.[3]

FAIRBANKS

Hess, Harriet Trimmer, 1877?–1951, Educator

Hess Hall and Hess Dining Commons, University of Alaska

During the early years of the twentieth century, Harriet Trimmer Hess recognized how desperately Alaskans needed a college of their own. As a school principal, she saw firsthand how disappointed students were when they could not continue their schooling because they could not afford to attend colleges in the states. She and her husband, Luther Hess, contributed time, energy, and financial resources to promote the establishment of higher education in Alaska. In 1916 she selected the site for the first building, and in 1917 she became one of the original members of the board of trustees of the Alaska Agricultural College and School of Mines. Five years later, it had a building and opened its doors to fifteen students. This school was to become the University of Alaska, and Hess actively participated in its growth and development for more than thirty years. She was secretary (without salary) to the board of regents until her death.[4]

GLACIER BAY HISTORICAL MONUMENT

Scidmore, Eliza Ruhamah, 1856–1928, Traveler and Writer

Scidmore Glacier. Mount Ruhamah

Eliza Ruhamah Scidmore first came to this area in 1883 as a tourist on the *Idaho*, the first passenger-carrying vessel to enter Glacier Bay. ''When the ship neared a green and mountainous island at the mouth of the bay,'' she wrote, ''the Captain and the pilot made me an unconditional present of the domain, and duly entered it on the ship's log by name.'' Her book, *Alaska* (1885), launched her on a career of travel and travel writing. She was long associated with the National Geographic Society, one of the few women invited to join at its formation, later acting as its correspondence secretary, then its foreign secretary.[5]

HAINES

Willard, Caroline McCoy Wright, 1853–1916, Missionary

Haines United Presbyterian Church

In 1881 Presbyterian missionaries Eugene S. Willard and Caroline McCoy Wright Willard arrived at this frontier settlement to serve the Chilkat Indians. During their first years here, the family suffered greatly from cold and hunger, and because the Indians themselves were poor and miserable they blamed the missionaries for their troubles and refused to help them. At length, however, they were won over by Willard's interest in their handicrafts. An artist herself, she appreciated their basketry and metalwork. She learned to speak and write the Tlingit language. Before she left Haines in 1890, the Indians adopted her into their tribe and gave her a name of honor. The settlement was named for Mrs. F. E. Haines, secretary of the Women's Executive Committee for Home Missions.[6]

JUNEAU

Drake, Marie, 1878–1965, Educator and Writer

Marie Drake School, 1250 Glacier Avenue

When Marie Drake became the first secretary to the Alaska Territory's Department of Education, there was not even a table or chair provided for her. There were no records showing how many schools or teachers she was to supervise. She found out by traveling to them by boat, dogsled, and plane, despite hazardous weather and uncomfortable conditions. In 1934 she was appointed assistant commissioner of education, a position she held for twenty years. She wrote ''Alaska's Flag,'' adopted as the territorial song, now the state song.[7]

LAWING

Lawing, Nellie Neal, 1874–1956, Roadhouse Operator

Alaska Nellie's Homestead, Mile 23, Seward-Anchorage Highway; NR

The town is named for Nellie Neal Lawing, popularly known as Alaska Nellie, who started as a cook for railroad crews in 1915. The federal government hired her as a roadhouse operator for railroad construction crews while they built the road from Seward to Fairbanks. Nellie was a hunter, trapper, dog-musher, miner, and postmistress. Near Seward, she converted a roadhouse into a natural history museum. In 1923 she married Bill Lawing and they opened the Lawing Roadhouse, a tourist resort on Lake Kenai. When Nellie got a mail contract two years later, the town was renamed Lawing. The trains used to stop there so passengers could hear her lecture on wildlife. The museum contains priceless mementoes of the early Alaska days, big game trophies, and some of the many letters Lawing received from all over the world.[8]

NOME

McLain, Carrie, 1895–1973, Teacher and Historian

Carrie McLain Memorial Museum, Kegayah Kosga Public Library Building, Front Street. Carrie McLain Home, Belmont Point (Private); NR

Carrie McLain came to Nome at the age of ten and spent the rest of her life in Alaska. Widowed in 1940, she won the post of city clerk and held it for fourteen years. As a teacher and historian, she found little time to write until she retired. Her *Gold Rush Nome* was published in 1969, *Pioneer Teacher* in 1970. The museum is open Mon. and Wed. 10–7, Tues., Thurs., and Fri. 10–5, Sat. 10–4.[9]

PAXSON

Barnette, Isabelle Cleary, 1862–1942, Pioneer Trader and Traveler

Isabel Pass, Highway 4

Isabelle Cleary Barnette traveled by dogsled over the Alaska Range from Fairbanks to Valdez, with the thermometer dropping to −40°F, and the impressed Alaskans named this pass for her (with a simplified spelling). She and her husband were founders of the town of Fairbanks, Alaska, first known as Barnette's Cache. It was established on the Chena River because the steamer on which they had their cargo of trade goods could go no farther. When they learned that gold had been found nearby, they happily unloaded and set up a trading post. The gold rush did the rest.[10]

SITKA

Paul, Tillie (Tamaree), 1864?–1952, Educator

Tillie Paul Manor, Jeff Davis Street, Sheldon Jackson College

Sheldon Jackson College began as a Presbyterian mission established in 1878 by John G. Brady (later territorial governor) and Fanny Kellogg (d. 1915).

Kellogg soon married S. Hall Young, the newly arrived missionary at Wrangell, and they joined forces there with Amanda Reed McFarland, q.v. The Sitka school, which occupied the old Russian guardhouse, burned down in 1882 and its replacement was named for the pioneer missionary and educator Sheldon Jackson. It is now a junior college.

Tillie Paul taught here for many years. The daughter of a Tlingit woman and a Scotch father, she had been one of the best students at McFarland's school. She married Louis Paul, and together they were sent to open a mission at Willard. Louis was drowned and Tillie, with her three sons, came to Sitka to teach. The early missionaries, like most whites of their generation, looked down on the natives. In the words of Jackson, natives were "God's children—to be pitied, loved, borne with and patiently tended as children." But Tillie felt that the ancient culture of her people was worth preserving. In time she became the most influential native woman in Alaska, helping to form the Alaska Native Sisterhood and fighting for the Alaskans' right to vote. She married William Tamaree in 1905.

Tillie Paul Manor was dedicated in her memory in 1979.[11]

Yaw, Caroline Witzigman, 1900–1983, Civic Worker

Caroline Yaw Chapel, Sheldon Jackson College

Caroline Witzigman Yaw first came to Sitka in 1924. She was born and grew up in Iowa. She met her husband, Leslie Yaw, at Cornell College in Mount Vernon, Iowa. Leslie served as president of Sheldon Jackson College, as superintendent of the Pioneers Home, and was in private business. Caroline raised five children. Both the Yaws were noted for their contributions to civic development and church work. The chapel was named for Caroline in 1979, while she was still living, in recognition of her years of service to Sheldon Jackson College and to Sitka's cultural life.[12]

SKAGWAY

Walsh, Mollie, 1873?–1902, Grub Tent Operator

Statue, 6th Street, Off Broadway

According to the inscription on this bust, "Alone without help this courageous girl ran a grub tent near log cabin during the gold rush of 1897–1898 she fed and lodged the wildest gold crazed men generations shall surely know this inspiring spirit murdered Oct. 27 1902." The bust of Mollie Walsh was erected in 1930 by Jack Newman, an early admirer. Walsh had married another man, Mike Bartlett, and moved to Seattle, Washington. There in a fit of jealousy, Bartlett shot to death his young wife. As for Newman, when he erected the statue he, too, was married, and to placate his wife he had to give her a memorial.

So a bronze medallion honoring Hannah Newman was attached to a building on the corner of 6th and Union Streets in Seattle.[13]

WRANGELL

McFarland, Amanda Reed, c. 1837–1912, Missionary

First Presbyterian Church

Amanda Reed McFarland came to Alaska in August 1877, under the auspices of the Presbyterian Board of Missions. She was a widow, ''two hundred pounds of good nature,'' when recruited for the Alaska mission by Sheldon Jackson. Not only was she teacher and administrator of the school, but she acted as physician, judge, marriage counselor, and lawyer. She interfered in cases of witchcraft and is reported to have saved two girls from being killed as witches. She was presiding officer of a constitutional convention called by the natives on February 23, 1878, to set up some civil government—since the United States provided none—and she wrote the constitution. In it, general authority was given to the U.S. Customs Officer and McFarland. She established an industrial home to shelter native girls, who were often sold by their mothers to white men for ''base purposes.'' The church in Wrangell, erected in 1879, was the first Protestant church in Alaska.[14]

NOTES

In addition to the sources mentioned below, I have had help from the Skagway Information Center; Alaska Travel Division; Evangeline Atwood of the *Anchorage Times*; the Loussac Library, Anchorage; the Elmer E. Rasmusen Library, University of Alaska; the Alaska Historical Commission, Department of Education; Jo Anne Wold, Fairbanks; and Mary Bowen Hall, Sacramento, California.

1. *Anchorage Times*, Jan. 1 and Nov. 29 and 30, 1965; correspondence and clippings, University of Alaska.
2. *Anchorage Times*, Dec. 18, 1953; correspondence, University of Alaska.
3. Nomination form, National Register; Kathryn Koutsky Cohen, ''Rika's—An Historic Roadhouse Park on the Richardson Trail,'' in Alaska Historical Society, *Transportation in Alaska's Past* (Alaska Department of Natural Resources, State Division of Parks, Office of History and Archaeology Publication No. 30, 1982).
4. *Alaska Journal* 4 (Autumn 1974); *Anchorage Times*, Apr. 3, 1951.
5. Isabel C. McLean, ''Eliza Ruhamah Scidmore,'' *Alaska Journal* 7 (Autumn 1977).
6. Caroline M. Willard, *Life in Alaska*, ed. Eva McClintock (Philadelphia, Pa.: Presbyterian Board of Publication, 1884); Sheldon Jackson, *Alaska and Missions on the Pacific Coast* (New York: Dodd, Mead & Co., 1883); Julia McNair Wright, *Among the Alaskans* (Philadelphia, Pa.: Presbyterian Board of Publication, 1883); brochures and correspondence, Elisabeth S. Hakkinen, the Sheldon Museum and Cultural Center, Haines.
7. H. Wendy Jones, *Women Who Braved the Far North*, vol. 1 (San Diego, Calif.: Grossmont Press, 1976).
8. ''Gracious Pioneer,'' *Alaska* 56 (July 1984); Nellie Neal Lawing, *Alaska Nellie*

(Seattle, Wash.: Seattle Printing and Publishing Co., 1940); Michael E. Smith, *Alaska's Historic Roadhouses* (Alaska Division of Parks, Department of Natural Resources, History and Archaeology Series No. 6, 1974).

9. *Alaska* 39 (Sept. 1973); David B. Wharton, *The Alaska Gold Rush* (Bloomington: Indiana University Press, 1972).

10. *Alaska Book: Story of Our Northern Treasureland* (Chicago, Ill.: J. G. Ferguson Publishing Co., 1960).

11. Wright, *Among the Alaskans*; *Sitka Sentinel*, Oct. 19, 1979; Mary Lee Davis, *We Are Alaskans* (Boston, Mass.: W. A. Wilde Co., 1931).

12. *Sitka Sentinel*, Oct. 22, 1979 and June 3, 27, and 28, 1983; correspondence, Susan McClear, curator, Isabel Miller Museum, Sitka Historical Society.

13. "A Skagway Bust Commemorates a Heroine of the Gold Trail," *National Geographic* 104 (Sept. 1953).

14. Jackson, op. cit; Jones, op. cit.

ARIZONA

FLAGSTAFF

Colton, Mary-Russell Ferrell, 1889–1971, Artist and Museum Founder

The Museum of Northern Arizona, Fort Valley Road

Mary-Russell Ferrell Colton was an artist with her own studio in Philadelphia, Pennsylvania, when she met Harold S. Colton, a scientist. They visited Arizona on their honeymoon in 1912 and returned in 1926 to make their home here. Two years later they founded the museum. As Curator of Art and Ethnology, Mary-Russell encouraged Arizona painters and sculptors to exhibit their work. Her Hopi craftsman exhibitions were instrumental in bringing back to the Hopi their traditional skills in pottery, baskets, textiles, and jewelry. In recognition of her work with the native craftsmen, she was given a Certificate of Award by the Indian Arts and Crafts Board, U.S. Department of the Interior. The Northern Arizona Society of Science and Art established a memorial fund in her name. The museum is open daily 9–5; closed some holidays; adm.[1]

GRAND CANYON

Colter, Mary Jane Elizabeth, 1869–1958, Architect

Hopi House. Hermit's Rest; NR. Lookout Studio. Phantom Ranch. Watchtower. Bright Angel Lodge

So much a part of the landscape, with their unworked rocks and rough logs, Mary Jane Elizabeth Colter's buildings appear to have been part of the Grand Canyon scene from time immemorial. She was commissioned to design Hopi House by the Fred Harvey Company, for which she had decorated some of the comfortable hotels, fine restaurants, and gift shops they had established along the Santa Fe Railroad beginning in the 1880s. Eschewing tacky, touristy decoration in favor of solid southwestern-style furniture, rugs, dishes, and ironwork, she designed a suitable background for the shops that sold the work of American Indians and other regional artists, potters, and weavers.

Colter learned architecture as an apprentice to a San Francisco, California, architect while attending art school, then taught in St. Paul, Minnesota, for fifteen years before the Harvey Company recruited her as a decorator. Hopi House was built in 1905; five years later the company put her on their payroll as a full-time designer. She worked for them almost forty years. Aside from the structures at the Grand Canyon, few of the many buildings she designed or decorated remain. See Winslow, AZ.[2]

OATMAN

Oatman, Olive, 1837?–1903, Indian Captive; NAW

Oatman, practically a ghost town, bears the name of a family attacked at this spot by Indians in 1851. They had unwisely pushed ahead of the California-bound wagon train and in the lonely desert were set upon by a band of Yavapai Indians. All were killed, except a son, left for dead, and two daughters, Olive and Mary Ann Oatman, taken captive. The girls were sold to Mojaves and taken to a village in the Colorado River Valley. Meanwhile the brother was rescued and began a long search for his sisters. Five years after the capture, Olive was found; Mary Ann was dead. It was months before Olive could readjust to life among the whites, and nothing could obliterate the tattoo marks the Indians left on her chin. Her story was published as *Life Among the Indians* (1857), and she lectured on her captivity and on Indian customs. Her accounts remain a source of information about the Mojaves before they came under white influence.[3]

PHOENIX

Heard, Maie Bartlett, 1868–1951, Art Collector and Patron

The Heard Museum, 22 E. Monte Vista Road

The Dwight B. Heards came to Phoenix in 1895 because Dwight Heard had developed lung trouble, and they fell in love with Arizona. Fascinated by the area's ancient Indian culture, they collected art and cultural objects not only from the Arizona Indians but from Alaska, the Nile, and pre-Columbian sites in Mexico. They donated the land and the building for a museum. Dwight died before the bulding was finished, but his wife, Maie Bartlett Heard, not only saw it to completion but worked with the museum for twenty-three years. It opened in 1929 and soon became one of the top anthropology and ethnic art museums specializing in the American Indian. Maie also gave land for a new building for the Phoenix Woman's Club, and the Phoenix Civic Center is built on land donated to the city from her family's estate. The museum is open Mon.-Sat. 10–4:45, Sun. 1–4:45; adm.[4]

Hughes, Josephine Brawley, 1839–1926, Suffragist

Tablet, State Capitol

When Josephine Brawley Hughes was elected president of the territorial suffrage association, she relinquished the presidency of the Woman's Christian Temperance Union (WCTU), which she had held since the WCTU was brought here by Frances Willard. "Let us secure the vote for women first," she said, "then the victory for the protection of our homes and for the cause of temperance will follow." She and her husband, Louis C. Hughes, established the *Arizona Star*, the first daily newspaper in Arizona, in 1878, and continued it for thirty years. Louis became territorial governor. In 1894 Josephine went to the national suffrage convention, taking her young son John with her. Susan B. Anthony dubbed him "the suffrage knight of Arizona." Eighteen years later John was a state senator, and it was he who introduced the resolution that added woman's suffrage to the Arizona constitution. The tablet reads: "Mother of Methodism, Founder of W.C.T.U., and Founder of the First Daily Newspaper in Arizona."[5]

PRESCOTT

Hall, Sharlot Mabridth, 1870–1943, Historian and Preservationist

Sharlot Hall Museum (Old Governor's Mansion), 415 W. Gurley Street; HABS, NR

Poet, historian, and traveler, Sharlot Mabridth Hall was a woman of wide interests, great talents, and energy that spent itself in interpreting the American westward movement. Appointed territorial historian of Arizona in 1909, she was the first woman in the territory to hold public office. She began by inventorying Arizona books and documents in public institutions and private hands, and she embarked on one of the earliest oral history programs. When Arizona became a state, Hall leased the old log house built for the first governor of the territory and restored it. Two additional period houses and the Sharlot Hall building along with the museum center are open to the public Tues.-Sat. 9–5, Sun. 1–5; closed some holidays.[6]

SEDONA

Schnebley, Sedona Miller, d. 1950, Farmer and Community Worker

Memorial Bell, Wayside Chapel

The town of Sedona is named for Sedona Miller Schnebley, a pioneer who came to the beautiful canyon among the red and white cliffs in 1901 with her husband

and children. They grew fine vegetables, which were needed by the people of Flagstaff, Arizona, but it took three days by stage, over a rough mountain road, to get them there. The Schnebleys and their neighbors donated money, matched by the county, to build the Sedona-Flagstaff road, thus opening the market for their farm produce. The family left their farm after one of the children was accidentally killed, but Sedona and her husband returned later in their lives, she to remain for another nineteen years of active community life. One of her greatest desires was to see a wayside chapel built, and just before her death she attended its dedication. She died with a request that instead of flowers she be remembered by donations for a bell to be hung in the chapel. On Mother's Day, 1951, the bell was dedicated to her memory.[7]

TOMBSTONE

Cashman, Nellie, 1851–1925, Miner and Hotel Owner

Nellie Cashman Apartments, 5th and Toughnut Streets

Nellie Cashman had two interests in life, mining and helping others. In the toughest diggings of Alaska and Arizona, she was respected as a mining expert and revered for her feeding, nursing, counseling, and grubstaking for the communities in which she lived. She traveled alone, yet she knew how to keep her reputation as a good woman among rough men. She kept a base in Tombstone for many years while visiting mining camps wherever there was gold—in Alaska, Nevada, Mexico, and even, it is claimed, in Africa. Never married, she brought up her sister's five children after they were orphaned. The Catholic Church in Tombstone is said to have been built with Cashman's gifts and fund-raising efforts. She ran a store in Tombstone after taking over the Russ House, renaming it the Nellie Cashman Hotel. It is now converted to apartments.[8]

Macia, Ethel Robertson, 1881–1964, Hotel Operator and Clubwoman

Rose Tree Inn Museum, 4th and Toughnut Streets

"Believe-it-or-Not" Ripley visited the hotel run by Ethel Robertson Macia and her husband, Burt Macia, and called the spreading white rose bush in the courtyard "the world's largest rose tree." The Macias, already well known for gracious hospitality and the family-style meals they served, benefited from the publicity and changed the name of the hostelry to the Rose Tree Inn. Macia, who represented the quiet, civic-minded people of Tombstone, was twice president of the Tombstone Woman's Club, held office in the State Federation of Woman's Clubs, and belonged to the Arizona Pioneers Historical Society. She was a charter member of the Tombstone Restoration Commission, formed to restore historical Tombstone to its "wild and woolly" splendor of the 1880s. The inn is now a museum, open daily 9–5; adm.[9]

TUCSON

Kitt, Edith Stratton, 1878–1968, Museum Director

Plaque, Lobby of Arizona Historical Society, 949 E. 2nd Street

The Arizona Pioneers Historical Society was ready to close in 1925 when its president persuaded Edith Stratton Kitt to take on the job of secretary. The position paid fifty dollars a month and looked unpromising. The secretary was in charge of a rundown club of aging pioneers, a library of sorts, and correspondence. By the time Kitt left the job in 1947 she had transformed it into a distinguished regional library and museum. She persuaded authors to donate their books and she solicited free subscriptions to newspapers and magazines. She recorded the reminiscences of old-timers. She built up the membership, moved the headquarters, and began to collect funds for the society's permanent home, a goal achieved in 1954. According to the plaque, ''It is her dream that has come true.'' The society is open Mon.-Fri. 8–5, Sat. 8–1, and Sun. 2–5.[10]

WINSLOW

Colter, Mary Jane Elizabeth, 1869–1958, Architect

La Posada, Division Headquarters of Santa Fe Railway

In 1957 the *Wall Street Journal* carried an advertisement reading: ''La Posada is for Sale! Santa Fe says losses make action necessary.'' The hotel, including 80 rooms, a coffee shop for 116, a dining room for 72, a bar and cocktail lounge, was put on the market for $400,000. Passenger traffic on the railroad had declined. The Harvey House hotels, restaurants, and gift shops built for the accommodation of Santa Fe travelers beginning in the 1880s could no longer make it; one by one they had been converted to other uses or torn down to make way for parking lots.

It was a sad day for Mary Jane Elizabeth Colter, the hotel's architect, then eighty-eight years old. La Posada was the favorite of all the buildings she designed and decorated over the years for the Fred Harvey Company (including those at the Grand Canyon, Arizona, q.v.) Fortunately, the railway decided to keep the building for a headquarters. Thus it remains a testament to the work of the remarkable woman who was one of the first architects to recreate the cultural heritage of the region instead of imitating European styles. Her close friend, Erna Fergusson, said of her, ''She has studied Southwestern architecture and all its variants from church to pueblo, from Moorish castle to Navajo hogan, and she has incorporated all their features into Harvey's hotels.''[11]

NOTES

In addition to the sources mentioned below, I have had assistance from the Arizona Historical Society, Arizona Women's Commission, University of Arizona Library, Springerville Public Library, Tombstone Chamber of Commerce, Hubbell Trading Post (U.S Department of the Interior), Tucson Public Library, and Virginia L. Grattan.

1. "Mary-Russell Ferrell Colton, 1889–1971," *Plateau* 44 (Fall 1971); correspondence, Museum of Northern Arizona.

2. Virginia L. Grattan, *Mary Colter, Builder Upon the Red Earth* (Flagstaff, Ariz.: Northland Press, 1980).

3. *The Women*, by the editors of Time-Life Books (Alexandria, Va.: Time-Life Books, 1978).

4. Pam Hait, "The Inheritor," *Arizona Highways* 55 (Jan. 1979); *Journal of Arizona History* 18 (Autumn 1977); correspondence, the Heard Museum.

5. C. Louise Boehringer, "Josephine Brawley Hughes—Crusader, State Builder," *Arizona Historical Review* 2 (Jan. 1930).

6. *Sharlot Hall on the Arizona Strip: A Diary of a Journey through Northern Arizona in 1911*, ed. C. Gregory Crampton (n.p., 1975); James J. Weston, "Sharlot Hall: Arizona's Pioneer Lady of Literature,"*Journal of the West* 4 (July 1965); correspondence, Sharlot Hall Museum.

7. R. J. Slade, "A Bell for Sedona," *Arizona Highways* 35 (May 1959).

8. John P. Clum, "Nellie Cashman," *Arizona Historial Review* 3 (Jan. 1931); Harriet Rochlin, "The Amazing Adventures of A Good Woman," *Journal of the West* 12 (Apr. 1973).

9. Dorothy G. Palmer, "Ethel Macia, First Lady of Tombstone," *Arizona Highways* 34 (Apr. 1958); correspondence, Rose Tree Inn Museum.

10. Odie B. Faulk, "A Tribute to Mrs. George F. Kitt," *Journal of Arizona History* 7 (Spring 1966); "In Memoriam, Edith Stratton Kitt," *Journal of Arizona History* 9 (Summer 1968).

11. Grattan, op. cit.

CALIFORNIA

ALPHA

Nevada, Emma, 1859–1940, Singer; NAW

Monument, Roadside Park on State 20, Between Grass Valley and Truckee

Alpha is less than a ghost town. It existed during the gold rush, somewhere near the present marker, and is only remembered because the singer Emma Nevada was born there. She was the daughter of William Wixon. She lived later in Nevada City, California, and then in Austin, Nevada. When she made her operatic debut in London, England, in 1880 she took the name of Emma Nevada to honor her western homes. A coloratura soprano with a voice of "flute-like purity," she delighted audiences. She toured Italy, made an impression on Verdi, sang at La Scala, then went to Paris, France. In 1884 she returned to America on tour and was overwhelmed by a heartwarming reception in San Francisco, California. On other American tours she was billed under the names of the Sagebrush Linnet or the Comstock Nightingale. She married an English physician, Raymond Palmer, and settled in England. She retired from a long operatic career in 1910, the year her daughter Mignon Nevada made her debut.

ANAHEIM

Modjeska, Helena, 1840–1909, Actress; NAW

Modjeska House, Santiago Canyon (Private); NR. Statue, Pearson Park, Lemon and Sycamore Streets. Modjeska Park, Nutwood Street and Woodworth Road

Helena Modjeska was tall and graceful, with dark eyes and beautiful features. As the leading actress of the Imperial Theatre in Warsaw, Poland, and then as a star on the American stage, she captivated audiences with her silvery, expressive voice. It was said that she could hold an audience spellbound by reciting the alphabet in Polish. She and her husband, Count Bozenta, came to southern California in 1876 to help a colony of Polish compatriots establish a utopian farm in the Santa Ana valley. When they failed to prosper, she decided to return to the theater. One of her first roles was Camille. She starred on the American and European stage for another twenty years. She and the count became American citizens and established a home in Santiago Canyon near the site of the ill-fated colony, naming it the Forest of Arden. They also bought a home in Newport Harbor on an island that was named for her. There is a Modjeska Peak in the Santa Ana Mountains.

BENICIA

Arguëllo, Maria de la Concepcion Marcela, 1791–1857, Romantic Heroine and Churchwoman

Monument, St. Dominic's Cemetery, Hillcrest Avenue

Maria de la Concepcion Marcela Arguëllo, known as Concha, was the heroine of one of the saddest romances of early California. Daughter of the Spanish comandante of the San Francisco presidio, she became engaged to the gallant Russian Count Rezanov. He sailed off to Russia to obtain permission for the marriage. No word came, and after many years of waiting Concha joined the Dominican Order of Monterey, taking the name of Mary Dominica. California's first native nun, she gave the rest of her life to caring for the poor and sick. A poem by Bret Harte describes the scene, forty years after she and her fiancé separated, when she learned that he had never reached Russia but was killed on the journey. Gertrude Atherton wrote a novel based on her life.

The monument was first placed in the gardens of St. Catherine's Academy in Benicia. When the school closed, it was moved next to the grave of Sister Dominica, in the sisters' section of the cemetery, to the left of the main entrance. Other writers have told her story, and other memorials, some in Monterey, California, have been erected to her.[1]

Atkins, Mary (Lynch), 1819–1882, Educator; NAW

Marker, Site of Benicia Female Seminary, 153 W. I Street; California Historic Landmark. Plaque and Monument, City Park, Facing Military Road

Mary Atkins, a feminist and a graduate of Oberlin College, wore bloomers on her voyage to California in 1854. A fellow traveler advised her to discard the costume if she wished to succeed in the new state. She did, and students at the prestigious Benicia Female Seminary she owned and headed would have been surprised if they had known of her adoption of the reform dress. They were even self-conscious wearing gymnasium costumes. Atkins has been called "one of the most individual characters among the American women who dedicated themselves to the work of education in the early and mid-nineteenth century." Under her leadership the school became well and favorably known.

In 1866, tiring of the demands on her time and energy, Atkins sold the seminary to the Reverend Cyrus T. and Susan Mills, who a few years later moved to Oakland with most of the faculty to establish Mills Seminary, now Mills College (see Oakland, CA). Atkins married John Lynch and eventually bought back the old school in Benicia and conducted it until her death; it was closed in 1886. Atkins-Lynch's imposing grave marker in the pioneer cemetery overlooking Benicia is inscribed "Solid blocks of pure marble best represent her."[2]

BERKELEY

University of California

A large number of women contributed to the development of the great center of learning here. The names of a few appear on buildings and plaques on the campus. The first in chronology and importance was Phoebe Apperson Hearst (1842–1919, NAW), whose name is given to the women's gymnasium. She was the wife of the mining engineer George Hearst and mother of the newspaper publisher William Randolph Hearst. In 1896 she financed an international competition for a comprehensive plan for the new Berkeley campus. She spent thousands of dollars to secure the design and begin its execution. She gave two buildings to the campus. The plaque on the Hearst Memorial Mining Building reads: "This building stands as a memorial to George Hearst, a plain, honest man and good miner." Hearst Hall, a social and athletic center for women, burned down in 1922 and was replaced by Hearst's son as a memorial to her. Hearst was the first woman regent of the university, serving from 1897 until her death. She supported archeological expeditions, gave the money to construct a university museum, and subsidized the Department of Anthropology. Other towns and cities which benefited from her generosity include San Francisco, California, Anaconda, Montana, and Lead, South Dakota.

The museums of paleontology and of vertebrate zoology were established by Annie Montague Alexander (1867–1950). She took up paleontology when failing eyesight forced her to give up ambitions to become an artist or a nurse. She began her many field trips in 1901 with a visit to the Fossil Lake region of Oregon. In 1905 she was in Nevada with a team that made an exciting discovery of saurian fossils. She spent half a century collecting hundreds of fossils for the university museum in many of the western states, Baja California, Alaska, and Hawaii (where she was born).[3]

Cheney Hall is named for May L. Cheney (d. 1942), who was the university's placement secretary for forty years. It is estimated that during those years she placed some twenty thousand persons—graduates and others—in positions, chiefly teaching, throughout the world.

Morgan Hall, housing the Department of Nutritional Sciences, College of Natural Resources, was named for Agnes Fay Morgan (1884–1968, NAWM), a nutritionist. She earned her college degree in chemistry and after teaching that subject for some time she realized that the new field of nutrition offered a real opportunity for a woman chemist. She introduced the first scientific human nutrition course at the university. She studied the nutrient content of food and the effect of processing, storage, and preparation on proteins and vitamins. She battled food faddists and quacks and set standards for human nutrition.

The Morrison Music Building was named for May Treat Morrison (1858–1939), an early graduate of the university (Ph.B., 1878). She gave the Alexander Morrison Memorial Library in memory of her husband and left the university ovcr onc million dollars. See San Francisco, CΛ.

The Sather Gate and the Sather Campanile, as well as two professorships, bear the name of Jane Krom Read Sather (1824–1911), widow of Peder Sather. Jane was a childless widow of fifty-eight when she marrried Peder, a widower of seventy-two. He had been in California since 1850 and had built up a fortune, chiefly through banking. He died four years after their marriage, leaving the money to his widow. The disposition of this wealth weighed heavily on her mind, and when she met the new president of the university, Benjamin Ide Wheeler, she was easily persuaded to donate to its support. She was still alive when the gate (which used to mark the campus boundary) was built, but she never had the joy of hearing the bells in the campanile, first played in 1917.[4]

Lucy Ward Stebbins (1880–1955) is memorialized in Stebbins Hall. She was dean of women for thirty-five years and also taught social work and economics, becoming a full professor in 1912. The first cooperative women's residence at the university was named for her.[5]

Wurster Hall is named for William and Catherine Bauer Wurster (1905–1964, NAWM, as Bauer), respectively dean and associate dean of the College of Environmental Design. Catherine, when a fledgling architect, won a prize for an essay on art in industry, published in the May 1931 issue of *Fortune*. It contrasted the picturesque old housing in Frankfort-am-Main with a modern housing development in New Frankfort. She pointed out that no matter how charming and romantic the medieval houses looked, the roofs leaked, the walls crumbled, the floors were rotten, and the air commemorated ancient beer and victuals. She much preferred the clean lines and simple surfaces of the new housing. Publication of the article won for the young woman the interest of housing experts. She helped prepare legislation that led to the 1937 U.S. Housing Act and to government subsidies for low-income housing; she was director of research and information for the U.S. Housing Authority. She married William in 1940; their connection with the University of California began in 1950.[6]

Morgan, Julia, 1872–1957, Architect; NAWM

Julia Morgan Center for the Arts (St. John's Presbyterian Church), 2640 College Avenue; NR

Julia Morgan studied with Bernard Maybeck at Berkeley and in 1898 became the first woman accepted as an architectural student at the Ecole des Beaux Arts in Paris, France. She worked with Maybeck on the Hearst memorial buildings at the University of California and developed a lifelong association with Phoebe Hearst and her son, William Randolph Hearst, for whom she designed Hearst Castle at San Simeon, California, q.v.

The art center was designed and built between 1908 and 1910 as a church. The rambling, shingled structure has been a Berkeley architectural landmark ever since. Extremely modest, Morgan avoided publicity, but the quality of her work spoke for her. Many women's groups, proud of her success, commissioned buildings; she designed residences for the Young Women's Christian Association throughout California, including the Asilomar Conference Center at Pacific Grove.[7]

BERRYVALE

Fellows, Sophia Jane Bullock Belden, 1822–1898, Businesswoman

Plaque, Opposite Old Post Office

A widow with two daughters, Sophia Jane Bullock Belden Fellows crossed the Isthmus of Panama to reach California, arriving in 1860 at Yreka, where she had a stepbrother. A year later she married Joseph S. Fellows and they bought a ranch in Berryvale. There they built a tub factory operated by water power and produced butter firkins and other kinds of tubs. Widowed again some years later, Fellows gave up the factory and operated the Mount Shasta Hotel on the main stage road. In addition, she was Berryvale's postmistress and ran a little store in the post office. Everybody called her Aunty Fellows. The plaque was erected in 1947 by the Siskiyou County Historical Society.[8]

CARMICHAEL

Yeaw, Effie, 1900–1970, Naturalist

Effie Yeaw Interpretive Center, Ancil Hoffman Park. Plaque, Carmichael Post Office, Palm Street

Effie Yeaw grew oaks from acorns in her backyard. Then she planted them where she thought oaks should be. She carried water in her car and whenever she thought her little oaklings needed water she gave it to them. In the classroom she taught little children about plants and animals, and she took them on walks through the woods, planting in receptive minds a love of nature and a reverence for growing things. When Yeaw died they named the nature center in the park for her, and each year thousands of people, young and old, walk the wooded trails that bring them close to the eternal yet fragile web of nature. The center is a gathering place for environmentalists who work to preserve the American River natural area. It is open weekdays except Wed., 1:30–5:30, Sat. and Sun. 11–5.

CHICO

Bidwell, Annie Ellicott Kennedy, 1839–1918, Humanitarian

Bidwell Mansion, 525 Esplanade; State Historic Park, NR.
Bidwell Park

In all we read of Annie Ellicott Kennedy Bidwell, she sounds too good to be true. A tiny, blue-eyed brunette, she was dainty, sweet natured, and merry; hardworking, charitable, and useful; a vivacious companion, a gracious hostess, an excellent manager, and a good sport. All these encomiums were bestowed on Bidwell by those who knew her, and all appear well deserved. Her husband, California pioneer John Bidwell, called her "Precious." She called him her "General Dear." He fell in love with her when he first saw her at her home in Washington, D.C., in 1865. For the next two years and more he dreamed of her, wrote her long letters, and built this elegant twenty-six room mansion for her.

The home became a mecca for visitors, including Governor Leland Stanford, Horace Greeley, President Ulysses S. Grant, President and Mrs. Rutherford B. Hayes, and John Muir. Annie's interest in the Women's Christian Temperance Union brought Frances E. Willard to visit. (A street near the mansion is named for her.) Phoebe Apperson Hearst came to discuss the National Indian Association. Annie worked long and hard to Christianize the Mechoopda Indians who lived on the ranch. Bidwell Park, Annie's gift to the city, was dedicated by Susan B. Anthony in a 1905 ceremony. In the 1960s the house was restored by the state as a memorial to the Bidwells. It is open daily, 10–5; closed some holidays; adm.[9]

CLAREMONT

Scripps, Ellen Browning, 1836–1932, Newspaperwoman and Philanthropist; NAW

Plaque, Entrance to Scripps College

The quotation from Ellen Browning Scripps inscribed on the plaque expresses her hopes for the college she founded, as well as epitomizing the qualities she felt important in her own life: "The paramount obligation of a college is to develop in its students the ability to think clearly and independently and the ability to live confidently, courageously and hopefully.'' A working newspaperwoman for twenty years, Scripps made a fortune, mainly by investing, in her early years, every spare cent in the newspapers run by her brothers in Detroit, Michigan, and other cities. Her writing talents and administrative energy also went into the papers, chiefly those of the youngest brother, E. W. Scripps, founder of the Scripps-Howard chain. She moved to southern California in the 1890s when E. W. bought property in La Jolla, California, q.v. She built a house there for herself and lived simply, even austerely, while she spent her wealth in schools, clinics, libraries, and parks, most of them in her adopted state. Scripps College, the climax of a lifetime of giving, opened in 1927, but she had reached the age of ninety and never was able to visit the school.

EUREKA

Clarke, Cecile, 1885–1978, Educator, Collector, and Museum Founder

Clarke Memorial Museum, 3rd and E Streets; NR

Cecile Clarke taught history at Eureka High School, 1914–50, and she was a teacher who could make history live. She was described as formal—addressed her students Mr. and Miss and demanded the best of them. What brought history to life in the classroom was her passion for collecting things of importance to the area, particularly Native American basketry. While still at home on the family's Mendocino County sheep ranch she began her collections. She brought many of the items to the classroom to liven up the discussion of local history. Cases in one of the classrooms were given to her to display some of the material. When the collection outgrew the cases a small building was used. In 1960 the school needed the space for classrooms and Clarke had to find a new home for the collection. Just at the right time, the Mendocino ranch was sold and the handsome old Eureka Bank building became available. Clarke did not hesitate. She used her inheritance to buy the building and opened a museum.

Shortly after her death, the museum was updated and reopened with a professional staff and the backing of the entire community. It has since acquired and put on permanent display the Hover Collection of Karok basketry, dance regalia, and stonework—one of the finest in the world. The museum is open Tues.-Sat. 10–4; closed holidays.[10]

Mexia, Ynes, 1870–1938, Plant Collector; NAW

Ynes Mexia Memorial Grove, Montgomery Redwoods State Reserve

Ynes Mexia took up a career in botany at the age of fifty-five while a student at the University of California at Berkeley. For some thirteen years she traveled in Alaska, Mexico, and South America collecting specimens for herbariums all over the world. Her searches took her into remote areas, where she got about on foot, in dugout canoes, by mule and oxen, almost always the only woman, with one or two native guides and carriers. One trip took her up to one of the sources of the Amazon River, where she lived for months with the still uncivilized Jivaro Indians, renowned as headshrinkers. She rafted down the white water of the Pongo de Manseriche on a balsa raft constructed by those same Indians. Although highly respected in the world of botany, she never had time to finish her college course and considered herself an amateur naturalist. She discovered several new genera and numerous species of plants, many of them named for her. Mexia, whose mother was American and whose father was a Mexican official, was at home in both countries. She left part of her estate to the Save-the-Redwoods League, which named the redwood grove in her memory.[11]

GLENDALE

Bond, Carrie Jacobs, 1862–1946, Song Writer; NAW

Plaque, Memorial Court of Honor, Forest Lawn Cemetery

Many a bride of an older generation left the altar with the words of Carrie Jacobs Bond's "I Love You Truly" ringing in her ears. Bond is the only woman to be singled out for commemoration here. The plaque honoring the composer bears President Herbert Hoover's tribute to her "heart songs that express the loves and longings, sadness and gladness of peoples everywhere." Her "Just a-Wearyin' for You" and "A Perfect Day" are part of America's musical heritage. She adopted southern California as her home, living here for the last thirty years of her life.

GRASS VALLEY

Montez, Lola, 1818–1861, Dancer; NAW

Lola Montez House, 248 Mill Street; State Historic Landmark

Although she lived in Grass Valley for only two years, from 1853 to 1855, Lola Montez's flamboyant reputation, undeniable beauty, and lovable eccentricities made her the town's most memorable resident. Here the dancer-actress kept a pet bear and numerous other wild animals, gardened, smoked cigars, and held weekly soirées for local young men and occasional notables from Europe and America. Born Eliza Gilbert in Ireland, she early broke away from her disapproving relatives, studied dancing briefly, and adopted the name of Lola Montez. Acclaimed as a dancer in Europe, Montez had several marriages and liaisons and was the mistress of King Ludwig I of Bavaria, who made her the countess of Landsfeld. When Ludwig was forced to abdicate in 1848, Montez was banished. She toured America, her titillating Spider Dance a sensation. She came to Grass Valley and this house as the wife of Patrick Hull, whose tenure as husband was brief.

Montez befriended a redheaded moppet who lived a few doors away (at 238 Mill Street) named Lotta Crabtree (1847–1924, NAW), and taught her a few dance steps. Crabtree learned her skills as a performer dancing before homesick miners in the gold camps of California and eventually became the highest paid and most popular actress in America. Her home (formerly a boardinghouse run by her parents) is still standing and is a state historical landmark. However, it is not marked and is not open to the public (see San Francisco, CA).

The Montez house has been rebuilt as it was when Montez owned it and is used for community projects.

Spencer, Dorcas James Barber, 1841–1933, Temperance Worker and Indian Rights Advocate

Plaque, Garden of the United Methodist Church, Church Street

In the winter of 1873 a spontaneous temperance movement spread across the Midwest. Bands of women knelt in the streets before saloons and prayed for the souls of the saloon keepers and patrons. Many saloons were closed as a result. Reading about the success of the movement, Dorcas James Barber Spencer was inspired to do something about the evils of liquor in Grass Valley. At a meeting in the Grass Valley Congregational church on March 25, 1874, she and her friends established a temperance union of women. It was the first such union in the state, the first in the West, and preceded by some months the national Women's Christian Temperance Union (WCTU). After her success here, Spencer helped to found similar groups throughout the state.

The power of organized women became known and Spencer was asked by the Hupa Indians in northern California to rid their reservation of a repressive military post. She visited the reservation, in a remote and almost inaccessible mountain valley, and wrote to the authorities about the conditions there. The post was removed and the agency put under civilian control.

The plaque "Commemorating the First Woman's Christian Temperance Union in California" was donated to the Congregational church by the state WCTU in 1926. Spencer was the honored guest at its dedication. When that church was demolished, the marker was moved to its present location.[12]

HEALDSBURG

Wightman, Hazel Hotchkiss, 1886–1974, Tennis Champion; NAWM

Monument, Healdsburg Plaza

Hazel Hotchkiss Wightman, a native of Healdsburg, saw her first tennis game in 1902 and from then on her game was tennis. When she lived in Berkeley,

California, there was only one asphalt tennis court, not open to females after eight in the morning, so she played from dawn until schooltime. She began winning matches at a young age and was still playing and winning at sixty-five. She inaugurated the Wightman Cup matches, the equivalent for women's tennis of the Davis Cup. In a *New Yorker* profile of her, she was called the Queen Mother of American Tennis, "a bouncy, warm, unpretentious accumulation of unnervous energy." At that time (1952) she had won forty-three national tennis titles. She taught many American champions, including Helen Wills, Helen Jacobs, and Sarah Palfrey. The original "little old lady in tennis shoes" won many honors, including election to the International Tennis Hall of Fame.[13]

HEMET

Jackson, Helen Hunt, 1830–1885, Writer and Indian Rights Advocate; NAW

Ramona Bowl and Pageant

"My life-blood went into it," Helen Hunt Jackson said of her novel *Ramona*: "all I had thought, felt and suffered for five years on the Indian question." A writer from Massachusetts and Colorado (see Colorado Springs, CO), Jackson took up the cause of the American Indian in 1881 after hearing Susette La Flesche (Bright Eyes) speak of the federal mistreatment of the Ponca Indians. Jackson wrote a documented history of government behavior toward Native Americans in *A Century of Dishonor*, a copy of which she sent to every congressman. One result was her appointment to survey the needs of the mission Indians in California, which led to the writing of an official report and also of the emotional novel. *Ramona* touched the hearts of readers and did more in changing public attitudes than any amount of documentation and lecturing. An annual presentation based on the novel is given in Ramona Bowl, late Apr.–early May, Sat. and Sun. afternoons. Apply for tickets and information to Ramona Pageant Association, P.O. Box 755, Hemet, CA 92343.

INDEPENDENCE

Austin, Mary, 1868–1934, Writer; NAW

Home, 253 W. Market Street; State Historic Landmark

Mary Austin was one of the first writers to point out the connection between man's needs and nature's resources and the necessity to conserve the latter. She is said to have designed and supervised the construction of the house in Independence, where she lived when she wrote her classic *The Land of Little Rain*. She wrote, "If ever you come beyond the borders as far as the town that lies in a hill dimple at the foot of Kearsarge, never leave it until you have knocked at the door of the brown house under the willow-tree at the end of the village street, and there you shall have such news of the land, of its trails and what is astir in them, as one lover of it can give to another.'' West of town is Mount Mary Austin. The house belongs to the city, but is not open to the public.

INGLEWOOD

Leitzel, Lillian Alize Elianore, 1892–1931, Circus Performer; NAW

Statue, Reunion, *Inglewood Park Cemetery, 720 E. Florence*

Lillian Alize Elianore Leitzel was for long the favorite aerialist with Barnum and Bailey's Greatest Show on Earth. She is described as having a disposition ''filled with bursting inner merriment.'' A tiny four feet nine inches, she appeared fairylike as she entered the arena heralded by a brass band and spotlights. The audience went wild as she spun rapidly and dizzily near the dome of the big top. She married Alfredo Codona, a performer on the flying trapeze. Six years after her death from a fall, Codona killed himself, but not until he had erected to her memory this twelve-foot-high marble statue of two figures in fond embrace.[14]

LA JOLLA

Scripps, Ellen Browning, 1836–1932, Newspaperwoman and Philanthropist; NAW

Scripps Institute of Oceanography. Ellen Browning

Scripps Memorial Park, and Other Memorials

In recognition of her many gifts to the city, La Jolla annually celebrates October 18, Ellen Browning Scripps' birthday. She was a woman of many interests, from marine biology to politics. She was wealthy, her wealth acquired not by inheritance or marriage but by hard work and wise investment. When her brothers went into newspaper work in Illinois, Scripps helped them with proofreading, writing, and editing. She wrote the first syndicated newspaper column, ''Miss Ellen's Miscellany.'' She worked much with her older brother, E. W. Scripps, who founded a chain of newspapers in which she invested. For the last forty years of her life she lived in La Jolla and contributed greatly to its social, economic, and cultural life. The Museum of Contemporary Art occupies her former home. A hospital and a clinic are named for her. She founded Scripps College in Claremont, California, q.v.

LASSEN PARK

Brodt, Helen Tanner, 1838–1908, Artist

Marker, Lake Helen

Helen Tanner Brodt is credited with being the first non-Indian woman to climb Lassen Peak. She made the climb on August 28, 1864, and one of her companions named the mountain lake for her. Brodt had recently arrived in California, after studying art in New York City, to join her husband in Red Bluff. It was not as a sportswoman that she made her mark, however, but as a painter. She lived in Tehama County and later in the San Francisco Bay Area, where she was able to combine her role as wife and mother with that of painter. Many of Brodt's paintings are in the Oakland Museum and other galleries.[15]

LAVA BEDS NATIONAL MONUMENT

Winema (Toby Riddle), c. 1848–1932, Modoc Indian Heroine

Winema's Chimneys

Toby Riddle, wife of Frank Riddle, was a Modoc Indian who played a heroine's role in the Modoc War of 1873. She saved the life of Alfred Meacham, superintendent of Indian affairs, when the Indians shot him and attempted to take his scalp. She then worked in the army hospital. Meacham wrote in defense of the Modocs in *Wi-ne-ma* (1876), originating the name, Winema, by which she was known thereafter. Her son, Jeff C. Riddle, also wrote of the war in *The Indian History of the Modoc War* (1914). See Winema National Forest, OR.

LOS ANGELES

Andrus, Ethel Percy, 1884–1967, Teacher and Advocate for the Aging; NAWM

Ethel Percy Andrus Gerontology Center, University of Southern California

Ethel Percy Andrus retired from a lifetime of teaching with a state pension of a little over sixty dollars a month. Fortunately, she did not have to live on that, but she knew that many teachers spent their last days struggling to keep alive on meager incomes. There was little in the way of health or accident insurance for those over retirement age. Prescription drugs were to many an expensive necessity. Even worse, from her point of view, was the low esteem in which ex-teachers were held and the retirees' resultant loss of faith in themselves. Believing and preaching that age is "not a defeat but a victory, not a punishment but a privilege," Andrus began to turn things around.

In 1947 she founded the National Retired Teachers' Association (NRTA). A handsome, stately woman, she was an eloquent speaker. The association soon had millions of members and won adequate health insurance, low-cost drug distribution, a retirement home, and other services for retired teachers. In 1958 she was persuaded to extend retiree benefits to others and formed the American Association of Retired Persons. She edited its journal, *Modern Maturity*, as well as the *NRTA Journal*. She believed that learning did not stop with retirement and founded the Institute for Lifetime Learning. The Gerontology Center, founded in 1973, is devoted to studies of aging.

Barnsdall, Louise Aline, 1882–1946, Philanthropist

Barnsdall Park, 4800 Hollywood Boulevard; HABS, NR

A lonely and eccentric woman whose crusades included freedom for Tom Mooney (convicted in 1916 of a bombing), EPIC (Upton Sinclair's program to End Poverty in California), and independence for India, oil heiress Louise Aline Barnsdall is remembered for her gift of the thirteen-acre park to the city of Los Angeles. True, she tried to repossess the property because the city refused to abide by some odd restrictions, but the city prevailed. Included in the park is her spectacular Hollyhock House, resembling a Mayan temple, the first house in the city to be designed by the noted Frank Lloyd Wright. Wright found her a difficult client.

The city restored the home in the 1970s, refurbishing it with many of the original Wright choices. A guided tour is offered Tues. and Thurs. 10–1, Sat. and the first and third Sun. of each month 12–3, on the hour; adm. Call for reservations (216–662–7272). The park, with its picnic facilities, is open and free.

Dorsey, Susan Almira Miller, 1857–1946, Educator; NAW

Dorsey High School, Farmdale Boulevard

In 1937 Susan Almira Miller Dorsey became the first living person in Los Angeles to have a school named for her. She came to California in 1881, where she engaged in social work until her husband—a Baptist clergyman—deserted her. She then taught in the public schools, moving up the administrative ladder to become in 1920 the superintendent of the Los Angeles city school system. During the nine years she held this position, she championed increased school building funds, higher teacher salaries, and teacher tenure. Regarded as a conservative, she was, however, open to such new educational practices as visual education, special classes for the handicapped, and vocational training.

Foy, Mary Emily, 1862–1962, Librarian

Foy House, 633 S. Witmer Street; National Cultural Monument

Mary Emily Foy's lifetime spanned a century of the city's dynamic history. She was born in Los Angeles when it was a sleepy pueblo; the house in which she grew up was "at the outskirts of town." Its original site, 7th and Figueroa Streets, is now occupied by the Hilton Hotel. The Los Angeles Public Library named its California Room for her, remembering not only her role in the city's history but her position as the first woman city librarian. She held the post from 1880 to 1884. She then attended the Normal School and taught for a number of years. She turned her attention to politics, worked for woman's suffrage, campaigned for Woodrow Wilson, and was a delegate to the Democratic national convention of 1920. She was a participating investor and secretary of the Adams Street Ladies' Woman's [*sic*] Investment Company. Her interest in local history led her to organize the California Parlor of the Native Daughters of the Golden West. In 1962 the Los Angeles High School Alumni Association placed a plaque on her house.[16]

McPherson, Aimee Semple, 1890–1944, Evangelist; NAW

Angelus Temple, 1100 Glendale Boulevard

When Aimee Semple McPherson, the colorful and eloquent evangelist, founded her Church of the Foursquare Gospel in 1922, a new pentecostal denomination came into being. Her sermons were dramas, complete with costumes, brass bands, choruses, lighting effects, and audience participation. She was reputed to heal the sick. She converted hundreds. She founded a Bible college which graduated some three thousand ordained missionaries, many of whom were women. During the Great Depression her commissary, with food contributed by parishioners, fed the hungry. She caused a sensation in 1926 when she disappeared, apparently into the ocean near Los Angeles. A month later she reappeared, with a story of having been kidnapped and kept prisoner in a desert shack in Mexico. Her church members believed her. The district attorney charged her with conspiracy, but the charges were dropped. The publicity only stimulated the growth of her church. At the time of her death the church had some four hundred branches in the United States and Canada, two hundred missions abroad, and twenty-two thousand members.[17]

Ross, Ida Haraszthy Hancock, d. 1913, Rancher

Plaque, Hancock Park, Wilshire Boulevard and Curson Avenue

Among the obligatory sights in Los Angeles are the La Brea Tar Pits, where the bones of large animals trapped in the tar eons ago form one of the most complete collections of Pleistocene fauna in the world. Up until the first years of this century, the tar in the pits was used only to finish roofs; the bones were considered of no value and many were thrown away. The pits were on Rancho La Brea, the property of Ida Haraszthy Hancock Ross. She was the daughter of the pioneer viticulturist Agostine Haraszthy of Sonoma, California. When Major Henry Hancock, her husband, died in 1883 she was left with two little boys to support and had to fight many legal battles to protect the ranch from squatters. In 1901 she had an oil well dug and the oil brought her from comparative poverty to wealth. It was about that time that the animal remains in the pits were recognized as of great value. They were excavated, cleaned, studied, and placed in a museum. In 1909 Ida married Judge Erskine Mayo Ross. The pits and the surrounding park were donated to the city by Ida's son, George Allen Hancock, in memory of his parents. The remains of the trapped animals are in the new George C. Page Museum, which is open Tues.-Sun. 10–5.[18]

St. Denis, Ruth, 1879–1968, Dancer, NAWM

Ruth St. Denis Foundation, 150 N. La Brea Avenue

"The Gods have meant that I should dance, And by the Gods I will!" These lines from a poem by Ruth St. Denis are engraved on her cemetery marker in Forest Lawn Cemetery. St. Denis began her career as a solo dancer after being inspired by Oriental motifs and mysticism, creating dances with such names as Egypta, Rahda, the Incense, the Cobras. With her husband, dancer Ted Shawn, she founded the Denishawn School in Los Angeles. The first university of the dance, it was the seedbed of modern dance, a training ground for choreographers, where individual development was stressed. Doris Humphrey and Martha Graham were among pupils who won fame.

Sterling, Christine, d. 1963, Preservationist

Avila Adobe and Paseo de la Plaza, Olvera Street, El Pueblo de Los Angeles State Historical Monument; NR

Olvera Street, colorful with Mexican shawls and pottery, redolent of candlemakers' wares and Mexican cookery, annually draws some two million visitors. In 1926, when Christine Sterling wandered into it, it was a filthy, rat-infested, crime-ridden alley. The Avila adobe, the oldest and one of the most historical houses in Los Angeles, had become a flophouse for derelicts, and was condemned by the health department. Sterling, a history buff, was shocked that a house and street that had played an important role in the city's history should be destroyed. She persuaded the city to begin its work of historical preservation here. It took years for the work to be done. In 1952 the state made the forty-acre district a joint state and city park. The alley was rebuilt by men from the jail; Sterling noted in her diary that she used to pray that bricklayers and plumbers would run afoul of the law, so that she would have good workmen on whom to call.

The Avila house, built in 1818 by Francisco Avila for his second wife, Encarnacion Sepulveda, is restored and furnished in the style of the early Spanish homes. It is open Tues.-Fri. 10–3, Sat.-Sun. 10–4:30.[19]

Wendt, Julia Bracken, 1871–1942, Sculptor

Art, Science, and History, *Sculpture, Rotunda of Los Angeles County Museum of Natural History, Exposition Park*

Julia Bracken Wendt was a well-established sculptor when she came to California from Chicago, Illinois, as the wife of the landscape painter William Wendt. She taught at the Otis Art Institute from 1918 to 1925 and served on the municipal art commission. She and William built a studio by the sea at Laguna Beach and sometimes exhibited together. Her eleven-foot-high bronze of three female figures representing art, history, and science was commissioned by the people of Los Angeles, who raised ten thousand dollars for it. In 1914 it was unveiled to admiring viewers. Later, by a quirk of misguided museumship, the Beaux-Arts statue was hidden from view for almost thirty years behind cases displaying minerals. In 1980 it was rediscovered and again proudly displayed in the newly furbished rotunda. The museum is open Tues.-Sun. 10–5; adm.; first Tues. of month, open 12–9, free.[20]

MILL VALLEY

Eastwood, Alice, 1859–1953, Botanist; NAWM

Camp Alice Eastwood, Mount Tamalpais

A self-taught botanist, Alice Eastwood served as curator of botany at the California Academy of Sciences for sixty years, known over the world for her contributions to horticulture. She was honored by the naming of this secluded park for her by the Tamalpais Conservation Club, with which she had hiked over the mountain trails. It was dedicated to her in 1949 on her ninetieth birthday. She also had a little home in Mill Valley with a cosmopolitan garden of trees and shrubs collected from throughout the world. It was burned to the ground. She had lost everything once before, in the 1906 earthquake and fire of San Francisco, California. Like the bulbs in her garden and some of the hardy trees, she survived the tragedies and only seemed to grow stronger and more beautiful. See San Francisco and Orick, CA.[21]

Kent, Elizabeth Thacher, d. 1952, Philanthropist and Suffragist

Muir Woods National Monument

William Kent and Elizabeth Thacher Kent bought a redwood grove in Marin County early in the twentieth century and later moved to California permanently, establishing a home in Kentfield, which was named for the family. Elizabeth was one of the most brilliant workers in the cause of suffrage in California's 1910 campaign. William was elected to Congress and served on President Woodrow Wilson's Tariff Commission. In Washington, D.C., Elizabeth joined the Woman's Party. In 1917 she took part in around-the-clock picketing of the White House in an effort to persuade Wilson to favor suffrage for women. She was arrested with other suffragists but escaped jail when her husband paid her fine.

The major part of their redwood grove was given to the nation in 1908 to establish the five-hundred-acre national park named for John Muir. The Kents also gave a large parcel of land for Mt. Tamalpais State Park.[22]

Norris, Kathleen Thompson, 1880–1966, Novelist; NAWM

Kathleen Norris Park, Molina and Wildomar Streets

One of six children in a happy Irish Catholic family, Kathleen Thompson Norris spent part of her childhood on the slopes of Mt. Tamalpais in Mill Valley. "Here," she said, "we ranged free." Later they moved back to San Francisco, California, her birthplace. Tragedy struck the family when she was nineteen. Both parents died, leaving less than five hundred dollars, and Norris and a brother took on the responsibility of supporting their younger siblings. Ten years later she went to New York, married, and was at last free to write. Her first novel, *Mother* (1911), was serialized in the *Ladies' Home Journal* and attracted many readers. She followed it by a novel a year for many years until she had produced almost a hundred. She was happy in her marriage to Charles G. Norris, also a writer, although their philosophies and products were as different as night and day. He was liberal and scholarly. She was conservative, prohibitionist, and isolationist. Her novels, on the whole, were frothy, sentimental, and supplied with happy endings. They carried a strong message to American women: marriage was life's greatest adventure.[23]

NEVADA CITY

Sargent, Ellen Clark, 1826–1911, Suffrage Leader

Sargent House, 449 Broad Street (Private); NR

Ellen Clark Sargent and Aaron Sargent lived here during their early married life. The house was recently designated a place of historical interest in a ceremony attended by descendants of the Sargents and Susan B. Anthony, grandniece and namesake of the great suffrage leader who was one of Ellen's close friends. The two women met in Washington, D.C., while Aaron was serving in Congress. It was he who introduced Anthony's suffrage amendment in Congress and was its strongest advocate all the years he was there. When he was appointed U.S. minister to Germany, his wife and daughters accompanied him to Berlin, where

Anthony visited them. After Ellen was widowed she continued to work for suffrage from her home in San Francisco, California, headquarters for the 1896 campaign to gain voter acceptance of a suffrage amendment to the California constitution. Fifteen years later, on the eve of victory for California women, Ellen died and the flags of the city were placed at half-mast in her honor.[24]

OAKLAND

Bates, Alta, d. 1955, Nurse and Hospital Administrator

Alta Bates Hospital, 1 Colby Plaza at Ashby

Alta Bates was the first registered nurse in Humboldt County when she graduated from Sequoia Hospital in Eureka, California, in 1903. She had stifled her indignation at the long hours and insensitive treatment there of nurses, and after graduation she learned that this was the common lot of nurses. "They were once not thought of as human," she said. In 1905 she founded a small hospital in Oakland and three years later the Alta Bates Sanitorium, precursor of the hospital, where nurses were treated with respect. She directed the sanitorium and hospital for forty-five years.[25]

Mills, Susan Lincoln Tolman, 1825–1912, College President; NAW

Mills College

Mills College had its beginning in the Young Ladies' Seminary in Benicia, California, q. v., purchased by John and Susan Lincoln Tolman Mills from Mary Atkins in 1866 and moved to Oakland in 1871. It thus dates its history back to the establishment of the seminary in 1852. Mills is not only one of the oldest women's colleges but is today one of the most eminent in the country. After it became a college, its board of trustees chose men as presidents until 1890, when they had the good sense to elect Susan. She remained as president until 1909, when she retired at eighty-four. She was the guide and confidante of generations of young California women.

Reinhardt, Aurelia Henry, 1877–1948, College President; NAW

Reinhardt House, Mills College

Aurelia Henry Reinhardt was offered the presidency of Mills College in 1916. She wrote to her friend Marian Stebbins, "It will interest you to learn that I have accepted the presidency of Mills College; which is, as you know, a moribund institution. Marian, will you come and help me make it live?" Mills' failure to make the transition from a girls' seminary to a women's college during a time of change had reduced its faculty, its student body, and its reputation. By providing a vital curriculum, a strong faculty, attractive buildings, and adequate equipment, Reinhardt was able to attract many more students, and during her years as president (she retired in 1943), she made the college known for excellence. In addition, she reared two boys, who were under the age of five when she undertook the job as a young widow. She said that she was the first college president to arrive on the campus pushing a perambulator. The women's history collection in the Bender Library is also named for Reinhardt.

OCEANO

LaDue, Francia, 1849–1922, Theosophist

Temple of the People

The Temple, or Halcyon Community, was founded as a utopian theosophical community in Syracuse, New York, and brought to Oceano in 1903 by Francia LaDue and William H. Dower. Some of the members formed a cooperative colony, the Temple Home Association, wherein "all the land will be owned all of the time by all of the people; where all the means of production and distribution . . . will be owned by the people." They established a newspaper, *The Temple Artisan*, which is still published. About half of the present members are theosophists. A Victorian building, known as the Rice (Coffee) House, I and 25th Street (private), was used by the community as a sanitarium. Former members are buried in Halcyon Cemetery, the Pike and Elm, where LaDue's gravestone identifies her as first guardian in chief, 1898–1922.[26]

ORICK

Eastwood, Alice, 1859–1953, Botanist; NAWM

Alice Eastwood Grove, Prairie Creek Redwoods State Park

A bronze plaque set in a great boulder at the grove, reads: "Alice Eastwood, 1859–1953, botanist, conservationist, teacher, Curator of Botany, California Academy of Sciences 1892–1949. Established by the California Spring Blossom and Wildflower Association and friends in cooperation with the California State Division of Parks and Beaches, 'ageless as the redwood trees she knew and loved.'" See Mill Valley and San Francisco, CA.[27]

PALO ALTO

Stanford, Jane Lathrop, 1828–1905, College Founder; NAW

Statue, Stanford University Campus

When the Leland Stanfords' only son died at the age of sixteen, Jane Lathrop Stanford adopted the children of California in his place, and the couple founded in his memory Leland Stanford, Jr., University. Senator Leland Stanford died two years after the college opened its doors in 1891, and although his widow was left with pressing financial problems, she completed the endowment of the university and aided it through its first troubled years. In a tribute to Jane, Stanford's first president said: "The future of the university hung by a single thread, the love of a good woman." All three of the Stanfords are buried on the campus. See Sacramento, CA.

PASADENA

Fenyes, Eva Scott, 1846–1930, Artist

Pasadena Historical Society Museum, 470 W. Walnut Street

The handsome mansion which now houses the historical society was the home of Eva Scott Fenyes and Adelbert Fenyes. Eva was the widow of Brigadier General William S. Muse when she married Adelbert, a distinguished physician, entomologist, and ornithologist. She was a world traveler and an accomplished artist. After she and Adelbert settled in Pasadena, she met Charles Lummis, of the Southwest Museum. At his suggestion, she began to visit historical California sites and to paint watercolors of the many old and crumbling adobe houses that still existed throughout the state from Sonoma to San Diego. She made hundreds of such watercolors, many of them now on display at the Southwest Museum, serving to illustrate California's romantic past. The Pasadena Historical Society owns albums containing over three thousand of her sketches, drawings, and paintings.

The Fenyes home, in a wooded, four-acre garden, with rare and valuable furnishings, was in the 1960s donated to the historical society by Eva's daughter, Leonora Muse Curtin, and granddaughter, Leonora Curtin Paloheimo, whose husband was the first Finnish consul in southern California. For a time the house served as the Finnish consulate, and on the grounds is a Finnish folk art museum, a recreated Finnish farmhouse, maintained by the Finlandia Foundation. Both the historical society museum and the Finnish museum are open for tours Tues., Thurs., and the last Sun. of each month, 1–4; adm.; the historical library is open daily.

Nicholson, Grace, 1879–1948, Art Collector

Pacific Asia Museum, Grace Nicholson Building, 46 N. Los Robles Avenue; NR

Grace Nicholson came to Pasadena in 1901 and established a private art gallery specializing in Oriental and Indian art. After many years of study she planned this building in the form of a traditional north Chinese courtyard. It incorporates materials imported from China and the handwork of Chinese tilesetters and gardeners. Nicholson deeded the building in 1943 to the city, and the Pasadena Art Institute became the lessee. When the institute's art museum moved to what is now the Norton Simon Museum, the building was leased to the Pacificulture Foundation. It is dedicated to preserving the art and cultures of the Asian and Pacific areas. It is open Wed.-Sun. 12–5; closed holidays; adm.; third Sat. of month free.

Robinson, Jane Bancroft, 1847–1932, and Her Sister Henrietta Ash Bancroft, 1842–1929, Methodist Deaconesses; NAW

Robinson Hall, Blackburn Estates, 275 Robincroft Drive

The residential care community was established in 1925 as a home for retired deacons and deaconesses of the Methodist Episcopal church. It was then named Robincroft, combining the names of its founders, Jane Bancroft Robinson and Henrietta Ash Bancroft. Robinson was a pioneer in the deaconess movement, by which laywomen, unsalaried but supported by the church, worked among the poor, the sick, and the homeless. As dean of women at Northwestern University, 1877–85 (before her marriage), she was a founder of the Western Association of Collegiate Alumnae, forerunner of the American Association of University Women. Bancroft was professor of English and dean of women at Albion College in Michigan and later field secretary for the deaconess department of the church.

The original Robinson Hall, called the Castle, is now used for administrative offices. Other buildings in the complex were named for Isabella Thoburn (1840–1901, NAW), missionary to India and active in the deaconess movement, and for Mabel Metzger, a deaconess, for twenty-five years administrator of Robincroft and after retirement its historian.[28]

PLACERVILLE

Johnson, Mary Jane Stroyers, fl. 1861, Pioneer

Plaque on Building, 489 Main Street

"Emigrant Jane drove a band of horses across the plains and from the proceeds of their sale she erected this building in 1861." So reads the plaque, erected in 1954 by the Native Daughters of the Golden West. For what use Mary Jane Stroyers Johnson made of the building is not noted, and little is known about her life, except that she came from Carthage, Illinois, was renowned as a horsewoman, and was seen about the countryside in a riding habit of black velvet. She could not read or write but was nevertheless a success at business.

POINT LOMA

Tingley, Katherine Westcott, 1847–1929, Theosophist; NAW

Greek Theater, Point Loma College

Katherine Westcott Tingley laid the cornerstone for the first building of what was to be an ideal community here in 1897. It was founded on theosophical beliefs, opposing materialism and working toward the brotherhood of man. A hotel sanitorium was domed with aquamarine glass, the temple with purple. The glittering domes, lit from within at night, created an architecture "noticeable even in southern California." The colony became a cultural mecca; arts and crafts flourished, Greek plays were produced in this theater; and a Raja-Yoga school attracted as many as three hundred children in one year. But Point Loma, once the most magnificent and exotic of utopian communes, ceased to flourish even before Tingley's death. It has been replaced by the Point Loma College campus and most of the original buildings are gone. The plaque on the theater reads: "First Greek Theater in America. Built A.D. 1901 by the Universal Brotherhood and Theosophical Society under leadership of Katherine Tingley. The Society occupied these premises from 1897 to 1942."[29]

RICH BAR

Clapp, Louise Amelia Smith, 1819–1906, Author; NAW

Rich Bar Historical Park, Feather River Highway (State 70), Near Belden

Louise Amelia Smith Clapp lived here with her physician husband during the early days of the gold rush and wrote letters under the pen name of Dame Shirley. Writing as a woman to another woman, her sister, Clapp gave graphic and amusing descriptions of a rough mining camp, full of details no man would notice or bother to write about: habitations of "round tents, square tents, plank hovels, log cabins"; food ranging from oysters and champagne to steak and onions; and culinary implements consisting of an iron dipper, a brass kettle, and a gridiron made of an old shovel. While she spoke poetically of the beauties of the Feather River canyon, Clapp did not forget to spice up her journal with details of drunken revelries, murders, fights, and accidents, all so much a part of camp life. The *Shirley Letters*, published in a newspaper during her life and in book form after her death, is a classic of early California literature.

The riverside park is undeveloped and hard to find. It is four miles southeast of Belden, near the Caribou Road. A plaque honoring Clapp was here once; later it was stored at the Plumas County Museum in Quincy, California.[30]

RIVERSIDE

Tibbets, Eliza, d. 1898, Gardener

Memorial, Magnolia and Arlington Avenues; State Historic Landmark

Eliza Tibbets raised the first navel orange trees in California. The trees were introduced from Brazil by the U.S. Department of Agriculture in 1870, buds were propagated, and young trees were distributed in the United States. Two went to Tibbets in 1873, and from these two budlings grew the great navel orange industry of the state. The trees were moved from the Tibbets home, once at Central Avenue and Navel Court. One was planted in this park, the other in the courtyard of the Mission Inn. The latter has not survived.[31]

SACRAMENTO

Coolbrith, Ina Donna, 1841–1928, Poet; NAW

Plaque, Rotunda of State Library and Courts Building

Ina Donna Coolbrith was made poet laureate of California in 1915. Her poems celebrate love, the beauty of nature, and the poignancy of loss, separation, and death. They are truly poetic, fresh, and clear-voiced. See San Francisco, CA.

Crocker, Margaret Rhodes, 1821–1901, Art Collector

Crocker Art Museum, 216 O Street; NR

Margaret Rhodes Crocker was born on an Ohio farm several months after her father's death, adding not a little to the burdens of her mother, who already had twelve children to raise. If Margaret did not share fully in the chores with the rest of the family, it was only because she was the baby; but in her later affluent years she remembered the hard times and remained sympathetic to the less fortunate.

She married Edwin B. Crocker, a widower, in 1852 and came with him to California. Their first years in Sacramento were anything but tranquil. Fires, floods, illness, and a succession of babies—four girls and a boy, the latter dying in infancy—filled Margaret's life with excitement, sadness, and joy. Edwin rose in the ladder of success as a railroad lawyer, and in 1863 was appointed chief justice of the California Supreme Court. Margaret gave generously of her time and money to many charities, including Marguerite Home, a residence for elderly women. The family moved into a mansion at 2nd and 0 Streets in 1869, after Edwin suffered a disabling stroke. They built the art gallery next door, then went to Europe to collect paintings for it. Margaret left the gallery to the city. It was the first art museum in the area and is today a flourishing cultural center. It is open Tues. 2–10, Wed.-Sun. 10–5; closed some holidays; adm.[32]

Stanford, Jane Lathrop, 1828–1905, College Founder; NAW

Stanford-Lathrop House, 800 N Street; State Historic Landmark, HABS, NR

Jane Lathrop Stanford persuaded her lawyer husband, Leland Stanford, to move to California from their home in New York in 1855 because the prospects were much better in the West. He had spent the preceding three years in the northern California mining country and had already made a modest fortune in merchandising. Jane's hunch was right; they prospered. Leland was governor of the state in 1862–63. They bought the mansion at that time. Jane was interested in the kindergarten movement in San Francisco, California, and in 1885 when Leland was elected to Congress, she enjoyed her role as a Washington, D.C., hostess. Tragedy struck the couple when their only son, Leland Stanford, Jr., died just before his sixteenth birthday. In his memory they founded Stanford University (see Palo Alto, CA).

The Sacramento home was presented by Jane to the Roman Catholic Diocese in 1900, and it has long been used as a residence for young people. It is now the property of the state.

ST. HELENA

White, Ellen Gould Harmon, 1827–1915, Church Founder; NAW

Elmshaven, 125 Glass Mountain Lane

Ellen Gould Harmon White was cofounder and lay leader of the Seventh-Day Adventist church. She was an itinerant minister from the age of eighteen, speaking about the imminent return of Christ and advocating observance of the seventh day (Saturday) as the Sabbath. After she married James White, both continued to spread the Advent message. They settled in Battle Creek, Michigan, the center of their work for many years. There the Seventh-Day Adventist Church was organized in 1860. She, who had always been frail, taught the importance of good health and was instrumental in establishing what later became the Battle Creek Sanitarium, pioneering in the development of cereal foods with J. H. Kellogg. Her lecturing occupied many years and her writings were voluminous (fifty-four of her books are still in print). Elmshaven was her home for the last fifteen years of her life. It can be reached by turning off Glass Mountain Road from the Silverado Trail and turning onto Glass Mountain Lane, where there is a marker. It is open daily 10–5, Sabbath (Sat.) 2–6.[33]

SAN DIEGO

Hulett, Alta M., c. 1854–1877, Lawyer

Marker, Mount Hope Cemetery, 3751 Market Street

For eighty years the grave of Alta M. Hulett, pioneer woman lawyer, went unmarked, overgrown with weeds and unkempt. Then the San Diego Women Lawyers' Association placed a marker over it. She was eighteen when she applied for admission to the bar in Chicago, Illinois, after studying for a year in the office of a lawyer. But women were not admitted to the practice of law in Illinois. Hulett prepared a bill providing that no person could be debarred from any occupation, profession, or employment except military, on grounds of sex. She and Myra Bradwell, another early lawyer, lobbied it through the Illinois legislature in March 1872. On her nineteenth birthday, Hulett became the first woman admitted to the bar in Illinois. She practiced only a few years, however, moving to San Diego shortly before she died of tuberculosis.[34]

Rice, Lilian, 1888–1938, Architect

Rancho Santa Fe

The tract of land northeast of San Diego, formerly called Rancho San Dieguito, was the property of the Santa Fe Railroad, which planted it with eucalyptus trees. It hoped to harvest them for railroad ties, and when this was found inexpedient it proposed to develop the property as a planned community. Lilian Rice, a graduate of the School of Architecture, University of California, designed the overall plan and some of its buildings, including Rancho Santa Fe Inn, the library, and the school. Among other designs that won her esteem were the Robinson House in La Jolla and the clubhouse for a women's rowing team. A Lilian Rice Trophy was donated to the club in her memory.[35]

Sessions, Kate, 1857–1940, Horticulturist; NAW

Marker, Balboa and Pico. Plaque, Hall of Nations, Balboa Park. Kate Sessions Elementary School, 2150 Beryl Street. Kate Sessions Park, Pacific Beach

Kate Sessions was a horticulturist who leased thirty acres of undeveloped land in a city park to grow plants, promising to plant at least a hundred trees a year and to donate three hundred more to the city. Many of the exotic trees that grace Balboa Park and San Diego's streets and gardens were first imported and propagated by Sessions. She was the first woman to receive the International Meyer Medal in Genetics. The plaque at Balboa and Pico, under a Tipuana tree, marks the site of her nursery. The marker in Balboa Park is at an incense cedar planted in her memory by the San Diego Floral Association. The school given her name was opened in 1956; behind it a nature trail has been named by the children Kate's Canyon Tumbleweed Trail. On November 8, 1957, the hundredth anniversary of her birth, the park in Pacific Beach was dedicated.

Waterman, Hazel Wood, 1865–1948, Architect

Wednesday Club Building, 540 Ivy Lane

Hazel Wood Waterman studied art at the University of California, where she met Irving Gill. As he worked on the design for her family home, he was impressed with her creativity and grasp of detail and suggested she study architecture. After her husband's death, she took Gill's advice, then joined his office as a draftsperson before opening her own office. During that first generation of women in architecture, many women's clubs sought female designers for their buildings. Waterman designed the Wednesday Club in 1910. This was followed by a number of commissions in San Diego, including the Children's Home building in Balboa Park.

SAN FRANCISCO

Children's Hospital, 3700 California Street

Children's Hospital was established in 1875 by a group of pioneer women physicians as the Pacific Dispensary for Women and Children. It was intended to provide women with medical care by doctors of their own sex and to give female physicians needed professional experience in a world dominated by male doctors and hospital administrators. Among the founders and early attending physicians were Charlotte Amanda Blake Brown, Cloe Annette Buckel, and Lucy Marie Field Wanzer.

Brown (1846–1904, NAW) earned her medical degree from the Woman's Medical College of Pennsylvania in 1874, taking her training after she was married and had three children. She had a busy obstetrics practice. She was the first woman on the West Coast to perform an ovariotomy. She pioneered the use of incubators for premature babies and designed a milk-sterilizing apparatus for the nursery. Her brother also practiced medicine in San Francisco, and two of her children, Philip King Brown and Adelaide Brown, became physicians.

Buckel (1833–1912, NAW) received her degree in 1858, also from the Woman's Medical College. A year later she joined another doctor in founding a dispensary for women and children in Chicago, Illinois. During the Civil War she set up field hospitals for soldiers (when she was always addressed as "Miss" rather than "Doctor"). She took a special interest in retarded children and left funds to study child psychology. A research fellowship at Stanford University is named for her.

Wanzer (1841–1930) was the first woman to get an M.D. from a Pacific Coast college (1876). She had to get a ruling from the Board of Regents of the University of California before they would admit her to Toland Hall, and then the dean and instructors tried to get rid of her. After graduation she practiced for over thirty years and won the respect of her colleagues, both men and women.

Bremer, Anne, 1872–1923, Artist

Anne Bremer Memorial Library, San Francisco Art Institute, 800 Chestnut Street. Plaque, Zen Center, Paige and Laguna Streets

Anne Bremer was one of the best-known artists of the Bay Area, especially noted for her murals. She was president of the San Francisco Sketch Club and a member of the board of the later San Francisco Art Association. Other memorials to Bremer include a bird fountain at Mills College and a chair at the Greek Theater in Berkeley, California. A statue of her by Jacques Schnier is at the memorial library.[36]

Brown, Charlotte. See Children's Hospital

Buckel, Cloe. See Children's Hospital

Cameron, Donaldina, 1869–1968, Humanitarian; NAWM

Cameron House, 920 Sacramento Street

Donaldina Cameron fought a forty-year battle to save young Chinese slave girls brought to San Francisco to serve as prostitutes in Chinatown. Reputable Chinese women were not allowed to accompany their husbands to America. Very young girls were sold to traders by their parents or kidnapped and forced into the short, cruel life of the cribs. Cameron raided the houses, kidnapped the girls, brought them to the mission established here, and gave them hope and health. In time the decent Chinese came to know and love her. They called her "Lo Mo," or the mother. Cameron House is now a community center.

Coit, Lillie Hitchcock, 1843–1929, Celebrity

Coit Tower, Top of Telegraph Hill

Saved from a disastrous hotel fire when she was eight years old, Lillie Hitchcock Coit adored the firemen who rescued her. It was the beginning of a lifetime love affair with the volunteers of Knickerbocker Company Number 5. Despite her parents' objections, Coit often joined the men as they rode to a fire, bells clanging. Number 5 adopted her as a mascot and later made her an honorary member. She grew up a society belle, eloped with a popular young man, Howard Coit, and for years delighted and scandalized San Franciscans with her lively escapades. When she died she left a third of her considerable estate to "add beauty to the city which I have always loved." After much debate, the tower named for her was constructed with some of the funds. The statue of three firemen in Washington Square was another gift to the city by Coit. The San Francisco Fire Department Pioneer Memorial Museum, 655 Presidio Street, has Coit memorabilia. It is open Thurs.-Sun. 1–4. Coit Tower is open daily, 10–4:30; closed some holidays; adm. to elevator.

Coolbrith, Ina Donna, 1841–1928, Poet; NAW

Coolbrith Park, Vallejo and Taylor Streets

Ina Donna Coolbrith was a brilliant poet whose output was small but who inspired and encouraged other writers who were working in San Francisco in the 1860s. To support herself and two motherless nieces, as well as a child left in her care by Joaquin Miller, she took a job as librarian of the Oakland Public Library. There she gave to young people—including Isadora Duncan and Jack London—a love of great literature. She became librarian of the San Francisco Mercantile Library in 1897, then of the Bohemian Club. The park is on the site of her home. Another memorial to her is Mount Ina Coolbrith, near Beckwourth Pass, by which she entered California, riding on the saddle of mountain man Jim Beckwourth. See Sacramento, CA.

Cooper, Sarah Brown Ingersoll, 1835–1896, Kindergartner; NAW

Cooper Fountain, Children's Playground, Golden Gate Park

"To be perpetually telling a little child . . . that there is no good thing in him, that he is vile and corrupt, is one of the very best ways of making a rascal out of him." These words were spoken by Sarah Brown Ingersoll Cooper when she addressed the 1893 Congress of Women. Her words do not sound radical today, but they did then, when babies were believed to be born sinners and when sending little children to school was a new idea. Cooper was influenced by Emma Marwedel in Oakland and Kate Douglas Wiggin in San Francisco, both early kindergarten workers. She founded her kindergarten for the slum children of the Barbary Coast in 1879. Under her direction some forty kindergartens were associated in the Golden Gate Kindergarten Association by 1895.

The fountain, a child figure standing by a pool, carved by Enid Foster, was erected in 1923 with funds raised by the Kindergarten Association. Like so many monuments, it has been neglected and vandalized.[37]

Crabtree, Lotta, 1847–1974, Actress; NAW

Lotta's Fountain, Market, Geary and Kearney Streets; NR

Lotta Crabtree grew up in Grass Valley, where her first instructor in the dance was Lola Montez. She began her career by dancing for miners in the gold camps of the Sierra foothills, and before she retired she had become one of the most popular of American actresses.

The fountain was given by the California comedienne to relieve the tired and thirsty horses of the city streets. Never a thing of beauty, the monument remains as dear to the sentimental San Franciscans of today as Crabtree was to those of the late nineteenth century. All efforts of traffic engineers to move it have been negated by preservationists. In 1910 Luiza Tetrazzini sang on Christmas Eve before thousands gathered around the fountain. In commemoration of this event a bas-relief portrait of Tetrazzini by Haig Patigian was added to the column. Sixty-eight-year-old Crabtree was there in 1915; November 6 was Crabtree Day at the Panama Pacific Exposition. She brought a carefully prepared speech, but when she was introduced to the throng around the monument, cheering "Lotta, Lotta, Lotta!" no words came. Tears coursed down her cheeks, and the crowd happily wept with her.

Duncan, Isadora, 1878–1927, Dancer; NAW

Plaque, Wall of Building, Taylor and Geary Streets

The tablet, installed in 1973, reads: "Daughter of California Pioneers, America's Genius of the Dance was born on this site. She created a new art form, liberating the dance as an expression of life."

Isadora Duncan's parents were divorced when she was an infant, and her mother tried to raise her four children on a meager income earned by playing and teaching piano. They lived in Oakland, California. The children early left school, learned to dance, staged their own plays, published a newspaper, and educated themselves at the Oakland Public Library. By the time they reached their teens, Duncan and her sister had their own dance school, first in Oakland, then in San Francisco. They danced to classical music, using natural movements, wearing loose-fitting and gauzy draperies, moving against a plain blue muslin backdrop—all to be characteristic of Duncan's dancing life. It was a life that meant grueling poverty, hard work, and tragedy, but it also brought rich rewards in wealth, love, and adoration. She has been described as an enigma, "a saint and a sinner, a spartan and a sybarite, an idler and a perfectionist, a teasing courtesan and a loving mother, a revolutionary who spouted Marxian ideology and an aristocrat who reveled in privilege." In Berkeley, California, the Temple of Wings keeps alive her dance philosophy.[38]

Eastwood, Alice, 1859–1953, Botanist; NAWM

Eastwood Hall of Botany, California Academy of Sciences, Golden Gate Park. Memorial Bench, Shakespeare Garden, Academy of Sciences

After the earthquake and fire of 1906, Alice Eastwood climbed six flights of broken marble stairs to the academy offices to rescue what she could of the valuable collections, while her own home and possessions were destroyed. She had come to the academy in 1893 and spent the rest of her life here as curator of botany and curator emerita. She collected plants in the field, organized the specimens, built up a botanical library, and made the academy known around the world as one of the finest institutions of its kind. She wrote and lectured and made friends of naturalists and conservationists throughout the Bay Area and the West. After the fire it was six years before the academy was rebuilt and could open its Department of Botany. Eastwood spent those free years studying in Massachusetts, New York, and Philadelphia, Pennsylvania, as well as London, England, Paris, France, and other European cities with botanical collections. See Mill Valley and Orick, California. The Academy of Sciences is open daily 10–5; adm., except on first Wed. of month.

Hearst, Phoebe Apperson, 1842–1919, Philanthropist; NAW

Hearst Memorial Fountain, Steinhart Aquarium, Golden Gate Park. Phoebe A. Hearst Preschool Learning Center, 1315 Ellis Street

Phoebe Apperson Hearst lived in San Francisco from 1826 until about 1896. Wife of George Hearst, she was noted for her entertainments, her interest in talented people, and her study of architecture, music, science, and education. An openhanded philanthropist, Hearst contributed to many institutions, particularly to the University of California (see Berkeley, CA). The Learning Center replaces the school on Union Street formerly named for Hearst in recognition of her efforts on behalf of early childhood education. It houses the headquarters of the Golden Gate Kindergarten Association. See Anaconda, MT, and Lead, SD.

Huntington, Anna Hyatt, 1876–1973, Sculptor; NAWM

El Cid Compeador *and* Joan of Arc, *Statues in Front of the Palace of the Legion of Honor, Lincoln Park*

Anna Hyatt Huntington was one of America's outstanding sculptors, and these massive pieces are ranked among the great equestrian statues of the world. The daughter of a naturalist, Huntington was always interested in animals, and her early statues were of tigers and lions. As a girl, she dreamed of doing a statue of Joan of Arc. She began work on this one in 1909, using a ground-floor studio in Paris, France, large enough to bring in carts and horses as models. With only a woman assistant, she made her own armature and massed a ton of clay for the statue. Replicas cast in bronze were placed in New York City and in San Diego, California, as well as other places. *El Cid Compeador*, which won her a Grand

Cross of Alfonso XII from Spain, was brought to California as a companion to *Joan of Arc* in 1937.

Kennedy, Kate, 1827–1890, Schoolteacher; NAW

Kate Kennedy School, 1670 Noe Street

An Irish girl who emigrated to California in 1856 and became a San Francisco schoolteacher, Kate Kennedy fought for equal pay for equal work in the school system. That battle won, she began another, which culminated in a state supreme court decision in 1890 virtually establishing teacher tenure in California: ''A teacher of any particular grade and with a proper certificate cannot be placed in a lower grade or dismissed except for misconduct or incompetency.''

Lambert, Rebecca, d. c. 1886, Seamen's Champion

Obelisk, Lincoln Park Golf Course

Rebecca Lambert, a sea captain's widow, became the champion of ill-treated sailors of San Francisco. She helped to found the Ladies Seamans Friend Society of the Port of San Francisco, the Sailors' Home on Rincon Hill, and the cemetery for those who died in port. The obelisk is near the fifteenth tee of the golf course, just below the balustrade in front of the Palace of the Legion of Honor. It was erected by Henry Cogswell, an odd San Francisco dentist known for his ugly monuments across the country. The cemetery itself is under the golf greens.[39]

Morrison, May Treat, 1858–1939, Philanthropist

May T. Morrison Auditorium, California Academy of Sciences, Golden Gate Park

May Treat Morrison graduated from the University of California in 1878 (see Berkeley, CA). She was thenceforth closely connected with the field of learning in the Bay Area. As the wife of Alexander Morrison, a prominent attorney, she gave her time to club work and a number of institutions to which she donated large sums. She was a trustee of the Academy of Sciences and knew of the need for an auditorium; she left $150,000 for its building. A plaque calls her a ''distinguished citizen and humanitarian.''

Pleasant, Mary Ellen, 1814?–1904, Civil Rights Advocate; NAW

Mary Ellen Pleasant Memorial Park, Octavia and Bush Streets

Black pioneer Mary Ellen Pleasant was one of San Francisco's most powerful women. Born a slave in Georgia, she was educated in Boston, Massachusetts, where she attained her freedom and married a wealthy black Bostonian. Inheriting fifty thousand dollars from him, she moved to California and opened a boarding house in 1849. She increased her wealth by lending money and speculating in real estate. She was variously accused of blackmailing clients, trading in stolen babies, and pilfering a fortune from the elderly banker with whom she lived. On the other hand, she was a known friend to the blacks of San Francisco, a strong abolitionist and philanthropist. The house in which she lived with her partner, Thomas Bell, was on this site. To later San Franciscans it was known as the "house of mystery." In 1976 the San Francisco African-American Historical and Cultural Society dedicated this park to her memory. In 1965 they marked her grave in Tulocay Cemetery, Napa, "She was a friend of John Brown" and "Mother of Civil Rights in California."[40]

Randall, Josephine, 1886–1968, Recreation Leader

Josephine Randall Junior Museum, 199 Museum Way, Off Roosevelt, Corona Heights

In 1928 Josephine Randall walked over vacant land on Corona Heights and dreamed of building there a museum and work center where children could create something. She was for twenty-five years director of recreation for the city of San Francisco. A stubborn fighter for improvement in recreational facilities for the city, she established a children's museum on Ocean Avenue. In 1951 it moved into this new building, surrounded by fifteen acres on top of the hill she had selected in 1928. She was the honored guest at the dedication ceremonies. The museum has workshops, tools, printing equipment, zoology and chemistry labs, a weaving room, and other facilities—enough to accommodate five hundred children each week where they can explore, tinker, and learn. It is open Tues.-Sat. 10–5.

Russell, Katherine (Mother Mary Baptist), 1829–1898, Churchwoman; NAW

Saint Mary's Hospital, 450 Stanyan Street

Katherine Russell (Mother Mary Baptist) and several other Sisters of Mercy were recruited in Ireland in 1854 to minister to the social needs of San Francisco. No place in the world, perhaps, needed their services more, for a layer of disease and poverty existed beneath the new wealth of the gold rush, and few charitable or educational organizations existed to care for the homeless, ill, and needy. They founded Saint Mary's, the first Catholic hospital on the Pacific Coast, in 1857. Initially it occupied a former marine hospital building, where the nuns had nursed cholera victims. The Sisters of Mercy were also kept busy setting up shelters for unemployed and "fallen" women and schools for girls and boys. Mother Mary Baptist and the others regularly visited the prisons, including Death

Row, and they set up kitchens for feeding the poor. When she died, San Francisco papers called Mother Mary Baptist "the best-known charitable worker on the Pacific Coast."

Spreckels, Alma de Bretteville, 1881–1968, Philanthropist

California Palace of the Legion of Honor, Lincoln Park

Alma de Bretteville Spreckels, a free-spirited young woman who developed into one of San Francisco's social leaders, married the sugar king, Adolph Spreckels. He built her a "sugar palace" in Pacific Heights. She had studied art at the Mark Hopkins Institute and after the 1906 earthquake helped to rescue some of its paintings and sculpture. In 1915 she visited Paris, France, where she bought one of the castings of Auguste Rodin's *The Thinker* and presented it to San Francisco. She then decided to have a museum built, patterned after the Palais de Legion d'Honneur in Paris. The museum, funded largely by Spreckels and her friends, opened in 1924. It is open daily 10–5; later in summer; adm.; free on 1st Wed. of month.

Stern, Rosalie Meyer, 1869–1956, Music Patron

Sigmund Stern Grove, Sloat Boulevard at 19th Street

One day John McLaren, superintendent of Golden Gate Park, was driving about San Francisco with Rosalie Meyer Stern, a member of the Playground Commission, in search of sites for playgrounds. He said, "I want to show you a place you should have," and took her to an "enchanted vale," a natural bowl sheltered by a grove of century-old eucalyptus trees. She bought it at once and presented it to the city as a memorial to her husband. The site was part of the historical Trocadero Ranch. She formed a group to sponsor outdoor summer concerts there, paying for most of them herself. Thousands of San Franciscans today throng to the Stern Grove Sunday concerts every summer. Among Stern's other gifts was Stern Hall, a residence hall at the University of California at Berkeley.[41]

Strybing, Helene Jordon, c. 1846–1926, Philanthropist

Strybing Arboretum and Botanical Gardens, 9th Avenue and Lincoln Way, Golden Gate Park

Helene Jordon Strybing was a longtime resident of San Francisco and a lover of flowers, especially those native to California. The daughter of a pastor in Romstedt, Germany, and widow of Christian Strybing, a silk merchant, she left over $100,000 to be used eventually for an arboretum and botanical garden in Golden Gate Park. She added the provision that the garden should include "a collection of trees, shrubs and plants indigenous to, or characteristic of California, also plants used for medicinal purposes.'' When the money became available in 1928, the city expanded its arboretum, which had been started late in the nineteenth century, and gave it her name. It consists of some seventy acres, including a library and a center for horticultural education and experiments. Strybing also left the city a collection of jewels—all glass. The arboretum is open weekdays 8–4:30; weekends and holidays 10–5. Tours leave the kiosk daily at 1:30 and Thurs.-Sun. 10:30.[42]

Wanzer, Lucy. See Children's Hospital

Willard, Frances, 1839–1898, Temperance Leader; NAW

Plaque, on Balustrade at Palace of the Legion of Honor, Lincoln Park

Frances Willard, national president of the Woman's Christian Temperance Union (WCTU), visited San Francisco in 1883 and what she saw in San Francisco's Chinatown shocked her into a realization that the fight to free women from oppression was an international one. ''But for the intrusion of the sea, the shores of China and the far East would be part and parcel of our land. We are one world of tempted humanity.'' She extended the WCTU into a worldwide organization of women working together for freedom. In 1938 the San Francisco WCTU dedicated this plaque commemorating Willard's visit.

SAN JOSE

Winchester, Sarah, d. 1922, Eccentric Builder

Winchester Mystery House, 525 S. Winchester Boulevard; State Historic Landmark, NR

Widow of William Winchester, who was the son of the Winchester Arms founder, Sarah Winchester was left with $20 million and an income of nearly $1,000 a day. But wealth did not make her happy. She had lost a baby daughter and the death of her husband soon afterward left her plunged in melancholy. A spiritualist counseled her to build, and her doctor also advised her to pursue a talent for design. In 1884 she moved to California and began construction of her Llanda Villa. Her health immediately improved.

She went on building—a bizarre collection of 160 rooms, 40 stairways, 47 fireplaces, 13 bathrooms. Doors opened to blank walls, stairways lead to a ceiling, useless chimneys stopped at the ceiling—a maze of rooms in which one could become lost without a guide. Yet Winchester had much ingenuity. She designed all the details of intricate parquetry, paneling, special window catches, Tiffany stained-glass windows, and innovations such as rock wool insulation that builders have since adopted. The present owners guide visitors through the house daily 9–5 (later in summer); closed Christmas; high adm.[43]

SAN RAFAEL

Boyd, Louise Arner, 1887–1972, Arctic Explorer

Boyd House, 1125 B Street; NR

"San Francisco Society Woman Back from Hunt in Polar Wilds" "San Francisco Huntress Victorious in Arctic Wilds"—such headlines kept San Franciscans au courant with the adventures of San Rafael's Louise Arner Boyd. Her Arctic expeditions, on her own chartered ships, were treated as the expensive hobby of a wealthy woman, and much was made of her skill in shooting polar bears. In 1929, after she assisted in the search for the lost explorer Roald Amundsen and was decorated by the governments of Norway and France, the headlines began to change. The stories were shifted from the society pages to the news section, and her expeditions were reported as scientific explorations. The real change came in 1931 when she met Isaiah Bowman and others from the American Geographical Society; from then on the society sponsored her trips.

She headed six expeditions to the polar regions, contributing significantly to knowledge of the Arctic and breaking a trail for other women in a career hitherto exclusively male-oriented. A portion of Greenland is called Louise Boyd Land.

The old Victorian house was built by Boyd's great-grandfather. It is now the headquarters of the Marin County Historical Society. Maple Lawn, the Boyd home, at 1312 Mission Avenue, is now the property of the Elks Club. Boyd Park, next to it, was a memorial to Boyd's two brothers, who died in young manhood. The historical society, which has Boyd memorabilia and papers, is open Wed.-Sun. 1–4.[44]

O'Donnell, Catherine (Mother Louis), 1852–1931, Churchwoman and College Founder

Dominican Convent and College, 1520 Grand Avenue

"If we don't leave Benicia," Mother Louis said, "we must die of hunger." It was 1887 and she had just been elected prioress provincial by the Dominican sisters of St. Catherine's in Benicia. The town, once known as the Athens of California because of its excellent schools, was dwindling in importance, and Mother Louis wished to move the motherhouse and novitiate to San Rafael, closer to San Francisco. The fact that the order had no money to finance the move did not deter the young and energetic nun. She begged, borrowed, and prayed, and in two years she was able to establish the College of the Holy Rosary, which grew into the present Dominican College, in San Rafael.

Mother Louis was the daughter of a gold miner in the Sierra town of Murphys,

California. She entered the Dominican order at the age of sixteen. Nineteen years later, after a distinguished career as a Catholic educator, she became mother provincial of the order.

The 1889 Italianate academy building is still in use as the motherhouse of the sisters. Adjoining it a small museum contains memorabilia and pictures of Mother Louis and others active in the early years of the school. Dominican College, now a four-year college, occupies the adjoining parklike campus of some eighty acres.[45]

SAN SIMEON

Morgan, Julia, 1872–1957, Architect; NAWM

Hearst Castle, Hearst San Simeon State Historic Park, State 1; NHL

For decades the publishing tycoon William Randolph Hearst had owned and loved this site overlooking the Pacific Ocean. He hiked and camped here and after his marriage brought his family for summer camping. He dreamed of building a castle on the site and began collecting art and furnishings for it. In San Francisco, Julia Morgan was building a reputation as one of the Bay Area's most competent architects (see Berkeley, CA). She had built homes for Hearst's mother, Phoebe Apperson Hearst. When the millionaire was ready to begin building his dream home, he called on Morgan.

The project was indeed a challenge. The spot was almost inaccessible. There was no port at which to land heavy equipment and materials. Water came from a spring five miles away from the bare knob the castle was to occupy. Morgan was equal to the task. For twenty years she worked on the estate, commuting almost weekly to San Simeon. She engineered the site, built a dock and warehouses and roads, and incorporated in the plans whole sections of dismantled palaces and cathedrals Hearst had brought from Europe. The shimmering castle, its guest houses, and its lavish gardens are as much a memorial to the architect as to the owner.

A plaque at the castle reads: "La Cuesta Encantada—Presented to the state of California in 1958 by Hearst Corporation, in memory of William Randolph Hearst who created this enchanted hill, and of his mother, Phoebe Apperson Hearst, who inspired it." San Simeon is open for conducted tours daily, 8–4 in summer, shorter hours in winter; reservations advised; apply at Ticketron outlets; high adm.[46]

SANTA ANA

Howe-Waffle, Willella Earhart, 1854–1924, Physician

Howe-Waffle House, Sycamore and Civic Center Drive; NR

"The enemy of the woman who pioneers in medicine is prejudice. While not as cruel as an Apache Indian, it is just as relentless." Willella Earhart Howe-

Waffle, the first southern California woman to practice medicine outside of the city of Los Angeles, spoke thus of her days as a physician in the 1880s and 1890s. The occasion was a reception given in her honor in 1921 by the people of Santa Ana. Hard work and a philosophical approach to life had brought the physician through her early years of struggle until she became one of the best-loved women of the community. She began the study of medicine after her first marriage, to Alvin Jared Howe, and read medical books while holding a child in her lap. She went to the Hahneman Medical College in Chicago, Illinois, studied homeopathic medicine, and returned to California to begin her practice. In 1898 she married Edson Dwight Waffle. Her house (and office) and carriage house, moved from their original site, have been restored by the Santa Ana Historical Preservation Society. Open by appointment (914–543–3086).[47]

SANTA BARBARA

Juana Maria, d. 1853, Indian Survivor

Plaque, on Cemetery Wall, Santa Barbara Mission

The Indian woman the padres named Juana Maria just before they baptized and then buried her is known as "the lone woman of San Nicolas." A female Robinson Crusoe, she lived for eighteen years without human companionship on the isolated, rocky island of San Nicolas, one of the Santa Barbara Islands, about sixty-five miles from the mainland. Rescued in 1853, she was unable to communicate her story. Other Indians were brought to talk to her but none could understand her language. Nor could she subsist on the food given her, and although she had appeared healthy when taken from the island, she soon sickened and died. There were no anthropologists nearby to study her, and the brief known accounts of her plight and rescue leave many questions as to how she was able to survive. It is clear, however, that she somehow retained to an extraordinary degree the human characteristics of patience, modesty, tact, gentleness, faith, and humor. Her story is the basis for Scott O'Dell's children's book *Island of the Blue Dolphins*. The plaque to her memory, erected in 1928 by the Santa Barbara Chapter, Daughters of the American Revolution, is just to the right of the exit gate.[48]

Lehmann, Lotte, 1888–1976, Singer

Lehmann Hall, University of California, Santa Barbara

Born in Prussia, Lotte Lehmann was a world-famous opera singer when she first came to the United States to sing with the Metropolitan Opera. Hermann Göring, the Nazi minister, had offered to make her the leading singer of Germany, provided she appeared only in Germany and sang only approved works. She refused the honor and in 1938 left her homeland forever to settle in the United

States. Here she was long the Met's leading lyric-dramatic soprano before turning to the concert stage. Santa Barbara claimed her as its own. It was here that she was naturalized in 1945. Here she taught at the Music Academy of the West. Here in 1951 she gave her last concert. The city celebrated her birthday in 1968, presenting her with a birthday cake in the shape of the Vienna Opera House. Her papers repose in the university library, and townspeople as well as students enjoy concerts in the hall named for her.

SANTA PAULA

Isbell, Olive Mann, 1824–1899, Teacher

Plaque, Isbell School, 221 S. 4th Street

According to the tablet at the school, Olive Mann Isbell was the "First American Schoolteacher in California." Many legends have grown up about this adventurous young woman and her "eccentric, jolly, queer old cuss" of a husband, Isaac Chauncey Isbell (or Isbel). She herself left a three-paragraph autobiography, written in 1893, in which she says she began teaching in December 1846 in a room without light or heat in the Santa Clara Mission. Soon afterward she moved to Monterey, California, where Thomas O. Larkin, the American consul, appointed her a teacher for three months, fitting up a schoolroom over the jail. She says she returned to Ohio in 1850, was in Texas 1857–63, in Santa Barbara, California, 1864, and in Santa Paula in 1872, "where I have resided ever since." Her house still stands, privately owned.[49]

SOQUEL

Parkhurst, Charlie, c. 1812–1879, Stage Driver

Plaque, Soquel Firehouse, 4747 Main Street

"The average stage driver," wrote historian H. H. Bancroft, "was above all, lord in his way, the captain of his craft, the fear of timid passengers, the admiration of the stable boys, and the trusted agent of his employer." He might have had in mind Charlie Parkhurst, a noted whip of gold rush days. He was high-strung and when held up by highwaymen—a common occurrence—he gave up the treasure box with an ill grace and sometimes shot it out with the robbers. He was an excellent shot as well as a dexterous driver. He lost an eye in an accident and was thereafter known as one-eyed Charlie. Not until he died was it discovered that the person who had masqueraded for most of his/her life as a man was a woman! The Soquel Fire Department's plaque states that "the first ballot by a woman in an American presidential election was cast on this site November 3, 1868, by Charlotte (Charlie) Parkhurst who masqueraded as a man for much of her life." Charlie was buried in the Odd Fellows Cemetery in

Watsonville, with a marker placed by the Pajaro Valley Historical Society in 1955.[50]

STOCKTON

Lewis, Tillie, 1901–1977, Businesswoman

Tillie Lewis Foods, Inc., 1405 S. Fresno Avenue

As a girl in New York, Tillie Lewis (then named Myrtle Ehrlich) noticed that the pear-shaped tomato had more flavor than the globular one. Although the New York Botanical Garden and other horticulturists told her the pomodoros would not grown in the United States, she still thought she would like to try. She found a grower in Italy willing to back up her experiment with a $10,000 loan. She planted the prized tomato seeds in the San Joaquin Valley. From this beginning she developed a $100 million enterprise, with a line of many varieties of regular and diet foods in addition to the tomatoes. By 1937 she was sole owner and manager of Flotill (her backer's name combined with hers) and was known locally as the tomato queen. In 1947 she married Meyer Lewis, who originally came to her canneries to settle a strike, and in 1961 she changed the corporate name to Tillie Lewis Foods. This was acquired by Ogden Food Products, which she served as president. In addition to managing the business, Lewis had time to serve on the Stockton Port Commission and to worry about the starving people of the world.[51]

UKIAH

Hudson, Grace Carpenter, 1865–1937, Artist

Sun House, 431 S. Main Street; State Historic Landmark, NR

Grace Carpenter Hudson's paintings of the Pomo Indians are treasured by the art collector for their artistic beauty and by the anthropologist for their documentation of many aspects of Pomo life. Hudson was born in Potter Valley, California, daughter of a newspaper editor and a schoolteacher and granddaughter of Clarina Howard Nichols (1810–1885, NAW), a longtime advocate of women's rights. Hudson painted portraits of the Indians in her area, producing over six hundred oils, plus watercolors and drawings. In Ukiah she was called the painter lady. John Hudson, her husband, also had a strong interest in the culture of the Native Americans. Most of his collection of Indian baskets was donated to the Smithsonian Institution in Washington, D.C., but some are displayed, along with Grace's paintings, in the museum attached to their former home, Sun House. Now the property of the city of Ukiah, it is open Wed.-Sun. 12–4.[52]

WEOTT

Edson, Katherine Philips, 1870–1933, Public Official, NAW

Katherine Philips Edson Memorial Grove, Avenue of the Giants, Humboldt Redwoods State Park

As a young mother in Los Angeles, California, Katherine Philips Edson launched a campaign for pure milk. Later she joined the Friday Morning Club and became chair of its committee on municipal problems. She uncovered a great many problems, and among those she brought to the attention of the city were public health matters, a revision of the city charter, and an eight-hour day for student nurses, then working twelve hours. She was a strong suffragist and a pacifist. She served on the advisory committee of the Washington Conference on Limitation of Armaments in 1921. Her greatest achievement was in the field of protective legislation for women and children. In 1913 she had a California State Industrial Welfare Commission established. She served on the commission for eighteen years, becoming executive commissioner in 1916 and chief of the State Division of Industrial Welfare in 1927. She was a regional director of the National League of Women Voters, and the California league set aside the redwood grove in her memory.[53]

WEST COVINA

Yaw, Ellen Beach (Lark Ellen), 1868–1947, Singer; NAW

Lark Ellen Street

In 1896 critics went to hear Ellen Beach Yaw sing at Carnegie Hall expecting to be disappointed. Her manager had claimed that she had the highest vocal range in history and could reach E above high C. To their surprise, they heard a well-trained voice of great color and character. Yaw had begun studying voice in Minneapolis, Minnesota, Boston, Massachusetts, and New York City and was hoping to finance European training. Sir Arthur Sullivan composed for her the leading soprano role in the opera *Rose of Persia*. It opened in London, England, in 1899 and made her a star. She began a highly successful operatic career in Europe and the United States. She was often called Lark Ellen.

Yaw first came to West Covina, in the foothills of the Sierra Madre, in the 1890s; later she designed and built the Lark's Nest, a home at 19101 E. Cameron Street. She added an outdoor auditorium, Lark Ellen Bowl, and from 1934 to 1945 gave summer concerts there. The proceeds of some of the concerts went to support a home for newsboys which honored her by changing its name to Lark Ellen Home for Boys (since closed). Still remaining here are a hospital and a retirement home, as well as the street, named for the tiny, sweet-faced singer.[54]

NOTES

In addition to sources mentioned below, I have had assistance from California State University, Fresno; the California Historical Society; Presidio of San Francisco; San Pedro Regional Branch, Los Angeles Public Library; Madera County Historical Society, Madera; Mills College Library; Inyo County Free Library, Independence; La Puente Valley Historical Society, Rowland Heights; Fresno City and County Historical Society; Southern California Visitors Council; Pat Murray, Fresno; Jessie V. Heinzman, Potter Valley; John M. Houston, San Pedro; Pacific Asia Museum, Pasadena; and Josephine Randall Junior Museum, San Francisco.

1. Correspondence, St. Dominic School, Benicia.

2. "Sherman Was There: The Recollections of Major Edwin A. Sherman," *California Historical Society Quarterly* 23–24 (Sept. 1944–Sept. 1945).

3. Janet Lewis Zullo, "Annie Montague Alexander: Her Work in Paleontology," *Journal of the West* 8 (Apr. 1969), 183–99.

4. Sterling Dow, *Fifty Years of Sathers* (Berkeley: University of California Press, 1965); correspondence, University of California Archives.

5. *San Francisco Chronicle*, Feb. 2, 1955.

6. Many of the campus buildings are treated in Albert G. Pickerell and May Dornin, *The University of California: A Pictorial History* (Berkeley: University of California Press, 1968).

7. Sara Boutelle, "The Long-Distance Dreamer Who Altered the Look of California," *California Monthly* 86 (Apr. 1976); Elinor Richey, *Eminent Women of the West* (Berkeley, Calif.: Howell-North Books, 1976); correspondence, Sara Boutelle, Julia Morgan Association, Santa Cruz.

8. Siskiyou County Historical Society, "The Siskiyou Pioneer in Folklore, Fact, and Fiction," pamphlet, 1950; correspondence, Siskiyou County Historical Society.

9. Richey, *Eminent Women*; correspondence, Bidwell Mansion.

10. Correspondence, clippings, and brochure, Clarke Museum.

11. Correspondence, Save-the-Redwoods League; Mexia MSS at Bancroft Library, University of California, Berkeley.

12. Dorcas Spencer, *A History of the Woman's Christian Temperance Union of Northern and Central California* (Oakland, Calif.: West Coast Printing Co., 1913); Byron Nelson, Jr., *Our Home Forever: A Hupa Tribal History* (Hoopa, Calif.: Hupa Tribe, 1978).

13. *New Yorker*, Aug. 30, 1952.

14. *New Yorker*, Apr. 21 and 28, 1956.

15. Correspondence and clippings, Virginia Wilson, Napa.

16. Brochure, Los Angeles Public Library.

17. "Miracles for a Dime," *California History* 57 (Winter 1978–79).

18. Thomas M. Heric, "Rancho La Brea: Its History and Fossils," *Journal of the West* 8 (Apr. 1969).

19. John D. Weaver, *El Pueblo Grande: A Nonfiction Book About Los Angeles* (Los Angeles, Calif.: Ward Ritchie Press, 1973).

20. Charlotte S. Rubinstein, *American Women Artists* (New York: Avon Books, 1982).

21. Carol G. Wilson, *Alice Eastwood's Wonderland: The Adventures of a Botanist* (San Francisco, Calif.: California Academy of Sciences, 1955).

22. *San Francisco Chronicle*, Aug. 16, 1952.

23. Lincoln Fairley, "Literary Associations with Mount Tamalpais," *California History* 61 (Summer 1982).

24. Reda Davis, *California Women: A Guide to Their Politics, 1885–1911* (San Francisco, Calif.: California Scene, 1976; Selina Solomons, *How We Won the Vote in California* (San Francisco, Calif.: New Woman Publishing Co., 1913).

25. *San Francisco Chronicle*, Dec. 2, 1955.

26. Paul Kagan, *New World Utopias: A Photographic History of the Search for Community* (New York: Penguin Books, 1975).

27. Correspondence and clippings, Save-the-Redwoods League.

28. Correspondence, Pasadena Public Library.

29. Kagan, op. cit.

30. Clapp, *The Shirley Letters* (Santa Barbara, Calif.: Peregrine Smith, 1970); information from State Department of Parks and Recreation and from Plumas County Museum.

31. Correspondence and clippings, Riverside City and County Library.

32. Barbara Lowney, "Lady Bountiful: Margaret Crocker of Sacramento," *California Historical Society Quarterly* 47 (June 1968).

33. Brochures and information, Elmshaven.

34. Herman Kogan, *The First Century: The Chicago Bar Association* (Chicago, Ill.: Rand McNally, 1970); *San Diego Union*, Aug. 16 and Oct. 21, 1957.

35. *Women in American Architecture*, ed. Susan Torre (New York: Whitney Library of Design, 1977).

36. *California Art Research*, no. 7 (San Francisco, Calif.: U.S. Works Progress Administration, 1937); Martin Snipper, *A Survey of Art Work in the City and County of San Francisco* (San Francisco, Calif.: Art Commission, 1975).

37. Caroline Drewes, "100 Years of Minding the Children," *San Francisco Examiner*, July 8, 1979, scene, p. 1.

38. Richey, *Eminent Women*.

39. Ella S. Mighels, *Life and Letters of a Forty-Niner's Daughter*, by Aurora Esmeralda (San Francisco, Calif.: Harr Wagner, 1929).

40. Kenneth R. Goode, *California's Black Pioneers* (Santa Barbara, Calif.: McNally & Loften, 1974); *Ebony*, May 1979.

41. Gertrude Atherton, *My San Francisco* (Indianapolis, Ind.: Bobbs-Merrill, 1946); *San Francisco Chronicle*, Feb. 9, 1956.

42. Elizabeth McClintock, "The Strybing Arboretum," *California Horticultural Journal*, May 9, 1980.

43. Elinor Richey, *Remain to Be Seen: Historic California Houses Open to the Public* (Berkeley, Calif.: Howell-North Books, 1973).

44. Clippings and correspondence, Marin County Historical Society.

45. *The Dominicans of San Rafael* (San Rafael, Calif.: Dominican College of San Rafael, 1941); *San Francisco Chronicle*, March 7, 9, and 10, 1931; clippings and MSS, Dominican Convent Archives.

46. Richey, *Eminent Women*.

47. Diane G. Stelley, "Laudable Ladies of the 1880s," *Dawn for the Orange County Woman*, 8 (Nov. 1981); correspondence, Santa Ana Historical Preservation Society and Santa Ana Public Library.

48. *Original Accounts of the Lone Woman of San Nicolas Island*, ed. Robert Heizer and Albert Elsasser (Ramona, Calif.: Ballena Press, 1973; repr. from Reports of the University of California Archaeological Survey, no. 55).

49. "Dr. and Olive Mann Isbel, Pioneers of 1846," *Ventura County Historical Society Quarterly* 1 (Nov. 1955); correspondence, Blanchard Community Library, Santa Paula.

50. Correspondence, Pajaro Valley Historical Society, Watsonville.

51. "Thoroughly Modern Tillie," *Sacramento Bee*, Feb. 1, 1976.

52. Searles R. Boynton, *The Painter Lady: Grace Carpenter Hudson* (Eureka, Calif.: Interface California Corporation, 1977) and "The Pomo Indian Portraits of Grace Carpenter Hudson," *American West* 14 (Sept.-Oct. 1977); correspondence, Mendocino County Historical Society.

53. Jean Lowey, "Katherine Philips Edson and the California Suffragette Movement, 1919–1920," *California Historical Society Quarterly* 47 (Dec. 1968); correspondence, Save-the-Redwoods League.

54. Clippings from Lark Ellen Home, West Covina.

COLORADO

BOULDER

Converse, Mary, 1872–1962, Navigator

Converse Room, High Altitude Observatory, Astro-Geophysics Building, University of Colorado.

This technical laboratory has given to one of its rooms the name of a technician from Denver, Colorado. Denver, the mile-high city, far from the sea, seems an odd place for navy recruits to study navigation. Even odder, the teacher was a woman, the first woman commissioned as a captain by the U.S. Merchant Marine. Mary Converse qualified herself to command seagoing vessels at the Washington, D.C., Technical College. She served in World War I, and during World War II she won citations from the navy, the merchant marine, and the Office of War Information. From her home in Denver, known as Annapolis Annex, she taught more than twenty-five hundred landlocked naval recruits, appearing before the class dressed in her captain's uniform with its gold stripes on the sleeves.

Converse was noted for other than her naval exploits. In 1947 she was awarded the University of Colorado Recognition Medal, and a musical scholarship was established in her name at Denver University.[1]

Rippon, Mary, 1850–1935, Educator

Mary Rippon Theater, University of Colorado

One of the first women in the country to be made a full professor in a university, Mary Rippon was appointed head of the Department of Germanic Languages and Literature at the University of Colorado in 1881, three years after she became the first woman faculty member here. She held the post for twenty-eight years, serving also as unofficial dean of women until 1901. In 1884 she founded the

Fortnightly Club, Boulder's oldest literary group. In recognition of her role in launching the university's first dramatic productions, this amphitheater, used principally for the summer Colorado Shakespeare festivals, was dedicated to her in 1936.[2]

Sabin, Florence Rena, 1871–1953, Medical Researcher; NAWM

Florence Rena Sabin Building for Research in Cellular Biology, University of Colorado

Colorado honored Florence Rena Sabin by choosing her one of two representative citizens of the state for Statuary Hall in the National Capitol. A book and a microscope, incorporated into the lifesize bronze statue of her by Joy Buba, are symbols of the "little doctor's" devotion to medical research. Her discoveries in cellular biology paved the way for a longer and healthier life for mankind. She earned her M.D. from Johns Hopkins University in 1900 and two years later was appointed the first woman on its faculty. She remained at the university many years, progressing from research fellow to full professor. Then she moved to the Rockefeller Institute of Medical Research in New York, heading a department of cellular studies. She was the first woman elected to the National Academy of Sciences. After she retired she began a new career in Denver, Colorado, q.v., where she used her medical training and experience to reform the state's health laws. See Greeley, CO.[3]

CENTRAL CITY

Brown, Clara, 1800?–1885, Pioneer

Memorial Chair, Opera House, Eureka Street. Plaque, St. James Methodist Episcopal Church, Eureka Street

"Aunt" Clara Brown, a freed slave, came West during the Colorado gold rush and was reputedly the first black woman to settle in Colorado. She grubstaked miners and was well repaid when some struck pay dirt. She had lost a twelve-year-old daughter, Eliza, when the slave auctioneer's gavel divided the family, and for many years she tried to locate the child. She searched in Missouri, Kentucky, and Kansas, and finally, just before Brown's death, Eliza was found in Council Bluffs, Iowa, and reunited with her mother. The plaque in the church notes that before it was built in 1872, "services were held in the home of 'Aunt Clara' Brown." The opera house is open June 1–Aug. 31, Tues.-Sun. 10–5; rest of year, Wed.-Sun. 1–5; adm. See Denver, CO.[4]

Florence Rena Sabin, of Colorado, was a medical researcher at Johns Hopkins University and the Rockefeller Institute. Colorado chose her as one of its representatives in Statuary Hall in the National Capitol, Washington, D.C. The sculptor was Joy Flinsch Buba. Courtesy Architect of the Capitol, Washington, D.C.

Evans, Anne, 1871–1941, Art Patron and Preservationist; NAW

Anne Evans Observation Point. Plaque, Teller House

Anne Evans was a leader in the movement to restore Central City, site of Colorado's first important gold discovery. She was the daughter of John Evans, second territorial governor of Colorado and founder of Denver University. She followed the family interest in art and was in 1904 appointed to the newly created Denver Art Commission, which was given the responsibility of approving all public monuments and paintings in public buildings. It was her interest in indigenous American art that stimulated the Denver Art Museum to emphasize folk art in its collections. She was also a founder and board member of Allied Arts, which provided financial aid to artists, and a member of the Denver Public Library Commission. The observation point is outside the city, overlooking the mountains.[5]

McFarlane, Ida Krus, 1873–1940, Teacher and Preservationist

Hilltop Memorial Cross, Off Spruce Street

Ida Krus McFarlane, chair of the English department at Denver University, was associated with Anne Evans in the movement to restore Central City in the 1930s. The women restored the old opera house and established the annual play festival. The cross that commemorates McFarlane was from the old St. Aloysius Academy. She is also honored by the naming of a residence hall for her at Denver University.[6]

COLORADO SPRINGS

Jackson, Helen Hunt, 1830–1885, Writer and Indian Rights Advocate; NAW

Memorial Rooms, Pioneers' Museum, 215 S. Tejon

The poet Helen Hunt ("H.H.") Jackson came to Colorado Springs in 1873 and two years later married one of its leading citizens, William S. Jackson. It was while she was living here that she first became aware of the injustice suffered by the Ute Indians of Colorado and the Ponca Indians of the Dakota-Nebraska area. After hearing Susette La Flesche, an Omaha Indian, speak on Indian rights, Jackson adopted the cause of the Native Americans and spent the rest of her life fighting for them. She wrote *A Century of Dishonor*, documenting government mistreatment of the Indians, and followed that by a novel, *Ramona*, about the California tribes (see Hemet, CA).

Her home, originally at Kiowa and Weber Streets, was torn down in the

1960s, but three of the rooms, rebuilt, may be seen at the museum, with some of the writer's original furnishings. Helen Hunt Falls, North Cheyenne Canyon, is named for her. Jackson's remains were first buried on Cheyenne Mountain but later removed to Evergreen Cemetery. The museum in the old courthouse is open Tues.-Sat. 10–5, Sun. 1–5.[7]

Taylor, Alice Bemis, 1877–1942, Art Collector and Philanthropist

Colorado Springs Fine Arts Center, 30 W. Dale Street

Alice Bemis Taylor collected southwestern folk art, much of it now in the Taylor Museum for Southwestern Studies, which she founded. She built the Fine Arts Center, and also gave the city a magnificent English-style country mansion, built for the Colorado Springs Day Nursery as a memorial to her father. She founded the Bemis Taylor child guidance clinic and maintained it for a decade. Among other gifts was a pipe organ for the Grace Episcopal church and a trust fund for organ concerts in memory of her husband, investment banker Frederick P. Taylor. Colorado College, for whom she was the first woman trustee, dedicated a building to her. The Fine Arts Center is open Tues.-Sat. 10–5, Sun. 1:30–5.[8]

Van Briggle, Anne Gregory (Ritter), 1868–1929, Artist

Van Briggle Art Pottery, 600 S. 21st Street

The brochure of this pottery describes the clay of Colorado as perpetuating "the skies of Colorado, ablaze with the colors of sunset" and "clothed in the mysteries of earth's darker palette." Anne Gregory Van Briggle, who was art director of the pottery for some years, was the widow of its founder, ceramicist Artus Van Briggle. She was one of the more important women artists of the state. Her second husband was the mining engineer Etienne Ritter. The pottery offers self-guided tours through the factory and exhibition rooms, Mon.-Sat. 8–5.[9]

DENVER

Blue, Virginia Neal, 1910–1970, State Officer and Feminist

Virginia Neal Blue Resource Center for Women, 1800 Pontiac. Memorial Window, State Capitol, E. 14th Avenue and Lincoln Street

Virginia Neal Blue was the first woman to be elected Colorado's state treasurer (in 1966) and made an excellent record. She had a background as a businesswoman (real estate), an educator (member of the board of regents of the University of Colorado), a politician (Republican), and a feminist (Colorado Commission on the Status of Women). The Resource Center was established with funds raised by the American Association of University Women to implement public service programs. A number of centers named for Blue were established in other cities of Colorado.[10]

Bonfils, Helen G. (Somnes), 1889–1972, Newspaperwoman and Theatrical Producer

Wood-Morris-Bonfils House, 707 Washington Street (Private); NR. Bonfils Theater, E. Colfax Avenue and N. Elizabeth Street

Helen G. Bonfils took over her father's control of the *Denver Post* when he died in 1933, eventually becoming chair of the board which guided the paper's change from a conservative to a more liberal stand. She carried on the work of the F. G. Bonfils Foundation and through it established the Bonfils Tumor Clinic and Bonfils Memorial Blood Bank. With her husband, George Somnes, she operated the Bonfils and Somnes Productions, New York City theatrical producers. In 1949 she was named Citizen of the Year by the American Legion Post, and many other honors testified to her dedicated service to the community. The theater is now part of the Denver Center for the Performing Arts.[11]

Bradford, Mary C. Craig, 1862–1938, State Officer and Suffragist

Memorial Tree, Grounds of State Capitol

After 1893, when Colorado won the vote for women, state and national suffrage associations often invited Mary C. Craig Bradford to speak. Not only was she a compelling speaker, but she had been a leader in the winning campaign and she loved to tell of the changes brought about by the woman's vote. "Equal suffrage has not only educated women and elevated the primaries," she said, "but it has given back to the State the services of her best men." In the 1901 national suffrage convention she expressed the wish that all her hearers could go out to Colorado "and see how subtly, yes, and how swiftly, the social transformation is going on. It is the home transforming the State, not the State destroying the home." She herself ran for public office and won; she was a county superintendent of schools and between 1913 and 1927 held the post of state superintendent of public instruction.[12]

Brooks, Nona Lovell, 1861–1945, Church Founder

Divine Science Church, E. 14th Avenue and Williams Street

Nona Lovell Brooks became interested in mental healing and trained for several months at the Home School of Divine Science in San Francisco, California, where she was ordained a minister in 1898. By 1918, when she became an honorary doctor of divine science, she had a large following and founded her own church, a college, and a monthly magazine. Denver's first woman pastor and religious founder, she remained active in her chosen work until her death.[13]

Brown, Clara, 1800?–1885, Pioneer

Memorial Window, North Wing, State Capitol

Aunt Clara Brown, born into slavery, was given her freedom after her owner died, and she set off for Colorado, where she heard that gold had been discovered. She worked as a cook for a wagon train. She settled in Central City, Colorado, q.v., where she worked at the scrub board, accumulated savings, invested in real estate, and grubstaked miners. She had time to give of herself, and she won the love and respect of the community. In Denver she was the first black woman member of the Colorado Pioneer Association.[14]

Brown, Margaret Tobin, 1867–1932, Heroine

Molly Brown House Museum, 1340 Pennsylvania Street; NR

Margaret (Molly) Tobin Brown was clerking in a store in Leadville, Colorado, when she met and married James J. Brown, who made a fortune in the mines. The newly rich Browns were snubbed by Denver society, so Molly went to New York and Europe to become refined. She studied dramatic technique in France, where she staged a performance of *L'Aiglon*. She came home in 1912, sailing on the S.S. *Titanic*, which hit an iceberg and sank, with tremendous loss of life. Molly helped to row a lifeboat and kept up the spirits of the shivering and terrified passengers by singing. When reporters asked about her survival techniques, she said, "Oh, I'm unsinkable!" She returned to Denver an international heroine. Her story was written as *The Unsinkable Mrs. Brown* (1956), made into a musical and then a movie.

The Brown home, built in the late 1880s and named the House of Lions for the sculptured beasts and sphinxes that adorn it, is now a museum operated by Historic Denver. Guided tours, Apr.-Sept., Tues.-Sat. 10–4, Sun 12–4; rest of year, Tues.-Sat. 10–3, Sun. 12–3; adm.[15]

Decker, Sarah Platt, 1852–1912, Clubwoman; NAW

Decker Library, 1501 S. Logan; Denver Historic Landmark. Platt Park, 1500 S. Grant

Elected president of the General Federation of Women's Clubs in 1902, Sarah Platt Decker made her views clear in her inaugural address: "Ladies, you have chosen me as your leader. Well, I have an important piece of news to give you. Dante is dead. He has been dead for several centuries, and I think it is time we dropped the study of his Inferno and turned our attention to our own." She guided the federation and the Woman's Club of Denver away from literary discussions into civic reform. She was proud of the part women's clubs took in establishing Mesa Verde and other national parks. Her activities were not confined to club work; she was on the Colorado Board of Charities and Corrections, was a member of the state Civil Service Commission, and presided over the Denver Civic Federation. Before her death she was spoken of as a candidate for the U.S. Senate—years before nationwide woman suffrage had been achieved. The library is a memorial to her third husband, Westbrook S. Decker, and the park to her second, James H. Platt.[16]

Griffith, Emily, 1880?–1947, Educator; NAW

Emily Griffith Opportunity School, 1250 Welton. Emily Griffith Boys Home, 1260 Franklin. Stained-Glass Portrait, State Capital. Drinking Fountain, Civic Center

In September 1916 a sign appeared over the doors of the old Longfellow Building in Denver: "Public Opportunity School. For All Who Wish to Learn." Within a week, 1400 persons had signed up to take the free day and evening courses in this new type of school. It was the realization of a dream for Emily Griffith, who taught public school in a poor neighborhood. There she became aware of the need to offer educational opportunity not just to youngsters but to all who wished to learn. This included people who worked during the day and pupils who wanted vocational skills. When Griffith resigned as principal of the Opportunity School seventeen years later, there were 8,670 students enrolled and the school facilities covered an entire city block.

Griffith herself had little formal education, yet she was a popular and effective teacher and a good administrator, sensitive to the changes in needs and opportunities over the years. She was appointed deputy state superintendent of schools in 1904 and again in 1910 and was given honorary degrees from several colleges. Her ideas came not from formalizations of educational psychology but from her warm appreciation of the worth of every person and the value of education in opening up a world of choices to the student. In 1934 the Denver school board renamed the Opportunity School to honor her.

Jacobs, Frances Wisebart, 1843–1892, Social Worker; NAW

Stained-Glass Portrait, Dome of State Capitol

Denver in its early years faced unusual health problems due to indigent health seekers, many afflicted with tuberculosis. It also had welfare problems because of the many disappointed and unemployed who had come seeking wealth. Frances Wisebart Jacobs, soon after she came to Denver in 1874, began to work among the poor. She served as president of the Hebrew Benevolent Ladies Aid Society, then as an officer in the Ladies Relief Society. She distributed relief funds herself, making many visits daily to needy families. She always brought a bar of soap with her, for she claimed that a household that needed food generally needed soap. In 1887 she helped form the Charity Organization Society, a federation of existing relief agencies, for the purpose of conducting joint fund drives. She then served as its secretary until her death. She was known as Colorado's Mother of Charities. On one of her trips to a needy family she caught cold which developed into pneumonia and caused her death at the age of forty-nine. In 1900 the state honored sixteen of its pioneers with portraits in the capitol dome; she was the first woman chosen.

Moore, Dora, c. 1855–1938, School Administrator

Dora Moore Elementary School, E. 9th Avenue and Corona Street; NR

When Dora Moore retired in 1929, after teaching school all her life—thirty-five years as principal of the Corona Street School—men and women who had been her pupils initiated a movement to have the name of the school changed to honor her. On the day when she saw her name engraved above the door of the school, she spoke of her love of teaching. "From these children I gain vitality and enthusiasm and hope for each day's work. What I have gained from my long service as teacher is an ever-deepening love of and faith in humanity, especially that portion of humanity we call youth. There is nothing discouraging about their attitude toward personal freedom. They know the way and will not be deceived."[17]

Sabin, Florence Rena, 1871–1953, Medical Researcher; NAWM

Statue, Colorado State Department of Health Building, 4210 E. 11th Street. Plaque, Denver General Hospital, W. 8th Avenue and Cherokee. Sabin School, 3050 S. Vrain

After a distinguished career in medical research at Johns Hopkins University in Baltimore, Maryland, and the Rockefeller Institute in New York City, Florence Rena Sabin retired to live with her sister in Denver. She was appointed to a position, intended to be honorary, on the Postwar Planning Commission to plan public health regulations. She took the appointment seriously and launched into a full-scale study of the state's health. She found shocking conditions: high infant mortality, high incidence of preventible diseases, raw sewage in the streams, almost no control of milk production. She stumped the state to inform the voters about health hazards, lobbied the legislature, and managed to get four bills passed to correct the worst conditions. She became manager of Denver's Division of Health and Welfare, a position she resigned only at the age of eighty. The statue is a replica of the one representing the state of Colorado in Statuary Hall in the National Capitol. See Boulder and Greeley, CO.[18]

FORT COLLINS

Stone, Elizabeth Hickok Robbins, 1801–1895, Pioneer

Aunty Stone Cabin, Museum Courtyard, Lincoln Park

Elizabeth Hickok Robbins Stone was the first white woman to become a permanent resident in Fort Collins, arriving in 1864 with her second husband, Lewis Stone. The cabin was used as a mess hall for the soldiers of Camp Collins, with Stone as cook. After the military post was disbanded in 1867, Stone, then a widow, ran the cabin as a hotel. According to a local historian, "Mrs. Stone used to entertain all the ministers that came along in the early days and was friendly to all the religious denominations, giving liberally of her means to their support." She was an organizer of a local Woman's Christian Temperance Union. She also expanded her business activities, built a flour mill, and later started a brickyard. The cabin has survived five moves, the last in 1975. It is open Tues.-Sat. 10–5, Sun. 12–5.[19]

GOLDEN

Cabrini, Saint Frances Xavier (Mother Cabrini), 1850–1917, Churchwoman; NAW

Mother Cabrini Shrine, Off I–70

In 1946 Frances Xavier Cabrini became the first American citizen to achieve sainthood. She was born in Italy and sent to the United States by the pope in 1889 to work among the Italian immigrants in New York City. Her work became international in scope when she opened schools in Central and South America, then in a number of European cities. She founded the Missionary Sisters of the Sacred Heart. She was naturalized in 1909 and the following year was made superior general of her order for life. She was in Denver, Colorado, in 1902 to establish a school. The shrine is a mile and a half from exit 259 of the freeway. It is open daily 6:30 A.M. to 8:30 P.M.

GREELEY

Sabin, Florence Rena, 1871–1953, Medical Researcher; NAWM

Sabin Hall, University of Northern Colorado

A residence hall built in 1936 was named in honor of Florence Rena Sabin, Colorado's most distinguished daughter. She was born in Central City and moved to Denver when she was four. Because her mother died when she was young, many of her early years were spent with relatives in Chicago, Illinois, and at school in New England. She returned to Denver after graduating from Smith College and taught mathematics for two years while she saved money to pay for a medical education. Her sister Mary and her father continued to live in Denver and she often visited them, although her work kept her in Baltimore, Maryland, and in New York City until 1938, when she retired and came back to live with her sister. She received numerous honors and awards throughout her life for her scientific studies. See Boulder and Denver, CO. [20]

LEADVILLE

Tabor, Elizabeth McCourt Doe, 1854–1935, Mine Owner

Matchless Mine Cabin, E. 7th Street Extended

Leadville was one of the richest mining centers during Colorado's early days. Horace Tabor was one of the silver millionaires who took a fortune out of the mines. When he struck it rich, he abandoned his wife of many years, Augusta, and took up with a pretty young girl who, to the townsfolk, was a ''shameless hussy,'' Elizabeth McCourt Doe Tabor. He divorced Augusta and married Baby Doe. They lived in luxury until the country went off the silver standard. He died almost bankrupt, cautioning her to hang onto the Matchless Mine, for he was sure it would once again be worth working. She hung onto it, in extreme poverty, and at the end was found in a cabin at the closed mine, frozen to death. Her rags-to-riches and riches-to-rags life inspired an opera, *The Ballad of Baby Doe*. The cabin is open May 30–Labor Day, daily 9–5; adm.

MANCOS

McClurg, Virginia Donaghé, 1857–1931, and Lucy Evelyn Peabody, 1865–1934, Clubwomen and Preservationists

Mesa Verde National Park

Virginia Donaghé McClurg first visited Mesa Verde as a young woman in 1882, guided by the Wetherills, ranchers who first discovered the spectacular Indian cliff dwellings. Four years later she organized her own expedition into the valley, where she is credited with the discovery of Balcony House. For years thereafter she lobbied and lectured for the protection of the ruins, which were being vandalized by treasure hunters. At last she persuaded the Denver Woman's Club to organize the Colorado Cliff Dwellings Association, which McClurg served as regent general from 1895 to 1930. The association not only persuaded the government to purchase the land from the Ute Indians and set it aside as a national monument but carried out negotiations with the Indian chiefs and built a road into the area.

Lucy Evelyn Peabody became a rival of McClurg when she insisted that the park be national instead of state. She then became the leading protagonist for the park and was known as the Mother of the Mesa Verde. For a while Square Tower House was called Peabody House in her honor.

After McClurg's death the women of Colorado hoped to erect a bronze plaque to her memory in Balcony House, but the Park Service ruled against placing markers in the ruins. A few mementoes of McClurg are preserved at the Pioneers' Museum in Colorado Springs. The park is open all year, on a limited basis in winter; adm. by permit.[21]

MEEKER

Meeker, Josephine, c. 1857–c. 1882, Indian Captive

Marker, Off State 64, Site of Meeker Massacre

Josephine Meeker was the daughter of Nathan Meeker, agent at the Ute White River Agency. An Oberlin College graduate, she taught a few of the Indians and was much more sympathetic with them than with her father's heavy-handed efforts to civilize them. On September 19, 1879, the Utes massacred all the men at the agency, including Nathan, and took into captivity his wife, Josephine, and the only other woman there, Flora Ellen Price, with her two children. Twenty-three days later, responding to pleas by the wife of Chief Ouray, the Indians returned the captives. An official investigation took place at the Meeker home in Greeley, Colorado, during which the three women reluctantly admitted to having been "outraged" by their captives. The result was just what the mining interests had wished for: the Utes were driven off their gold-rich territory. Josephine, given a secretarial job in Washington, D.C., as indemnification, died there three years later. Mementoes of the family are in the Meeker Museum in Greeley, a town founded by Nathan Meeker in 1869.[22]

MONTROSE

Chipeta, 1843–1924, Ute Heroine

Grave, Ouray Memorial Park

Chipeta was supposed to have persuaded the renegade Ute Indians to release the Meeker women after their capture in 1879. She was the wife of Chief Ouray, and in her youth was called the laughing maiden of the Utes. In cold fact, her life represents the tragedy of the Indians. After happy and peaceful years she was forced to move to the Ute Reservation in Utah, where she died poor and blind. In 1925 her body was brought from Utah to this spot, where she and Chief Ouray had lived. The Ute Memorial Site is listed in the National Register; the Chief Ouray State Historical Monument was erected in 1949. A Ute Indian

Museum, administered by the Colorado Historical Society, displays the history of the Utes. It is open Memorial Day–Labor Day, daily 9–5; adm. [23]

NOTES

In addition to the sources mentioned below, I have had correspondence with the Mamie Doud Eisenhower Library in Broomfield and the National Park Service. The Western History Department of the Denver Public Library has supplied a great deal of information.

1. Elinor Bluemel, *One Hundred Years of Colorado Women* (Denver, Colo.: 1973).

2. *Women's History Sources*, ed. Andrea Hinding and others (New York: R. R. Bowker Co., 1979).

3. Elinor Richey, *Eminent Women of the West (Berkeley, Calif.: Howell-North Books, 1975); Current Biography*, 1945 and 1954; correspondence, Denver Public Library.

4. Kathleen Bruyn, *Aunt Clara Brown, Story of a Black Pioneer* (Boulder, Colo.: Pruett Publishing Co., 1970).

5. Bluemel, op. cit.

6. James Alexander Semple, *Representative Women of Colorado* (Denver, Colo.: Alexander Art Publishing Co., 1911).

7. Dolores Stark, "The Historic Jackson House," pamphlet (Colorado Springs, 1969); Virginia McConnell, " 'H.H.,' Colorado, and the Indian Problem," *Journal of the West* 12 (Apr. 1973); correspondence, Pioneers' Museum.

8. *Denver Post*, June 23, 1942; *Rocky Mountain News*, June 26, 1942; correspondence, Denver Public Library and Colorado Springs Fine Arts Center.

9. Correspondence and brochure, Van Briggle Art Pottery; correspondence, Colorado Springs Fine Arts Center.

10. Bluemel, op. cit.; *Colorado Hidden Heroines* (Denver, Colo.: Girl Scouts Mile Hi Council, 1975).

11. Bluemel, op. cit.; *New York Times*, June 7, 1972.

12. Bluemel, op. cit.; *History of Woman Suffrage*, vol. 4, ed. Susan B. Anthony and Ida B. Harper (Rochester: Susan B. Anthony, 1902), pp. 282–83, and scattered references in vols. 4 and 5.

13. Bluemel, op. cit.; *Women of the West*, ed. Max Binheim (Los Angeles, Calif.: Publishers' Press, 1928); Semple, op. cit.

14. *Denver Post*, Jan. 19, 1977.

15. Grace Ernestine Ray, *Wily Women of the West* (San Antonio, Tex.: Naylor Co., 1972); Caroline Bancroft, *The Unsinkable Mrs. Brown* (Denver, Colo.: Golden Press, 1956).

16. *From Parlor to Prison: Five American Suffragists*, ed. Sherna Gluck (New York: Vantage Books, 1976).

17. Clippings and correspondence, Western History Department, Denver Public Library.

18. Elinor Richey, op. cit.

19. Correspondence and clippings, Pioneer Museum, Fort Collins.

20. Correspondence, University of Northern Colorado.

21. *Women of the West*; Virginia McClurg, "The Making of Mesa Verde into a National

Park,'' *Colorado Magazine* 7 (Nov. 1930); Mary S. Logan, *The Part Taken By Women in American History* (New York: Perry-Nalle, 1972).

22. Marshall Sprague, ''The Bloody End of Meeker's Utopia,'' *American Heritage* 8 (Oct. 1957).

23. Bluemel, op. cit.; correspondence, Colorado Historical Society, Ute Indian Museum.

HAWAII

EWA (OAHU)

Burke, Katherine Macintosh, 1861–1938, Teacher

Katherine Burke Building (Administration Building), Ewa Elementary School

Katherine Macintosh Burke was principal of Ewa School from 1919 to 1927. When she died, she left eight thousand dollars to have a statue of President Abraham Lincoln placed at the school to serve as an inspiration to the pupils. Avard T. Fairbanks made the life-size bronze statue of Lincoln the Frontiersman which stands on the school campus, erected in 1944. The building was named in Burke's honor in 1967.[1]

HANA (MAUI)

Kaahumanu, d. 1832, Queen; NAW, NWH[2]

Plaque on Boulder, Ocean Side of Kauiki Head

Kaahumanu was the favorite wife of Kamehameha I, who unified the islands. After his death she married King Kaumualii, the ruler of Kauai, the last island to hold out, thus peaceably completing the unification. It was Kaahumanu who broke the ancient religious custom by which men and women were forbidden to eat together, and some foods, such as pork, bananas, coconuts, or certain fish, were denied to women. She and Keopuolani, mother of the young King Liholiho, in 1819 persuaded the king to break the taboo. He openly ate with the women at a public banquet, and when no terrible event followed, the king began toppling the old idols and disregarding the ancient religious customs. When the American missionaries came to the islands the following year, Kaahumanu became friendly with them, learned to read and write, and adopted Christianity.

She was born in a cave at this site, the birthdate variously given as 1768, 1773, or 1777. See Honolulu and Wailuku, HI.

HILO (HAWAII)

Kanaka'ole, Edith, 1913–1979, Hawaiian Cultural Leader; NWH

Edith Kanaka'ole Hall, University of Hawaii

The music building is named for one of Hawaii's "Living Treasures"—an expert in Hawaiian dance, a chanter, singer, poet, and composer. Born at a time when she saw the Hawaiian culture and language on the decline, Edith Kanaka'ole immersed herself in their study. In 1953 she founded a dance school where the ancient and modern hula, as well as other Polynesian dances, were taught. In the 1950s she toured western Canada, the U.S. mainland, and the Orient giving concerts. From 1973 to 1979 she taught at the University of Hawaii. Only a few months before her death she was given the Governor's Award of Distinction for Cultural Leadership.

Liliuokalani, 1838–1917, Queen; NAW, NWH

Liliuokalani Garden, Banyan Drive

Lydia Kamakaeha, destined to be the last monarch of Hawaii, was adopted at birth by Abner Paki and his wife, Konia, granddaughter of Kamehameha I. She was educated by American missionaries at the Royal School, then married an American trader, John Dominis, governor of the islands of Oahu and Maui. In 1891, on the death of her brother David Kalakaua, she succeeded to the throne of Hawaii as Queen Liliuokalani. Kalakaua had been forced by the American traders and ministers to accept a constitution that weakened the power of the crown. His sister was determined to restore the monarchy to its former prestige, but when she proclaimed a new constitution in 1893, a strong group of residents took possession of the government and applied for annexation to the United States. See Honolulu, HI.

HONOLULU (OAHU)

Kamehameha Schools, Kapalama Heights

The Kamehameha Schools were established by Bernice Bishop, q.v., who left her property to establish two schools, one for girls and one for boys of Hawaiian ancestry. Such children still have first preference. The administration building is named for Bishop. Many of the other buildings perpetuate the names of royal Hawaiian women.

Classrooms are named for Chiefess Kapiolani (c. 1781–1841, NAW—not to be confused with the later Queen Kapiolani). She was one of the first converts to Christianity after the missionaries arrived in the islands and is said to have changed from a dissolute and imperious woman to a model of decorum. In 1824 she walked the hundred miles from her home on the Kona coast to the volcanoes. The goddess Pele supposedly resided in the crater and caused its eruptions. Despite the pleas of her fearful attendants, Kapiolani went some five hundred feet into Kilau Crater, refusing to make the usual sacrifices of berries and proclaiming that the power of the Christian God would protect her. When no fiery bursts or eruptions followed, Pele's power toppled from superstition into folklore.

Queen Keopuolani (1778?–1823) was the highest ranking wife of Kamehameha I and mother of his three surviving royal children. After the king died she began to break some of the taboos and with Kaahumanu and her son Liholiho she ate meals with men and ate the foods heretofore forbidden to women. She accepted western ways and was baptized a Christian just before she died. The conference center bears her name.

Princess Nahienaena (c. 1815–1836) was caught in the cross-currents of change that began at the death of her father, Kamehameha I. She was the daughter of Keopuolani, who sent her to the missionaries to be educated. The chiefs wanted her to marry Kauikeaouli, heir to the throne (he would reign as Kamehameha II), but as he was her brother, this shocked the missionaries who were in charge of her education. In 1834 the marriage took place, but it was not recognized by the missionaries or by the court. She died shortly after bearing a child in 1836.

Princess Ruth Keelikolani (1826–1883) lost her mother at birth and grew up under the kindly Queen Kaahumanu. She was too old to attend the Royal School when it was established for the chiefs' children, and although she learned English she chose to speak Hawaiian and never converted to Christianity. In 1881 the volcano Mauna Loa threatened to destroy Hilo and Ruth was sent to Hawaii to appease Pele. She prayed and sacrificed to the goddess, and the lava flow stopped, making her a heroine. Hawaiian women were noted for their size, and Princess Keelikolani grew to a fearsome four hundred pounds. She inherited a very large estate, which she willed to her cousin Bernice Pauahi Bishop. The swimming pool is named for her.

Princess Victoria Kamamalu (1838–1866) was in 1850 officially voted the heir of Queen Kaahumanu, giving her title to many acres throughout the islands. Though an heir to the throne, she never occupied it, dying unmarried at twenty-seven. A government office building at 1010 Richards Street and a playground on Vineyard Boulevard and Queen Emma Street are also named for her.

A dormitory bears the name of High Chiefess Kinau (c. 1805–1839), coruler during the reign of Kamehameha II. She was one of the earliest pupils of the American missionaries, became a Christian, and was much influenced by Kaahumanu, who named Kinau her successor. She was responsible for many reform programs. A state government office building, Kinau Hale, at 1250 Punchbowl Street, also perpetuates her name.

The dining hall is named for Queen Kalama (c. 1820–1870), the wife of

Kamehameha III. The first Iolani Palace was built for her. Still young when her husband died, she retired from court circles and developed some of her lands as a sugar plantation. She was a good manager and at the time of her death held a large estate in Oahu. She established a collection of exotic grasses, ferns, and palms, still to be seen at the Foster Botanic Garden, 18 N. Vineyard Boulevard.

High Chiefess Kekauluohi (1794–1845) was coruler with Kamehameha III. Although he already had several wives, she was married to him at fifteen. She was kept in a guarded house where she studied ancient arts and customs under teachers who knew the old proverbs, legends, and songs. After the arrival of the missionaries, she was converted to Christianity. She is remembered for her famous edict of religious toleration, issued in 1839 soon after she had come to power. A dormitory bears her name.

Princess Kaiulani (1875–1899) might have been Queen of Hawaii had not Liliuokalani been deposed. She was groomed for the position and sent to school in London. On August 12, 1898, the Stars and Stripes replaced the Hawaiian flag over Iolani Palace, and the princess had no throne. She presided with dignity over ceremonial functions and worked for the Red Cross and the Hawaiian Relief Society. Mourners believed her death at twenty-five was caused by a broken heart. Besides the dormitory here, a school, a hotel, and Kaiulani Square perpetuate her name.[3]

Allyn, Edna Isabel, 1861–1927, Librarian; NWH

Children's Room, State Library, 478 S. King Street

Edna Isabel Allyn was chief librarian of the Library of Hawaii, where she served for twenty years. When she began her work here in 1907 it was the small private Honolulu Library and Reading Room Association, which had itself developed out of an 1879 Honolulu Workingman's Reading Room Association. She placed small depositories of books in community centers, schools, and homes in the other islands, which some years later formed a territorial and then a state library system. Her special interest was in children's books, and the children's room completed in 1929 was named for her.

Bilger, Lenore, 1893–1975, Chemistry Professor; NWH

Bilger Hall, University of Hawaii

Atomic energy, chemotherapy, and the flouridation of water were among the topics on which Lenore Bilger lectured or wrote while teaching chemistry at the university. She came to Hawaii first in 1925 as dean of women. A few years later she married Earl M. Bilger, a biochemist. In 1943 she was head of the department of chemistry and when she retired in 1954 she was made professor emerita. In 1959 the biochemical laboratory, which she had planned, was formally dedicated in honor of both Lenore and Earl Bilger.

Bishop, Bernice Pauahi, 1831–1884, Princess; NAW, NWH

Bernice Bishop Museum, 1525 Bernice Street; NR

Bernice Pauahi Bishop was the last direct descendant of Kamehameha I, and before her death she inherited the landed estates of the chiefly family, as well as those of her parents, Abner and Konia Paki. Bishop was given to another high chiefess at birth, according to custom, and returned to her parents at the age of seven. The Pakis, meanwhile, had become the adoptive parents of Lydia Kamakaeha—later Queen Liliuokalani—and the two were brought up as sisters, both attending the Royal School. When Bishop married Charles Bishop, American collector of customs, she elected not to take part in political life. She left her property to establish the Kamehameha Schools, where a building is named for her. A building on the Punahou School campus was also given her name. Her husband established the museum, devoted to Hawaiian and Polynesian ethnology, as a memorial. It is open Mon.-Sat. 9–5, Sun. 12–5.

Chamberlain, Maria Patton, 1803–1880, Missionary; NWH

Chamberlain House, 553 S. King Street

Maria Patton Chamberlain arrived in Hawaii on the *Parthian* in 1828, one of four single women who came to the islands as missionaries, and was assigned to a mission in Lahaina. She married Levi Chamberlain, a missionary who had preceded her to Hawaii. Chamberlain House, built of coral blocks, was completed several years later. It became the center of mission activity, where missionaries from the neighbor islands and mission stations came to transact business and enjoy each other's company. This was to be Chamberlain's home for the rest of her life. After 1849 she was a widow, supporting herself by hard work in the mission and taking in a few boarders. Besides her own children she often cared for motherless and orphaned children of other missionaries.

Chamberlain House is one of three mission houses, where some of the first Protestant missionaries lived. It is now the headquarters of the Hawaiian Mission Children's Society, which maintains the mission houses as a museum. It is open daily 9–4; closed some holidays; adm. The library is open Mon.-Fri. 10–4.

Cooke, Anna Charlotte Rice, 1853–1934, Art Patron; NAW, NWH

Honolulu Academy of Arts, 900 S. Beretania Street; NR

Anna Charlotte Rice Cooke was born in Hawaii, the daughter of American missionaries. She was brought up on a sugar plantation in Kauai, where her father was manager. She married Charles Cooke, son of another missionary couple who were close friends of the Rices. He was a successful businessman, and they were able to travel extensively in Europe and the Orient, bringing back many art objects. They added to their collections Hawaiian paintings and sculpture. They founded the Aquarium at Waikiki, Rice Hall and the Cooke Library at Punahou School, and established the Charles M. and Anna C. Cooke Trust. Charles died in 1909. In her years of widowhood Anna planned the art museum, which was built on the site of the small frame house in which the Cookes had lived for years. It opened its doors in 1927. It is open Tues.-Sat. 10–4:30, Sun. 2–5; closed some holidays. Tours Tues.-Sat. at 11, Thurs. and Sun. at 2.

Cooke, Juliette Montague, 1812–1896, Missionary Educator; NWH

Tablet, Kawaiahao Church, 957 Punchbowl Street

Amos Starr and Juliette Montague Cooke were selected by the high chiefs in 1840 to assume responsibility for the education of the highest ranking children of the islands. They had arrived in Hawaii in 1837 as newlyweds. What became known as the Royal School began with six uninhibited students, none used to restrictions of any kind, all of them bringing their attendants to school with them. The couple ran the school for eleven years, retiring after Bernice Pauahi married. The memorial tablet contains the names of the sixteen pupils, including two queens and four kings. It was placed in the church on the centennial of Cooke's birth and unveiled by Queen Liliuokalani. Montague Hall on the Punahou School campus is named for Cooke and her daughter, Juliette Atherton.[4]

The Kawaiahao church, "the Westminster Abbey of Hawaii," was built by converts under the direction of the first missionaries. It was the royal chapel for Hawaiian monarchs for two decades and still has services in English and Hawaiian. It is in the National Register and is open Mon.-Sat. 8:30–4, Sun. services at 10:30.

Dillingham, Louise Gaylord, 1885–1964, Social and Civic Leader; NWH

Memorial Fountain, Kapiolani Park

For most of her fifty-three years of marriage, Louise Gaylord Dillingham, the wife of Walter Dillingham, was Hawaii's hostess without portfolio, entertaining scores of official visitors at their home, La Pietra, below Diamond Head. She was an outspoken activist on behalf of parks, art, music, and civic betterment. She organized the Friends of the Honolulu Academy of Arts to purchase outstanding paintings for the gallery, and she left her furnishings to it. She was a founding member of the League of Women Voters in Honolulu and was on the Board of Parks and Recreation for thirty years. The Dillinghams willed La Pietra to Punahou School. It was sold by Punahou and became the Hawaii School for Girls at La Pietra. After her death friends contributed funds for the fountain in her memory.

Earhart, Amelia, 1897–1937, Aviator; NAW

Tablet, Diamond Head Road

Amelia Earhart, the plucky aviator from Kansas, made the first solo flight from Hawaii to the American mainland in January 1935. She landed in Oakland, California, eighteen hours and fifteen minutes after takeoff, to the cheers of enthusiastic admirers. The public loved the tall, tomboyish woman with tousled blond hair, a flashing smile, and an unaffected manner. There was general consternation, disbelief, and then mourning when she disappeared while on a world flight in 1937. Extensive searches never found a trace of her plane or the pilot and copilot.

Emma, 1836–1885, Queen; NAW, NWH

Queen Emma Summer Palace, 2913 Pali Highway; HABS, NR. Queen Emma Center, 224 Queen Emma Square. Queen's Medical Center, 1301 Punchbowl Street

Young Emma Rooke, of mixed Hawaiian and English ancestry, attended the Royal School, where she learned English and the ideals of morality of the New England missionaries. After she married Kamehameha IV she joined him in bringing Anglican Episcopalianism to Hawaii. She visited England, following the death of Kamehameha, to raise funds for the education of native Hawaiian girls. There she met and became a close friend of Queen Victoria, who wrote of Emma in her diary: "nothing could be nicer or more dignified than her manner." The two widowed queens corresponded until Emma's death.

The hospital named for her opened in 1860 as the first public hospital in Hawaii. She acquired the summer palace in 1857, the year after her marriage, and lived there after her husband's death. The house is open daily 9–4; closed holidays; adm.

Kaahumanu, c. 1772–1832, Queen; NAW, NWH

Judiciary Building, Punchbowl and Halekauwila Street. Kaahumanu School, 1141 Kinau Street

Kaahumanu was one of the most powerful persons in Hawaii during the period when it was emerging from an isolated island kingdom. She led in breaking some of the ancient taboos and was one of the first of the chiefly class to accept the missionaries' teachings. She promulgated what amounted to the islands' first code of laws, forbidding murder, theft, and violence, providing for observance of the Sabbath, and calling for general education. See Hana and Wailuku, HI.

Kapiolani, 1834–1899, Queen and Philanthropist; NWH

Kapiolani Park, from Kapahulu Avenue to Diamond Head Street. Queen Kapiolani Rose Garden, 3625 Leahi Avenue. Kapiolani Women's and Children's Center, 1319 Punahou Street

Kapiolani was the wife of David Kalakaua, who came to the throne in 1874. One of her great concerns was for the children of the Hawaiian race. She traveled from island to island collecting donations for the establishment of a maternity home, which opened in 1890, the forerunner of the women's and children's center. The queen also sponsored the Kapiolani Home for girls in Kakaako, to care for nonleprous children of leprous parents. Kapiolani went with her sister-in-law, Liliuokalani, to England for Queen Victoria's golden jubilee. In America she was the guest of President Grover Cleveland. After Liliuokalani became ruler, the widowed Kapiolani lived quietly at Waikiki. Her home was at the spot now occupied by the Hyatt Regency Hotel.

Liliuokalani, 1838–1917, Queen; NAW, NWH

Washington Place, 320 S. Beretania Street (Private); HABS, NR.
Iolani Palace State Monument, 364 S. King Street; HABS, NR.
Statue, State Capitol Grounds

Liliuokalani, the last monarch of Hawaii, was deposed in 1893 and imprisoned in her former royal mansion, Iolani Palace (see Hilo, HI). After the United States annexed the islands in 1898, the ex-queen was allowed to live in her home, Washington Place, on a government pension. Bitter and angry at her treatment, she gradually mellowed and became popular as a link between Hawaii's past and present. She composed songs, including the famous "Aloha-Oe," and worked on the epic Hawaiian creation chant *Kumulipo*. A children's center at 1300 Halona Street, established with funds she left, was named for her. She also established the Liliuokalani Trust for the benefit of orphaned and destitute children. Liliuokalani Gardens, School Street and Waikahalulu Lane, was also given her name. In 1982 a bronze statue of her was erected on the grounds of the capitol, the work of Marianne Pineda, dedicated as "a symbol of the character and spirit of Hawaii." Washington Place is now the executive mansion for the state of Hawaii, not open to the public. Iolani Palace is open for guided tours, Wed.-Sat. 9–2:15; closed holidays; reservations required; adm.

Rice, Mary Sophia Hyde, 1816–1911, Missionary and Civic Leader; NWH

Mother Rice Preschool and Kindergarten, 2707 S. King Street

Mary Sophia Hyde Rice was born and brought up near the Seneca Indian Reservation in New York State, where her father was a missionary to the Senecas.

In 1840 she married William H. Rice, also a New York native. They sailed almost immediately for Hawaii, under auspices of the American Board of Commissioners of Foreign Missions. They began their work in Hana, and several years later were assigned as teachers to Punahou School. It was established in 1841 for the education of mission children. "Mother Rice" was much loved by the children and by the other teachers. She had five children of her own, three born at Punahou. Anna Charlotte Cooke, q.v., was her youngest. After ten years at Punahou, William accepted a position as manager of a sugar plantation on Kauai.

In 1917 the Mother Rice Playground was dedicated to her memory. It had been established near a stone church close to Punahou School. The playground then became the site of the preschool and kindergarten still bearing her name.

Smyth, Mabel Leilani, 1892–1936, Public Health Nurse; NWH

Mabel Smyth Memorial Building, Beretania and Punchbowl Streets

A native of Honolulu, daughter of a Celtic father and Polynesian mother, Mabel Leilani Smyth became a recognized leader among women of Hawaiian blood. She trained at the Springfield Hospital Training School for Nurses in Massachusetts and on her return to Honolulu became the first director of nurses at Palama Settlement. For nine years, up until the time of her death at forty-three, she was supervising nurse of the territorial health services, known as the Florence Nightingale of Hawaii. She was active in many organizations in the field of public health. The memorial building was opened in 1941. It includes an auditorium and headquarters of several medical and nurses associations.

Tennent, Madge, 1889–1972, Artist; NWH

Tennent Art Foundation Gallery, 201–203 Prospect Street

Madge Tennent's warm, understanding interpretations of the native Hawaiians she painted are so vital and glowing that it has been said that even if they vanished as a race, the people would live forever in her art. She saw the Hawaiians as "having descended from gods of heroic proportion." She and her husband, Hugh Tennent, established the gallery in 1954. It displays her work and also that of other island artists whom she encouraged.

KAAAWA (OAHU)

Swanzy, Julie Judd, 1860–1941, Philanthropist and Civic Leader; NWH

Swanzy Park, Kamehameha Highway

Julie Judd Swanzy was born at Sweet Home, her grandparents' home in Nuuanu Valley. Her grandparents were Gerrit Parmele Judd and Laura Fish Judd, early missionaries to Hawaii and part of the court circle of Kamehameha III. In 1887 she married Francis Mills Swanzy in Honolulu, Hawaii. She gave some of her beachfront property at Kaaawa for use as a public park, now called Swanzy Park. She was a regent of the Daughters of Hawaii, which encouraged cultural and historical preservation. They were instrumental in saving Queen Emma's Summer Palace in Honolulu, as well as Hulihee, a royal vacation retreat in Kona, both now museums important to Hawaiian history.

KALAUPAPA (MOLOKAI)

Cope, Barbara (Mother Marianne), 1838–1918, Missionary Nurse; NWH

Monument, Kalaupapa Leprosy Settlement; NHL

Barbara Cope (Mother Marianne) nursed lepers at Kalaupapa from 1888 until her death. Born in Germany (her name also appears as Kopp or Koob), she first came to Honolulu in 1883 with several sisters of the order of Saint Francis from Syracuse, New York. She and two other nuns were the first women to be stationed at Kalaupapa, and they carried on some of the work of Father Damien, who died of leprosy just six months after their arrival. Robert Louis Stevenson visited Molokai and wrote a poem dedicated to Mother Marianne. The monument was erected by the people of the settlement.

WAILUKU (MAUI)

Kaahumanu, c. 1772–1832, Queen; NAW, NWH

Kaahumanu Church, High Street; NR

Kaahumanu was "a woman of remarkable character, with strong passions and great failings." She is remembered today as the woman who broke through the sex barrier of ancient custom and won for Hawaiian women the power to take part in political decisions. See Hana and Honolulu, HI.

NOTES

In addition to the sources listed below, I am indebted to the Hawaii Visitors Bureau, the Women's Commission, and the Hawaii State Library. Agnes Conrad, Foundation for Hawaii Women's History, has given me much information on all the women and sites in the state.

1. Honolulu *Star Bulletin*, Mar. 20, 1967.

2. NWH appears next to the names of women whose biographies are included in *Notable Women of Hawaii*, ed. Barbara B. Peterson (Honolulu: University of Hawaii Press, 1984).

3. Biographies of all the women noted at Kamehameha Schools are in NWH; many more buildings are named for members of the royalty, but it was not feasible to include them all.

4. Amos Starr Cooke, *The Hawaiian Chiefs' Children's School* (Rutland, Vt.: Charles E. Tuttle Co., 1970).

IDAHO

BOISE

Ailshie, Margaret Cobb, 1883–1964, Newspaperwoman

Old Statesman Building, 6th and Main Streets

The *Idaho Statesman* has existed since a year before Idaho became a state. Its editor and publisher for almost forty years was Calvin Cobb, who made it an important factor in the state's development. His daughter Margaret Cobb Ailshie grew up with the country and the paper. On Cobb's death in 1928 she inherited the *Statesman* and continued to publish it for many years. She was married to James F. Ailshie, Jr. Boise is indebted to Ailshie not only for her dissemination of news but for her contributions to the city. They include funds for reconstruction of the pioneer village in Julia Davis Park (named for another Boise pioneer) and the stadium at Boise Junior College.

When the paper moved to its new home at 5th and Bannock, the old building, a replica of buildings in Philadelphia's lower Chestnut Street, was given to the Red Cross in her memory.[1]

Campbell, Clara, 1847–1930, Legislator

Memorial Tree, Statehouse Lawn, 8th and Jefferson Streets

In 1898 three women were elected to the state legislature, including Clara Campbell, an Idaho pioneer and an energetic promoter of woman suffrage and temperance. She sponsored the bill creating the University of Idaho. The tree was planted in her honor a year before her death.[2]

Green, Emma Edwards, d. 1942, Teacher and Artist

Idaho State Seal, 4th Floor of Capitol

The Idaho State seal, designed by Emma Edwards Green, depicts a man and woman side by side in support of the state, said to be symbolic of the equal participation of the sexes in Idaho's growth. Whether or not Green, a young schoolteacher, really meant the symbolism is a question. Certainly women teachers in that day were paid far less than men, though it is equally certain that they contributed their share to the development of social institutions. Green, the daughter of Governor John C. Edwards of Missouri, came to Idaho Territory in 1887. Her design was approved four years later. She married a Mr. Green in 1905.[3]

CALDWELL

Dorion, Marie, c. 1790–1850, Iowa Indian Traveler; NAW

Monument, US 80

A young woman of the Iowa Indian tribe, Marie Dorion was the only woman on the famed overland trip of the Astorians, a party that went from St. Louis to Astoria, on the Pacific Coast, in 1811–12. She was the wife of Pierre Dorion, interpreter for the party. The leader of the expedition, Wilson Price Hunt, wrote of Dorion: "We cannot but notice the wonderful patience, perseverance, and hardihood of the Indian woman, as exemplified in the poor squaw of the interpreter. She was now far advanced in her pregnancy, and had two children to take care of: one four and the other two years of age. The latter of course she had frequently to carry on her back, in addition to the burden usually imposed upon the squaw, yet she had borne all her hardships without a murmur, and throughout this weary and painful journey had kept pace with the best of the pedestrians. Indeed on various occasions in the course of this enterprise, she displayed a force of character that won the respect and applause of the white men."

The monument is at a rest area adjacent to the highway, about a mile northwest of town. See Corbett, Gervais, Milton-Freewater, North Powder, and Woodburn, OR.[4]

Strahorn, Carrie Adell, 1854–1925, Writer and Traveler

Carrie Adell Strahorn Memorial Library, College of Idaho; NR

Carrie Adell Strahorn and Robert Strahorn lived in Caldwell in its very early days. The founder of the college, W. J. Boone, credited Carrie with having started the college and the music school, as well as with organizing Caldwell's First Presbyterian Society and building its church. She was instrumental in bringing Boone to Caldwell in 1887 and, he said, she "put some stiffness into his spinelessness" when the going got rough. "She was energy personified," he said. "The radiance of her, her wonderful good cheer in unfavorable circumstances, her power to recover from defeat were all there."

Robert had been hired to study the resources of the West and to write promotional literature for the railroad which would induce settlers to come to the area. Carrie traveled with him, and her book, *Fifteen Thousand Miles by Stage*, with illustrations by Charles Russell, is graphic, sometimes hilarious, and an unfailingly more realistic account of conditions in the West than were Robert's pieces.[5]

GRANGEVILLE

Nathoy, Lalu (Polly Bemis), 1853–1933, Chinese Pioneer

Monument, Prairie View Cemetery

Lalu Nathoy (later called Polly Bemis), a Chinese woman, came to the Idaho gold regions in 1872, when she was nineteen. She had been sold by her impoverished parents in China and then by procurers in San Francisco, California, to be a slave and mistress to a tavernkeeper in Warrens, Idaho. She found in the mining camp something better than gold, a good man. Charlie Bemis bought her from her owner. Although slavery was illegal in America, the Chinese could not defend themselves, as they were not allowed to testify in court. When Polly wanted to buy land to farm, Charlie told her a Chinese person could not own land, so he bought some for her. In return, she gave him her devotion and nursed him through a near-fatal shooting. Eventually they married and lived long and happily together. On their farm near Warrens, Polly raised flowers and vegetables. Polly Creek bears her name, and the cabin where she last lived still remains. At a time when the Chinese had few rights and little respect in America, Polly's sweet nature, industry, and natural dignity won her the affection of the community. Memorabilia of Lalu-Polly are in the museum at St. Gertrude's Convent in Cottonwood, Idaho.[6]

IDAHO FALLS

Mitchell, Rebecca Brown, 1834–1908, Missionary

First Baptist Church, 665 Adams Parkway. Fountain, Rose Hill Cemetery

Rebecca Brown Mitchell came to Idaho in 1882 as a Baptist missionary. When her husband died, she had been left penniless by discriminatory property laws. She wrote, "[I] took in the legal restrictions of my sex, which has been as a fire shut up in my bones, permeating my whole being." She opened a day school, the first in Idaho Falls. She established the church, the only one in eastern Idaho, in an abandoned saloon. She organized a Woman's Christian Temperance Union and lectured for liquor control. But her greatest effort was for suffrage—"not for myself . . . but for womanhood." During the first Idaho General Assembly after women won the vote, Mitchell proudly served as chaplain of the House of Representatives. A portrait of her hangs in the church she founded, and her grave has been marked by the clubwomen of the state with a fountain.[7]

KAMIAH

McBeth, Susan Law, 1830–1893, and Her Sister Kate McBeth, 1833–1915, Missionaries; NAW (under Susan McBeth)

Sue McBeth Cabin, US 12; NR

Susan Law McBeth was sent west by the American Board of Missions in the early 1870s, after she had served as a missionary among the Choctaw Indians. She was a prim, plainly dressed Scotchwoman in her forties, the first unmarried white woman to come to the Nez Percé Reservation. She mastered the language and compiled a dictionary. (Left unfinished at her death, the calico-bound, waterstained manuscript is now in the Smithsonian Institution.) She spent twenty years among the Indians at Kamiah and Lapwai and finally at Mount Idaho, making rigorous attempts to change their morals, tribal customs, and beliefs according to strict Presbyterian precepts.

Kate McBeth joined her sister in 1879 and continued the work of the mission. For two independent women taking care of themselves in a primitive and sometimes dangerous place and time, the sisters were remarkably out of tune with feminist thought. Kate was opposed to woman suffrage, citing biblical texts to show that man was the protector of women. Men, she said, "do not like to marry women who want to vote." She wrote an account of the mission in *The Nez Percés Since Lewis and Clark* (1908), dedicated to "my sainted sister, Miss S. L. McBeth, who had so much to do with the success of the Gospel among the Nez Percés." Both sisters are buried near the mission church.[8]

Smith, Sarah Gilbert White, 1813–1855, Missionary

Kamiah Mission Church (First Presbyterian Church); NR

The church on the Clearwater River is near the site of the mission established in 1838 by Sarah Gilbert White Smith and her husband, Asa Smith. They had hurried their wedding in Massachusetts so that they could accept an appointment as missionaries to the Oregon Indians. With three other missionary couples they traveled overland through a roadless wilderness and across the Rocky Mountains. Sarah had never before ridden a horse and was not in robust health, yet she gamely accepted the challenge. When they arrived at Waiilatpu (now Walla

Walla, Washington), where Marcus and Narcissa Whitman had established a mission two years earlier, the Smiths chose to go to Kamiah, among the Nez Percés. While Asa built a three-room cabin, Sarah wrote her family that "we lived in a lodge of buffalo hides 3 weeks and 3 days." Their high hopes and religious fervor evaporated when Asa decided that the Indians had wicked hearts and were "immodest, using outrageous language." Sarah had a serious spinal affliction and was in constant pain. In the spring of 1842 they left Kamiah, Sarah so ill that she had to be carried in a hammock, and went to Honolulu, Hawaii.[9]

MOSCOW

French, Permeal Jane, 1869–1954, Educator

Residence Hall, University of Idaho

Permeal Jane French was the first dean of women at the University of Idaho, where she oversaw the health and behavior of women students from 1908 to 1936, paying special attention to dress and table manners as well as the emotional well-being of her charges. She had one trait that endeared her to all—she could remember their names after once meeting them. When the new dormitory was dedicated in 1955, a speaker likened French to Mr. Chips of *Good-bye, Mr. Chips*. "Neither had any children of their own, but each in reality had thousands of them—the students to whom they devoted their lives."[10]

MOUNT IDAHO

Aleblemot, Tolo, fl. 1877, Nez Percé Indian Heroine

Monument, Red Rock Canyon

Tolo Aleblemot became a heroine to the whites when she warned the Slate Creek settlers of the outbreak of the Nez Percé war of 1877 and rode twenty-seven miles over the mountains to Florence to get help. The Nez Percés repudiated her, but the whites gave her an allotment of land off the reservation (under the name Tola-Tsomy), the only Indian so honored. The Slate Creek rodeo arena is built on her land. A Lake Tolo on Camas Prairies is named for her. The monument was placed in 1939 by the American Legion Auxiliary.[11]

SALMON

Sacajawea, c. 1786–1812, Shoshoni Indian Guide; NAW

Marker on Boulder, State 28

The supposed birthplace of Sacajawea, one of the most famous of Native Americans, is marked by the boulder, fourteen miles south of Salmon. Monuments to her may be found in nearly all the northwestern states and in other parts of the country as well. The only woman in the Lewis and Clark Corps of Discovery expedition to the Pacific Coast in 1805–6, she served as interpreter and at times a guide. This part of Idaho was the home of the Lemhi group of Shoshonis to which she belonged. She was captured here as a young girl, taken eastward by the Hidatsa Indians, and finally sold to a French-Canadian trapper, Toussaint Charbonneau. Meriwether Lewis and William Clark wintered at the Mandan villages on the Missouri River, where they hired Charbonneau as a guide; he insisted on taking with him Sacajawea and their two-month-old baby. When they learned that she was a Shoshoni and could interpret for them when they reached the West, the expedition leaders agreed to take her.

She proved her worth to the expedition many times over. She was cool in danger and always cheerful. She was able to supplement their diet with edible roots and could sew moccasins and buckskins. Her infant son was a source of amusement to the homesick men. Most important, she helped them find the Shoshoni and to get from them badly needed horses and supplies. The meeting of the expedition with Sacajawea's people and her recognition of the chief, Cameahwait, as her own brother, is one of the most touching moments in the Lewis and Clark saga. For other monuments to the Bird Woman, see Montana, North Dakota, Oregon, South Dakota, Washington, and Wyoming.

SPALDING

Spalding, Eliza Hart, 1807–1851, Missionary; NAW

Spalding Memorial Park, Nez Percé National Historical Park

Eliza Hart Spalding, a New York schoolteacher, came here with her husband, Henry Harmon Spalding, in 1836 to establish a mission among the Nez Percés. She was one of two white women in a vast territory inhabited by wilderness tribes. She and her friend Narcissa Whitman (see Walla Walla, WA) were the first white women to cross the Rocky Mountains, riding sidesaddle through plains and mountains to minister to the Indians of the Oregon country. At this place, known then as Lapwai, Eliza worked alongside her husband. She learned the Nez Percé language and wrote a book in it for him to use in his teaching. Printed on a press brought from Hawaii in 1839, it was the first book printed West of the Rockies. Eliza is credited, too, with being the first artist of the Northwest, illustrating Bible stories for the Sunday school. In 1847, after the tragic massacre of the Whitmans and others at Walla Walla (then called Waiilatpu), the mission was closed. Eliza moved to the Willamette Valley in Oregon. Her remains are now buried with those of Henry, near the old mission site. The Spalding Memorial was made a state park in 1936 and in 1968 became part of the Nez Percé National Historical Park. See Casper, Daniel, and South Pass, WY.[12]

NOTES

In addition to sources mentioned below, I have had correspondence with the Public Library of Salmon and the Pocatello Public Library and the use of the Idaho Historical Society's valuable clipping and newspaper files.

1. Clippings, Idaho Historical Society; *A Victorian Gentlewoman in the Far West: Reminiscences of Mary Hallock Foote*, ed. Rodman Paul (San Marino, Calif.: Huntington Library, 1972).

2. *Idaho Statesman*, Oct. 23, 1929.

3. *The Women*, by the editors of Time-Life Books (Alexandria, Va.: Time-Life Books, 1978) has a color photograph of Green's design.

4. *The Discovery of the Overland Trail, Robert Stuart's Narrative of His Overland Trip Eastward from Astoria in 1812–13 with Wilson Price Hunt's Diary of His Overland Trip Westward to Astoria in 1811–12*, ed. Philip Ashton Rollins (New York: Edward Eberstadt & Sons, 1935), appendix A, journal of Mr. Hunt; Washington Irving, *Astoria*, ed. Edgeley M. Todd (Norman, Okla.: University of Oklahoma Press, 1964); correspondence, Caldwell Public Library.

5. "The passing of Mrs. Robert E. Strahorn. A few of the news excerpts, editorial comments and sketches of her remarkable career in Pacific Coast papers," leaflet, 1925, copy in William Andrews Clark Library, University of California, Los Angeles.

6. Ruthanne Lum McCunn, *Thousand Pieces of Gold* (San Francisco, Calif.: Design Enterprises, 1981); correspondence, R. L. McCunn.

7. Rebecca Brown Mitchell, *Historical Sketches: Pioneer Characters and Conditions of Eastern Idaho* (Idaho Falls: B. P. Mill, 1905); clippings, Idaho State Historical Society.

8. Hope Holway, "A Report on Research for the Record of Sue McBeth, Missionary," *Chronicles of Oklahoma* 44 (Summer 1966); Kate McBeth, *The Nez Percés Since Lewis and Clark* (New York: F. H. Revell Co., 1908); *Women's History Sources*, ed. Andrea Hinding and others (New York: R. R. Bowker Co., 1979), quoting a MS in University of Missouri Library.

9. Clifford M. Drury, *First White Women Over the Rockies*, vols. 1 and 3 (Glendale, Calif.: Arthur H. Clark Co., 1963–66); State Historical Society of Idaho, *8th Biennial Report*, quoting a letter of Feb. 16, 1837.

10. Rafe Gibbs, *Beacon for Mountain and Plain* (Caldwell, Idaho: Caxton Printers, 1962); correspondence, Moscow-Latah County Library System.

11. Sister M. Alfreda Elsonsohn, *Pioneer Days in Idaho County*, vol. 2 (Caldwell, Idaho: Caxton Printers, 1947), p. 14, quoting *Lewiston Morning Tribune*, c. 1938.

12. Drury, op. cit., vol. 1.; Howard M. Ballou and George R. Carter, "The History of the Hawaiian Mission Press," *Papers of the Hawaiian Historical Society*, no. 14 (1908); Cornelius J. Brosnan, *History of the State of Idaho* (New York: Charles Scribner's Sons, 1948).

MONTANA

ANACONDA

Hearst, Phoebe Apperson, 1842–1919, Philanthropist; NAW

Hearst Free Library, 4th and Main Streets; NR

Phoebe Apperson Hearst at seventeen was teaching in a rural school in Missouri when she met George Hearst. Twenty-two years her senior, he had returned to his home state for a visit after years of mining for gold and silver in California and Nevada. He and Phoebe were married and moved to a new home in San Francisco, California. As their fortunes increased, Phoebe made a career out of supporting educational and charitable ventures. She endowed libraries and child care centers in those towns from which part of their wealth came, such as Anaconda. The Anaconda library, a fine brick building, was built in 1898. See Berkeley and San Francisco, CA, and Lead, SD.

AVALANCHE GULCH

Rankin, Jeannette, 1880–1973, Congresswoman and Pacifist; NAWM

Rankin Ranch National Historic Landmark (Private)

"I wish to stand by my country, but I cannot vote for war. I vote No." It was April 6, 1917. The speaker was Jeannette Rankin, the first woman in America elected to Congress and in office only a few days. She voted with the minority against war with Germany. America entered World War I.

On December 8, 1941, Rankin was again in Congress when President Franklin D. Roosevelt called for a declaration of war against Japan. This time hers was the only dissenting vote. America entered World War II.

In 1968 the eighty-six-year-old crusader led the "Jeannette Rankin Brigade" to Washington to protest the Vietnam War. Rankin's star had risen with her struggle to win the vote for women in Montana in 1914. Her stand against war lost her a chance for reelection to Congress (until 1940), but during her first term she guided the suffrage amendment through the House. Her second term was won on her record as a pacifist, but Pearl Harbor changed the nation's feeling; she was criticized, even reviled, for her stand. By 1968 she had a large part of the nation, including most of its women, agreeing with her abhorrence of war. Rankin remained steadfast throughout her life. "We cannot settle disputes by eliminating human beings."

Rankin Ranch was the home of her brother and chief advisor, Wellington Rankin, and her home during many summers.[1]

DAYTON

Ronan, Mary Sheehan, b. 1852, Pioneer

Mary Ronan Lake

Mary Sheehan Ronan and her husband, Peter Ronan, lived on the Flathead Indian Reservation for sixteen years, through the Nez Percé march under Chief Joseph in 1876, the Bannack War, and the moving of Chief Charlot and his Bitter Root band in 1891. Peter was the respected superintendent of the Confederated Tribes. Mary in her later years was besieged by interviewers who wanted to hear her stories of the exciting pioneer days, and she once sighed, "I'm so tired of being a pioneer." Her daughter thereupon began collecting Mary's reminiscences, triggered by long-kept letters, articles, and papers. The result is *Frontier Woman: The Story of Mary Ronan*, published in 1973. It is a wide-ranging account of western travel, mining, education, religion, and reservation life, in the words of a capable and charming woman. The lake is a State Recreation Area.[2]

FORT BENTON

Sacajawea, c. 1786–1812, Shoshoni Indian Guide; NAW

Statue, Fort Benton National Historic District

The heroic-sized bronze statue, by Robert Scriver, shows Lewis, Clark, Sacajawea, and her child, Jean Baptiste. When the Lewis and Clark expedition reached Montana on their westward march in 1805, Sacajawea began to recognize many landmarks, for they were approaching her tribe's territory. She knew Beaverhead Rock (near Dillon, MT). This gave the party hopes of getting horses and guides for the remainder of their journey. Pompey's Pillar, near Bozeman, is named for the baby, who was called Pompey by William Clark. Helena, Livingston, Missoula, and Three Forks, Montana, also have memorials to Sacajawea, as have many other western states. The statue here was dedicated in 1976.

HARDIN

Custer, Elizabeth Bacon, 1842–1933, Army Wife and Writer

Custer Battlefield National Monument

The monument marks the field where General George A. Custer died at the Battle of the Little Bighorn in 1876. His widow, Elizabeth Bacon Custer, donated mementoes now shown at the Visitor Center. The love Elizabeth had for her "Autie" lasted far beyond his death. She spent her fifty-seven years of widowhood memorializing George. For the twelve years of their marriage she had traveled with him from army camp to army camp. When he was killed she was left with no home and a pension of thirty dollars a month. Eventually she grew wealthy from her books. *Tenting on the Plains* (1887) covers the years from her marriage in 1864 until 1867; *Following the Guidon* (1890) covers 1867–69; and *Boots and Saddles* (1885) brings the story up to the time of George's death. All are well worth reading. Elizabeth is buried beside George at West Point, New York. The museum and monument are open daily, June-Aug., 7–7, rest of year 8–4:30.[3]

HELENA

Sacajawea, c. 1786–1812, Shoshoni Indian Guide; NAW

Memorials, Montana Historical Society, 225 N. Roberts, and State Capitol

A sculpture of Sacajawea, the Indian Bird Woman, by Henry Lion is at the Montana Historical Society. A mural in the House of Representatives at the capitol, by Edgar S. Paxson, shows the Lewis and Clark expedition at Three Forks, Montana. Another, in the senate chamber, is by Charles M. Russell; it shows Lewis and Clark meeting the Flathead Indians.

LIVINGSTON

Sacajawea, c. 1786–1812, Shoshoni Indian Guide; NAW

State Marker, US 10, at Bozeman Pass; Sacajawea Park

Thirteen miles west of Livingston stands the monument commemorating the day, July 15, 1806, when the Lewis and Clark party reached this point on their eastward journey. A park on an island in the Yellowstone River is named for Sacajawea.

MISSOULA

Sacajawea, c. 1786–1812, Shoshoni Indian Guide; NAW

Memorials

A statue of the Shoshoni girl Sacajawea surmounts a fountain in front of the old Northern Pacific Railroad Depot, north end of Higgins Avenue. A painting of Sacajawea by Edgar S. Paxson is on the third floor of the library, University of Montana. Missoula also has a Sacajawea Park.

THREE FORKS

Sacajawea, c. 1786–1812, Shoshoni Indian Guide; NAW

Marker, US 10. Sacajawea Hotel, 5 Main Street; NR

The marker indicates the site of Sacajawea's capture, while a young girl, by Indians hostile to the Shoshoni. She was sold by her captors to the Hidatsa Indians and taken to the Mandan village on the Missouri River. There she became the property of a French-Canadian trapper, Toussaint Charbonneau. When in 1805 Meriwether Lewis and William Clark were looking for a guide for their expedition to the Pacific Coast, they visited the Mandan village and hired Charbonneau. He insisted on taking his young wife. Although she had a newborn son and would be the only woman on the expedition, Lewis and Clark found that she was from a western tribe and could speak Shoshoni, so they consented to take her. It was a fortunate choice, for she proved of great value. She was cheerful, hardworking, knew of many edible roots, and could serve as a guide when they reached territory she knew. She and the papoose made the journey westward and back again. After their return, Clark sent her son, Jean Baptiste, to school in St. Louis. One of the most famous of Native American heroines, Sacajawea has more memorials across the country, especially in the western states, than any other American woman.

NOTES

I have been helped by correspondence with the Fort Benton Community Improvement Association, the Montana Historical Society in Helena, Richard Rollins of Carroll College in Helena, the University of Montana Library, and the State Parks Department.

1. Elinor Richey, *Eminent Women of the West* (Berkeley, Calif.: Howell-North Books, 1976); Hope Chamberlin, *A Minority of Members: Women in the U.S. Congress* (New York: New American Library, 1973); Ronald Schaffer, "The Montana Woman Suffrage Campaign, 1911–14," *Pacific Northwest Quarterly* 55 (Jan. 1964).

2. *Frontier Woman*, ed. H. G. Merriam (Missoula: University of Montana, 1973).

3. Jay Monaghan, *Custer, The Life of General George Armstrong Custer* (Boston, Mass.: Little, Brown & Co., 1959); Elizabeth Custer, *Tenting on the Plains*, "Introduction" (Norman: University of Oklahoma Press, 1971).

NEBRASKA

BEATRICE

Freeman, Agnes Suiter, 1843–1931, Homesteader

Freeman Homestead and Freeman School, Homestead National Monument

The site is the first land acquired by a settler under the 1862 Homestead Act. Daniel Freeman, a Civil War soldier on furlough, filed his claim on January 2, 1863, and after the war he returned to take up his land, with Agnes Suiter Freeman as his bride. Agnes learned enough medicine from her husband to get a license to practice as a physician. She also raised six children, earning the title on her monument, ''A True Pioneer Mother.'' The 162-acre site includes an 1867 cabin, moved here in 1950, like that in which the Freemans lived. It is open Memorial Day-Labor Day, daily 8–8; rest of year Mon.-Fri. 8–5, Sat.-Sun. 8:30–5.[1]

CHADRON

Smith-Hayward, Mary E., 1842–1938, Businesswoman

Fountain, Courthouse Square

Mary E. Smith-Hayward came to Nebraska in 1885, preempted land near White River, and established a millinery and dry-goods store in Chadron. By the turn of the century she was the foremost merchant in western Nebraska. Known for her many kindnesses to the unfortunate victims of droughts and other disasters, Smith-Hayward was a beloved resident of the city. She was responsible for much of the work in beautifying the grounds around the courthouse. She belonged to the National Woman's Suffrage Association and was a friend of Susan B. Anthony and Elizabeth Cady Stanton. For a short time she was married to William Hayward and attached his name to hers.[2]

ELMWOOD

Aldrich, Bess Streeter, 1881–1954, Novelist

The Elms, Off State 1 (Private); NR. Marker, Elmwood Park

Bess Streeter Aldrich, a native of Iowa, moved to Nebraska after her marriage to Charles Aldrich. She wrote a few stories and one novel, *The Rim of the Prairie*, published in 1925. Her husband died that year, leaving her with four dependent children. She then needed to write as a means of support. Her best novel, *A Lantern in Her Hand* (1928), was inspired by her mother's stories of pioneer life. She had appealed in a radio talk for stories of early days and was sent a large number of clippings, news stories, scrapbooks, and diaries which gave color and reality to the story. She went on to write other novels capturing the spirit and flavor of the Midwest's small towns and prairies. They commanded high prices, brought her movie contracts, and won for her numerous literary and academic honors, including election to the Nebraska Hall of Fame (see Lincoln, NE).[3]

GORDON

Sandoz, Mari, 1896–1966, Writer; NAWM

Museum, State 27

In 1933, after painful years of learning to write, Mari Sandoz sent to an *Atlantic Monthly* nonfiction contest *Old Jules*, a biography based on the struggles of her Swiss-German father and other Nebraska pioneers. When it was rejected, she went back to the family homestead and burned the manuscripts of her stories. She spared that of *Old Jules*, and two years later she tried again and won a five-thousand-dollar prize and fame. Through this book and other works chronicling the drama of man on the great plains, she became internationally known as the historian and interpreter of the area. Her achievement was recognized by the establishment of the Mari Sandoz Heritage Society and the Mari Sandoz Center for the Study of Man, both at Chadron State College. In 1974 she was elected to the Nebraska Hall of Fame (see Lincoln, NE). The museum is a recreation of the Greenwich Village, New York City, apartment where she did much of her writing after 1943. A historical marker in a nearby roadside park also commemorates the writer. Her grave is two and a half miles off the highway.[4]

GRAND ISLAND

Abbott, Edith, 1876–1957 (NAWM), Her Sister Grace Abbott, 1878–1939 (NAW), Social Workers, and Their Mother Elizabeth Abbott, 1845–1941, Civic Worker

Edith Abbott Memorial Library. Grace Abbott Park

Elizabeth Abbott had a heritage of service to others. She was born in a log house in Illinois used as part of the abolitionist underground railroad. She came to

Nebraska in 1873, the wife of a lawyer, and immediately began to improve the town. She put through the legislation that established the Veterans Home, organized the Women's Park Association to raise funds to improve the city park, served as honorary president of the Grand Island Woman's Club when it was founded in 1919, and was a founder of the city library. She was an officer of the state woman's suffrage association and a delegate to the 1886 National Conference of Corrections and Charities. She raised two sons who became attorneys and two daughters who achieved national recognition in social welfare, Edith and Grace Abbott.[5]

Edith graduated from the University of Nebraska and went to the University of Chicago on a fellowship in economics. With a Ph.D., she went on to study at the London School of Economics, where she was influenced by Beatrice Webb, a social activist. Soon after her return she joined Jane Addams at Hull House in Chicago, Illinois. She studied and published books on many aspects of society—tenements, women in industry, the treatment of offenders, immigration, and public relief. From 1913 she taught at the University of Chicago and in 1924 became dean of its School of Social Service Administration. In her many years there, she earned for the school a high reputation, especially for its influence on public welfare administration.[6]

Grace graduated from Grand Island College and then followed her sister to Chicago and Hull House. She worked with immigrants who were victimized by phony employment agencies, travel bureaus, and others who preyed on their ignorance. She went to the federal Children's Bureau in 1917 and in 1921 became its director. She held this post for thirteen years, the pride and heroine of women who were just beginning to find a place in public affairs after winning the vote. Toward the end of her career in Washington, D.C., Grace helped to draft the Social Security Act. In 1934 she joined Edith again in Chicago, becoming professor of social welfare at the School of Social Service Administration. She is in the Nebraska Hall of Fame (see Lincoln, NE).[7]

LINCOLN

Nebraska Hall of Fame, State Capitol

Four women, three of them writers, are included in the Nebraska Hall of Fame. Grace Abbott, of Grand Island, Nebraska, spent her life in the field of social service. The three writers all reflect in their works their western orientation. Bess Streeter Aldrich, of Elmwood, Nebraska, drew many of the characters for her popular short stories and novels from her knowledge of life on the great plains. Willa Cather, of Red Cloud, Nebraska, is considered one of the most distinguished of American writers. She, too, drew much inspiration from the lives of Nebraska pioneers, although her themes were by no means confined to this area. Mari Sandoz, of Gordon, Nebraska, used not only her own life and that of her family but serious historical research in her series of studies of the trans-Missouri West.[8]

Bryan, Mary Elizabeth Baird, 1861–1930, Reformer

Fairview, 4900 Summer Street, on Grounds of Bryan Memorial Hospital; NHL

Though overshadowed by the fame of her husband, William Jennings Bryan (congressman, secretary of state, and three times candidate for U.S. president), Mary Elizabeth Baird Bryan was an unusual woman and just the right wife for an unusual man. She studied law and passed the state bar examination in 1888. She never practiced law, but it proved useful as she campaigned with her husband. She also studied German, for the German language papers were powerful in the Midwest. Besides helping William through his political campaigns, she worked for women's rights, the eight-hour day, currency reform, prohibition, the graduated income tax, and international peace. She passed on to her daughter, Ruth Bryan Owen (later Rohde, 1885–1954, NAWM), her strong views on these questions. Owen was the first congresswoman from Florida—and from the South. As ambassador to Denmark, she was also the first woman envoy from the United States to a foreign power.

The former Bryan home, Fairview, is open Mar. 1–Nov. 30, daily 1:30–5; rest of year, Sat.-Sun. only; closed some holidays.[9]

Dolan, Elizabeth Honor, 1887–1948, Muralist

Mural, State Capitol

Elizabeth Honor Dolan spent some years in the 1920s and 1930s in Nebraska, where she painted "The Spirit of Nebraska," the mural in the capitol. It depicts in glowing light a barefooted woman standing on a golden prairie with a child in her arms, her skirt billowing in the breeze. One critic thought it was "worth a trip to Nebraska" to see it. A native of Fort Dodge, Iowa, Dolan studied at the University of Nebraska, the Art Students League in New York City, the Chicago Art Institute, and the School of Fine Arts in Fontainebleau, France. Among her notable works were a frescoe for a thirteenth-century cathedral at Fourquet, France, a frescoe in a theater in Fontainebleau, and a stained-glass window for Tiffanys in New York City. Several of her paintings are in Nebraska galleries.[10]

Pound, Laura Biddlecombe, 1841–1928, Civic Worker, and Her Daughter, Louise Pound, 1872–1958 (NAWM), Folklorist

Pound Junior High School, 4740 S. 45th Street

Laura Biddlecombe Pound was the wife of Judge Stephen Bosworth Pound and moved with him to Lincoln in 1869. Lincoln, thanks to the presence of the University of Nebraska, offered cultural opportunities which Pound grasped. She studied German literature, was an amateur botanist, ran the public library as a volunteer when the city fathers declined to appropriate money for a librarian, belonged to the state historical society, and was a founder of at least two women's clubs. She taught her three children at home and all of them achieved distinction. Roscoe Pound became dean of Harvard Law School. Olivia Pound (1874–1961) was assistant principal of Lincoln High School from 1918 to 1943.[11]

Louise Pound was long associated with the University of Nebraska, first as a student, then as a faculty member, becoming a full professor in 1912. Her chief academic interest was American folklore. She was president of the American Folklore Society and the author of works on linguistics. She was also a noted devotee of sport, a tennis champion, winning golfer, ice skater, and basketball coach. When the sport of bicycling was at its height she won a medal for cycling five thousand miles. At the age of eighty-two she won double honors: election as thc first woman president of the Modern Language Association and election to the Nebraska Sports Hall of Fame—the only woman on the roster.[12]

NEBRASKA CITY

Morton, Caroline Joy French, 1833–1881, Ecologist

Arbor Lodge State Historical Park; NHL

J. Sterling Morton, who was U.S. secretary of agriculture, originated Arbor Day as a school holiday devoted to the planting of trees. Caroline Joy French Morton, his wife, was a pioneer ecologist, a musician and artist, and during her husband's frequent absences from home she managed the home farm and orchards. The Mortons imported many shade and fruit trees to plant around their home on the treeless prairie. Arbor Lodge eventually grew from a four-room house to a fifty-two-room mansion, and the surrounding sixty-five-acre park is a sylvan paradise. The park, with its arboretum, prairie garden, and rare trees, is open daily 8–sunset, all year. The mansion is open daily Memorial Day-Labor Day, daily 10–5; Apr. 22–Memorial Day, and Labor Day-Oct. 31, daily 1–5; adm. for mansion only.[13]

NELIGH

White Buffalo Girl, d. 1877, Ponca Indian

Monument, Neligh Cemetery

White Buffalo Girl was a child of the Ponca tribe who died when her people were removed from their homeland on the Niobrara River to Indian Territory in present-day Oklahoma. The route became known as the Ponca Trail of Tears. In 1913 a marble monument was erected over the grave by the people of Neligh in memory of the Poncas.

OMAHA

Joslyn, Sarah Selleck, 1851–1940, Philanthropist

Joslyn Memorial Art Museum, 2200 Dodge Street. Joslyn Mansion, 3902 Davenport Street (Private); NR

Sarah Selleck Joslyn and her husband, George A. Joslyn, arrived in Nebraska in 1880 with nine dollars and plenty of ambition. They opened two small hotels, and from that beginning they accumulated a fortune. George founded the Western Newspaper Union. When he died in 1916 he left Sarah a comfortable income and the thirty-two-room mansion, with a pipe organ, ballroom, and greenhouses. For some years she considered how best to use her wealth for the benefit of the community. ''The money was made in Omaha,'' she said, ''and it will be spent in Omaha.'' She began construction of the art museum in 1928 as a memorial to her husband and her own gift to the city. A modest woman, Sarah shunned publicity. She refused to sit for her portrait, and the artist who painted the one that hangs in the museum had to work from photographs. The museum is open Tues.-Sat. 10–5, Sun. 1–5; closed holidays; adm., except Sat. 10–12. Lectures, gallery talks, and chamber music programs are offered.[14]

ORD

Freeman, Minnie, fl. 1888, Heroine

Marker, State 70

Minnie Freeman, a teenaged schoolteacher, is honored for heroism while on duty. During the blizzard of 1888, when the wind tore the roof off the sod schoolhouse, she tied the children to each other with twine and led them half a mile through the blinding storm to a farmhouse. A song, ''Thirteen Were Saved; or, Nebraska's Fearless Maid,'' celebrated her bravery.[15]

Sharp, Evelyn Genevieve, 1919–1944, Aviator

Marker, Ord Airport

Though she lived a short life, Evelyn Genevieve Sharp became Nebraska's best-known woman aviator. She got her pilot's license at the age of eighteen and at twenty was an instructor. She was the nation's first woman airmail pilot and the first to fly the A–20 from coast to coast. In 1943 she enlisted to ferry bombers from the factory to posts in the United States and Canada, becoming a squadron commander in the Women's Auxiliary Ferrying Squadron. At twenty-four she was killed in the crash of a P–39 pursuit plane.[16]

RED CLOUD

Cather, Willa, 1873–1947, Novelist; NAW

Cather Home, 3rd and Cedar Streets; NHL. Willa Cather Memorial Prairie, US 281; NR

Of all her memorials, Willa Cather would have been most pleased with the 610 acres of native grassland set aside in 1974 by the Nature Conservancy, for she loved the prairies. Even though she was not a native Nebraskan—she was born in Virginia—and spent much of her active life far from the Midwest, she was a spiritual daughter of the state. Some of her greatest novels deal with the people of the Nebraska plains. The heroine of *My Antonia* was "a rich mine of life, like the founders of early races," who could "make you feel the goodness of planting and tending and harvesting at last." Cather also wrote novels set in other places and periods. Her *Shadows on the Rock* won the first annual Prix Femina Americaine, and *One of Ours* won the Pulitzer Prize.

The museum and the Cather home, as well as four additional Cather sites, are administered by the Nebraska State Historical Society as the Willa Cather Historical Center. The museum is open Tues.-Fri. 8–12 and 1–5, Sun. 1–5, except Nov.-Apr. closed Sun. Tours of the Cather home are offered at 9:30, 11, 1:30, 2:45, and 4 on days that the museum is open. The Willa Cather Pioneer Memorial and Educational Foundation, 326 N. Webster Street, offers tours of Willa Cather's Red Cloud, including the Cather house, by appointment only; adm. for guided tours. See the Hall of Fame in Lincoln, NE.[17]

WALTHILL

Picotte, Susan La Flesche, 1865–1915, Omaha Indian Physician, and Her Sister Susette La Flesche Tibbles, 1854–1903, Lecturer on Indian Rights; NAW

Picotte Hospital

The La Flesche sisters were the daughters of Iron Eye, an Omaha chief who had become a Christian and adopted many of the white man's ways. The year Susette La Flesche Tibbles was born the tribe gave up their hunting grounds in northeastern Nebraska and reserved a small tract on the Missouri River. She was brought up on this reservation, went to a school in New Jersey, and returned to teach in a government school. In 1877 an event occurred that aroused her indignation and changed the course of her life. The federal government forcibly removed the Poncas from their land to Indian Territory, where a third of them died. Their chief, Standing Bear, tried to lead the remnant of the tribe back to their homeland, whereupon the military authorities arrested him. He was defended by an Omaha newsman, Thomas H. Tibbles, who won his release. Then Standing Bear, Thomas, and Susette, with her brother, Francis La Flesche, went

The Willa Cather Memorial Prairie near Red Cloud, Nebraska, was set aside in 1974 to honor the writer, many of whose novels deal with the pioneers' struggle to tame the wild grasslands.
Courtesy Willa Cather Memorial Collection, Nebraska State Historical Society.

on a lecture tour publicizing the wrongs done to the western Indians. Susette was the first woman to speak publicly for Indian rights. She became an eloquent speaker on the lecture platform, using her Indian name, Bright Eyes. She married Tibbles in 1881 and went with him to lecture in England, where she was received as the very embodiment of an Indian princess.

Susan La Flesche Picotte, eleven years younger than Susette, chose a profession. She went East for her education and, with the help of the Women's International Indian Association, entered the Woman's Medical College of Pennsylvania. After receiving her M.D. in 1889, she returned to become a physician to the Indian children of her tribe and later to marry Henry Picotte. During her twenty-five years of medical practice she treated almost every member of the tribe and became virtual leader of the Omahas. In 1913 she established a hospital in Walthill, which after her death was given her name.[18]

NOTES

In addition to the sources mentioned below, I have had assistance from the State Department of Economic Development and the Nebraska Commission on the Status of Women.

1. *The Women*, by the editors of Time-Life Books (Alexandria, Va.: Time-Life Books, 1978).

2. C. Raymond Woodward, Jr., "A Frontier Leader of Men and Women," *Nebraska History* 18 (July-Sept. 1937).

3. Bess Streeter Aldrich, "The Story Behind *A Lantern in Her Hand*," *Nebraska History* 56 (Summer 1975); A. Mabel Meier, "Bess Streeter Aldrich, A Literary Portrait," *Nebraska History* 50 (Spring 1969).

4. LaVerne Harrell Clark, "A Dedication to the Memory of Mari Sandoz, 1896–1966," *Arizona and the West* 18 (Winter 1976); *Nebraska's Highway to Adventure* (Stuart, Neb.: National Highway 20 Association, n.d.).

5. *Mothers of Achievement in American History, 1776–1976*, comp. American Mothers Committee (Rutland, Vt.: Charles E. Tuttle Co., 1976).

6. *Current Biography*, 1941 and 1957.

7. Edith Abbott, "Grace Abbott: A Sister's Memories," *Social Service Review* 13 (Sept. 1939) and "Grace Abbott and Hull-House, 1908–21," *Social Service Review* 24 (Sept.-Dec. 1950); Lela B. Costin, "Grace Abbott of Nebraska," *Nebraska History* 56 (Summer 1975); J. R. Johnson, *Representative Nebraskans* (Lincoln, Neb.: Johnson Publishing Co., 1954).

8. Correspondence, Nebraska State Historical Society. A Nebraska Hall of Fame, prepared for International Women's Year, 1976, consisted of a weekly series of biographical sketches for Nebraska newspapers and collected for publication in a booklet. Three of the women so honored are Elizabeth Abbott, Mari Sandoz, and Bess Streeter Aldrich.

9. *Mothers of Achievement*.

10. *Nebraska History* 56 (Summer 1975).

11. *Mothers of Achievement*.

12. J. R. Johnson, op. cit.

13. *Mothers of Achievement*; correspondence, Arbor Lodge State Historical Park.

14. *New York Times*, Feb. 29, 1940; correspondence, Joslyn Memorial Art Museum.

15. *The Women*, p. 94.

16. "Evelyn Sharp, Pilot from Ord," *Nebraska History* 25 (Apr.-June 1944).

17. Mildred R. Bennett, "Willa Cather and the Prairie," *Nebraska History* 56 (Summer 1975) and *The World of Willa Cather* (Lincoln: University of Nebraska, 1961); correspondence and brochures, Willa Cather Historical Center.

18. Margaret Crary, *Susette La Flesche, Voice of the Omaha Indians* (New York: Hawthorne Books, 1973); Norma Kidd Green, "Four Sisters: Daughters of Joseph La Flesche," *Nebraska History* 45 (June 1964).

NEVADA

CARSON CITY

Clapp, Hanna Kezia, 1824–1908, and Her Partner Eliza Babcock, d. 1899, Educators and Businesswomen

Fence Surrounding Old Capitol Grounds

Hanna Kezia Clapp opened the first school for girls in Nevada, but she is remembered more by the fact that she won a contract to build a fence. When the state appropriated money in 1875 to beautify the capitol grounds, the best bid for the iron fencing came from two women who were principals of Sierra Seminary. According to the local paper, "Let there be no more complaints about the non-enjoyment of their rights by the women of Nevada. The contract . . . has been awarded to the Misses Clapp and Babcock." They had bid $5,500 for the job, some hundreds of dollars below any other bids, and they made $1,000 profit.

Clapp founded the seminary in 1860 and Eliza Babcock joined her four years later, beginning a friendship that lasted for thirty-five years. Clapp was strong-featured, gray-haired, commonsensical, and slightly masculine. Babcock was delicate, soft, and feminine. During the centennial year, the two traveled extensively in the East and South, and Babcock took the opportunity to investigate the kindergarten system then being introduced from Germany. On her return in 1877 she opened the first kindergarten in Nevada. The women moved in 1887 to Reno, where Clapp was on the first faculty of the fledgling University of Nevada. The capitol fence was so well designed and constructed that it remains in place today, one of the state's treasures.[1]

Dat So La Lee, c. 1835–1925, Washoe Indian Basketmaker

Markers, Stewart Cemetery Entrance, Off Snyder Avenue, and at Proctor and Division Streets

Dat So La Lee was also known as Dabuda (her given name) and as Louisa Keyser (after marriage to Charley Keyser). She learned to weave baskets as a child, but for years did not practice the art. She returned to the craft only when she was in her sixties and was living in Carson City. Abe Cohn, a Carson City businessman, recognized the artistic value of her baskets and arranged for their inventorying and sale. By the time of her death she had created a rich heritage of imaginative and perfectly formed baskets. Buildings at the nearby Indian school are named for her. Her workshop stood at the corner of Proctor and Division Streets. The State Museum has a collection of her baskets on display. It is open May 1–Oct. 31, daily 8:30–4:30; rest of year, Wed.-Sun.[2]

LAS VEGAS

Frazier, Maude, 1881–1963, Educator and Public Official; NAWM

Frazier Building, University of Nevada, 4505 S. Maryland Parkway

As deputy state superintendent of public instruction from 1921 to 1927, Maude Frazier became locally famous, driving her little roadster over the dreadful roads of Lincoln, Clark, Esmeralda, and Nye counties in Nevada to investigate school conditions. She followed this by nineteen years as superintendent of the Las Vegas Union School District. After her retirement she was elected to the state assembly, where she served for ten years. Her sharp mind, great vigor, and interest in quality education won the respect of her fellow lawmakers. In 1962, when she was eighty-one, she was appointed lieutenant governor of Nevada.[3]

Stewart, Helen J. Wiser, 1854–1926, Rancher

Helen J. Stewart School, 2375 E. Viking Road

Helen J. Wiser Stewart was the largest landowner in the Las Vegas area when she took over management of the two-thousand-acre property left by her husband, Archibald Stewart. He was murdered in 1884, leaving a family of five children. In addition to managing the property, she helped to found the historical society and a woman's club, was elected to the county school board, and in 1916 became one of the first women in Nevada to serve on a jury. In 1903 her ranch was sold to the Los Angeles and Salt Lake Railroad Company and became the townsite of Las Vegas. She had a granddaughter and namesake who was mentally handicapped, and the school for special children was in fact named for the granddaughter.[4]

McDERMITT

Winnemucca, Sarah, c. 1844–1891, Paiute Indian Leader; NAW

Marker on Circle Drive Around Fort McDermitt Reservation

Sarah Winnemucca was the daughter of Chief Winnemucca. She was well educated and as a young woman took up the cause of Indian rights, trying to serve as a peacemaker between Indians and whites. She wrote to the commissioner of Indian Affairs in 1870 detailing the problems the Paiutes had with the Indian agents. "If the Indians have my guarantee," she said, "that they can secure a permanent home on their own native soil and that our white neighbors can be kept from encroaching on our rights, after having a reasonable share of ground allotted to us as our own and giving us the required advantage of learning etc. I warrant that the savage as he is called today will be a law-abiding member of the community." In spite of her efforts, she met with confusion, frustration, and despair instead of justice for her people. At her death she was called the "most famous Indian woman of the Pacific Coast."[5]

RENO

Bowers, Eilly Orum, 1826–1903, Mine Owner

Bowers Mansion, Off US 395; NR

Eilly Orum Bowers and her husband, Sandy Bowers, built their mansion in the 1860s after they struck it rich in the mines near Virginia City, Nevada. For years they traveled in Europe buying luxurious treasures to furnish their home. As Sandy said, they had "money to throw at the birds." But riches failed to bring happiness. Their precious adopted daughter, Persia, died at the age of twelve. Sandy died in 1868. The mines played out, and Eilly supported herself by telling fortunes. The "Washoe Seeress" was finally forced to sell her treasures and her house. The mansion, after being sold many times, each time for less, was bought in 1946 by the state, through the efforts of the Reno Women's Civic Club, and used as a playground for the children of Nevada. The park is open mid-May to Oct. 31, daily 8–8; rest of year 8–5:30. Guided tours of the house mid-May to Oct. 31, daily 11–1 and 1:30–4:30; adm.

Mack, Effie Mona, 1888–1969, History Professor

Mack Building, University of Nevada

To read Effie Mona Mack's *Mark Twain in Nevada* (1947) is to wish you had been one of her students. History to her was an exciting and colorful view of the past, and she had the ability to transmit this excitement and color. She taught history in Reno High School for forty years. She was coauthor of the state's standard school text on Nevada and wrote the first history of the state by a professional historian. Not until 1954, when a campus of the University of Nevada was opened at Las Vegas, did she win an appointment to the university faculty. The social science building was given her name.[6]

Mackay, Marie Louise Hungerford, 1843–1928, Philanthropist

Mackay School of Mines, University of Nevada; NR

Marie Louise Hungerford Mackay's mother, born in France, named her Marie Louise Antoinette and brought her up to speak French as well as English. Her father went to California to hunt for gold and instead became a barber in the Sierra town of Downieville, where Mackay grew up and at sixteen married the local doctor. Some seven years later she was a widow, living in genteel poverty in Virginia City, Nevada, earning a living for herself and a child by sewing and teaching French. There she met and married John Mackay, who soon made one of the richest strikes of the Comstock Lode. Mackay found herself wealthy beyond her wildest dreams. Most of her life after that was spent abroad as a member of the international set. She had a Paris mansion near the Champs Elysées, where she entertained ex-President Ulysses S. Grant and his party at a grand ball that launched her into society. Her daughter married a prince. Meanwhile John Mackay remained in America, engaged in money-making ventures, until his death. The School of Mines was his wife's memorial to him and her gift to Nevada.[7]

Martin, Anne Henrietta, 1875–1951, Suffragist; NAWM

Plaque, Near Holiday Hotel, Mill and Center Streets

Anne Henrietta Martin became a feminist when her advice was rejected in family councils following the death of her father; she tried to expose his partners' mismanagement of the estate, but her brothers' advice was followed, while hers was ignored. She took her share of the inheritance in 1903, left her position as head of the history department of the University of Nevada, and went abroad to study.

While in England she worked shoulder to shoulder with the militant suffragists under Emmeline Pankhurst. On her return to Nevada in 1911 she became president of the state Equal Franchise Society, which began an exhausting fight to have a state suffrage amendment ratified. Martin traveled over three thousand miles and talked to almost every one of the voters in the state. Nevada won the vote for women in 1914. Martin then worked for suffrage on the national level and was among the women arrested for picketing the White House in 1918. She was the first woman candidate in any state for the U.S. Senate, running unsuccessfully in 1918 and 1920.

The plaque marks the site of her home.

VIRGINIA CITY

Bulette, Julia, 1832–1867, Prostitute

Monument, C Street

In 1877 Miriam F. Leslie (wife of the publisher Frank Leslie) visited the West, her trip including a stop in the mining town of Virginia City. "To call a place dreary, desolate, homeless, uncomfortable, and wicked is a good deal," she wrote, "but to call it God-forsaken is a good deal more, and in a tolerably large experience of this world's wonders, we never found a place better deserving the title than Virginia City." The town now considers itself a showplace of boomtown prosperity, if not of decorum. One of its star attractions is the monument to Julia Bulette, the Queen of Sporting Row. She was called the Angel of Miners, Friend of Firemen, and Administrator to the Needy. She was a genuine favorite with the men of Virginia City and was always ready to help out the volunteer firefighters. She was made an honorary member of the Virginia Engine Company No. 1. One night she was murdered for her jewels, and the town's largest funeral procession, led by the firemen, followed the hearse to her grave. Some three miles from the town, the grave is enclosed by a fence resembling bedposts.[8]

NOTES

In addition to the sources listed below, I have had the help of Ellen Glass, of the University of Nevada, and the librarians at the Nevada State Library, as well as the staff at the Old State Capitol.

1. Kathryn Dunn Totton, "Hannah Kezia Clapp: The Life and Career of a Pioneer Nevada Educator," *Nevada Historical Society Quarterly* 20 (Fall 1977); Mary Matrille, "Hannah Kezia Clapp," *Nevada Magazine* 36 (1976); Carson City *Daily Appeal*, May 4, 1875; correspondence, Nevada Historical Society.

2. Jane Green Hickson, *Dat So La Lee, Queen of the Washoe Basketmakers* (Carson City: Nevada State Museum, 1967); Russell E. Ewing, "Her Crown Was Willow," *Nevada Magazine* 43 (Jan.-Feb. 1983).

3. Mary Ellen Glass, "Nevada's First Lady Lawmakers: The First Half Century," *Nevada Public Affairs Report*, Bureau of Governmental Research, University of Nevada, Reno, vol. 14 (Oct. 1975).

4. Carrie Miller Townley, "Helen J. Stewart, First Lady of Las Vegas," *Nevada Historical Society Quarterly* 16 (Winter 1973); *Mothers of Achievement, 1776–1976*, comp. American Mothers Committee (Rutland, Vt.: Charles E. Tuttle Co., 1976).

5. Patricia Stewart, "Sarah Winnemucca," *Nevada Historical Society Quarterly* 14 (Winter 1971); Mary Ellen and Al Glass, *Touring Nevada* (Reno: University of Nevada Press, 1983).

6. James W. Hulse, *The University of Nevada* (Reno: University of Nevada Press, 1974).

7. Ellin Berlin, *Silver Platter* (Garden City, N.Y.: Doubleday & Co., 1957); Ellin (Mrs. Irving Berlin) was the granddaughter of Louise Mackay.

8. Miriam F. Leslie, *California: A Pleasure Trip from Gotham to the Golden Gate* (New York: G. W. Carleton & Co., 1877); Dee Brown, *The Gentle Tamers* (New York: Bantam Books, 1958), pp. 64–69.

NEW MEXICO

ALBUQUERQUE

Fergusson, Erna, 1888–1964, Writer

Fergusson Library, 3700 San Mateo, N.E.

Erna Fergusson was born in New Mexico and lived here all her life, never having any desire to live elsewhere. A teacher and reporter, she formed a partnership with Ethel Hickey to guide tourists to Indian pueblos, the Navajo Reservation, and the Hopi Indian dances. Her brother Harvey Fergusson, who was a successful writer, told her any fool could write a book. ''I proceeded to prove him right,'' she joked. Her first book, *Dancing Gods* (1931), was an immediate success. She made a serious study of the Indian, Spanish, and Anglo cultures intermixed in the state, and for thirty years she wrote books interpreting New Mexico and the Latin American countries. In the year before her death the governor of New Mexico proclaimed Erna Fergusson Day to honor New Mexico writers. Her former family home at 1801 Central Avenue, N.W., was later occupied by the Manzano Day School. The branch library was dedicated to her memory in 1966.[1]

FOLSOM

Rooke, Sarah J., d. 1908, Heroine

Monument, Folsom Cemetery

In 1908 a flood inundated the town of Folsom. Sarah J. Rooke, sixty-eight, was a telephone switchboard operator who remained at her post warning inhabitants of the rising flood waters. She saved the lives of all but seventeen, who ignored her warning, and her own. She was carried away on the crest of the flood. Telephone workers all over the territory contributed to the monument, erected in 1926.[2]

NEWCOMB

Newcomb, Franc Johnson, 1887–1970, Trader to the Indians and Writer

The town is named for Arthur Newcomb and Franc Johnson Newcomb, who established a trading post here early in the twentieth century. On the Blue Mesa, in the Navajo Reservation some forty miles from Gallup, it was originally called Pesh-do-clish. When a U.S. post office was established here, it was named for the traders. They ran the post for some twenty-five years, becoming absorbed in the Navajo culture. They worked with the Indian weavers to improve their rugs and, to get quality wool, taught them to improve the livestock. They also found a market for the Navajo silverwork.

In 1936 fire destroyed the trading post, including Franc's collection of prehistoric pottery of the Southwest and four hundred pressed specimens of herbs and medicinal plants used by medicine men. Though the post was rebuilt, the Newcombs moved to Albuquerque, New Mexico. There Franc wrote on the Native American culture and religion. She had a great talent for remembering exactly what she saw and heard and was able to reproduce from memory many sand paintings for the Wheelwright Museum in Santa Fe, New Mexico. She and Gladys Reichard preserved a valuable record of a Navajo ceremonial in *Sand Paintings of the Navajo Shooting Chant* (1937). Among her other books is *Hosteen Klah, Navaho Medicine Man and Sand Painter* (1964).[3]

SANTA FE

Fletcher, Alice Cunningham, 1838–1923, Interpreter of Indian Culture; NAW

Tablet, Courtyard of Museum of Fine Arts, the Plaza

The tablet quotes Alice Cunningham Fletcher's words: "Living with my Indian friends I found I was a stranger in my native land. As time went on the outward aspect of nature remained the same but a change was wrought in me. I learned to hear the echoes of a time when every living thing even the sky had a voice. That voice devoutly heard by the ancient people of America I desired to make audible to others." She did this by translating Indian songs and writing scholarly monographs.

Fletcher grew up in New York, taught school, and studied archeology. Inspired by hearing the Omaha speaker Susette Tibbles (see Walthill, NE), she visited the Omaha tribe and dedicated herself to helping them preserve their tribal lands. In 1883 Fletcher was appointed a special agent to the Omahas, in which capacity she supervised the granting of land allotments. She formed a mother-son relationship with Tibbles' brother, Francis La Flesche, which lasted all her life. She was the prime mover in the establishment of the School of American Research in Santa Fe (first called the School of American Archaeology).[4]

Henderson, Alice Corbin. See Wheelwright, Mary

Spiegelberg, Flora Langerman, 1857–1943, Civic Worker

Spiegelberg House, 237 E. Palace Street (Private); NR

Flora Langerman Spiegelberg, the wife of Willi Spiegelberg, is believed to be the first Jewish woman to arrive in New Mexico. She came here from Colorado as a bride. She organized the first nonsectarian school for girls in Santa Fe, where she taught classes in needlework, gardening, and nature study. Flora and Willi (who was mayor of Santa Fe) later lived in New York City. There she was horrified by the garbage and flies in the streets and the pollution of the Hudson River and the ocean shores. She made a thorough study of waste disposal methods used in other cities and abroad and suggested the garbage collection and incineration plan adopted by the city in 1911.[5]

Wheelwright, Mary Cabot, 1878–1958, Museum Founder

Wheelwright Museum of the American Indian, 704 Camino Lejo

Mary Cabot Wheelwright, a Bostonian, visited Gallup, New Mexico, in 1921 and purchased a tapestry by Hosteen Klah, a famous Navajo weaver and medicine man. Then she visited the Canyon de Chelly in Arizona and was entertained by the Newcombs at their trading post (see Newcomb, NM). She returned often, made a serious study of Navajo religion and art, and bought many sand-painting tapestries. In 1936 she drew up plans for the museum, fulfilling a dream of interpreting Navajo culture. First called the Museum of Navajo Ceremonial Art, it was dedicated to the memory of Klah, who died in 1937 and was buried on a nearby knoll. The museum has the largest collection in the world of reproductions of Navajo sand paintings. In 1975 the sacred medicine bundles entrusted to it were given to the Ned Hatathli Cultural Center at Navajo Community College. The name of the museum was changed after Wheelwright's death to honor her.[6].

The librarian and curator of the museum was Alice Corbin Henderson (1881–1949), who moved from Chicago, Illinois, to Santa Fe in 1916 seeking recovery from tuberculosis. She had been associate editor of *Poetry* in Chicago, and her presence in Santa Fe brought visits from poets with whom she had worked in Chicago, including Carl Sandburg, Robert Frost, and Vachel Lindsay. She studied and recorded Indian songs; her *Red Earth*, a volume of Indian and New Mexican verse, was published in 1920.

The museum is open Mon.-Sat. 10–5, Sun. 1–5; winters, closed Mon.; donations.[7]

White, Amelia Elizabeth, 1884–1972, Student of Indian Culture

Laboratory of Anthropology, Camino Lejo, Off the Old Santa Fe Trail; NR

Amelia Elizabeth White was an expert on American Indian art and a leader in calling public attention to the artistic achievements of Native Americans. She gave the land for the laboratory as well as for the Wheelwright Museum and the International Folk Art Foundation. She left her estate to the School of American Research. At her death, the board of the school passed a resolution recognizing her many unusual contributions to the community since her arrival in Santa Fe in 1923: restoring a historical building for a youth club, developing the park and rose garden along the Santa Fe Trail, founding an animal shelter, and supporting art and music. They paid tribute to "her gentle strength, delicate persuasiveness and generous heart." The laboratory is part of the Museum of New Mexico and is open Mon.-Fri. 9–4:45.[8]

TAOS

Blumenschein, Mary Shepherd Greene, 1869–1958, Artist

Blumenschein House, Ledoux Street; NHL

Mary Shepherd Greene Blumenschein and her husband, Ernest Blumenschein, moved to Taos from New York in 1918. Ernest had discovered the beauties of Taos twenty years earlier and spent many summers here. He was one of the first of many artists who chose to live and work in Taos, and he became a leader in the Taos Society of Artists. But Mary found that a married woman swam against the tide in trying to have an independent career. Ernest saw her as his attractive wife, a "capable" artist, and the mother of his delightful daughter, rather than as a creative artist with ambitions of her own. After a time she turned to jewelry design. Her work can be seen at the Harwood Foundation and other galleries. The house is open Apr. 1–Oct. 31, daily 9–5, winters 10–4; closed some holidays; adm.[9]

Harwood, Elizabeth, 1867–1938, Artist and Philanthropist

Harwood Foundation, Ledoux Street; NR

At the outbreak of World War I, artists Burt and Elizabeth Harwood left Paris, France, and moved to Taos. They purchased the old home of Captain Smith H. Simpson, a friend of Kit Carson. Over the years it became a gathering place for other artists. After Burt's death in 1923, Elizabeth began a lending library and offered the house for community meetings, art classes, and exhibits. She formally organized the foundation so that she could accept donations of art and financial help from others in the community. In 1936 she gave the foundation to the University of New Mexico, to be maintained in perpetuity in Taos as an educational, cultural, and art center. In the permanent collections are portraits of Elizabeth and Burt and paintings by both. It is open Mon.-Fri. 10–5, Sat. 10–4; closed holidays.[10]

Luhan, Mabel Dodge Sterne, 1879–1962, Writer and Art Patron; NAWM

Mabel Dodge Luhan House, Luhan Lane (Private); NR

When Mabel Dodge Sterne Luhan visited Santa Fe in 1916 it seemed to her the end of the earth; she came from Greenwich Village in New York City. Then she discovered Taos, which she described as a tiny, dusty hamlet with few white inhabitants, but she stayed here for the rest of her life, finding meaning in its peaceful, earthy atmosphere. She spent much of her time with the women of the Indian pueblo and fell in love with an Indian, Tony Luhan. She divorced her husband at the time, artist Maurice Sterne, to marry Tony.

In New York she had made her apartment the meeting place for writers, artists, and any interesting people she came across. She invented radical chic by inviting to her evenings at 23 Fifth Avenue anarchists Emma Goldman and Alexander Berkman, the daring advocate of free love and modern dancing Isadora Duncan, and the socialist writer John Reed. In Taos her life changed, but she still attracted interesting people, including D. H. Lawrence. She gave Kiowa Ranch at San Cristobal to him and his wife, Frieda, who in turn gave it to the University of New Mexico. Mabel also brought modern art to Taos, gave the town a hospital, a bandstand, and many books. She wrote here several volumes of her fascinating autobiography.[11]

TRUTH OR CONSEQUENCES

Tingley, Carrie Wooster, d. 1961, Philanthropist

Carrie Tingley Hospital

Carrie Wooster Tingley, wife of New Mexico's Governor Clyde Tingley, was interested in the treatment of children who were victims of infantile paralysis (polio). She persuaded her husband to appeal to President Franklin D. Roosevelt for federal funds to build a treatment center in New Mexico. Roosevelt not only promised to help but offered to get the services of the architect who designed the Warm Springs Foundation hospital in Georgia. This site was chosen because of its hot thermal springs. The town, originally Hot Springs, adopted the name of a popular radio program once broadcast from here. Clyde dedicated the hospital in 1937.[12]

NOTES

In addition to the sources mentioned below, I am indebted to the University of New Mexico Library for much assistance, as well as to the New Mexico Commission on the Status of Women and the Roswell Public Library.

1. William A. Keleher, ''Erna Mary Fergusson,'' *New Mexico Historical Review* 39 (Oct. 1964); Al Lowman, ''A Dedication to the Memory of Erna Fergusson,'' *Arizona and the West* 14 (Spring 1972).

2. Clippings furnished by the Zimmerman Library, University of New Mexico.

3. Franc Newcomb, *Hosteen Klah* (Norman: University of Oklahoma Press, 1964); *Mothers of Achievement in American History*, comp. American Mothers Committee (Rutland, Vt.: Charles E. Tuttle Co., 1976).

4. Helen Addison Howard, ''Literary Translators and Interpreters of Indian Songs,'' *Journal of the West* 12 (Apr. 1973); correspondence, School of American Research.

5. *New York Times*, Dec. 9, 1943.

6. Newcomb, op. cit.; Linda Monacelli, ''Mary Cabot Wheelwright's Hogan,'' *New Mexico Magazine* 61 (Feb. 1983); correspondence, Wheelwright Museum.

7. Howard, op. cit.; T. M. Pearce, *Alice Corbin Henderson* (Austin, Tex.: Southwest Writers Series, no. 21, 1969).

8. *New York Times*, Aug. 29, 1972; correspondence and clippings, School of American Research.

9. Erna Fergusson, *New Mexico: A Pageant of Three Peoples* (New York: Alfred A. Knopf, 1964); Patricia J. Broder, *Taos: A Painter's Dream* (Boston, Mass.: New York Graphic Society, 1980).

10. Dorothy L. Kethler, ''History of the Harwood Foundation,'' MS, 1975; brochure and correspondence, Harwood Foundation.

11. Claire Morrill, *A Taos Mosaic* (Albuquerque: University of New Mexico Press, 1973).

12. *New York Times*, Nov. 8, 1961; William A. Keleher, *Memoirs, 1892–1969* (Santa Fe, N.Mex.: Rydal Press, 1969).

NORTH DAKOTA

BISMARK

Anderson, Elizabeth Preston, 1861–1954, Temperance Leader

Portrait, State Capitol Lobby

The North Dakota legislature closed the saloons in 1890, a year after Elizabeth Preston Anderson, wife of a Methodist minister in Fargo, North Dakota, organized the state Woman's Christian Temperance Union (WCTU). The bars did not open until national prohibition was repealed. But eternal vigilance was needed to keep the law on the books, and Anderson was the WCTU watchdog for many years. She was president of the state organization and recording secretary for the national WCTU. The largest women's organization in the state, it labored for much more than liquor control. It fought the ninety-day divorce law, which made Fargo a divorce mill where a single judge heard 350 cases in a year. It also sought laws banning pornography, limiting child labor, and giving women equal voting rights.[1]

Sacajawea, c. 1786–1812, Shoshoni Indian Guide; NAW

Statues, East Side of Capitol Grounds and West Bank of Missouri River

Here the Bird Woman's name is spelled Sakakawea. She was a local heroine because the Mandan Village is nearby, where she was living when Lewis and Clark hired her husband, Toussaint Charbonneau, as guide. The first statue is a 12-foot bronze by Leonard Crunelle, sponsored by the North Dakota Federation of Women's Clubs, unveiled in 1910. The other is a more recent 530-foot-high statue of concrete, steel, and glass, by Lincoln Borglum. The State Historical Society, in Liberty Memorial Building, on the capitol grounds, has a painting by Verne Erickson of Lewis and Clark meeting Charbonneau and Sacajawea. In Riverdale a lake formed by Garrison Dam is named Lake Sakakawea. There are many memorials to her in most of the northwestern states.

CENTER

Miner, Hazel, d. 1920, Heroine

Monument, Courthouse Square

On March 15–16, 1920, a violent blizzard struck the area. Sixteen-year-old Hazel Miner and a younger brother and sister were caught without shelter in the storm. She covered the two children with blankets and wraps and lay on top of them to keep them warm. When found, the two children were alive, but Miner had frozen to death. The granite marker was erected by former Governor L. B. Hanna.

ELBOWOODS

Hall, Susan Webb, 1850–1922, Mission Teacher

Memorial Chapel

Susan Webb Hall spent most of her adult years as a missionary to the Indians of the Mandan, Hidatsa, and Arikara tribes. She and her husband, Charles Hall, went first to Fort Berthold. When the Indians moved to their government allotments, the Halls traveled among them. When an agency was established at Elbowoods—on the prairie fifteen miles south of Pashall— the Indians took down the former mission house and rebuilt it at the new location. Parents who had attended the first mission school now sent their children to the second one. The chapel was dedicated to her memory in 1925–26.[2]

GRAND FORKS

Cable, Margaret Kelly, 1884–1960, Ceramicist

Pottery Display, Ceramics Department, University of North Dakota

Brought into the ceramics department in 1910 to teach pottery making, Margaret Kelly Cable remained at the University of North Dakota for four decades. She became nationally known for her ceramics. She had worked with the Handcraft Guild in Minneapolis and in the potteries of East Liverpool, Ohio. Later she studied with other master potters. She produced many outstanding pieces herself, some of them signed Maggie Mud. She was asked to design and produce a number of special presentation works, including vases for Queen Marie of Rumania, for Crown Princess Martha of Norway, and for President John F. Ken-

Margaret Cable of the University of North Dakota was an artist who worked in clay. This bowl, made to commemorate the 1805 journey of Lewis and Clark, has one panel depicting Sacajawea, their Shoshoni Indian woman companion, and her papoose. Courtesy University of North Dakota.

nedy. After her retirement, she was given one of the most coveted national honors in the field of ceramics, the Charles Fergus Binns medal. It is due to Cable and a number of potters and designers she recruited (many of them women) that the University of North Dakota is ranked as outstanding for ceramics.[3]

Page, Alice Nelson, 1872–1916, Printer and Newspaper Publisher

Washburn Printing Center, 1440 S. Washington

After a stint as society editor for the *Grand Forks Herald*, Alice Nelson Page established a print shop, with the name Page Printerie, and made it a success. She began in 1915 to publish a weekly paper, the *Grand Forks Independent*, but did not live to carry it on and it ceased publication two years later. Although she did not expect to reform the community, much less the nation, with her views, Page's paper was influential during its short life. She was well known to the politicians of the state as an active and dedicated suffragist and an enthusiastic supporter of the Grand Forks Civic League. The Page Printerie is now the Washburn Printing Center.[4]

MEDORA

De Mores, Medora von Hoffman, Marquise, d. 1920, Celebrity

Chateau de Mores Historic Site, Off I–94; NR

The town bears the name of a woman who lived in it for less than two years. Medora von Hoffman, Marquise De Mores, was the daughter of a wealthy New York banker and the wife of Antoine de Vallambrosa, the Marquis de Mores. The Marquis came to the Badlands to set up a packing plant. The tiny, titian-haired Medora arrived in the town late in 1883 to move into the chateau he had built for her. She furnished it with sturdy, locally made tables and chairs; fur rugs, mixed with Oriental rugs; fine European furniture; and a piano. Sèvres and Limoges china, fine wines, and champagne were imported for the family's use. The Marquis built for his wife St. Mary's Chapel, at 4th Street and 3rd Avenue (also in the National Register). The meat-packing business was not a success, and the family left for Europe. The adventurous Marquis was killed by Touaregs in Algeria in 1896. Medora brought her three children to North Dakota for a six-week visit in 1903, but the chateau was never again used by the family. It is open for conducted tours May 1–Oct. 31, daily 8:30–4:30; rest of year by appointment (701–623–4355); adm.[5]

NOTES

In addition to the sources listed below, I am grateful to the University of North Dakota for assistance; to the North Dakota Highway Department; and to Margaret Barr, Emma

Lou Hariman, Elizabeth Hampsten, and Jean Vivian, editor of the *Plainswoman*, all of Grand Forks.

1. Helen E. Tyler, *Where Prayer and Purpose Meet: The WCTU Story* (Evanston, Ill.: Signal Press, 1949); Erling Nicolai Rolfsrud, *Extraordinary North Dakotans* (Alexandria, Minn.: Lantern Books, 1954).

2. *Mothers of Achievement in American History*, comp. American Mothers Committee (Rutland, Vt.: Charles E. Tuttle Co., 1976).

3. Margaret Libby Barr and others, *University of North Dakota Pottery: The Cable Years* (Fargo, N.Dak.: Knight Printing Co., 1977).

4. Walter Kaloupek, "Alice Nelson Page: Pioneer Career Woman," *North Dakota History* 13 (Jan.–Apr. 1946).

5. Donald Dresden, *The Marquis de Mores, Emperor of the Badlands* (Norman: University of Oklahoma Press, 1970).

OREGON

ASTORIA

Owens-Adair, Bethenia, 1840–1926, Physician; NAW

Monument, Ocean View Cemetery

The grave of this pioneer woman doctor, Bethenia Owens-Adair, went unmarked until 1975, when the citizens of Clatsop County erected a granite memorial, with the words: "Only the enterprising and the brave are actuated to become pioneers." Owens-Adair crossed the plains with her family in 1843. She worked hard on the farm, married at fourteen, and five years later was divorced, with a young son and almost no formal schooling. She ran a millinery and dress shop in Roseburg and waited until her son finished college before she went east to study medicine. When she returned, male physicians in Roseburg sought to frighten her out of practice. She did not frighten easily. After further training, she earned an M.D. and practiced in Portland and Warrenton, Oregon, and in North Yakima, Washington. She married Colonel John Adair, a West Point graduate. In her autobiographical *Dr. Owens-Adair, Some of Her Life Experiences*, she reveals herself as a somewhat opinionated egocentric and an advocate of sterilization of the unfit. She is remembered for her work for temperance and women's rights, as well as her pioneering in the medical field.

Sacajawea, c. 1786–1812, Shoshoni Indian Guide; NAW

Fort Clatsop National Memorial, US 101A

The party led by Meriwether Lewis and William Clark spent the winter of 1806 here, after arriving on the coast from their long westward journey. The reconstructed fort includes the quarters occupied by Sacajawea, who had been so valuable to the Corps of Discovery as guide, interpreter, and general camp helper (see Salmon, ID). After traveling so far, the Bird Woman was anxious to see the ocean and a beached whale. She got her wish to see ''that monstrous fish'' on January 6, 1806, shortly before the party started the return journey to the Mandan village on the Missouri. Many other memorials exist to Sacajawea, mainly in the Northwest. In the Whitman National Forest there is a Mount Sacajawea.

From mid-June to Labor Day a living history program is presented at the fort, which is open daily 8–8, in winter 8–5.

CORBETT

Dorion, Marie, c. 1790–1850, Iowa Indian Traveler; NAW

Plaque, Vista Point, Crown Point State Park

Marie Dorion, ''the red heroine of the West,'' traveled from St. Louis to the West Coast with her husband, interpreter for the Astorians, in 1811–12. This was the second party of Americans to traverse the plains and mountains to reach the coast. Dorion had with her two children, and another was born and died on the trail. Her story was told in Washington Irving's *Astoria*, who said that Dorion, ''for the most part of the time, trudged on foot, like the residue of the party; nor did any of the men show more patience and fortitude than this resolute woman in enduring fatigue and hardship'' (see Caldwell, ID). Two years later Marie went through a harrowing winter alone with her two boys, living in a makeshift shelter and eating smoked horsemeat, and brought them through the ordeal alive and well. See Gervais, Milton-Freewater, North Powder, and Woodburn, OR.[1]

EUGENE

Kerns, Maude I., 1876–1965, Artist

Maude I. Kerns Art Center, 10 E. 15th Avenue

Maude I. Kerns was head of the University of Oregon's School of Architecture and Fine Arts from 1921 to 1947 and afterward professor emerita. Long after she left the classroom, she continued an interest in teaching. In 1961 she gave to the community the building in which the center is located. Once the Fairmount Presbyterian church, it is the oldest church building in Eugene, completed in 1895. Kerns' own work is represented in a number of art galleries. The center is open Tues.-Fri. 10–5, Sat. 12–5.[2]

FLORENCE

Honeyman, Jessie M., 1852–1948, Preservationist

Jessie M. Honeyman Memorial State Park, US 101

Oregon is famed for its many public parks and roadside rests. This one is a memorial to a woman who was for years president of the Oregon Roads Council, which was established to beautify the highways. Jessie M. Honeyman was a longtime resident of Portland, Oregon, born in Glasgow, Scotland, who loved her adopted home and was dedicated to preserving its natural beauty.

FOREST GROVE

Brown, Tabitha Moffat, 1780–1858, Educator

Tabitha Brown Hall, Pacific University

Tabitha Moffat Brown reached Oregon in 1846, after one of the most harrowing journeys in the annals of the Oregon Trail. She was in her late sixties, the widow of the Reverend Clark Brown, of Brimfield, Massachusetts. (He was a member of the Brown family who founded Providence, Rhode Island, and were patrons of Brown University.) On arrival in the Oregon Territory, Tabitha used her whole cash resources, six and a half cents, to buy three needles. She traded some of her clothes to the Indian women for buckskins and worked the skins into gloves for sale. At West Tualatin Plains—now Forest Grove—she worried about the many orphans left to be cared for by strangers after losing one or both parents on the trail. She boarded and taught the orphans in what grew to be Tualatin Plains Academy and then the four-year Pacific University. Old College Hall, a museum displaying among its treasures mementoes of Brown, is listed in the National Register.[3]

Walker, Mary Richardson, 1811–1897, Missionary

Monument, Forest Grove Cemetery

The seven-foot monument to Mary Richardson Walker and her husband, Elkanah Walker, is inscribed: "Missionaries of the A.B.C.F.M. Surely goodness and mercy have followed me all the days of my life." The Walkers had traveled to the Oregon country in 1838 as one of four missionary couples appointed by the American Board of Commissioners of Foreign Missions to carry the gospel to the Indians. They set up a mission at Tshimakain, "place of the springs," about twenty-five miles northwest of Spokane Falls (now Ford, Washington, q.v.). Mary had a child four months after she arrived in the West, and by the time she left Tshimakain, after the Whitman massacre in 1847 put an end to the mission, she had six. The family moved to Forest Grove and spent the rest of their lives here, working and preaching. Elkanah was one of the first trustees of Pacific University. Mary was the last survivor of the Protestant missionaries who crossed the Rocky Mountains in 1836–38.[4]

GERVAIS

Dorion, Marie, c. 1790–1850, Iowa Indian Traveler; NAW

Plaque, St. Louis Church

For many years the later life of Marie Dorion, who had trudged across the country with the Astorians in 1811–12 (see Corbett, OR), was obscure. She was commonly known as Marie Iowa or its French equivalent, "L'Aguivoise." Church records establish the dates of a second marriage, to Jean Baptiste Toupin, and her death and burial here. See Caldwell, ID, and Milton-Freewater, North Powder, and Woodburn, OR.

MARYLHURST

Gleason, Caroline (Sister Miriam Theresa), 1886–1962, Social Worker

Lounge, Shoen Library, Marylhurst Education Center

In 1912, the year Oregon women won the vote, the state Consumers League commissioned Caroline Gleason to survey the wages, hours, conditions of labor, and standards of living of women wage earners in Oregon. Determined to get at the truth, she went into the factories herself as a worker. She found shocking conditions. The average pay was far below the amount needed for bare subsistence, which meant that girls had to have allowances from home or take on extra domestic work. If that was impossible, they had other options: to go without medical care, walk miles to work, wear threadbare clothes, go into debt, starve, or become "charity girls"—living on money from men. Industry, Gleason concluded, was parasitic, living off the bodies of young women.

Her report caused a sensation among clubwomen and gave them a strong reason to exert their newly won political power. In 1913 the legislature established an Industrial Welfare Commission with power to regulate industry, the first enforceable wage-and-hour law in the country.

Gleason soon afterward entered the Society of the Sisters of the Holy Names of Jesus and Mary, adopted the name of Sister Miriam Theresa, and became dean of the School of Social Work at Marylhurst College. Her picture and mementoes of her life are displayed in the lounge dedicated to her. She is buried on the campus.[5]

MILTON-FREEWATER

Dorion, Marie, c. 1790–1850, Iowa Indian Traveler; NAW

Marie Dorion Historical Park, Near Old Milton Power Plant, On the Walla Walla River

In 1814 some men who had been with the Astorians in 1811–12 were surprised to be greeted in French by an Indian woman. It was Marie Dorion. She told them a tale of fortitude that far surpassed their previous experiences. She had been on a trapping party with Pierre Dorion and several others near the Snake River. All but one of the men were killed by hostile Indians. She caught two horses, put the surviving, badly wounded man on one and mounted the other, with her two children. Gathering a few clothes and provisions, they fled. The man died, and Dorion knew she was alone in the wilderness, except for unfriendly Indians. They rode westward, but before they reached the upper Walla Walla River, winter snows made travel impossible. With buffalo skins, bark, and branches, she made a wigwam for shelter. She killed the two horses and smoked the meat. The children and the mother spent fifty-five bitter cold days in their shelter. In March, almost destitute of food, they set out again toward the West and managed to reach a band of friendly Walla Walla Indians.

This park may be near the place where Dorion reached shelter after her ordeal. See Corbett, Gervais, North Powder, and Woodburn, OR.[6]

NORTH POWDER

Dorion, Marie, c. 1790–1850, Iowa Indian Traveler; NAW

Marker, State 237 Between North Powder and Union

This marker commemorates one of many episodes in the story of Marie Dorion. By the time the Astorian expedition reached this point on their journey to the West, they were starving; they had killed and eaten all their horses except the one belonging to Marie's husband, Pierre Dorion. With unaccustomed consideration, he had refused to give up the last horse, claiming that Marie, far gone in pregnancy, could no longer walk and carry all her burdens—including two other children. About dawn of December 30, 1811, she gave birth to a child. All that day, while the rest of the party pushed on, the Dorion family remained here. The next day they traveled twenty-one miles to catch up, Dorion "on horseback with her newborn infant in her arms; another . . . slung at her side. One would have said, from her air, that nothing had happened to her." Washington Irving, in his version of the story, comments: "so easy is nature in her operations in the wilderness, when free from the enfeebling refinements of luxury, and the tamperings and appliances of art." If Dorion's labor and recovery were indeed so easy, it was probably because malnutrition had produced a tiny baby. Eight days later, on January 7, one of the party recorded simply, "Dorion's baby died." See Caldwell, ID, and Corbett, Gervais, Milton-Freewater, and Woodburn, OR.[7]

OREGON CITY

McLoughlin, Marguerite Wadin, 1775–1860, Pioneer

McLoughlin House National Historic Site, McLoughlin Park, 713 Center, at 7th Street; HABS, NR

Marguerite Wadin McLoughlin, a beautiful, well-educated woman, half Cree Indian, was the widow of Alexander McKay when she married John McLoughlin, the factor of the Hudson's Bay Company. They lived in this house after John resigned his position and moved away from Fort Vancouver. The missionaries Narcissa Whitman and Eliza Spalding had been guests of the McLoughlins at the fort in 1836. Whitman found Marguerite "one of the kindest women in the world" and reported that she spoke a little French and had a fine ear for music. The house is open Tues.-Sat. 10–5, Sun. 1–5; winters, 1–4; closed Jan. and holidays; adm.[8]

PORTLAND

Duniway, Abigail Scott, 1834–1915, Newspaper Publisher and Suffragist; NAW

Portrait, Water Tower, John's Landing, 5331 S. W. Macadam Street

Abigail Scott Duniway became aware of the legal inequity suffered by married women when her husband endorsed a note for a friend. The friend defaulted and the Duniways lost their land. "When that obligation was made," she said, "I was my husband's silent partner—a legal nonentity—with no voice or power for self protection under the sun; but when penalty accrued I was his legal representative." She came to the conclusion that women could control their lives only when they could take part in making the laws. She established and published for sixteen years (1871–87) the *New Northwest*, a weekly devoted to women's rights. The vote was won for Oregon women in 1912, and although Duniway was then seventy-eight and almost retired from politics, she was selected to write the suffrage proclamation and cast the first woman's vote. The portrait in the elevator's etched glass front is part of a photo collage depicting bits of area history.[9]

Sacajawea, c. 1786–1812, Shoshoni Indian Guide; NAW

Statue, Washington Park

The Portland Woman's Club undertook to raise funds for a statue of the Bird Woman for the Lewis and Clark Exposition held in Portland in 1905. Eva Emery Dye (1855–1947) was the instigator of the project. When her book, *The Conquest, The True Story of Lewis and Clark*, appeared in 1902, somewhat exaggerating the role of the Indian girl in the exploration of the West, suffragists seized on Sacajawea as a popular heroine. At the statue's unveiling, speakers were Susan B. Anthony and Anna Howard Shaw, revered leaders of the woman suffrage movement. After the exposition the statue, by Alice Cooper, was given a permanent home in Washington Park. See Salmon, ID, and other memorials throughout the western states.

Victor, Frances Fuller, 1826–1902, Historian; NAW

Marker, Riverview Cemetery, 8421 S. W. Macadam Street

Frances Fuller Victor was Oregon's foremost woman historian, although the work on which she spent twelve years of her life was published without acknowledgment of her authorship—several volumes of Hubert Howe Bancroft's *History of the Pacific States*. Bancroft, who prepared his monumental histories by hiring competent researchers and writers to work under his direction, persuaded her to join his staff in San Francisco, California, where she worked between 1878 and 1890. After her return to Oregon, Victor wrote on Oregon history and was commissioned by the legislature to write on the native Indians. She had spent her early writing years in New York City with her sister, Metta Fuller Victor, also an author. They married brothers. Metta, who remained in the East, made a great deal of money writing Beadle Dime Novels, while Frances's far more important historical works brought her a very modest living.

For years her grave was unmarked, but in 1947 the Portland chapter of the Daughters of the American Revolution and the Board of the Oregon Historical Society erected a marker.

SALEM

Sacajawea, c. 1786–1812, Shoshoni Indian Guide; NAW

Statue, North Entrance of State Capitol, Court and Summer Streets

The statue, by Leo Friedlander, is of Meriwether Lewis, William Clark, and Sacajawea, interpreter and guide. It was erected in 1938. In the capitol is a mural showing the same figures at Celilo Falls on the Columbia River, Oregon; another, by Barry Faulkner and F. H. Schwarz, shows Narcissa Whitman (see Walla Walla, WA) and Eliza Spalding (see Spalding, ID) being welcomed at Fort Vancouver in 1836.

THE DALLES

Ferguson, Belle Cooper Rinehart, 1862–1945?, Physician

The Dalles General Hospital Building

In 1893 Belle Cooper Rinehart was left a widow with four small boys. She decided that the best way to earn their support would be through a medical practice. She had already served an apprenticeship in medicine under her husband, a graduate of Bellevue Medical College of New York. She enrolled in medical school in Portland, Oregon, graduated in 1897, and returned to The Dalles to practice, the first woman physician in eastern Oregon. She married another doctor, Elmer Ferguson, and together they established the hospital and operated it for some years before moving their practice to Portland. The old hospital building was later used for county offices.[10]

WINEMA NATIONAL FOREST

Winema (Toby Riddle), c. 1848–1932, Modoc Indian Heroine

Winema Forest. Winema Pinnacles. Winema County

Winema, wife of Frank Riddle, was the heroine of the Modoc War, when fifty-two warriors, holding out against the whites, retreated into the Lava Beds just across the northern boundary of California in 1872–73 (see Lava Beds National Monument, CA). With them were 150 old men, women, and children. A U.S. Army peace commission, including Colonel A. B. Meacham, went to treat with the warriors, despite warnings of treacherous intent on the part of the Indians. When they shot and attempted to scalp Meacham, Winema shielded him with her body and then nursed him back to health. Her cousin, "Captain Jack," was executed for his part in the assault, and at the time of the execution he appealed to Meacham to tell the Indians' side of the story. Meacham's book about the war in defense of the Modocs was entitled *Wi-Ne-Ma*. Winema herself went east in 1875 and toured the country in a play about her life. Winema Pinnacles is above the Columbia River Highway near Multnomah Falls. Her name was also given to a town in Klamath County. Her grave is in Schonchin Cemetery, Sprague River Road, in Beatty, with a marker erected by the Daughters of the American Revolution to "Winema—a strong heart."[11]

WOODBURN

Dorion, Marie, c. 1790–1850, Iowa Indian Traveler; NAW

Plaque

Still another memorial to the intrepid Marie Dorion, of the Astorian party, was erected here in 1975. See Caldwell, ID, and Corbett, Gervais, and Milton-Freewater, OR.

NOTES

In addition to the sources mentioned below, I have had help from the University of Oregon, the Oregon State Library, Oregon Historical Society, Library Association of

Portland, State Highway Division, Governor's Commission for Women, Josephine County Library System in Grants Pass, Elgin Public Library, and the School of Medicine Alumni Association of the University of Oregon Health Sciences Center.

1. Washington Irving, *Astoria*, ed. Edgeley M. Todd (Norman: University of Oklahoma Press, 1964, first published 1836).

2. Mike Helm, *Eugene, Oregon, A Guide* (Eugene, Oreg.: Rainy Day Press, 1979); MS obituary, Lane County Museum, Eugene.

3. Ella Brown Spooner, *The Brown Family History* (Laurel, Mont.: Laurel Outlook, 1929), quotes Brown's letter of Aug. 1854 describing her westward trip and the establishment of the college.

4. Clifford M. Drury, "Wilderness Diaries: A Missionary Couple in the Pacific Northwest, 1839–48," *American West* 13 (Nov.-Dec. 1976).

5. Consumer's League of Oregon, Social Survey Committee, *Report . . . on the Wages, Hours, and Conditions of Work and Standards of Living of Women Wage Earners in Oregon with Special Reference to Portland* (Portland, Oreg.: Consumers' League, 1913); correspondence and clippings, Convent of the Holy Names, Marylhurst.

6. Correspondence and brochures, Russell Blackler, Milton-Freewater.

7. Irving, op. cit.

8. Richard C. Montgomery, *The White-Headed Eagle: John McLoughlin, Builder of an Empire* (New York: Macmillan, 1935); Clifford M. Drury, *First White Women Over the Rockies* (Glendale, Calif.: Arthur H. Clark Co., 1963–66).

9. Correspondence, Joan Salisbury, manager, the Water Tower Building, Johns Landing, Portland.

10. *An Illustrated History of Central Oregon* (Spokane, Wash.: Western Historical Publishing Co., 1905); William H. McNeal, *History of Wasco County, Oregon* (Oxon Hill, Md.: Silesia Printing and Publishing Co., 1974); correspondence, The Dalles-Wasco County Library.

11. E. A. Brininstool, *Fighting Red Cloud's Warriors* (Columbus, Ohio: Hunter-Trade-Trapper Co., 1926).

SOUTH DAKOTA

CUSTER

Tallent, Annie Donna, 1827–1901, Pioneer Teacher and Writer

Monument, Gordon Stockade, Custer State Park, US 16A

Annie Donna Tallent was the first white woman to enter the Black Hills, arriving with the Gordon expedition in 1874. They spent a miserable winter here, holed up in a stout stockade built as a defense against the Indians while they dug for gold. They had violated a treaty with the Sioux in entering land considered sacred. They were arrested and forced by a military guard of U.S. soldiers to return to Iowa. There, news of the gold discoveries started a gold rush that forced the Sioux to cede the territory to the United States in 1877. Tallent felt no compunction about violating the rights of the Indians. In her day—and until recently—most white Americans agreed with her that settlement was a righteous attempt to bring civilizing forces to a country of savages. She returned to South Dakota in 1876 and was identified with it as teacher and writer for the rest of her life. Schools in the state have been named for her, and an annual teacher's award is presented in her name. The friends who erected the marker here wrote: "The world is better because she lived and worked in it." The Sioux feel differently (see Sturgis, SD). The park is open all year; park entrance permit required.[1]

DE SMET

Wilder, Laura Ingalls, 1867–1957, and Her Daughter, Rose Wilder Lane, 1886–1968, Writers; NAWM (under Wilder)

Ingalls House, 210 3rd Street, West; NR

De Smet is the "Little Town on the Prairie" made famous by the much-loved children's stories by Laura Ingalls Wilder. It was the homestead site of her parents, Charles and Caroline Ingalls. Wilder wrote her first book when she was sixty-five and continued with a series of popular stories based on recollections of prairie life. The books were Newbery honor books. They have been reprinted, translated into many languages and into Braille, and formed the basis for a popular television series. The American Library gives a Laura Ingalls Wilder award every five years for contributions to children's literature; Wilder was the first recipient.

Rose Wilder Lane, her daughter, was born in De Smet, and it was she who encouraged her mother to write down the memories of pioneer days. A successful journalist, she served as agent, editor, and collaborator on her mother's books.

De Smet has a memorial tour, including the Wilder family's church and home. A pageant based on the Little House books is presented here annually in June and July. The house is open June 1–Sept. 15, daily 9–5; rest of year by appointment (605–854–3383); adm.

DEADWOOD

Burk, Martha Cannary (Calamity Jane), 1852?–1903, Frontierswoman; NAW

Grave, Mount Moriah Cemetery

Martha Cannary Burk (Calamity Jane) was one of the West's most famous "wild women." She ended up in this historical gold mining town, and her grave is one of the spots visitors must see. Some picture Calamity Jane as a devoted nurse to the sick, a scout for the army, a pony express rider, and a stagecoach driver. Others dismiss her as a picturesque prostitute and camp follower. She could ride, shoot, drink, and chew tobacco with the men in her life. Dime novels built up the folklore of the indomitable and beautiful Calamity Jane, and she herself wrote a largely fictitious autobiography. She claimed to have been married to Wild Bill Hickok and probably was married to Clinton Burk. The cemetery is open daily, 9–7; adm. June 1–Oct. 31; rest of year free.

HURON

Pyle, Mary Isabel Shields, 1866–1949, Suffrage Leader

Pyle House, 376 Idaho Avenue, S.E. (Private); NR

The 1918 campaign which won the vote for women in South Dakota was well planned and carried out by an army—a small but determined one—of women like Mary (Mamie) Isabel Shields Pyle. She was the hardest-working suffragist in the state. She was elected president of the Universal Franchise League in 1910 and served until the federal suffrage amendment was ratified in 1920. She expended energy in other fields as well: she was on the board of trustees of Huron College and president of the College Women's Association which raised money to build the first permanent building on the campus. In 1938 she had the pleasure of driving to Washington, D.C., with her daughter, Gladys Pyle, when Gladys went to the U.S. Senate after serving as the state's first woman legislator and as secretary of state. Mamie Pyle was chosen state mother of South Dakota in 1947.[2]

LEAD

Hearst, Phoebe Apperson, 1842–1919, Philanthropist; NAW

Phoebe Apperson Hearst Library, 309 W. Main Street

Phoebe Apperson Hearst was the wife of George Hearst, the mining engineer whose "vision and organizing genius built a small mining claim into the mightiest gold mine in the world—the Homestake"; he founded the Hearst family fortune. George was known as a somewhat ruthless man, not well liked because of sharp business practices. Phoebe, however, was a true philanthropist, interested in the welfare of the miners. In addition to donating the library to Lead, she founded the first free kindergarten in town. The Hearst Highway is dedicated to the memory of the Hearsts. See Berkeley and San Francisco, CA, and Anaconda, MT.

MOBRIDGE

Sacajawea, c. 1786–1812, Shoshoni Indian Guide; NAW

Statue, Dakota Memorial Park. Marker at Burial Site of Sitting Bull

The statue is on a hilltop west of the Missouri River, across the Mobridge bridge, south of US 12. Sacajawea, the interpreter and guide for the Lewis and Clark expedition, is believed to be buried near here. A claim has been made, however, that a Sacajawea who died in 1884 and was buried at the Wind River Reservation in Wyoming was really the Bird Woman (see Lander, WY). In support of South Dakota's claim, it may be said that Clark's 1828 diary noted beside the name of Sacajawea "Dead." Also a clerk at Fort Manuel noted on December 20, 1812, "This evening the wife of Charbonneau, a Snake Squaw, died." The statue erected here in 1929 by the original Hickory Stick Club is a replica of the Alice Cooper statue in Portland, Oregon. The burial site of Sitting Bull, where there is a marker to Sacajawea, is six miles west on US 12, then four miles south. Many memorials exist to the Bird Woman in the Northwest and other parts of the country.

RAPID CITY

Gossage, Alice R., 1861?–1929, Newspaper Publisher

Monument, Skyline Drive

Alice R. Gossage was a suffragist, prohibitionist, and newswoman. She began her news career by setting type on the *Vermilion Standard* and other papers. She married the owner of the *Rapid City Journal*, and in 1890 his illness forced her to assume management of the paper. She was editor, reporter, proofreader, and foreman of the job room for three decades.[3]

REDFIELD

Gardner, Abbie (Sharp), c. 1844–1921, Indian Captive

Marker, US 281

Abbie Gardner was in her teens when she was captured by Sioux Indians at the time of the Spirit Lake Massacre in Iowa, near the Minnesota border, on March 8, 1857. She was delivered to her rescuers at this spot after eighty-three days of captivity. Her story was published shortly after the rescue by Lorenzo Lee, and in 1885, as Abigail Sharp, she herself published the popular *History of the Spirit Lake Massacre and Captivity of Miss Abbie Gardner*. The family's log cabin was still in her possession at her death and has been preserved at Arnolds Park, Iowa.

STURGIS

Tallent, Annie Donna, 1827–1901, Pioneer Teacher and Writer

Annie D. Tallent House, 1603 Main Street (Private); NR

Annie Donna Tallent came to South Dakota in 1874 with other gold seekers, in defiance of the U.S. government and in grave danger of Indian attack (see Custer, SD). She walked all the way from Sioux City, Iowa, to near Custer, wearing out two pairs of shoes, then donning moccasins. In spite of great hardships, she fell in love with the Black Hills, describing them as "one continuous poem, replete with all that is grand, sublime and beautiful." She lived in South Dakota from 1876 until her death, teaching, superintending schools, and writing.

In 1897 she wrote *The Black Hills: or, The Last Hunting Ground of the Dakotahs*, in which she defended the whites' invasion of the Sioux' sacred hunting grounds in violation of treaties with the Indians. She fully believed that "such treaties as tend to arrest the advance of civilization, and retard the development of the rich resources of our country," should not have been entered into. Recently, her book was reprinted as a valuable source of local history. The publishers bravely included an introduction by a Sioux, Virginia Driving Hawk Sneve, who bitterly described Tallent's work as a ''malicious, bigoted'' book that ''would best serve mankind if it were burned.'' The tribe is still trying to have their sacred Black Hills returned to them.[4]

Tubbs, Alice Ivers (Poker Alice), 1853–1930, Gambler

Tubbs House, North Junction, Adjacent to Bear Butte Creek (Private); NR

Like Calamity Jane, Poker Alice has been considered a typical woman of the wild West—a good shot, possessed of a colorful vocabulary, growing rich as a gambler, and spending her wealth on the unfortunate. It is difficult to separate fact from fiction, but it appears that Alice Ivers Tubbs was born in England, had a college education, and moved to the United States as a young woman. When her husband, Frank Duffield, was killed, she took to gambling to support herself. She drifted from camp to camp, winning and losing, always maintaining the inscrutable expression that won her the nickname. She ran a gaming house in Deadwood, South Dakota, where she married W. G. Tubbs. She was once sentenced to the penitentiary for running a house of ill repute, but the governor pardoned her because of her age—she was in her seventies. The house where she ended her days was acquired by the city under the Deadman Gulch Urban Disaster Project and entered in the National Register of Historical Sites.[5]

NOTES

In addition to the sources listed below, I have had correspondence with the South Dakota State Library, the South Dakota Department of Economic and Tourism Development, and the Department of Education and Cultural Affairs.

1. Annie Donna Tallent, *The Black Hills* (Sioux Falls, S.D.: Brevet Press, 1974); *South Dakota History* 3 (Spring 1973), back cover.
2. *History of Woman Suffrage*, vol. 6, ed. Ida Husted Harper (New York: National American Woman Suffrage Association, 1922), p. 593; ''Dakota Images,'' *South Dakota History* 8 (Winter 1977); Hope Chamberlin, *A Minority of Members: Women in the U.S. Congress* (New York: New American Library, 1973), under Gladys Pyle; correspondence, Huron Public Library.
3. *South Dakota History* 4 (Fall 1974), back cover.
4. Tallent, op. cit.
5. Grace E. Ray, *Wily Women of the West* (San Antonio, Tex.: Naylor Co., 1972); James D. Horan, *Desperate Women* (New York: G. P. Putnam's Sons, 1952); *Rushmore News*, June 18, 1975.

UTAH

HELPER

Magafan, Jenne, 1916–1952, Painter

Mural, Post Office

Jenne Magafan and her twin sister Ethel Magafan worked closely together and were companions until Jenne's untimely death. Their first artistic successes came through the federal mural projects of the depression years. They lived in Colorado, where they studied at the Fine Arts Center in Colorado Springs. Jenne's "Western Town," painted about 1940 for the Helper Post Office, exhibits her mastery of technique and boldness of style. Both twins were married to artists, Jenne to Edward Chavez, Ethel to Bruce Currie. Jenne won a Fulbright Fellowship and went to Italy in 1952. On her return she died suddenly of a cerebral hemorrhage.[1]

HUNTSVILLE

Hammond, Mary Jane Dilworth, 1831–1877, Teacher

Monument, Huntsville School Grounds

The monument, a plaque mounted on a large granite boulder, reads: "In honor of the first school teacher in Utah, Mrs. Mary Jane Dilworth Hammond. Taught first school in Salt Lake City, October 1847. Came to Huntsville with her husband, Bishop Francis A. Hammond, 1865, where she resided until her death, 1877." Hammond taught in a military tent in Salt Lake City, Utah, using a Noah Webster speller, a few readers, a Bible, and an arithmetic book. In Huntsville, she was president of the Relief Society. The monument was erected by the Daughters of the Utah Pioneers.[2]

Smith, Mary Heathman, 1818–1895, Physician

Monument, Public Square

Across the road from the Hammond monument, q.v., is a tall stone pillar, whose plaque reads: "In memory of Mary Heathman Smith, lovingly known as Granny Smith. Born in England, January 21, 1818, where she was trained in a Maternity Hospital. She came to Utah in 1862. A doctor, surgeon, midwife and nurse for thirty years. In storm or sunshine during the bleakest winters or the darkest night with little or no remuneration, she attended the people of Ogden Valley with a courage and faithfulness unexcelled, in addition to raising her own family of nine. Under her skill and attention she brought into the world more than 1500 babies. She died in Huntsville, Utah, December 15, 1895." The monument was erected by the Daughters of Ogden Valley in 1937.[3]

OGDEN

Eccles, Bertha Jensen, 1857–1935, Businesswoman and Social Leader

Bertha Eccles Community Art Center, 2580 Jefferson Avenue; NR

Bertha Jensen Eccles was born in Denmark; at age ten she and her family moved to Utah where she met David Eccles. He was a native of Scotland, the son of a blind woodworker. In the Horatio Alger tradition David rose to become a significant financier with interests in lumber, land, railroads, and banking. Their Ogden home became a center of cultural festivities and social life. Bertha was one of the founders of the Girl Scout movement in Utah. She left her home as a community center. It is used by many civic and cultural groups, and is open Mon.-Fri. 9–5, Sat. 10–4.[4]

PROVO

Heritage Halls, Brigham Young University

Brigham Young University has named its group-living apartments, Heritage Halls, for noted women of the Mormon faith, and their names constitute a veritable Mormon women's hall of fame. Emma Lucy Gates (1889–1951), later the wife of A. E. Bowen, was the daughter of Susa Young Gates and a granddaughter of Brigham Young. A coloratura soprano, she studied voice in Germany and sang many operatic roles during her four years there. She was known as Utah's First Lady of Music. World War I ended her international career. With her brother, who had studied conducting, she formed the Lucy Gates Opera Company in Salt Lake City, Utah.

Susa Gates (1856–1933), Emma's mother, contributed so much to the religious, civic, and political life of Salt Lake City that she earned the title the "thirteenth apostle." She founded and edited for forty years the *Young Women's Journal*, organ of the National Young Ladies' Mutual Improvement Association. She also founded the *Relief Society Magazine* and wrote *Women of the Mormon Church*. Her name is given to awards presented to women who have worked to elevate the status of women.

Romania B. Pratt (later Penrose, 1839–1932) was the first Mormon woman to go East to attend medical school. She received her degree in 1877 from the Women's Medical College in Pennsylvania. She was the first woman specialist in Utah in eye and ear surgery. At the time of the state constitutional convention she was one of a committee of women who asked that the new constitution provide that "the rights of citizens of the state of Utah to vote and hold office shall not be denied or abridged on account of sex." In 1882 she and other concerned Mormon women worked together to establish a hospital in Salt Lake City for doctors and patients of the Latter Day Saints. It was planned, staffed, and directed entirely by women. Pratt was president of the board of directors and resident physician. The hospital was forced to close in 1893 for lack of funds, and some time later Pratt married Charles W. Penrose.

Ellis Reynolds Shipp (1847–1939) received her M.D., also at the Women's Medical College, in 1878. She was married at age nineteen, supported four children while her husband was away on a two-year church mission, and then went off to Philadelphia, Pennsylvania, for study. Her husband visited her there and almost put an end to her training by leaving her pregnant. But she continued in school and bore her fifth child the day after the final examinations. On her return to Utah she founded a school of obstetrics and nursing. She practiced medicine for over sixty years and was also active in church work. She was chosen for the Utah Hall of Fame.[5]

Emily Sophia Tanner Richards (1850–1929) was the wife of Franklin S. Richards, an attorney who went on numerous occasions to Washington, D.C., to argue cases before the Supreme Court. She accompanied him on these visits and became acquainted with leaders in the women's movement. They were at first inclined to shun Mormon women as being degraded by plural marriage and as victims of exploitation. Richards was given an opportunity to speak at the first International Council of Women, held at the national capital just at the time when statehood for Utah was being considered. In an atmosphere of denunciation of polygamy and hostility to Mormons, an immense crowd assembled to hear her speak. They were surprised to see a delicate, refined woman on the platform, presenting a scholarly, well-reasoned speech about Utah and its people. In 1896 she was proposed as Utah's first woman state senator, but she declined the honor.

Zina Huntington Young (1821–1901) went East to speak at temperance meetings in 1881, but because of the feeling against the Mormons at the time, she was refused permission to represent the women of Utah at the Woman's Congress in Buffalo, nor was she allowed to address the National Woman's Suffrage Association in New York City. At the time of the 1893 Columbian Exposition, however, the climate of opinion had changed (thanks to women like Emily

Richards) and Young was able to represent Utah on the platform. She was married three times, including ties to Joseph Smith and to Brigham Young.

Heritage Halls are also named for Eliza Roxey Snow, Emmeline Wells, and Alice Merrill Horne, all of Salt Lake City, Utah, q.v.[6]

Kimball, Sarah Melissa Granger, 1818–1898, Churchwoman

Kimball Hall, Wymount Terrace, Brigham Young University

Sarah Melissa Granger Kimball was described by her biographer as a strong-minded woman who ''maintained the principle of equality of the sexes and contended for it with all the advantages pertaining thereto. She did not believe in half measures.'' When her first son was born, she asked her husband, Hiram Kimball, who was not a Mormon, if he thought she was half owner of the child. He agreed. She then asked if her half might be considered worth five hundred dollars. Again he agreed. She said she would give her half to the church. When Hiram related this to Joseph Smith, the prophet said he could either give the five hundred dollars in cash and keep possession or collect that amount and give possession. Hiram gracefully gave the sum (in land) and kept his son. The Relief Society was organized in 1842 in Sarah's kitchen. In 1857, after the move to Utah, she was made president of the ward Relief Society and remained its president all her life. She was one of three women in the Utah Constitutional Convention of 1882.[7]

Reynolds, Alice Louise, 1873–1938, English Teacher

Rare Book Collection, Brigham Young University Library.
Reynolds Hall, Wymount Terrace

Alice Louise Reynolds is remembered chiefly for her contributions to the Brigham Young University Library. She taught English literature at BYU for forty-four years, giving her students a rich mixture of Chaucer, Shakespeare, Tennyson, and Browning. She was instrumental in securing for the university many rare books, including a fine liberal arts library from Judge Whitecotton. In addition to her work at the university, she was active in the L.D.S. church, editing for some time the *Relief Society Magazine*.[8]

SALT LAKE CITY

Babcock, Maud May, 1867–1954, Professor

Little Theater, Pioneer Memorial Theater, University of Utah

Maud May Babcock was an elocutionist and physical culturist, the first woman professor at the University of Utah. A few years after she accepted the position in 1892, she was made a trustee of the university. She opened its first gymnasium and began theatrical performances in the form of "educational gymnastics," which soon developed into drama. A convert to Mormonism, Babcock left her real estate, valued at ten thousand dollars, to the church. She was elected to the Utah Hall of Fame in 1943.[9]

Horne, Alice Merrill, 1868–1948, Art Patron

Alice Art Collection, Utah Arts Council, 617 East South Temple

Alice Merrill Horne, a member of the third state legislature, wrote the bill establishing a state art institute "to advance the interests of the fine arts, including literature and music, in all their phases within the state of Utah." The bill provided for the collection of art works, which was named for her, and for annual art exhibits. Horne and her husband, George Horne, entertained artists at their home, sold paintings by local artists, and financed art exhibitions. For her work in promoting Utah art she was proposed by the Federation of Women's Clubs to the Utah Hall of Fame. The Utah Arts Council, successor to the State Institute of Fine Arts, is open Mon.-Fri. 8–5.[10]

Snow, Eliza Roxey (Smith), 1804–1887, Churchwoman; NAW (under Smith)

Statue, Rose Garden of Pioneer Memorial Museum, 300 North Main Street

Eliza Roxey Snow was one of the most influential, creative, and dedicated women of the Mormon church. When the Women's Relief Society was created in 1842 she was its secretary. Later, in Utah, she directed the organization from 1866 to 1887. She founded women's cooperative stores, a women's hospital, a kindergarten, and a woman's newspaper. She defended the church against attacks by those who accused it of subjecting women. In 1880 she was ordained president of the L.D.S. women's organizations throughout the world. She was a serious student of the Bible and a poet, author of the most lofty of Mormon hymns, "O, My Father." The song—words and music—is reproduced in bronze at her grave in Brigham Young's private cemetery, First Avenue between North State and A Streets. She had been the wife, successively, of both Joseph Smith and Brigham Young.

Wells, Emmeline Woodward, 1828–1921, Journalist and Churchwoman; NAW

Marble Bust, State Capitol

Emmeline Woodward Wells was editor, from 1877 to 1914, of the *Woman's Exponent*, one of the first long-lasting women's journals in the West. It cham-

Eliza Roxey Snow, Mormon woman leader, is memorialized by a statue at the Pioneer Memorial Museum in Salt Lake City, Utah.
Courtesy Daughters of Utah Pioneers.

pioned women's rights and brought news of women from all parts of the world to those of Utah. When Congress threatened to repeal woman suffrage for the territory in 1885–86, she was one of the leaders who lobbied, unsuccessfully, for its retention. She and others then formed the Woman Suffrage Association of Utah. Widely known and respected, ''Aunt Em'' was a model for Utah women. She presided over the Relief Society, which had some fifty thousand members. She wrote the words to the hymn ''Our Mountain Home So Dear.'' When she died the flags of Utah flew at half-mast. Seven years later the bust was placed in the capitol rotunda by the women of Utah.[11]

Young, Harriet Decker, 1803–1871, and Other Pioneer Women

Monument, This Is the Place, *Sunnyside Avenue, at Emigrant Canyon*

The three women who were included on the famous Mormon monument came with the first settlers to what was to become Salt Lake City in 1847. Harriet Decker Young was the wife of Lorenzo D. Young. At their arrival, after the long westward journey, she was seven months pregnant. ''Lorenzo,'' she said, ''we have traveled fifteen hundred miles over prairies, deserts and mountains, but feeble as I am I would rather go a thousand miles farther than stay in such a desolate place.'' Stay she did, and bore the first Mormon child in Utah.

Clara Decker Young (1828–1889) was Harriet's daughter by a previous marriage. She was the wife of Brigham Young, whom she married in Nauvoo, Illinois, when she was sixteen.

Ellen Sanders Kimball (1824–1869) was one of six orphans who came from Norway to America. She and her sister Harriet both were married in Nauvoo to Heber C. Kimball (who during his life had forty-five wives). Brigham Young's twenty-seven wives included Clara Young's sister Lucy.[12]

NOTES

In addition to sources mentioned below, I have had assistance from the Division of State History, State of Utah; Utah Travel Council; Daughters of the Utah Pioneers Museum; University of Utah Library; the Kanab Public Library; and the late Kate B. Carter.

1. Charlotte S. Rubinstein, *American Women Artists* (New York: Avon Books, 1982).
2. Orson F. Whitney, *History of Utah* (Salt Lake City, Utah: George Q. Cannon & Sons Co., 1904); correspondence, Huntsville Town Historians.
3. Correspondence, Huntsville Town Historians.
4. Nomination form, National Register of Historic Places; correspondence, Ogden Community Arts Council.
5. The Salt Lake City Council of Women has a centennial list of women elected to the Utah Hall of Fame.
6. *Brigham Young University: The First Hundred Years*, ed. Ernest L. Wilkinson

(Provo, Utah: Brigham Young University, 1975), vol. 3, app. 21; Whitney, op. cit.; Leonard Arrington, ''Blessed Damozels: Women in Mormon History,'' *Dialogue* 6 (Summer 1971); Kate B. Carter, *Our Pioneer Heritage* (Salt Lake City, Utah: Daughters of the Utah Pioneers, 1936); Claudia Bushman, *Mormon Sisters: Women in Early Utah* (Salt Lake City, Utah: Olympics Publishing Co., 1976).

7. Jill C. Mulvay, ''The Liberal Shall Be Blessed: Sarah M. Kimball,'' *Utah Historical Quarterly* 44 (Summer 1956); Andrew Jenson, *Latter Day Saints Biographical Encyclopedia* (Salt Lake City, Utah: Andrew Jenson Memorial Association, 1936), vol. 2.

8. *Brigham Young University*; Jenson, op. cit., vol. 4.

9. Ray Price, ''Utah's Leading Ladies of the Arts,'' *Utah Historical Quarterly* 38 (Winter 1970).

10. Ibid.; correspondence, Utah Arts Council.

11. Sherilynn Cox Bennion, ''*The Woman's Exponent*: Forty-two Years of Speaking for Women,'' *Utah Historical Quarterly* 44 (Spring 1976).

12. Whitney, op. cit., vol. 4.

WASHINGTON

BELLINGHAM

Higginson, Ella Rhoads, 1862–1940, Poet

Higginson Hall, Western Washington University, 516 High Street

The college hall was named in honor of Russell C. Higginson and Ella Rhoads Higginson because he was a member of the first board of trustees, 1895–99, and she was a ''neighbor and friend of the college for more than fifty years.'' The site of their home is now occupied by the Viking Union. Ella was a writer all her life, but recognition came slowly. She tried poems, short stories, a novel, a travel book, and was at last recognized as Washington's poet laureate. Her most famous poem, ''Four Leaf Clover,'' was many times set to music and was adopted as the official song of the General Federation of Women's Clubs.[1]

Wilson, Mabel Zoe, c. 1880–1964, Librarian

Mabel Zoe Wilson Library, Western Washington University

Mabel Zoe Wilson was Western Washington University's librarian from 1902 until her retirement in 1946. When she began, the first professionally trained librarian to be appointed, she found a single room with a few reference books, a pile of magazines, some outdated textbooks, and a few records. Long before her retirement, her energy and enthusiasm had resulted in a new library building with tens of thousands of books, pamphlets, and periodicals. At the dedication ceremony in 1964 in which the present building was given her name she was recognized as the ''true founder and creator of the library.''[2]

ENUMCLAW

Montgomery, Catherine, d. 1958, Conservationist

Interpretive Center, Federation State Forest, State 410, Near Greenwater

The State Forest, over six hundred acres of virgin timber, was acquired largely through the efforts of the Washington State Federation of Women's Clubs and presented to the state in 1964. Catherine Montgomery, an outstanding conservationist and educator, left part of her fortune to the state for park improvements, and when the center was built it was named for her. The park is open Apr. 15–Oct. 15, daily 6:30 A.M. to 10 P.M. The center is open June 15–Sept. 15, Wed.-Sun. 10–7.[3]

FORD

Eells, Myra Fairbanks, 1805–1878, and Mary Richardson Walker, 1811–1897, Missionaries

Monument, State 231

This is the site of Tshimakain, a mission established for the Spokane Indians in 1838 by Elkanah Walker and Cushing Eells and their wives. The four had traveled together across the plains and Rocky Mountains, even sharing a tent. As both women had been married just before the journey began, this must have caused them some problems in adjustment. Mary Richardson Walker, from a farm in West Baldwin, Maine, and Myra Fairbanks Eells, from Holden, Massachusetts, both kept journals on the long trek, and poignant reading they make. Both tell of one incident when they sat in a leaking tent in a downpour, the buffalo robe on the floor soaking wet. "We sit with our Indian rubber shoes, shawls and hoods on, it is so cold," wrote Myra. "Mrs. Walker has been crying. I asked her why she cried. She said to think how comfortable her father's hogs were. This made us both laugh and cry together."

The missionaries, sent by the American Board of Commissioners for Foreign Missions, entered on their work of Christianizing the Indians with high hopes, but the hard work and apparent failure of their attempts to change the ways of the Spokanes discouraged them. They held out here until 1847, when the Whitman mission at Waiilatpu (see Walla Walla, WA) was attacked and the Whitmans massacred. That put an end to all mission work for a time. The Eells and Walker families went to Oregon (see Forest Grove, OR). Cushing and Myra Eells later returned to Washington and were active in promoting Whitman Seminary, now Whitman College, in Walla Walla. The Tshimakain monument was dedicated in 1908 by the Washington State Historical Society and the Congregational churches of the state.[4]

OLYMPIA

Klager, Hulda, 1863–1960, Horticulturist

Memorial Plaque, Capitol Grounds

Hulda Klager was an experimental horticulturist, a nationally recognized authority on the hybridizing of lilacs. The plaque is surrounded by bushes from her lilac gardens in Woodland, Washington, q.v.

PASCO

Sacajawea, c. 1786–1812, Shoshoni Indian Guide; NAW

Sajawea State Park and Museum, Off US 12. Lake Sacajawea

The park named for the Bird Woman who accompanied the Lewis and Clark expedition of 1805–6 is a bird refuge. Lake Sacajawea, formed by Ice Harbor Dam on the lower Snake River, covers over nine thousand acres. The museum in the park is open June 16–Labor Day, Wed.-Sun. 10–6, May 1–June 15, 10–5; rest of year by appointment (509–545–2361). See Salmon, ID, and many memorials to Sacajawea throughout the Northwest.

SEATTLE

Cornish, Nellie C., 1876–1956, Musician and School Founder

Cornish School of Allied Arts, 710 E. Roy Street; NR

Nellie C. Cornish established a school of music in 1914 in a rented room containing a piano, a blackboard, and three chairs. A year later she had expanded her space to an entire floor and her curriculum to piano, violin, folk dancing, singing, French, painting, and eurythmics. Soon she added ballet, drama, composing, and a marionette department. Her aim was to include all of the arts—a pioneer venture not only in the Northwest but in the world. Ground was broken in 1921 for the present School of Allied Arts. Aunt Nellie, as she was affectionately called, sparked the cultural life of the area, and her school continues to act as a feeder institution for symphonies, ballets, galleries, and theaters.[5]

Leary, Eliza Ferry, 1851–1935, Social Leader and Antisuffragist

Leary House, 1551 10th Avenue East; NR

Eliza Ferry Leary was one of Washington's wealthiest women, the daughter of the first governor of the state and the wife of the mayor of Seattle. She was a prominent clubwoman and society leader, a founder of the local Daughters of the American Revolution. Among her charities were the Seattle Childrens Home and the Childrens Orthopedic Hospital, both of which she helped found. Due to her social position, she was chosen to represent the National Association Opposed to Woman Suffrage. However, she did nothing, and thus endeared herself to the active campaigners for the vote. The house was occupied by the American Red Cross after Leary died, and in 1948 it became the property of the Episcopal church and serves as the headquarters of the diocese.[6]

Ryther, Ollie, fl. 1880s–1920s, Social Worker

Ryther Child Center, 2400 N. E. 95th Street

Ollie Ryther organized a home for orphans in 1883. She kept no records, case studies, or financial accounts. She simply welcomed to her home any child who had no place to go. In 1920 the people of Seattle built a home for "Mother" Ryther and her children. She estimated that during her fifty-one years of caring for children she mothered more than three thousand. The present center treats maladjusted children.[7]

SPOKANE

Hutton, May Arkwright, 1860–1915, Humanitarian

Hutton Settlement, E. 9907 Wellesley; NR

May Arkwright Hutton and her husband, Levi Hutton, were both orphans who had made their own way in the rough world of mining in Idaho. There they found each other and were married, invested in silver mines, and grew wealthy. They moved to Spokane, and May, already known for her practical humanitarianism, threw herself wholeheartedly into working for better city government, jail reform, day nurseries, and training for women in housekeeping. An uneducated, rough-speaking, homely woman who weighed almost three hundred pounds and sometimes dressed in men's suits and smoked cigars, May was something of an embarrassment to the suffrage leaders when she joined their ranks. She believed the women's rights movement was not for the educated woman alone but for the sales girl, office girl, farm wife, and household worker, and she fought to have them represented in the suffrage organization. Levi and May together planned the Hutton Settlement as a happy, homelike place where orphaned children could grow as individuals. After May's death, Levi built the home as her memorial.[8]

STEILACOOM

Perkins, Mary, c. 1859–1941, Physician

Perkins Park, Union and Martin Streets

The likeness of Mary Perkins appears on a stone and brick monument in the park, which was dedicated in 1972. A native of Kentucky, Perkins graduated from nursing school and then earned an M.D. from the University of Michigan. She married another physician, Luther Perkins, and after the arrival of three children the family moved to Steilacoom. She practiced medicine from 1903 until three years before her death, first here and then in Tacoma, Washington. Luther was too ill to continue his work and died in 1911, which left Mary with the burden of raising and supporting the children. In Tacoma she was a school physician, and in 1918 she became the first woman doctor at Western State Hospital. Her soft southern speech, her dignified bearing, her fashionable dress, and her strict professionalism are remembered. The land for Perkins Park was donated to the city by her son in her memory.[9]

VANCOUVER

Pariseau, Esther (Mother Joseph of the Sacred Heart), 1823–1902, Churchwoman and Builder

Providence Academy, 400 E. Evergreen; NR

Esther Pariseau (Mother Joseph) came to Vancouver in 1856 from Montreal, Canada. She was one of five Sisters of Charity of Providence sent to minister to the needs of children and the poor. Soon after her arrival she supervised the building of a residence and a schoolroom and the first hospital in the Pacific Northwest, St. Joseph's, which opened in 1858. She had learned from her carriage-maker father to use woodworking tools and understood the basics of good construction. In 1873 she designed the academy building, supervised construction, and herself made the chapel woodcarvings. It is the earliest extant building of the many she designed.

With tireless energy, Mother Joseph and her sister nuns established schools and hospitals throughout the Northwest, raising the money themselves by traveling through the mining country and begging from the miners. After her death she was acclaimed by the American Institute of Architects as the first architect of the Pacific Northwest and honored by the Coast Lumbermen's Association as the first Northwest artist to work with wood. In 1977 the state legislature passed a bill to place a statue of Mother Joseph in Statuary Hall in the National Capitol to represent the state.

The Providence Academy building is now used for shops and offices.[10]

Short, Esther, 1806–1862, Pioneer and Town Developer

Esther Short Park, Columbia and W. 8th Streets

Esther Short and her husband, Amos Short, took up land near Fort Vancouver in 1845. When British representatives of the Hudson's Bay Company tried to evict them, Amos shot one of them. He was acquitted of murder. Shortly after, however, he was drowned and Esther was left with ten children. She developed the land and sold home sites, in effect founding the town of Vancouver. Part of the land was set aside for this public park. The statue here is not of Esther but is an idealized pioneer woman, by Avard Tennyson Fairbanks, given to the city by E. G. Crawford.

WALLA WALLA

Whitman, Narcissa Prentiss, 1808–1847, Missionary; NAW

Whitman Mission National Historic Site, US 12

Narcissa Prentiss Whitman, one of the first two white women to cross the Rocky Mountains, spent eleven years here at Waiilatpu, "the place of the rye grass." She taught and supervised the domestic economy of the mission she and her husband, Marcus Whitman, established in 1836. Her partner on the westward journey, Eliza Spalding, went with her husband, Henry Spalding, to Lapwai to establish a mission among the Nez Percés (see Spalding, ID). Narcissa's only child, a daughter, was tragically drowned here at the age of two. Over the years the Whitmans took in eleven foster children, including seven from one family whose parents had died on the Oregon Trail. Narcissa's initial enthusiasm and missionary zeal were deadened by the realities of pioneer life. Despondency over the loss of the baby, failing eyesight, lack of communication with her family back home, and finally repugnance at the intrusion into her home of the flea-ridden Indians made her life anything but joyous. That life was snuffed out in 1847 by the Cayuse Indians to whom she had already given all she could.

Marcus's enthusiastic reports of the opportunities for settlers in the West were in large part responsible for the great wave of western migration that began about 1843. The immigrants generally stopped at the Whitman mission for rest and guidance. Late in 1847 they brought an epidemic of measles. Marcus was able to treat the white children, who recovered, but the Indians had no immunity and did not respond to his medicine. The Indians believed he was poisoning their children. On November 19 a band of Cayuse men set upon the Whitman household, killed Marcus and Narcissa and twelve others, and took forty-seven prisoners. That tragedy effectually put an end to mission activity in the Northwest for some years. News of the massacre was carried East and Congress the following year created the Oregon Territory and sent a governor to establish law and order.

Narcissa's enduring fame rests less on her mission activity than on the remarkable journey across the country, much of it through a trackless wilderness uninhabited except by Indians and a few trappers, where no white woman had ever gone. She and Eliza kept accounts of their trip which are epics of American history. A number of markers trace their route through the West (see Casper, Daniel, and South Pass, WY).

A mass grave for the victims of the massacre is on a hillside above the mission site. Whitman College in Walla Walla and Whitman National Forest in Oregon perpetuate the name. Narcissa's childhood home in Prattsburg, New York, has been restored as a memorial to her.[11]

One tall shaft was placed on the grave site in memory of Mary Augusta Dix Gray (1810–1881) and her husband, William Gray. William had accompanied the Whitman and Spalding party westward in 1836 and two years later returned from a trip East with Mary, his bride, and three other missionary couples, including the Cushing Eellses and the Elkanah Walkers (see Ford, WA), and the Asa Smiths (see Kamiah, ID). The Grays were soon disillusioned by their lack of success in changing the ways of the Indians and left the mission in 1842 for Oregon. In 1916 their bodies were removed here from Warrenton, Oregon, and buried in the mass grave with the victims of the 1847 massacre.[12]

The mission site here is open June 1–Aug. 31, daily 8–8, winters 8–4:30; closed some holidays.

WOODLAND

Klager, Hulda, 1863–1960, Horticulturist

Hulda Klager Lilac Garden, 115 S. Pekin Road; NR

Hulda Klager was fascinated with lilacs and in her fifty-five years of work she is credited with developing over 250 new varieties. In addition to the lilacs, she hybridized dahlias, roses, apples, crabapples, peonies, magnolias, azaleas, and colored broom. She opened her gardens, her laboratory and showplace, to visitors, and instituted Lilac Week each May when the lilacs are in full bloom. The garden is off I–5 at exit 21, a mile and a half south of town. It is open daily, dawn to dusk; donations. Klager's home, restored by the Woodland Federated Garden Club, is open during Lilac Week or by appointment. See Olympia, WA.[13]

YAKIMA

Carbonneau, Belinda Mulrooney, 1872–1967, Businesswoman

Carbonneau Castle, 620 S. 48th Avenue, NR

Belinda Mulrooney Carbonneau was one of the colorful figures of the Yukon Gold Rush. She was working as a stewardess on a steamship between Seattle, Washington, and Skagway, Alaska, when she heard of the gold strike. She was there early, with a cargo of cotton goods and hot water bottles. When she went through the Chilcoot Pass and reached Dawson, in Yukon Territory, she made 600 percent profit on her goods. She opened a restaurant, erected cabins, and twenty miles from Dawson built the Grand Forks Hotel. Later she put up the Fair View, a luxury hotel in Dawson City, boasting electric lights, Turkish baths, and steam-heated rooms with brass beds. She married Count Charles Eugene

Carbonneau, a champagne merchant, who took her to Paris on a honeymoon. About 1910, by then millionaires due to Belinda's business acumen, the couple moved to Yakima and built the mansion people call the Castle. It is privately owned, part of it being used as a gift shop and art gallery, and the owners arrange tours for interested groups.[14]

NOTES

In addition to the sources mentioned below, I have had much assistance from Florence K. Lentz, State Office of Archaeology and Historic Preservation, Olympia, who supplied nomination forms; Marci Whitney, Tacoma; Tacoma Public Library; Washington State Library; Seattle Public Library; Seattle Historical Society; Eastern Washington State Historical Society; and the State Department of Commerce.

1. Lelah J. Edson, *The Fourth Corner, Highlights from the Early Northwest* (Bellingham, Wash.: the Author, 1951); Washington State Federation of Women's Clubs, "Ella Higginson, A Tribute" (1974).

2. Correspondence and clippings, Western Washington University.

3. Mildred Wells, *Unity in Diversity: The History of the General Federation of Women's Clubs* (Washington, D.C.: General Federation of Women's Clubs, 1953); correspondence and clippings, State Parks and Recreation Commission.

4. Clifford M. Drury, *First White Women Over the Rockies* (Glendale, Calif.: Arthur H. Clark Co., 1963–66); Opal Sweazea Allen, *Narcissa Whitman* (Portland, OR: Binfords & Mort, 1959).

5. *Miss Aunt Nellie: The Autobiography of Nellie C. Cornish*, ed. Ellen V. Browne and Edward N. Beck (Seattle: University of Washington Press, 1964); nomination form, National Register of Historic Places.

6. Laura V. Wagner, *Through Historic Years With Eliza Ferry Leary* (Seattle, Wash.: F. McCaffrey, Dogwood Press, 1934); nomination form, National Register.

7. Marci Whitney, *Notable Women* (Tacoma, Wash.: Tacoma News Tribune, 1977), a reprint of a series of articles on noted Washington women.

8. Benjamin H. Kizer, "May Arkwright Hutton," *Pacific Northwest Quarterly* 57 (Apr. 1966); James W. Montgomery, *Liberated Woman: A Life of May Arkwright Hutton* (Spokane, Wash.: Gingko House Publishers, 1974); nomination form, National Register.

9. Whitney, op. cit.

10. Sister Mary McCrosson and others, *The Bell and the River* (Palo Alto, Calif.: Pacific Books, 1975); John G. Brougher, "Mother Joseph, Great Humanitarian of the Northwest," *Pacific Northwesterner*, Summer 1975; correspondence, Clark County Historical Museum, Vancouver, and Sisters of Providence, Seattle; nomination form, National Register.

11. Drury, op. cit.; Allen, op. cit.; nomination form, National Register; brochure, Whitman Mission National Historic Site.

12. Drury, op. cit.

13. Nomination form, National Register. Clippings, brochure, and correspondence, Ardis R. Dye, Woodland Federated Garden Clubs.

14. Ibid.

WYOMING

CASPER

Hebard, Grace Raymond, 1861–1936, Historian and Educator; NAW

Plaque, Independence Rock National Monument, State 220, Near Alcova

Independence Rock is a 193-foot-tall rock covering 27 acres. It was a natural landmark for westward bound travelers, and passersby left numerous inscriptions on its surface. Even after the great flood of immigrants ceased to come by road, the rock was used as a handy place to erect markers. Grace Raymond Hebard's plaque is inscribed: "In memory of Dr. Grace Raymond Hebard, 1861–1936, Wyoming historian, author, educator." She was a teacher and administrator at the University of Wyoming (see Laramie, WY).

Whitman, Narcissa Prentiss, 1808–1847, and Eliza Hart Spalding, 1807–1851, Missionaries; NAW

Plaque, Independence Rock National Monument

Narcissa Prentiss Whitman and Eliza Hart Spalding came through here in 1836 with their husbands, bound for the Oregon country to serve as missionaries to the Indians. They were the first white women to approach the coast by way of the Rocky Mountains. See Spalding, ID, Walla Walla, WA, and Daniel and South Pass City, WY.[1]

CHEYENNE

Morris, Esther Hobart, 1814–1902, Suffragist and Justice of the Peace; NAW

Statue, State Capitol, Capitol Avenue. Marker at House, 2114 Warren Avenue (Private)

Esther Hobart Morris is credited with proposing the bill giving Wyoming its distinction as "the 1st government of the world to grant women equal rights"—a claim not entirely true. The story is that she entertained several members of the first territorial legislature and got them to promise to introduce a bill giving women the vote. They did so, and the bill passed the legislature in December 1869. Shortly afterward Morris was appointed justice of the peace in South Pass City, a position equivalent in frontier days to that of a judge. She held the position for less than a year, but in that time she presided over a large number of cases and felt she had proved that women were capable of holding public office.

In 1960 a statue honoring Morris was placed in Statuary Hall in the National Capitol as one of Wyoming's two representative citizens. The statue here is a replica. Historians have disputed the importance claimed for Morris as well as the boast that Wyoming women were the first in the country to vote. However, she stands as a symbol of independent western womanhood, equal to man and indispensable to him in public as well as private life. See South Pass City, WY.[2]

Ross, Nellie Tayloe, 1876–1977, State Governor

Governor's Mansion, 300 E. 21st Street; NR

In 1925 Nellie Tayloe Ross became the first woman to govern a state in the United States. Although elected on the same day, "Ma" Ferguson of Texas was inaugurated sixteen days later than Ross, to become the second woman state governor. Both were chosen to fill out the terms of their husbands. Ross had had no experience of public life and no preparation for addressing a legislature except that gained as president of the Cheyenne Woman's Club. Her two-year term was efficient if not spectacular, and although defeated for reelection she continued to be active in Democratic politics. In 1933 President Franklin D. Roosevelt appointed her director of the U.S. Mint, the first woman appointed to this position. She served in the office twenty years and saw the building of three new structures, the Fort Knox Bullion Depository, the West Point Depository, and a new mint in San Francisco, California, all bearing her name on their cornerstones. Her likeness was placed on a mint medal. She was universally liked, particularly by the women of her generation. On her hundredth birthday she received tributes from all over her state.[3]

Esther Hobart Morris, of South Pass, Wyoming, persuaded legislators to add a woman's suffrage clause to the territorial constitution of Wyoming. Wyoming women were the first American women to vote legally in a national election since 1807. Wyoming chose Morris to represent the state in Statuary Hall in the National Capitol in Washington, D.C. The sculptor was Avard Fairbanks.
Courtesy Architect of the Capitol, Washington, D.C.

CODY

Sacajawea, c. 1786–1812, Shoshoni Indian Guide; NAW

Statue, Buffalo Bill Historical Center, 720 Sheridan Avenue

This larger-than-life statue, by Harry Jackson, was unveiled July 3, 1980, one of the latest in the many tributes to Sacajawea, the Indian woman who was of inestimable help to the Lewis and Clark expedition of 1805–6 on their journey to the Pacific Coast and back. See Salmon, ID, and many memorials throughout the northwestern states.

Whitney, Gertrude Vanderbilt, 1875–1942, Sculptor; NAW

Whitney Gallery of Western Art, Statue of William F. Cody, Buffalo Bill Historical Center; NR

The Whitney Gallery, containing one of the finest collections of western art in America, was a gift from C. V. Whitney as a memorial to his mother, Gertrude Vanderbilt Whitney. The Historical Center is a memorial to William F. Cody, Buffalo Bill. In 1942 the first component of the center was delivered to the site in the form of a huge equestrian statue of Cody by Gertrude, its creator. The center now includes a museum, a Plains Indian Museum, and a Winchester Museum, the latter a collection of guns from the Winchester factory in New Haven, Connecticut.

Gertrude began to study art after her marriage to the wealthy sportsman, Harry Payne Whitney. To forestall "inaccurate and prejudicial judgements" of her work, she began to exhibit under an assumed name. But she was proud to use the name after she won honors and awards for her work. Well-known statues by her are to be seen in many cities of the United States and other countries. Her name is also commemorated by the Whitney Museum in New York City, which she founded. The statue of Buffalo Bill is considered one of her best surviving works.

The center is open June-Aug., daily 7–10; May and Sept., 8–5; Mar.-Apr. and Oct.-Nov., Tues.-Sun. 1–5; adm.[4]

DANIEL

Whitman, Narcissa Prentiss, 1808–1847, and Eliza Hart Spalding, 1807–1851, Missionaries; NAW

Plaque, Green River Rendezvous; NHL

The rendezvous, an annual meeting between fur traders and Indian trappers, usually celebrated with much drinking and noisy jubilation, was held at various places in the West. When the Whitman and Spalding party came through in

Ten-foot-high statue of Sacajawea, at the Buffalo Bill Historical Center, in Cody, Wyoming. © Harry Jackson, 1980. Photography by Ed Leikam.
Courtesy Wyoming Foundry Studios, Cody, Wyoming.

1836 on their way to the Oregon country, it was held here. The site is now in almost the same natural state as it was then.

Narcissa Prentiss Whitman and Eliza Hart Spalding were the cause of much wonder when they arrived at the rendezvous. The Indians had never seen white women and the Native American women were especially fascinated by their clothing and housekeeping methods. As for the missionaries, they observed that the tribeswomen did all the work, such as getting the wood, preparing food, pitching the lodges, packing and driving the animals, ''the complete slaves of their husbands.'' See Casper and South Pass City, WY, Walla Walla, WA, and Spalding, ID.[5]

LANDER

Sacajawea, d. 1884, Indian; NAW

Monument, Wind River Reservation

The monument was dedicated to Sacajawea in 1941, with some of her direct descendants present. Their belief was that the Sacajawea who lived to be almost a hundred years old, dying in April 1884, and was buried here, was the same woman who accompanied Lewis and Clark on their western journey to the Pacific in 1805–6. But other historians disagree and say that the Bird Woman actually died in 1812 and is buried in Mobridge, South Dakota, q.v. On the wall of the Bishop Randall Chapel, Shoshoni Cemetery, is a marker to Sacajawea.

LARAMIE

Downey, June Etta, 1875–1932, Psychologist; NAW

Downey Hall, University of Wyoming

June Etta Downey was a native of Laramie. Her father was largely responsible for the legislation creating the University of Wyoming and was on the board of trustees. Downey graduated from the university and went to Chicago, Illinois, to study philosophy and psychology. She returned to join the university as an instructor in English and remained here for the rest of her life, eventually heading the department of psychology and philosophy. She was a world authority on right- and left-handedness and handwriting and developed a personality test which gave her a place as a pioneer in clinical psychology. She was the first woman elected to the Society of Experimentalists, was a member of the council of the American Psychological Association, and was included in *American Men of Science* (now appropriately renamed *American Men and Women of Science*). The hall named for her was constructed in 1965 for the housing of women students; it is now coeducational.[6]

Hebard, Grace Raymond, 1861–1936, Historian and Educator; NAW

Hebard Room, American Heritage Center, University of Wyoming

Grace Raymond Hebard was a maverick from the start. She attended Iowa State University when it was "entirely a man's college" and studied civil engineering, a male occupation. Her B.S. degree earned her a job as a draftsperson for the U.S. surveyor general, a job she held for nine years while working for a master's degree. She was the first female admitted to the Wyoming bar (1898). Four years after the University of Wyoming opened its doors in 1887, she became a trustee and secretary to the trustees. In 1893 she received a Ph.D. and in 1906 was an associate professor. She served as librarian and taught subjects ranging from international law to children's literature. She was active in the woman's suffrage movement, promoted the marking of historical trails, and won the Wyoming tennis championship. Her chief intellectual interest was history, primarily western history, and she wrote seven books on the early history of the West and Wyoming. She was uncritical and tended to romanticize history, and it is largely due to her enthusiastic feminism that Sacajawea's role in western history and Esther Morris's in Wyoming have been given somewhat more importance than the facts justify. But as a teacher and administrator, her renown was well earned. See Casper, WY.[7]

Knight, Emma Howell, d. 1928, Educator

Knight Hall, University of Wyoming

In 1889 Emma Howell Knight married the territorial geologist Wilbur Knight and went with him to Keystone mining camp. There were sixteen brides in the camp that year and sixteen babies were born during the summer and fall, one of them to the midwife who delivered all the others. The rest of Emma's career seems less eventful. Wilbur was teaching at the University of Wyoming when he died in 1903. Emma was elected county superintendent of schools the following year. From 1911 to 1920 she was dean and advisor to women students at the university. After that she continued active in city affairs. The building named for her was first a woman's dormitory, built in 1941; it is now an office building.[8]

Stevens, Alice Hardie, 1900–1975, Civic Leader

Stevens Community Center, Ivinson Mansion, Between 6th and 7th and Ivinson and University; NR

The historical Edward Ivinson mansion was saved from destruction by a group of citizens headed by Alice Hardie Stevens, a charter member of the Laramie

Plains Museum Association (now housed in the mansion). Her preservation efforts were only a small part of her services to the community, which won her a Distinguished Community Service Award in 1965. As founder, officer, or member she served numerous organizations—the Laramie League of Women Voters, a chapter of the American Association of University Women, the Laramie Women's Club, local Camp Fire Girls, and Public Health Nurses. She was unpaid publicity writer for the Community Chest, Cancer Fund, Salvation Army, United Nations Association, and United Service Organizations. Besides teaching speech and journalism, she reported for the *Laramie Boomerang* and edited its women's page. The museum is open daily 10–12 and 1–4.[9]

LUSK

Shephard, Charlotte, d. 1879, Outlaw

Roadside Monument

The stone slab, on a gravel road some twelve miles southwest of town, is near the old Cheyenne–Black Hills stage road, on the south slope of Demmon Hill. It is inscribed: "Here lies Mother Featherlegs Shephard. So called, as in her ruffled pantalettes she looked like a feather-legged chicken in a high wind. She was a road house ma'am. An outlaw confederate, she was murdered by 'Dangerous Dick Davis the Terrapin' in 1879 for a $1500 cache." That tells it all, except why the citizens of Lusk in 1964 wished to commemorate Charlotte Shephard, the red-headed bandit queen. Road agents and outlaws were a colorful, if dangerous, part of the stagecoach scene, and the monument was intended to preserve a small bit of the American westward movement, a validation of the wildness of the wild West. Mother Featherlegs went with the territory.[10]

SOUTH PASS CITY

Morris, Esther Hobart, 1814–1902, Suffragist and Justice of the Peace; NAW

Esther Morris Home and Office, South Pass City State Historical Site

Esther Hobart Morris, credited with being coauthor of the first equal suffrage act in the country in 1869 and the first woman justice of the peace in 1870, lived in South Pass from 1869 to 1873. Later she lived in Cheyenne, Wyoming, q.v. She is described as a large woman, nearly six-feet tall, "with a craggy countenance, and blunt and explosive in speech." Carrie Strahorn, who knew her in later years, remembered her cheerfulness, kindness, and wisdom.

A commission as justice of the peace was issued at the same time for Morris and for Caroline Neil of Point of Rocks, Wyoming. It took Neil longer to qualify because she was born in England; there is no record that she ever heard any cases, while Morris heard many. If one can credit *Frank Leslie's Illustrated Newspaper* for June 25, 1870, the two women justices of the peace were "the terror of all rogues" and afforded "infinite delight to all lovers of peace and virtue." Morris herself made no claim that she was the mother of suffrage in Wyoming. It was made for her after her death by her son, a newspaper editor.

South Pass City is now part of the state's recreation system, and several of its buildings have been restored or reconstructed for visitors to explore. The Morris cabin is a reconstruction and it is not certain that it occupies the original site. The historical site is open May 15-Oct. 15, daily 9–6.[11]

Whitman, Narcissa Prentiss, 1808–1847, and Eliza Hart Spalding, 1807–1851, Missionaries; NAW

Marker, State 28

South Pass was the natural gateway to the Continental Divide. The marker in memory of the 1836 journey of the Whitmans and Spaldings, first missionaries to the Oregon country to cross the Rocky Mountains, mentions the women only as "wives" of Marcus Whitman and Henry Spalding. Three miles to the east of the highway, in the middle of a barren plain, is a neatly chiseled boulder reading: "Narcissa Prentiss Whitman. Eliza Hart Spalding. First White Women to Cross This Pass July 4, 1836." See Casper and Daniel, WY, Walla Walla, WA, and Spalding, ID.

NOTES

1. The story of these remarkable women is told in Clifford L. Drury's *First White Women Over the Rockies*, 3 vols. (Glendale, Calif.: Arthur H. Clark Co., 1963–66).
2. Lynne Cheney, "It All Began in Wyoming," *American Heritage* 24 (Apr. 1973); Taft A. Larson is the chief critic of the claim that Morris proposed the legislation for suffrage; see his "Woman Suffrage in Wyoming," *Pacific Northwest Quarterly* 56 (Apr. 1965), and other articles on suffrage in the state.
3. *Current Biography*, 1940; *New York Times*, Dec. 21, 1977.
4. Gene Ball, "Preserving the Western Legacy: The Buffalo Bill Historical Center," *Journal of the West* 20 (Jan. 1981); *American West* 17 (Mar.-Apr. 1980); correspondence, Wyoming State Archives, Museums and Historical Department.
5. Drury, op. cit.
6. Correspondence, Archives of Contemporary History, University of Wyoming.
7. Ibid.
8. Wilburta Knight Cady, "A Family Portrait," *Annals of Wyoming* 32 (Apr. 1961); correspondence, University of Wyoming.
9. *Laramie Daily Boomerang*, Aug. 26, 1975; *Mothers of Achievement in American History*, comp. American Mothers Committee (Rutland, Vt.: Charles E. Tuttle Co., 1976); correspondence, University of Wyoming and Laramie Plains Museum.

10. *Denver Post*, Empire Magazine, Nov. 19, 1978; correspondence, University of Wyoming.

11. Larson, op. cit.; Carrie Adell Strahorn, *Fifteen Thousand Miles by Stage* (New York: G. P. Putnam's Sons, 1911); correspondence, Wyoming State Archives, Museums and Historical Department.

Appendix I

CLASSIFIED LISTS OF WOMEN

Each region has been analyzed according to the fields in which the biographees were primarily active. Though a woman might fit into more than one category, each has been listed only once. Most of the headings and subheadings are self-explanatory. ''Communications'' includes lecturers, librarians, editors, publishers, and museum workers. ''Pioneer Life and Unusual Experience'' is a catchall group of women who do not fit into other fields: frontier women, Indian captives, victims, and heroines. The groupings vary somewhat from one region to another, which reflects not so much the strength of the region in a particular field but the type of activity for which women were honored in their own communities.

NEW ENGLAND WOMEN

Travel, Transportation, and Exploration

Peck, Annie
Workman, Fanny

Business and Labor

Auerbach, Beatrice
Boit, Elizabeth
Davis, Hannah
Greene, Catherine
Larcom, Lucy
Lewis, Ida
Rudkin, Margaret
Troup, Augusta

Communications

Goddard, Sarah
Hale, Sarah
Hewins, Caroline

Education

College Founders and Administrators

Agassiz, Elizabeth
Blunt, Katharine
Clapp, Margaret
Comstock, Ada
Cronkhite, Bernice
Doyle, Sarah
Irwin, Agnes
Lyon, Mary
Palmer, Alice
Smith, Constance
Smith, Sophia
Warren, Constance
Wheelock, Lucy
Woolley, Mary

Teachers and School Administrators

Baldwin, Maria
Beecher, Catharine

Chase, Mary
Crandall, Prudence
Crocker, Lucretia
Farmer, Fannie
Longfellow, Alice
Phelps, Almira
Pierce, Sarah
Porter, Sarah
Shaw, Pauline
Willard, Emma

Educators of the Handicapped

Cogswell, Alice
Keller, Helen
Macy, Anne
Rogers, Harriet
Yale, Caroline

Government and Politics

Knox, Lucy
Pepperrell, Lady
Rogers, Edith

Health

Physicians

Dimock, Susan
Jordan, Sara
Zakrzewska, Marie

Health Workers and Crusaders

Abbe, Penelope
Barton, Clara
Cutter, Carrie
Locket, Molly
Mahoney, Mary
Palmer, Sophia
Parsons, Emily

Performing Arts

Performers and Theater Workers

Crabtree, Lotta
Flanagan, Hallie
Kemble, Frances
Sanderson, Julia
Vincent, Mary

Musicians and Music Patrons

Cary, Annie
Coolidge, Elizabeth
Daniels, Mabel
MacDowell, Marion
Norton, Lillian

Religion and Philanthropy

Churchwomen

Dyer, Mary
Eddy, Mary
Hutchinson, Anne
Lathrop, Rose
Lee, Ann

Philanthropists

Fletcher, Mary
Harkness, Mary
Heller, Florence
Hemenway, Mary
McCormick, Katharine

Science and Nature

Bingham, Millicent
Cannon, Annie
Carson, Rachel
Draper, Mary
Fenwick, Lady Alice
Ferguson, Margaret
Fleming, Williamina
Hamilton, Alice
Ilg, Frances
Mitchell, Maria
Patch, Edith
Richards, Ellen
Shattuck, Lydia
Stanwood, Cordelia
Todd, Mabel
Whiting, Sarah
Whitney, Mary

Social Science and Reform

Adams, Abigail
Anthony, Susan
Belmont, Alva
Blackwell, Alice
Crowninshield, Louise
Dix, Dorothea
Dudley, Helena
Fayerweather, Sarah
Foster, Abigail
Freeman, Elizabeth
Fuller, Margaret
Hooker, Isabella
May, Abigail
Murray, Judith
Peabody, Elizabeth
Roosevelt, Anna Eleanor
Scudder, Vida
Sears, Clara
Smith, Abby
Smith, Hannah
Smith, Julia
Smith, Virginia
Stevens, Lillian
Stone, Lucy

Sports and Recreation

Allerdice, Ellen
Atkinson, Juliette
Berenson, Senda
Brinker, Maureen
Bundy, May
Lenglen, Suzanne
Mallory, Mollie
Moore, Elisabeth
Payson, Joan
Roosevelt, Ellen
Ryan, Elizabeth
Sears, Eleanora
Toulmin, Bertha
Wagner, Marie
Wallach, Maud
Wightman, Hazel

Visual Arts

Artists and Architects

Ames, Blanche
Anderson, Erica
Bulman, Mary
Day, Katharine
Hawthorne, Sophia
Moses, Anna
Nichols, Rose
Riddle, Theodate

Art Collectors and Patrons

Choate, Mabel
Gardner, Isabella
Griswold, Florence
Roberts, Elizabeth
Rockefeller, Abby
Webb, Electra

Sculptors

Cresson, Margaret
Fuller, Meta
Hosmer, Harriet
Huntington, Anna
Judson, Sylvia
Kitson, Theo
Longman, Evelyn
Whitney, Anne
Yandell, Enid

Writing

Writers for Children

Alcott, Louisa
Clarke, Rebecca
Lothrop, Harriet
Wiggin, Kate

Nonfiction Writers

Caulkins, Frances
Davis, Varina
Fisher, Dorothy
Hamilton, Edith
Richards, Laura
Ripley, Sarah

Schlesinger, Elizabeth
Tyler, Mary

Novelists and Storytellers

Cather, Willa
Glaspell, Susan
Howe, Julia
Jewett, Sarah
Kent, Louise
Stowe, Harriet
Wharton, Edith
Wood, Sally

Poets

Bates, Katharine
Bradstreet, Anne
Branch, Anna
Dickinson, Emily
Millay, Edna
Sigourney, Lydia
Tappan, Caroline
Thaxter, Celia

Pioneer Life and Unusual Experience

Alden, Priscilla
Duston, Hannah
Gaylord, Katherine
Hendee, Hannah
Johnson, Susannah
Nurse, Rebecca
Pabodie, Elizabeth
Rowlandson, Mary
Sampson, Deborah
Stark, Elizabeth
Story, Ann
Weston, Hannah
Willard, Mary
Winslow, Mary

SOUTHERN WOMEN

Travel, Transportation and Exploration

Berry, Harriet
Earhart, Amelia
Fort, Cornelia
Sacajawea
Stinson, Katherine
Stinson, Marjorie
Thaden, Louise

Business and Labor

Atkinson, Susie
Beal, Mattie
Duncan, Anne
Gentry, Ann
Gleason, Kate
Long, Jane
Patton, Mary
Pontalba, Micaëla
Riggs, Annie
Robins, Margaret
Sidbury, Charlotte
Turnbo-Malone, Annie
Tuttle, Julia
Walker, Maggie

Communications

Babcock, Bernie
Canton, Ruby
Culver, Essae
Dacus, Ida
Dixon, Margaret
Douglas, Mary
Ferguson, Elva
Ferguson, Lucia
Fulbright, Roberta
Gorgas, Amelia
Henry, Carmelite
Ideson, Julia
Johnson, Edith
Lane, Rose
McCullar, Bernice
McManus, Jane
Nicholson, Eliza
O'Keefe, Quincy
Perkerson, Medora
Royall, Anne
Speed, Hattie
Susong, Edith

Education

College Founders and Administrators

Baldwin, Mary
Berry, Martha
Bethune, Mary
Cottey, Virginia
Cruikshank, Margaret
Giles, Harriet
Lloyd, Alice
Morgan, Mary
Packard, Sophia
Read, Florence
St. Clair, Louella
Sibley, Mary
Wright, Elizabeth

Teachers and School Administrators

Albright, Ann
Baldwin, Alice
Benton, Alice
Blow, Susan
Brown, Charlotte
Butler, Susan
Cahalan, Mary
Camp, Cordelia
Campbell, Olive
Dickey, Sarah
Dobbs, Ella
Eaton, Rachel
Elliot, Margaret
Elliott, Harriet
Forten, Charlotte
Fox, Susie
Goodrich, Frances
Gray, Wil
Greenleaf, Mary
Harris, Agnes
Hester, Elizabeth
Kavanaugh, Rhoda
Laney, Lucy
Lyndon, Mary
McKee, Gertrude
McKimmon, Jane
Marshall, Ann
Mather, Rachel
Michael, Moina
Moore, Elizabeth
Morgan, Lucy
Munford, Mary-Cooke
Pettit, Katherine
Peyton, Annie
Randolph, Virginia
Robertson, Alice
Schofield, Martha
Sloop, Mary
Spencer, Cornelia
Stanley, Louise
Stewart, Cora
Stone, May
Stranahan, Ivy
Tevis, Julia
Towne, Laura
Turner, Hallie
Tutwiler, Julia
Washington, Margaret
Withers, Sarah
Wood, Edwina

Educators of the Handicapped

Keller, Helen
Macy, Anne
Wright, Sophie

Government and Politics

Caraway, Hattie
Davis, Alice
Davis, Varina
Dunn, Loula
Felton, Rebecca
Ferguson, Miriam
McCurtain, Jane
Mesta, Perle
Rogers, Edith
Tunstall, Loraine
Wallace, Lurleen
Ward, Nancy

Health

Physicians

Berrey, Ruth
Carroll, Delia

Dimock, Susan
Guion, Connie

Health Workers and Crusaders

Barton, Clara
Bass, May
Breckinridge, Mary
Crawford, Jane
Dix, Dorothea
Fletcher, Pauline
Goldsmith, Grace
Hancock, Cornelia
Mann, Celia
Moynahan, Sister Chrysostom

Musicians

Bilbro, Anne
Moore, Grace
Smith, Bessie
Williams, Mary

Law and Justice

Davis, Katherine
Harris, Mary
Mitchell, Edwina
Moore, Jessie
Price, Annie
Willebrandt, Mabel

Organization and Club Work

Birney, Alice
Browne, Maimee
Cotten, Sallie
Cunningham, Ann
Desha, Mary
Ellis, Lizzie
Gibbs, Henrietta
Goodlet, Caroline
Jarvis, Anna
Korn, Anna
Lawson, Roberta
Low, Juliette
Lumpkin, Mary
Waterhouse, Mary

Performing Arts

Performers and Theater Workers

Bankhead, Tallulah
Burson, Kalita
Hoblitzelle, Esther
Jones, Margo
Kemble, Frances
Mabie, Louise
Niggli, Josefina
Russell, Annie

Religion and Philanthropy

Churchwomen

Bennett, Belle
Bennett, Sue
Brent, Margaret
Brent, Mary
Crawford, Isabel
Eddy, Mary
Fillmore, Myrtle
Mallory, Kathleen
Moore, Martha
Neel, Isa-Beall
Robertson, Ann
Shuck, Henrietta
Tift, Bessie

Philanthropists

Bellingrath, Bessie
Biddle, Mary
Cole, Anna
Hearst, Phoebe
Hogg, Ima
Humphreys, Geraldine
Jeanes, Anna
Newcomb, Josephine
Stern, Edith
Vanderbilt, Edith

Science and Nature

Cox, Gertrude
Dormon, Caroline
Moore, Edith
Semple, Ellen
Taylor, Charlotte

Social Science and Reform

Reformers and Social Workers

Alderman, Carlotta
Barrett, Janie
Barrett, Kate
Breckinridge, Madeline
Brooke, Mary
Butler, Selena
Cannon, Ruth
Chapin, Sarah
Clay, Laura
Cone, Laura
Correjolles, Coralie
Farmer, Hallie
Gordon, Jean
Gordon, Kate
Haughery, Margaret
Hunt, Elayn
Ingram, Frances
Jacobs, Pattie
Johnson, Johnnie
Johnston, Elizabeth
McLendon, Mary
McMain, Eleanor
Marshall, Louise
Monroe, Lilla
Nation, Carry
Neville, Linda
Scott, Mary
Shaw, Anna
Terry, Adolphine
Tubman, Emily
Tuggle, Carrie
Valentine, Lila
Webster, Delia
Weil, Sarah
White, Eartha
Wisner, Elizabeth
Wright, Frances
Zande, Ethel

Preservationists and Conservationists

Baruch, Belle
Cate, Margaret
Cook, Fannye
Davis, Eva
DeZavala, Adina
Driscoll, Clara
Dwelle, Mary
Kellenberger, May
Latham, Maude
Orton, Dorothy
Porter, Gladys

Society and Public Life

Astor, Lady Nancy
Clay-Clopton, Virginia
Cruger, Lydia
LeVert, Octavia
Madison, Dolley
Murat, Catherine
Pickens, Lucy
Whistler, Anna

Sports and Recreation

Lewis, Ann
Montgomery, Margaret
Mulhall, Lucille
Shelton, Reine
Steele, Fannie
Thurman, Sissy
Woodyard, Sydna
Zaharias, Mildred

Visual Arts

Artists

Busbee, Juliana
Clark, Kate

Goldthwaite, Anne
Greenwood, Marion
Hambidge, Mary
Metcalfe, Augusta
Parrish, Clara
White, Elizabeth

Art Collectors and Patrons

Blaffer, Sarah
Clubb, Laura
Cummer, Ninah
High, Harriett
McNay, Marion
Peters, Susan
Ringling, Mable
Rockefeller, Abby
Seebold, Nettie
Stewart, Euphan

Sculptors

Fraser, Laura
Hahn, Nancy
Hosmer, Harriet
Huntington, Anna
Lander, Louisa
Ney, Elisabet
Scholz, Belle
Yandell, Enid

Writing

Writers for Children

Burnett, Frances
Calhoun, Frances
Johnston, Annie

Nonfiction Writers

Andrews, Eliza
Chesnut, Mary
Connor, Jeanette
Dawson, Sarah
Dorsey, Sarah
Foreman, Carolyn
Gregorie, Anne
King, Grace
Lewis, Anna
Owen, Marie
Tartt, Ruby
Wright, Muriel

Novelists and Storytellers

Bonner, Katharine
Buck, Pearl
Cather, Willa
Chopin, Kate
Davis, Rebecca
Fitzgerald, Zelda
French, Alice
Furman, Lucy
Glasgow, Ellen
Harris, Corra
Hurston, Zora
Keyes, Frances
Mitchell, Margaret
Murfree, Mary
O'Connor, Flannery
O'Neill, Rose
Rawlings, Marjorie
Rice, Alice
Rives, Amélie
Stowe, Harriet
Tiernan, Frances
Wilder, Laura
Wilson, Augusta
Woolson, Constance

Poets

Montgomery, Roselle
Reed, Ida
Spencer, Anne
Weeden, Marie
Wheatley, Phillis
Whitson, Beth

Pioneer Life and Unusual Experience

Atzeroth, Juliann
Babb, Bianca
Boone, Rebecca
Brown, Margaret

Burk, Martha
Cole, Hanna
Crockett, Elizabeth
Crockett, Polly
Dare, Virginia
Daugette, Annie
Francis, Milly
Gibson, Irene
Inglis, Mary
Jai, Anna
Journeycake, Sally
Labiche, Emmeline
MacDonald, Flora
Martus, Florence
Musgrove, Mary
Otahki
Parker, Cynthia
Pocahontas
Sage, Caty
Sevier, Catherine
Starr, Belle
Troutman, Joanna
Whitney, Ann
Wiley, Jenny

Revolutionary War Figures

Bailey, Anne
Barker, Penelope
Barry, Kate
Bell, Martha
Geiger, Emily
Hart, Nancy
Motte, Rebecca
Slocumb, Mary
Turner, Kerenhappuck
Zane, Elizabeth

Civil War Figures

Boyd, Belle
Greenhow, Rose
Hart, Nancy
Murphree, Celia
Murphree, Winnie
Sansom, Emma
Turner, Lizabeth
Tynes, Mary
Van Lew, Elizabeth

Agriculture and Horticulture

Armstrong, Henrietta
Burns, Mamie
Combs, Loula
Greene, Catherine
King, Henrietta
Leigh, Frances
Matthews, Sallie
Metoyer, Marie
Miller, Ellen
Pinckney, Eliza
Pringle, Elizabeth
Scull, Sarah
Selby, Marie

MID-ATLANTIC WOMEN

Business and Labor

Ames, Elizabeth
Brent, Margaret
Brett, Cathryna
Dreier, Mary
Estaugh, Elizabeth
Grossinger, Jennie
Kellor, Frances
Knox, Rose
Loehmann, Frieda
Lukens, Rebecca
Moody, Lady Deborah
O'Reilly, Leonora
Roebling, Emily
Schneiderman, Rose
Shaver, Dorothy
Smith, Catherine
Walker, Sarah

Communications

Askew, Sarah
Briggs, Emily
Folger, Emily

Giffin, Etta
Harper, Frances
Meyer, Agnes
Meyer, Annie
Ottendorfer, Anna
Reid, Helen
Royall, Anne
Swisshelm, Jane
Tarbell, Ida
Wallace, Lila
Zenger, Anna

Education

College Founders and Administrators

Bethune, Mary
Douglass, Mabel
Lyon, Mary
Palmer, Alice
Scribner, Lucy
Thomas, Martha
Watteville, Henrietta

Teachers and School Administrators

Baldwin, Maria
Birch, Louise
Burroughs, Nannie
Carnell, Laura
Cook, Alice
Coppin, Fanny
Howland, Emily
Knipp, Anna
Miner, Myrtilla
Mitchell, Lucy
Moten, Lucy
Packer, Harriet
Richman, Julia
Richmond, Sarah
Sanford, Maria
Simpson, I. Jewell
Slowe, Lucy
Tall, Lida
Valle, Marta
Willard, Emma

Educators of the Handicapped

Benson, Elizabeth
Cogswell, Alice
Eustis, Dorothy
Hanson, Agatha
Holt, Winifred
Katzenbach, Marie
Keller, Helen
Lowman, Alto
Switzer, Mary

Government and Politics

Aliquippa, Queen
Davis, Vera
Montour, Madam
Perkins, Frances

Health

Physicians

Bassett, Mary
Blackwell, Elizabeth
Blackwell, Emily
Bodley, Rachel
Cleveland, Emeline
Greene, Cordelia
Guion, Connie
L'Esperance, Elise
Longshore, Hannah
Lozier, Clemence
Macfarlane, Catharine
Marshall, Clara
Preston, Ann
Sabin, Florence
Tracy, Martha
Winslow, Caroline

Nurses

Delano, Jane
Dock, Lavinia
Hancock, Cornelia
Maass, Clara
Maxwell, Anna
Palmer, Sophia
Spencer, Elmina

Health Crusaders

Barton, Clara
Bissell, Emily
Breckinridge, Aida
Dix, Dorothea
Sanger, Margaret
Van Rensselaer, Martha

Organization and Club Work

Desha, Mary
Lockwood, Mary
Simms, Sallie
Smyth, Alice
Walworth, Ellen
Washington, Eugenia
Webb, Aileen

Performing Arts

Performers and Theater Workers

Cornell, Katharine
Cushman, Charlotte
Flanagan, Hallie
Isaacs, Edith
Mills, Florence

Musicians and Music Patrons

Braslau, Sophie
Coolidge, Elizabeth
Diller, Angela
Mannes, Clara
Pons, Lily
Ponselle, Rosa
Quaile, Elizabeth
Sembrich, Marcella
Ward, Justine
Whittall, Gertrude
Zimbalist, Mary

Law and Justice

Donlon, Mary
Gillett, Emma
Mussey, Ellen

Religion and Philanthropy

Churchwomen

Cabrini, Saint Frances
Cannon, Harriet
Drexel, Katharine
Heck, Barbara
Hutchinson, Anne
Lee, Ann
McGroarty, Susan
Pariseau, Esther
Regan, Agnes
Reifsnyder, Elizabeth
Seton, Saint Elizabeth
Shipley, Elizabeth
Spalding, Eliza
Swain, Clara
Tekakwitha, Kateri
Thoburn, Isabella
Whitman, Narcissa
Wilkinson, Jemima

Philanthropists

Caldwell, Mary
Harkness, Rebekah
Hearst, Phoebe
McCormick, Katharine
Post, Marjorie
Sage, Margaret
Schenley, Mary
Terry, Julia
Warburg, Frieda
Wilson, Sarah

Science and Nature

Cannon, Annie
Carson, Rachel
Colden, Jane
Earhart, Amelia
Henry, Mary
Horney, Karen
Mead, Margaret
Mitchell, Maria
Robinson, Winifred

Social Science and Reform

Women's Rights Leaders

Anthony, Mary
Anthony, Susan
Belmont, Alva
Bloomer, Amelia
Boissevain, Inez
Burns, Lucy
Garrett, Mary
Hunt, Jane
McClintock, Mary
Morris, Esther
Mott, Lucretia
Paul, Alice
Rogers, Julia
Shaw, Anna
Stanton, Elizabeth

Reformers and Social Workers

Addams, Jane
Boardman, Mabel
Cary, Mary Ann
Crandall, Prudence
Dodge, Grace
Douglass, Helen
Einstein, Hannah
Green, Gretchen
Grimké, Charlotte
Jackson, Lillie
Kelley, Florence
Lampkin, Daisy
Lewisohn, Irene
Loeb, Sophie
Lowell, Josephine
Matthews, Victoria
O'Neill, Margaret
Palmer, Ellen
Parkhurst, Marion
Peter, Sarah
Pratt, Anna
Rice, Julia
Roosevelt, Anna Eleanor
Seward, Olive
Simkhovitch, Mary
Szold, Henrietta
Terrell, Mary
Towle, Charlotte
Truth, Sojourner
Tubman, Harriet
Wald, Lillian
Warner, Emalea
Willard, Frances
Wise, Louise
Woerishoffer, Emma

Preservationists and Conservationists

Crowninshield, Louise
Edge, Mabel
Ridgeley, Mabel
Rittenhouse, Sarah

Society and Public Life

Bonaparte, Elizabeth
Churchill, Jennie
Hayes, Lucy
Johnston, Harriet
Madison, Dolley
Roosevelt, Sara
Wilson, Edith

Visual Arts

Artists and Architects

Adams, Marian
Austen, Elizabeth
Barney, Alice
Bethune, Louise
Bliss, Mildred
Farrand, Beatrix
Greenwood, Marion
Oakley, Violet
Wright, Patience

Art Collectors and Patrons

Bliss, Lizzie
Cone, Claribel
Cone, Etta
Force, Juliana

Havemeyer, Louisine
Lang, Florence
Marchais, Jacques
Rockefeller, Abby
Stevenson, Christine
Sullivan, Mary

Sculptors

Callery, Mary
Cohen, Katherine
Farnham, Sally
Foley, Margaret
Frishmuth, Harriet
Huntington, Anna
Johnson, Adelaide
Longman, Beatrice
Mears, Helen
Nevin, Blanche
Putnam, Brenda
Ream, Vinnie
Scaravaglione, Concetta
Stebbins, Emma
Turnbull, Grace
Vonnoh, Bessie
Whitney, Gertrude

Writing

Writers for Children

Burnett, Frances
Warner, Susan

Nonfiction Writers

Cooper, Susan
Lippincott, Sara
Trask, Kate
Warner, Anna

Novelists and Storytellers

Barr, Amelia
Buck, Pearl
Freeman, Mary
Kerr, Sophie
Porter, Katherine
Stein, Gertrude
Stowe, Harriet
Wilder, Laura

Poets

Doolittle, Hilda
Ferguson, Elizabeth
Lazarus, Emma
Millay, Edna
Moore, Marianne
Reese, Lizette
Stockton, Annis
Wheatley, Phillis

Pioneer Life and Unusual Experience

Carroll, Anna
Freeman, Hannah
Fritchie, Barbara
Jemison, Mary
Knight, Kitty
Pickersgill, Mary
Slocum, Frances
Surratt, Mary
Swetland, Hannah
Wade, Jennie
Wright, Susanna

Revolutionary War Figures

Arnett, Hannah
Caldwell, Hannah
Corbin, Margaret
Livingston, Susan
Ludington, Sibyl
Murray, Mary
Pitcher, Molly
Ross, Elizabeth
Whitall, Ann

Agriculture and Horticulture

Haines, Jane
King, Louisa
Penn, Hannah
Steele, Cecile

MIDWESTERN WOMEN

Travel, Transportation, and Exploration

Earhart, Amelia
Johnson, Osa

Business and Labor

Helbing, Cleora
Jones, Mary
La Framboise, Madeline
Logan, Sallie
Miller, Bina
Newbury, Mollie
Palmer, Nelle
Savery, Annie
Walker, Sarah

Communications

Boyd, Anne
Countryman, Gratia
Doren, Electra
Eastman, Linda
Eddy, Mary
Gaar, Julia
Halsted, Gertie
Leslie, Annie
Massee, May
Patterson, Eleanor
Spencer, Mary
Strauss, Juliet
Swisshelm, Jane
Watson, Carrie

Education

College Founders and Administrators

Comstock, Ada
Guerin, Anne
Gurney, Eliza
Ireland, Ellen
McHugh, Anne
Morgan, Mary
Shimer, Frances

Teachers and School Administrators

Baker, Edna
Beecher, Catharine
Booth, Ellen
Bradford, Mary
Brown, Hallie
Harrison, Elizabeth
Hilleboe, Gertrude
Hogrefe, Pearl
Larson, Agnes
Mellby, Agnes
Meyers, Sister Anna
Mortimer, Mary
Parkhurst, Helen
Pennell, Rebecca
Porter, Eliza
Sabin, Ellen
Samuelson, Agnes
Sanford, Marie
Schurz, Margarethe
Sudlow, Phoebe
White, Helen
Young, Ella

Educators of the Handicapped

Baker, Laura
Trader, Florence
Trader, Georgia

Government and Politics

Bolton, Frances
Meir, Golda
Miller, Ola
O'Neill, Lottie
Pendray, Carolyn
Salter, Susanna

Health

Physicians

Dodds, Susan
Hill, Elizabeth

Longstreet, Martha
Minoka-Hill, Lillie
Newcomb, Kate
Ripley, Martha
Thompson, Mary
Van Hoosen, Bertha

Nurses and Health Crusaders

Barton, Clara
Bevier, Isabel
Bickerdyke, Mary
Brooks, Marguerite
Harvey, Cordelia
Hay, Helen
Taylor, Lucy

Organization and Club Work

Adams, Mary
Doggett, Kate
Fauntleroy, Constance
Fox, Emma
Houghton, Dorothy
Lewis, Julia
Logan, Mary
Morris, Lucy
Solomon, Hannah
Stone, Lucinda
Walworth, Ellen

Performing Arts

Performers and Theater Workers

Bonstelle, Jessie
Castle, Irene

Musicians and Music Patrons

Bond, Carrie
Densmore, Frances
Hackley, Emma
Jackson, Mahalia
Price, Florence
Schumann-Heink, Ernestine
Swensson, Alma
Von Elsner, Marie

Law and Justice

Bartelme, Mary
Bedell, Virginia
Bradwell, Myra
Mansfield, Arabella

Religion and Philanthropy

Churchwomen

Bishop, Harriet
Crane, Caroline
Dempsey, Julia
Dudzik, Josephine
Hayden, Margaret
Kittlesby, Agnes
Meyer, Lucy
Molloy, Mary
Peter, Sarah
Segale, Rose
Smith, Emma
Tank, Mrs. Neils
White, Ellen

Philanthropists

Bradley, Lydia
Buckingham, Kate
Garrett, Eliza
Kohler, Ruth
McCormick, Nettie
Palmer, Lizzie
Rotch, Charity
Watkins, Elizabeth

Science and Nature

Braun, Emma
Kendrick, Pearl
Stratton-Porter, Gene

Social Science and Reform

Women's Rights Leaders

Bloomer, Amelia
Brown, Olympia
Catt, Carrie

Darwin, Mary
Hooper, Jessie
Monroe, Lilla
Shaw, Anna
Stone, Lucy
Truth, Sojourner
Ueland, Clara

Reformers and Social Workers

Binford, Jessie
Coffin, Catharine
Cowles, Betsy
DeCleyre, Voltairine
Flynn, Elizabeth
Goldman, Emma
Gomon, Josephine
Gordon, Anna
Haviland, Laura
Hillis, Cora
Holley, Susan
Jacobs, Mary
Kander, Lizzie
Muller, Eliza
Nation, Carry
Nelson, Julia
Parsons, Lucy
Rankin, Jean
Smith, Ida
Stewart, Eliza
Thompson, Eliza
Wells-Barnett, Ida
Willard, Frances
Wittenmeyer, Annie
Woods, Mehitable
Wright, Frances

Settlement House Workers

Addams, Jane
Bowen, Louise
Flower, Lucy
Gilman, Catheryne
Lathrop, Julia
McDowell, Mary
Stansbury, Margaret
Starr, Ellen

Society and Public Life

Eisenhower, Mamie
Palmer, Bertha

Sports and Recreation

Bauer, Sybil
Oakley, Annie

Visual Arts

Artists and Architects

Murdock, Louise
Storer, Maria
Stratton, Mary

Art Collectors and Patrons

Meredith, Anna
Rogers, Grace
Spencer, Helen
Taft, Anna
Thayer, Sallie

Sculptors

Eberle, Mary
Hoffman, Malvina
Kitson, Theo
Longman, Evelyn
Mears, Helen
Ream, Vinnie
Walker, Nellie
Wendt, Julia

Writing

Bolton, Sarah
Cary, Alice
Cary, Phoebe
Chandler, Elizabeth
Custer, Elizabeth
French, Alice
Gág, Wanda
Gale, Zona
Glaspell, Susan

Hansberry, Lorraine
Kinzie, Juliette
Sawyer, Ruth
Stowe, Harriet
Suckow, Ruth
Thorpe, Rose
Wilcox, Ella
Wilder, Laura
Woolson, Constance

Pioneer Life and Unusual Experience

Gardner, Abbie
Jenkins, Mary
Keller, Annie
Shelley, Kate
Slocum, Frances
Zane, Elizabeth

Agriculture and Horticulture

Jones, Sarah
Opel, Anna
Peck, Roseline
Sayre, Ruth
Shambaugh, Jessie
Wilson, Matilda

WESTERN WOMEN

Travel, Transportation, and Exploration

Boyd, Louise
Converse, Mary
Dorion, Marie
Earhart, Amelia
Parkhurst, Charlie
Sacajawea
Scidmore, Eliza
Sharp, Evelyn
Strahorn, Carrie

Business and Labor

Barnette, Isabelle
Carbonneau, Belinda
Cashman, Nellie
Fellows, Sophia
Lawing, Nellie
Lewis, Tillie
Macia, Ethel
Newcomb, Franc
Smith-Hayward, Mary
Stone, Elizabeth
Wallen, Erika

Communications

Journalists and Lecturers

Ailshie, Margaret
Gossage, Alice
Page, Alice
Scripps, Ellen
Tibbles, Susette
Wells, Emmeline
Winnemucca, Sarah

Librarians and Museum Workers

Allyn, Edna
Colton, Mary-Russell
Fletcher, Alice
Foy, Mary
Hall, Sharlot
Henderson, Alice
Kitt, Edith
Wheelwright, Mary
White, Amelia
Wilson, Mabel

Education

College Founders and Administrators

Brown, Tabitha
Mills, Susan
Reinhardt, Aurelia

Stanford, Jane
Stebbins, Lucy

Teachers and School Administrators

Andrus, Ethel
Atkins, Mary
Babcock, Eliza
Burke, Katherine
Cheney, May
Clapp, Hanna
Clark, Orah
Clarke, Cecile
Cooke, Juliette
Cooper, Sarah
Dorsey, Susan
Drake, Marie
Frazier, Maude
French, Permeal
Griffith, Emily
Hammond, Mary
Hess, Harriet
Isbell, Olive
Kennedy, Kate
Knight, Emma
McLain, Carrie
Mears, Jane
Paul, Tillie
Pound, Louise
Reynolds, Alice

Government and Politics

Blue, Virginia
Campbell, Clara
Edson, Katherine
Emma, Queen
Kaahumanu
Kaiulani, Princess
Kalama, Queen
Kamamalu, Victoria
Kapiolani, Chiefess
Kapiolani, Queen
Keelikolani, Ruth
Kekauluohi, Chiefess
Keopualani, Queen
Kinau, Chiefess
Lilioukalani
Moore, Dora
Nahienaena, Princess
Rankin, Jeannette
Ross, Nellie

Health

Physicians

Brown, Charlotte
Buckel, Cloe
Ferguson, Belle
Howe-Waffle, Willella
Owens-Adair, Bethenia
Perkins, Mary
Picotte, Susan
Pratt, Romania
Sabin, Florence
Shipp, Ellis
Smith, Mary
Wanzer, Lucy

Health Workers and Crusaders

Bates, Alta
Morgan, Agnes
Smyth, Mabel

Organization and Club Work

Decker, Sarah
Lambert, Rebecca
Peabody, Lucy

Performing Arts

Performers and Theater Workers

Babcock, Maud
Bonfils, Helen
Crabtree, Lotta
Duncan, Isadora
Kanaka'ole, Edith
Leitzel, Lillian
Modjeska, Helena
Montez, Lola

Rippon, Mary
St. Denis, Ruth

Musicians and Music Patrons

Bond, Carrie
Bowen, Emma
Cornish, Nellie
Lehmann, Lotte
Nevada, Emma
Yaw, Ellen

Law and Justice

Hulett, Alta

Religion and Philanthropy

Churchwomen

Arguëllo, Maria
Bancroft, Henrietta
Brooks, Nona
Cabrini, Saint Frances
Cope, Barbara
Gates, Susa
Gleason, Caroline
Kimball, Ellen
Kimball, Sarah
LaDue, Francia
McPherson, Aimee
Mitchell, Rebecca
O'Donnell, Catherine
Pariseau, Esther
Richards, Emily
Robinson, Jane
Russell, Katherine
Snow, Eliza
Tingley, Katherine
White, Ellen
Young, Clara
Young, Harriet
Young, Zina

Missionaries

Chamberlain, Maria
Eells, Myra
Gray, Mary
Hall, Susan
McBeth, Kate
McBeth, Susan
McFarland, Amanda
Rice, Mary
Smith, Sarah
Spalding, Eliza
Walker, Mary
Whitman, Narcissa
Willard, Caroline

Philanthropists

Barnsdall, Louise
Bidwell, Annie
Bishop, Bernice
Crocker, Margaret
Hearst, Phoebe
Kent, Elizabeth
Mackay, Marie
Morrison, May
Sather, Jane
Spreckels, Alma
Stern, Rosalie
Swanzy, Julie
Tingley, Carrie

Science and Nature

Alexander, Annie
Bilger, Leonore
Downey, June
Eastwood, Alice
Mexia, Ynes
Yeaw, Effie

Social Science and Reform

Women's Rights Leaders

Bradford, Mary
Duniway, Abigail
Hughes, Josephine
Hutton, May
Martin, Anne
Morris, Esther
Pyle, Mary
Sargent, Ellen

Reformers and Social Workers

Abbott, Edith
Abbott, Elizabeth
Abbott, Grace
Anderson, Elizabeth
Bryan, Mary
Cameron, Donaldina
Jacobs, Frances
Pleasant, Mary
Pound, Laura
Ryther, Ollie
Spencer, Dorcas
Spiegelberg, Flora
Stevens, Alice
Willard, Frances
Yaw, Caroline

Preservationists and Conservationists

Evans, Anne
Honeyman, Jessie
McClurg, Virginia
McFarlane, Ida
Montgomery, Catherine
Sterling, Christine

Society and Public Life

Coit, Lillie
De Mores, Medora
Dillingham, Louise
Leary, Eliza

Sports and Recreation

Randall, Josephine
Wightman, Hazel

Visual Arts

Artists and Architects

Blumenschein, Mary
Bremer, Anne
Brodt, Helen
Cable, Margaret
Colter, Mary
Dat So La Lee
Dolan, Elizabeth
Fenyes, Eva
Green, Emma
Hudson, Grace
Magafan, Jenne
Morgan, Julia
Rice, Lilian
Tennent, Madge
Van Briggle, Anne
Waterman, Hazel
Wurster, Catherine

Art Collectors and Patrons

Cooke, Anna
Eccles, Bertha
Harwood, Elizabeth
Heard, Maie
Horne, Alice
Joslyn, Sarah
Kerns, Maude
Luhan, Mabel
Nicholson, Grace
Taylor, Alice

Sculptors

Huntington, Anna
Wendt, Julia
Whitney, Gertrude

Writing

Aldrich, Bess
Austin, Mary
Cather, Willa
Clapp, Louise
Coolbrith, Ina
Custer, Elizabeth
Fergusson, Erna
Hebard, Grace
Higginson, Ella
Jackson, Helen
Lane, Rose
Mack, Effie
Norris, Kathleen
Sandoz, Mari

Victor, Frances
Wilder, Laura

Pioneer Life and Unusual Experience

Bowers, Eilly
Brown, Clara
Freeman, Agnes
Johnson, Mary
McLoughlin, Marguerite
Nathoy, Lalu
Ronan, Mary
Short, Esther
Tallent, Annie
Walsh, Mollie

Heroines and Celebrities

Aleblemot, Tolo
Brown, Margaret
Bulette, Julia
Burk, Martha
Chipeta
Freeman, Minnie
Gardner, Abbie
Juana Maria
Meeker, Josephine
Oatman, Olive
Rooke, Sarah
Sacajawea
Shephard, Charlotte
Tabor, Elizabeth
Tubbs, Alice
White Buffalo Girl
Winchester, Sarah
Winema

Agriculture and Horticulture

Klager, Hulda
Morton, Caroline
Ross, Ida
Schnebley, Sedona
Sessions, Kate
Stewart, Helen
Tibbetts, Eliza

Appendix II

SOME SIGNIFICANT DATES IN WOMEN'S HISTORY

1607 English settle in Jamestown (Virginia)
1620 First pilgrims arrive in Plymouth (Massachusetts) on the *Mayflower*
1626 Peter Minuit buys Manhattan Island from the Indians
1637 Ann Hutchinson banished from Massachusetts Bay Colony for heresy
1660 Mary Dyer hanged on Boston Common for her Quaker faith
1692 Men and women tried as witches in Salem, Massachusetts
1774 First Continental Congress meets in Philadelphia, Pennsylvania; Declaration of Independence adopted
1787–90 New U.S. Constitution adopted and ratified
1792 Sarah Pierce establishes in Litchfield, Connecticut, first institution in America for the higher education of women; Mary Wollstonecraft publishes *A Vindication of the Rights of Women*
1821 Emma Willard opens Troy Female Seminary in Troy, New York
1833 Oberlin College established, admitting blacks, Native Americans, and women
1836 Narcissa Whitman and Eliza Spalding first white women to cross the Rocky Mountains
1837 Mount Holyoke Female Seminary established by Mary Lyon in Massachusetts
1838 Mobs angered by antislavery lecturers burn newly built Pennsylvania Hall in Philadelphia
1842 Augusta Female Seminary founded in Staunton, Virginia (now Mary Baldwin College)
1843 Miss Porter's School founded in Farmington, Connecticut; Dorothea Dix memorializes Massachusetts legislature on plight of mentally ill
1844 Mormon leaders lynched; Mormons leave Nauvoo, Illinois, for the West
1845 Margaret Fuller publishes feminist manifesto *Women in the Nineteenth Century*; Elias Howe invents sewing machine; Female Labor Reform Association founded
1846 Maine adopts nation's first prohibition against alcohol (on books until 1934)
1847 Maria Mitchell discovers a new comet
1848 Seneca Falls Convention; Boston Female Medical College established by Samuel Gregory
1849 Elizabeth Blackwell becomes first woman in America to graduate from an established medical school; Mormons establish State of Deseret (Utah)

1850 Woman's Medical College of Pennsylvania opens; first national women's rights convention held in Worcester, Massachusetts; Land Donation Act in Oregon gives a man and wife 640 acres, a single woman 320 in her own right
1851 Singer sewing machine patented; Bloomer costume adopted; Myrtilla Miner founds first teacher-training school for black women in Washington, D.C.
1852 Antioch College established in Yellow Springs, Ohio, admitting women; Harriet Beecher Stowe publishes *Uncle Tom's Cabin*
1855 Elmira College established in Elmira, New York
1857 New York Infirmary for Women and Children opened by Elizabeth and Emily Blackwell
1860 South Carolina secedes from United States, thus precipitating the Civil War.
1862 New England Hospital for Women and Children founded in Boston, Massachusetts, by Marie Zakrzewska; Homestead Act brings settlers to Kansas
1863 Dakota Territory opened to homesteaders; New York Medical College and Hospital for Women opened by Clemence Lozier
1865 Vassar College opens as a female seminary in Poughkeepsie, New York; Lee surrenders to Grant at Appomatox, ending Civil War
1866 Young Women's Christian Association founded in Boston, Massachusetts
1868 Sorosis woman's club founded in New York City; New England Women's Club founded in Boston, Massachusetts; Women's Typographical Union founded
1869 Wyoming Territory gets woman's suffrage; National Woman's Suffrage Association founded; first transcontinental railroad completed
1870 Arabella Mansfield of Iowa becomes the first woman regularly admitted to the practice of law in the United States; Utah Territory adopts woman's suffrage
1874 Typewriter invented; Woman's Christian Temperance Union founded
1875 Smith College opens in Northampton, Massachusetts; Wellesley College opens in Wellesley, Massachusetts
1877 Mary Baker Eddy publishes *Science and Health* and establishes a new religion
1878 Senator Aaron Sargent introduces in Congress the Anthony amendment giving women the vote (passed in 1919)
1879 Belva Lockwood becomes first woman admitted to practice before U.S. Supreme Court
1881 Helen Hunt Jackson's *A Century of Dishonor* calls attention to the unjust treatment of Native Americans
1882 Association of Collegiate Alumnae formed (predecessor of American Association of University Women); Clara Barton founds American Red Cross
1883 Washington Territory women win the vote (lost in 1889, when Washington became a state)
1885 Bryn Mawr College founded
1888 International Council of Women founded
1889 Hull House established in Chicago, Illinois, by Jane Addams and Ellen Starr
1890 General Federation of Women's Clubs founded; Daughters of the American Revolution founded; two suffrage organizations merged as National American Woman's Suffrage Association; Mormons prohibit polygamy
1892 Women's basketball devised by Senda Berenson at Smith College
1893 Henry Street Settlement established in New York City by Lillian Wald; Colorado adopts woman's suffrage; World's Columbian Exposition opens in Chicago, Illinois

1895 National Organization of Negro Women's Clubs organized in Boston, Massachusetts
1896 Utah joins the Union, with woman's suffrage; Idaho adopts woman's suffrage
1898 Hawaii annexed by United States; Washington, D.C., College of Law established by women
1903 Women's Trade Union League founded
1904 Ida Tarbell publishes *History of the Standard Oil*, first of the muckraking books
1910 Washington State women regain the vote
1911 Triangle Shirtwaist Company fire in New York City results in protective legislation
1912 Hadassah organized
1916 Jeanette Rankin becomes first woman elected to U.S. House of Representatives
1917 United States enters World War I
1919 Nineteenth (woman's suffrage) Amendment passes Congress; League of Women Voters founded
1920 Mary Anderson made first director of Woman's Bureau in U.S. Department of Labor; suffrage amendment ratified; Margaret Sanger publishes *Family Limitation* with explicit birth-control information
1921 Sheppard-Towner Act allows states to establish clinics for women and children
1922 Rebecca Felton becomes first woman seated in U.S. Senate
1923 Alice Paul proposes Equal Rights Amendment
1925 Nellie Tayloe Ross becomes first woman governor of a state (Wyoming); Miriam Ferguson elected governor of Texas
1929 Stock market crash begins Great Depression
1930s Dust Bowl destroys economy of many western states
1931 Jane Addams wins Nobel Peace Prize
1932 Amelia Earhart makes first transcontinental nonstop flight by a woman; Babe Didrikson wins gold and silver medals in Olympics; Frances Perkins becomes first woman in U.S. cabinet
1934–40 Hattie Caraway is first woman to serve a full term in U.S. Senate
1938 Fair Labor Standards Act passed
1941 United States enters World War II
1960 Enovid, first birth-control pill, goes on market
1962 Rachel Carson's *Silent Spring* calls attention to danger of agricultural pesticides
1963 Betty Friedan's *Feminine Mystique* sounds beginning of a new feminist movement
1965 Voting Rights Act passed
1966 National Organization for Women started
1975 Ella Tambussi Grasso elected governor of Connecticut
1976 Dixie Lee Ray elected governor of Washington State
1981 Sandra Day O'Connor is first woman named to U.S. Supreme Court
1984 Geraldine Ferraro is first woman on a major party ticket to run for vice president of United States

BIBLIOGRAPHIC ESSAY

For the history of American women, the best guide to current literature is Barbara Haber, *Women in America: A Guide to Books, 1963–1975* (Boston, Mass.: G. K. Hall, 1978). It is arranged by subject categories, ''according to those issues that have naturally emerged from the writings,'' and includes evaluations.

Much current material is found in periodicals, the learned journals published by historical societies and professional organizations as well as popular magazines. These can be found by consulting *America: History and Life* (Santa Barbara, Calif.: American Bibliographic Center–Clio Press, 1964–65 to date). It covers U.S. and Canadian history and is published in four parts: *A*. Article abstracts and citations (three issues annually); *B*. Index to Book Reviews (twice annually); *C*. American History Bibliography, citations of books, dissertations, and articles (annually); and *D*. Index to the preceding three parts by author and a subject profile index by subject and biographical, and geographic terms. Some libraries have computer access to the data base. Abstracts of articles of value to the historian of women, 1964–77, were separately published by the same press in *Women in American History: A Bibliography*, edited by Cynthia E. Harrison (1979).

The most recent and comprehensive source of biographical information on women in America is *Notable American Women, 1607–1950*, 3 vols., edited by Edward T. and Janet Wilson James and Paul S. Boyer (Cambridge, Mass.: Belknap Press of Harvard University Press, 1971). This is supplemented by *Notable American Women: The Modern Period*, edited by Barbara Sicherman and Carol Hurd Green (1980). The first includes women who died before January 1, 1951, the latter women who died between that date and December 31, 1975. Each biography in those volumes contains a listing of the principal printed, documentary, and manuscript sources.

A useful finding list for biographies of non-contemporary American women is Kali Herman's *Women in Particular: An Index to American Women* (Phoenix, Ariz.: Oryx Press, 1984). It lists women by field and career; by religious affiliation; by ethnic and racial origin; and geographically. Each entry refers to one or more of a selected list of biographical dictionaries or indexes.

For manuscript material, a recent and comprehensive guide is *Women's History Sources: A Guide to Archives and Manuscript Collections in the United States*, 2 vols., edited by Andrea Hinding and others (New York: R. R. Bowker Co., 1973). It not only locates papers of women and women's organizations in public collections but includes some valuable biographical information. It gives full citations to guides published by individual libraries to their own collections.

Microfilm publication has made the resources of great collections available to researchers who have access to large libraries. *History of Women*, published by Research Publications, Inc., in cooperation with nine distinguished women's history archives, is unequaled in scope. It includes printed books through 1920, pamphlets, periodicals not already available in microfilm, selected manuscripts, and a sampling of photographs. It encompasses holdings of the Schlesinger Library at Radcliffe College, the Sophia Smith Collection at Smith College, the Jane Addams Memorial Collection at the University of Illinois, the Galatea Collection of Books at the Boston Public Library, the private collection of Miriam Y. Holden, the Ida Rust Macpherson Collection at Scripps College, and further materials from the New York Public Library, the Widener Library at Harvard University, and the Yale University libraries. Research Publications (New Haven, Conn.) also publishes in microfilm H. Carleton Marlow's *Bibliography of American Women*, part I, covering the period to 1900.

The *Biography Index*, published periodically since 1946 by the H. W. Wilson Company, covers current books and articles on American men and women appearing in over fifteen hundred periodicals and professional journals, including some obituaries in the *New York Times*. It has an index by professions and occupations.

The *Biography and Genealogy Master Index: A consolidated index to more than 3,200,000 biographical sketches in over 350 current and retrospective biographical dictionaries*, edited by Miranda C. Herbert and Barbara McNeil (Detroit, Mich.: Gale Research Co., current edition) covers the world. Biographies appearing in collections (rather than one-woman biographies) up to 1968 are indexed in *Index to Women of the World from Ancient to Modern Times*, by Norma Olin Ireland (Westwood, Mass.: F. W. Faxon Co., 1970). It includes some magazine series and is particularly useful in locating material suitable for young readers. A revision is in preparation.

A Personal Name Index to the New York Times Index, 1851–1974, by Byron A. and Valerie R. Falk (Succasunna, N.J.: Roxbury Data Interface, 1976) gives access to the vast amount of biographical information in the *New York Times*, microfilm of which is available in most large libraries. The *New York Times* has also published annually since 1969 a biographical edition, containing all biographical articles, including obituaries, excerpted from its pages.

There is no comprehensive guide to historical sites. Raymond Pisney, *Historical Markers, A Bibliography* (Verona, Va.: McClure Printing Co., 1977) lists a great many separate guides, many of them not easily obtainable. States occasionally issue guides to historical markers placed under state auspices, and for a few states comprehensive works on historical sites are available. The Federal Writers' Guides prepared during the depression years for most of the states are indispensable, though outdated except for a few that have been brought up-to-date and reissued. Tour guides issued by auto clubs generally confine themselves to places along freeways or the larger cities. *The National Register of Historic Places* (Washington, D.C.: National Park Service, 1976) lists sites determined to be National Historic Landmarks, historical areas in the National Park Service, Natural Landmarks, and buildings in the Historic American Buildings Survey. The responsible government agency is the Department of the Interior, National Park Service. The list is kept up-to-date by a section in the *Federal Register* (Washington, D.C.: Government Printing Office), generally in the issue for the first Tuesday of February in each year, with monthly supplements.

In addition to regional and state guidebooks, a number of specialized travel guides have been published. *The American Woman's Gazetteer*, by Lynn Sherr and Jurate Kazickas (New York: Bantam Books, 1976), was the first to catalog sites associated with women and has been an invaluable starting point for the present volume. The "Discovering Historic America" series published by E. P. Dutton includes volumes for California and the West, the Mid-Atlantic states, and the Southeast. William Morrow & Company publishes Literary Tour Guides, one each for the Northeast, the West and Midwest, and the South and Southeast. Alice Hamilton Cromie compiled *A Tour Guide to the Civil War* (New York: E. P. Dutton, 1975). Bernard Postal and Lionel Koppman prepared *A Jewish Tourist's Guide to the U.S.* (Philadelphia, Pa.: Jewish Publication Society of America, 1954), and Marcella Thum, *Exploring Black America* (New York: Atheneum, 1975) and *Exploring Literary America* (New York: Atheneum, 1979). Margaret Hobbie compiled *Museums, Sites and Collections of Germanic Culture in North America* (Westport, Conn.: Greenwood Press, 1980). More such guides may be found by consulting Jon Heise's *The Travel Book: Guide to the Travel Guides* (New York: R. R. Bowker Co., 1981).

Guides to museums, outdoor sculpture, music festivals, gardens, wildlife preserves, and a host of other things to see and do yield much information about places associated with women.

General and local histories deal so little with women that the reader must look to specialized material. The most useful are histories of movements in which women were active—education, medicine, law, literature, science; the settlement movement, kindergarten, and early childhood education; and histories of women's clubs and organizations such as the Young Women's Christian Association. *The History of Woman Suffrage* is invaluable. The first three volumes were prepared by Elizabeth C. Stanton, Susan B. Anthony, and Matilda J. Gage; the fourth by Anthony and Ida Husted Harper; the fifth and sixth by Harper. Volumes I and II were published in New York by Fowler and Wells, 1881, 1882; III and IV, in Rochester, New York, by Susan B. Anthony, 1886, 1902; V and VI, in

New York by the National American Woman's Suffrage Association, 1922. All have been reprinted in New York by Arno and the New York Times, 1969.

A valuable single volume on the women's rights movement is Eleanor Flexner's *Century of Struggle*, rev. ed. (Cambridge, Mass.: Belknap Press of Harvard University Press, 1975).

Useful for regional background are such works as Laurel T. Ulrich, *Good Wives* (New York: Alfred A. Knopf, 1982); Julia Cherry Spruill, *Women's Life and Work in the Southern Colonies* (New York: Norton, 1972; first publ. 1938); and Ann Firor Scott, *The Southern Lady: From Pedestal to Politics, 1830–1930* (Chicago, Ill.: University of Chicago Press, 1970). Sandra L. Myres, *Westering Women and the Frontier Experience* (Albuquerque: University of New Mexico Press, 1982) summarizes the recent literature on western women and offers a new interpretation of women's role in the West, not forgetting that of the Native American, Mexican, French, and Afro-American woman.

Since in many ways memorials to women may be regarded as an aspect of popular culture, a useful key to understanding images of women is provided by Katherine Fishburn, *Women in Popular Culture: A Reference Guide* (Westport, Conn.: Greenwood Press, 1982).

INDEX

About the Author

Marion Tinling is a free-lance writer based in Sacramento, California. She edited *The Correspondence of the Three William Byrds of Westover, Virginia* and has published in such journals as *The Historian*, *Historic Preservation*, and the *William and Mary Quarterly*.